TRADE UNION LAW AND
EMPLOYMENT RIGHTS

TRADE UNION LAW AND COLLECTIVE EMPLOYMENT RIGHTS

Nick Humphreys

LLB, LLM Solicitor and Barrister (Non practising)
Associate, Bircham Dyson Bell, Westminster

JORDANS
2005

Published by
Jordan Publishing Limited
21 St Thomas Street
Bristol BS1 6JS

British Library Cataloguing-in-Publication Data

A catalogue record for this book is available from the British Library.

ISBN 0 85308 960 4

Typeset by Columns Design Ltd, Reading, England

Printed and bound in Great Britain by Antony Rowe Limited

PREFACE

This book owes its origins to *Trade Union Law*, which was previously published by Blackstone Press (1999). However, it is very far from being a second edition of that title and is much more in the nature of a wholly new title.

In this regard, very much has changed in the collective employment law landscape since *Trade Union Law* was published. This has come, at national level, principally as a result of the Employment Relations Act 1999 and the introduction of the concept of statutory trade union recognition (the principles of which have been amended by the Employment Relations Act 2004). Consequently, a completely new chapter has had to be written to cover this highly complex area. A by-product of the high take-up by trade unions of the statutory right to be recognised by employers is the new lease of life which has been given to the Central Arbitration Committee.

Further, this title has now progressed beyond simply dealing with trade unions, their members and the various legal relationships, rights and obligations that can be spun out of the existence of trade unions. Instead, this title recognises the importance of non-trade union collective employment law in the guise of European works councils (incorporated into United Kingdom national law by the Transnational Information and Consultation of Employees Regulations 1999, SI 1999/3323, from the European Works Council Directive, Directive 94/45/EC), together with the most recent form of promoting 'social dialogue' between management and employees by means of a standing body of employee and employer representatives under the Information and Consultation of Employees Regulations 2004, SI 2004/3426 (derived from the European Information and Consultation of Employees Directive, Directive 2002/14/EC). The trend for non-trade union consultation in this area has, therefore, been very much driven by Europe. A further new chapter has been written covering these areas.

Another potential trend which is starting to appear is the increase in prominence of trade unions generally. For the first time in nearly 20 years, industrial action (the *Gate Gourmet Limited* dispute) has been high-profile headline news and the relevant principles to emerge from the litigation from that case are included in this title. Additionally, trade unions have been active in seeking to use the human rights of their members as a means to wring concessions from employers. A good example of this is the *Wilson and Palmer* litigation which is covered extensively in this title. Going forwards, there is the possible merger of three of this country's largest trade unions, which, if it happens, will undoubtedly increase the profile of trade unions in the United Kingdom even further and, at a political level, increase trade union negotiating power with central government.

Quite apart from this, there have been numerous case law developments (especially in relation to the law relating to collective redundancies) which have continued to show this as an area of the law which does not stand still for long. Indeed, at some point in the (hopefully) not too distant future, new Transfer of Undertakings (Protection of Employment) Regulations will be issued (at the time of writing, April 2006 is the proposed roll-out for the new Regulations, but this is a piece of legislation that has repeatedly slipped). The principles of these long-promised new Regulations are set out in the text, albeit that there may still be some fine tuning before the final Regulations are eventually commenced.

In writing this book, inevitably, I have incurred a number of debts of gratitude, principally, to Tony Hawitt at Jordan Publishing for putting up with me as deadlines slipped due to legislative and case law developments, and to Kate Kelleher of Goldsmiths Chambers, a specialist criminal law barrister, for updating **Chapter 12** on the criminal law aspect of trade union law (although any errors in the final text are mine and not Kate's).

Last, but not least, I must also thank my wife, Fenella, and children, Lucinda and Isabelle, for having the patience to put up with me early in the morning, in the evenings and at weekends when I have been writing and not as otherwise attentive as perhaps I might have been.

The law is set out as at 6 September 2005.

Nick Humphreys
Bircham Dyson Bell, Westminster
October 2005

CONTENTS

TABLE OF CASES

TABLE OF STATUTES

References are to paragraph number.

TABLE OF STATUTORY INSTRUMENTS AND CODES OF PRACTICE

References are to paragraph number.

TABLE OF EUROPEAN AND INTERNATIONAL MATERIALS

References are to paragraph number.

TABLE OF ABBREVIATIONS

Legislation

IRA 1971	Industrial Relations Act 1971
TULRA 1974	Trade Union and Labour Relations Act 1974
EPA 1975	Employment Protection Act 1975
EPCA 1978	Employment Protection (Consolidation) Act 1978
EA 1980	Employment Act 1980
TUPE 1981	Transfer of Undertakings (Protection of Employment) Regulations 1981
EA 1982	Employment Act 1982
TUA 1984	Trade Union Act 1984
EA 1988	Employment Act 1988
EA 1990	Employment Act 1990
TULRCA 1992	Trade Union and Labour Relations (Consolidation) Act 1992
TURERA 1993	Trade Union Reform and Employment Rights Act 1993
ERA 1996	Employment Rights Act 1996
ERA 1999	Employment Relations Act 1999
EA 2002	Employment Act 2002
ERA 2004	Employment Relations Act 2004

Courts

EAT	Employment Appeal Tribunal
ECJ	European Court of Justice
ECHR	European Court of Human Rights

Chapter 1

INSTITUTIONS AND SOURCES OF TRADE UNION LAW

THE HISTORY AND SOURCES OF TRADE UNION LAW

1.1 Trade unions have been subject to legal regulation for much of their history. Indeed, it was only in the twentieth century that trade unions were allowed a relatively free hand in the way that they were able to conduct affairs between their members and with employers or employers' associations. Understanding the history of trade unions is important in order fully to understand the current legislative framework relating to trade unions and the perceived need for intervention in almost every facet of trade union activity. The following is a brief history of trade unions which can be broken down into six phases, these being:

- the position pre-1824;
- the reform of trade unionism up to the Trade Disputes Act 1906;
- the Industrial Relations Act 1971 (IRA 1971);
- the 'Social Contract' of 1974–1979;
- the reforms of trade union law between 1979 and 1997; and
- the changes to collective rights introduced between 1997 and the current date.

THE HISTORY OF TRADE UNIONS

The position pre-1824

1.2 Before 1824, trade unions were regulated by a total ban on the recognition of workers' collectives. This regulation was provided by, variously, the Statute of Labourers 1351, the Statute of Artificers 1563, the Poor Law 1601, the Master and Servant Acts and the Combination Acts. This legislation collectively empowered Justices of the Peace (usually employers) to fix rates of pay for servants, to prevent the withdrawal of labour by servants and to make combinations of workers unlawful.

1.3 The Master and Servant Acts were introduced initially to ensure that skilled workers could not take advantage of the consequences of the Great Plague (which inevitably substantially reduced the workforce available to employers) to drive up wages. The legislation provided that all able-bodied workers could be compelled to work at rates of pay in line with those prior to the Great Plague.

1.4   The main feature of the Master and Servant Acts was the absence of a contract of employment upon which to frame the working relationship between a master and servant. A servant could be compelled to work by the local Justices of the Peace and a failure of a servant to work could result in criminal penalties being imposed on the servant. However, to the extent that a master refused to provide work, he could only be punished by civil sanctions.

1.5   The Combination Acts of 1799 and 1800 had a different aim, being passed against a social and political background of the then recent French Revolution. The aim of the Combination Acts was to outlaw any combination of the working classes with a view to preventing the sort of revolutionary turmoil that had occurred in France. To this end, the Combination Act 1800 outlawed all agreements proposed by workers to bring about changes in such matters as working conditions and rates of pay. The legislation was again enforced by criminal sanctions before Justices of the Peace.

1.6   Another feature of this period was the attitude of the judiciary to organisations of workers, where the prevailing view was that, even with the body of legislation hemming workers in, any organisation of workers attempting to bring about changes in working conditions was, of itself, a criminal conspiracy. An example was *R v Mawbey*[1] where it was held in relation to combinations of workers, that:

> '... each may insist on raising his wages if he can, but if several meet for the same purpose it is illegal and the parties may be indicted for a conspiracy.'

1.7   One of the main engines of change for the legalisation of workers' combinations was the Industrial Revolution, where one of the consequences of new manufacturing processes was an increase in the hardship associated with working conditions, particularly industrial injuries. Consequently, social thinking was forced to adapt and take a more liberal stance. Many changes came about for trade unions in the period between 1800 and 1906, including an acceptance that trade unions should be legalised as they acted to protect the interests of workers in the face of capitalism. The decriminalisation of trade unions came in the form of the Combination of Workmen Act 1824 and the Combination Laws Repeal Amendment Act 1825 (the Combination Acts). The Combination Acts recognised that combinations of workers were of themselves lawful but that such combinations could still commit criminal offences. In particular, the Combination Laws Repeal Amendment Act 1825, s 3, created a loosely worded collection of offences that could be committed by combinations, in the form of threats, molestation, intimidation or obstruction, in relation to which prosecutions were regularly brought since the Combination Acts only allowed combinations the right to attempt to change the conditions of employment at particular individual establishments; any attempt to influence the working conditions at other places of employment was capable of being a criminal offence under the Combination Laws Repeal Amendment Act 1825, s 3.

1.8   In spite of the Combination Acts, trade unions continued to prosper. This was largely due to increasing professionalism in their organisation which in turn led to their social acceptability. Rather than acting and being seen as

---

[1]   (1796) 6 TR 619.

'secret societies', trade unions started to build funds for their members, to appoint professionals to look after their members' interests and to lobby for change in the law for the benefit of their members. Consequently, it became accepted that the overriding aim of trade unions was to change working conditions and not to change society (as had happened, for example, in France).

Reform of the Combination Acts

1.9 Further reforms followed to the law relating to trade unions. The Molestation of Workmen Act 1859 was passed, which restricted the meaning of 'molestation' under the Combination Laws Repeal Amendment Act 1825, s 3, by providing that 'molestation' did not occur where a combination of workers attempted peacefully to persuade workers to leave their work and take industrial action for the purpose of changing working hours or conditions of employment in situations where the workers would not be in breach of their contract of employment by leaving their employment.

1.10 Changes under the Master and Servant Act 1867 followed which resulted in imprisonment of workers for individually breaching their contracts of employment becoming an exceptional punishment rather than the usual punishment that it had been under the Master and Servant Act 1823. However, despite the Master and Servant Act 1867, prosecutions still continued to follow in large numbers due to largely conservative judicial attitudes where trade unions were concerned.

1.11 In spite of these legislative changes, the common law was slow to catch up. For example, in *Hornby v Close*,[2] it was held that trade unions were unlawful if they had as one of their objects the raising of wages and the organisation of labour, since such aims were in restraint of trade.

1.12 However, further legislative changes continued to be enacted. In 1867, a Royal Commission was set up to investigate the disturbances arising out of an industrial dispute that escalated into what became known as the 'Sheffield Outrages'. The Royal Commission examined, inter alia, whether more should be done to protect combinations of workers. Two schools of thought emerged from the Royal Commission's report: a majority expressed the view that trade unions should be legalised in return for which they would be required to abandon rules that were perceived to be in restraint of trade; and a minority expressed the view that trade unions should be legalised and provided with an immunity relating to their acting in restraint of trade together with the criminal consequences of any conspiracy which might arise from their actions.

Developments following the Royal Commission 1867

1.13 Whilst legislative change did not immediately follow the report of the Royal Commission 1867, the minority finding of the Royal Commission gradually became accepted as being the means by which changes to the law affecting trade unions should progress. Further reforms followed between 1871 and 1875 in the form of the Criminal Law Amendment Act 1871, the Trade Union Act 1871 and the Conspiracy and Protection of Property Act 1875.

---

[2]   (1867) 10 Cox CC 393.

1.14   The Criminal Law Amendment Act 1871 made a number of changes, including:

- repealing the last remaining traces of the Combination Acts and the Molestation of Workmen Act 1859;
- confining cases of 'molestation' to threats of violence; and
- removing liability for criminal conspiracy where the alleged conspiracy consisted of doing an act which was not of itself illegal.

1.15   However, the Criminal Law Amendment Act 1871 was not entirely good news for trade unions as it also introduced new offences in the nature of criminal harassment (which still exist today under Trade Union and Labour Relations (Consolidation) Act 1992 (TULRCA 1992), s 241) and recreated a criminal offence of picketing.

1.16   The Trade Union Act 1871 was a milestone as regards the constitution and civil status of trade unions. In particular, it provided[3] that 'the purposes of a trade union' were not to be viewed as unlawful simply because a trade union acted in restraint of trade. Unfortunately, the Trade Union Act 1871, s 4 also provided that the courts could not 'enforce directly large parts of the union's agreements with members ... or ... with other unions'. Thus, the internal affairs of trade unions were effectively removed from the jurisdiction of the courts.

1.17   Another major change was the Trade Union Act 1871, s 6 which created the Administrative Register. The Administrative Register provided for registration of trade unions with the Registrar of Friendly Societies. Although certain minor tax benefits arose as a result of trade unions being registered in this way, it was also believed that the Trade Union Act 1871, s 6 did nothing to change the legal status of trade unions as unincorporated associations. As will be seen below at **2.69** et seq, the courts were eventually to hold otherwise.

1.18   The Conspiracy and Protection of Property Act 1875, s 17 repealed the Master and Servant Acts thereby making it no longer a criminal offence for workers to withdraw their labour from their employer save in relation to certain prescribed cases (these being where the strikes would endanger life or property[4] or where the strike occurred in the workforce one of the former public utilities[5]). The Conspiracy and Protection of Property Act 1875 also provided the basis of the right to strike by removing criminal liability from the acts of a conspiracy of workers acting in furtherance or contemplation of a trade dispute unless the acts would of themselves be criminal in nature.

1.19   By the end of the Victorian era, trade unions were generally regarded for legislative purposes as being lawful bodies. However, matters were not finished with regard to the way that trade unions operated so far as the common law was concerned. The case of *Quinn v Leathem*[6] required a further consideration of whether trade unions were immune from the consequences of their actions. In *Quinn*, the claimant was an employer of non-union labour. The defendant was a trade union activist keen to establish a closed shop. He

---

3   Trade Union Act 1871, s 3.
4   Conspiracy and Protection of Property Act 1875, s 5.
5   Conspiracy and Protection of Property Act 1875, s 4 – repealed by IRA 1971.
6   [1901] AC 495.

informed the claimant and one of the claimant's main customers that unless their non-union employees were dismissed, they would suffer industrial action. The threat of industrial action caused the customer to terminate its purchase agreement with the claimant. Consequently, the claimant sued the defendant for common law conspiracy in relation to the loss that it had suffered. On appeal, the case ultimately was heard by the House of Lords which found in favour of the claimant, holding in relation to the issue of the lawfulness of trade unions and acts carried out in their name that:[7]

'... [a] combination not to work is one thing, and is lawful. A combination to prevent others from working by annoying them if they do is another, and is prima facie unlawful ... A threat to call men out given by a trade union official to an employer of men belonging to the union and willing to work with him is a form of coercion, intimidation, molestation or annoyance to them and to him very difficult to resist, and, to say the least, requiring justification. None was offered in this case.'

1.20 Following the commencement of the Trade Disputes Act 1906, *Quinn v Leathem*[8] largely became a footnote to the history of this area as trade unions were provided with a statutory immunity from the consequences of certain economic torts committed in the course of industrial action. The Trade Disputes Act 1906 had to be supplemented by further statutory modifications on a number of occasions (see, generally, **Chapter 8**) but otherwise, apart from the Trade Disputes Act 1906 and the Trade Union Act 1913 (providing for trade union financing of political objects), successive governments actively refrained from legislating to interfere with industrial relations (save in relation to the provision of certain minimum standards for employers and employees as regards safety, compensation and the like), until the passing of IRA 1971. Regulation of the workplace was instead left to trade unions and employers operating by means of collective bargaining at a local or national level for the purposes of workforces as a whole, rather than for individuals, a system which became known as 'collective *laissez faire*'.

IRA 1971

1.21 IRA 1971 was introduced in response to a perceived need for widespread trade union reform at that time. Between 1906 and 1971, much changed in both the workplace and the economy in Britain due to factors such as:

- inflation and unemployment, which had been marginal in the economy for years, both of which had started to increase; and
- an increase in the number of people looking for jobs in the economy due in part to the baby boom, immigration and increasing numbers of women moving full-time into the workplace.

1.22 However, the ability of the economy to absorb this influx in workers decreased due to increasing mechanisation of workplace processes. Against this background, successive governments tried to maintain full employment policies. Further, one of the key industrial relations problems facing employers in the British manufacturing workforce as a whole (which at that point was a major contributor to the British economy) towards the end of the 1960s

---

7   [1901] AC 495 at 538.
8   [1901] AC 495.

occurred at local level due to the power that local trade union officials had. This resulted in these local officials seeking to negotiate changes to terms and conditions of employment with employers who either by themselves, or acting through an employers' association, had negotiated national level collective agreements. Local level trade union officials, for various reasons, would use what became known as 'wild cat' strikes as a negotiating ploy. These strikes would take place at short notice upon the breakdown of negotiations between the local trade union representative and employer. The employer's unionised staff would immediately stop work and the employer was then forced to negotiate against a background of economic pressure.

1.23   The problems with this form of industrial action were so damaging to the economy as a whole that a Royal Commission, chaired by Lord Donovan,[9] was convened to examine them. The Royal Commission examined private sector manufacturing-based industries. It came to the conclusion that reform of factory-level collective bargaining was necessary but that this should be achieved through the education of trade union activists. The Commission, with one member dissenting, rejected calls for full legal intervention in the area of industrial relations. However, in 1971, the Government implemented wholesale 'corporatist' trade union policies in the form of IRA 1971 as part of a prices and incomes policy.

1.24   IRA 1971 worked at two levels, these being, first, the granting of individual rights to employees and, secondly, the attempted control of collective activity by trade unions. IRA 1971 made a number of changes to the law as it had evolved up to this point, one of the central features being the registration of trade unions. Registration provided corporate status to trade unions and made them liable to have their rulebooks subject to the supervision of the courts. Registration under IRA 1971 was a voluntary process but as part of a 'stick and carrot' approach, in return for registration, trade unions received exclusive collective bargaining rights in relation to pay and conditions, collective bargaining information, tax benefits and immunity from action in tort.

1.25   The main consequence of the 'stick' side of IRA 1971 was that unregistered unions were liable in full for the torts that they committed in the course of industrial action and received none of the other benefits afforded to registered unions.

1.26   Another feature of IRA 1971 was that collective agreements between employers and/or employers' associations and trade unions were conclusively presumed to be binding unless they contained a written clause expressing them not to be so. Further, employers could enforce the provisions of IRA 1971 in the National Industrial Relations Court (NIRC) as could the government in an emergency situation, by applying for a 'cooling-off order' before industrial action could commence.

1.27   In spite of all the 'carrots' that were offered to trade unions to register under IRA 1971, most refused to do so. In a further attempt to undermine IRA 1971, the TUC instructed its members sitting as members on industrial

---

9   Donovan Report of the Committee on Trade Unions and Employers Associations, Cmnd 3623 (1968).

tribunals to resign, which a large number of them did. Additionally, notwith-
standing the resolve of trade unions not to comply with IRA 1971, employers
refused to use the powers that they were given to seek redress in the NIRC.
Furthermore, the Government only used its new emergency powers in one case,
Secretary of State for Employment v ASLEF (No 2),[10] where railworkers had
introduced an overtime ban and a work-to-rule as a result of a dispute over pay.
The action caused severe train timetabling problems which resulted in the
Government making an application to the NIRC for a cooling-off order. The
argument advanced by ASLEF was that its members in withdrawing their
goodwill were not actually in breach of their contracts of employment. The
Court of Appeal ultimately held otherwise[11] and granted the requested cooling-
off order. A ballot was then held which provided overwhelming support for the
union and a pay settlement was then negotiated on very favourable terms to the
union. Despite substantial trade union provocation to use the cooling-off
powers again (most notably in the case of the Miners' Strike of 1974), the
Government refrained from making any further applications to the NIRC so as
to exercise them.

The Social Contract

1.28   Following a change in government in 1974, IRA 1971 was repealed and
the new Labour Government then attempted to promote a 'Social Contract'.
The gist of this 'contract' was that the Government would operate a policy of
full employment and couple it with the provision of certain social and
employment benefits, in return for which a prices and incomes policy would be
instituted with the TUC helping to keep the incomes end of the bargain
through a non-inflationary wage policy.

1.29   The first piece of employment-related legislation as part of the Social
Contract was the Trade Union and Labour Relations Act 1974 (TULRA 1974)
which, inter alia, repealed IRA 1971 and restated much of the pre-IRA 1971
era law whilst adding a few modifications culled from IRA 1971. Notably, the
blanket exemption in relation to trade union liability in tort was reintroduced
as TULRA 1974, s 14. Further, registration of trade unions was abolished
(TULRA 1974, s 8) and collective agreements were once more deemed to be
non-legally binding as between the collective parties (save to the extent that a
written collective agreement contained a clause stating that it was to be legally
binding upon the parties (TULRA 1974, s 18)).

1.30   Further employment legislation was also introduced under the Social
Contract. The Employment Protection Act 1975 (EPA 1975) introduced a
number of new employment institutions, notably the Advisory, Conciliation
and Arbitration Service (ACAS) (EPA 1975, ss 1–6); the Certification Officer
(EPA 1975, s 7); the Central Arbitration Committee (CAC) (EPA 1975, s 10);
and the Employment Appeal Tribunal (EAT) (EPA 1975, s 87).

1.31   Furthermore, EPA 1975 granted extensive new rights to trade unions
and their members, some of which are still in existence today (albeit with many
of these rights having been modified over time), in particular:

---

[10]   [1972] ICR 19.
[11]   See now the comments of the Privy Council in *Burgess v Stevedoring Services Limited* [2002]
IRLR 810, which doubts the correctness of this view.

- the introduction of compulsory arbitration for the recognition of trade unions (EPA 1975, ss 11–16);
- the duty for employers to disclose bargaining information to recognised trade unions (EPA 1975, ss 17–21);
- the introduction of procedural limits on the employer's right to make compulsory redundancies (EPA 1975, Part IV);
- the right for members of a trade union during their working hours to participate in the actions of an independent trade union (EPA 1975, ss 53–56); and
- the right for officials of a trade union to take time off work for trade union duties (EPA 1975, ss 57–58).

1.32   More rights were granted to trade union members under the Trade Union and Labour Relations (Amendment) Act 1976, including making the dismissal of an employee who was not a member of a closed shop automatically fair.

1.33   However, in spite of these incentives, trade union members, acting through their unions, continued to press for inflationary pay rises. The response of the Executive Committees of many trade unions to protests that, through making requests for pay rises, trade unions were not keeping their side of the Social Contract despite the introduction of the social measures provided by the Government, was to protest that they could not keep their members from asking for pay rises and to state that the Government had not gone far enough in relation to its side of the bargain under the Social Contract since not enough legislation had been introduced to protect the disadvantaged in society and the very low paid (a problem caused in part by the International Monetary Fund which helped Britain out of its economic problems by providing financial help at a cost: cutting back on public spending).

1.34   Ultimately, trade unions continued to strike, particularly in very low paid public sector employment. The Social Contract capitulated into meltdown in the infamous 'Winter of Discontent' of 1978.

1.35   By this time, trade unions had reached the high-water mark of the protection afforded to them by the law: they were immune from liability in tort in respect of the consequences of industrial action organised by them (including against third parties), and they had no restrictions on their taking of industrial action (save for that contained within their union rulebooks).

1.36   Following the 1979 General Election, a package of reforms was introduced by the incoming Conservative Government to change the way in which trade unions operated. Trade unions were perceived by the incoming Government to be a corrupting effect on the operation of free markets, setting wage levels higher than they would be if left to negotiations between employers and individual employees.

The 1979–1997 reforms

1.37   The changes that were made to trade union law in the period 1979–1997 were introduced, significantly, on a piecemeal basis rather than *en bloc* as IRA 1971 had been. The first major reform came in the form of the Employment Act 1980 (EA 1980), the main effects in relation to the activities of trade unions of which were:

- the provision of central government funds for secret ballots and workplace ballots for trade unions (EA 1980, ss 1–2);
- a power for the Secretary of State to issue Codes of Practice on industrial relations (EA 1980, s 3);
- a right for individuals not to be unreasonably excluded or expelled from a trade union (EA 1980, ss 4–5);
- the repeal of immunity in tort for secondary picketing, and limiting immunity for picketing to picketing at employees' place of work only (EA 1980, ss 16–17); and
- the repeal of certain trade union recognition machinery (EA 1980, s 19).

1.38 More legislation was to follow in the form of the Employment Act 1982 (EA 1982) which made further inroads into the rights which trade unions had enjoyed in the 1970s by:

- narrowing the closed shop exceptions relating to unfair dismissal and increasing the compensation available to employees dismissed as a result of the closed shop (EA 1982, ss 2–9);
- preventing the use of trade union membership or recognition requirements in supply contracts and, to the extent that they existed, removing immunity from liability in tort for inducing a contractor to introduce these requirements (EA 1982, ss 12–14);
- removing the immunities that existed in tort actions against trade unions whilst at the same time protecting union assets held in provident benefit funds and political funds, and capping the amount of damages that could be awarded against a trade union found to have committed a tort (EA 1982, ss 15–19); and
- narrowing the definition of 'trade dispute' (EA 1982, s 18).

1.39 Next came the Trade Union Act 1984 (TUA 1984) which, as one of its cornerstones, had the principle that trade unions should be democratic and exist for the benefit of their members. In this regard, the thrust of TUA 1984 was the introduction of new balloting requirements for trade unions in respect of:

- the holding of elections for trade union leadership offices (TUA 1984, Part I);
- the requirement to confirm the calling of industrial action by means of a ballot (TUA 1984, Part II);
- the requirement to confirm the retention of a union's political fund by means of a ballot (TUA 1984, ss 12–16) and provisions concerning the meaning of 'political objects' in this regard (TUA 1984, s 17); and
- provisions governing the regulation of check-off arrangements (TUA 1984, s 18).

1.40 TUA 1984 was enacted in the midst of the Miners' Strike 1984–1985. The strike provided the catalyst for further legislation, this time taking the shape of the Employment Act 1988 (EA 1988). It seized upon the dissatisfaction of individual mineworkers and the litigation that had taken place between them and their union. With this in mind, the EA 1988 made changes to the existing rights that individuals enjoyed, and introduced new rights for individuals against trade unions. In effect, EA 1988 reshaped the landscape for individuals in connection with their membership or non-membership of a trade union in the following ways:

- it required the holding of a ballot in favour of the taking of industrial action by trade union members before taking such action (EA 1988, s 1);
- it provided trade union members with the right not to be denied access to the courts (EA 1988, s 2);
- it provided trade union members with the right not to be unjustifiably disciplined by their trade union (EA 1988, ss 3–5);
- it provided a right to members of a trade union to inspect their union's accounting records (EA 1988, s 6);
- it provided a right for employees to require their employer to stop a trade union from making deductions (EA 1988, s 7);
- it allowed trade union members the right to control the expenditure of trade union funds by trustees of the union (EA 1988, ss 8–9);
- it repealed the provisions of the Trade Union and Labour Relations (Amendment) Act 1976 allowing for the automatically fair dismissal of an employee as a consequence of an employer's 'closed shop' policy (EA 1988, s 10);
- it provided a cause of action for employees who had other discriminatory action short of dismissal taken against them as a result of their membership of a trade union (EA 1988, s 11); and
- it contained detailed provisions relating to elections for non-voting trade union office, ballots on political funds and ballots on industrial action affecting different workplaces, including a power to issue Codes of Practice on balloting (EA 1988, ss 12–18).

1.41   Still further changes followed. These came in the form of the Employment Act 1990 (EA 1990) which attempted to remedy a number of matters. The most important of the reforms under EA 1990 were:

- the bringing of government policy on trade union membership to its logical conclusion by making discrimination by employers due to job applicants' membership or non-membership of a trade union unlawful (EA 1990, ss 1–3);
- introducing further reforms to the law relating to balloting of industrial action by making trade unions vicariously liable for the unlawful action of trade union officials (which concept was widely defined) where a union failed to condemn industrial action called by a union official in the union's name without the union's authority and dealing with the effect of dismissal of those taking part in unofficial industrial action (EA 1990, ss 4–9); and
- extending the power of the Secretary of State to issue Codes of Practice (EA 1990, s 12).

1.42   By now, the law relating to trade unions had become a complex bundle of rights and obligations for trade unions, trade union members and employers alike which were comprised in a number of different statutes. Consolidation followed in the form of TULRCA 1992. Having enacted TULRCA 1992, yet further reforms were implemented almost immediately afterwards in the shape of the Trade Union Reform and Employment Rights Act 1993 (TURERA 1993) (which introduced certain amendments to, inter alia, TULRCA 1992, most notably under TURERA 1993, s 14, in the form of the introduction of the right for individuals not to be denied membership of a trade union as TULRCA 1992, s 174).

The changes to collective rights introduced between 1997 to the current date

1.43 Probably the main driver for change to collective rights since 1997 has been the desire of the European Union to implement new collective consultation rights. Whereas previously the main arena for the collective rights of workers had been that between trade unions and employers, the new arena is defined by Europe as being one of information being passed to employees and consultation through either specific or ad hoc bodies or representatives of the employees.

1.44 In this regard, employees are now entitled to receive information and be consulted collectively in a number of different situations (albeit that in some of these situations trade unions are granted rights to be recognised by an employer), as follows:

- in the case of collective redundancies, under the provisions of the Collective Redundancies Directive[12] (as enacted in the United Kingdom by TULRCA 1992, s 188 et seq);
- in the case of transfers of undertaking, under, first, the Acquired Rights Directive,[13] and now the Business Transfers Directive[14] (as enacted in the United Kingdom by the Transfer of Undertakings (Protection of Employment) Regulations 1981[15] (TUPE 1981), regs 10–11;
- in the case of Pan-European Works Councils, under the European Works Councils Directive[16] (as enacted in the United Kingdom by the Transnational Information and Consultation of Employees Regulations 1999[17]); and
- in the case of the information and consultation of national workforces, under the Information and Consultation Directive[18] (enacted in the United Kingdom by the Information and Consultation of Employees Regulations 2004[19]).

1.45 Furthermore, changes have inevitably continued to be made to the rights of trade unions and their members. The first such changes were introduced under the provisions of the Employment Relations Act 1999 (ERA 1999), which introduced the following main provisions in relation to trade unions:

- the right to statutory recognition of trade unions under ERA 1999, s 1 and Sch 1 (implemented as TULRCA 1992, s 70A and Sch A1, in respect of which see, generally, **Chapter 4**);
- certain amendments to the right not to suffer a detriment on grounds of trade union membership under ERA 1999, s 2 and Sch 2 (introducing amendments to TULRCA 1992, s 146);
- the right for members of trade unions not to be placed on blacklists by employers under ERA 1999, s 3 (this right is still to be implemented under regulations to be issued under ERA 1999);

---

[12] Council Directive 75/129/EEC, as replaced by Council Directive 98/59/EC.
[13] Council Directive 77/187/EEC.
[14] Council Directive 2001/23/EC.
[15] SI 1981/1794.
[16] Council Directive 94/45/EC.
[17] SI 1999/3323.
[18] Council Directive 2002/14/EC.
[19] SI 2004/3426.

- certain amendments to the law relating to the balloting of trade unions and the giving of notice to employers under ERA 1999, s 4 and Sch 3 (in respect of which see **9.5** et seq);
- the introduction of new rights for training in relation to the statutory recognition of trade unions under ERA 1999, s 5 (introduced as TULRCA 1992, ss 70B and 70C);
- the enhancement of unfair dismissal protection in relation to interim relief applications for the purposes of statutory trade union recognition under ERA 1999, s 6 (amending the Employment Rights Act 1996 (ERA 1996), ss 128 and 129);
- the introduction of unfair dismissal protection for employees taking industrial action under ERA 1999, s 16 and Sch 5 (introducing rights in the form of TULRCA 1992, s 238A in respect of which see **7.127** et seq);
- amendments to the constitution of the CAC under ERA 1999, ss 24 and 25 (amending TULRCA 1992, ss 260, 263 and 264 and introducing a new TULRCA 1992, s 263A);
- minor amendments to the constitution of ACAS under ERA 1999, ss 26 and 27; and
- the abolition of the Commissioner for the Rights of Trade Union Members and the Commissioner for the Protection Against Unlawful Industrial Action and the enhancement of the powers of the Certification Officer under ERA 1999, ss 28, 29 and Sch 6.

1.46 Additionally, under the Employment Act 2002 (EA 2002), s 43, a right was introduced for trade union learning representatives to take paid time off work in relation to the rights under TULRCA 1992, ss 70B and 70C introduced under ERA 1999 (see TULRCA 1992, s 168A in this regard).

1.47 Bringing matters up to date, yet more changes have been introduced under the Employment Relations Act 2004 (ERA 2004), which focus on the following:

- certain improvements to the statutory trade union recognition and derecognition process under ERA 2004, ss 1–9, 11–12, 14–16 and 18–20, amending TULRCA 1992, Sch A1 (in respect of which see, generally, **Chapter 4** where the amended provisions are included generally in the text);
- a new provision under ERA 2004, s 21 relating to the information required by ACAS for ballots and ascertaining union membership (in the form of a new TULRCA 1992, s 210A);
- measures to tackle the intimidation of workers during statutory trade union recognition and derecognition ballots under ERA 2004, ss 10, 13 and 17, amending TULRCA 1992, Sch A1 (in respect of which see **4.158** et seq);
- amendments under ERA 2004, s 25 to the information about employees to be contained in the notice of industrial action provided by a trade union to an employer who will be affected by that industrial action (in respect of which see the amendments made to TULRCA 1992, s 234A, discussed at **9.90** et seq);
- the introduction under ERA 2004, ss 26–28 of provisions to increase the protection provided to employees undertaking properly constituted industrial action for the purposes of TULRCA 1992, s 238A et seq (in respect of which see **7.127** et seq);
- the introduction under ERA 2004, ss 29–32 of measures to implement the

effects of the decision of the European Court of Human Rights (ECHR) in *Wilson and Palmer v The United Kingdom*[20] (in respect of which see **7.17** et seq);

- the amendment under ERA 2004, s 33 of provisions relating to the right not to be excluded or expelled from a trade union under TULRCA 1992, s 174 (in respect of which see **6.49** et seq);
- amendments under ERA 2004, s 34 to the provisions relating to the forum for applications for compensation for infringement of the rights of trade union members not to have unreasonable disciplinary action taken against them, and the rights of individuals not to be excluded or expelled from a trade union (in respect of which see **6.56**);
- the introduction under ERA 2004, s 42 for a power to make regulations[21] relating to information and consultation of representatives of employees (in respect of which see, generally, **Chapter 5**);
- the introduction under ERA 2004, ss 48–51 of new powers for the Certification Officer to strike out weak or vexatious applications made to him under various of the provisions under TULRCA 1992;
- amendments under ERA 2004, ss 52 and 53 to the governance rules relating to trade unions in connection with the election of senior officers of a union (now incorporated as TULRCA 1992, s 46(4A) (in respect of which see **6.151**)) and the removal of the rule under TULRCA 1992, s 34 that an auditor of a trade union could not be a body corporate;
- the introduction under ERA 2004, s 54 of a power for regulations to be issued amending the way that any ballot or election in relation to a trade union under TULRCA 1992 may be conducted; and
- the introduction under ERA 2004, s 55 of a new TULRCA 1992, s 116A under which regulations may be issued for the provision of public money for trade union modernisation (this being a controversial provision during the passage of the Employment Relations Bill through Parliament) – at the time of writing, no regulations have been issued.

1.48 Finally, there are the amendments which will be made under the proposed new Transfer of Undertakings (Protection of Employment) Regulations (due in April 2006), inter alia, to the law relating to the provision of information relating to employees in connection with the transfer of an undertaking (in connection with which see **3.110** et seq).

1.49 The area of law relating to trade unions, their members and to collective consultation more generally, is a dynamic one which does not stand still for long: therefore, trade unions, employers and employees constantly have to keep one eye to the future and further change. Indeed, all that can be said with any certainty with regard to the future legal position in this area is that further changes will inevitably be made.

INSTITUTIONS OF TRADE UNION LAW

1.50 A number of different institutions exist which have an impact upon trade unions and which exercise various functions under either statute, agreement or convention. The following are the most important of the bodies.

---

[20]   [2002] IRLR 568.
[21]   The current regulations being the Information and Consultation of Employees Regulations 2004, SI 2004/3426.

The Advisory, Conciliation and Arbitration Service (ACAS)

1.51 ACAS was created by EPA 1975 and derives its continued existence from TULRCA 1992, ss 247–253. ACAS is a body corporate (TULRCA 1992, s 247(2)) and is separate from the government, having the power to appoint its own staff (being such number as it thinks fit, subject to the consent of the Secretary of State: TULRCA 1992, s 250(2)).

1.52 The primary management body of ACAS is the Council, consisting of nine ordinary members (with three coming from employers' organisations and three from organisations representing workers) and a chairman, all of whom are appointed by the Secretary of State (TULRCA 1992, s 248). The Council is empowered to determine its own procedure (including the quorum necessary for meetings: TULRCA 1992, s 248(5)). The terms of appointment of members of the Council are set out in TULRCA 1992, ss 249–250 but members cannot be appointed for a term exceeding 5 years (TULRCA 1992, s 249(3)).

1.53 ACAS was created to facilitate the use and, where necessary, reform of collective bargaining between employers and trade unions.

1.54 ACAS has been given a power to levy charges for the work that it provides under TULRCA 1992, s 251A and exercises this power in relation to some of its minor activities (such as conferences which it provides). ACAS does not charge for its industrial trouble-shooting roles though.

1.55 Being a creature of statute, ACAS is subject to judicial review where, in exercising any of its functions, it acts in a way that no reasonable body charged with the particular function in question would.[22]

1.56 In the case of collective disputes, the powers of ACAS to act will only be exercised where the protagonists are 'parties' to a 'trade dispute' as defined in TULRCA 1992, s 218, this being a definition which is wider in scope than that relating to the calling of industrial action under TULRCA 1992, s 244.

1.57 The distinction between the definition of trade dispute in TULRCA 1992, s 218 and TULRCA 1992, s 244 is that the s 218 definition is necessarily wider (covering as it does disputes between workers and employers, rather than workers and *their* employer), so as to allow ACAS to intervene and head off potential industrial disputes before they crystallise into industrial action.

1.58 TULRCA 1992, s 218 defines 'a trade dispute' as being one between employers and workers or workers and workers in respect of a particular list of reasons, these being identical to those in TULRCA 1992, s 244 (see **9.7**). Under TULRCA 1992, s 218(4), a dispute to which a trade union or employer's association is a party is treated as if it were a dispute between workers or employers. Thus, where a trade union consisting of workers for one or more different employers is in dispute with a particular employer, workers of the other employers are treated as being in dispute with the particular employer subject to the dispute.

1.59 TULRCA 1992, s 218 does no more than require that the dispute is connected with one of the list of reasons and therefore any connection, provided that it is not contrived, will be enough for ACAS to become involved.

---

[22]   See *ACAS v UKAPE* [1980] IRLR 124.

1.60 In many collective agreements there exists an automatic reference to ACAS in the event of a trade dispute. Of the 1,245 references to ACAS in 2003/04 for collective conciliation, 348 references came from unions, 172 came from employers, 581 were joint references (explained partially by the use of automatic reference clauses in collective agreements) and the remainder were instituted by ACAS of its own volition.

1.61 As regards the duties of ACAS, its main statutory duty now under TULRCA 1992, s 209 is 'to promote the improvement of industrial relations'.

1.62 However, in addition to this general duty, ACAS is required to carry out certain other specific statutory functions under TULRCA 1992, Part IV, Chapter IV, as amended, and, in the context of trade unions, this extends to four matters, these being:

- the issuing of Codes of Practice (TULRCA 1992, s 199);
- the provision of conciliation services under TULRCA 1992, s 210;
- the undertaking of arbitration services under TULRCA 1992, ss 212 and 212A; and
- the giving of advice (TULRCA 1992, s 213).

1.63 As regards these services, some expansion in details is required, as follows.

Issuing of Codes of Practice

1.64 Under TULRCA 1992, s 199(1), ACAS may issue Codes of Practice containing such practical guidance as it thinks fit for the purpose of promoting the improvement of industrial relations or for purposes connected with trade union learning representatives. In particular, ACAS has a duty under TULRCA 1992, s 199(2) to issue such Codes of Practice where they affect any of:

- time off for trade union officials under TULRCA 1992, s 168 (including guidance on the circumstances in which a trade union official is to be permitted to take time off under TULRCA 1992, s 168 in respect of duties connected with industrial action: TULRCA 1992, s 199(3));
- time off for trade union members to carry out trade union activities under TULRCA 1992, s 170 (including guidance on the question whether, and the circumstances in which, a trade union member is to be permitted to take time off under TULRCA 1992, s 170 for trade union activities connected with industrial action: TULRCA 1992, s 199(3)); and
- disclosing information to trade unions for the purposes of collective bargaining under TULRCA 1992, ss 181–182.

1.65 The procedure for issuing Codes of Practice is set out at TULRCA 1992, s 200. A draft Code of Practice must first be prepared for general public comment and ACAS may make any modifications it thinks fit in the light of comments that it receives following that consultation (TULRCA 1992, s 200(1)). Thereafter, the draft Code of Practice is sent to the Secretary of State, who either approves the same and lays it before the two Houses of Parliament or, alternatively, he rejects it and gives his reasons for doing so (TULRCA 1992, s 200(2)).

1.66 Under TULRCA 1992, s 200(3), a Code of Practice containing practical guidance must not be issued unless the draft has been approved by a resolution of each House of Parliament where the draft Code of Practice concerns any of the following matters:

- time off to be permitted to a trade union learning representative in accordance with TULRCA 1992, s 168A (ie time off for training and carrying out functions as a learning representative);
- training that is sufficient to enable a trade union learning representative to carry on the activities under TULRCA 1992, s 168A(2) (ie activities for which time off is to be permitted); or
- any of the matters referred to in TULRCA 1992, s 199(2).

1.67   If a Code of Practice is approved in this way, ACAS must issue the Code of Practice in the form of the draft (TULRCA 1992, s 200(3)). However, in all other cases, under TULRCA 1992, s 200(4), the procedure to be applied is as follows:

- If, within 40 days beginning with the day on which the draft is laid before Parliament or, if copies are laid before the two Houses on different days, with the later of the 2 days, where either House so resolves, no further proceedings are to be taken in respect of that draft Code of Practice. This is without prejudice to the laying before Parliament of a new draft of the Code of Practice.
- If no such resolution is passed by either House, ACAS must issue the Code in the form of the draft.

1.68   Under TULRCA 1992, s 200(5) a Code of Practice issued in accordance with TULRCA 1992, s 200 comes into effect on the day that the Secretary of State may appoint by order made by statutory instrument.

1.69   Once issued, a Code of Practice can be revised by ACAS, but all revision must take place under the approval of Parliament, again in the form of laying the revised Code of Practice and waiting for 40 days to see whether an objection of either House is raised (TULRCA 1992, s 201).

1.70   Powers for amendment and revocation of Codes of Practice exist under TULRCA 1992, ss 201 and 202 respectively.

1.71   The effect of ACAS Codes of Practice is that they are not law themselves but can be used as evidence in any proceedings before an employment tribunal or the CAC (TULRCA 1992, s 207(2)).

1.72   The Secretary of State also has powers to issue Codes of Practice under TULRCA 1992, s 203. The procedure for issuing such Codes of Practice requires the Secretary of State to consult with ACAS in formulating such a Code of Practice (TULRCA 1992, s 204(1)) and again requires the approval of both Houses of Parliament in issuing, revising and/or revoking the Code of Practice (TULRCA 1992, ss 204–206). Codes of Practice issued by the Secretary of State are likely to be issued where ACAS feels unable to issue a Code of Practice in a particular area, for example, the Code of Practice on Picketing (First Revision).

1.73   The effect of a Code of Practice issued by the Secretary of State is that it can be used in evidence in proceedings before a court, employment tribunal or the CAC (TULRCA 1992, s 207(3)). In other words, the evidential scope of a Code of Practice issued by the Secretary of State is wider as Codes of Practice issued by ACAS are not stated to be admissible as evidence in court proceedings.

1.74   Where Codes of Practice are issued either by ACAS or the Secretary of State, their evidential effect can be highly persuasive. For example, in a case arising from the Miners' Strike 1984–1985,[23] groups of picketing mineworkers attended picket lines at colliery gates on a daily basis. Six members of the group were selected to stand at the gates and another, larger group was placed back from those pickets at the colliery gates from where they shouted abuse at other mineworkers who had decided to return to work. An injunction was sought to prevent harassment of the returning mineworkers. In granting the injunction, the effect of which was to limit the number of pickets at the colliery gates, the High Court relied on the Code of Practice on Picketing, 1980, stating that para 31 of that version of the Code:[24]

'... does not make it a criminal offence or tortious to have more than six persons on a picket line. Nor is less than six any guarantee of lawfulness. The paragraph simply provides a guide as to a sensible number ... in order that the weight of numbers should not intimidate those who wish to go to work. [The court is] directed by [TULRCA 1992, s 207(3)] to take this guidance into account ... [The court does] so and [proposes], therefore, to restrain the South Wales Union ... from organising picketing or demonstrations at colliery gates by more than six persons.'

Conciliation

1.75 Conciliation services can be provided where a 'trade dispute' exists or is apprehended. In such a case ACAS may, at the request of one or more parties to the dispute or otherwise, offer the parties to the dispute its assistance with a view to bringing about a settlement (TULRCA 1992, s 210(1)). As regards the types of assistance which may be provided, this is dealt with under TULRCA 1992, s 210(2), which provides that assistance may be by way of conciliation or 'by other means'.

1.76 In this regard, 'assistance' is specifically defined as including the appointment of a person (other than an officer or servant of ACAS) to offer assistance to the parties to the dispute with a view to bringing about a settlement of the trade dispute. Further, when providing conciliation services under TULRCA 1992, s 210, ACAS must have regard to the desirability of encouraging the parties to a dispute to use any appropriate agreed procedures for negotiation or the settlement of disputes.

1.77 Furthermore, following amendments inserted by ERA 2004 (incorporating a new TULRCA 1992, s 210A), where ACAS is exercising its functions under TULRCA 1992, s 210 with a view to bringing about a settlement of a trade union recognition dispute relating to any of the matters covered under TULRCA 1992, s 218, the parties to the recognition dispute may jointly request ACAS or a person nominated by ACAS to do either or both of holding a ballot of the workers involved in the dispute and ascertaining the union membership of the workers involved in the dispute (TULRCA 1992, s 210A(2)).

1.78 In such a case, under TULRCA 1992, s 210A(4)–(6), ACAS or its nominated person may (but is not bound to: TULRCA 1992, s 210A(9)), at any time after ACAS has received such a request, require any party to the recognition dispute to supply ACAS with specified information concerning the workers involved in the dispute within such period as it may specify.

---

23   *Thomas v NUM (South Wales Area)* [1985] IRLR 136.
24   [1985] IRLR 136 at 151.

1.79   ACAS may impose such a requirement only if it considers that it is necessary to do so to bring about a settlement of a trade union recognition dispute (TULRCA 1992, s 210A(5)). In such a case the recipient of a requirement must, within the specified period, supply ACAS with such of the specified information as is in the recipient's possession (TULRCA 1992, s 210(6)). It is possible for the request to be withdrawn by any party to the recognition dispute at any time and, if it is withdrawn, ACAS cannot take any further steps to hold the ballot or to ascertain the union membership of the workers involved in the dispute (TULRCA 1992, s 210A(7)).

1.80   ACAS is given a statutory power under TULRCA 1992, s 211 to appoint conciliation officers.

Arbitration

1.81   The power for ACAS to refer a matter to arbitration is given under TULRCA 1992, s 212. Arbitration can be provided where a trade dispute exists or is apprehended. However, in order for a reference to arbitration to take place, there must have been a request for arbitration by one or more of the parties to the dispute and all of the parties to the dispute must consent to the referral (TULRCA 1992, s 212(1)). ACAS is then empowered to refer the matter either to an ACAS-appointed arbitrator or to the CAC. ACAS is not allowed to make a reference to arbitration where there are agreed procedures for negotiation or resolution of trade disputes in place between the parties unless it is satisfied that either the procedures have broken down or that there are special reasons justifying the reference (TULRCA 1992, s 212(3)). In any event, prior to referring to arbitration, ACAS should consider whether the dispute could be adequately resolved by conciliation (TULRCA 1992, s 212(2)).

1.82   Conciliation is a valuable stage in the proceedings. If it is successful, there is no need for the parties to go to arbitration and unnecessary time and cost can thereby be saved. Further, the conciliation officer can also help the parties in deciding what terms of reference will be provided to the arbitrator in the event that the arbitration is ultimately unsuccessful.

1.83   ACAS has a panel of arbitrators that it chooses from and in most cases the arbitration will be carried out by one arbitrator acting alone. Under TULRCA 1992, s 212A (inserted by the Employment Rights (Dispute Resolution) Act 1998, s 7), ACAS is empowered to prepare a scheme providing for arbitration in the case of disputes involving proceedings, or claims which could be the subject of proceedings, before an employment tribunal arising out of a contravention or alleged contravention of the unfair dismissal provisions of ERA 1996 and any other enactment that the Secretary of State specifies. The idea behind this scheme was to remove cases from the ambit of the employment tribunals. There has, however, been a very poor take-up of this service. Further, in certain, more complex cases, a panel of arbitrators can be appointed. In such a case, under TULRCA 1992, s 212(4)(a), one of the panel must act as the chairman of the panel.

1.84   The procedure at arbitration is left to the arbitrator. It is unusual to have legal representation (it is discouraged) and the manner of arbitration is usually designed so as to avoid legal formality.

1.85   Finally, it should be noted that, under TULRCA 1992, s 212(5), the result of the arbitration is not binding upon the parties in dispute unless they consent to it being so.

Provision of advice

1.86 The power to provide advice is given under TULRCA 1992, s 213(1), which allows ACAS to provide advice on request or otherwise to employers, employers' associations, workers or trade unions. ACAS also has a power under TULRCA 1992, s 213(2) to issue such publications as it thinks are likely to affect industrial relations.

Inquiries

1.87 Inquiries are all aimed at resolving the causes of trade disputes, or trade disputes likely to take place or in progress. Under TULRCA 1992, s 214, ACAS is empowered, if it thinks fit, to enter into an inquiry for the purposes of looking at industrial relations generally, in a specific industry or even in a particular undertaking or part thereof (TULRCA 1992, s 214(1)). The findings of the inquiry and any advice given may be published by ACAS if it appears to ACAS that publication is desirable for the improvement of industrial relations, either generally or in relation to the specific question inquired into, and after sending a draft of the findings to all parties appearing to be concerned and taking account of their views, if it thinks fit (TULRCA 1992, s 214(2)).

1.88 Further, under TULRCA 1992, s 215(1), where a trade dispute exists or is apprehended, the Secretary of State may inquire into the causes and circumstances of the dispute and may appoint a Court of Inquiry in relation to it if he thinks fit. The Court of Inquiry will have referred to it any matters appearing to the Secretary of State to be connected with or relevant to the trade dispute. Under TULRCA 1992, s 215(2), the Court of Inquiry is required to inquire into the matters referred to it and report on them to the Secretary of State. It may also make interim reports if it thinks fit. Additionally, the Court of Inquiry is required to lay any report, and any minority report, before both Houses of Parliament as soon as possible (TULRCA 1992, s 215(3)). Under TULRCA 1992, s 215(4) the Secretary of State has a power to publish any information obtained or conclusions arrived at by the court before or after the report has been laid before Parliament. TULRCA 1992, s 216 provides for the constitution and procedure of Courts of Inquiry.

1.89 Courts of Inquiry are rarely used as a means of establishing the cause of an industrial dispute. The most notable exception to this was the court chaired by Lord Scarman in the dispute at the Grunwick photographic company.[25]

The Central Arbitration Committee (CAC)

1.90 The CAC was created in 1975 and took over the functions of the former Industrial Arbitration Board. The CAC is now governed by TULRCA 1992, Part VI. Under TULRCA 1992, s 259, it is the duty of ACAS to provide staff (from the officers and employees of ACAS), accommodation, equipment and other facilities for the CAC.

---

[25] Reported as *Grunwick Processing Laboratories Limited v ACAS* [1978] ICR 231 in the subsequent litigation that followed ACAS's recommendation to allow recognition of the union at the centre of the dispute.

1.91   The CAC has a permanent seat in London, is composed of members experienced in industrial relations appointed by the Secretary of State (TUL-RCA 1992, s 260(1) and (3)) and is chaired by a chairman appointed from amongst the members by the Secretary of State (TULRCA 1992, s 260(2)). Other members of the CAC may also be appointed as deputy chairmen (TULRCA 1992, s 260(2)). The appointment of members and the chairman can only take place after consulting with ACAS (TULRCA 1992, s 260(3A)).

1.92   The CAC members may be appointed for terms of a maximum of 5 years' duration (TULRCA 1992, s 261(2)). TULRCA 1992, s 261 deals generally with the terms of appointment for members of the CAC and TULRCA 1992, s 262 deals with provisions relating to remuneration of CAC members.

1.93   The CAC can only hear cases referred to it by ACAS where both sides have consented to a referral and will hear cases involving industrial disputes or in a case where another statute provides for specific referral of a matter to the CAC. In this regard, the areas in which the CAC operates have been extended greatly since 1999. In addition to its general duties, under TULRCA 1992, the following additional jurisdictions for the CAC are now provided:

- First, the CAC is now required to determine statutory recognition disputes under the provisions of TULRCA 1992, s 70A and Sch A1. This is now one of the mainstays of the CAC's work and is dealt with generally in **Chapter 4**.
- Secondly, the CAC has been given the task of determining a number of matters in connection with certain disputes relating to the establishment and operation of both United Kingdom-based European works councils (under the Transnational Information and Consultation of Employees Regulations 1999[26]), and employee information and consultation procedures (under the Information and Consultation of Employees Regulations 2004[27]). This is discussed generally in **Chapter 5**.

1.94   The ordinary proceedings of the CAC are dealt with under TULRCA 1992, s 263 (ie those other than in relation to requests for statutory trade union recognition disputes under TULRCA 1992, s 70A and Sch A1). In such ordinary proceedings, the CAC sits with the chairman and such other members as the chairman directs. It can sit in two or more divisions if the chairman thinks it expedient and, to the extent that a division is sitting without the chairman, the functions of the chairman are carried out by a deputy chairman (TULRCA 1992, s 263(1)). Under TULRCA 1992, s 263(2), the CAC may, at the discretion of the chairman, where it appears expedient to do so, call in the aid of one or more assessors, and may settle the matter wholly or partly with their assistance.

1.95   The CAC generally takes a proactive approach to the referrals it hears. It is usual for a chairman or deputy chairman, together with an ACAS concilia-tion officer, to approach the parties at the start of a case to attempt to reach a joint result in the case rather than having the CAC sitting as would a judge in normal adversarial proceedings.

---

[26]   SI 1999/3323.
[27]   SI 2004/3426.

1.96 In determining the outcome of a referral, the CAC can determine its own procedure (TULRCA 1992, s 263(5)) and can sit in private where it considers it expedient to do so (TULRCA 1992, s 263(3)).The CAC has no power to administer oaths or to compel the attendance of witnesses.

1.97 To the extent that the CAC is not unanimous in its decision, the chairman is entitled to act in a case with the full powers of an umpire (TULRCA 1992, s 260(4)). Upon the CAC making a decision, it has a duty to publish the decision (TULRCA 1992, s 264(3)). Arbitration decided upon by the CAC is not binding upon the parties except to the extent that they agree that it will be so.

1.98 As regards trade union recognition disputes under TULRCA 1992, s 70A and Sch A1, there is a special set of procedures provided under TULRCA 1992, s 263A. In this regard, under TULRCA 1992, s 263A(1), the CAC sits in panels for each recognition dispute it deals with. Panels are appointed by the chairman of the CAC and each panel consists of three people, being the chairman of the CAC or a deputy chairman, who sits as chairman of a panel, together with two members, one having experience as a representative of employers and one having experience as a representative of employees (TULRCA 1992, s 263A(2)). Panels may sit in private if they consider it expedient to do so (TULRCA 1992, s 263A(4)) and may reach decisions on a majority basis (TULRCA 1992, s 263A(5)). Where a panel is deadlocked in relation to an issue the chairman is given a casting vote (TULRCA 1992, s 263A(6)). Further, panels are generally free to determine their own procedure subject to any other statutory limitations (TULRCA 1992, s 263A(7)).

1.99 TULRCA 1992, s 264 provides for certain minor, interpretive provisions relating to CAC awards. Under TULRCA 1992, s 264(1) the CAC may correct in any award, or in any of its decisions or declarations of the Committee under TULRCA 1992, Sch A1, any clerical mistake or error arising from an accidental slip or omission. If a question arises as to the interpretation of an award of the CAC, or of a decision or declaration of the CAC under TULRCA 1992, Sch A1, any party may apply to the CAC for a decision; and the CAC must decide the question after hearing the parties or, if the parties consent, without a hearing. Once the CAC has made its decision, it is required to notify the parties (TULRCA 1992, s 264(2)). Further, the CAC is required to publish its decisions under TULRCA 1992, s 264(3).

1.100 The CAC also has a duty to publish an annual report and prepare financial accounts for submission to ACAS in order that ACAS can report to the Secretary of State (TULRCA 1992, s 265).

The Trades Union Congress (TUC)

1.101 The TUC is the collective body for trade unions. It was established in 1868. It has no overall power to bind member unions with regard to TUC policy.

1.102 Under its constitution, the TUC has the power to become involved in disputes between member unions. The principles relating to inter-union disputes were agreed at the 1939 TUC Conference at Bridlington (commonly referred to as the Bridlington Principles). The Bridlington Principles cover such matters as union influence, membership recognition of other bodies and transfers of member from union to union. The introduction to the Bridlington

Principles states that they are not contractual in effect but that all affiliated unions accept the principles as a binding commitment for their continued affiliation to the TUC.

1.103 The TUC has a specialist division constituted to hear claims between trade unions under the Bridlington Principles, the TUC Disputes Committee. Prior to 1993, the Bridlington Principles prevented trade unions from recruiting new members where it was the case that the potential member was a clearly ascertainable member of another affiliated union, was under discipline from such a union or where there was good reason not to have the member otherwise accepted by the union. An example of the way in which the Disputes Committee operated prior to 1993 was the case of *Cheall v APEX*,[28] where the claimant requested a right to be heard by the Disputes Committee after he joined APEX from the TGWU. The TGWU objected to the Disputes Committee about APEX granting membership to the claimant. The Disputes Committee ordered the termination of the claimant's membership and denied the claimant the opportunity of putting forward representations to the Disputes Committee. The House of Lords upheld the right of the Disputes Committee to order expulsion, notwithstanding the lack of an opportunity being granted to the claimant to appear before the Disputes Committee. Their Lordships held that trade union decisions concerning membership of the union were entirely within the bounds of the union's discretion. The position has now changed following the creation of the statutory right to membership of a trade union under TULRCA 1992, s 174 (dealt with at **6.48** et seq). Accordingly, the Bridlington Principles had to be modified so as to take account of those changes.

1.104 Members of the TUC are now required to attempt to resolve disputes amicably before referring a matter to the Disputes Committee with a 'poaching' union making, where necessary, any appropriate payment for loss of income to the union suffering the poaching. However, if the parties cannot agree their dispute, the matter is then referred to the Disputes Committee which can make such order for compensation as it thinks fit if the case is proven. Ultimately, if a trade union which has actively engaged in poaching fails to adhere to a decision of the Disputes Committee, it can be excluded from the TUC.

The Certification Officer

1.105 The statutory scheme covering the Certification Officer is contained in TULRCA 1992, Part VI. The Certification Officer is appointed by the Secretary of State after consulting with ACAS (TULRCA 1992, s 254(1) and (2)). Assistant Certification Officers can be appointed by the Certification Officer and he can delegate to the appointed assistants such powers within his remit as he thinks fit (TULRCA 1992, s 254(3)). Facilities for the Certification Officer have to be provided by ACAS, including staff and accommodation (TULRCA 1992, s 254(5)). ACAS is also required to pay to the Certification Officer any sums needed for the performance of his duties (TULRCA 1992, s 254(5A)). Further, ACAS is also obliged to pay to the Certification Officer and any assistant appointed such sums as are necessary for remuneration, pension, travelling and retirement gratuities as are approved by the Secretary of State and the Treasury (TULRCA 1992, s 255).

---

[28]   [1983] IRLR 215.

1.106   The Certification Officer is required to undertake the following duties:

- to maintain lists of trade unions and employers' associations (TULRCA 1992, s 2);
- to determine the independence of trade unions (TULRCA 1992, s 6);
- to keep annual returns and accounts from trade unions (TULRCA 1992, s 32);
- to act as a decision-making body in matters relating to the alleged non-compliance with rules relating to elections to trade union office (TULRCA 1992, s 55);
- to act as a decision-making body in matters relating to the alleged non-compliance with rules relating to the proper application of trade union funds (TULRCA 1992, s 72A);
- to approve a trade union's political ballot rules (TULRCA 1992, s 74);
- to act as a decision-making body in matters relating to the alleged non-compliance with rules relating to trade union political funds (TULRCA 1992, s 82);
- to secure observance of the statutory procedures on transfers of engagements, amalgamations and changes of name by unions, and to deal with disputes in relation thereto (TULRCA 1992, ss 97–108);
- to hear claims that there has been a breach or threatened breach of the rules of a trade union relating to certain matters which were previously within the remit of the Commissioner for the Rights of Trade Union Members (before that office was abolished under ERA 1999), these matters being:
  – the appointment or election of a person to, or the removal of a person from, any office;
  – disciplinary proceedings by the union (including expulsion) (but not dismissal or disciplinary proceedings taken against members of the union by their employer);
  – the balloting of members on any issue other than industrial action;
  – the constitution or proceedings of any executive committee or of any decision-making meeting; and
  – such other matters as may be specified in an order made by the Secretary of State (TULRCA 1992, s 108A);
- to keep and maintain a list of employers' associations (TULRCA 1992, ss 124–126);
- to secure observance of certain administrative requirements by employers' associations, and to deal with disputes in relation thereto (TULRCA 1992, ss 131–134); and
- to retain custody of documents submitted under earlier enactments in respect of annual returns, accounts, copies of rules and other documents that were required under the Trade Unions Acts 1871–1964, IRA 1971 or TULRA 1974 (TULRCA 1992, s 257).

1.107   The Certification Officer is allowed to create such procedures as he thinks fit in the discharge of matters conducted before him (TULRCA 1992, s 256(1)) but is required to have regard to whether he will make known the identity of any individual lodging a complaint (TULRCA 1992, s 256(2)). This latter provision is designed to provide some measure of secrecy for 'whistle-blowing' trade union members. In the ordinary course of matters, the Certification Officer is required to disclose the identity of an individual to the trade union in connection with which the complaint has been made and to such other third parties as the Certification Officer thinks fit (TULRCA 1992, s 256(2A)). To the extent that expenses are incurred in the course of hearings held by the Certification Officer, the Secretary of State can make provision for the payment of them although consent from the Treasury is required (TULRCA 1992, s 256(3)).

1.108   Further, the Certification Officer is granted extensive powers to strike out applications and complaints on the grounds that:

- they are scandalous, vexatious, misconceived or otherwise unreasonable (there is a power for the Certification Officer to order amendment of proceedings for these reasons too), or that proceedings before him have been conducted in a way that is scandalous, vexatious or unreasonable (TULRCA 1992, s 256ZA(1)); or
- there has been an excessive delay in proceeding with the application or complaint (TULRCA 1992, s 256ZA(2)).

1.109   The strike out power can be exercised in the event of an application by a party to proceedings before the Certification Officer or by the Certification Officer of his own initiative, and it can be exercised against either party to proceedings before the Certification Officer (TULRCA 1992, s 256ZA(1) and (3)). The Certification Officer can only exercise the strike out powers granted to him where he advised the party against whom he proposes to exercise the power to state that he is proposing to exercise the power and to give that party the opportunity to contest the exercise of that power (TULRCA 1992, s 256ZA(4)). A right of appeal on any point of law lies to the EAT against any exercise of these powers by the Certification Officer (TULRCA 1992, s 256ZA(7)).

1.110   Further, the Certification Officer is granted powers under TULRCA 1992, ss 256A and 256B to refuse to entertain complaints made by vexatious litigants (as defined under TULRCA 1992, s 256A(4)).

The International Labour Organization (ILO)

1.111   The ILO was founded in 1919 by the Treaty of Versailles, Arts 387–427. The ILO works by having representatives from three different fields within a Member State, these being workers, employers and government. The Constitution of the ILO was revised in 1944 by the Declaration of Philadelphia and makes a number of important policy statements about employment law generally, most notably, that:

- '... labour is not a commodity ...';
- '... freedom of expression and of association are essential to sustained progress ...'; and
- '... poverty anywhere constitutes a danger to prosperity everywhere ...'

1.112   Above all, the ILO states that the yardstick for governments in formulating labour law policy is that '... all human beings irrespective of race, creed or sex, have the right to pursue both their material well-being and their spiritual development in conditions of freedom and dignity, of economic security and equal opportunity'.

1.113   The United Kingdom was one of the countries that played a founding role in the creation of the ILO and a substantial amount of early twentieth-century employment law in the United Kingdom was created as a result of ILO

Conventions or ILO Recommendations (for example, the Employment of Women, Young Persons and Children Act 1920, the Hours of Employment (Conventions) Act 1936 and the Merchant Shipping (International Conventions) Act 1936).

1.114 The ILO has three main bodies, these being the International Labour Conference, the Governing Body and the International Labour Office. The International Labour Conference (the Conference) normally meets once a year and is attended by four representatives of each Member State, these being two government members, one member representing employers and one representing employees (ILO Constitution, Art 3(1)).

1.115 The Governing Body consists of government officials from Member States and equal numbers of worker and employer representatives, with the distribution of the seat-holders being on a geographical basis. Members of the Governing Body are elected every three years at the Conference, although a number of seats are reserved for states of industrial importance, one of which is the United Kingdom. The Governing Body arranges such matters as the activities of the ILO, the agenda of the Conference and appoints various committees and the Director-General of the International Labour Office.

1.116 The International Labour Office is the secretariat of the ILO and has its base in Geneva.

1.117 There are two sources of law that come from the ILO, these being Conventions and Recommendations. Recommendations are used most commonly as a device for fleshing out Conventions. Under the ILO Convention, Art 19(5) and (6), each Member State must submit Conventions and Recommendations within 18 months of Conference to the national authority competent to enact legislation. The national body cannot '… bur[y] or set aside without due consideration …' an instrument put forward in this fashion (per ILO Official Bulletin 1944).

1.118 The United Kingdom complies with its obligations by the laying of White Papers before Parliament setting out the views of the government of the day. To the extent that the views are not adopted by Parliament, no further obligation falls upon the United Kingdom, save for certain reporting requirements as may be required by the Governing Body from time to time. Similar requirements exist in relation to Recommendations.

1.119 A Member State that ratifies a Convention is required to take such action as may be necessary to make effective the content of the Convention. Ratification must be unconditional. In order for a Convention or Recommendation to be ratified a two-thirds majority of delegates at the Conference is required and this is normally only after the matter has been heard by Conference at two successive sessions.

1.120 Conventions of the ILO contain powers for Member States to denounce previously adopted Conventions. The power is contained, usually, in the final articles of a Convention. Denunciation is not usually possible in the first 10 years following adoption and thereafter, if a Member State has not exercised the right, it will be bound for further periods of 5 years. In order to denounce a Convention, it is necessary to inform the International Labour Office and the denunciation becomes effective one year after receipt by that body.

1.121 Enforcement of ILO law takes place by either referring the Constitution or a Convention to the International Court of Justice. The International Labour Office tends to be the main interpreting body. Interpretations are placed in the Official Bulletin. There also exists a Committee on Freedom of Association composed of nine members appointed by the Governing Body dealing with failures to comply with this principle. Complaints can be made by either a Member State against another Member State, by the Governing Body or by employers' or worker's organisations, to the Committee.

1.122 The position of United Kingdom governments in relation to ILO Conventions has changed in the years since 1979. Prior to 1979, successive governments had ratified over 80 ILO Conventions. Following the change of government in 1979, a number of Conventions have been denounced in the United Kingdom (to make way for changes to the law on wages policy in public sector contracts, wages councils and places and hours of working). Perhaps the biggest problem area in recent years in the United Kingdom has been the incompatibility of the free market approach with unionised labour. Examples of the tensions are the complaint put forward by the TUC in 1981 following the unilateral revocation of the Civil Service Pay Agreement and the subsequent refusal by the then Government to refer the matter to the Civil Service Arbitration Tribunal. It was alleged that this action violated Conventions nos 87 of 1948 (Freedom of Association), 98 of 1949 (Right to Organise and Collective Bargaining) and 151 of 1978 (Right to Organise in the Public Sector). The complaint was upheld in part by the Committee on Freedom of Association, as were complaints in 1984 concerning the Government's decision to remove trade union membership rights at GCHQ (alleged breach of Convention 87 of 1948, complaint again made by the TUC) and, additionally, in 1987, that the Teachers Pay and Conditions Act 1987 contained provisions that would be in breach of Conventions 98 of 1949 and 151 of 1978 (the complaint here being made by the National Union of Teachers and the World Confederation of Organisations of the Teaching Profession).

1.123 Whilst a decision of an ILO Committee that a complaint is justified carries substantial moral weight against a non-complying Member State, no sanctions exist for failure to comply with the decision. Therefore, to the extent that a Convention is not enshrined in domestic legislation, failure to comply with it causes no problems for the government. This said, there is an increasing move on the part of the European Court of Justice (ECJ) to follow generally accepted principles of international law in determining the outcome of employment cases referred to it and there is the possibility that the United Kingdom may ultimately be influenced by the ILO in this way, if not by the fact that the Government since 1997 has moved away from a rigid adherence to free market employment policies.

The Confederation of British Industry (CBI)

1.124 The CBI is the central business organisation in Britain. It represents employers both to the public in the United Kingdom and also at an international level in the European Union.

1.125 The CBI is chaired by a part-time elected President who serves for 2 years. The President is elected by members who are companies or business

associations. Ultimately, it is the Director General of the CBI and the permanent staff of the CBI who deal with day-to-day policy issues, meetings with
ministers and the like.

1.126　The CBI maintains contact with the TUC through a variety of
different formal channels including ACAS. Informal links also exist between
the CBI and the TUC but the CBI does not engage in collective bargaining on
its own account.

The Department of Trade and Industry (DTI)

1.127　The DTI is responsible, inter alia, for implementing employment policy
insofar as it concerns ACAS, industrial relations policy, pay and redundancy
issues. The DTI has a substantial employment relations website providing clear
DTI guidance on employment legislation which is found at http://
www.dti.gov.uk/er.

1.128　The DTI used to carry out the functions of conciliation and arbitration
until these functions were transferred to ACAS in 1974 by TULRA 1974.

The European Union

1.129　European law has a part to play in the regulation of trade unions
following the adoption of the Social Chapter of the European Community
(passed at the inter-governmental summit at Maastricht in November 1991).
The Social Chapter has three key themes, these being to clarify the right of the
European Union to engage in matters relating to social policy, to extend the
concept of qualified majority voting and to stimulate the development and
growth of dialogue between workers and managers. Article 1 provides for:

> '... the promotion of employment, improved living and working condi-
> tions, proper social protection, dialogue between management and labour,
> the development of human resources with a view to lasting high employ-
> ment and the combating of exclusion.'

1.130　Where measures are introduced under the Social Chapter, some of
them can be dealt with on the basis of qualified majority voting (these being
health and safety, working conditions, information and consultation of workers, equality between the sexes and integration of excluded groups[29]), whilst
other matters require unanimity of Member States to invoke change (these
being social security, protection of workers faced with termination of employment, representation and collective defence of the interests of workers, rights of
third country nationals legally resident in the European Union and financial
provision for promoting employment and job creation[30]).

1.131　The Social Chapter does not apply to pay, the right of workers to
associate or the right to strike or impose lock-outs.[31]

1.132　Articles 3 and 4 of the Social Chapter aim at promoting consultation
between workers and managers in the public and private sector on issues that

---

[29]　Articles 2(1) and 2(2).
[30]　Article 2(3).
[31]　Article 2(6).

affect social policy. If Member States cannot make progress in terms of this policy development, the European Commission is empowered to put forward proposals to achieve this aim.

Chapter 2

THE NATURE AND STATUS OF COLLECTIVE ORGANISATIONS

TRADE UNIONS

2.1   The definition of a 'trade union' is provided by the Trade Union and Labour Relations (Consolidation) Act 1992 (TULRCA 1992), s 1 which states that a trade union is:

'... an organisation (whether temporary or permanent)—

(a) which consists wholly or mainly of workers of one or more descriptions and whose principal purposes include the regulations of relations between workers of that description or those descriptions and employers or employers associations; or

(b) which consists wholly or mainly of—

(i) constituent or affiliated organisations which fulfil the conditions in paragraph (a) (or themselves consist wholly or mainly of constituent or affiliated organisations which fulfil those conditions), or

(ii) representatives of such constituent or affiliated organisations,

and whose principal purposes include the regulation of relations between workers and employers or between workers and employers' associations, or the regulation of relations between its constituent or affiliated organisations.'

EXPLANATION OF THE DEFINITION

2.2   The definition under TULRCA 1992, s 1 needs to be examined as regards a number of different points, as follows.

Organisation

2.3   The concept of an 'organisation' confers some notion of a body with a structure. In considering what this was, the National Industrial Relations Court held[1] that a mere body of workers claiming to be a trade union for the purposes of claiming sole bargaining rights under the Industrial Relations Act 1971 (IRA 1971) was not an organisation since it had no name, no constitution, no

---

[1]   *Frost v Clarke & Smith Manufacturing Co Limited* [1973] IRLR 216.

rules, it held no meetings, kept no minutes, had no offices, had no property and had no funds. Indeed, as the court concluded, it had none of the attributes of an organisation.

Regulation of workers as a principal purpose

2.4 The requirement under TULRCA 1992, s 1 that a trade union has as one of its 'principal purposes' the regulation of relations between workers and employers or employers' associations, was considered in *Midland Cold Storage Limited v Steer*[2] where the issue arose as to whether a body of shop stewards of two unions at the Port of London could amount to a trade union. The case arose from the claimant suing the defendant shop stewards for 'blacking' incoming goods destined for it which caused the claimant substantial disruption in its business. The court had to determine whether the defendants (as members of what was termed a Joint Shop Stewards Committee) were a union capable of having proceedings served against that Committee. The High Court held that the defendants, as members of the Committee, were not a trade union. In particular, the court held that it was:[3]

> '... far from satisfied by the evidence ... that the "principal objects" of the Committee include the regulation of relations between workers of that description or those descriptions and employers or organisations of employer ... There [was] little satisfactory evidence about the composition or activities of the Committee, apart from some evidence relating to "blacking"; and although the Committee appears to intend to secure the employment of registered dockworkers by the claimants, [the court could not] infer that, once this [was] achieved, the Committee has any ambition to "regulate relations" thereafter ...'

2.5 This said, where there is satisfactory evidence of organisation and the desire to regulate activities, this is often adequate to establish a trade union. A good example in this regard is *British Association of Advisers and Lecturers in Physical Education v National Union of Teachers*.[4] The case concerned the claimant's exclusion from a national pay-negotiating body for four categories of local authority education employees called the Soulbury Committee. The background to the exclusion was that, in 1961, the claimant had entered into an agreement with the defendant for its members to become members of the defendant at a reduced subscription rate. It was also agreed at this time that the claimant would at all times retain its autonomy. In 1982, the claimant wrote to the defendant withdrawing its collective membership. In 1985, the defendant put forward a motion to the Soulbury Committee that the claimant should be removed from the Committee. The motion was carried and it was at this point that the claimant sued for breach of contract relating to its exclusion and asked for an injunction and damages. In the High Court, the claim was struck out on the grounds that the claimant was not a trade union and therefore had no locus standi to bring the proceedings. The main issue was whether the claimant had as one of its principal objects the regulation of relations between workers and

---

2   [1972] ICR 435.
3   [1972] ICR 435 at 443.
4   [1986] IRLR 497.

employers. The claimant appealed to the Court of Appeal which allowed the appeal on two points. First, the court dealt with the Constitution of the claimant, which stated that:

> 'The Association shall be concerned with the professional interests of its members ...'

in relation to which the court held that:[5]

> '... when one is dealing with persons who are of professional standing and one speaks of the professional interests of the members, one is not confining one's attention simply to the status of the profession to which they belong, but is dealing in a wider context with the interests of the individual members in their profession. It seems ... that in the context of this constitution the phrase "professional interests" is apt to cover the interests of individual members in their profession including their interests vis-à-vis their employers.'

2.6   Secondly, the court looked at the language used in the Constitution of the claimant so as to establish whether it demonstrated as a principal purpose of the claimant the regulation of relations between workers and employers. In this regard, the court held:[6]

> 'We are concerned with an association that has a total membership of 402. [TULRCA 1992] does not require, for an association to qualify as a trade union, that it be of any particular size or that it demonstrate any particular capacity or effectiveness or frequency of intervention in its role of regulation of the relations between its members and their employers. It qualifies if it demonstrates that it has a principal purpose to regulate those relations and is an association wholly or mainly of workers.'

Representative unions and divisions of unions

2.7   The definition under TULRCA 1992, s 1 also makes provision for bodies representative of a collection of trade unions to be categorised as a trade union (TULRCA 1992, s 1(b)), such as, for example, the Trades Union Congress. The converse is equally true. Where a union is a collective of different trades or exists in a number of different regions, it is possible to have separate unions within a main union.[7]

2.8   The consequences of being found to be a smaller union are important under TULRCA 1992, s 22(2) with regard to the issue of remedies and the quantum of damages that can be awarded against a union by reference to its size (see **10.80**).

ENTRY ON THE LIST OF TRADE UNIONS

2.9   Once a body complies with the definition of a 'trade union' under TULRCA 1992, s 1, it can apply to be included on the list of trade unions. 'Listing' is a mechanical process dealt with in TULRCA 1992, ss 2–5. The duty to keep a list of trade unions is imposed upon the Certification Officer by

---

5   [1986] IRLR 497 at 500.
6   [1986] IRLR 497 at 501.
7   *Thomas v NUM (South Wales Area)* [1985] IRLR 136.

TULRCA 1992, s 2(1). The bodies to be kept on the list are those which were included on the list under the Trade Union and Labour Relations Act 1974 (TULRA 1974), s 8, and other organisations satisfying the criteria of TULRCA 1992, Part I (per TULRCA 1992, s 2(1)).

2.10   The list of trade unions is a public document and can be inspected by members of the public at all reasonable hours without payment of charge (TULRCA 1992, s 2(2)).

2.11   The Certification Officer is bound to include a copy of the list in his annual report (TULRCA 1992, s 2(3)).

The procedure for listing

2.12   The statutory listing procedure is set out in TULRCA 1992, s 3. An application by an unlisted trade union is initially made to the Certification Officer (TULRCA 1992, s 3(1)). The Certification Officer can specify a model form to be used in the listing process. Organisations requesting to be listed must supply a copy of their rules, a list of their officers, the address of the main or head office of the body and the name that the body is to be known by, together with the fee for registration from time to time (TULRCA 1992, s 3(2)).

2.13   In the event that a body making an application to be included on the list of trade unions complies with these criteria, the Certification Officer must list the body if:

- he is satisfied that the body is a trade union as defined in TULRCA 1992, s 1;
- the matters in TULRCA 1992, s 3(2) (as set out at **2.12**) have been complied with; and
- registration of the name of the body is not prohibited due to its similarity with either another listed organisation, a body that was registered as a trade union under the Trade Union Acts 1871–1964 or with one registered under IRA 1971 as a trade union (TULRCA 1992, s 3(3)–(4)).

Removal from the list of trade unions

2.14   The Certification Officer also has a power to remove from the list of trade unions a body where:

- although the body is listed, it appears in fact that it is not a trade union (TULRCA 1992, s 4(1));
- he is requested to remove the body from the list by the body (TULRCA 1992, s 4(3)(a)); or
- he is satisfied that the body no longer exists (TULRCA 1992, s 4(3)(b)).

2.15   In a case where the Certification Officer has decided to remove a body from the list, he is required to give the body notice of this fact and must consider any representations made to him by the body where they are received by him during the notice period. The notice period cannot be less than 28 days (TULRCA 1992, s 4(2)).

Appeals against refusal to list or removal from the list

2.16   To the extent that an organisation is either refused entry to the list of trade unions or has its entry removed by the Certification Officer, an appeal against the decision of the Certification Officer lies to the Employment Appeal Tribunal (EAT) on either a point of fact or law (TULRCA 1992, s 9).

2.17   The Certification Officer should not be called as a witness in any appeal. In *The Certification Officer v Squibb UK Staff Association*, a case involving a refusal to grant a Certificate of Independence (in connection with which see **2.22** et seq), the Court of Appeal held in relation to the function of the Certification Officer that:[8]

> 'The Certification Officer is a judicial position. He has to be impartial and independent. He has to give his determination and support it with written reasons. [We] cannot believe it is right that he should be cross-examined on those reasons. He should not be cross-examined any more than a justice of the peace or a planning inspector or arbitrator or any of the many people who have to make decisions from which there is an appeal. Such a person can be asked to supplement his reasons and to give further reasons: or the matter can be remitted to him for reconsideration ... No doubt on any appeal there is public interest involved. So there should be someone present to support the decision of the Certification Officer ... In one of these cases I think that the public interest should be safeguarded by the Treasury Solicitor.'

The benefits of being included on the list of trade unions

2.18   Listing is important to a trade union in a number of ways. First, it provides evidence that a trade union is a trade union (TULRCA 1992, s 2(4)) and a certificate can be issued by the Certification Officer to a body claiming to be a trade union that it has been included on the list of trade unions (TULRCA 1992, s 2(5)).

2.19   Secondly, to the extent that a listed trade union provides provident benefits to its members, those benefits are exempt from income tax, corporation tax and capital gains tax.

2.20   Thirdly, under TULRCA 1992, s 12, the property of the union, which is required to be held by union trustees, can be vested in new trustees or transferred by the process in TULRCA 1992, ss 13–14, which relies on the resolution of appointment of a trustee as being sufficient to vest the property in the trustee and thereby dispenses for the need for a vesting deed to transfer the property.

2.21   Finally, once a union has been listed, it can apply for a Certificate of Independence which is important in the context of the various statutory rights given to trade unions.

CERTIFICATES OF INDEPENDENCE

2.22   The grant of a Certificate of Independence is of fundamental importance to a trade union from the point of claiming trade union rights. The formulation of the main trade union statutory rights requires that trade unions

---

8   [1979] IRLR 75 at 77.

must be both independent and, in some cases, recognised by an employer as well (see **Chapter 3** with regard to recognition rights generally) in order to be able to benefit from any given right.

2.23   The requirement of independence for the grant of rights to trade unions is to ensure that collective rights are exercised by truly independent bodies as opposed to staff associations (which, for example, may otherwise provide a means for an employer's own human resources department to impose informal control over the workforce).

2.24   Further, since the rights afforded to trade unions include, inter alia, the power to bargain away the right of trade union members to take industrial action[9] (this being a measure of last resort for trade unions), the use of the Certification Officer as an external measure to gauge independence ensures that union members are protected from interference from their employers that could otherwise deprive them of their ability to take such action. As the point was put in one case:[10]

> 'Parliament will not tolerate the recognised and certificated existence of a band of people claiming to be an independent trade union when in reality they are unable to offer a vigorous challenge to the employers on behalf of their members whether collectively or individually.'

Independence

2.25   As with listing, TULRCA 1992 provides statutory criteria to be fulfilled in order for a Certificate of Independence to be granted. The first requirement for a trade union applying for a Certificate of Independence is to demonstrate that the trade union is, in fact, independent. TULRCA 1992, s 5 provides a definition of what amounts to 'independence' for these purposes, which states that a trade union will be independent where it:

> '(a) is not under the domination or control of an employer or group of employers or of one or more employers' associations, and
> (b) is not liable to interference by an employer or any such group or association (arising out of the financial or material support or by any other means whatsoever) tending towards such control ...'

2.26   The test works at two levels asking in effect, first, whether the union is simply an emanation of an employer and, if not, secondly, whether the union could be forced to defer to the wishes of an employer. Further comment is required in relation to each of these points as follows.

Limb 1 – Independence from employers

2.27   As to the first limb of the test, the Certification Officer publishes a booklet 'Guidance for trade unions wishing to apply for a Certificate of Independence' (2005), which deals essentially with two issues, these being the procedure for obtaining a Certificate of Independence and the criteria used for determining independence. The criteria set out in the booklet are broadly similar to those approved by the EAT in *Blue Circle Staff Association v The*

---

[9]   TULRCA 1992, s 180.
[10]   *Association of HSD (Hatfield) Employees v Certification Officer* [1978] IRLR 261 at 262.

Certification Officer.[11] In this case, the appellant trade union was appealing against the refusal by the Certification Officer to grant it a Certificate of Independence. The appellant had been formed in 1971 to provide representation to salaried staff of the Blue Circle Group of Companies. In 1975, it had made constitutional changes to attempt to make it independent of management, but under its Constitution the body was dominated by management of the employer at all levels. The Certification Officer rejected the application for a Certificate of Independence and set out eight criteria which he had considered in refusing to grant the Certificate of Independence, the six main ones of which are now provided as formal guidance by the Certification Officer, as follows:

- *The history of the union* In this regard, the union should not have a recent history of having been created by management. If the union was created by management but has since evolved and is effectively the author of its own destiny, the origin of the union can be ignored.
- *The membership base of the union* Applications from unions deriving their membership solely from one employer may be more closely examined by the Certification Officer since a limited membership base makes the union more vulnerable to pressure from an employer; ultimately, independence requires an ability to withstand pressure.
- *The organisation and structure of the union* This head examines whether the union can be said to be truly independent; in other words, the union should not be infiltrated by management and should be able to make its own decisions. Of particular importance is whether senior employees are able to be members, since this potentially allows a degree of management interference.
- *The finances of the union* The union must be financially self-supporting. In the case of a union receiving a direct subsidy from an employer this is probably enough to be fatal to a claim of independence. However, independence also requires a sound asset base which allows a union to ward off the withdrawal of any facilities provided by an employer (such as check-off).
- *Whether the union receives any employer-provided facilities* This will include any administrative support that is provided to the union whilst also dealing with such matters as time off for members. In the case of single-employer bodies, the Certification Officer considers the cost of the provision of any facilities provided by the employer at market rates to see if the union could cope financially in the event that the employer were to withdraw the facilities provided. The provision of facilities should not necessarily be determinative of the grant of a Certificate of Independence. Employers should consider as a matter of good industrial relations practice the ACAS Code of Practice No 3, *Time Off for Trade Union Duties and Activities* (2003), which recommends, at para 38, that employers should provide to unions facilities such as notice boards (including electronic notice boards on internets or intranets), accommodation for meetings, a telephone and office space.
- *The negotiating record of the union* Under this head, the Certification Officer considers whether the union is able to influence management through negotiation. In this regard, a weak success rate in negotiations is

---

[11]   [1977] IRLR 20.

not necessarily proof of a lack of independence but a strong success rate can help to outweigh defects in any of the above factors. According to the Certification Officer, negotiation is the point at which independence and success overlap; an effective union is likely to be an independent one.

2.28　Good examples of cases involving applications for Certificates of Independence based on these criteria are *A Monk & Co Staff Association v Certification Officer*[12] and *Association of HSD (Hatfield) Employees v Certification Officer*.[13] In the *Monk* case, the union in question was a staff association drawing its membership from one employer which had evolved from a union initially formed to combat interest in recruitment at the firm by an established trade union (the Association of Clerical and Transport Staff). The union previously had made two unsuccessful applications to the Certification Officer for a Certificate of Independence when it made the application leading to the appeal. The Certification Officer turned down the application holding that the union was not independent and was likely to suffer from interference from the employer. The union appealed and the EAT granted the appeal. The EAT held that although the union was not as strong as some (having a membership of 481 and small cash holdings at the bank), the union had the determination to carry on in the event that the employer withdrew facilities that it provided. Further, it had an established record of negotiations with the employer. To the extent that it was prepared and able to carry on in the event of the employer withdrawing facilities, it was independent.

2.29　In the *Association of HSD (Hatfield) Employees* case,[14] the union was formed out of the workers at Hawker Siddeley Dynamics (HSD) at Hatfield. The union had a membership base of some eight hundred employees. Following nationalisation of the United Kingdom aerospace industry, the union became fiercely independent of the management of HSD. The HSD Hatfield plant was subsequently visited by the new head of British Aerospace who refused to have dealings with the union on the grounds that he believed it was not a trade union. Following this snub, the union applied for a Certificate of Independence but the application was refused by the Certification Officer. On hearing the appeal, the EAT held that following the nationalisation of HSD, it was clear that, factually, the union was opposed to the management of the business, that the union could be classed as independent and could therefore be provided with a Certificate of Independence.

Limb 2 – The likelihood of interference

2.30　The second limb of the test (TULRCA 1992, s 5(b)) focuses upon a union's ability to resist external pressure from an employer. Two possibilities exist as to the point in time at which the test posed by TULRCA 1992, s 5(b) of a union being 'liable to interference by an employer' is to be considered. The first is that liability to interference has to be considered at the time that the union applies for a Certificate of Independence (this view being favourable to an applicant union). The second is that a union could be considered to be liable to interference at some point in the future (this view is obviously unfavourable

---

[12]　[1980] IRLR 431.
[13]　[1978] IRLR 261.
[14]　*Association of HSD (Hatfield) Employees v Certification Officer* [1978] IRLR 261.

to applicants as it requires an element of 'crystal ball-gazing' on the part of the Certification Officer so as to consider the various eventualities which may arise in the future, for example, the attempted calling of industrial action by the union).

2.31 The leading case on the correct test to be applied is *The Certification Officer v Squibb UK Staff Association.*[15] Here, the union in question had evolved as a union drawing its membership from a single employer (it had a membership of 231 and had funds of around £1,100). The union had subsequently sought independence from the employer. The employer recognised the union as having sole negotiating rights for members of staff. The employer also provided a number of facilities for the association such as check-off, office facilities and time off for officials of the union. The Certification Officer refused to grant a Certificate of Independence to the union following its application on the grounds that the union was liable to interference. The union successfully appealed to the EAT but on a further appeal to the Court of Appeal, the Certification Officer's decision was reinstated with the Court of Appeal holding:[16]

> 'The phrase "liable to" when used otherwise than in relation to legal obligations has an ordinary and well-understood meaning, namely, "subject to the possibility of". Counsel for the union has in fact contended that it means "subject to the likelihood of" … I see no warrant in the context of the legislation or in practical common-sense for so limited a construction of the words "liable to". If adopted, it would impose upon the Certification Officer the need for an exercise in clairvoyance with much uncertainty developing in the outcome.'

2.32 Another good example of the issue of what is capable of amounting to interference was *Government Communications Staff Federation v Certification Officer.*[17] The case arose out of the decision of the Government to ban outside trade unions at GCHQ. Staff at GCHQ were allowed to form their own departmental staff association provided that the same was approved by the Director of GCHQ. The appellant union was created as a result. The union was accorded sole negotiation rights for its members. In time the union made an application for a Certificate of Independence which was refused. The union appealed and on appeal, the EAT upheld the decision of the Certification Officer, holding that the union's continued existence was always contingent on the permission of the Director of GCHQ and therefore it could never be an independent union.

Granting and revoking the Certificate of Independence

2.33 The grant of a Certificate of Independence is dealt with at TULRCA 1992, ss 6–9. The Certification Officer may not come to a decision on the application before the end of the period of one month after it has been made. Before coming to his decision the Certification Officer must make such inquiries as he thinks fit and must take into account any relevant information

---

15   [1979] IRLR 75.
16   [1979] IRLR 75 at 79.
17   [1993] IRLR 260.

submitted to him by any person before making a determination on the matter and entering it on to the record (TULRCA 1992, s 6(4)–(5)).

2.34 The Certification Officer is bound to give reasons for any refusal to grant a Certificate of Independence (TULRCA 1992, s 6(6)), and must keep a record of all Certificates of Independence granted and allow free public access to that record at all reasonable hours (TULRCA 1992, s 6(2)).

2.35 Once the Certification Officer has granted a Certificate of Independence to a trade union, the Certification Officer can review his decision and withdraw the Certificate of Independence at a later date if he is of the opinion that the union is no longer independent (TULRCA 1992, s 7(1)). If the Certification Officer does review the grant of a Certificate of Independence, he must inform the union to whom it was granted of his decision and enter a notice of the proposal in the record kept by him (TULRCA 1992, s 7(2)). Since the function being exercised by the Certification Officer in such a case is quasi-judicial in nature, the Certification Officer is required to make such inquiries as he thinks fit and to take into account any representations that are submitted to him before making a decision. Once the Certification Officer has made his decision, he must either confirm that the Certificate of Independence remains granted or withdraw the Certificate of Independence and provide his reasons for doing so (TULRCA 1992, s 7(3)–(6)).

Evidential effect of the Certificate of Independence

2.36 A Certificate of Independence or the absence of it (including where it has been revoked), is conclusive evidence as to whether or not a trade union is independent, and any document purporting to be a Certificate of Independence signed by either the Certification Officer or a person appointed by him to sign such Certificates is presumed to be a Certificate of Independence unless the contrary is proved (TULRCA 1992, s 8(1)–(2)). Certified copies of a Certificate of Independence are presumed to be valid evidence of the independence of a union (TULRCA 1992, s 8(3)).

2.37 To the extent that proceedings are issued which require a determination of whether a trade union is independent before the courts, the EAT, the Central Arbitration Committee (CAC), the Advisory, Conciliation and Arbitration Service (ACAS) or an employment tribunal, if no Certificate of Independence can be provided and no entries exist on the record kept by the Certification Officer as to the independence of the union in question, the case must be stayed pending a determination by the Certification Officer under the procedure for an initial grant of a Certificate of Independence (TULRCA 1992, s 8(4)).

Appeals relating to the Certificate of Independence

2.38 As with a refusal to enter a trade union on the list of trade unions or a decision to remove a trade union from the list, an appeals procedure exists in the event that a trade union is dissatisfied with a decision to refuse to grant, or to revoke, a Certificate of Independence. The appeal lies to the EAT either on grounds of fact or law.

RECOGNITION OF TRADE UNIONS

2.39 After a trade union has been issued with a Certificate of Independence by the Certification Officer, the next important hurdle in relation to access to the main statutory rights for trade unions is to be recognised by an employer, or two or more associated employers (dealt with generally in **Chapter 3**).

2.40 Apart from the situation discussed generally in **Chapter 4** in relation to the statutory recognition of trade unions, recognition of a trade union cannot be imposed upon an employer save for one situation (albeit, as is discussed in **Chapter 5**, employers can be required to recognise worker representatives in the case of certain pan-European businesses and required to inform and consult with employee representatives of undertakings (initially from April 2005, those employing 150 or more employees, but falling by April 2007 to those undertakings employing 50 or more employees)). This is where a transfer of an undertaking, or part of one, occurs where the transferor employer recognised one or more trade unions in relation to the employees of that undertaking, or part of it, being transferred. In such a case, where after the transfer the undertaking or part thereof retains its identity within the transferee's organisation, the transferee is bound to recognise the union or unions to the same extent as it/they were recognised by the transferor, and any collective agreements that were entered into between the transferor and the union or unions are deemed to be modified to that effect (Transfer of Undertakings (Protection of Employment) Regulations 1981, reg 9[18]).

2.41 Recognition in relation to a trade union is defined by TULRCA 1992, s 178(3) as meaning:

'... the recognition of the union by an employer, or two or more associated employers, to any extent, for the purposes of collective bargaining; and "recognised" and other related expressions shall be construed accordingly.'

2.42 Collective bargaining is defined by TULRCA 1992, s 178(2) and covers negotiations relating to or connected with:

- terms and conditions of employment, or the physical conditions in which any workers are required to work;
- engagement or non-engagement, or termination or suspension of employment or the duties of employment, of one or more workers;
- allocation of work or the duties of employment between workers or groups of workers;
- matters of discipline;
- a worker's membership or non-membership of a trade union;
- facilities for officials of trade unions; and
- machinery for negotiation or consultation, and other procedures, relating to any of the above matters, including the recognition by employers or employers' associations of the right of a trade union to represent workers in such negotiation or consultation or in the carrying out of such procedures.

2.43 Consequently, 'recognition' for the purposes of the rights provided to trade unions under TULRCA 1992 will arise where an employer or associated employers recognise one or more trade unions for one or more of these purposes.

---

[18]   SI 1981/1974.

2.44 Furthermore, since TULRCA 1992, s 244(1)(g) provides that a trade dispute can also arise out of a trade union's claim to be recognised by an employer, the effect is to allow lawful industrial action in relation to recognition-related trade disputes, an important point in the context of the statutory immunity from claims in tort against trade unions which exists in the context of industrial action (discussed at **9.7**).

2.45 As to when a trade union can be taken to have been recognised by an employer, three general propositions have emerged from case law.

Proposition 1

2.46 Recognition can be achieved by the parties either expressly or impliedly. For example, in *National Union of Tailors v Charles Ingram & Co Limited*,[19] the employer laid off a large number of staff without consulting the claimant trade union, which it would have been required to do in the event that the union was recognised (under the predecessor to what is now the right for appropriate representatives of employees to be consulted in the case of a collective redundancy under TULRCA 1992, s 188). Central to the claim by the claimant, therefore, was whether it was recognised, a point considered on appeal by the EAT, which held:[20]

> ' "Recognition" plainly, we think, implies agreement – which, of course, involves consent. That is to say it is a mutual process by which the employers recognise the union, which obviously agrees to be recognised and it may come about in a number of different ways. There may [be] a written agreement that the union should be recognised. There may be an express agreement not in writing. Or, as we think, it is sufficient if neither of those exist but the established facts are such that it can be said of them that they are clear and unequivocal and give rise to the clear inference that the employers have recognised the union. This will normally involve conduct over a period of time. Of course, the longer that state of facts has existed the easier it is in any given case to reach a conclusion that a proper interpretation of them inevitably leads to the conclusion that the employers have recognised the union.'

2.47 A further example is *National Union of Gold, Silver and Allied Trades v Albury Bros Limited*.[21] Here, the question of whether a claimant trade union was recognised arose out of a collective redundancy situation. On the facts, the claimant had broached tentatively with the employer the issue of recognition but no steps had been taken between the employer and the union to finalise relations between them. The claimant tried to argue that since tentative steps had been taken by it to discuss recognition with the employer, it was entitled to rely on what is now TULRCA 1992, s 178(3) as being recognised by the employer, since this contemplated recognition occurring 'to any extent'. The EAT, which was upheld by the Court of Appeal, held that the words 'to any extent' were used to denote recognition for a particular purpose or purposes,

---

[19] [1977] IRLR 147.
[20] [1977] IRLR 147 at 148.
[21] [1977] IRLR 173; affd [1978] IRLR 504, CA.

rather than recognition arising out of limited contact between an employer and a trade union. The Court of Appeal added that recognition to any extent:[22]

> '... entails not merely a willingness to discuss but also to negotiate in relation to one or more [of the matters set down in TULRCA 1992, s 178(2)]. That is to say, to negotiate with a view to striking a bargain upon an issue ...'

2.48   Other examples of a failure to recognise include:

- *Amalgamated Union of Engineering Workers v Sefton Engineering Co Limited*,[23] where meetings between an employer and two union representatives as workers representatives were held not to constitute recognition;
- *Transport and General Workers Union v Dyer*,[24] where one previous negotiated ending to a strike did not amount to recognition; and
- *Cleveland County Council v Springett*,[25] where courteous replies by an employer to questions raised by a trade union was held not to amount to recognition of that union.

2.49   Examples of cases in where the courts have held unions to be recognised are *National Union of Tailors v Charles Ingram & Co Limited*[26] (see **2.46**); *Union of Shop, Distributive and Allied Workers v Sketchley Limited*[27] (see **2.50**); and *Joshua Wilson & Bros Limited v Union of Shop, Distributive and Allied Workers*,[28] where the employer was found to have recognised a trade union through observing Joint Industrial Council conditions, allowing a union representative to post notice of wage changes on a notice board and allowing a union representative to collect union subscriptions whilst on the employer's premises.

Proposition 2

2.50   The second issue that arises from the cases is that once an employer is taken to have recognised a union, the employer cannot, in the absence of formal withdrawal of recognition, argue that it did not intend to recognise the union. An example of this point is *Union of Shop, Distributive and Allied Workers v Sketchley Limited*.[29] Here, a collective agreement had been entered into between the claimant union and employer, granting the claimant certain limited rights of worker recognition, check-off and other rights. Under the terms of the collective agreement, the claimant was stated not to have rights in relation to the negotiation of terms and conditions of employment and this point was reiterated to the claimant in various pieces of correspondence. In January 1980, the employer implemented a programme of redundancies and again informed the claimant in correspondence that it would not be able to take part in any negotiations relating to the redundancies. On 28 February 1980, the claimant held a meeting of its members and informed the employer that its

---

22   [1978] IRLR 504 at 506, CA.
23   [1976] IRLR 318.
24   [1977] IRLR 93.
25   [1985] IRLR 131.
26   [1977] IRLR 147.
27   [1981] IRLR 291.
28   [1978] IRLR 120.
29   [1981] IRLR 291.

members would be taking strike action unless the claimant was granted the right to represent the employees' interests. On 29 February, a written agreement was entered into allowing the claimant a right of audience in relation to the proposed redundancies. However, the employer then undertook the redundancy programme without consulting the claimant. The claimant presented proceedings for protective awards for the affected employees following the employer's failure to consult with it. The EAT held that the claimant had been recognised by the employer, holding:[30]

> 'In our view, an employer who enters into an agreement with a union relating to the terms and conditions of employment of members of their union runs a severe risk that the inference will be drawn that such an employer has recognised the union as having negotiating rights in that field.'

2.51   Practically, in order to avoid such an outcome, it is open to the parties to restrict the context of such an agreement by a clause expressly stating that a union is not recognised for the purposes of negotiating terms and conditions. However, as the *Sketchley* case[31] shows, where such a clause is contained in an agreement, it should be observed by the employer.

Proposition 3

2.52   Recognition also raises the question as to whether or not an employers' association can enter into a collective agreement binding all of its members to deal with a particular trade union or unions. This point was examined in *National Union of Gold, Silver and Allied Trades v Albury Bros Limited*,[32] where one of the issues facing the EAT was whether the employer was bound by a collective agreement that had been entered into by the North Area Goldsmiths' and Jewellers' trade section of the British Jewellers' Association. The EAT stated:[33]

> 'We do not think that the mere fact that a trade association has negotiated with a union an agreement relating to terms and conditions of employment, etc is by itself sufficient to establish that an employer who is a member of the association has, for that reason alone, recognised the union within the meaning of [what is now TULRCA 1992, s 178(3)]. Such a conclusion would seem to us to be contrary to the generally accepted meaning of recognition in industrial circles, where it is understood to postulate some kind of direct contact between the unions and the employers for the purpose of negotiating terms and conditions of employment, etc.'

2.53   Accordingly, without more, mere membership of a trade association that has signed a collective agreement with a trade union will not impose a duty to recognise that trade union upon an employer who is a member of the trade association.

---

30   [1981] IRLR 291 at 295.
31   *Union of Shop, Distributive and Allied Workers v Sketchley Limited* [1981] IRLR 291.
32   [1977] IRLR 173; affd [1978] IRLR 504.
33   [1977] IRLR 173 at 175.

Withdrawal of recognition

2.54 Save in the case of a statutory recognition agreement under TULRCA 1992, Sch A1 (see, generally, **Chapter 4**), or in the case of a collective agreement which takes effect as a legally binding contract (of which there are very few), there is no legal duty to carry on recognising a trade union pursuant to a common law collective agreement dealing with recognition between an employer and a trade union. Consequently, in such a case the employer is free to withdraw its recognition of the union as and when it chooses.

2.55 The foregoing is qualified by four points, as follows:

- first, it is good industrial relations practice to honour the terms of a collective agreement during any notice period which the employer is required to give to the union under the terms of the collective agreement;
- secondly, the employer should honour the statutory recognition rights which the union would have as a consequence of recognition during any period of notice which may have to be given to the union under the collective agreement;
- thirdly, where a collective agreement which provides for terms and conditions of employment for individual employees has been revoked, the employer is bound to honour those terms and conditions of employment to the extent that they have to be incorporated into individual employees' contracts of employment;[34] and
- finally, employers need to be aware of the practical danger of withdrawing common law recognition from a trade union – the act of withdrawing recognition may trigger a request for statutory recognition under TULRCA 1992, Sch A1 (in respect of which see, generally, **Chapter 4**).

STATUS AND LEGALITY OF TRADE UNIONS

2.56 The legal status of trade unions is dealt with under TULRCA 1992, s 10. This grants trade unions a special status as a collection of individuals who are able to do, or have done to them, a specific category of things in the collective name of the union. They are therefore effectively distinguished from both incorporated and unincorporated associations. In arriving at this unusual status, it is necessary to bear in mind the history surrounding the origins of trade unions, as follows.

2.57 Prior to the Trade Union Act 1871, trade unions were treated as just another form of unincorporated association. In this respect, if a union was to be sued or was itself to sue, it had to do so by way of a collective action. It was thought that the introduction of the Trade Union Act 1871, which had introduced the concept of registration for trade unions (see **1.17**) made no difference to this position. However, in *Taff Vale Railway Co v Amalgamated Society of Railway Servants*,[35] the House of Lords held that trade unions enjoyed a somewhat different status to ordinary unincorporated associations. The case arose out of the alleged victimisation of a member of a trade union,

---

[34] See *Robertson v British Gas Corporation* [1983] IRLR 302 and *Whent v T Cartledge Limited* [1997] IRLR 153; but, to contrary effect on its facts, see *Cadoux v Central Regional Council* [1986] IRLR 131.
[35] [1901] AC 426.

who had presented a claim for a pay rise to the employer, the same eventually resulting in a strike being called by the union. The employer hired strike-breakers to carry on its business and sought an injunction to prevent union members from harassing its members of staff who were still working. The injunction was granted against the union at first instance, but on appeal, the Court of Appeal quashed the injunction holding that, since the union did not have any legal capacity, it could not be sued. The employer appealed to the House of Lords which unanimously reinstated the injunction, albeit for different reasons. Two reasons emerged for the decision. First, it was held that proceedings against a trade union were simply an extension of a representative action and therefore it was possible to sue a union in its own name. Secondly, two of the Law Lords held that upon registering under the Trade Union Act 1871, the consequence was to create a quasi-corporate body whose status could be lost upon de-registration.[36]

2.58 Whatever the position, it was at last possible to sue not only the individual members of a trade union but also the trade union itself with the consequence that, between 1901 and 1906 (when the Trade Disputes Act 1906 was commenced), trade union funds were open to attack when enforcing judgments against unions for their tortious conduct during industrial action. Following the commencement of the Trade Disputes Act 1906, this remained the position until the commencement of IRA 1971. One of the central themes of IRA 1971 was formal registration of trade unions in order for them to receive rights. The effect of such registration was to confer corporate status on trade unions so registering. Unions that chose not to register were treated as unincorporated associations (although having some benefits of corporate status). IRA 1971 was repealed and replaced by TULRA 1974 which created the current position (consolidated under TULRCA 1992, s 10), this being that trade unions are not to be treated as bodies corporate, save that they can do the following things in their own name:

- make contracts;
- sue or be sued in proceedings relating to property, founded on tort or contract or any other cause of action; and
- bring or have brought against them proceedings for a criminal offence alleged to have been committed by them, or in their name.

2.59 The current position has therefore moved away from the position postulated by the House of Lords in the *Taff Vale* case:[37] it ties in with neither of the two theories previously espoused in that case in that TULRCA 1992, s 10 now expressly states that trade unions are not bodies corporate. Further, it is not strictly correct to talk in terms of an action brought or taken being representative since trade unions directly benefit or suffer from such proceedings.

---

[36] See though the case of *Lawlor v Union of Post Office Workers* [1965] Ch 712 where an unregistered union was sued in its own name.

[37] *Taff Vale Railway Co v Amalgamated Society of Railway Servants* [1901] AC 426.

Particular points relating to actions by or against trade unions

Matters arising in tort

2.60   In *News Group Newspapers Limited v SOGAT 82 and others*,[38] injunctions were sought against branches of the first defendant union and another union for torts committed in the course of the *Times* newspaper Wapping industrial dispute. The employer alleged that the litigation ought to take the form of a representative action since a dispute existed as to whether the local branches of the defendant unions were, in fact, trade unions in their own right under the definition in TULRCA 1992, s 1. The High Court, whilst accepting that a representative action could be maintained in an appropriate case, held, on the facts, that a representative action was inappropriate since the members of the unions clearly had divergent views from those of the unions of which they were members. As to the problems that can arise with representative action when dealing with a large class of members, the High Court held:[39]

> 'Only a small proportion of any one branch are directly involved in the dispute. Some of those who are will have taken an active part in the commission of torts, others may have disapproved and condemned such conduct in their colleagues. Of those who are not directly involved some may approve or authorise such tortious action on the part of the branch committee, which pending a delegate meeting of the branch is empowered to act for the branch, others may not; even on the committee itself opinion and action may be divided.'

2.61   Consequently the representative action was dismissed. Further, in most cases the appropriate method of commencing proceedings by, or against, a trade union will be for the union to sue, or be sued, in its own name.[40]

Trade unions and defamation

2.62   The second problem that arises in the context of trade unions in the context of proceedings in the law of tort is the question of whether a trade union can sue for defamation. The most recent case directly on point is *Electrical, Electronic, Telecommunications and Plumbing Union v Times Newspapers Limited*.[41] The case concerned an allegedly libellous article published by the defendant in November 1977. A preliminary issue was raised in the proceedings, this being whether, under TULRA 1974, a trade union could have a personality capable of being defamed. The matter was heard in the High Court which held that, since TULRA 1974 stated that trade unions were not to be treated as bodies corporate, they were to be treated differently to previous decisions on the point (notably *National Union of General and Municipal Workers v Gillian*,[42] which relied on the concept of trade union status derived from the *Taff Vale Railway* case[43] under the Trade Union Act 1871, namely that unions were quasi-corporate bodies and therefore could have personalities).

---

38   [1986] IRLR 337.
39   [1986] IRLR 337 at 354.
40   This principle has been confirmed by the High Court in *Gate Gourmet Limited v Transport and General Workers Union and others* [2005] EWHC 1889.
41   [1980] QB 585.
42   [1946] KB 81.
43   *Taff Vale Railway Co v Amalgamated Society of Railway Servants* [1901] AC 426.

Accordingly, the High Court held that since trade unions were unincorporated associations with certain rights to sue or be sued, they did not have legal personalities beyond this and they could not be sued for defamation in relation to a non-existent personality. The High Court further held that it would not be possible to use a representative action to further the claims of union members either since each member would have different interests in the outcome of the case if damages were recovered.

2.63   It is submitted that the decision in the *Times Newspapers* case[44] is flawed in a number of respects. First, the issue of legal personality distinct from membership was not addressed by the House of Lords in the *Taff Vale* case[45] in either of its formulations of the legal status of trade unions: their Lordships treated trade unions in that case as juridical persons at best. If this is so, the law did not change from that as decided in *Taff Vale* following TULRA 1974 (as now consolidated in TULRCA 1992).

2.64   Secondly, although the court in the *Times Newspapers* case[46] dealt with the issue of whether trade unions' interests are representative of the interests of their members in the case of a representative action, by refusing to accept that this is so (on the grounds that, individually, each member of a trade union may have a different interest in the outcome of proceedings and therefore the use of a collective action is inappropriate in such cases), the High Court did not go on to consider whether a collective reputation could be damaged: indeed, it has long been held that it is possible to damage a collective reputation, for example, in the case of partnerships.[47]

2.65   Thirdly, in *Derbyshire County Council v Times Newspapers Limited*,[48] the House of Lords appear to have accepted, albeit obiter dicta, that a trade union can be defamed. The case dealt with a libel action brought against a local authority. In the course of submissions, their Lordships were referred to the *Gillian* case[49] in the course of proceedings (although, regrettably, not the *EETPU* case[50]), with Lord Keith, stating of trade union defamation cases that they:[51]

> '... are understandable upon the view that defamatory matter may adversely affect the union's ability to keep its members or attract new ones or maintain a convincing attitude towards employers.'

2.66   On this basis whilst the *EETPU* case[52] is directly decided on the basis of defamation, it seems that there may yet be some mileage left in trade unions arguing that they can be defamed.

---

[44]   *Electrical, Electronic, Telecommunications and Plumbing Union v Times Newspapers Limited* [1980] QB 585.

[45]   *Taff Vale Railway Co v Amalgamated Society of Railway Servants* [1901] AC 426.

[46]   *Electrical, Electronic, Telecommunications and Plumbing Union v Times Newspapers Limited* [1980] QB 585.

[47]   See, for example, *Cook v Batchelor* (1802) 3 Bos & Pul 150.

[48]   [1993] AC 534.

[49]   *National Union of General and Municipal Workers v Gillian* [1946] KB 81.

[50]   *Electrical, Electronic, Telecommunications and Plumbing Union v Times Newspapers Limited* [1980] QB 585.

[51]   [1993] AC 534 at 547.

[52]   *Electrical, Electronic, Telecommunications and Plumbing Union v Times Newspapers Limited* [1980] QB 585.

Criminal proceedings

2.67 TULRCA 1992, s 10(1)(c) allows criminal proceedings to be issued by, or against, a trade union. Since (as stated at **2.59**) trade unions have no legal personality beyond that prescribed under TULRCA 1992, the qualification is required because unincorporated associations are otherwise treated as being a collection of their members, and therefore without more, a trade union would not be able to prosecute or be prosecuted.

SPECIAL REGISTER BODIES

2.68 Special Register bodies are carried over from IRA 1971, ss 84–86. The Special Register was created to allow professional bodies who, as a minor part of their functions, entered into collective agreements for their members with employers or employers' associations. IRA 1971 allowed those bodies powers to register so as to gain the benefits of registration without raising the question of whether such bodies were trade unions. The Special Register was closed when registration under IRA 1971 was abolished under TULRA 1974. However, provision was made for bodies that had registered to stay on the Special Register. Very few such bodies now remain and those that do must be either registered under the Companies Act 1985 or have been granted letters patent or a charter (TULRCA 1992, s 117). Special Register bodies are bodies corporate.

LEGALITY OF TRADE UNIONS

2.69 From their inception, trade unions were treated as being illegal due to their purposes being contrary to public policy in that they act in restraint of trade (the restraint of trade arising as a result of trade union members divesting themselves of their ability individually to negotiate their own terms and conditions of employment[53]). The consequences of the restraint of trade doctrine were removed by the Trade Union Act 1871, ss 2–3. However, following the commencement of the Trade Union Act 1871, the restraint of trade doctrine was still to play an important part in the history of trade unions. This was due to the Trade Union Act 1871, s 4, which made trade union rules unenforceable before the courts.

2.70 The reasoning behind the Trade Union Act 1871, s 4 was that whilst Parliament was happy for trade unions to exist for the benefit of their members, it was felt that it would be wrong if a trade union could rely on its rulebook to create a binding contract between itself and a member which it could then enforce through the courts by means, for example, of an injunction, so as to force a strike. As a result, the courts initially took the view that they would not enforce rulebook provisions.[54]

2.71 However, other areas of the law had shown that not all restraint of trade was, per se, unlawful. For example, in *Nordenfelt v Maxim Nordenfelt Guns and*

---

[53] Per *Hornby v Close* (1867) LR 2 QB 153.
[54] See, for example, *Russell v Amalgamated Society of Carpenters and Joiners* [1912] AC 42, where a union member's widow tried to enforce a requirement in the defendant's rules in order to receive a provident benefit and the House of Lords held that where some of the rules of the union were in restraint of trade, the rules that were not could not be severed.

Ammunition Co Limited,[55] the House of Lords had held that whilst, as a general principle, restraint of trade was prima facie unlawful, reasonable restraint of trade could be justified under the common law. This view ultimately filtered through into trade union cases when the courts came to consider trade union rulebook disputes. What the courts did was to ask whether a trade union itself was acting in restraint of trade at common law. If the union was not so acting, the Trade Union Act 1871, s 4 was not necessary to legalise the union's conduct and it was therefore possible to enforce the union's rulebook in any dispute arising out of it. This much appeared to be beyond dispute after *Osbourne v Amalgamated Society of Railway Servants*[56] and *Amalgamated Society of Carpenters and Joiners v Braithwaite*.[57] Ultimately, however the Trade Disputes Act 1871, s 4 was repealed by IRA 1971.

2.72   The modern position in this regard is now set out in TULRCA 1992, s 11(1)–(2) which provides that the purposes and rules of a trade union are not to be treated as unenforceable or unlawful merely because they are in restraint of trade.

2.73   It is worth noting though that the courts are still prepared to use the doctrine of restraint of trade in an appropriate case. For example, in *Bodding-ton v Lawton*,[58] members of the Prison Officers Association sought a declaration that they were allowed to use funds of the Association to pay towards the defence of members being sued for trespass, false imprisonment and breach of duty. The claims arose as a result of industrial action taken by the Association which had resulted in patients at a mental hospital being locked in their rooms for longer than usual. In an earlier case involving the Association, it had been held that the Association could not engage in a trade dispute. This arose due to the fact that prison officers are not 'workers' under the definition in TULRCA 1992, s 296; rather they are officeholders.[59] It was held in *Boddington* that the rules of the Association were in restraint of trade and therefore constituted an unlawful contract. When faced with the argument that, due to evolution over a period of years, the rules of a trade union were in the public interest, the High Court rejected it and held that cases such as *Hornby v Close*[60] and *Goring v British Actors Equity Association*[61] had held union rulebooks to be in restraint of trade and that:[62]

> 'It would be most undesirable for judges now to hold that, to reflect changes in social conditions, the common law in this field has developed and is now to the contrary effect of what has been established and acted on for so many years.'

2.74   The court went on to hold that since the Association's rules were unenforceable as a contract in any event, it did not matter if the trustees carried on funding the defences of the members who were being sued.

---

55   [1894] AC 535.
56   [1911] 1 Ch 540.
57   [1921] 2 AC 440.
58   [1994] ICR 478.
59   *Home Office v Evans* (unreported) 18 November 1993.
60   (1867) LR 2 QB 153.
61   [1987] IRLR 122.
62   [1994] ICR 478 at 487.

2.75 Ultimately, it would appear that, at common law, trade unions may be taken to act in restraint of trade, but the problems created by the common law can, in the case of enforcing trade union rulebook disputes, to some extent be avoided by TULRCA 1992, s 11.

EMPLOYERS' ASSOCIATIONS

2.76 Employers' associations were created to perform a fundamentally different role to that of trade unions. Whereas trade unions were created to provide collective bargaining and representation power for workers, employers have always been holders of collective power in the form of capital. Employers' associations evolved after the First World War into bodies that took part in national level collective bargaining, but when national level bargaining broke down as the predominant method of negotiating terms and conditions of employment in the 1960s, the role of employers' associations changed to providing knowledge and expertise in dealing with unions to small businesses. The role of employers' associations has continued to decline and in the modern era they tend to act so as to:

- provide advice and consultancy services to their members;
- lobby politically on behalf of their members; and
- represent members' interests at a national and international level.

Definition and status of employers' associations

2.77 Employers' associations are regulated under TULRCA 1992, Part II. An employers' association is defined by TULRCA 1992, s 122(1) as to be:

'... an organisation (whether temporary or permanent)—

(a) which consists wholly or mainly of employers or individual owners of undertakings of one or more descriptions and whose principle purposes include the regulation of relations between employers of that description or those descriptions and workers or trade unions; or

(b) which consists wholly or mainly of—
(i) constituent or affiliated organisations which fulfil the conditions in paragraph (a) (or themselves consist wholly or mainly of constituent or affiliated organisations which fulfil those conditions) or
(ii) representatives of such constituent or affiliated organisations,

and whose principal purposes include the regulation of relations between employers and workers or between employers and trade unions, or the regulation of relations between its constituent or affiliated organisations.'

2.78 The definition in TULRCA 1992, s 122 shows that an employers' association must fulfil two criteria, these being as to membership and purpose.

Membership

2.79 One of three types of membership is available to an employers' association, these being employers or individual proprietors; constituent or affiliated organisations which are themselves employers' associations; or representatives of constituent or affiliated organisations which are themselves employers' associations.

2.80   In order to rank as an employers' association, as one of its principal purposes the body has to carry out the regulation of relations between either employers and workers or trade unions, or, in the case of organisations consisting of constituent or affiliated organisations, regulation between the constituent or affiliated members.

2.81   When looking at whether a body regulates relations between employers and workers, it has to be considered whether the association is responsible to the members for these purposes. In *Greig v Insole*,[63] the defendant was a member of the Committee of the Test and County Cricket Board (TCCB), which had denied the claimant the right to work in the United Kingdom as a professional cricketer as a result of his taking part in the infamous Kerry Packer 'Cricket Circus'. The TCCB claimed that it was immune from action in tort as it was an employers' association (this was a possible defence at the time under TULRA 1974). The High Court held that the TCCB was an association comprising employers, but it was not accountable to its members in relation to the way it carried out regulation of working conditions; instead it was accountable to the International Cricket Council. Further, since it had power to prevent employment arising in the first place, the court doubted whether such rules could fall within the requirement of regulating relations between workers and employers. Consequently, the court held that the TCCB was not an employers' association and therefore could not be sued as such.

2.82   Unlike trade unions, under TULRCA 1992, s 127(1), employers' associations can be either incorporated or unincorporated bodies. Further, where such an association is unincorporated, it has the same rights and obligations as a trade union in relation to matters arising in contract, tort, property and the bringing of proceedings for an offence in its name (TULRCA 1992, s 127(2)).

Listing of employers' associations

2.83   As with trade unions, it is possible for an employers' association to be included on the list of employers' associations maintained by the Certification Officer ('listing'). The mechanics of listing are dealt with under TULRCA 1992, ss 123–126. The associations entitled to be listed are those satisfying the definition of an employers' association in TULRCA 1992, s 122 together with associations which were listed under the provisions of TULRA 1974 (per TULRCA 1992, s 123(1)). The list, as with the list of trade unions, is a public document and can be inspected by anyone at all reasonable hours free of charge (TULRCA 1992, s 123(2)).

2.84   The effect of an employers' association being listed is that it provides proof that the association is an employers' association and a certificate can be issued to the association to this effect which can be admitted in evidence where the matter is in dispute (TULRCA 1992, s 123(4)). The Certification Officer is bound to attach a copy of the list of employers' associations to his annual report (TULRCA 1992, s 123(3)).

The listing process

2.85   The process of listing is dealt with by TULRCA 1992, s 124. Any employers' association, whenever formed, which is not included on the list

---

[63]   [1978] 1 WLR 302.

compiled by the Certification Officer is entitled to apply for listing (TULRCA 1992, s 124(1)). Applications to be listed should be in the form specified by the Certification Officer from time to time. As a minimum under TULRCA 1992, s 124(2), the Certification Officer must require that an employers' association applying to be listed supplies:

- a copy of the rules of the association;
- a list of the association's officers;
- the address of the main or head office;
- the name by which the association is known; and
- the prescribed fee set by statutory instrument from time to time.

2.86 When an employers' association supplies the information and fee required for it to be listed, the Certification Officer, provided that he is satisfied that the organisation is an employers' association and entry on the list is not prohibited by reason of the association having the same or a similar name to a body registered under either the Trade Union Acts 1871–1964, IRA 1971 or currently listed under TULRCA 1992, must list the association (TULRCA 1992, s 124(3)).

Removal of an employers' association from the list

2.87 As with trade unions, it is possible for the Certification Officer to remove an employers' association from the list. This can occur where either the Certification Officer is satisfied that the association does not satisfy the statutory definition of an employers' association, or where the Certification Officer is either requested by the association to remove it from the list, or is satisfied that the association no longer exists (TULRCA 1992, s 125(1) and (3)). If the reason for removal from the list is that the Certification Officer believes that the association is not an employers' association, he must give the body at least 28 days' notice of his decision to remove the association from the list and consider any representations made by the association within that period (TULRCA 1992, s 125(2)).

Appeals against decisions of the Certification Officer

2.88 Employers' associations are entitled to appeal to the EAT against decisions of the Certification Officer to remove them from the list (TULRCA 1992, s 126(1)). Appeals may be made in relation to questions of law only (TULRCA 1992, s 126(1) and (3)).

2.89 If the EAT is satisfied that an association either is an employers' association or should remain on the list, the EAT must declare accordingly and order the Certification Officer to take such steps as are necessary to ensure that the association is reinstated on the list or remains on the list, as appropriate (TULRCA 1992, s 126(2)).

The advantages of listing

2.90 A number of advantages from being listed arise under TULRCA 1992 for an employers' association. First, there is the simple procedure for vesting of property in the trustees of an employers' association. The procedure is the same as for trade unions and regard should be had to **2.20** in relation to this procedure.

2.91   Employers' associations gain two other advantages as a result of being listed. First, under TULRCA 1992, s 129(3), benefits accrue under the Friendly Societies Acts in relation to insurance on the lives of children under 10 and also in relation to charitable subscriptions and contributions to other registered societies.

2.92   Secondly, under TULRCA 1992, s 130, to the extent that judgment is awarded against an employers' association, the members, trustees and officials of the association are not liable to satisfy the judgment out of their own assets, even if the association is unincorporated (TULRCA 1992, s 130). Unlike trade unions, since changes made by the Employment Act 1982, employers' associations have had no immunity in tort whatsoever.

Administrative obligations of employers' associations

2.93   Employers' associations are subject to a number of administrative obligations. These are the same as would apply to a trade union and TULRCA 1992 makes reference to the provisions applying in like manner. The provisions imposed under TULRCA 1992, s 131 are the following:

- the duty to supply copies of their rules to any person (TULRCA 1992, s 27);
- the duty to keep accounting records (TULRCA 1992, s 28);
- the duties in respect of annual accounts, returns and audits (TULRCA 1992, ss 32(1), (2), (3)(a)–(c), (4)–(6) and 33–37);
- the investigation of financial affairs (TULRCA 1992, ss 37A–37E);
- matters relating to members' superannuation schemes (TULRCA 1992, ss 38–42);
- the exemption in relation to certain reporting obligations for newly formed associations (TULRCA 1992, s 43(1));
- the discharge of duties in the case of an association having branches or sections (TULRCA 1992, s 44(1), (2) and (4)); and
- the offences in relation to non-compliance with the administrative provisions under TULRCA 1992 (TULRCA 1992, ss 45 and 45A)).

2.94   Employers' associations incorporated under the Companies Act 1985 do not have to comply with TULRCA 1992, ss 33–35 in relation to the appointment of auditors (since auditors have to be appointed under the Companies Act) but TULRCA 1992, ss 36 and 37 apply as to the rights and duties of the auditors.

2.95   Where an employers' association is made up wholly or mainly of constituent or affiliated organisations or representatives thereof (a federated employers' association (TULRCA 1992, s 135(1)), the matters in the first five list points in **2.93** do not apply (TULRCA 1992, s 135(1)–(3)).

2.96   Finally, in relation to the administration of employers' associations, unlike trade unions, they do not have to disclose in their annual return details of the salaries and benefits paid to their officers (as defined in TULRCA 1992, s 136) and neither are they caught by increased disclosure provisions relating to accounts introduced under the Employment Act 1988.

Political objects of employers' associations

2.97   Employers' associations are entitled to have political objects and to the extent that they do they are bound by the same rules as trade unions in relation to such matters as balloting (per TULRCA 1992, s 132), in respect of which see **6.95** et seq.

2.98   If an employers' association is a federated association and has voted not to operate a political fund, there is nothing to prevent a component association from collecting contributions towards a political fund from such of its members as are not exempt from contributing to the fund (TULRCA 1992, s 135(4)).

Amalgamations and changes of name

2.99   An unincorporated employers' association is able to merge with another association in the same way that unions are capable of merging and the rules on mergers are drafted in similar terms to the provisions relating to trade unions (see **11.24** et seq). The rules in this regard are provided under TULRCA 1992, s 133 (although some minor changes to the rules exist in relation to the balloting provisions under TULRCA 1992, s 133(2)).

2.100   Changing the name of an employers' association is dealt with in TULRCA 1992, s 134. In the first instance, the association must either have a name-changing provision in its rules or must use the association's rules to procure a power to change the name of the association (TULRCA 1992, s 134(1)). A change of name cannot take effect in the case of either an incorporated or unincorporated association until such time as the Certification Officer is notified of the change (TULRCA 1992, s 134(2)). The Certification Officer has a power to refuse a name change where it is the case that the association is proposing to adopt a name that is the same or similar to either an existing employers' association or trade union (TULRCA 1992, s 134(3)). A change of name does not affect any existing legal liability of an unincorporated association (TULRCA 1992, s 134(4)).

Chapter 3

RIGHTS OF RECOGNISED TRADE UNIONS

3.1 Trade unions are provided with certain legally protected rights under various pieces of legislation, as follows:

- to have relevant information disclosed to facilitate collective bargaining;
- to be consulted in respect of large-scale redundancies;
- to be consulted in relation to a transfer of an undertaking;
- to be consulted in respect of health and safety matters;
- to be recognised in respect of negotiations for pay, hours and holiday in relation to certain bargaining units (dealt with in **Chapter 4**); and
- to be consulted in the case of a trade union representing workers of a public authority where a previous practice of consultation exists.

3.2 Rights and obligations in respect of trade unions can also arise by way of collective agreements between an employer or employers and one or more trade unions. Each will be examined in turn.

THE RIGHT TO INFORMATION FOR COLLECTIVE BARGAINING PURPOSES

3.3 The duty to provide information to a trade union recognised for the purpose of collective bargaining was introduced by the Employment Protection Act 1975 (EPA 1975, s 17) and is now consolidated as the Trade Union and Labour Relations (Consolidation) Act 1992 (TULRCA 1992), Chapter 1, Part IV.

3.4 The aim of the legislation is to provide a level playing field in collective bargaining. However, a trade union cannot claim unlimited information from an employer under TULRCA 1992, Chapter 1, Part IV.

3.5 When the duty was originally enacted under EPA 1975, it was possible for all independent trade unions to enforce the right to be given collective bargaining information by means of a statutory mechanism established by EPA 1975, ss 11–16 which provided a duty to recognise independent trade unions. Once recognition was granted to a trade union, an employer was bound to provide the types of information required under EPA 1975, s 17. In 1977, the Advisory, Conciliation and Arbitration Service (ACAS) issued a Code of Practice on the Disclosure of Bargaining Information which dealt with the type of information that should be disclosed to recognised trade unions in collective bargaining situations (see **3.15** with regard to this Code of Practice generally).

3.6   The duty to recognise trade unions was repealed by the Employment Act 1980 but upon coming to power in 1997, the current Government introduced proposals (now enacted as TULRCA 1992, Sch A1), which impose a duty on an employer to recognise an independent trade union (usually where, following a ballot, a specified proportion of workers within a bargaining unit and the majority of those voting are in favour of recognition as shown by that ballot, unless there is a proven majority of workers within the bargaining unit who are in favour of recognition, in which case recognition is afforded automatically). These procedures are dealt with fully in **Chapter 4**.

3.7   Whilst the duty to provide information to an independent recognised union under TULRCA 1992, s 181 et seq still exists, it can be circumvented relatively easily by an employer failing either initially to recognise, or subsequently de-recognising, a trade union (although as regards a trade union that is currently recognised, an employer cannot escape an existing duty to provide information simply by saying that it no longer recognises that trade union). An act of derecognition will only apply to future duties to disclose collective bargaining information.[1]

3.8   The duty to disclose collective bargaining information is available to both Crown staff (TULRCA 1992, s 273) and parliamentary staff (TULRCA 1992, ss 278–279), although the right to enforce the duty is not available to either group (TULRCA 1992, ss 184–185).

The general duty of disclosure

3.9   The duty to disclose collective bargaining information is contained in TULRCA 1992, s 181 which provides that an employer shall disclose, on the request of representatives of an independent trade union recognised by the employer, the information required thereunder. The duty arises at all stages of the collective bargaining process. Requests to an employer for information must be in writing (TULRCA 1992, s 181(3)). An employer is only bound to disclose information within its possession or within the possession of an associated employer (TULRCA 1992, s 181(2)).[2]

3.10   Whilst TULRCA 1992, s 181 states that collective bargaining information should be provided to a recognised trade union upon request by the union, it does not provide a time-limit for an employer to comply with the request and, theoretically, there is nothing to stop an unscrupulous employer from withholding information until such time as it suits the employer to disclose up to the point where a union presents a claim to the Central Arbitration Committee (CAC).

3.11   The types of collective bargaining information to be disclosed to a recognised independent trade union are dealt with at TULRCA 1992, s 181(2) which creates a conjunctive two-limb test, as follows.

---

[1]   See, for example, Selfridges Limited and the Manufacturing Science Finance Union (CAC Award 91/1); and Ackrill Newspapers Limited and the National Union of Journalists (CAC Award 92/1).

[2]   For the definition of 'associated employer', see TULRCA 1992, s 297. See also *Ayrshire Bus Owners (A1 Service) Limited and the Transport and General Workers Union* (CAC Award 91/2) in this regard.

Limb 1 – Material disadvantage

3.12 The first limb focuses on the level playing field ideal and requires consideration of whether a recognised trade union would be impeded to a material extent if the requested information was not supplied to the union (TULRCA 1992, s 181(2)(a)). In addressing this limb of the test, the CAC has stated that what must be looked at is whether a trade union would be hampered generally without provision of a particular type of information rather than whether a failure to provide specific information will be harmful in a particular instance of collective bargaining.[3] Thus, TULRCA 1992, s 181(2) looks to the general nature of the information sought and addresses the question of whether the union will be able to prepare to bargain adequately.

3.13 It has been argued in *BL Cars Limited, MG Abingdon Plant and the General and Municipal Workers Union and the Transport and General Workers Union* that if an employer refuses to take part in collective bargaining with an independent trade union which it has recognised then the union cannot be materially disadvantaged as a result of the employer failing to provide information to the union since there are no negotiations in which to use that information.[4] In the *BL Cars* case,[5] the CAC agreed that the failure of the employer to consult with the trade union deprived the union of the statutory right to receive collective bargaining information and the union therefore was not entitled to the information claimed.

3.14 However, the position was revisited in *BP Chemicals and the Transport and General Workers Union*.[6] Here, the employer and union were in disagreement over the provision of information relating to the employer's pension scheme. The employer argued before the CAC that it was not bound to disclose the requested information since even if it did disclose the information it would not negotiate over it. On the evidence before it, the CAC ordered disclosure. It held that the employer had recognised the union for the purposes of negotiation over pensions and since the information related to pensions, the union was entitled to that information. In short, the provision of the collective bargaining information did not relate to a discretion of management (which the CAC stressed was the point of the *BL Cars* case,[7] which related to a factory closure, a matter entirely within management discretion).

Limb 2 – Good industrial relations practice

3.15 The second limb of the test requires a consideration of whether it would be in the context of good industrial relations generally to release the requested information. In considering this issue, ACAS has issued Code of Practice No 2, *Disclosure of Information to Trade Unions for Collective Bargaining Purposes* (2003) (the Code of Practice on Disclosure), which can be used as evidence of what is good practice, but is expressly stated not to be conclusive evidence

---

[3]   See Daily Telegraph Limited and the Institute of Journalists (CAC Award 78/353); Beecham Group Limited and the Association of Scientific, Managerial and Technical Staffs (CAC Award 79/337); and BP Chemicals and the Transport and General Workers Union (CAC Award 86/1).

[4]   CAC Award 80/65.

[5]   See **n 4**.

[6]   CAC Award 86/1.

[7]   See **n 4**.

(TULRCA 1992, s 181(4)). ACAS has also published an advisory booklet, 'Employee Communications and Consultation' (2005), which provides practical guidance to employers in relation to the issue of consultation.

3.16   The Code of Practice on Disclosure, at para 11, provides some examples of the types of information that should be disclosed. Paragraph 11 starts with a general caveat stating:

'Collective bargaining within an undertaking can range from negotiations on specific matters arising daily at the workplace affecting particular sections of the workforce, to extensive periodic negotiations on terms and conditions of employment affecting the whole workforce in multiplant companies ... Consequently, it is not possible to compile a list of items that should be disclosed in all circumstances.'

3.17   Paragraph 11 then goes on to list certain types of information that it is generally considered good practice to disclose, these being:

- information in relation to pay and benefits;
- conditions of service;
- manpower resources;
- performance of the undertaking; and
- finance of an undertaking.

Paragraph 12 of the Code of Practice on Disclosure states that the requirements are not exhaustive.

3.18   Although TULRCA 1992, s 181(2)(b) talks in objective terms by referring to 'good industrial relations practice', if a dispute arises as to what amounts to good practice in a particular case, it is desirable that evidence should be provided in support. Provided that the evidence is relevant, it is possible to adduce evidence as to what is considered to be good industrial relations practice at other firms or in other industries.[8] For cases where it has been decided that no duty to disclose collective bargaining information exists, see *Daily Telegraph Limited and the Institute of Journalists*[9] and *Standard Telephone and Cables Limited and the Association of Scientific, Technical and Managerial Staffs.*[10]

Exceptions to the duty to disclose

3.19   Whilst TULRCA 1992, s 181 creates a general duty to disclose collective bargaining information to independent recognised trade unions, the duty can be avoided under TULRCA 1992, s 182(1) which provides six categories of cases where disclosure will not be ordered against an employer, as follows:

- Where it would not be in the interests of national security to disclose information. It is possible for a Minister of the Crown or a person acting on his behalf to certify that the disclosure of information would be

8   For examples of the types of information, see Tyne and Wear Passenger Transport Executive and the General Municipal Workers Union (CAC Award 82/10); and BP Chemicals and the Transport and General Workers Union (CAC Award 86/1).
9   CAC Award 78/353.
10   CAC Award 79/484.

prejudicial to national security. Further, if such a Certificate is provided, it is conclusive proof of its contents (TULRCA 1992, s 183(6)).

- Where disclosure would contravene an enactment.
- Where the information requested was originally disclosed to an employer in confidence and, therefore, to disclose the same would amount to a breach of confidence by the employer. It should be noted that an employer cannot simply claim that information is confidential and therefore be immune from disclosure. However, if information is provided to the employer from a third party, there seems to be nothing to stop the employer from requesting that the person passing the information to the employer passes it on the understanding that the employer has a duty to keep the information confidential.[11]
- Where the information specifically relates to an individual. Whilst it is the case that a union is prevented from making inquiries about named individuals, it is entitled to information relating to particular posts. It used to follow that if only one person occupied such a post, the union would be entitled to the information notwithstanding that it relates clearly to that person occupying the post.[12] However, this position needs to be considered in the light of the Data Protection Act 1998 (DPA 1998), which, subject to the exceptions under DPA 1998, would prevent an employer, as a data controller, disclosing personal data about an individual data subject if the data subject could be identified from that data or that and other data. Arguably, the exception that would apply here is in DPA 1998, Sch 2, para 3 which allows data to be processed where it is necessary due to the data controller being subject to a legal obligation other than a contract (this being TULRCA 1992, s 181).
- Where disclosure of the requested information would cause substantial harm to an undertaking other than any effect which might arise through collective bargaining. As regards this head, the CAC has been willing to take a pragmatic view as to what will cause substantial harm. This is reflected in the fact that disclosure orders which have been granted show that the CAC will often allow some, but not all, of the information requested by a union to be disclosed in an appropriate case. Sensitive information is information that is objectively sensitive, not information that is claimed to be sensitive by the employer.[13]
- Where the information has been obtained by the employer for bringing, prosecuting or defending any legal action.

---

[11] See Joint Credit Card Co Limited and the National Union of Bank Employees (CAC Award 78/212); Ministry of Defence and the Civil Service Union (CAC Award 80/73); and Seifert Sedley & Co and Association of Scientific, Technical and Managerial Staffs (CAC Award 80/152).

[12] See University of Lancaster and the Association of University Teachers (CAC Award 79/300); British Aerospace, Dynamics Group, Space and Communications Division, Site B, and the Association of Professional, Executive, Clerical and Computer Staff (CAC Award 80/69); and Chloride Legg Limited and the Association of Clerical, Technical and Supervisory Staffs (CAC Award 84/15).

[13] See *Hoover Limited and the General and Municipal Workers' Union* (CAC Award 79/507), a claim that unit cost and unit price information was sensitive if it fell into the hands of a competitor. The CAC took the view that certain categories of information relating to manufacturing cost, budgeted expenditure and the basis for budget forecasts should not be disclosed.

Complaints of failure to disclose

3.20   To the extent that an employer fails to comply with the duty to disclose collective bargaining information, a trade union can present a complaint under the procedure set out in TULRCA 1992, s 183. A complaint lies to the CAC and may be presented where an employer either fails to disclose the information requested (TULRCA 1992, s 183(1)(a)), or fails to confirm information that has been communicated in writing (TULRCA 1992, s 183(1)(b)).

3.21   Upon receipt of a claim, the CAC is required to consider whether it thinks that the complaint could be disposed of by way of a conciliated settlement. If the CAC believes this is likely, it is bound to refer the matter to ACAS and to notify the union and employer of the referral (TULRCA 1992, s 183(2)). It is then the duty of ACAS to resolve the dispute. If, after a referral to ACAS, the complaint cannot be resolved, ACAS is required to inform the CAC of this fact (TULRCA 1992, s 183(2)).

3.22   In the event that a complaint is either not referred to ACAS or ACAS decides that a case that has been referred cannot be dealt with by conciliation, then the CAC must proceed to hear and determine the complaint and make a declaration after hearing the case stating whether or not the complaint is well founded. A decision can be wholly or partly favourable to a claimant union (TULRCA 1992, s 183(3)).[14]

3.23   In the course of proceedings before it, the CAC is entitled to hear evidence from anyone other than a trade union or employer who has an interest in the outcome of the proceedings. TULRCA 1992, s 183(4) adds that, to the extent that an interested third party is not heard in the proceedings, the validity of the proceedings is not affected.

3.24   In the event of deciding in favour of a trade union, TULRCA 1992, s 183(5) requires that the CAC's declaration must specify the following matters:

● What information it has been found necessary to disclose.
● The date on which the employer either refused to supply the requested information or refused to confirm the information in writing.
● A period of time within which the employer is bound to make good its failure to supply or to confirm the information. In specifying a time-limit, the CAC must allow a period of at least one week from the date of the declaration.

3.25   The CAC cannot specify what matters it thinks ought to be disclosed in the future as between the parties and, to the extent that it tries to do so, it can be judicially reviewed.[15]

Enforcing a declaration

3.26   Where an employer fails to comply with the terms of a CAC declaration within the time specified for compliance, a trade union is able to present a further complaint to the CAC under TULRCA 1992, s 184(1). As with the initial complaint, the further complaint must be in writing in such form as the

---

[14]   See Hoover Limited and the General and Municipal Workers' Union (CAC Award 79/507).
[15]   See, for example, *R v Central Arbitration Committee, ex p BTP Trioxide Limited* [1981] ICR 843.

CAC determines. Upon receiving the subsequent complaint, the CAC is bound to hear the claim and determine whether it finds the complaint well founded, whether wholly or in part (TULRCA 1992, s 184(2)). The CAC is again entitled to hear evidence from anyone it thinks has a legitimate right to be heard in a dispute. As with the initial complaint, a failure to allow a non-party to be heard does not affect the validity of the proceedings (TULRCA 1992, s 184(3)). To the extent that the CAC finds wholly or partly for a claimant union, a declaration is required to this effect.

3.27 As the purpose of collective bargaining information to be disclosed is usually to negotiate terms and conditions for employees, after a declaration has been granted, it is possible for a trade union in whose favour a declaration has been granted to request in writing from the CAC an order that one or more employees (but not workers) have the terms and conditions of their contracts of employment modified in the form of the request made by the trade union (TULRCA 1992, s 185(1)). If the employer discloses or confirms in writing the information requested by the union, the right to modified terms and conditions is lost. Any claim that has been presented by a union is treated as being withdrawn where the information is supplied at any time prior to the CAC determining the claim (TULRCA 1992, s 185(2)).

3.28 If the CAC does not consider the terms and conditions claimed in any such application to be appropriate, it may substitute its own terms and conditions in an order. A Terms and Conditions Order can be expressed to take effect at any point in time back to the date of the original complaint giving rise to the Terms and Conditions Order (TULRCA 1992, s 185(3)). Terms and conditions of employment so modified take place as implied terms of the contract of employment of the employees being represented for the purposes of collective bargaining and continue in effect until such time as:

- they are varied by a new Terms and Conditions Order;
- they are varied by a collective agreement between a trade union and the employer incorporated into the contract of employment of the employees; or
- they are replaced by terms and conditions of employment agreed individually between an employee and the employer (TULRCA 1992, s 185(5)).

3.29 Two qualifications need to be considered when requesting a Terms and Conditions Order from the CAC. First, the CAC can only order amended terms and conditions in favour of a trade union commensurate with the extent of its recognition by the employer (TULRCA 1992, s 185(4)). Therefore, if a trade union is only partially recognised by an employer, for example, for the purposes of dealing with an employer's pension scheme, the union cannot seek an order modifying terms and conditions of employment in respect of matters such as pay, hours of work, holiday and the like. Secondly, the CAC cannot impose a Terms and Conditions Order in respect of terms and conditions of employment fixed by statute (TULRCA 1992, s 185(7)), although in the case of terms and conditions of employment where minimum standards are fixed by statute, it is possible for the CAC to order an increase over the statutory minimum.

3.30 It should be noted that these provisions do not apply to Crown employees (TULRCA 1992, s 273(2)).

CONSULTATION RELATING TO LARGE-SCALE REDUNDANCIES

3.31   The duty to consult with trade unions in respect of large-scale redundancies was introduced by EPA 1975, s 99 (now TULRCA 1992, s 188) and was the method used to adopt the European Collective Redundancies Directive.[16] The Collective Redundancies Directive was subsequently amended by Directive 92/56/EEC.

3.32   Despite the commencement of EPA 1975, s 99 (as consolidated into TULRCA 1992, s 188), it was alleged, and subsequently confirmed in proceedings in the European Court of Justice (ECJ) by the European Commission, that the United Kingdom had failed to implement the original form of the Collective Redundancies Directive.[17] In order to comply with the Collective Redundancies Directives, the Government took remedial steps by enacting the Trade Union Reform and Employment Rights Act 1993 (TURERA 1993) and the Collective Redundancies and Transfer of Undertakings (Protection of Employment) (Amendment) Regulations 1995,[18] which had the combined effect of both extending and reducing the duty of employers to consult in cases of collective redundancies. In this regard, EPA 1975 envisaged consultation in *all* cases of redundancy and laid down minimum periods of consultation in respect of larger scale redundancies. The changes enacted by TURERA 1993 and the Collective Redundancies and Transfer of Undertakings (Protection of Employment) (Amendment) Regulations 1995 moved the duty away from collective consultation in relation to single or smaller group redundancies towards consultation in the case of larger-scale redundancies only. Since part of the changes were enacted by statutory instrument under the European Communities Act 1972, s 2(2)(b) (which empowers the government to implement matters arising out of or related to European Union rights or obligations), there followed, in *R v Secretary of State for Trade and Industry, ex p UNISON*,[19] a challenge to these amendments. The basis of this challenge was that the removal of the right to consultation in respect of single redundancies arose only under national law and therefore using regulations under the provisions of the European Communities Act 1972 was ultra vires. However, the Divisional Court dismissed the application.

3.33   The main thrust of the amended legislation in TULRCA 1992 with regard to the duty to consult in situations of collective redundancy is that an employer must consult with 'appropriate representatives' of the affected employees, these being either representatives of an independent trade union recognised by the employer for the purposes of consulting in the context of collective redundancies, or employees' representatives elected for the purposes of the consultation.[20] If there is more than one independent trade union recognised by the employer, the employer can only discharge its duty to consult by consulting all of those unions.[21] In a case where the employer specifically

---

16   Directive 75/129/EEC.
17   *EC Commission v United Kingdom* [1994] IRLR 412.
18   SI 1995/2587.
19   [1996] IRLR 438.
20   TULRCA 1992, s 188(1B).
21   See *Governing Body of the Northern Ireland Hotel and Catering College v National Association of Teachers in Further and Higher Education* [1995] IRLR 83.

recognises a trade union or unions for the purposes of collective redundancy consultation, the employer must consult with those trade union representatives rather than with employee representatives elected for that purpose.[22] Employers should also take into account the ACAS advisory booklet 'Redundancy Handling' (August 2005) when proposing to dismiss employees by reason of a collective redundancy.

Scope of the duty

3.34 Consultation must take place 'in good time' where it is the case that the employer is proposing to dismiss 20 or more employees over a period of 90 days at the same establishment.[23] What amounts to 'good time' depends upon the degree of redundancy measures being implemented.

3.35 Problems have arisen in relation to the formulation of TULRCA 1992, s 188(1) in that it does not appear to implement properly the Collective Redundancies Directive, Art 2. This states that an employer is bound to consult where it is 'contemplating collective redundancies'. Under TULRCA 1992, s 188(1), this is enacted as arising where an employer is 'proposing to dismiss'. An argument exists that the duty under the Collective Redundancies Directive arises *before* an employer has made a definite decision to dismiss (a broad formulation of the duty), and that the obligation under UK national law arises *after* the decision has been taken (a narrower formulation). In spite of the fundamental nature of this point, there had been no European law decision directly on the point prior to 2005 (although in *Dansk Metalbejderforbund v H Nielsen*,[24] Advocate General Lenz had stated that the broader formulation was to be favoured).

3.36 The matter had been considered extensively in the English courts and tribunals in a number of cases though, these being *Hough and APEX v Leyland DAF Limited*;[25] *Re Hartlebury Printers*;[26] *R v British Coal Corporation, ex p Vardy*;[27] *Griffin v South West Water Services Limited*;[28] *GMB v Man Truck & Bus UK Limited*;[29] *Scotch Premier Meat Limited v Burns*;[30] *MSF v Refuge Assurance plc*;[31] and *Hardy v Tourism South East*.[32]

3.37 In *Hough*,[33] the case was brought under the original formulation of EPA 1975, s 99, and the Collective Redundancies Directive. The facts involved the dismissal of the respondent's security staff and consultation with APEX some 4 months after an initial decision to implement the redundancy programme had been taken. The Employment Appeal Tribunal (EAT) held that there was a difference between the formulation of the Collective Redundancies Directive

---

[22] TULRCA 1992, s 188(1B)(a).
[23] TULRCA 1992, s 188(1A).
[24] [1986] CMLR 91.
[25] [1991] IRLR 194.
[26] [1992] IRLR 516.
[27] [1993] IRLR 104.
[28] [1995] IRLR 15.
[29] [2000] IRLR 636.
[30] [2000] IRLR 639.
[31] [2002] IRLR 324.
[32] [2005] IRLR 242.
[33] *Hough and APEX v Leyland DAF Limited* [1991] IRLR 194.

and EPA 1975, s 99 and that 'contemplating' under the Collective Redundancies Directive was an elastic concept covering a multiplicity of circumstances
(ie at one end of a spectrum, an idea that change might be necessary, moving to
having a firm idea as to how to implement change, at the other end). The EAT
considered that the term 'proposing' as used in the Collective Redundancies
Directive was certain in nature. This said, since 'contemplating' was elastic, it
was possible to read the Collective Redundancies Directive in line with UK
national law by consulting at the stage of having made a decision (the narrow
formulation).

3.38   The next case, *Re Hartlebury Printers*,[34] involved a claim against admin-
istrators for a failure to consult trade unions when a decision to wind up a
company in administration was taken. The EAT again favoured the narrow
view of the formulation of 'contemplating' under the Collective Redundancies
Directive, holding, in effect, that UK national law did comply with the
Collective Redundancies Directive due to the flexible interpretation of the word
'contemplating'.

3.39   Further, in *Ex p Vardy*,[35] a judicial review was requested of the decision
of British Coal to close 31 collieries without consulting with representatives of
trade unions recognised by the employer. The decision of the President of the
Board of Trade to close the collieries was ultimately quashed with the Divisional Court holding, obiter, that the duty to consult under the Collective
Redundancies Directive was not a duty to consider how to implement the
redundancies proposed by an employer (the narrow formulation) but rather
whether there should be redundancies in the first place (the broad formulation).
The Divisional Court was therefore willing to construe UK national law in the
light of the Collective Redundancies Directive.

3.40   In *Griffin v South West Water Services Limited*,[36] the claimant commenced an action against the defendant for failing to consult in the context of
collective redundancies. The defendant had received a report in November 1993
recommending that a reorganisation should take place that would lead to
large-scale redundancies. The defendant decided that proposals would be
discussed with employee representatives in May 1994. A claim was launched
under the Collective Redundancies Directive contending that since the
employer was a successor to the former South West Water Authority, it was an
emanation of the state, and that therefore the Collective Redundancies Directive could be directly relied upon against the employer. Further, it was argued
that since the Collective Redundancies Directive was wider in scope than UK
national law, the Directive had not been complied with, because consultation
had not taken place in good time. An injunction was therefore sought by the
claimant to prevent breaches of the duty to consult. The High Court held that
the duty to consult arises only at the time that the employer has identified the
employees to be made redundant (the narrow formulation), and is able to give
them the information in the Collective Redundancies Directive, Art 2(3)
(covering such matters as the reasons for the redundancies, the number and
categories of workers to be dismissed and the time frame over which the

---

[34]   [1992] IRLR 516.
[35]   *R v British Coal Corporation, ex p Vardy* [1993] IRLR 104.
[36]   [1995] IRLR 15.

redundancies are to take place). Consequently, the court failed to follow the judgment in *Ex p Vardy*.[37] The court also held that it was not possible to rely on the Collective Redundancies Directive due to it being insufficiently precise and unconditional and therefore not capable of direct effect.

3.41 Problems arise from the decision in *Griffin*,[38] most notably that the information required under the Collective Redundancies Directive, Art 2(3) does not envisage that individual employees have been identified. It also does not appear that the High Court was directed to the opinion of the Advocate General in *Nielsen*.[39]

3.42 Following this, in *MSF v Refuge Assurance plc*,[40] the EAT was required to consider the situation arising from the merger of two companies, Refuge and United Friendly, each of which had field staff operating out of a network of branch offices. The claimant trade union had members at each of Refuge and United Friendly. The merger terms included the closure of the United Friendly London head Office and that within 3 years of the completion of the merger, the combined workforce would be reduced by somewhere in the region of one-quarter, to be achieved, so far as possible, through voluntary redundancies. Following the merger being announced, MSF was involved in seeking approval for the redundancies and an agreement was reached in this regard on 9 December 1996. The merger received shareholder approval on 16 October 1996. On 14 January 1997, MSF was told that the steering group established in relation to the redundancies was working towards an initial presentation to the merged board concerning the implementation of the redundancies. MSF made it clear that once a framework had been established, it expected consultation to begin. MSF was told that consultation would begin in February 1997, but MSF raised no objection. On 29 January 1997, a detailed proposal was put to the merged board and this was approved in principle. These plans were put to the union on 18 February 1997. Subsequently, on 17 March 1997, the two companies notified the Department of Trade and Industry (DTI). Thereafter, on 31 March 1997, the first redundancy took place at Southwark and the majority of the redundancies at that site took place that July. The remainder of the redundancies of the field staff took place in November and December 1997, with the result that some 1,777 staff in total were dismissed by reason of redundancy. On 30 March 1998, MSF presented an application to the employment tribunal arguing that the employer had failed in its statutory duty to consult with the union about the redundancies which it was proposing. At the employment tribunal hearing, the tribunal dismissed the claim, holding that the words 'proposing to dismiss' under TULRCA 1992, s 188(1A) did not cover the situation where the employer was 'thinking about dismissal'. The employment tribunal specifically drew a distinction between the employer forming and reaching a provisional decision on a business plan that could result in dismissals, and the employer's proposal to act upon that plan.

3.43 The union appealed to the EAT which held that the employment tribunal had not erred in finding that the employer had consulted in good time. In particular, the EAT approved the distinction drawn by the tribunal as to the

---

[37] *R v British Coal Corporation, ex p Vardy* [1993] IRLR 104.
[38] *Griffin v South West Water Services Limited* [1995] IRLR 15.
[39] *Dansk Metalbejderforbund v H Nielsen* [1986] CMLR 91. See **3.35**.
[40] [2002] IRLR 324.

duty to consult under TULRCA 1992, s 188 not applying to a case where there was a mere contemplation or consideration of dismissal. The EAT went on to hold that an employer is taken to first 'contemplate' collective redundancies when the employer envisages the possibility that it may have to make employees redundant, that it then has a view at least as a contingency, that the numbers, the period and the establishment or establishments involved amount to a collective redundancy for the purposes of the Collective Redundancies Directive, Art 1(1). The EAT went on to adopt the test from *Ex p Vardy*[41] that where an employer 'proposes' to dismiss, this relates to a state of mind which is more certain down the line than mere 'contemplation'.

3.44 In *GMB v Man Truck & Bus UK Limited*,[42] the EAT had to consider whether the employer was proposing to dismiss its workforce in a case where, leaving aside issues with regard to the Transfer of Undertakings (Protection of Employment) Regulations 1981[43] (TUPE 1981), two previously independent businesses merged and issued notice to terminate their existing employees' contracts of employment with an offer to employ the employees on new terms and conditions of employment in a situation where the employer had failed entirely to comply with the consultation requirements under TULRCA 1992, s 188 (the employer's argument being that there was no proposal to dismiss as redundant any of the employees and none of them had been so dismissed). Although an employment tribunal accepted the employer's argument, the decision was overturned on appeal, with the EAT holding that the employer was proposing to dismiss as redundant the workforce. The EAT stressed that the broader definition of redundancy under TULRCA 1992, s 195 had to be considered in such a case. Further, it was not open to the employer to argue that the dismissals were mere 'technical' dismissals in the sense that the employees did not actually lose their jobs as when the employer implemented the new terms, it effected a blanket dismissal and re-engagement of the workforce.

3.45 Further, in *Scotch Premier Meat Limited v Burns*,[44] the EAT in Scotland considered a case involving a decision by the owners of a slaughterhouse, which had lost a major contract, to sell the business either as a going concern or as a development site. In the case of the latter course of action being adopted some 155 employees would be dismissed. The options had been arrived at on 15 April 1998. On 28 April 1998, the employees were offered a voluntary redundancy package, but no mention was made of a possible business sale. A briefing paper was given to employee representatives on 1 May 1998 and this, too, failed to include the possibility of a sale as a going concern. A number of employees accepted the voluntary redundancy package and the remainder were dismissed on 1 June 1998. The employees presented claims for a protective award. In its decision, the EAT focused on whether the employer's two options (to sell as a going concern or to sell as a development site) meant that, as at 15 April 1998, the employer was not proposing to dismiss the employees. The EAT held that the word 'proposing' connotes an intention in the mind of the employer, this being a question of fact. The EAT also held that the employment tribunal was

---

[41] *R v British Coal Corporation, ex p Vardy* [1993] IRLR 104.
[42] [2000] IRLR 636.
[43] SI 1981/1794.
[44] [2000] IRLR 639.

entitled to conclude that the two options proposed arrived at by the employer on 15 April, one of which was the closure and sale as a development site, indicated that the employer was proposing redundancies as at that date. Consequently, protective awards were payable.

3.46 *Hardy v Tourism South East*[45] required the EAT to consider whether a protective award should be made in a case where an employer had decided to undertake a collective redundancy round, but formed the view that it did not need to consult with the appropriate representatives because it believed that it would not dismiss the employees due to the employer being able to offer alternative employment to the majority of the employees concerned, thereby bringing the number to be dismissed below 20. The EAT held that in such a case, the employer would still be proposing to dismiss as redundant more than 20 employees and therefore must engage in collective consultation. A failure to consult would leave the employer open to the potential of having to make protective awards to the employees in such a case.

3.47 This is a point which will have profound consequences in cases of business restructuring, or indeed even where the employer is proposing to terminate contracts on notice and give all employees a new contract of employment (a case which would be caught due to the extended definition of what amounts to a redundancy for the purposes of TULRCA 1992, s 195).

Time-limits for collective consultation

3.48 The provisions of TULRCA 1992, s 188(1) require that an employer shall consult the appropriate representatives of the affected employees in 'good time'. This phrase is taken directly from the Collective Redundancies Directive, Art 2(1) and replaces the original requirement in EPA 1975 that consultation should begin 'at the earliest opportunity'.

3.49 The meaning of 'good time' must be considered in the light of the purpose of the duty to consult, ie to see whether job losses are actually required. In *Transport and General Workers Union v Ledbury Preserves (1928) Limited*,[46] the EAT said of the duty:[47]

> 'It seems to us ... that there must be sufficient meaningful consultation before notices of dismissal are sent out. The consultation must not be a sham exercise; there must be time for the [appropriate] representatives who are consulted to consider properly the proposals that are put to them.'

3.50 TULRCA 1992, s 188(1A) sets down the minimum periods of consultation required stating that, in any event, the requirements of consultation are:

'(a) where the employer is proposing to dismiss 100 or more employees as mentioned in subsection (1), at least 90 days, and
(b) otherwise, at least 30 days

---

[45] [2005] IRLR 242.
[46] [1985] IRLR 412.
[47] [1985] IRLR 412 at 413. Similar views were expressed in *National Union of Teachers v Avon County Council* [1978] IRLR 55; *Spillers French (Holdings) Limited v USDAW* [1979] IRLR 339; and *E Green & Son Castings v Association of Scientific, Technical and Managerial Staffs* [1984] IRLR 135.

before the first of the dismissals takes effect.'

3.51	As to when the dismissals 'take effect', this has been considered by the EAT on a number of occasions. In *E Green & Son Castings v Association of Scientific, Technical and Managerial Staffs*,[48] the EAT considered that the phrase 'takes effect' should mean the point in time at which the first of the dismissals is proposed to actually happen, holding that:[49]

> '... [i]t is implicit ... that the reference in [TULRCA 1992, s 188(1A)] to a period "before the first of those dismissals takes effect" is a reference to the first of the proposed dismissals. The whole section is concerned with looking forward to projected dismissals at a future date and with imposing upon the employer the requirement to disclose information about his plans for those dismissals. In the event, not all of those dismissals may occur; or they may occur at different dates from that originally proposed. Clearly, however, the employer cannot reasonably be required to provide information and to consult [appropriate representatives] other than what he anticipates at the outset of the 90 day period.'

3.52	On this basis, if employees were to attempt to take advantage of the notice requirements, for example, by alleging that an employer had agreed to allow workers to leave by reason of redundancy at a date within the protected period, they ought not to be able to claim the remedies provided for by TULRCA 1992.

3.53	However, in *Association of Scientific, Technical and Managerial Staffs v Hawker Siddeley Aviation Limited*,[50] the employer had proposed to make redundant 320 employees on 18 August 1976 with the first of the proposed redundancies taking effect not before 15 November 1976 so as to comply with the 90-day consultation period. An employee asked to be able to leave on 27 August 1976 on the grounds that he was not actually doing any work for the employer. He was duly allowed to go, whereupon the trade union presented a claim for a protective award. The industrial tribunal held that the employer had breached the consultation requirements by not consulting 90 days prior to the first dismissal but, ultimately, did not make a protective award.

3.54	The ECJ has recently considered when dismissals 'take effect' for the purposes of the Collective Redundancies Directive in *Junk v Kuhnel*,[51] a case concerning the dismissal of more than 100 employees of an insolvent German business. Under the Collective Redundancies Directive, Art 4(1), collective redundancies may not take effect earlier than 30 days after notification is given to the competent public authority (CPA) for the purposes of the national enactment of the Directive. The notification in *Junk* was given to the CPA more than 30 days before the redundancies were due to take place but some 2 months after the works council had been advised of the redundancies, this being the point in time at which the redundancy notices had been served on the employees in the workforce. A point of construction arose under the Collective Redundancies Directive, Art 3(1), this being that since this refers to the redundancies being 'effected', were the redundancies so effected when the

---

48	[1984] IRLR 135.
49	[1984] IRLR 135 at 140.
50	[1977] IRLR 418.
51	Case C-188/03 [2005] IRLR 310.

employer gave notice or when the notice expired and the contract came to an end (the argument backed by the United Kingdom Government). The ECJ held that the point in time at which redundancies 'take effect' is when notice of the redundancies is given. Further, it went on to hold that since the consultation had to be with a view to reaching agreement under the Collective Redundancies Directive, Art 2(1), this meant that there must be negotiation with the employee representatives before notice of dismissal could be given.

3.55 The point is of relevance in that under TULRCA 1992, s 188(1A), consultation (ie negotiation) must take place in good time (subject to the minimum time-limits) and in any event before notice of the first of the dismissals is given. This is heaped upon the requirement that the duty to consult arises where the employer is 'proposing' to dismiss. Consequently, in the case of collective redundancies, this will mean that employers will have to consult for the full period of 30 or 90 days (as relevant) before giving notice of redundancy. This will inevitably add very substantially to the cost of a redundancy exercise (in the region of one or 3 months' extra pay per employee depending upon the scale of the redundancy).

3.56 In attempting to calculate the period of consultation, an employer is not bound to take into account employees in respect of whose proposed dismissal consultation has already begun (TULRCA 1992, s 188(3)). However, this subsection only applies where an employer discovers a genuine need to implement further redundancies after an initial batch has been decided upon.

3.57 Further, if an employer were to attempt to take advantage of TULRCA 1992, s 188(3) by attempting to impose redundancies in two or more batches so as to comply with the lesser of the two minimum consultations periods only (for example, where 100 employees are to be dismissed and the employer attempts to introduce the dismissal in two separate batches of, say, 50 each), the employer's actions will be examined closely by an employment tribunal if a failure to consult complaint is presented to it.

Failure to comply with time-limits where no appropriate representatives

3.58 In a case where collective redundancies are contemplated, an employer is required, in the absence of a trade union recognised by it, to invite any of the employees who may be dismissed to elect employee representatives. TULRCA 1992, s 196 provides a definition of what amounts to a representative which, in broad terms, provides that the representatives can be either ad hoc for the purposes of the redundancy or can be recognised generally by the employer.

3.59 As regards the machinery for electing employee representatives, this is set out at TULRCA 1992, s 188A and requires the employer to take the following steps:

- The employer must make such arrangements as are reasonably practical to ensure that the election is fair.
- The employer must determine the number of representatives to be elected so that there are sufficient representatives to represent the interests of all the affected employees having regard to the number and classes of the employees.
- The employer must determine whether the affected employees should be represented either by representatives of all the affected employees or by representatives of particular classes of the employees.

• Before the election the employer must determine the term of office as employee representatives. This must be of sufficient length to enable information to be given and consultations under TULRCA 1992, s 188 to be completed.

• The employer must ensure that candidates for election as employee representatives are affected employees on the date of the election.

• The employer must ensure that no affected employee is unreasonably excluded from standing for election.

• The employer must ensure that all affected employees on the date of the election are entitled to vote for employee representatives.

• The employer must ensure that the employees entitled to vote may vote for as many candidates as there are representatives to be elected to represent them or, if there are to be representatives for particular classes of employees, may vote for as many candidates as there are representatives to be elected to represent their particular class of employee.

• The employer must ensure that the election is conducted so as to secure that:

– so far as is reasonably practicable, those voting do so in secret; and
– the votes given at the election are accurately counted.

3.60 To the extent that employees facing dismissal by reason of a collective redundancy fail to elect employee representatives, the employer is able to comply with the obligations imposed in relation to consultation by following the requirements of TULRCA 1992, s 188(7A). This provides that where an employer has issued an invitation to elect representatives and the invitation was issued 'long enough' before the consultation is required under TULRCA 1992, s 188(1A) (ie either at least 30 or 90 days as the case may be), the employer is deemed to have complied with the requirements of notice if, after the employees subsequently elect representatives, the employer provides the representatives with the information required to be given in a reasonable time. Where, however, the employees fail to elect representatives having been given the opportunity of doing so by their employer in reasonable time for the purposes of the consultation, the employer is provided with a defence under TULRCA 1992, s 188(7A), provided that the employer individually notifies each of the affected employees of the information which it is required to provide them with under TULRCA 1992, s 188(7B).

Failure to comply with time-limits in 'special circumstances'

3.61 Another category of case exists in which it is possible for an employer to fail to comply with the time-limits for collective redundancy consultation, this being where 'special circumstances' exist which render it not reasonably practicable to comply with the consultation requirements (TULRCA 1992, s 188(7)). TULRCA 1992 does not provide a definition of what amounts to 'special circumstances'. However, case law has attempted to provide some guidance to this end. In *The Bakers Union v Clarkes of Hove Limited*,[52] the appellant company had dismissed nearly its entire workforce of 368 on the same day for redundancy without following the statutory consultation procedures. The respondent trade union had presented proceedings to the industrial tribunal for

---

[52]   [1978] IRLR 366.

a protective award which the employer defended on the grounds that special circumstances existed, namely that the company was insolvent. The tribunal held that this did not amount to special circumstances by itself. On appeal, the Court of Appeal held that 'special circumstances' were matters out of the ordinary run of events. Insolvency per se was neutral and the cause of the insolvency would have to be looked at to determine whether the case was special or not.[53] In *Association of Patternmakers & Allied Craftsmen v Kirvin Limited*,[54] the Scottish EAT held that an employer cannot claim 'special circumstances' where it is the case that he has shut his eyes to the obvious. The EAT added:[55]

'Insolvency by itself is not a special circumstance and it may well be foreseeable. What can be a special circumstance, however, may be the fact, if proved, that the employer has continued trading in the face of adverse economic pointers in the genuine but nonetheless reasonable expectation that redundancies will be avoided.'

3.62 Other examples of special circumstances have been:

- *Hamish Armour v Association of Scientific, Technical and Managerial Staffs*,[56] the refusal of a government loan;
- *USDAW v Leancut Bacon Limited*,[57] the unexpected withdrawal of banking facilities and appointment of a receiver;
- *GMB v Rankin and Harrison*,[58] the appointment of receivers and sudden redundancy of part of the workforce in order to achieve a sale of the business of the employer as a going concern; and
- *AEEU and GMB v Clydesdale Group plc*,[59] the dismissal of employees for redundancy following a court order to wind up the employer.

3.63 Conversely, in *Middlesbrough Borough Council v TGWU*,[60] 'financial difficulties' were held not to excuse the employer from consulting. Likewise, in *GMB and Amicus v Beloit Walmsely Limited*,[61] the EAT held that a case in which a parent company had unexpectedly withdrawn financial support resulting in the sudden collapse of a UK subsidiary did not fall within the 'special circumstances' exemption since under TULRCA 1992, s 188(7), it is specifically provided that:

'Where the decision leading to the proposed dismissals is that of a person controlling the employer (directly or indirectly), a failure on the part of that person to provide information to the employer shall not constitute special circumstances rendering it not reasonably practicable for the employer to comply with such a requirement.'

---

[53]   NB: the Court of Appeal held in *Kranser v McMath* [2005] EWCA Civ 1072 that protective awards which become payable in the event of a dismissal by an administrator do not enjoy super-priority to the expenses of the administration.

[54]   [1978] IRLR 318.

[55]   [1978] IRLR 318 at 319.

[56]   [1979] IRLR 24.

[57]   [1981] IRLR 281.

[58]   [1992] IRLR 514.

[59]   [1995] IRLR 527.

[60]   [2002] IRLR 332.

[61]   [2004] IRLR 18.

3.64   However, establishing 'special circumstances' is not by itself enough and an employer also has to show that it was not reasonably practicable to comply with the duty to consult because of those special circumstances. The issue of reasonable practicability is generally left to the discretion of employment tribunals but guidance on what amounts to reasonable practicability was given in the case of *Union of Construction, Allied Trades and Technicians v H Rooke & Son (Cambridge) Limited*, where the EAT held that:[62]

'... [w]hat is in issue here is the compliance with a binding obligation of the law imposing substantive legal obligations in favour of third parties. In such cases, for example under the Factories Acts, the words "reasonably practicable" are often used as a formula for justification, if the circumstances warrant it, of non-compliance with some such obligation. But it would be extraordinary if it could be held that it was not reasonably practicable to comply with such a statutory provision merely because the person upon whom the obligation lay was, even if for good reason, ignorant of the existence of the provision.'

3.65   Finally, if an employer seeks to assert that there were special circumstances, it is up to the employer to show that they did exist and that it took all reasonable steps to comply with the consultation requirements (TULRCA 1992, s 189(6)).

Varying time-limits

3.66   Under TULRCA 1992, s 197 the Secretary of State retains a power to vary the minimum notice periods. If the power is exercised, it cannot be varied below the 30-day minimum prescribed by the Collective Redundancies Directive, Art 4(1) (TULRCA 1992, s 197(1)).

The place of employment at which the right can be claimed

3.67   TULRCA 1992 imposes the duty to consult only where an employer proposes to dismiss the requisite number of employees and the employees are employed at one establishment. No definition of what amounts to an 'establishment' is contained in either TULRCA 1992 or the Collective Redundancies Directive. This said, extensive case law exists at both national and European level on this point. It was held by Lord Parker in *Secretary of State for Employment v Vic Hallam Limited* that an 'establishment' can be defined in the following way:[63]

'... [it is] quite impossible to give any exclusive definition or test as to what constitutes an establishment. The tribunal said that they approached the matter as one of broad common sense. For my part I think that is the correct approach in deciding whether as a matter of fact and degree any particular premises do constitute an establishment. But it seems to me there are certain indications which help in the matter. The first is one to which I have already referred, exclusive occupation of premises; secondly some degree of permanence ... and thirdly, as it seems to me, some organisation on the premises, an organisation of the men who are working

---

[62]   [1978] IRLR 204 at 205.
[63]   (1969) 5 ITR 108 at 110.

there. Finally, the question whether a particular premises is an establish-ment is bound up with the question of where the men who are working there are being employed in or from ... When one finds, as here, a place in which there is no organisation of staff whatsoever, no administration is carried out, there is a strong pointer, as it seems to me, to it not being an establishment.'

3.68 This dicta was approved by the House of Lords in *Lord Advocate v Babcock and Wilcox Limited.*[64]

3.69 Further, the position has been considered by the ECJ in *Rockfon A/S v Specialarbejderforbundet i Danmark*, where it held that:[65]

'... the term "establishment" appearing in art. 1(1)(a) of Directive 75/129/EEC must be understood as meaning, depending on the circum-stances, the unit to which the workers made redundant are assigned to carry out their duties. It is not essential, in order for there to be an "establishment", for the unit in question to be endowed with a manage-ment which can independently effect collective redundancies.'

3.70 An establishment, it seems, is a local employment centre bearing the hallmarks of organisation yet not necessarily having its own independent management.

3.71 One of the problems with the requirement of having the redundancies from a single establishment is that it is possible for an employer with a number of different establishments to implement a redundancy programme involving more than 20 employees in a 90-day period that does not require consultation by simply choosing staff to be selected as redundant from the different sites. Since it may be the case that each different site will be treated as being a different establishment for the purposes of TULRCA 1992, the duty to consult would not arise in such cases.

The content of consultation

3.72 The general nature of consultation is set down in TULRCA 1992, s 188(2). This requires the employer and the appropriate representatives to discuss ways of avoiding the proposed dismissals, reducing the numbers of employees to be dismissed and mitigating the consequences of the dismissals.

3.73 The employer is bound to undertake the consultation with a view to reaching agreement with the appropriate representatives. TULRCA 1992, s 188(4) provides details of specific information that an employer is required to provide to appropriate representatives, as follows:

- the reasons for the employer's proposals;
- the numbers and descriptions of employees whom the employer is propos-ing to dismiss as redundant;
- the total number of employees of any such description employed by the employer at the establishment in question;
- the proposed method of selecting employees who are to be dismissed as redundant;

---

64   [1972] 1 All ER 1130.
65   [1996] IRLR 168 at 174.

- the proposed method of carrying out the dismissals, with due regard being given to any existing procedure, including the period of time over which the dismissals are to be implemented; and
- the proposed method of calculating the amount of any redundancy payments to be made (if the same deviates in any way from an existing enactment) to the employees who are to be dismissed.

3.74   In *Middlesbrough Borough Council v TGWU*,[66] the EAT held that the duties are disjunctive and, on the facts, that the Council had failed in its duty under TULRCA 1992, s 188(2) to consult about ways of avoiding redundancies, albeit it accepted that the Council had consulted about ways of reducing the numbers to be dismissed and about mitigating the effects of the dismissals.

3.75   The above information is required to be provided in writing (TULRCA 1992, s 188(4)) and must be given to each of the appropriate representatives by being delivered to them, or sent by post to an address notified by them to the employer or, in the case of trade union representatives, sent to the union at the address of the union's main or head office (TULRCA 1992, s 188(5)).

3.76   As regards when the information under TULRCA 1992, s 188(4) is required to be given, this was considered in *Securicor Omega Express Limited v GMB*.[67] Here, the employer had decided that two of its branches must be closed, one at Droitwich and one at Hams Hall, and there needed to be redundancies at another branch in Lichfield. All three of these branches were in the same operations area, namely the Midlands area. A senior representative of the union was given notice of a meeting on 10 December 2001 at Hams Hall to discuss redundancies, but was given no other information. The meeting duly went ahead and lasted for one hour and 15 minutes during which the employer's proposal in the light of its decision to make the closures of the two branches and to make some redundancies at Lichfield was that there should be 28 redundancies, namely the entire personnel at Hams Hall, 15 redundancies at Droitwich and out of the employees at Lichfield, which was not to close, there was proposed to be 12 redundancies, making a total number across the three operations of 55. The employer accepted that Hams Hall and Droitwich were one 'establishment', which therefore triggered the consultation requirements under TULRCA 1992, s 188 in respect of both sites. There were no further meetings between the respondents and union representatives in respect of the closure of Hams Hall and the redundancies at Droitwich. Notices of the impending redundancies were posted at each branch at or around 13 December 2001. On 13 December, copies of the minutes of the meeting on 10 December were sent to the senior union official. Redundancy notices were then posted to the affected employees, whereupon the union presented a claim for a protective award.

3.77   The employment tribunal accepted that the employer had not consulted with the union, holding that the 10 December meeting was not a consultation meeting. However, on appeal, the EAT overturned the tribunal's decision and held that although consultation must be fair and meaningful, it does not extend to the economic background or context in which redundancies take place.

---

66   [2002] IRLR 332.
67   [2004] IRLR 9.

Rather, the EAT held that the question to be addressed was whether there was adequate consultation in relation to the consequences of the employer's decisions, with a view to reducing, or possibly even avoiding entirely, the redundancies which would follow as a consequence. The employer had in the case before the EAT met with the union following a decision to close two sites, but had not decided upon the numbers of employees to be dismissed, or even who the employees should be. The employer was required to consult about ways of avoiding the dismissals and mitigating the consequences of the dismissals, and this is precisely what had happened. The EAT stated that there was no requirement to serve a notice under TULRCA 1992, s 188(4) containing the information to be supplied to the appropriate representatives prior to the start of the consultation exercise. Indeed, the Collective Redundancies Directive (from which TULRCA 1992, s 188(4) is derived) requires only that the information to be supplied is supplied in good time 'during the course of consultations', which the EAT accepted had happened.

3.78 In order that the appropriate representatives are able to consult adequately with the affected employees, the employer is required to give the appropriate representatives access to the employees they represent. Further, the employer is under a duty to provide the representatives with accommodation and such other facilities as it may be appropriate to provide (TULRCA 1992, s 188(5A)).

Remedies for failure to consult

3.79 Where an employer fails to consult with appropriate representatives in good time, the remedy provided is initially in the form of a complaint to an employment tribunal (TULRCA 1992, s 189(1)). The persons who can present a complaint to the tribunal are:

- in the case of a failure relating to the election of employee representatives, any of the affected employees or any of the employees who have been dismissed as redundant;
- in the case of any other failure relating to employee representatives, any of the employee representatives to whom the failure related;
- in the case of failure relating to representatives of a trade union, the trade union; and
- in any other case, any of the affected employees or any of the employees who have been dismissed as redundant.

3.80 If an employment tribunal finds that a claim is well founded, it is obliged to make a declaration to that effect and may also make a protective award (TULRCA 1992, s 189(2)).

3.81 Protective awards are defined by TULRCA 1992, s 189(3) as to mean an order requiring an employer to pay remuneration to employees who have been dismissed as redundant without consultation during the protected period.[68] That remuneration must be paid for the duration of the protected period.

3.82 The protected period is defined in TULRCA 1992, s 189(4) as beginning on the earlier of the date on which the first of the dismissals to which the

---

[68] See, in this regard, the comments of the EAT in *Securicor Omega Express Limited v GMB* [2004] IRLR 9.

complaint relates takes effect, or the date of the award, and it lasts for such period as the tribunal decides is just and equitable in all the circumstances having regard to the seriousness of the employer's default but is not more than 90 days in duration. The 90-day period of the protective award was introduced under the Collective Redundancies and Transfer of Undertakings (Protection of Employment) (Amendment) Regulations 1999[69] which provided for, inter alia, a flat rate of 90 days' pay as the amount of the protective award, where previously the length of the protected period varied according to the length of the consultation period.

3.83   Any complaint under TULRCA 1992, s 189 has to be presented to an employment tribunal either before the date on which the last of the dismissals to which the claim relates takes effect, within 3 months beginning with that date or within such period as the employment tribunal shall consider reasonable if it is not reasonably practicable to comply with that requirement (TULRCA 1992, s 189(5)).

3.84   As to which of these dates should be used, if dismissals have actually taken place, the actual date of dismissal is the one to be used for considering the protected pay period. If it is the case that an employer is proposing to ignore the consultation obligation and is to make employees collectively redundant, the end of the protected period is the date of the employment tribunal award.[70] It has been suggested that the correct dates to use should in fact be the same dates as those for the period of consultation referred to in TULRCA 1992, s 188.[71] It is submitted that the better view is the former in that it has the advantage of imposing a clear, literal construction on TULRCA 1992 rather than twisting the wording of TULRCA 1992 to find one protected period when, on the face of it, TULRCA 1992 envisages two separate periods and provides different definitions for each.

3.85   The amount of the protective award is dealt with under TULRCA 1992, s 190(2). An employer is obliged to pay a week's pay to each employee for each week of the period. To the extent that fractions of a week are brought in to the calculation, a week's pay is reduced proportionately (TULRCA 1992, s 190(2)).

3.86   Some provisos to the payment of and amount of an award do exist, as follows.

Exercise of the tribunal's just and equitable discretion

3.87   First, there is the issue of the 'just and equitable' discretion open to the employment tribunal. When focusing on the length of the period of the protective award, the tribunal is bound to take into account the loss of the chance of consultation and therefore the possibility of avoiding redundancies through consultation rather than any immediate financial loss that employees suffer as a result of the employer's failure to consult. In other words, the protective award is compensation for an employer's failure to consult. In this regard, the EAT held in *Sovereign Distribution Services Limited v Transport and*

---

69   SI 1999/1925.
70   See *GKN Sankey Limited v National Society of Metal Mechanics* [1980] IRLR 8.
71   See to this effect *General and Municipal Workers Union v British Uralite Limited* [1979] IRLR 413; and *E Green & Son (Castings) Limited v Association of Scientific, Technical and Managerial Staffs* [1984] IRLR 135.

General Workers Union[72] that even though an employer might be able to show that consulting with appropriate representatives would not have made a difference, a protective award could still be ordered. This is because the purpose of the legislation is to ensure that consultation takes place.

3.88 Following the changes to the amount of the compensatory award after the implementation of the Collective Redundancies and Transfer of Undertakings (Protection of Employment) (Amendment) Regulations 1999,[73] the EAT was required, in *TGWU v Morgan Platts Limited*[74] to consider whether the nature of the protective award should be compensatory or penal. The EAT held that the particular factor to be taken into account is the seriousness of the employer's default. The EAT added that employees are to be compensated for the loss of their right to be collectively consulted, not their loss of earnings, if any, arising from the dismissal.

3.89 The amount of compensation to be awarded under the protective award was considered by the Court of Appeal in *Susie Radin Limited v GMB*.[75] The court had to consider in making a protective award whether the purpose of the protective award was compensatory or punitive. The court rejected the employer's argument that the purpose of the protective award was compensatory, holding that in making protective awards, employment tribunals must consider the following points:

- the purpose of the protective award is to provide a sanction for breach by the employer of its obligations under TULRCA 1992, s 188 – it is not to compensate the employees for loss which they had suffered in consequence of the breach;
- employment tribunals have a wide discretion to do what is just and equitable in all the circumstances, but the focus should be on the seriousness of the employer's default;
- the default of an employer in a given case might vary in seriousness from the technical to a complete failure to provide any of the required information and to consult;
- the deliberateness of the failure might be relevant, as might the availability to the employer of legal advice about its obligations under TULRCA 1992, s 188; and
- how an employment tribunal assesses the length of the protected period is a matter for the tribunal, but a proper approach in a case where there has been no consultation is to start with the maximum period and reduce it only if there are mitigating circumstances justifying a reduction to an extent which the tribunal considers appropriate.

3.90 Following the *Susie Radin* case,[76] the EAT was required to consider in *Smith v Cherry Lewis Limited*[77] whether an employment tribunal was justified

---

[72] [1989] IRLR 334.

[73] SI 1999/1925.

[74] EAT/0646/02/TM.

[75] [2004] IRLR 400.

[76] *Susie Radin Limited v GMB* [2004] IRLR 400.

[77] [2005] IRLR 86. See too *Newage Transmission Limited v Transport and General Workers Union*, UKEAT/031/05/MAA, where the EAT held that an employment tribunal is justified in making a 90-day protective award for failure to consult in a case where only the 30-day

in refusing to grant a protective award in circumstances where the employer had flagrantly failed to comply with the statutory duty to consult under TULRCA 1992, s 188 due to the insolvency of the employer, in a case where the employment tribunal had decided that there would be no purpose in ordering such an award due to the employer's insolvency. In overturning the employment tribunal's decision, the EAT held that the mere fact that the employer did not have the funds to pay the protective award (with the result that the affected employees would have to have recourse to government funds), did not stop such an award being ordered. Indeed, as the EAT pointed out, there are many cases in which employers become insolvent and fail to comply with the statutory procedure, and the effect of the tribunal's decision would be to deny employees the right to recover a payment which was due as a deterrent punishment for the employer's failure to comply with the statutory procedures.

3.91   As regards the amount of a protective award, employers can ask an employment tribunal to take into consideration when assessing the seriousness of the employer's breach the fact that the employer tried to find alternative employment for the employees who are to be made redundant.[78] This seems logical since an employer taking these steps is attempting to reduce the seriousness of its breach of duty and is thereby behaving equitably towards the claimants. It follows that an employer should receive credit from the employment tribunal when the tribunal exercises its discretion. Likewise, the EAT has held in *AMICUS v GBS Tooling Limited*[79] that where an employer fails to consult during the relevant consultation period but has consulted prior to this, the employer is entitled to receive credit in the form of a reduction from the amount of the protective award ordered. In short, the key to the amount of compensation to be awarded is the degree of seriousness of the employer's failure to consult and not the number of employees who are affected.

Termination of employment during the protected period

3.92   Protective awards may be affected by a number of factors depending upon the way in which employment of any of the affected employees terminates during the protected period. Depending upon how such termination arises, this may have the effect either of terminating the right for employees to receive a protective award or merely reducing the amount of the award.

3.93   The first way in which termination of employment may affect the right to a protective award is where an employee dies during the protected period. In such a case, TULRCA 1992, s 190(6) provides that the protective award is reduced by treating the protected period as if it had ended on the date of the employee's death.

3.94   A second possibility is that an employee is either fairly dismissed for a reason other than redundancy during the protected period or that the employee unreasonably terminates the contract of employment during the notice period.

---

consultation period applied. In doing so, the EAT rejected the employer's argument that a 90-day protective award was disproportionate on the basis that, following *Susie Radin Limited v GMB* [2004] IRLR 400, the purpose of the protective award was punitive, not compensatory.

78   *Spillers-French (Holdings) Limited v Union of Shop, Distributive and Allied Workers* [1979] IRLR 339.

79   [2005] IRLR 683.

The definition of redundancy under TULRCA 1992, s 195 is used for these purposes (as opposed to the definition set down in the Employment Rights Act 1996 (ERA 1996), s 139). Where termination of employment arises in either of these cases, the right to a protective award is lost in any period where, but for the dismissal or termination, the employee would have continued to have been employed during what would have been the protected period (TULRCA 1992, s 191(1)).

3.95 Thirdly, an employer may make an offer either to renew an employee's contract of employment or to re-engage the employee. The offer does not have to be in writing (TULRCA 1992, s 191(2)). Where the renewal or re-engagement would take effect before the end of the protected period with the contract of employment being either the same, substantially the same or where the renewal or re-engagement would amount to a suitable offer of employment to the employee, then if the employee unreasonably refuses that offer of employment, he is not entitled to a protective award in any period during which, but for his refusal, he would have continued to have been employed by the employer (TULRCA 1992, s 191(2)–(3)).

3.96 If the contract of employment is renewed and the employee is re-engaged in suitable alternative employment, the employee is entitled to a trial period of 4 weeks beginning on the date on which he starts work under the contract of employment as renewed or substituted, or for such longer periods as the parties may agree in writing (TULRCA 1992, s 191(4)–(6)). Any agreement entered into providing for a longer trial period is required to be entered into before the employee starts work under the new contract of employment and is required to specify the end of the trial period and the terms and conditions that apply after the end of that period. Where an employee terminates a renewed contract of employment or one that he has been re-engaged under during a trial period, or the employer gives notice to the employee for a reason arising out of the new terms of the contract, the employee will remain entitled to a protective award unless the employee has acted unreasonably in terminating the contract of employment. Since these provisions are similar to those relating to trial periods in cases of redundancy under ERA 1996, regard should be had to the redundancy cases on the meaning of the unreasonable rejection of an offer of re-employment or re-engagement, in particular, *Carron Co v Robertson*[80] and *Hindes v Supersine Limited*.[81]

Excluded employees

3.97 The next group of cases in which an employee cannot claim a protective award is where the employee falls within a class of persons who are not eligible to receive a protective award due to being excluded either by statute or voluntarily.

3.98 The categories of statutory exclusion are short-term employees (TULRCA 1992, s 282), share fishermen (TULRCA 1992, s 284), overseas

---

[80]   (1967) 2 ITR 484.
[81]   [1979] ICR 517.

employees (TULRCA 1992, s 285) and persons in the police service due to their not being deemed 'employees' for the purposes of TULRCA 1992.[82]

3.99   Further, it is possible by means of a collective agreement to contract out of the statutory scheme for the provision of protective awards where a collective agreement provides for a scheme that is at least as favourable as the statutory scheme and has been approved by the Secretary of State (TULRCA 1992, s 198(1)–(2)). However, under TULRCA 1992, s 198(3), approval cannot be given unless the collective agreement provides for the following:

• a grievance procedure in cases where employees allege that an employer has not followed a collective agreement; and
• machinery for referring a dispute to arbitration or allowing a claim to be made to an employment tribunal.

Enforcing protective awards

3.100   Where an employer has been ordered to make a protective award and has failed to comply with the order, it is possible for an employee to apply to an employment tribunal for an order to pay the remuneration due under the protective award (TULRCA 1992, s 192(1) and (3)). An employee must present a claim within a 3-month time-limit beginning with the date of the employer's alleged failure to pay the protective award, although the employment tribunal retains a power to extend the time-limit if it is satisfied that it was not reasonably practicable for an applicant to present the claim in that time (TULRCA 1992, s 192(2)). In this regard, the EAT considered in *Howlett Marine Services Limited v Bowlam*[83] whether, where a claim for an order for a protective award was sought some 10 months after the employer's failure to pay the award, the employment tribunal was correct to hold that it had not been reasonably practicable to make the application for an order within this 10-month period. At the appeal hearing, the Secretary of State was given the opportunity to make representations as to the proper construction of the limitation period within which the 3-month period ran (on the basis that most applications for such orders would potentially be time-barred). The Secretary of State argued that the 3-month period should run from the date being 3 months after the making of the protective award. This argument was rejected by the EAT which went on to hold that the plain literal meaning of TULRCA 1992, s 192 had to be followed and that the employment tribunal had been right to hold that it had not been reasonably practicable to present claims within the ordinary 3-month limitation period. Further, the EAT went on to hold that it must always not be reasonably practicable in terms of TULRCA 1992, s 192(2)(b) to present a complaint of failure to pay remuneration under a protective award in respect of a period where no award has yet been made, adding that it was not only not reasonably practicable, it was impossible for an employee to present a claim under TULRCA 1992, s 192 in such circumstances. The EAT concluded on the point by holding that no employment tribunal, properly instructing itself, could conclude other than that throughout that period it was not reasonably practicable for a complaint to be presented.

---

[82]   TULRCA 1992, s 280.
[83]   [2001] IRLR 201.

3.101 The remedy is available only under TULRCA 1992, s 192 and not under ERA 1996, Part II as a claim for unlawful deduction of wages (per TULRCA 1992, s 192(4)).

Protective awards and recoupment of benefits

3.102 For the purposes of social security legislation, in particular, the Employment Protection (Recoupment of Jobseekers' Allowance) Regulations 1996,[84] a protective award is treated as 'earnings' and is therefore subject to the provisions relating to recoupment when assessed by an employment tribunal. A payment of a protective award for a period therefore excludes the employee from being able to claim jobseekers' allowance for any period covered by the protective award. A discussion of the law relating to recoupment is beyond the scope of this book and regard should be had to more general social security law texts.

Protection for appropriate representatives

3.103 Protection is provided to appropriate representatives from being either victimised or unfairly dismissed as a result of being an appropriate representative. In the case of victimisation, the protection provided to trade union representatives is provided under TULRCA 1992, s 146 (see **Chapter 7**), whereas with non-trade union employee representatives, the protection is provided under ERA 1996, s 47.

3.104 Further, if an employer unfairly dismisses an appropriate representative for acting in that capacity, protection for trade union representatives is provided by TULRCA 1992, s 152 (see **Chapter 7**) and for employee representatives under ERA 1996, s 103.

3.105 Finally, appropriate representatives have the right to paid time off work to carry out their functions as such under TULRCA 1992, ss 168–169 for trade union representatives and ERA 1996, s 61 in the case of employee representatives.

Notification to the Department of Trade and Industry

3.106 Where an employer is proposing to dismiss a group of employees as redundant in circumstances to which the duty to collectively consult would apply, an obligation to inform the Department of Trade and Industry also arises. If an employer is proposing to dismiss as redundant 100 or more employees at the same establishment, the duty on the employer is to inform the Secretary of State at least 90 days before the first of the dismissals. Where an employer is proposing to dismiss 20 or more but less than 100 employees, the employer is bound to notify at least 30 days before the first dismissal (TULRCA 1992, s 193(1)–(2)).

3.107 The notice is required to be in writing and must be delivered to the Secretary of State at such address as the Secretary of State directs. The notice is required to state who the appropriate representatives are for the purposes of consultation and also when consultation started. It can also contain such other particulars as the Secretary of State declares relevant (TULRCA 1992,

---

[84]   SI 1996/2349.

s 193(4)). The Secretary of State can request such further information as he thinks fit upon receiving the employer's notice. The Secretary of State is required to send a copy of the employer's notice to each of the appropriate representatives named in the employer's notice (TULRCA 1992, s 193(5)–(6)). The current form of notice is a Form HR 1, copies of which can be obtained from the DTI website, http://www.dti.gov.uk/er.

3.108   Employers can deviate from the procedure to notify the Secretary of State where 'special circumstances' exist. These are the same types of circumstances for failing to consult with appropriate representatives as have already been discussed at **3.61**. If an employer fails to notify the Secretary of State due to not being provided with necessary information by a person controlling the employer either directly or indirectly, that will not constitute special circumstances (TULRCA 1992, s 193(7)).

3.109   Failure to notify the Secretary of State is a criminal offence and can be punished on summary conviction by a fine not exceeding scale 5 (TULRCA 1992, s 194(1)). Where an employer is found guilty and the employer is a company, if the company has committed the offence with the consent or connivance of an officer of the company, the officer can also be prosecuted (TULRCA 1992, s 194(3)). Only the Secretary of State or an officer appointed by him may issue criminal proceedings for this offence.

THE DUTY TO CONSULT ARISING ON THE TRANSFER OF AN UNDERTAKING

3.110   As with the duty to consult in the event of large-scale redundancies, the duty to consult in respect of the transfer of an undertaking is a product of European law. In this case, the duty arises under the Acquired Rights Directive 77/187/EEC, as amended by the Business Transfers Directive 98/50/EC. The Directives are currently implemented into United Kingdom national law as the Transfer of Undertakings (Protection of Employment) Regulations 1981 (TUPE 1981).[85] Following long-term public consultation, a new version of the Transfer of Undertakings (Protection of Employment) Regulations is to be commenced to replace the 1981 Regulations.

3.111   As with many other pieces of national legislation which owe their origins to European law, TUPE 1981 did not meet the standards of the Acquired Rights Directive[86] introducing it when it was commenced. Consequently, it was widely anticipated that the European Commission would launch infringement proceedings against the United Kingdom on the basis that the United Kingdom had failed to implement a duty to consult with appropriate representatives of the employer's workforce in the event of a transfer of an undertaking. The proceedings duly appeared (in the form of *EC Commission v United Kingdom*[87]) which the Government was so confident of losing that it had already taken remedial steps in the form of TURERA 1993 by the time of the ECJ hearing. The outcome of the case, however (coming after the enactment of TURERA 1993), went further than the Government had anticipated.

---

85   SI 1981/1794.
86   Directive 77/187/EEC.
87   [1994] IRLR 392.

It required that appropriate representatives of workers should have the right to be consulted in the absence of a recognised, independent trade union. To this end, it was necessary to remedy the omission in TUPE 1981 by introducing the Collective Redundancies and Transfer of Undertakings (Protection of Employment) (Amendment) Regulations 1995.[88]

3.112 Following the passing of the Business Transfers Directive 98/50/EC, the Government has been involved in a number of measures to ensure that it has scope to implement new regulations for the purposes of ensuring that the United Kingdom is compliant with its obligations under the Business Transfers Directive. First, it passed the Employment Relations Act 1999, s 38 (ERA 1999) which gives the government powers to implement regulations for the purposes of compliance with the Business Transfers Directive. Secondly, in September 2001, the DTI published a public consultation document setting out its policy proposals for the reform of TUPE 1981. Thirdly, in February 2003, the DTI announced that it intended to implement all of its proposed changes, but that provisions relating to occupational pension schemes would be dealt with separately through pensions legislation. The pensions legislation duly followed in the form of the Pensions Act 2004. Further consultation was then undertaken in March 2005 (closing in June 2005) with regard to whether the Government's published draft of the new TUPE Regulations correctly and effectively implemented the Government's policy views from the September 2001 public consultation. It was anticipated that the March 2005 public consultation would result in new Transfer of Undertakings (Protection of Employment) Regulations in October 2005. However, this deadline has been pushed back to April 2006.

3.113 Following the extensive consultation procedure (which will result in what is likely to be TUPE 2006), relatively little has changed with regard to the previous established principles under TUPE 1981. Given the Government's statement in the March 2005 public consultation that the principles underpinning the proposed new TUPE Regulations are fixed (albeit that the content may change from the first draft of those Regulations provided with the March 2005 public consultation), it is likely that the following key changes will be made to TUPE 1981:

- The introduction of the concept of a 'service provision change', which is designed to provide certainty in outsourcing situations by ensuring that all service provision changes are deemed to be transfers of undertakings.
- The introduction of the non-assignment of certain classes of financial liability in the case of a relevant transfer arising in the course of 'relevant insolvency proceedings' (ie insolvency proceedings under the supervision of an insolvency practitioner which will not result in the liquidation of the undertaking). For these purposes, the classes of financial liability which will not transfer are proposed to be statutory redundancy payments under ERA 1996, Part XI and the statutory insolvency payments provisions under ERA 1996, Part XII. The provision is aimed at promoting the rescue of insolvent business by ensuring that those debts which are subject to a statutory guarantee pursuant to the Insolvency Payments Directive[89] are

---

88 SI 1995/2587.
89 Directive 80/987/EEC.

met by the National Insurance Fund, thereby allowing a potential rescuer of the business to buy the business clear of potentially deal-breaking liabilities.

- The introduction of the right for the transferee and 'appropriate representatives' of the employees assigned to the undertaking to agree 'permitted variations' to the contracts of employment of the affected employees in a case where a relevant transfer occurs in the event of 'relevant insolvency proceedings' (defined as in the point above). For these purposes, 'appropriate representatives' will be any representatives of an independent trade union recognised by the employer in respect of the employees, or, in other cases, employee representatives generally recognised by the employer who have authority to agree 'permitted variations' or employee representatives recognised pursuant to the TUPE 1981 employee election procedures. In the case of non-trade union employee representatives, the permitted variations must be agreed in writing and a copy of the agreement provided to each of the employees. 'Permitted variations' for these purposes are variations to a contract or contracts of employment otherwise than for an economic, technical or organisational reason entailing changes in the workforce, where the change is designed to safeguard employment opportunities by ensuring the survival of the undertaking, business or part of the undertaking or business. In short, the purpose of this right is to facilitate a rescue culture in failing businesses by allowing the rescuer to negotiate more commercially realistic terms with the appropriate representatives of the employees of the undertaking whose jobs may be saved.

- A duty on the transferor in the case of a relevant transfer (which would include a case of a service provision change) for the transferor to provide certain minimum information relating to the transferring employees ('transferring employee information'). Whilst the reality is that in many transfers of an undertaking occurring in the case of a first generation outsourcing or a business sale, information relating to the transferring employees tends to be provided as part of the commercial due diligence process, it is much rarer in the case of a second or subsequent generation outsourcing for the outgoing service provider to provide information relating to the transferring employees to the incoming service provider, and the requirement to provide transferring employee information pursuant to a legal obligation will therefore be of most practical benefit in the case of a service provision change. The transferring employee information is to be provided in writing and is information which is or ought to be known by the transferor as to the transferor's rights, powers, duties and liabilities under or in connection with any contract of employment of any employee who is assigned to the undertaking transferring (including the identity of the employees transferring).

- So as to enable the enforcement of the right to transferring employee information, the introduction of a right for a transferee to present an application to the High Court for a penalty of up to £75,000 to be paid by the transferor to the transferee in a case where the transferor has not provided the transferring employee information to the transferee. Whether this proposed legal requirement will have an impact in the case of a large service provision change where thousands of employees may transfer is another matter. Indeed, the Government specifically sought clarification in the March 2005 public consultation of whether it was accepted that the provisions of the Business Transfers Directive[90] would be complied with in this regard.

3.114 Although the draft new TUPE Regulations have a number of potentially interesting new features, the key one for the purposes of the law relating to collective consultation is the proposed ability for a transferee collectively to negotiate changes to transferring employees' terms and conditions of employment in the case of a business failure. This is likely to prove a fruitful source of litigation going forward when the draft new TUPE Regulations are commenced.

The scope of the duty to consult

3.115 The following provisions relate to the law as it stands at the date of publication of this book under TUPE 1981.

3.116 The duty to inform and consult arises under TUPE 1981, reg 10 when a relevant transfer takes place. A relevant transfer is one under which the whole or part of an undertaking is transferred from one employer to another where that undertaking, or part thereof, retains its own identity after the transfer. A full discussion of when a transfer of an undertaking occurs is beyond the scope of this book and regard should be had generally to specialist practitioner works on this subject although, for the general principles of when an undertaking is transferred, regard should be had to *Spijkers v Gebroeders Benedik Abbatoir CV*[91] and, depending upon the nature of the undertaking, *Suzen v Zehnacker Gebaudereinigung GmbH*[92] (in the case of labour intensive undertakings) and *Oy Liikenne AB v Liskojärvi*[93] (in the case of asset intensive undertakings).

3.117 The duty to inform and consult under TUPE 1981 falls on the transferor employer but the transferor is required to be provided with assistance by the transferee employer. The obligation in respect of the transferor employer is a duty to consult appropriate representatives of the employees of their workforces where the employees may be affected by the transfer or the measures proposed to be taken in connection with it, whether or not the affected employees are employed in the undertaking or the part of it to be transferred (TUPE 1981, reg 10(1)).

3.118 Appropriate representatives will be either employee representatives elected by the employees (whether on an ad hoc basis or generally), or representatives from an independent trade union recognised by the employer for those purposes (TUPE 1981, reg 10(2A)). Where an employer recognises one or more trade unions for the purposes of consultation, the employer must consult with representatives of that or those unions in respect of that part of the population of the affected employees within the undertaking in respect of whom the trade unions are recognised. In the event that no trade union is recognised by the employer, or a trade union or unions is/are recognised in respect of a part only of the affected employees in the undertaking, the

---

[90] Directive 98/50/EC.
[91] [1986] 2 CMLR 296.
[92] [1997] IRLR 255.
[93] [2001] IRLR 171.

employer is required to afford the opportunity to elect employee representatives to the affected employees who do not have trade union representatives recognised (TUPE 1981, reg 10(2A)).

3.119   A further point to note is that, as with consultation in the case of collective redundancies, there are detailed provisions dealing with how elections for appropriate representatives are to be carried out, these having been introduced under the Collective Redundancies and Transfer of Undertakings (Protection of Employment) (Amendment) Regulations 1999.[94] These provisions now take effect as TUPE 1981, reg 10(2A) and they are in identical terms to those discussed above in relation to collective redundancy-related dismissals.

THE CONTENT OF TUPE 1981 CONSULTATION

3.120   The information to be provided to the appropriate representatives is dealt with by TUPE 1981, reg 10(2)(a)–(d), under which the employer must provide to the appropriate representatives information as to:

- the fact that a transfer is to take place, the approximate time of the transfer and the reasons for the transfer;
- the legal, social and economic implications of the transfer on the employees who are likely to be affected by the transfer;
- the measures that an employer envisages will be taken in connection with the transfer in relation to the affected employees and, if it does not envisage any measures being taken, the employer is required to inform the appropriate representatives of this fact; and
- if the employer is the transferor, the measures which the transferee envisages it will take in relation to employees transferred under TUPE 1981 and if no measures are to be taken, this must be stated.

3.121   Employers are also required to consult with the appropriate representatives as to the matters in the second and third list points at **3.120**. ACAS has published an advisory booklet, 'Employee Communications and Consultation' (2005), which provides practical guidance to employers in relation to the issue of consultation.

3.122   Where a transferee proposes 'measures' the effect of which will be adversely and detrimentally to change the terms and conditions of employment of the transferring employees' contracts of employment, any employee so affected may seek to argue that they have been constructively dismissed by the transferring employer prior to the transfer under TUPE 1981, reg 5(5). There must, however, have been a repudiatory breach of the claimant's contract of employment contemplated by the transferee's proposed measure or measures.[95]

3.123   In order for the transferor to carry out the consultation required by TUPE 1981, reg 10(2)(d), the transferee must inform the transferor at such time as will enable the transferee employer to comply with the duty of consultation (TUPE 1981, reg 10(3)).

---

[94]   SI 1999/1925.
[95]   See *University of Oxford v Humphreys* [2000] IRLR 183; and *Rossiter v Pendragon plc* [2002] IRLR 483.

3.124 The method by which the information is to be delivered is dealt with by TUPE 1981, reg 10(4). This requires, in the first instance, that the information shall be given to the appropriate representatives in writing. In the alternative, it can be sent to them by post at an address notified by them to the employer. Further, if the appropriate representative is a trade union representative, the employer can discharge the duty to provide information by delivering the information by post to the union at the address of the union's main or head office.

3.125 Appropriate representatives have no say over the way in which information is provided to them. Provided that the employer meets with the requirements of TUPE 1981, reg 11(2), representatives are not entitled to ask for originals of documents or request that information should be delivered to them in a particular format.[96]

Timescale for consultation

3.126 The timescale for the provision of information under TUPE 1981 is vague. The Acquired Rights Directive[97] requires that consultation shall be 'in good time'. TUPE 1981, reg 10(2) translates this into a requirement that the necessary information shall be provided 'long enough before a relevant transfer' to enable consultation with appropriate representatives of the affected employees to take place. In *Institution of Professional Civil Servants v Secretary of State for Defence*,[98] the High Court held that the duty to consult can only take place after the employer has decided to transfer but long enough before the transfer for the consultations to be meaningful. What amounts to 'long enough before' is, therefore, a question of fact in each particular case.

Purpose of consultation

3.127 If measures are to be taken by an employer in relation to a transfer, the duty of the employer is to consult the appropriate representatives of those employees affected by the proposed measures with a view to securing the agreement to those measures (TUPE 1981, reg 10(5)). In the course of the consultation, the employer is bound to listen to and reply to any proposals that are put forward by the appropriate representatives (TUPE 1981, reg 10(6)).

Defences for an employer who has failed to consult

Special circumstances

3.128 As with the duty to consult in the case of a collective redundancy, a 'special circumstances' defence may exist for an employer who has failed to consult 'long enough before' a relevant transfer. Before attempting to rely upon this defence, the employer is required to carry out all reasonable steps to ensure that consultation does take place (TUPE 1981, regs 10(7) and 11(2)).

3.129 As to what can amount to special circumstances, regard should be had to **3.61**.

---

[96] See in this regard *Institution of Professional Civil Servants v Secretary of State for Defence* [1987] IRLR 373.

[97] Directive 77/187/EEC.

[98] [1987] IRLR 373.

Failure to elect appropriate representatives

3.130   An employer is only bound to consult with appropriate representatives. If none exist, the duty does not arise. To this end, if an employer has issued an invitation to elect appropriate representatives 'long enough before' the time that the employer was bound to consult, and the invitation has not been acted upon, the employer is treated as having complied with the provisions of TUPE 1981 insofar as they relate to the duty to consult provided that the employer issues the information individually to each of the affected employees within a reasonable time (TUPE 1981, reg 10(8A)) and, in the case of elected representatives who do not request information, as soon as is reasonably practicable after the election of the representatives (TUPE 1981, reg 10(8)).

Facilities

3.131   Appropriate representatives are entitled to be provided with accommodation and other facilities necessary for their needs and are entitled to be provided with access to the affected employees (TUPE 1981, reg 10(6A)).

Remedy for failure to consult

3.132   Under TUPE 1981, reg 11(1), where an employer is alleged to have failed to provide the required information to, or consult with, appropriate representatives of the affected employees, an application can be presented to an employment tribunal by any of the following categories of persons:

- any employees affected by the employer's failure to arrange elections for employee representatives;
- any employee representative not consulted;
- any trade union representative not consulted; or
- any of the employees who are affected by the transfer.

3.133   Where an issue arises that a transferor employer has failed to consult about the measures that are to be taken by a transferee employer, the transferor will be in breach of the consultation duty unless the transferor can show that he gave notice of the fact that he was going to disclose the required information to the appropriate representatives of the transferee employer and that the transferee employer did not comply with the duty to disclose under TUPE 1981, reg 10(3) (per TUPE 1981, reg 11(3)).

3.134   If an employment tribunal finds that a complaint is well founded, it must make a declaration to that effect and may award 'appropriate compensation' (TUPE 1981, reg 11(4)). Appropriate compensation is such sum as the tribunal finds just and equitable but TUPE 1981 provides a cap on the maximum amount awarded, this being fixed at 13 weeks' pay (TUPE 1981, reg 11(11)).

3.135   With regard to the factors an employment tribunal should consider when ordering compensation to be paid, these are likely in many cases to turn around the loss of the chance to consult. It would seem that, as with the requirement to consult in the case of collective redundancies,[99] where an employer is in default in relation to the consultation requirements under TUPE

---

99   In relation to which the Court of Appeal has held that the making of a protective award is a

1981, regs 10 and 11, the employer should be required to pay the maximum compensation for failure to consult unless good reason can be shown by the employer as to why this should not be so.

3.136 Either the transferor or, in the case of a transferee who has failed to comply with the obligation to disclose the measures that it is proposing to take, the transferee, can be ordered to pay compensation (TUPE 1981, reg 11(5)). However, following a series of decisions in the EAT,[100] it seems that the obligation to pay compensation in the case of a default of the transferor, transfers to the transferee. Practically, where there is either a business sale, or a first generation outsourcing, the transferee will usually seek in the negotiation of the commercial terms between the parties, a specific indemnity covering the risk of a failure by the transferor to comply with its obligations to inform and consult under TUPE 1981, reg 10(2).

3.137 If either the transferor or transferee fails to comply with an order to pay compensation, a fresh complaint can be made to an employment tribunal alleging failure to comply (TUPE 1981, reg 11(5)). If the tribunal finds that the complaint is well founded it can order that the compensation is paid (TUPE 1981, reg 11(6)).

3.138 In the case of either a claim under TUPE 1981, reg 11(1) or (5), the claim must be brought within a 3-month period beginning with the date on which the transfer is completed (in a claim under TUPE 1981, reg 11(1)), or the date of a tribunal's TUPE 1981, reg 11(1) order (in a claim brought under TUPE 1981, reg 11(5)). It is possible in a TUPE 1981, reg 11(1) claim to present a claim prior to the transfer taking place.[101]

3.139 Finally, it is possible for an employment tribunal to extend the 3-month period limitation where it considers that it was not reasonably practicable for the claimant to present a claim within the 3-month period (TUPE 1981, reg 11(8)).

Protection of appropriate representatives

3.140 Appropriate representatives are protected against being either victimised or unfairly dismissed as a result of their being an appropriate representative or performing any of the duties connected with that status. In the case of victimisation, the remedies provided to trade union representatives are provided by means of TULRCA 1992, s 146, whereas with employee representatives, the protection is provided under ERA 1996, s 47.

3.141 If an employer unfairly dismisses an appropriate representative where the reason for the dismissal is because the representative acted in that capacity, the protection is provided by TULRCA 1992, s 152, in the case of a trade union representative so dismissed, and ERA 1996, s 103, in the case of an employee representative.

---

penal sanction in connection with which the maximum award should be ordered unless there is good reason not to make such an award (*Susie Radin Limited v GMB* [2004] IRLR 400).

[100] *Kerry Foods Limited v Creber* [2000] IRLR 10; *TGWU v James McKinnon JR, (Haulage) Limited* [2001] IRLR 597; and *Alamo Group (Europe) Limited v Tucker* [2003] IRLR 266.

[101] See in this regard *South Durham Health Authority v UNISON* [1995] IRLR 407.

3.142   Appropriate representatives also have the right to paid time off work to carry out their functions, under TULRCA 1992, ss 168–169, in the case of trade union representatives, and ERA 1996, s 61, in the case of employee representatives.

Excluded employees

3.143   The right to be consulted in respect of the transfer of an undertaking does not arise in the case of an employee who ordinarily works outside the United Kingdom under the terms of his contract of employment (TUPE 1981, reg 13(1)).

Appeals

3.144   It is possible to appeal a decision of an employment tribunal on a point of law only, the appeal lying in the first instance to the EAT (TUPE 1981, reg 11(10)).

CONSULTATION IN RESPECT OF HEALTH AND SAFETY MATTERS

3.145   A full-scale review of the law relating to health and safety consultation in employment is beyond the scope of this book and regard should be had to more specialist texts generally. A brief review of the law relating to consultation on health and safety consultation is therefore all that will be undertaken.

The duty to consult

3.146   A duty exists for all employers to consult with their employees 'fully and effectively' in all matters relating to health and safety at work. The duty arises under the Health and Safety (Consultation with Employees) Regulations 1996[102] (HS(CE)R 1996), reg 3. Prior to this, it was possible for recognised trade unions to appoint union safety representatives under the provisions of the Safety Representatives and Safety Committees Regulations 1977[103] (SRSCR 1977), under which a duty to consult has existed since 1 January 1993 (SRSCR 1977, reg 4A). SRSCR 1977 has continued in force but applies solely to recognised trade unions (SRSCR 1977, reg 3(1)). ACAS has published an advisory booklet, 'Employee Communications and Consultation' (2005), which provides practical guidance to employers in relation to the issue of consultation.

3.147   An employer must be notified in writing before a union safety representative can start to exercise his statutory functions (SRSCR 1977, reg 3(2)). The statutory functions of safety representatives are set out in SRSCR 1977, reg 4. Various other statutory rights and duties exist, as follows:

- upon the giving of written notice by a safety representative to an employer, there is a right for safety representatives to inspect the workplace in relation to which they are appointed (SRSCR 1977, reg 5);
- upon the giving of notice, a right exists for safety representatives to inspect

---

[102]   SI 1996/1513.
[103]   SI 1977/500.

the workplace where a notifiable accident or dangerous occurrence has taken place or where a notifiable disease has broken out (SRSCR 1977, reg 6); and

● upon the giving of reasonable notice, a right exists for safety representatives to inspect and take copies of documents which an employer is bound to keep in order to comply with the Health and Safety at Work etc Act 1974, save to the extent that the document relates to an identifiable individual.

3.148 If a trade union is not recognised by an employer, the employer is bound to consult either directly through the workforce or it can consult with a representative of the workers (known as 'representatives of employee safety': HS(CE)R 1996, reg 4(1)(b)).

3.149 Employers bound by HS(CE)R 1996 are required to provide such information within their knowledge on health and safety matters as is necessary to enable representatives of employee safety to participate fully and effectively in consultation (HS(CE)R 1996, reg 5(1) and (2)(a)). Representatives of employee safety have slightly wider rights to be provided with information under HS(CE)R 1996 than union safety representatives due to HS(CE)R 1996, reg 5(2)(b) allowing them access to information under the Reporting of Injuries, Diseases and Dangerous Occurrences Regulations 1995.[104]

3.150 The information that is provided should be such as to allow the representatives to carry out their functions under HS(CE)R 1996, reg 6, these being:

● to make representations on behalf of employees to the employer relating to potential hazards and dangerous occurrences;
● to make representations to the employer on general matters relating to the health and safety of employees who the representative represents; and
● to represent the interests of employees in consultations with inspectors under the provisions of the Health and Safety at Work etc Act 1974.

3.151 Representatives of employee safety are entitled to time off for training and employers are bound to provide facilities to such representatives for their functions as such representatives (HS(CE)R 1996, reg 7). Union safety representatives do not have similar statutory rights under SRSCR 1977, but are able to use their bargaining position to gain facilities. Union safety representatives are usually trained by their union in this regard in any event.

Right to pay for time off

3.152 Both union safety representatives and representatives of employee safety are entitled to paid time off to carry out their functions. In the case of union safety representatives, the right arises under SRSCR 1977, reg 4(2) and the Schedule thereto and, in the case of representatives of employee safety, the right arises under HS(CE)R 1996, reg 7(3) and Sch 1.

Protection for health and safety representatives

3.153 Protection against dismissal and victimisation is afforded to both classes of health and safety representatives under ERA 1996. As regards

---

[104] SI 1995/3163.

victimisation, an employee representative of either description is allowed to present a claim to an employment tribunal where his employer subjects the representative to a detriment short of dismissal, under ERA 1996, s 44. The right not to be unfairly dismissed for health and safety reasons arises under ERA, s 100. The one-year continuous service requirement and upper age limit are both removed in cases arising under this section (ERA 1996, ss 108(2) and 109(2) respectively, as is the cap on the maximum amount of compensation which may be awarded for unfair dismissal (ERA 1996, s 100)).

THE COMMON LAW RIGHT TO CONSULTATION IN PUBLIC AUTHORITY CASES

3.154   This right arises under the common law right where a previous practice of consultation has existed between a public body and a trade union representing employees employed by that public body. The right arises on the basis of a legitimate expectation of consultation. In *Council of Civil Service Unions v Minister for the Civil Service*,[105] for reasons of national security, the Minister for the Civil Service issued an Order in Council denying workers at Government Communications Headquarters (GCHQ) the rights to join or belong to a trade union. The claimant trade union sought a review of the decision and the case was ultimately heard on appeal by the House of Lords which held that, but for the justifying factor of national security, the union might have succeeded in its claim. In particular, their Lordships held:[106]

> '... even where a person claiming some benefit or privilege has no legal right to it, as a matter of private law, he may have a legitimate expectation of receiving the benefit or privilege, and, if so, the courts will protect his expectation by judicial review as a matter of public law.'

Legitimate expectation

3.155   As to what amounts to a legitimate expectation, the House of Lords then went on to hold in the *Council of Civil Service Unions* case[107] that it arises where a state of affairs exists between a decision-maker and another person which has arisen either because the person claiming the right:

● had in the past been permitted by the decision-maker to enjoy the right and therefore can legitimately expect to be permitted to continue to do so until there has been communicated to him some rational ground for withdrawing the right on which he has been given an opportunity to comment; or
● has received assurance from the decision-maker that the right will not be withdrawn without giving him the opportunity of advancing reasons for contending that they should not be withdrawn.

3.156   It follows from what the House of Lords held in the *Council of Civil Service Unions* case[108] that although it is possible to withdraw 'rights' based upon legitimate expectation, a public body can do so prospectively only after it

---

[105]   [1985] ICR 14.
[106]   [1985] ICR 14 at 28.
[107]   *Council of Civil Service Unions v Minister for the Civil Service* [1985] ICR 14.
[108]   *Council of Civil Service Unions v Minister for the Civil Service* [1985] ICR 14.

has given the person or body having the legitimate expectation notice of its intention to do so and has given that person or body a right to comment upon the withdrawal of the expectation.

Examples of legitimate expectations

3.157 *R v British Coal Corporation and Secretary of State for Trade, ex p Vardy*[109] concerned a review of the decision of the President of the Board of Trade to close down a number of collieries without consulting the mine-workers' unions recognised by British Coal, the employer and operator of the mines. Upon an application for judicial review being presented, it was held that the unions indeed had a legitimate expectation of consultation based upon previous such consultations. The consultation procedure could therefore not simply be withdrawn on the whim of the President of the Board of Trade and, following the quashing of the decision, the matter was remitted to him for a full and proper determination.

3.158 *Re NUPE and COHSE's Application*[110] is a further example of the principle, where it was held that a public body's failure to consult over redundancies could be judicially reviewed on the grounds of denial of a legitimate expectation. This would be so where the unions concerned could show that they had the expectation that they were claiming, and that as a result of the public authority's failure to consult, they would suffer substantial hardship.

COLLECTIVE AGREEMENTS

3.159 Collective agreements are agreements that exist between trade unions and employers (or collectives of either or both groups), for the purposes of regulating the procedures that are to be adopted by a trade union and employer, or terms and/or terms and conditions for workers.

3.160 Collective agreements can be either those falling within the statutory definition of a collective agreement under TULRCA 1992, s 178 or those falling outside that statutory definition. Collective agreements can either be contractual in effect or non-contractual depending upon the point in time that the collective agreement was reached, the intention of the parties and the content of the collective agreement. Collective agreements can also bind individual employees provided that they are incorporated in whole or in part in the contracts of employment of those employees.

Collective agreements defined

3.161 The statutory definition of a collective agreement is contained in TULRCA 1992, s 178 which provides:

'(1) ... "collective agreement" means any agreement or arrangement made by or on behalf of one or more trade unions and one or more employers or employer's associations and relating to one or more of the

---

[109] [1993] IRLR 104.
[110] [1993] IRLR 202.

matters specified below; and "collective bargaining" means negotiating relating to or connected with one or more of those matters.

(2)   The matters referred to above are—

(a) terms and conditions of employment, or the physical conditions in which any workers are required to work;
(b) engagement or non-engagement, or termination or suspension of employment or the duties of employment, of one or more workers;
(c) allocation of work or the duties of employment between workers or groups of workers;
(d) matters of discipline;
(e) a worker's membership or non-membership of a trade union;
(f) facilities for officials of trade unions; and
(g) machinery for negotiations or consultation, and other procedures, relating to any of the above matters, including the recognition by employers or employers' associations of the right of a trade union to represent workers in such negotiation or consultation or in the carrying out of such procedures.

(3)   In this Act "recognition" in relation to a trade union, means the recognition of the union by an employer, or two or more associated employers, to any extent, for the purposes of collective bargaining, and "recognised" and other related expressions shall be construed accordingly.'

3.162   Whilst this definition is wide, it is possible for collective agreements to fall outside its parameters and in such cases the collective agreements are not covered by TULRCA 1992.[111]

3.163   When looking at the content of a collective agreement, terms cannot be implied into such agreements in the same way as with normal contracts. A presumption, it seems, exists that, where a collective agreement is silent as to a particular point, the point was left out of the collective agreement on purpose on the grounds that it was either too controversial or too complicated to justify any variation of the collective agreement. Therefore rather than having judicial correction of such agreements (as might occur with other contracts and agreements), they are left as they are found by the courts.[112]

Status of collective agreements

3.164   The legal status of collective agreements can fall into one of three categories. The first category deals with agreements concluded before 1 December 1971 or outside the statutory definition of a collective agreement under TULRCA 1992, s 178. The last two categories deal with agreements concluded under either the Industrial Relations Act 1971 (IRA 1971) or by the regime that replaced it. Each will be looked at in turn.

Collective agreements prior to 1 December 1971 or outside the statutory definition

3.165   The legal status of the first category of collective agreements is governed by the common law rules relating to the construction of contracts

---

[111]   See, for example, *Universe Tankships Inc of Monrovia v ITWF* [1982] IRLR 200, where a payment of money by an employer as a goodwill gesture was held not to fall in the list in TULRCA 1992, s 178(2).
[112]   Per *Ali v Christian Salvesen Food Services Limited* [1997] IRLR 17.

which focus on, inter alia, whether the parties to the collective agreement intended that it should be legally binding as between them. The leading case on the point is *Ford Motor Co Limited v AEF*.[113] The case concerned collective agreements entered into between Ford and the defendant union which governed various matters relating both to dealings with trade unions at Ford and terms and conditions of employment for employees. The defendant union represented a minority of the workers at Ford and, after agreement was reached in respect of new terms between Ford and the majority of the other unions, the defendant called strike action so as to hold out for better terms. Ford sued for breach of contract (the collective agreements) and sought an injunction. In order to determine whether the defendant had breached the terms of an enforceable collective agreement, it was necessary that the collective agreements were intended to be legally binding. The High Court held that when determining whether the parties to a collective agreement had intended it to be legally binding, it was necessary to look at all of the facts of the case. After reviewing numerous cases, articles and Donovan Commission evidence, the court held that:[114]

> '... the general climate of opinion on both sides of industry has over-whelmingly been in favour of no legal obligation from collective agreements ... If one applies the subjective test and asks what the intentions of the various parties were, the answer is that so far as they had any express intentions they were certainly not to make the agreement enforceable at law. If one applies an objective test and asks what intention must be imputed from all the circumstances of the case, the answer is the same. The fact that the agreements prima facie deal with commercial relationships is outweighed by the other considerations, by the wording of the agreements, by the nature of the agreements, and by the climate of opinion voiced and evidenced by the extra-judicial authorities. Agreements such as these, composed largely of optimistic aspirations, preventing grave practical problems of enforcement and reached against a background of opinion adverse to enforceability, are, in my judgment, not contracts in the legal sense and are not enforceable at law. Without clear and express provisions making them amenable to law, they remain in the realm of undertakings binding in honour.'

3.166 Therefore, as between the parties, ordinarily it is necessary to construe collective agreements to be binding in honour only unless a clause is included making them into a legally binding agreement which can be reviewed by the court. This is not necessarily true though where the terms (or some of them) of a collective agreement are incorporated into individual contracts of employment and regard should be had to **3.180** on this point.

Agreements after 30 November 1971 and prior to 16 September 1974

3.167 Collective agreements covered by this period would fall into the regime created by IRA 1971, s 34(2), which provided that, if a collective agreement as defined under IRA 1971 was created, it was conclusively presumed to be binding as between the parties.

---

[113] [1969] 2 QB 303.
[114] [1969] 2 QB 303 at 330.

3.168   This said, it was possible to contract out of IRA 1971, s 34(2) by having a clause inserted into a written collective agreement which conclusively presumed that the agreement was to be non-binding (IRA 1971, s 34(1)).

3.169   IRA 1971 was introduced against a spirit of non-co-operation by trade unions and, as a result, the vast majority of collective agreements from that era included an IRA 1971, s 34(1) clause.

Collective agreements made after 16 September 1974

3.170   Any collective agreements (as now defined by TULRCA 1992, s 178) entered into after 16 September 1974 fall to be governed by the provisions of the Trade Union and Labour Relations Act 1974 and, latterly, by TULRCA 1992. The consolidated provisions with regard to enforceability are set down in TULRCA 1992, s 179, and there is now a presumption that, unless a collective agreement is in writing and contains a clause stating that it is intended to be binding as between the parties, it is conclusively presumed to be non-binding (TULRCA 1992, s 179(1)). To the extent that a collective agreement complies with these requirements, it is conclusively presumed to be binding (TULRCA 1992, s 179(2)).

Non-binding clauses in binding collective agreements

3.171   Whilst, as was discussed at **3.169–3.170**, some collective agreements are presumed to be binding as between the parties, not all clauses contained in such agreements are capable of being enforced by a court. These clauses fall into two categories, discriminatory clauses and clauses preventing the calling or taking of industrial action.

Discriminatory clauses

3.172   To the extent that a clause in a collective agreement seeks to discriminate against a person on grounds of sex, race, disability, religion or religious belief or sexual orientation, it is void under the provisions of, respectively, the Sex Discrimination Act 1975, s 77; the Race Relations Act 1976, s 72; the Disability Discrimination Act 1995, Sch 3A, Part 2; the Employment Equality (Religion or Religious Belief) Regulations 2003,[115] Sch 4, Part 2; and the Employment Equality (Sexual Orientation) Regulations 2003,[116] Sch 4, Part 2. Similar provisions will also apply in respect of the Employment Equality (Age) Regulations when these come into effect on 1 October 2006.

No industrial action clauses

3.173   Clauses in a collective agreement entered into between an employer and a trade union which contain a clause preventing the union from calling or taking industrial action are presumed to be non-binding as between the employer and individual employee members of the trade union unless they conform to the requirements of TULRCA 1992, s 180. This requires that the following criteria are observed, that:

- the collective agreement which contains the clause must be in writing;

---

[115]   SI 2003/1660.
[116]   SI 2003/1661.

- the collective agreement must contain a clause expressly stating that the clause or clauses are to be incorporated into individual contracts of employment of employees;
- the collective agreement itself must be reasonably accessible to employees at their place of work and employees must be able to inspect the collective agreement during their working hours; and
- the trade union entering into such a collective agreement must be an independent union.

3.174 Any such clause must also be actually incorporated into individual contracts (TULRCA 1992, s 180(2); see **3.180** as to incorporation of provisions of collective agreements).

3.175 It is not possible to contract out of the provisions of TULRCA 1992, s 180 (per TULRCA 1992, s 180(3)).

3.176 TULRCA 1992, s 180 exists as a safeguard to workers who would otherwise lose their right to take industrial action in the event that it is necessary to bring about a change in working practices. In practical terms, collective agreements of this nature should be entered into only after a trade union has thought long and hard about the implications of what it is giving up. The requirement of independence on the part of a trade union also stops staff associations (over which an employer might exert considerable pressure) from negotiating away the right to take industrial action thereby providing the employer with a 'tame' workforce.

Collective agreements and transfers of undertakings

3.177 Where a collective agreement has been entered into between an employer and a trade union and the employer then transfers the undertaking or part thereof containing members of the trade union with which the collective agreement has been made with the result that the undertaking retains its identity post transfer, a question arises as to whether a transferee employer is bound by the collective agreement. TUPE 1981, reg 6 (which enacts Transfer of Undertakings Directive,[117] Art 3(2)), provides that:

'Where at the time of a relevant transfer there exists a collective agreement made by or on behalf of the transferor with a trade union recognised by the transferor in respect of any employee whose contract of employment is preserved by Regulation 5(1) above, then,—

(a) without prejudice to the 1974 Act or Article 63 of the 1976 Order (collective agreements presumed to be unenforceable in specified circumstances) that agreement, in its application in relation to the employee, shall, after the transfer, have effect as if made by or on behalf of the transferee with that trade union, and accordingly anything done under or in connection with it, in its application as aforesaid, by or in relation to the transferor before the transfer, shall, after the transfer, be deemed to have been done by or in relation to the transferee; and

(b) any order made in respect of that agreement, in its application in

---

[117] Directive 77/187/EEC.

relation to the employee, shall, after the transfer, have effect as if the transferee were a party to the agreement.'

3.178   The effect of the provision is that where a collective agreement exists, its obligations are transferred upon the undertaking being transferred. There is a certain amount of window-dressing in this provision. Most collective agreements are non-binding as between a trade union and an employer. The effect of a transfer of an undertaking is that a transferee will be bound by a collective agreement to the same extent as a transferor; in other words, in practical terms, the transferee steps into the shoes of the transferor. It follows that if a transferor was not legally bound to observe a collective agreement, a transferee stepping into the transferor's shoes is not so bound either and is therefore free to ignore any such collective agreement if it thinks fit (subject to complying with any notice provisions in the collective agreement). The downside to abandoning collective agreements in this fashion is that the newly de-recognised trade union may seek compulsory recognition under TULRCA 1992, Sch A1.

3.179   One caveat needs to be added to the foregoing and this is that a transferee can only terminate a collective agreement with regard to a trade union which is a party to the collective agreement. However, to the extent that a collective agreement has incorporated terms into individual employees' contracts of employment, the transferee is bound to honour those terms due to TUPE 1981, reg 5. For example, in *Whent v T Cartledge Limited*,[118] in the course of an outsourcing arrangement, the respondent transferee had taken over the contract of carrying out the street lighting services for a local authority. The local authority was a party to a national level collective agreement which incorporated into the contracts of employment of its employees certain terms and conditions of employment. Upon the undertaking being transferred, the transferee wrote to the trade union representing the transferred employees informing it that recognition of the union was being withdrawn and that the respondent was terminating its membership of the national level collective agreement. The respondent also wrote to individual employees who had transferred with the undertaking and informed them that the collective agreements would no longer have any effect with regard to the setting of their terms and conditions of employment. The applicants lodged claims under the Wages Act 1986 (now ERA 1996, Part II) claiming that, since their individual contracts of employment contained terms and conditions set from time to time by the collective agreement, they were entitled to rely on those terms and conditions with regard to their pay. The respondent transferee argued that, to the extent that an obligation had transferred under TUPE 1981 in respect of the national-level collective agreements, it was an obligation to honour only the last collective agreement to which the local authority had been a party and not any new national collective agreements that were subsequently created. The EAT held that the respondent employer had an obligation to honour new national collective agreements as updated from time to time since the contracts of employment of the individual employees referred to terms and conditions being set by reference to the national level collective agreements: it was therefore not possible for the employer to claim that new collective agreements had no effect. Consequently, to the extent that the employer wanted to vary the terms and conditions of employment of the employees, it would have to be

---

[118]   [1997] IRLR 153.

done by individual agreement with each employee (although, obviously, it would not be possible to vary the terms and conditions of employment under TUPE 1981, reg 5(1) for a reason connected with the transfer[119]).

Incorporation of collective agreements into individual contracts of employment

3.180   As to when a collective agreement becomes incorporated into an individual contract, this is very much a question of fact in a particular case.[120] The fact that a clause in a collective agreement is non-binding as between a trade union and an employer does not stop the clause becoming incorporated by reference as a term in an individual employee's contract of employment.[121]

3.181   This said, not every term that is referred to in a collective agreement is capable of becoming incorporated into an employee's contract of employment. Terms of collective agreements which operate in relation to the collective rights and obligations of an employer and trade union are generally not thought appropriate to be incorporated into individual contracts.[122]

3.182   This said, each case in this area very much depends on the particular facts. Different courts have come to different results with regard to the incorporation of terms and conditions from collective agreements into contracts of employment, as follows.

3.183   In *Young v Canadian Northern Railway Co*,[123] the Privy Council held that a collective agreement relating to redundancy procedures was not incorporated into the claimant's contract of employment. In *Alexander v Standard Telephones & Cables Limited*,[124] the High Court dismissed an application for an injunction preventing a breach of a redundancy procedures agreements on the grounds that it would compel the employer to employ those it did not wish to employ. However, the court recognised that there was a serious issue to be tried in the case.

3.184   Further, in *Anderson v Pringle of Scotland Limited*,[125] the Scottish Court of Session held that an interdict could be granted where a last in, first out redundancy agreement between an employer and a union was breached on the ground that the agreement was capable of being incorporated into individual contracts of employment. Commenting upon the authorities generally,

---

[119]   See in this regard *Berriman v Delabole Slate Limited* [1985] IRLR 305; *Foreningen af Arbejdsledere i Danmark v Daddy's Dance Hall A/S* [1988] IRLR 315; and *Wilson v St. Helens Borough Council* [1998] IRLR 706.

[120]   See, for example, *Robertson v British Gas Corporation* [1983] IRLR 302; *Cadoux v Central Regional Council* [1986] IRLR 131; *Marley v Forward Trust Group Limited* [1986] IRLR 369; *Whent v T Cartledge Limited* [1997] IRLR 153; and *Burke v Royal Liverpool University Trust Hospital* [1997] ICR 730.

[121]   *Whent v T Cartledge Limited* [1997] IRLR 153.

[122]   See, for example, *R v Industrial Disputes Tribunal, ex p Portland UDC* [1955] 3 All ER 18 (where a disputes procedure was held not to have become incorporated); *Gallagher v Post Office* [1970] 3 All ER 712 (a requirement for union recognition was held not to have been incorporated); and *Lee v GEC Plessey Telecommunications* [1993] IRLR 383 (an agreement for enhanced redundancy packages was held not to have been incorporated).

[123]   [1931] AC 83.

[124]   [1990] IRLR 55.

[125]   [1998] IRLR 65.

the court stated that it could not see a difference between the position under English law and that under Scots law adding that it was satisfied that in principle it is a matter of circumstances rather than law.

3.185   More recently, in *Kaur v MG Rover Group Limited*,[126] the Court of Appeal had to consider a case where the claimant had sought to rely upon provisions of various collective agreements entered into between the employer and unions recognised by it in order to argue that the cumulative effect was to provide that no employee would be subject to compulsory redundancy (a point that would have been tested by the subsequent well-publicised insolvency of the employer). The court relied upon the decision in *Alexander v Standard Telephones and Cables Limited*[127] to find that the test of whether the collective agreements had become incorporated into the claimant's contract of employment was to consider whether they were 'apt' for incorporation. In this regard, the court found that the terms of the collective agreements were largely aspirational statements of objectives in nature. Consequently, although there was a provision which stated that there would be no compulsory redundancies, this was coloured by the remainder of the collective agreements. In the circumstances, the terms were found not to be 'apt' for incorporation. Indeed, the presumption in relation to the incorporation of terms from collective agreements seems to be against incorporation, a trend which goes back to *Ford Motor Co Limited v AEF*.[128]

---

[126]   [2004] EWCA Civ 1507.
[127]   See [1990] ICR 291 for the interlocutory proceedings, in which it was held to be 'arguable' that a last in, first out redundancy clause in a collective agreement had become incorporated into individual contracts of employment. However, the argument failed at the trial of the action: [1991] IRLR 286.
[128]   [1969] 2 QB 303.

Chapter 4

STATUTORY RECOGNITION OF TRADE UNIONS

4.1 Statutory trade union recognition was introduced following the coming to power of the Labour Government in 1997. In a review of a number of employment practises under the White Paper *Fairness at Work*,[1] the Government proposed that statutory trade union representation and recognition should be provided where a majority of workers wanted it. Following the *Fairness at Work* White Paper and its subsequent consultation, the Employment Relations Act 1999 (ERA 1999) was passed. It provided for, inter alia, the statutory recognition scheme under the Trade Union and Labour Relations (Consolidation) Act 1992 (TULRCA 1992), s 70A and Sch A1 and the training consultation provisions under TULRCA 1992, s 70B.

4.2 TULRCA 1992, Sch A1 has itself been substantially amended by the Employment Relations Act 2004 (ERA 2004) (most notably in connection with initial recognition and derecogniton of unions). The statutory recognition process is now contained in TULRCA 1992, Sch A1. It is a highly regulated piece of machinery for determining whether one or more independent trade unions may be afforded the right to be recognised by an employer (or group of employers) in relation to one or more 'bargaining units'. The process governs all aspects of trade union recognition, from making an application, through the application being considered, accepted, machinery being put in place for recognition during the life of the recognition agreement, through to the termination of recognition. The result is a huge volume of tightly drafted provisions and timetable requirements worthy of a whole separate Act rather than being tagged on as an afterthought to TULRCA 1992. Indeed, the provisions have been described in *R v Central Arbitration Committee, ex p Kwik-Fit (GB) Limited*[2] as being of 'Byzantine complexity'.

4.3 The following provisions take in the amendments under ERA 2004. All references to paras are references to paras of TULRCA 1992, Sch A1.

BASIC CONCEPTS

4.4 As to the procedure to be adopted in a recognition application under TULRCA 1992, Sch A1, it relies, so far as possible, on agreement between the parties. There is, however, a mechanism whereby any disputes can be arbitrated.

---

[1]   Cm 3968, 1998.
[2]   [2002] IRLR 395.

The body principally responsible for dealing with statutory recognition claims under TULRCA 1992 is the Central Arbitration Committee (CAC). In exercising its functions under TULRCA 1992, Sch A1, the CAC is required to have regard to the object of encouraging and promoting fair and efficient practises and arrangements in the workplace, so far as it is possible taking account of the other duties it owes under TULRCA 1992, Sch A1, para 171.[3]

4.5   TULRCA 1992, Sch A1, para 1 provides that a trade union (or trade unions) seeking recognition to be entitled to conduct collective bargaining on behalf of a group or groups of workers[4] may make a request to be recognised in accordance with TULRCA 1992, Sch A1.

4.6   TULRCA 1992, Sch A1, para 3(3) provides that references to collective bargaining are to negotiations relating to pay, hours and holidays. This has effect subject to para 3(4) which provides that if the parties agree matters as the subject of collective bargaining, references to collective bargaining are to negotiations relating to those agreed matters (and this is the case at whatever stage the parties reach agreement (para 3(4)). Additionally, para 3(6) specifically provides that this definition of 'collective bargaining' for the purposes of TULRCA 1992, Sch A1 does not apply for the purposes of paras 35 or 44 (where the CAC check to see whether another union is recognised in respect of collective bargaining as defined under TULRCA 1992, s 178).

4.7   Further, in *UNIFI and the National Bank of Nigeria*,[5] the CAC concluded that pensions were becoming increasingly included as a negotiating item in voluntary agreements under TULRCA 1992, Sch A1. Consequently, it concluded that the term 'pay' under Sch A1 included all matters relating to the levels or amount of employer's pension contributions. However, following this decision, a change has been implemented under ERA 2004, introducing a new para 171A, which now provides that 'pay' does not include any rights relating to membership of an occupational pension scheme (as defined under the Pension Schemes Act 1993, s 1) or to a personal pension scheme.

4.8   References to a 'bargaining unit' are to those specified in the request for recognition but those references to an 'appropriate bargaining unit' are to that or those units decided by the CAC as being the appropriate bargaining unit (TULRCA 1992, Sch A1, para 3(3) and (3A)).

4.9   Additionally, under TULRCA 1992, s 70B, where a trade union (or unions) is/are recognised, in accordance with TULRCA 1992, Sch A1 as entitled to conduct collective bargaining on behalf of a bargaining unit, and a method for the conduct of collective bargaining is specified by the CAC under TULRCA 1992, Sch A1, para 31(3) (and is not the subject of an agreement

---

3   See, for an example of how the obligations under para 171 are to be exercised, *R (on the application of Ultraframe (UK) Limited) v Central Arbitration Committee* [2005] EWCA Civ 560, [2005] IRLR 641.

4   As regards the definition of 'workers' for these purposes, this was considered in *R (on the application of the British Broadcasting Corporation) v Central Arbitration Committee* [2003] IRLR 460, which draws a distinction between the status of freelance contractors who were held by the CAC to be workers but, upon being judicially reviewed, were found to be 'professionals' (and therefore not entitled to claim the right to statutory recognition), and workers (who are entitled to claim the right).

5   [2001] IRLR 712.

under para 31(5)(a) or (b)), the employer must from time to time invite the trade union to send representatives to a meeting in relation to the following training-related matters:

- consulting about the employer's policy on training for workers within the bargaining unit;
- consulting about its plans for training for those workers during the period of 6 months starting with the day of the meeting; and
- reporting about training provided for those workers since the previous meeting.

4.10   The first such meeting must be held within 6 months of the union becoming recognised for the purposes of TULRCA 1992, s 70B and subsequent meetings must take place no more than 6 months apart (per TULRCA 1992, s 70B(3)). Additionally, at least 2 weeks before each such meeting, the employer must provide to the trade union any information without which the union's representatives would be to a material extent impeded in participating in the meeting and which it would be in accordance with good industrial relations practice to disclose for the purposes of the meeting (s 70B(4)). The CAC can specify what type of information should be provided (s 70B(5)).

4.11   The employer is required to take account of any written representations about matters raised at a meeting which it receives from the trade union within the period of 4 weeks starting with the date of the meeting (TULRCA 1992, s 70B(6)).

4.12   In the event that an employer fails to comply with its obligations under TULRCA 1992, s 70B, under TULRCA 1992, s 70C, a trade union (or unions) recognised for the purposes of s 70B may present a complaint to an employment tribunal that the employer has failed to comply with its obligations under s 70B in relation to the relevant bargaining unit. Where an employment tribunal finds such a complaint to be well founded it must make a declaration to that effect and may make an award of compensation to be paid by the employer to each person who was, at the time when the failure occurred, a member of the bargaining unit (s 70C(3)). The amount of compensation to be awarded may not exceed 2 weeks' pay (capped at the rate from time to time in force under the Employment Rights Act 1996 (ERA 1996)) per worker (TULRCA 1992, s 70C(4) and (5)). Proceedings under this head must be presented to an employment tribunal within 3 months of the employer's alleged breach (s 70C(2)). Enforcement proceedings in respect of a failure to pay any compensation so ordered can only be brought by a worker or workers in whose favour a compensation order has been granted (s 70C(6)).

REQUESTS FOR RECOGNITION

4.13   TULRCA 1992, Sch A1, para 4 provides that a union (or unions) seeking recognition must make a request for recognition to the employer in accordance with TULRCA 1992, Sch A1, paras 5–9. 'Employer' for these purposes means a single employer (albeit that a single employer can, in certain circumstances, be an employer spread out across a group of companies[6]).

---

6   As regards the definition of an employer for these purposes, this was considered in *Graphical, Paper and Media Union v Derry Print Limited* [2002] IRLR 380, in which the CAC held that

Furthermore, the request must specify the correct employer, which can include the correct employer albeit incorrectly particularised.

4.14   Where an application for recognition is made jointly by two or more trade unions, under TULRCA 1992, Sch A1, para 37, the unions must be able to satisfy the CAC that they will be able to operate together in manner that it is likely to secure collective bargaining arrangements which are stable and effective and, that if the employer wishes, they will enter into arrangements under which collective bargaining is conducted by the unions acting together on behalf of the workers constituting the relevant bargaining unit (para 37(2)). In this regard, the CAC may rely upon the industrial relations experience of its panel members to determine whether they believe that the unions will co-operate and the unions may seek to give appropriately drafted undertakings that they will co-operate with each other.[7]

4.15   Where applications are made by a number of different trade unions at the same time in respect either of the same bargaining unit, or overlapping bargaining units (the overlap can be in respect of as little as one employee[8]), and the CAC has not accepted any of the applications, the CAC must decide whether either none or more than one of the applications has the prima facie support of at least 10 per cent of the workers constituting the proposed bargaining unit (the 10 per cent test). Where this is the case, under TULRCA 1992, Sch A1, para 14(7) the CAC cannot accept any of the applications. If, however, only one of the competing applications passes the 10 per cent test, the CAC can consider that application provided it complies with the request of the criteria under TULRCA 1992, Sch A1, para 14(8).

4.16   These provisions in the case of multiple applications require the competing unions to determine from amongst themselves which is the appropriate union (if any) to represent the workers within the bargaining unit.

4.17   Where, however, an application has been presented to the CAC and accepted in respect of one trade union in relation to a defined bargaining unit, if another trade union subsequently makes an application in relation to the same, or an overlapping, bargaining unit, the application must be refused by the CAC under TULRCA 1992, Sch A1, para 38(2).[9]

4.18   A further issue arises in the case of an application for recognition where a union merges with another union either by means of an amalgamation or by undertaking a transfer of engagements (see **Chapter 11**) whilst in the course of making an application for recognition. In such a case, the union amalgamating or transferring its engagements ceases to exist upon completion of the merger.

notwithstanding the general aggregation provisions under TULRCA 1992 for associated employers, a bargaining unit can only be at a single employer rather than across the whole spectrum of associated employers which might exist in a group of companies. However, the CAC also went on to hold that, in exceptional cases (such as the instant one), it might be correct to 'lift the corporate veil' where two companies in a group were in reality only one and the technical appearance of separation concealed the reality of a unified employer. See also *NUMAST v Hoverspeed Limited* TUR1/433/05 for an example of this principle.

7   See, for example, TGWU and GMB and Gala Casinos Limited TUR1/206/02.
8   See, for example, the *Polypipe Building Products Limited* applications TR1/197/02 and TUR1/199/02.
9   See, for example, *GMB and Faccenda Group Limited* TUR1/209 and 210/02.

The way that the CAC has treated such matters has differed. In *MSF and Unipart Group of Companies Limited*,[10] the CAC provided two alternative solutions:

● That a union is simply a group of individuals who will themselves survive the merger, albeit under a different name. Therefore, in such cases, the benefit of the application made by a union merging into another union will pass to the merging body.

● That in any event, it was more likely than not that Parliament's intention was that where an application had been made by a merging union, the benefit of the application should transfer to the merged body.

4.19 However, in *Amicus-AEEU and GE Caledonian Limited*,[11] the CAC approached the question of how to deal with the merger of the applicant for recognition by treating the application made by AEEU as having been made by the merged Amicus-AEEU.[12]

4.20 The position in the case of a union merging by receiving a transfer of engagements (see **Chapter 11**) is less complicated in that the transferee union continues to exist both before and after the transfer and therefore the merger in this form is of no effect to the application for recognition.[13]

4.21 This matter has now been addressed under ERA 2004, which has inserted at TULRCA 1992, Sch A1, para 169A a power for the Secretary of State to make provision for cases where unions amalgamate or transfer all or any of their engagements, including in relation to an amalgamated union, or union to which engagements are transferred, which does not have a Certificate of Independence under TULRCA 1992, s 6.

Content of the request for recognition

4.22 A request for recognition is not valid unless:

● It is received by the employer (TULRCA 1992, Sch A1, para 5).
● The union (or each of the unions) making the request has a Certificate of Independence under TULRCA 1992, s 6 (TULRCA 1992, Sch A1, para 6).
● The employer, taken with any associated employer or employers, employs at least 21 workers on the day the employer receives the request or an average of at least 21 workers in the 13 weeks ending with that day (TULRCA 1992, Sch A1, para 7, in particular para 7(2)–(8) with regard to calculating the average number of workers). In this regard, all workers are to be counted (whether they are full-time, part-time, temporary or casual).
● It is in writing, identifies the union or unions and the bargaining unit and states that the request is made under TULRCA 1992, Sch A1.[14]

---

[10]   TUR1/94/01.
[11]   TUR1/120/01.
[12]   See also *Amicus and Britton Gelplas Limited* TUR1/171/02 for a similar example of attribution to a merged union.
[13]   See, for example, Amicus & GMB and Alan Worswick Engineering Limited TUR1/157/02.
[14]   See *NUMAST v Hoverspeed Limited* TUR1/374/04 in relation to the importance of the union putting forward a consistent bargaining unit in the written request and the subsequent application for recognition.

4.23   The request is required to be made on a form prescribed by statutory instrument (TULRCA 1992, Sch A1, para 9).

4.24   Upon receipt of a request for recognition, an employer has three options, as follows:

- If, within the period of 10 working days (the first period) starting with the day after that on which the employer receives the request for recognition, the employer accedes to the request for recognition, the union is (or unions are) to be recognised as entitled to conduct collective bargaining on behalf of the bargaining unit and no further steps need to be taken (TULRCA 1992, Sch A1, para 10(1)).
- If before the end of the period of 10 working days starting with the day after that on which the employer receives the request for recognition, the employer informs the union (or unions) that it does not accept the request but is willing to negotiate, the parties may conduct negotiations with a view to agreeing a bargaining unit and the union is (or unions are) to be recognised as entitled to conduct collective bargaining on behalf of the bargaining unit. The parties are then given 20 working days, starting with the day after that on which the first period ends or such longer period as they may agree (TULRCA 1992, Sch A1, para 10(2) and (3)), to negotiate.
- the employer may reject the application, or the negotiations under TULRCA 1992, Sch A1, para 10 may come to nothing, in which case matters are dealt with as follows:
    - In the case of an employer rejecting the request (either by failing to respond to the request or by rejecting it), the matter is dealt with under TULRCA 1992, Sch A1, para 11. In such cases, the union (or unions) may apply to the CAC to determine whether a bargaining unit proposed by the union is appropriate and/or whether the union has (or unions have) the support of a majority of the workers constituting the appropriate bargaining unit (para 11(2)).
    - In the case of negotiations under TULRCA 1992, Sch A1, para 10 failing, the matter falls to be dealt with under para 12 which allows the same questions as in para 11(2) to be put to the CAC (per para 12(2)).
    - It is also possible that the employer may accept the bargaining unit proposed by the union but reject that the union should be recognised in relation to it. In such a case, the union (or unions) may apply to the CAC to determine the question whether the union has (or unions have) the support of a majority of the workers constituting the bargaining unit (TULRCA 1992, Sch A1, para 12(4)).

4.25   However, no application may be made under TULRCA 1992, Sch A1, para 12 if within the period of 10 working days (starting with the day after that on which the employer informs the union (or unions) under para 10(2)), the employer proposes that ACAS is requested to assist in conducting the negotiations and the union rejects (or unions reject) the proposal, or the union fails (or unions fail) to accept the proposal within the period of 10 working days (starting with the day after that on which the employer makes the proposal: para 12(5)).

Applications to the CAC

4.26   Under TULRCA 1992, Sch A1, para 11 or 12, in the event that a union (or unions) make an application to the CAC, the CAC must give notice to the parties of receipt of the application.

4.27 Under TULRCA 1992, Sch A1, para 16, it is possible for a union (or unions) to request at any time up to a declaration by the CAC that a union is, or unions are, recognised under para 22(2), that the application made to the CAC is withdrawn. In such a case, the CAC must give notice of the withdrawal of the application to the employer and no further steps are then taken under that Part of TULRCA 1992, Sch A1.

4.28 Alternatively, under TULRCA 1992, Sch A1, para 17, it is open to the union(s) and the employer jointly to present a notice to the CAC to cease considering a recognition application at any time before the first of the CAC issuing a declaration under para 22(2) that a union or unions is/are recognised under para 22(2), or the period of 10 working days notice of the holding of a recognition ballot, starting with the day on which the union(s) (or the last of them in the case of multiple unions) or employer receives that notice. In such a case, no further steps are to be taken.

4.29 In the event that there is no such application, or no notice to withdraw is presented to the CAC, and the CAC accepts the application, the CAC must then move to consider the application.

4.30 Consideration of the application occurs under TULRCA 1992, Sch A1, para 15. In order for the CAC to accept an application, it must satisfy itself that the request for recognition to which the application relates is valid within the terms of paras 5–9 (as set out at **4.22**) and that the application is admissible within the terms of paras 34–42 (as set at **4.32**).

4.31 Consideration takes place within the period of 10 working days starting with the day after that on which the CAC receives the application or such longer period as the CAC may specify to the parties by notice containing reasons for the extension. The application must also be in the form specified by the CAC and be accompanied by such documents as the CAC specifies (TULRCA 1992, Sch A1, para 33).

4.32 The matters in TULRCA 1992, Sch A1, paras 34–42 are as follows:

- An application is not admissible unless the union gives (or unions give) to the employer notice of the application and a copy of the application and any documents supporting it (para 34).[15]
- The CAC must be satisfied that there is not already 'in force'[16] a collective

---

[15] See, for example, *NUMAST v Hoverspeed Limited* TUR1/383/04.

[16] See, in particular, *R (on the application of the National Union of Journalists) v Central Arbitration Committee and MGN Limited* [2005] IRLR 28, where the NUJ submitted an application seeking recognition in respect of the employer's sport division journalists. The employer contested the application on the grounds that another union was already voluntarily recognised by it, which the CAC accepted was the case. On a judicial review application, the union contended, first, that the collective agreement with the other union was not 'in force' as it had not been used to set terms and condition of employment of members of the bargaining unit and, secondly, that TULRCA 1992, Sch A1, para 35 was contrary to the European Convention on Human Rights, Art 11 in that it prevented freedom of association. The High Court rejected the application on both grounds holding that from the moment that a voluntary recognition agreement is signed, it is 'in force' for the purposes of para 35. As regards the freedom of association point, the court held that all the majority union's freedoms and those of the workers in that union are preserved, including the right to take industrial action and that Art 11 does not impose any positive obligation on a state to grant a union 'the

agreement under which a union is (or unions are) recognised as entitled to conduct collective bargaining on behalf of any workers (even one such worker) falling within the relevant bargaining unit. In this regard, a collective agreement can include a national collective agreement to which the employer is a party if that collective agreement confers collective bargaining rights (para 35).[17]

- The CAC must be satisfied that members of the union (or unions) amount to at least 10 per cent of the workers constituting the relevant bargaining unit, and a majority of the workers constituting the relevant bargaining unit would be likely to favour recognition of the union (or unions) as entitled to conduct collective bargaining on behalf of the bargaining unit (para 36). It is often the case that the CAC will require proof of union membership within a proposed bargaining unit and details of the names of employees within a bargaining unit to be supplied, respectively, by the union and the employer on a confidential basis. As for other evidence, petitions can be produced (both for the employer and the union) to demonstrate support (or lack of it) for the union and letters from employees showing that they would welcome union recognition for statutory collective bargaining purposes. Conversely, the union can be required to demonstrate that workers are members of the union in accordance with the union's own membership rules in cases where the union has offered free or reduced-rate memberships in the context of a pre-recognition claim recruitment drive.
- In the case of a joint union application, the union (or unions) must show to the CAC that they will co-operate with each other in a manner likely to secure and maintain stable and effective collective bargaining arrangements and that, if the employer wishes, they will enter into arrangements under which collective bargaining is conducted by the unions acting together on behalf of the workers constituting the relevant bargaining unit (para 37).
- The union (or unions) cannot present an application for recognition in relation to a bargaining unit which comprises at least one worker who is a member of a bargaining unit already recognised by the employer (para 38).
- The union (or unions) cannot present an application for recognition in relation to a bargaining unit which is the same, or substantially the same, as one in respect of which an application has been made in the 3 years starting with the day after that on which the CAC gave notice of acceptance of the application (para 39).

---

right' to conduct collective bargaining with any particular employer. See also *NUMAST v Hoverspeed Limited* TUR1/433/05, where the CAC held that an Italian collective agreement which potentially applied to a number of employees within the bargaining unit was not in force as the employer did not comply with its terms.

[17] See *Transport and General Workers' Union v Asda* [2004] IRLR 836, dealing with the provisions of para 35, where the applicant union submitted that a 'partnership agreement' between the employer and another union was not a collective agreement falling within para 35 because it did not cover pay, hours and holiday. The CAC rejected the application on the basis that the definition of 'collective bargaining' for the purposes of para 3 (which provides the general TULRCA 1992, Sch A1 definition), was specifically disapplied in relation to para 35. Therefore, the general definition of collective bargaining under TULRCA 1992, s 178 applied. Consequently, notwithstanding that the other union was not recognised for the purposes of pay, hours and holidays, it was still recognised for the purposes of para 35 and the application was therefore rejected.

• Likewise, it is not possible to gain recognition in respect of a bargaining unit in relation to which in the preceding 3 years the CAC has issued a declaration that a union is not entitled to be recognised following either an unsuccessful recognition (para 40), or a derecognition (para 41), ballot.

4.33 In this regard, the CAC is required to make a determination of compliance with the factors under TULRCA 1992, Sch A1, paras 5–9 and 34–42 as at the date of its decision on the most recent evidence available to it.

The bargaining unit

4.34 Under TULRCA 1992, Sch A1, para 18, if the CAC accepts an application under para 11(2) or 12(2), it must try to help the parties within the period of 20 working days (starting with the day after that on which the CAC gives notice of acceptance of the application (or such longer period as the CAC may specify to the parties by notice containing reasons for the extension)), to reach an agreement as to what the appropriate bargaining unit is. The 20-day period may be varied in three cases, as follows:

• first, if, during that period, the CAC concludes that there is no reasonable prospect of the parties' agreeing an appropriate bargaining unit before the time when (apart from this subparagraph) the 20-day period would end, the CAC may, by a notice given to the parties, declare an end to the period of negotiations effective on the date of that notice (para 18(3));

• secondly, if, during the 20-day period, the parties apply to the CAC for a declaration that the period is to end with a date (specified in the application) which is earlier than the date with which it would otherwise end, the CAC may, by a notice given to the parties, declare that the period ends with that specified date (para 18(4)); or

• thirdly, if the CAC has declared under para 18(4) that the 20-day period ends with a specified date, it may before that date by a notice given to the parties specify a later date on which the appropriate period ends (para 18(5)).

4.35 If the parties are unable to determine the appropriate bargaining unit within the timescale set out by the CAC, then, under TULRCA 1992, Sch A1, para 18A, within 5 working days (starting with the day after that on which the CAC gives the employer notice of acceptance of the application), the employer must, as accurately as is reasonably practicable in the light of the information in the possession of the employer at the time, supply the following information to the union (or unions) and the CAC in exactly the same format:

• a list of the categories of worker in the proposed bargaining unit;

• a list of the workplaces at which the workers in the proposed bargaining unit work; and

• the number of workers the employer reasonably believes to be in each category at each workplace.

4.36 Under TULRCA 1992, Sch A1, para 19, if the CAC accepts an application under para 11(2) or 12(2), the parties have not agreed an appropriate bargaining unit at the end of the 20-working day period under para 18 and at the end of that period no request under para 19A (see **4.37**) has been made, or a request has been made but the condition in para 19A(1)(b) (see **4.37**) has not been met, then, within the period of 10 working days (starting after the day on which the 20-working day period under para 18 comes to an end, or such longer period as the CAC may state), the CAC must decide whether the proposed bargaining unit is appropriate. It has been held by the Court of Appeal in *R v Central Arbitration Committee, ex p Kwik-Fit (GB) Limited*[18] that if the CAC determines that the union's proposed bargaining unit is appropriate, it must stop there and not consider whether there are other alternative bargaining units which might be appropriate.

4.37   Under TULRCA 1992, Sch A1, para 19A, if:

- the CAC accepts an application under para 11(2) or 12(2), during the 20-working day period (set out in para 18);
- the CAC is requested by the union (or unions) to make a decision under para 19A; and
- either at the time the request is made or at a later time during that 20-working day period the CAC is of the opinion that the employer has failed to comply with the duty imposed by para 18A,

the CAC must decide whether the proposed bargaining unit is appropriate.

4.38   In this regard, the CAC is given a period of 10 working days (starting with the day after the day on which the request is made to the CAC, or such longer period as the CAC shall specify). Further, if the CAC decides that the proposed bargaining unit is not appropriate, it must also decide within that period what bargaining unit is appropriate (TULRCA 1992, Sch A1, para 19A(3)).

4.39   Under TULRCA 1992, Sch A1, para 19B, if the CAC has to decide whether a bargaining unit is appropriate for the purposes of para 19(2) or (3) or 19A(2) or (3), under para 19B(3) and (4), the CAC must take into account the following matters:

(a)   the need for the bargaining unit to be compatible with effective management; and
(b)   insofar as they do not conflict with the bargaining unit being compatible with effective management:
    (i)   the views of the employer and of the union (or unions);
    (ii)   existing national and local bargaining arrangements;
    (iii)   the desirability of avoiding small fragmented bargaining units within an undertaking;
    (iv)   the characteristics of workers falling within the proposed bargaining unit and of any other employees of the employer whom the CAC considers relevant; and
    (v)   the location of workers.

4.40   Further, in taking account of the employer's views when deciding whether the bargaining unit is appropriate, the CAC must take into account any view the employer has about any other bargaining unit which it considers might be appropriate (TULRCA 1992, Sch A1, para 19B(4)).

4.41   Having considered these matters, the CAC must give notice of its decision to the parties as to the appropriate bargaining unit (TULRCA 1992, Sch A1, para 19B(5)).

---

[18]   [2002] IRLR 395.

Union access to the workers in the bargaining unit

4.42   Where the CAC accepts an application under TULRCA 1992, Sch A1, para 19B, a revised statutory regime exists (which was brought in by ERA 2004) under para 19C with regard to communication by the union (or unions) with workers in the appropriate bargaining unit after the CAC has accepted an application in relation to those workers. In this regard, during the 'initial period', the union (or unions) may apply to the CAC for the appointment of a suitable independent person (termed by para 19C(8) as 'the appointed person'), to handle communications between the union (or unions) and the 'relevant workers'. As soon as reasonably practicable after receiving the request, the CAC is required to make the appointment and it must inform the parties of the name of the appointed person (para 19C(7)).

4.43   'Relevant workers' are defined by TULRCA 1992, Sch A1, para 19C(3) as being in the case of an application under para 11(2) or 12(2):

- in relation to any time before an appropriate bargaining unit is agreed by the parties or decided by the CAC, those workers falling within that proposed bargaining unit; and
- in relation to any time after an appropriate bargaining unit is so agreed or decided, those workers falling within the bargaining unit agreed or decided upon.

4.44   In the case of an application under TULRCA 1992, Sch A1, para 12(4), the relevant workers are those falling with the bargaining unit agreed by the parties (para 19C(4)).

4.45   Under TULRCA 1992, Sch A1, para 19C(5), the 'initial period' is a movable concept starting with the day on which the CAC informs the parties of the name of the independent person and ending on the first day that any of the following occur:

- the application for recognition under para 11 or 12 is withdrawn;
- the CAC gives notice to the union (or unions) of a decision under para 20 that the application is invalid;
- the CAC notifies the union (or unions) of a declaration issued under para 19F(5) or 22(2); or
- the CAC informs the union (or unions) under para 25(9) of the name of the person appointed to conduct a ballot.

4.46   For the purposes of TULRCA 1992, Sch A1, para 19C(6), a person is qualified to be the appointed person if he would be capable of being appointed under para 25 (see **4.62**), and there are no grounds for believing either that he will carry out any functions arising from his appointment otherwise than competently or that his independence in relation to those functions might reasonably be called into question.

4.47   Once the appointed person has been appointed and the appointment has been notified to the employer, under TULRCA 1992, Sch A1, para 19D, the employer is required to comply with four duties, as follows:

- to give to the CAC, within the period of 10 working days starting with the day after that on which the employer is informed under para 19C(7)(b), the names and home addresses of the relevant workers;
- if the relevant workers change as a result of an appropriate bargaining unit being agreed by the parties or decided by the CAC, to give to the CAC,

within the period of 10 working days starting with the day after that on which the bargaining unit is agreed, or the CAC's decision is notified to the employer, the names and home addresses of those workers who are now the relevant workers;

- to give to the CAC, as soon as reasonably practicable, the name and home address of any worker who joins the bargaining unit after the employer has complied with the preceding two points; and
- to inform the CAC, as soon as reasonably practicable, of any worker whose name has been given to the CAC under the preceding three points and who ceases to be a relevant worker (otherwise than by reason of a change mentioned in the second point above).

4.48　The CAC is required to pass on information received from the employer to the appointed person as soon as possible after its receipt by the CAC (TULRCA 1992, Sch A1, para 19C(4)). None of the duties listed at **4.47** require the employer to give any such information to the CAC after the end of the 'initial period' (as defined under para 19C(5)).

4.49　Under TULRCA 1992, Sch A1, para 19F(1), if the CAC is satisfied that the employer has failed to fulfil a duty under para 19(D), the CAC may make a 'Remedial Order' requiring the employer to:

- take such steps to remedy the failure as the CAC considers reasonable and specifies in the Remedial Order; and
- do so within such period as the CAC considers reasonable and specifies in the Remedial Order.

4.50　Under TULRCA 1992, Sch A1, para 19F(2) and (3), if the CAC is satisfied that the employer has failed to comply with a Remedial Order before the end of the initial period, the CAC is required, as soon as is reasonably practicable, to notify the employer and the union (or unions) that it is satisfied that the employer has failed to comply and must also draw the employer's attention to the fact that the CAC may issue a declaration that the union is (or unions are) recognised as entitled to conduct collective bargaining on behalf of the workers constituting the bargaining unit in the event that the employer continues to fail to comply with its duties under para 19D (paras 19F(3)–(5)).

4.51　Further, under TULRCA 1992, Sch A1, para 19E(1) during the initial period, the appointed person, if asked to do so by the union or unions, must send to any worker whose name and address has been passed on to the appointed person and who is (so far as the appointed person is aware) still a worker within the appropriate bargaining unit, any information supplied by the union to the appointed person. There are also provisions dealing with the costs that the appropriate person may incur in this regard, which are to be borne by the union or, if more than one, rateably by the unions (para 19E(2)), and the method of recovering those costs (para 19E(3)–(7)).

TRADE UNION RECOGNITION

4.52　A quirk of the CAC being required to consider the issue of recognition arises where a trade union has made an application for recognition which has been accepted by the CAC under TULRCA 1992, Sch A1, para 15(5) and a subsequent application is made by another trade union in respect of a different proposed bargaining unit. If the CAC accepts the second application (because, under para 38, the proposed bargaining unit in such a case is different and it otherwise satisfies the criteria for acceptance), it may be the case that the bargaining unit in relation to the second application is then challenged by the employer and the CAC may then be called upon to determine the appropriate bargaining unit under para 19B. If so, and the CAC determines that the bargaining unit should be amended, it is possible that the CAC may redefine the bargaining unit so that it includes one or more workers covered by the first application. In such a case, the second application has to be rejected by the CAC under para 46(2).

4.53 Furthermore, in such a case, there is a possibility under TULRCA 1992, Sch A1, para 51(3) that the original application may itself be rejected by the CAC if that application was referred to the CAC in order to determine the bargaining unit *and* the question of whether the first union should be recognised, provided that the second application satisfies the 10 per cent test under para 14. In such a case, the CAC must reject the original application.[19] However, if the second application does not satisfy the 10 per cent test, then the second application has to be rejected but the original application is unaffected (per para 51(2)(c)).

4.54 In the event that the CAC decides that a different bargaining unit is appropriate having considered the matters it is required to take into account under TULRCA 1992, Sch A1, para 19B, under para 20 the CAC is then required to consider whether it is precluded from dealing with an application for recognition in respect of the revised bargaining unit taking into account the factors in paras 43–50, these being because:

- there is already in force a collective agreement under which an independent union, or independent unions (other than the union(s) making the application where that/those union(s) are not recognised in respect of all of pay, hours and holiday), is/are recognised to conduct collective bargaining on behalf of the workers within the bargaining unit (para 44);
- the CAC is not satisfied that at least 10 per cent of the workers constituting the bargaining unit and a majority of the workers in the bargaining unit would be likely to favour recognition of the union (or unions) in respect of the bargaining unit (para 45);
- at least one worker in the proposed bargaining unit falls within another bargaining unit in respect of which the CAC has already accepted an application (para 46);
- the application is made within the period of 3 years starting with the day after that on which the CAC gave notice of acceptance of an application in respect of the bargaining unit or a substantially similar one by the same union or unions (para 47);
- the CAC issues a declaration under para 27D(4) or 29(4) that a union is (or unions are) not entitled to be recognised as entitled to conduct collective bargaining on behalf of a bargaining unit, where the application is made within the period of 3 years starting with the date of the declaration, the relevant bargaining unit is the same or substantially the same as the bargaining unit mentioned in the first point above and the application is made by the union (or unions) which made the application leading to the declaration (para 48); or

---

[19] See, for example, *ISTC and Corus Living Solutions* TUR1/295/03.

- the CAC issues a declaration under para 119D(4), 119H(5) or 121(3) that bargaining arrangements are to cease to have effect (whether or not the ballot concerned is arranged under TULRCA 1992, Sch A1, Part IV or V), the application is made within the period of 3 years starting with the day after that on which the declaration was issued in respect of the same or substantially the same bargaining unit and the application is made by the union or unions which was or were a party or parties to the proceedings leading to the declaration (para 49).

4.55   This consideration is required because the CAC will not have considered the factors in respect of the revised bargaining unit. The CAC is required to make a decision as to whether it can accept the application within the period of 10 working days starting with the day after that on which the parties agree an appropriate bargaining unit or the CAC decides an appropriate bargaining unit (TULRCA 1992, Sch A1, para 20(6)). In relation to these matters, it is the CAC which is required to determine whether a bargaining unit is the same or substantially the same as another (para 50).

4.56   In the event that the CAC decides that it cannot accept the application, the CAC must give notice of its decision to the parties, the CAC must not proceed with the application and no further steps are to be taken by the CAC under TULRCA 1992, Sch A1 in connection with that matter (para 20(4)).

4.57   In the event that the CAC decides that the application is not invalid, it must proceed with the application and give notice to this effect to the parties (TULRCA 1992, Sch A1, para 20(5)). Likewise, it must proceed if the bargaining unit is the same as that originally proposed (para 21) and the CAC is not otherwise required to reject the application.

4.58   In the event that the CAC accepts an application and is satisfied that a majority of the workers constituting the bargaining unit are members of the union (or unions), the CAC *must* issue a declaration that the union is (or unions are) recognised as entitled to conduct collective bargaining on behalf of the workers constituting the bargaining unit (TULRCA 1992, Sch A1, para 22(2)), unless any of the three 'qualifying conditions' is/are fulfilled, in which case it will be necessary to hold a ballot to determine whether the union should be recognised (para 22(3)). The 'qualifying conditions' are as follows:

- The CAC is satisfied that a ballot should be held in the interests of good industrial relations.
- The CAC has evidence, which it considers to be credible, from a significant number of union members within the bargaining unit that they do not want the union (or unions) to conduct collective bargaining on their behalf.
- Membership evidence is produced which leads the CAC to conclude that there are doubts whether a significant number of the union members within the bargaining unit want the union (or unions) to conduct collective bargaining on their behalf. In this regard, such evidence is evidence about the circumstances in which union members became members and/or evidence about the length of time for which union members have been members of the union, in a case where the CAC is satisfied that such evidence should be taken into account (paras 22(4)(c) and 22(5)).

4.59 In *Fullarton Computer Industries Limited v Central Arbitration Committee*,[20] the Court of Session considered under TULRCA 1992, Sch A1, para 22(4) the issue of whether there was a majority of workers within the proposed bargaining unit at the claimant employer who were in favour of recognition. Due to a redundancy exercise and recruitment programme for new staff, the number of workers in the bargaining unit who were members of the union fluctuated between just below a majority (which, at the request of the union, required a re-checking of the workers in the bargaining unit), and just above a majority. Upon establishing that a majority of workers in the bargaining unit were members of the union, and having considered the qualifying conditions, the CAC proceeded to grant a declaration of recognition of the union in favour of the bargaining unit on the basis of a majority of workers in the bargaining unit being members of the union. The employer applied for a judicial review, on the basis that the re-checking of the evidence was a breach of natural justice as it had not been disclosed to the employer, and that the CAC panel had taken into account matters that were not relevant but also not taken into account other matters that were relevant when making its decision. The Court of Session rejected the application and held that the CAC had applied its mind to the right test in relation to each of the three conditions and had reached conclusions which it was entitled to reach without there being any manifest error or flaw upon the face of the record. Consequently, the decision would be upheld.

Secret ballot

4.60 If the CAC decides that a ballot is necessary and it has not issued a declaration under TULRCA 1992, Sch A1, para 19F(5) that the union (or unions) is/are entitled to be recognised in relation to the bargaining unit because of the employer's default under para 19D, it must give notice to the parties that it intends to arrange for the holding of a secret ballot in which the workers constituting the bargaining unit are asked whether they want the union (or unions) to conduct collective bargaining on their behalf (para 23(2)).

4.61 Under TULRCA 1992, Sch A1, para 24(2), it is possible where the CAC has given notice of acceptance of an application for the union (or unions), or the unions (or unions) and employer, to notify the CAC that they do not want the application to proceed to a secret ballot. In such a case, the CAC is required to act upon the request (notifying the parties of the reason why it is acting), provided that the CAC is notified within the period of 10 working days starting with the day on which the last of the parties receives the CAC's notice under para 22(3) or 23(2) (or such longer period as the CAC may specify) (para 24(3)–(7)).

4.62 A secret ballot must be conducted by a qualified independent person appointed by the CAC and must be conducted within the period of 20 working days starting with the day after that on which the qualified independent person is appointed, or such longer period (so starting) as the CAC may decide. The ballot is to be at a workplace or workplaces decided by the CAC, by post or by a combination of these methods depending on the CAC's preference. In deciding how the ballot is to be conducted the CAC must take into account the

---

20   [2001] IRLR 752.

likelihood of the ballot being affected by unfairness or malpractice if it were conducted at a workplace or workplaces, costs and practicality, and such other matters as the CAC considers appropriate (TULRCA 1992, Sch A1, para 25).

4.63   However, the CAC may not decide that the ballot is to be both workplace and postal unless there are special factors making such a decision appropriate, including factors arising from the location of workers or the nature of their employment and factors put to the CAC by the employer or the union (or unions) (TULRCA 1992, Sch A1, para 25(5) and (6)).

4.64   Further, if the CAC decides that the ballot must be conducted, wholly or partly, at a workplace (or workplaces), it may require arrangements to be made for workers who, but for the arrangements, would be prevented by the CAC's decision from voting by post, and/or who are unable for reasons relating to those workers as individuals, to cast their votes in the ballot at the workplace (or at any of them), to be given the opportunity (if they request it far enough in advance of the ballot for this to be practicable) to vote by post (TULRCA 1992, Sch A1, para 25(6)).

4.65   Under TULRCA 1992, Sch A1, para 25(9), as soon as is reasonably practicable after the CAC is required to arrange for the holding of a ballot, it must inform the parties:

- that the ballot is required;
- the name of the person appointed to conduct the ballot and the date of his appointment;
- whether the ballot is to be conducted by post or at a workplace or workplaces; and
- the workplace or workplaces concerned (if the ballot is to be conducted at a workplace or workplaces).

4.66   Under TULRCA 1992, Sch A1, para 26, an employer who is informed by the CAC of the need for a ballot must comply with five duties, as follows:

- The first and overriding duty is to co-operate generally, in connection with the ballot, with the union (or unions) and the person appointed to conduct the ballot.
- The second duty is to give to the union (or unions) such access to the workers constituting the bargaining unit as is reasonable to enable the union (or unions) to inform the workers of the object of the ballot and to seek their support and their opinions on the issues involved. For these purposes, TULRCA 1992, Sch A1, para 26(4D) provides that an employer is taken to have failed to comply with this duty if it does any of the following:
    - it refuses a request for a meeting between the union (or unions) and any or all of the workers constituting the bargaining unit to be held in the absence of the employer or any of its representatives (other than one who has been invited to attend the meeting) and it is not reasonable in the circumstances for the employer to do so;
    - the employer or a representative of it attends such a meeting without having been invited to do so;
    - it seeks to record or otherwise be informed of the proceedings at any such meeting and it is not reasonable in the circumstances for the employer to do so; or
    - the employer refuses to give an undertaking that it will not seek to

record or otherwise be informed of the proceedings at any such meeting unless it is reasonable in the circumstances for the employer to do either of these things.

- The third duty is to do the following (so far as it is reasonable to expect the employer to do so):
  - to give to the CAC, within the period of 10 working days starting with the day after that on which the employer is informed of the need for the ballot, the names and home addresses of the workers constituting the bargaining unit;
  - to give to the CAC, as soon as is reasonably practicable, the name and home address of any worker who joins the unit after the employer has complied with the point above; and
  - to inform the CAC, as soon as is reasonably practicable, of any worker whose name has been given to the CAC under para 19D(a) or (b) but who ceases to be within the bargaining unit.
- The fourth duty is to refrain from making any offer to any or all of the workers constituting the bargaining unit which has or is likely to have the effect of inducing any or all of them not to attend any 'relevant meeting' between the union (or unions) and the workers constituting the bargaining unit, and is not reasonable in the circumstances.
- The fifth duty is to refrain from taking or threatening to take any action against a worker solely or mainly on the grounds that he attended or took part in any relevant meeting between the union (or unions) and the workers constituting the bargaining unit, or indicated his intention to attend or take part in such a meeting.

4.67 In connection with the above, a 'relevant meeting' in relation to a worker is one which is organised in accordance with any agreement reached concerning the second duty above, or as a result of a step ordered by the CAC to be taken under TULRCA 1992, Sch A1, para 27 to remedy a failure to comply with that duty, and which the employer is required to permit the worker to attend (para 26(4C)). Further, it is specifically provided under para 26(4E) that the fourth and fifth duties do not confer any rights on any worker.

4.68 As soon as is reasonably practicable after the CAC receives any such information, it must pass it on to the person appointed to conduct the ballot (TULRCA 1992, Sch A1, para 26(5)). Further, if the person appointed to conduct the ballot is not the same person appointed under para 19D, the CAC must, as soon as is reasonably practicable, pass on to the person appointed to conduct the ballot the names and addresses given to it under para 19D (para 26(4H)).

4.69 Each of the Advisory, Conciliation and Arbitration Service (ACAS) and the Department of Trade and Industry (DTI) are entitled to issue Codes of Practice on balloting (TULRCA 1992, Sch A1, para 26(8)) and the DTI has issued a new Code of Practice *Access and Unfair Practices during Recognition and Derecognition Ballots*, which came into effect on 1 October 2005.

4.70 If the CAC is satisfied that the employer has failed to fulfil any of the duties imposed by TULRCA 1992, Sch A1, para 26, and the ballot has not been held, the CAC may order the employer to take such steps to remedy the failure as the CAC considers reasonable and specifies, and to do so within such period as the CAC considers reasonable (para 27(1)). If, after the issue of such an order, the CAC is satisfied that the employer has failed to comply with the order and the ballot has not been held, the CAC may issue a declaration that the union is (or unions are) recognised as entitled to conduct collective bargaining on behalf of the bargaining unit (para 27(2)).

4.71   Further, under TULRCA 1992, Sch A1, para 27A, each of the parties must refrain from using any 'unfair practices' in relation to a ballot. These measures carry stringent penalties for the employer or union (as the case may be). In this regard, para 27A(2) defines unfair practices as to mean:

- Offering to pay money or give money's worth to a worker entitled to vote in the ballot in return for the worker's agreement to vote in a particular way or to abstain from voting.
- Making an 'outcome-specific offer' to a worker entitled to vote in the ballot. Paragraph 27A(3) states that an 'outcome-specific offer' is an offer to pay money or give money's worth which is conditional on the CAC issuing a declaration that the union is (or unions are) or is/are not (as the case may be) recognised as entitled to conduct collective bargaining on behalf of the bargaining unit, or is unconditional in relation to anything which is done or occurs as a result of the CAC declaration.
- Coercing or attempting to coerce a worker entitled to vote in the ballot to disclose whether he intends to vote or to abstain from voting in the ballot, or how he intends to vote, or how he has voted, in the ballot.
- Dismissing or threatening to dismiss a worker.
- Taking or threatening to take disciplinary action against a worker.
- Subjecting or threatening to subject a worker to any other detriment.
- Using or attempting to use undue influence on a worker entitled to vote in the ballot.

4.72   In the event that a party believes that the other has failed to comply with TULRCA 1992, Sch A1, para 27A, it may present a complaint to the CAC on the first working day after the day of the ballot or the last day of balloting (if there is more than one day) (para 27B(1) and (2)). The CAC is then required to decide within 10 working days (or such longer period as it may specify) whether the claim is well founded (para 27B(3) and (5)). In order for a claim to be well founded, under para 27B(4), the CAC must find that the party complained against used an unfair practice and that the use of that practice changed or was likely to change, in the case of a worker entitled to vote in the ballot any of:

- the voter's intention to vote or to abstain from voting;
- the voter's intention to vote in a particular way; or
- how the voter voted.

4.73   If the CAC decides in respect of a complaint that unfair practices have been used, then under TULRCA 1992, Sch A1, para 27C(2) and (3), the CAC must issue a declaration to that effect as soon as reasonably practicable and, additionally, may do either or both of the following:

- order the party concerned to take any action specified in the order within such period as may be so specified; or
- give notice to the employer and to the union (or unions) that it intends to arrange for the holding of a secret ballot in which the workers constituting the bargaining unit are asked whether they want the union (or unions) to conduct collective bargaining on their behalf.

4.74 More than one such declaration can be issued under TULRCA 1992, Sch A1, para 27C.

4.75 Furthermore, under TULRCA 1992, Sch A1, para 27D, if the CAC issues a declaration that unfair practices have been used:

- the unfair practice consisted of either the use of violence or the dismissal of a union official; and/or
- in a case where the CAC has issued an order under para 27C(3)(a) requiring either that specified steps are taken, or that a secret ballot is held, and the CAC is satisfied that the party subject to the order failed to comply with it, or it makes a further declaration in relation to that party,

depending upon which party is at fault, one of two possible declarations may be issued by the CAC, as follows.

4.76 If the employer is the party in breach of TULRCA 1992, Sch A1, para 27C, under para 27D(3), the CAC may issue a declaration that the union is (or unions are) recognised as entitled to conduct collective bargaining on behalf of the bargaining unit. Conversely, if the union (or unions) is/are at fault, under para 27D(4), the CAC may issue a declaration that the union is (or unions are) not entitled to be so recognised.

4.77 Likewise, if the CAC has issued a declaration that a complaint under TULRCA 1992, Sch A1, para 27B is well founded and either gives notice under para 27C(3)(b) that this is so, or issued one of the declarations under para 27D, the CAC is required to cancel the ballot in respect of which the application is being made or, if the ballot has been held, it is a nullity (para 27E).

4.78 If the CAC has issued a notice under TULRCA 1992, Sch A1, para 27C(3)(b) (ie a notice that a secret ballot is to be held as a result of the employer engaging in 'unfair practices', under para 27F), the provisions of paras 24–29 then apply in relation to the ballot save that:

- A minor modification applies in relation to the notification period under para 24, in that it is reduced to 5 working days (para 27F(3)).
- The scope of the employer's duty under para 26(4)(a) (to give to the CAC the names and home addresses of workers in the bargaining unit) is limited to:
  - giving the CAC the names and home addresses of any workers in the bargaining unit which have not previously been given to it in accordance with that duty;
  - giving the CAC the names and home addresses of those workers who have joined the bargaining unit since the employer last gave the CAC information in accordance with that duty;
  - informing the CAC of any change to the name or home address of a worker whose name and home address have previously been given to the CAC in accordance with that duty; and
  - informing the CAC of any worker whose name had previously been given to it in accordance with that duty who has ceased to be within the bargaining unit (para 27F(4)).
- The costs of the ballot in such a case are borne by the parties in the proportions determined by the CAC rather than being dealt with under para 28 (para 27F(6)) so that half is borne by the employer and half by the union (para 28(2)). In the case of more unions making a joint application

for recognition, they are required to bear the union half share in such proportions as they jointly indicate to the person appointed to conduct the ballot, or in default of such indication, in equal shares (para 28(3)). There are also provisions dealing with the recovering of costs from parties under para 28(4)–(7).

4.79   Unless the ballot has been ordered by the CAC under TULRCA 1992, Sch A1, para 27C(3)(b), as soon as is reasonably practicable after the CAC is informed of the result of a ballot by the person conducting it, the CAC must inform the employer and the union (or unions) of the result of the ballot (para 29(1) and (2)). In order for a ballot to be passed in favour of union recognition, a majority is needed of the workers voting and at least 40 per cent of the workers constituting the bargaining unit must vote in favour of the union(s) being recognised (para 29(3)). Where such a majority is achieved, the CAC must issue a declaration that the union is (or unions are) recognised as entitled to conduct collective bargaining on behalf of the bargaining unit. If the result is otherwise, the CAC must issue a declaration that the union is (or unions are) not entitled to be so recognised (para 29(4)). This is subject to the CAC's general duties under paras 24 and 25 to be responsible for all matters in and around the ballot and the CAC's duty under para 171 when exercising its functions to have regard to its object of encouraging and promoting fair and efficient practices and arrangements in the workplace (including any failure to ensure that all of the bargaining unit are balloted, a matter which has been held to allow the CAC to 'go behind' the result of a ballot and to require a fresh ballot to be held[21]).

Consequences of recognition

4.80   If the CAC issues a declaration that the union is (or unions are) recognised as entitled to conduct collective bargaining on behalf of a bargaining unit, the parties may, in the period of 30 working days starting with the day after that on which the parties are notified of the declaration (or such longer period as the parties may from time to time agree), conduct negotiations with a view to agreeing a method by which they will conduct collective bargaining (TULRCA 1992, Sch A1, para 30).

4.81   If an application for assistance is made to the CAC under TULRCA 1992, Sch A1, para 30, the CAC must, in the period of 20 working days from the date of receipt of the application or such longer period as the CAC may decide with the consent of the parties (the agreement period), try to help the parties to reach an agreement on a method by which they will conduct collective bargaining. If at the end of the agreement period the parties have not made such an agreement, the CAC must specify to the parties the method by which they are to conduct collective bargaining, such method being deemed to be enforceable by way of specific performance as a contract (para 31).[22] However, the parties are free to agree in writing that the whole or part of the

---

[21]   *R (on the application of Ultraframe (UK) Limited) v Central Arbitration Committee* [2005] EWCA Civ 560, [2005] IRLR 641.

[22]   In respect of which the CAC will usually specify the method in the Trade Union Recognition (Method of Collective Bargaining) Order 2000, SI 2000/1300.

CAC stated procedure shall not apply and that written agreement shall itself then apply as a written contract between the parties enforceable by specific performance.

4.82 The above provisions also apply to a case where the CAC issues a declaration that the union is (or unions are) recognised as entitled to conduct collective bargaining on behalf of a bargaining unit, the parties agree a method by which they will conduct collective bargaining, one or more of the parties fails to carry out the agreement and the employer or the union (or unions) applies to the CAC for assistance (TULRCA 1992, Sch A1, para 32).

4.83 It seems that once a union is recognised for the purposes of TULRCA 1992, Sch A1 and a collective bargaining arrangement has been either negotiated or imposed by the CAC in relation to the bargaining unit, the employer is bound not to negotiate individually with workers within the bargaining unit. Indeed, to do so may expose such workers to claims by the union that they have induced the employer to breach either or both of a contract (the recognition agreement) or its statutory duty (under TULRCA 1992, Sch A1) under the principle in *Lumley v Gye*.[23]

4.84 In the event that a union or unions is/are granted recognition under TULRCA 1992, Sch A1 and the CAC has specified a means of collective bargaining under para 31, then, in addition to consulting about pay, hours and holiday in relation to the bargaining unit (para 3), the employer is also required to consult with the union(s) about the employer's training plans for members of the bargaining unit (TULRCA 1992, s 70B), in respect of which see **4.9**.

OTHER ISSUES ON THE ROAD TO RECOGNITION

4.85 The foregoing analysis assumes that the parties to a recognition dispute contest the matter through to a ballot. However, other possibilities also exist which may result in an application not reaching the stage of a recognition ballot.

4.86 First, under TULRCA 1992, Sch A1, para 16, it is possible for a trade union unilaterally to withdraw its application after the CAC has accepted that it has jurisdiction to hear the matter. This can be done at any time prior to the point either that:

- the CAC issues a declaration under para 22(2) that a union is recognised (in a case where the union can demonstrate that more than 50 per cent of the bargaining unit are members of the union who support recognition); or
- the CAC announces that a ballot is to be held under para 22(3) or 23(2).

4.87 Secondly, it is possible under TULRCA 1992, Sch A1, para 17 for the employer and the union to make a joint request to the CAC that an application for compulsory recognition under Sch A1 should be discontinued. The application can be made at any time after the CAC has received an application but before:

- the CAC has accepted the application;

---

[23]   (1853) 2 E & B. See too *Read v Friendly Society of Operative Stonemasons of England, Ireland and Wales* [1902] 2 KB 732.

- the CAC has issued a declaration that the union is recognised without the need for a ballot; or
- the last day of the 2-week notification period after the CAC has announced that a ballot is to be held to determine whether a union is to be recognised.

VOLUNTARY RECOGNITION AFTER COMMENCING THE STATUTORY PROCEDURES

4.88   Not all applications commenced under TULRCA 1992, Sch A1 result in a ballot. In many cases the parties agree that a union or unions should be recognised in relation to a bargaining unit. Indeed, the whole scheme of Sch A1 is designed to allow the parties to recognise a union or unions voluntarily. In this regard, TULRCA 1992, Sch A1, Part 2, paras 52–63 caters for the situation where an application is made under Sch A1 but is withdrawn so as to allow for voluntary recognition.

4.89   Voluntary recognition for these purposes arises where there is an 'agreement for recognition' (as defined under TULRCA 1992, Sch A1, para 52(2)), this being where:

- the agreement has been made in the time-limits provided under para 52(3) in consequence of a valid request for recognition made under para 4 and complying with the requirements of paras 5–9; and
- under the resulting agreement, the union(s) is/are recognised as entitled to conduct collective bargaining on behalf of a group of workers employed by the employer.

4.90   Upon an agreement for recognition being established, the parties are provided with a negotiation period of 30 working days, or such longer period as they may agree (the negotiating period), to agree a method by which they will conduct collective bargaining. In the event that at the end of the negotiating period it has not been possible for the parties to agree a method for collective bargaining, they may refer the matter to the CAC which is then empowered under TULRCA 1992, Sch A1, para 58 to determine the method of collective bargaining.[24]

4.91   Likewise, under TULRCA 1992, Sch A1, para 59, in the event that the agreed collective bargaining arrangements do not work in practice, it is possible to apply to the CAC in order for the CAC to determine a collective bargaining structure going forward.

4.92   Where an application is made to the CAC under either TULRCA 1992, Sch A1, para 58 or 59, under paras 60 and 61, the CAC can only consider the application provided that:

- the employer (together with any associated employers) employs 21 or more workers at the date of the application to the CAC and employed an average of at least 21 workers in the 13 weeks ending on the day of the application;
- the union (or every union recognised in relation to the bargaining unit) has a Certificate of Independence; and
- the application is made to the CAC in the form specified by the CAC.

---

[24]   In respect of which the CAC will usually specify the method in the Trade Union Recognition (Method of Collective Bargaining) Order 2000, SI 2000/1300.

4.93   Where the application complies with the requirements under TULRCA 1992, Sch A1, paras 60 and 61, the CAC is then required to consider the application under para 62 to see if it may accept the application. The CAC is required to make a determination in this regard within 10 working days or such longer period as the CAC may specify to the parties (notifying the parties of the reason for the extension of time where an extension is granted: para 62(5) and (6)).

4.94   Where the application is accepted by the CAC, the CAC must, within the period of 20 working days or such longer period as the parties may agree (the acceptance period), try to help the parties reach an agreement on a method by which collective bargaining may be carried out (TULRCA 1992, Sch A1, para 63(1) and (8)). If by the end of the acceptance period, the parties cannot agree on a method of collective bargaining, the CAC is required to specify to the parties the method by which collective bargaining is to be conducted (para 63(2)).[25] Under para 63(6), it is open to the party making the application to withdraw it at any time before the end of the acceptance period (usually this would occur where the parties determine a method by which collective bargaining will be performed). Any method specified by the CAC takes effect between the parties as if it were a contract enforceable by specific performance only (para 63(4) and (5)).

4.95   Further, where an agreement for recognition exists, the employer may not terminate the agreement for a period of 3 years commencing on the date of the agreement (TULRCA 1992, Sch A1, para 56). At any time after the end of the 3-year period, the employer may terminate the agreement for recognition with or without the consent of the union (para 56(2)).

4.96   Conversely, a union may terminate an agreement for recognition at any time, with or without the consent of the employer (TULRCA 1992, Sch A1, para 56(3)). In this regard, the CAC is given a power under para 55 to determine whether a collective bargaining agreement with a trade union is an 'agreement for recognition' for the purposes of para 52.

4.97   In the event that an agreement for recognition is terminated in accordance with TULRCA 1992, Sch A1, para 56, under para 57, any provisions relating to the collective bargaining method also cease to have effect.

CHANGES AFFECTING THE BARGAINING UNIT AFTER RECOGNITION IS GRANTED

4.98   TULRCA 1992, Sch A1 recognises that the business of an employer (including its workforce) is not a static concept and therefore TULRCA 1992, Sch A1, Part 3, paras 64–95, deals with issue of changes affecting the bargaining after recognition has been granted to a union or unions. In this regard, the provisions only apply where the CAC has issued a declaration that a union or unions is/are to be recognised as being entitled to conduct collective bargaining on behalf of a bargaining unit (para 64(1)). Changes to the bargaining unit in a case where a union or unions are voluntarily recognised

---

[25]   In respect of which the CAC will usually specify the method in the Trade Union Recognition (Method of Collective Bargaining) Order 2000, SI 2000/1300.

under TULRCA 1992, Sch A1, Part 2 are not covered. In the event that there is no formal declaration of recognition, TULRCA 1992, Sch A1, Part 3 cannot be relied upon by the parties.[26]

4.99   Two situations are covered in this regard. First, in cases where TULRCA 1992, Sch A1, Part 3 applies, either party may make an application to the CAC to argue that the bargaining unit is no longer appropriate due to any of the three matters in para 67(2), these being that there has been:

- a change in the organisation or structure of the business carried on by the employer;
- a change in the activities pursued by the employer in the course of the business carried on by the employer; and
- a substantial change in the number of employees employed by the employer.

4.100   Secondly, it may be possible for the employer to argue that the bargaining unit no longer exists. Each of these points will be examined in turn.

Bargaining unit is no longer appropriate

4.101   Where an application is made, the purpose of the application is for the CAC to determine what the appropriate bargaining unit is (TULRCA 1992, Sch A1, para 66(2)).

4.102   Upon receiving an application, the CAC is required to consider whether:

- the application has been made in the correct form and copied to the other party (TULRCA 1992, Sch A1, para 92); and
- any of the conditions in para 67(2) is satisfied (per para 68(2)).

4.103   Within the period of 10 days from receiving the application, the CAC is required to consider whether it can accept the application (TULRCA 1992, Sch A1, para 68(6)). If none of the conditions are satisfied, the application must be rejected by the CAC and it must notify the parties of the decision and no further steps are then taken in relation to the application (para 68(4)).

4.104   If the CAC accepts the application, it is required to notify the parties of this fact (TULRCA 1992, Sch A1, para 68(5)), and the parties are then given a period of 10 working days (or such longer period as the parties may agree) (the first period) after the CAC notification to them, to attempt to agree a new bargaining unit (para 69(1)). In the event that the parties agree a new bargaining unit, the CAC is required to consider whether it contains any workers already within a bargaining unit with the employer. If so, no further steps are to be taken under TULRCA 1992, Sch A1, Part 3 (per para 69(2)). If the CAC is satisfied that no worker within the proposed new bargaining unit falls within another existing bargaining unit recognised by the employer, the CAC is required to issue a declaration to this effect, recognition is then transferred to the new bargaining unit and the existing method of collective bargaining is then applied in relation to the new bargaining unit (para 69(3)).

---

[26]   See, for example, *Bank Tejarat and UNIFI* TUR3/1/02.

4.105 In the event that the parties reach a decision as to the new bargaining unit which does not contain any workers in another bargaining unit of the employer, but does not cover some of the workers covered in the existing bargaining unit, the CAC is required to approve the bargaining unit under TULRCA 1992, Sch A1, para 69(3), but as regards the workers not covered by the new bargaining unit, the CAC is required to issue a declaration that the existing bargaining arrangements are to cease to have effect from a date to be specified by the CAC in the declaration. The existing arrangements then cease to have effect as regards the workers from that date (para 73).

4.106 In the event that at the end of the first period, the parties have not reached a decision, then under TULRCA 1992, Sch A1, para 70(2):

- the CAC must, within a period of 10 working days or such longer period as the CAC shall specify to the parties (para 70(7)), decide whether or not the original unit continues to be an appropriate bargaining unit;
- if the CAC decides that the original unit does not so continue, it must decide what other bargaining unit, is or units are, appropriate; and
- the CAC must give notice to the parties of its decision or decisions.

4.107 In deciding whether or not the original bargaining unit continues to be appropriate, the CAC must take into account only the following:

- any change in the organisation or structure of the business carried on by the employer;
- any change in the activities pursued by the employer in the course of the business carried on by it; and
- any substantial change in the number of workers employed in the original unit.

4.108 Further, in deciding what other bargaining unit(s) is/are appropriate, under TULRCA 1992, Sch A1, para 70(4) and (5), the CAC must take these matters into account:

- the need for the bargaining unit or units under consideration to be compatible with effective management;
- the views of the employer and of the union (or unions);
- existing national and local bargaining arrangements;
- the desirability of avoiding small, fragmented bargaining units within an undertaking;
- the characteristics of workers falling within the original unit and of any other employees of the employer whom the CAC considers relevant; and
- the location of workers.

4.109 Of these matters, the need for the bargaining unit or units under consideration to be compatible with effective management is stated in TULRCA 1992, Sch A1, para 70(4) to be of most importance. Further, in the event that, following its consideration, the CAC decides that two or more bargaining units are appropriate for the employer, the CAC must be satisfied that there is no overlap for any worker into more than one of the bargaining units (para 70(6)).

4.110 The CAC may make a determination that the original bargaining unit continues to be appropriate. In such a case, no further steps are taken under TULRCA 1992, Sch A1, Part 3 (para 71). However, if the CAC decides that a new bargaining unit is appropriate, the CAC must then consider the matters in para 82 (per para 72), in relation to which see **4.121**.

Bargaining unit no longer exists

4.111   The other possibility for applying to the CAC arises where the employer believes that the bargaining unit no longer exists and wishes the bargaining arrangements to come to an end. In such a case, the employer may give the union 35 working days' notice of this fact (TULRCA 1992, Sch A1, para 74(1) and (2)). The notice must be copied to the CAC. Further, under para 74(2), the notice must state the following points:

- the details of the bargaining unit and the bargaining arrangements;
- the date on which the notice is given;
- the fact that the bargaining unit has ceased to exist; and
- the fact that the bargaining arrangements will cease to have effect at the end of the notice period (which starts on the date that the notice is given).

4.112   Within 10 working days of receiving a copy of the notice (or such longer period as the CAC may specify by notice to the parties), the CAC is required to decide whether the notice given by the employer complies with the requirements of TULRCA 1992, Sch A1, para 74(2) (per para 74(3) and (7)). If the CAC decides that the employer's notice is defective, the CAC must notify the parties of this fact and the notice is then treated as if it was not given (para 74(4)). Conversely, if the CAC decides that the notice complies with para 74(2), it must give the parties notice of this fact (para 74(5)).

4.113   If, upon receiving the CAC's notice under TULRCA 1992, Sch A1, para 74(5), the union fails to make an application to the CAC contesting the notice, the bargaining arrangements will cease to have effect on the date given in the employer's notice (para 74(6)). However, under para 75, it is possible for a union in receipt of a valid notice under para 74(2) to object to it. In doing so, the union is required to make an application to the CAC asking it to determine whether the bargaining unit has ceased to exist and whether the original bargaining unit is no longer appropriate.

4.114   The CAC is required to give notice to the parties of the receipt of the union's application (TULRCA 1992, Sch A1, para 76(1)). The CAC is then required to consider within 10 working days (or such longer period as it may specify in a notice to the parties) whether the application (including any evidence provided with it or by the employer) is admissible (para 76(3)). If the CAC decides that the union's application is not admissible, it must give notice of its decision to the parties, it must not accept the application and it must take no further steps (para 76(4)). However, if the CAC decides that the application is admissible, it must accept the application and give notice of this fact to the parties (para 76(5)).

4.115   Having accepted an application, the CAC must give the employer and the union (or unions) an opportunity to put their views in relation to the questions raised by the union's TULRCA 1992, Sch A1, para 75 application and must decide the questions within 10 working days starting on the day that the CAC accepts the application or such longer period as the CAC may specify by notice to the parties (per para 77(1) and (5)). In this regard, one of three outcomes is possible, as follows:

- First, the CAC may decide that the original bargaining unit has ceased to exist. In such a case, the CAC is required to notify the parties of this decision and the bargaining arrangements will then come to an end on the date specified in the employer's notice under para 74(2)) (per para 77(2)).

- Secondly, the CAC may decide that the original bargaining unit has not ceased to exist and that the bargaining unit is still appropriate. In such a case, the CAC must give notice to the parties of its decision and the employer's notice is treated as not having been given (para 77(3)).
- Thirdly, the CAC may decide that the original bargaining unit has not ceased to exist but that that bargaining unit is no longer appropriate by reason of any of the matters in para 75(3) (para 77(4)).

4.116 In the event that the CAC decides that the original bargaining unit has not ceased to exist but that that bargaining unit is no longer appropriate, the parties are given the chance to attempt to agree a new bargaining unit or units. In this regard, the parties are given 10 working days, starting with the day after that on which the CAC first gave notice under para 77(4) or such longer period as the parties may agree and have notified to the CAC (TULRCA 1992, Sch A1, para 78(1) and (4)).

4.117 If the parties decide upon a new bargaining unit or units, they must refer it/them to the CAC which is required to consider whether there is an overlap with any worker in another existing bargaining unit. If the CAC believes this to be the case, it is required to cease working on the application (TULRCA 1992, Sch A1, para 78(2)). If, however, there is no such overlap, the CAC must issue a declaration that the union is recognised in relation to the new bargaining unit/units and the original method of collective bargaining continues in relation to the new unit/units (para 78(3)). As regards any workers who then fall outside the new bargaining unit/units, the collective bargaining arrangements cease to have effect in relation to those workers (para 81).

4.118 In the event that the parties are unable to agree a new bargaining unit within the period of 10 working days, under TULRCA 1992, Sch A1, para 79, the CAC is required to consider what other bargaining unit or units is appropriate. In this regard, the CAC is given a period of 10 working days commencing on the date that the parties' 10-working day negotiation period under para 78(4) lapses (para 79(2)). In deciding whether a bargaining unit or units might be appropriate, under para 79(3) and (4), the CAC is principally required to take into account the need for the bargaining unit or units to be compatible with the needs of effective management and (to the extent that they do not conflict with that requirement) must also consider the following points:

- the views of the employer and of the union (or unions);
- any existing national and local bargaining arrangements;
- the desirability of avoiding small fragmented bargaining units within an undertaking;
- the characteristics of workers falling within the original bargaining unit and of any other employees of the employer whom the CAC considers relevant; and
- the location of workers in the proposed bargaining unit(s).

4.119 If having considered these factors, the CAC decides that two or more bargaining units are appropriate, it must ensure that no worker falls into more than one of the units (TULRCA 1992, Sch A1, para 79(5)).

4.120   In the event that the CAC decides that a new bargaining unit or units is appropriate, as with the issue of changes to the bargaining unit, the CAC is then required to consider the matters in TULRCA 1992, Sch A1, para 82.

Position where the CAC decides a new bargaining unit

4.121   In a case where the CAC is required to decide upon a new bargaining unit (either because the original bargaining unit is no longer appropriate or because the original bargaining unit no longer exists), one of the principal problems which will arise is that the CAC has to take into account any pre-existing bargaining units so as to ensure that there is no problem with the new bargaining unit or units overlapping with other existing statutory collective bargaining units. In this regard, under TULRCA 1992, Sch A1, para 82 where on investigation the CAC decides that there is at least one worker in another bargaining unit, the CAC is required to issue a declaration that the bargaining arrangements relating to both the original bargaining unit which is the subject of the application, together with the bargaining unit which is the subject of the overlap, are to cease to have effect within the period of 65 working days starting with the day after that on which the declaration is issued or earlier if the CAC believes this is required due to the existing bargaining arrangements being impracticable or contrary to the interests of good industrial relations (TULRCA 1992, Sch A1, paras 83(3) and (8)).

4.122   The effect of such a declaration by the CAC is that when the bargaining arrangements come to an end in the bargaining unit in respect of which the application has been made and the bargaining unit which is the subject of the overlap, no union is then recognised in respect of those parts of the employer's workforce (TULRCA 1992, Sch A1, para 83(2)).

4.123   Furthermore, under TULRCA 1992, Sch A1, para 84, if the CAC believes that its proposed new bargaining unit overlaps with any worker in any bargaining units voluntarily recognised by the employer, it is required to hold that the bargaining unit giving rise to the application to the CAC must come to an end within a period of 65 working days starting with the day after that on which the declaration is issued or earlier if the CAC believes this is required due to the existing bargaining arrangements being impracticable or contrary to the interests of good industrial relations (paras 84(2) and (5)). However, as regards the voluntary arrangements, these continue in effect and will do so even where the effect of this would be that the new CAC bargaining unit comes into effect so that the 'overlapped' worker is, or workers are, effectively a member, or members, of more than one bargaining unit.

4.124   Once the CAC decides upon a proposed new bargaining unit, it is then required to consider whether the difference between the bargaining unit giving rise to the application to the CAC and the proposed new bargaining unit is such that the support of the union (or unions) recognised in respect of the bargaining unit giving rise to the application needs to be assessed and the CAC is then required to give the parties notice of its decision in this regard (TULRCA 1992, Sch A1, para 85(1)).

4.125   If the CAC decides that the support of the union or unions does not need to be assessed, the CAC must issue a declaration that the union is, or unions are, recognised as entitled to conduct collective bargaining on behalf of the workers in the new bargaining unit. The union is, or unions are, then treated as being recognised in respect of the workers who fall within the new bargaining unit and the original method of collective bargaining carries on in effect in relation to the new bargaining unit subject to any modifications which the CAC considers necessary to take account of the change of bargaining unit (TULRCA 1992, Sch A1, para 85(2)). The collective bargaining arrangements between the parties then take effect as a legally binding contract save to the extent that the parties agree otherwise (para 95).

4.126 If, however, the CAC decides that the support of the union (or unions) needs to be proved by a ballot, under TULRCA 1992, Sch A1, para 86(2), the CAC must decided whether:

- the union (or unions) enjoys the support of at least 10 per cent of the workers in the bargaining unit; and
- a majority of workers in the bargaining unit would be likely to favour recognition of the union (or unions).

4.127 If the CAC decides either or both these questions in the negative, the CAC must issue a declaration that the bargaining arrangements are to cease to have effect from a date specified in the declaration and the bargaining arrangements will then come to an end accordingly (TULRCA 1992, Sch A1, para 86(2)). Conversely, if the CAC decides both of the questions in the positive, it must issue a declaration that the union is, or unions are, recognised as entitled to conduct collective bargaining in relation to the revised bargaining unit. This will be so unless any of the three conditions in para 87(4) are satisfied, in which case the CAC is required to arrange a secret ballot of the workers constituting the bargaining unit to determine whether they want the union or unions to be recognised to conduct collective bargaining on their behalf. The three conditions are that:

- the CAC is satisfied that it would be in the interests of good industrial relations;
- the CAC has evidence, which it considers to be credible, from a significant number of union members within the new bargaining unit that they do not want the union or unions to conduct collective bargaining on their behalf; or
- membership evidence (being either about the circumstances in which workers became members of the union or evidence as to the length of time which members have been members of the union: para 87(5)) is produced to the CAC which leads it to doubt whether a significant number of members within the new bargaining unit want the union to be recognised for the purposes of collective bargaining.

4.128 The union is, or unions are, given a period of 10 working days in which to notify the CAC of whether it/they require a ballot to be held (TULRCA 1992, Sch A1, para 89(1)). If the union(s) confirm that it/they do not require a ballot, the CAC informs the parties that no ballot will be held and is required to issue a declaration that the old bargaining arrangements will cease to have effect (para 89(2)). Conversely, if the union(s) either confirm(s) that it/they want the ballot to be held, or do not notify the CAC that it/they want the ballot to be held, the CAC must arrange for a ballot to be held (para 89(3)). In the event that a ballot is held, the same procedures as those in relation to an initial recognition ballot under paras 24–29 apply but as if the references to para 26(4F)–(4H) were omitted (para 89(4) and (5)).

4.129   Following the outcome of the ballot, in the case of a ballot result in favour of recognition of the union(s), under TULRCA 1992, Sch A1, para 89(6), the CAC is required to endorse the old bargaining arrangements in respect of the new bargaining unit(s) together with such modifications as the CAC considers necessary to take account of the change in bargaining unit. The collective bargaining arrangements between the parties then take effect as a legally binding contract save to the extent that the parties agree otherwise (para 95).

4.130   As regards any workers who were covered under the original bargaining arrangements who now fall outside the revised bargaining unit, the CAC must issue a declaration that those workers are no longer recognised for the purposes of collective bargaining from a date to be specified by the CAC (TULRCA 1992, Sch A1, para 90).

4.131   If the ballot resolves against the unions(s) being recognised for the purposes of collective bargaining, the CAC must issue a declaration as to the date upon which the old recognition arrangements are to come to an end and they will do so accordingly on that date (TULRCA 1992, Sch A1, para 89(7)).

DERECOGNITION

4.132   TULRCA 1992, Sch A1 also provides for a number of situations in which the relationship between the collective parties to the bargaining arrangements change over the course of time and an application to end the bargaining arrangements is made. In this regard, there are two sub-groups of cases, the first of which arises where a union has been recognised following a declaration by the CAC, and which covers the following situations:

- where the employer ceases to employ 21 or more workers at the end of the period of 3 years;
- where, at the end of the period of 3 years for which a period of statutory recognition must be granted, the employer requests to end the bargaining arrangements; or
- where, within the bargaining unit at the end of the period of 3 years for which a period of statutory recognition must be granted, the workers request to end the bargaining arrangements.

4.133   In these cases, where an application for derecognition is granted, the derecognition of the union or unions occurs within the timeframe allowed for the particular case, but only after the initial 3-year period of validity for the bargaining arrangements has come to an end (TULRCA 1992, Sch A1, para 97).

4.134   A further ad hoc category of cases exists covering the cases where:

- a trade union was recognised compulsorily under TULRCA 1992, Sch A1 without the need for a ballot due to it having a majority of members in the bargaining unit;
- a trade union is recognised by the employer but does not have a Certificate of Independence under TULRCA 1992, s 6; or
- an independent trade union which has been granted statutory recognition under TULRCA 1992, Sch A1 loses its Certificate of Independence.

Each will be examined in turn.

4.135   In the case of an independent trade union which has been recognised outside the scheme of TULRCA 1992, Sch A1, where the employer decides that it is no longer prepared to recognise the union, this is not catered for under Sch A1. The only avenue open to the union is to seek statutory recognition under Sch A1.

The employer ceases to employ 21 or more workers

4.136   Where an employer, together with any associated employers, ceases to employ more than an average of 21 workers in any period of 13 weeks, the employer may give the union or unions recognised by it 35 working days' notice that it wishes to cease the bargaining arrangements. Any notice (which must be compliant with the matters listed in TULRCA 1992, Sch A1, para 99(3)) so given must be copied to the CAC (para 99(1) and (2)). The matters listed in para 100(3) are that the notice must:

- not be invalidated under para 99A;
- identify the bargaining arrangements;
- specify the period of 13 weeks in question;
- state the date on which notice is given;
- be given within 5 working days starting with the day which is the day after the last day of the 13-week period;
- state that the employer, taken with all of its associated employers, employed fewer than an average of 21 workers throughout the 13-week period; and
- state the date upon which the bargaining arrangements are to cease to have effect.

4.137   Under TULRCA 1992, Sch A1, para 99A(1), a notice given under para 99 is invalidated where a 'relevant application' was made relating to the same bargaining unit, or an earlier notice under para 99(2) was given, within the period of 3 years prior to the date in a case where the CAC accepted the relevant application or decided under para 100 that the earlier notice under para 99(2) complied with para 99(3). For these purposes, a 'relevant application' is one given by the employer under any of paras 106, 107 or 128, or a notice given by a worker (or workers) under para 112.

4.138   Although the employer cannot terminate the bargaining arrangements in the initial 3-year period, the notice of termination can be given so as to expire at the end of that 3-year period (TULRCA 1992, Sch A1, para 99(3)(f)).

4.139   If an employer gives notice under TULRCA 1992, Sch A1, para 99(2), within the period of 10 working days (commencing on the day after notice is served on the CAC or such longer period as the CAC may specify: para 100(5)) of the CAC receiving a copy of the notice, the CAC must decide whether the notice so given is admissible and notify the parties of its decision in this regard (para 100(1)). If the CAC decides that the notice is defective, it must notify the parties and the notice is treated as not having been given (para 100(2)).

4.140   If the CAC determines that the notice is compliant with the requirements of TULRCA 1992, Sch A1, para 99(3), it must give the parties notice of that decision and, unless the union objects, the bargaining arrangements cease to have effect on the date specified in the employer's notice (para 100(3) and (4)).

4.141   A union in receipt of an employer's notice is allowed to make an application to the CAC, copied to the employer, within 10 working days starting with the day after the date on which notice is given to it. The union's application must comply with the form prescribed for the application by the CAC from time to time and be supported by such documents as the CAC shall specify (TULRCA 1992, Sch A1, para 101(2)). Under para 101(2), in its application, the union can challenge whether:

- the 13-week period stated by the employer was wholly within the protected 3-year period of recognition, or came to an end after that period; and/or
- the employer, when together with associated employers, in fact employed less than 21 workers.

4.142   Upon receipt of the union's application, the CAC is required within 10 working days starting on the day after the CAC receives the application (or such longer period as the CAC shall specify), to notify the parties of receipt and to determine whether the union's application is admissible (TULRCA 1992, Sch A1, para 102(1) and (2)). In the event that the CAC decides that the application is not admissible, it must give notice to the parties of that decision, it must not accept the application and no further steps are to be taken by the CAC with the result that the bargaining arrangements cease at the expiry of the employers notice under para 99(3) (para 102(3) and (4)).

4.143   However, if the CAC decides that the application is admissible, it must accept the application and give notice of acceptance to the parties (TULRCA 1992, Sch A1, para 102(4)). The CAC must then give the parties the opportunity to put their views on the two matters stated above and must decide those questions within the period of 10 working days starting on the day after the CAC gives notice of acceptance of the application (or such longer period as the CAC may specify) (para 103(1) and (4)).

4.144   If the CAC decides for the employer in relation to both of the questions above, the bargaining arrangements cease to have effect on the later of the termination date set out in the employer's notice under TULRCA 1992, Sch A1, para 99, or the day after the CAC's period for deciding the questions comes to an end (para 103). However, if the CAC decides in favour of the union in respect of either or both of the questions, the employer's notice is treated as not having been given (para 103(3)), save that this does not prevent notice from treated as having been given for the purposes of paras 99A(1), 109(1), 113(1) and 130(1) (para 103(3A) and (3B)).

The employer's request to terminate bargaining arrangements at the end of the period of 3 years

4.145   At the end of the initial 3-year bargaining period in a case of statutory recognition, the employer may apply to end the bargaining arrangements. In this regard, the procedure is very much a mirror image of the application for recognition. In the first instance, the employer has to make a request to the union for the bargaining arrangements to end. This request is made under TULRCA 1992, Sch A1, para 104 and, in order to be valid, the request has to be in writing, be received by the union, identify the bargaining arrangements and state that the request is made pursuant to TULRCA 1992, Sch A1 (para 104(2)).

4.146 If within the period of 10 working days starting with the day after the union receives the employer's request (or, in the event of multiple unions being recognised in relation to the bargaining unit, the day on which the last of the unions receives the request), the parties agree to end the bargaining arrangements, nothing more is done under TULRCA 1992, Sch A1 and that is the end of the statutory procedure (para 105(1)). The parties may also seek to negotiate an end to the collective bargaining arrangements. If they choose this route, the parties are granted a further period of 20 working days (or such longer period as they may agree between them) to negotiate an end to the procedure (para 105(3) and (7)). If the parties achieve a resolution to the negotiations in favour of ending the bargaining arrangements within this timeframe, then nothing else needs to be done under TULRCA 1992, Sch A1 and the statutory bargaining arrangements come to an end. Further, in order to help the collective parties come to a negotiated outcome, it is possible for a reference to be made to ACAS to help with the negotiations (para 105(5)).

4.147 If, however, the union or unions fails to reply to the employer's request to discontinue the bargaining arrangements, or the union(s) wish(es) to contest the request, the employer may apply to the CAC for a ballot under, respectively, TULRCA 1992, Sch A1, para 106 or 107. However, in a case where the union(s) has/have indicated that it/they wish to negotiate the employer's request, it is possible for the union(s) to inform the employer that it/they wish to involve ACAS, and the employer is then prevented from making an application to the CAC if the employer rejects the union(s) request, or fails to accept it within a period of 10 working days starting the day after the union's proposal is made (para 107(3)).

4.148 In the event that the employer makes a request to the CAC for a ballot, it must comply with the requirements as to the form of the request under TULRCA 1992, Sch A1, para 108(1) and supply a copy of the application together with any supporting documents to the union(s) (para 108(2)). Further, the employer cannot make an application to the CAC if within the previous 3 years:

- the employer has previously made an unsuccessful application for derecognition under para 106 or 107;
- the union(s) has/have made an application to defeat a 'small employer' application under para 101; or
- the workers within the bargaining unit have made an application to the CAC under para 112.

4.149 Under TULRCA 1992, Sch A1, para 109(1), an application under para 106 or 107 is not admissible if another 'relevant application' relating to the same bargaining unit was made, or a notice under para 99(2) was given, within the period of 3 years prior to the date of the application under para 106 or 107 and the CAC, as relevant, either accepted that application or decided under para 100 that the notice complied with para 99(3). Paragraph 109(2) defines a 'relevant application' for these purposes as being one made to the CAC by the employer under para 106, 107 or 128, or by a worker (or workers) under para 112.

4.150 The CAC is also required to consider whether at least 10 per cent of the workers constituting the bargaining unit are in favour of ending the bargaining arrangements and a majority of workers in the bargaining unit would be likely to be in favour of ending the bargaining arrangements (TULRCA 1992, Sch A1, para 110).

4.151 Upon receipt of the employer's application, the CAC is required to give notice to the parties of its receipt of the employer's request under TULRCA 1992, Sch A1, para 106 or 107, and must, within the period of 10 working days (or such longer period as the CAC may specify) determine whether the application is valid taking into account the foregoing (para 111(1) and (2)). If the CAC determines the application is not valid, it must notify the parties, it must not accept the application and no further steps are to be taken (para 111(4)). If, however, the CAC determines that the application is valid, it must accept the application and notify the parties of its acceptance (para 111(6)).

4.152 In the event that the CAC accepts the application, the matter is then dealt with under TULRCA 1992, Sch A1, para 117 (see **4.158**).

Workers' application to end bargaining arrangements

4.153 It is also possible for the workers or any of them within the bargaining unit to apply to the CAC to have the bargaining arrangements ended under TULRCA 1992, Sch A1, para 112. In this regard, the worker or workers must apply in the form specified by the CAC (para 112(2)) and send a copy of the application sent to the CAC to the employer and the union (para 112(3)).

4.154 Under TULRCA 1992, Sch A1, para 113 an application is not admissible if within the previous 3 years an application has been made to, and accepted by, the CAC concerning the same bargaining unit by either of:

- the employer (by means of a previous unsuccessful application for derecognition under para 106 or 107); or
- a worker or workers within the bargaining unit under para 112.

4.155 As with an employer's application for derecognition, the CAC cannot accept the application unless at least 10 per cent of the workers constituting the bargaining unit are in favour of ending the bargaining arrangements and a majority of workers in the bargaining unit would be likely to be in favour of ending the bargaining arrangements (TULRCA 1992, Sch A1, para 114).

4.156 The CAC must give notice to the worker (or workers), the employer and the union (or unions) of the receipt of an application under TULRCA 1992, Sch A1, para 112 and must within the period of 10 working days (or such longer period as the CAC may specify) determine whether the application is valid taking into account the foregoing (para 115(1) and (2)). If the CAC determines the application is not valid, it must notify the parties, it must not accept the application and no further steps are taken (para 115(4)). If, however, the CAC determines that the application is valid, it must accept the application and notify the parties of its acceptance (para 115(6)).

4.157 In the event of the acceptance of an application, the CAC must provide help to the employer, the union(s) and the worker(s) for a period of 20 working days (starting with the day after that on which the CAC gives notice of acceptance of the application or such longer period as the CAC may decide with the consent of the worker(s), the employer and the unions(s)), with a view to the employer and the union(s) agreeing to end the bargaining arrangements or the worker(s) withdrawing the application (TULRCA 1992, Sch A1, para 116). In the event that the parties cannot agree on an outcome, the matter is dealt with by way of a ballot under the provisions of para 117 et seq.

Balloting on continued recognition of bargaining arrangements

4.158   The balloting arrangements in both the case of an employer seeking to derecognise a union under TULRCA 1992, Sch A1, para 106 and of a worker or workers seeking to derecognise a union under para 112 are dealt with under TULRCA 1992, Sch A1, paras 117–121. These are almost identical to the provisions relating to independently scrutinised ballots for the initial recognition of a union or unions, including with regard to the provisions introduced by ERA 2004 dealing with the use of 'unfair practices' by any of the employer or the union (under paras 119A–119F) and in relation to applications by workers under para 112 (by paras 119G–119I). In respect of these provisions though, the 40 per cent threshold and a majority of those voting must be for those workers in the workforce not in favour of continued recognition (which, if achieved, will result in the union(s) being derecognised (para 121)).

4.159   Where 'unfair practices' relating to the termination of the bargaining unit (as defined by TULRCA 1992, Sch A1, para 119A) are used, it depends upon which provision for the request for derecognition is being used as to what the CAC may do in relation to those unfair practices. If the provision in respect of which derecognition is sought is either of para 106 or 107, then where the unfair practices are committed by:

● the employer, ultimately, the CAC may refuse the employer's application that recognition in relation to the bargaining unit is to come to an end (para 119D(3)); or
● the union (or unions), ultimately, the CAC may issue a declaration that the bargaining arrangements in respect of the bargaining unit shall cease to have effect from a specified date (para 119D(4)).

4.160   In the case of an application by workers in the bargaining unit in respect of the incumbent union continuing to be recognised under TULRCA 1992, Sch A1, para 112, the ultimate sanction by the CAC for the use of unfair practices is varied under para 119H according to the party undertaking the unfair practices and provides that where the unfair practices are committed by:

● the employer, the CAC may order the employer to refrain from further campaigning in relation to the ballot (para 119H(4));
● the union (or unions), the CAC may issue a declaration that the bargaining arrangements are to cease to have effect from a specified date; or
● the worker (or workers), the CAC may refuse the application under para 112.

4.161   Furthermore, where a ballot has been arranged in consequence of an application under TULRCA 1992, Sch A1, para 112, the CAC has given the employer an order under para 119(1), 119C(3) or 119H(4), and the ballot for the purposes of which the order was made (or any other ballot for the purposes of which it has effect) has not been held, the applicant worker (or each of the applicant workers) and the union (or each of the unions) are entitled to enforce obedience of the order in the same way as an Order of the County Court (para 119I).

Derecognition where recognition of a union was automatic

4.162   Where a trade union has been granted recognition automatically under TULRCA 1992, Sch A1, para 22 or 87 in relation to a bargaining unit due to a preponderance of members in the bargaining unit, a further set of provisions exist to deal with derecognition of the union. These arise under TULRCA 1992, Sch A1, paras 122–133. In such a case, the employer cannot make a request to end the bargaining arrangements that have been entered into in the first 3 years from the date of recognition (para 125).

4.163   In the event that the employer wishes to end the bargaining arrangements, the employer must follow the procedure under TULRCA 1992, Sch A1, para 127. This requires the employer to make a written request to the union or unions asking it/them to agree to end the bargaining arrangements. The request must be received by the union or each of the unions, identify the bargaining arrangements, state that the application is made under TULRCA 1992, Sch A1 and state that fewer than half of the workers constituting the bargaining unit are members of the union or those unions (para 127(1) and (2)). As to what constitutes 'bargaining arrangements' for these purposes, a different definition applies depending upon whether:

- the CAC imposed recognition but the employer and the union agreed their own bargaining arrangements (para 122);
- the CAC imposed recognition and specified the bargaining arrangements (para 123); or
- the CAC imposed recognition in relation to a revised bargaining unit under para 87 and the bargaining arrangements from the previous bargaining unit were transposed either with or without CAC modification (para 124).

4.164   Once the employer's request is received by the union(s), the parties are granted a period of 10 working days (or such longer period as the parties may agree), to negotiate with regard to the ending of the bargaining unit (TULRCA 1992, Sch A1, para 128(1) and (3)). Two possibilities arise during this period. First, the parties may agree during the negotiating period that the bargaining arrangements will come to an end. If this is the case, then the bargaining arrangements terminate in accordance with the parties' agreement (para 128(1)). However, if no such agreement is reached, the employer may apply to the CAC for the holding of a secret ballot to decide whether the bargaining arrangements should continue (para 128(2)). The application must be in the form specified by the CAC from time to time and a copy must be provided to the union(s) (para 129).

4.165   Under TULRCA 1992, Sch A1, para 130, the CAC cannot accept an application by the employer if another application has been made to, and accepted by, the CAC in respect of the same bargaining unit in the previous 3 years by any of:

- the union(s) (to defeat a small employer application under para 101);
- the employer (in respect of an application for derecognition under para 106, 107 or 128); or
- the workers within the bargaining unit where an application to the CAC has been made under para 112.

4.166   Further, the CAC cannot accept the application unless it is satisfied that less than half of the members of the bargaining unit are members of the union (TULRCA 1992, Sch A1, para 131).

4.167 Having received the application, the CAC is required to give notice of receipt of the application to the parties and determine within a period of 10 working days (or such longer period as it shall determine), whether it will accept the application (TULRCA 1992, Sch A1, para 132(2)). In the event that it decides not to accept the application, the CAC is required to notify the parties and that is then the end of the application (para 132(4)). If, however, the CAC accepts the application, it is required to notify the parties (para 132(5)) and then move on to the holding of a ballot under para 133.

4.168 Under para 133, a derecognition ballot then takes place in the same format as described above with a threshold of 40 per cent and a majority of those voting against continued recognition needed to end recognition of the union in respect of the bargaining unit.

Derecogniton in the case of a non-independent trade union

4.169 A further different form of procedure is provided in the case where an employer has recognised a trade union which does not have a Certificate of Independence under TULRCA 1992, s 6. In such a case, the procedure is set out under TULRCA 1992, Sch A1, paras 134–146. An application for derecognition under this procedure can be made by a worker or workers within the bargaining unit to the CAC under para 137. The application must be in the form specified by the CAC and supported by such documents as the CAC requires (para 137(2)).

4.170 The application cannot be accepted by the CAC if any of the unions which have been afforded recognition under the bargaining arrangements have a Certificate of Independence (TULRCA 1992, Sch A1, para 138). Further, the CAC cannot accept an application if the union(s) recognised in relation to the bargaining unit have made an application to the Certification Officer for a Certificate of Independence under TULRCA 1992, s 6 and the Certification Officer has not made a decision in relation to that application (para 140)).

4.171 Furthermore, the application cannot be accepted by the CAC unless it decides that at least 10 per cent of the workers in the bargaining unit do not support recognition and that it would be likely that a majority of workers in the bargaining unit would not support continued recognition (TULRCA 1992, Sch A1, para 139(1)). In so deciding, the CAC is required to give reasons for its decision (para 139(2)).

4.172 Having received an application, the CAC is required to give notice of this fact to the worker (or workers), the employer and the union (or unions) and must decide within the period of 10 working days (or such longer period as the CAC may specify) whether to accept the application (TULRCA 1992, Sch A1, para 141(1) and (6)). If the CAC decides that the application is not valid, it must notify the worker(s), the employer and the union(s), it must not accept the application and no further steps are then taken (para 141(4)). If the CAC decides that the application is admissible, it must notify the worker(s), the employer and the union(s) and must, within the period of 20 working days (or such longer period as the CAC shall decide with the consent of the parties) (the negotiating period) commencing on the day after the CAC accepts the application, help them with a view either to ending the bargaining arrangements or to the worker(s) withdrawing the application (para 142).

4.173   If, having accepted an application and before the end of the negotiating period, the CAC is satisfied that one or more of the unions recognised in relation to the bargaining unit presented an application to the Certification Officer for a Certificate of Independence under TULRCA 1992, s 6, prior to the making of the application to the CAC (but not otherwise) and the matter awaits to be determined by the Certification Officer, the CAC cannot proceed with the application TULRCA 1992, Sch A1, para 143.

4.174   Under TULRCA 1992, Sch A1, para 144, if the CAC subsequently decides that one or more of the unions subject to the bargaining arrangements is independent, then the application must be brought to an end. A similar provision exists under para 146(1) and (2) in the case where the CAC has accepted an application under para 137 and it comes to the attention of the CAC at any time prior to the happening of:

- any agreement between the employer and the union as to the ending of the bargaining arrangements;
- any withdrawal of the application by the worker or workers; or
- the CAC being informed of the result of a derecognition ballot.

4.175   Conversely, if it is brought to the attention of the CAC that the Certification Officer has rejected an application for a Certificate of Independence, then the negotiation process is restarted with a further period of 20 working days being granted to the parties to complete their negotiations (TULRCA 1992, Sch A1, para 145).

4.176   In the event that the parties cannot agree on derecognition or the withdrawal of the application, and no application for a Certificate of Independence was made prior to the derecognition application to the CAC, then the matter must proceed to a derecognition ballot under TULRCA 1992, Sch A1, para 147, which is carried out in accordance with paras 117–121. The usual requirements of TULRCA 1992, Sch A1 for the approval of 40 per cent of the bargaining unit and a majority of those voting apply.

Loss of independence

4.177   A further possible way in which bargaining arrangements ordered by the CAC may come to an end is where:

- a union, in respect of which the CAC has issued a recognition declaration in relation to a particular bargaining unit (TULRCA 1992, Sch A1, para 149(1)); or
- where the parties have agreed that a union is, or unions are, recognised, the CAC has specified a bargaining unit under para 63 and the parties have not changed the bargaining unit (para 150),

and the union, or more than one union, loses its or their Certificate of Independence.

4.178   In such a case, statutory recognition in relation to the union, or those unions, ceases (TULRCA 1992, Sch A1, para 152) and the union or unions are treated as being voluntarily recognised only. It should be noted that if only one of a panel of independent trade unions loses its Certificate of Independence, then this does not affect all of the unions; in such a case, statutory recognition will still exist unless all of the union in the panel lose their Certificates of Independence (para 152(2) and (3)).

4.179 If, on appeal under TULRCA 1992, s 9, the Certification Officer reissues the Certificate of Independence, then under TULRCA 1992, Sch A1, para 153, the bargaining arrangements have effect again on the day after the Certification Officer reissues the Certificate of Independence.

RIGHTS OF WORKERS IN BARGAINING UNITS

4.180 In order to protect workers within a bargaining unit, the workers are given the rights not to be subjected to victimisation or unfairly dismissed. Each will be looked at in turn.

Victimisation

4.181 The rights in relation to victimisation are set out in TULRCA 1992, Sch A1, paras 156–60. Under para 156, victimisation occurs where an employer, by any act or deliberate failure to act, subjects a worker to a detriment for any of the following reasons:

- the worker acted with a view to obtaining or preventing recognition of a union (or unions) by the employer under TULRCA 1992, Sch A1;
- the worker indicated that he supported or did not support recognition of a union (or unions) by the employer under TULRCA 1992, Sch A1;
- the worker acted with a view to securing or preventing the ending under TULRCA 1992, Sch A1 of bargaining arrangements;
- the worker indicated that he supported or did not support the ending under TULRCA 1992, Sch A1 of bargaining arrangements;
- the worker influenced or sought to influence the way in which votes were to be cast by other workers in a ballot arranged under TULRCA 1992, Sch A1;
- the worker influenced or sought to influence other workers to vote or to abstain from voting in such a ballot;
- the worker voted in such a ballot; or
- the worker proposed to do, failed to do, or proposed to decline to do, any of the things referred to in the above.

4.182 When considering what amounts to a 'detriment' for the purposes of the victimisation provisions, a worker is not allowed to argue that a dismissal is a detriment if the worker is an 'employee', since the employee can then pursue the right not to be unfairly dismissed (see **4.187**) (TULRCA 1992, Sch A1, para 156(4)).

4.183 The right not to be victimised is available to all workers as defined by TULRCA 1992, s 296. There is no minimum period of continuous service which is necessary to qualify for the right. In the event that a worker believes that he has been victimised, the worker may present a claim to an employment tribunal (para 156(5)). The claim must be presented within 3 months starting with the date of the act or failure to act or the last such incident in a series of acts or omissions (TULRCA 1992, Sch A1, para 157). The worker is also required, under the Employment Act 2002 (EA 2002), ss 31 and 32, to comply with the requirement to present a grievance (and to appeal that grievance) if the worker is to be able to present a claim to the tribunal and not to have any compensation reduced (by a factor of between 10 and 50 per cent).

4.184   Where a claim is presented to an employment tribunal, it is for the employer to show the reason why it acted or failed to act (TULRCA 1992, Sch A1, para 158).

4.185   In the event that an employment tribunal finds a worker's claim to be well founded, it is required to make a declaration to that effect and can award compensation on a just and equitable basis taking into account the loss suffered by the worker (TULRCA 1992, Sch A1, para 159(1) and (2)). This formulation of loss is probably sufficiently broad to include an award for injury to feelings. In particular, the tribunal is required to compensate the worker for any expenses reasonably incurred by the worker in consequence of the employer's breach, together with the loss of any benefit which might reasonably be expected to have accrued to the worker but for the employer's breach (para 159(3)). In all cases, the worker is required to mitigate his loss (para 159(4)) and the tribunal can reduce compensation where the worker caused or contributed to the act or omission complained of (para 159(5)).

4.186   The amount of compensation which can be awarded depends upon the worker's status and the nature of the claim. If the worker is an employee or worker, and the nature of the complaint is that the employer has taken action short of dismissal against that worker, the compensation is unlimited. However if the worker is not an 'employee' for the purposes of ERA 1996, s 230 and the nature of the claim is that the worker has been dismissed, the compensation is subject to a cap equivalent in amount to the total of the basic and compensatory awards from time to time in force (TULRCA 1992, Sch A1, para 160).

Unfair dismissal

4.187   In the case of unfair dismissal, it is automatically unfair to select a worker who is an employee for dismissal (TULRCA 1992, Sch A1, para 161) or to select the employee for redundancy (para 162) for a recognition-related reason. In such a case, the dismissal is not subject to the qualifying period or upper age limit requirements for general unfair dismissal cases (para 164). Further, interim reinstatement is also available as a remedy under ERA 1996, s 128. Finally, as with victimisation, the employee must comply with the statutory dispute resolution requirements under EA 2002 if the employee is to present a claim to an employment tribunal arising out of the dismissal.

GENERAL

4.188   A number of general changes have been made by ERA 2004 to the procedures under TULRCA 1992, Sch A1, most notably with regard to the detailed provisions which now exist in relation to powers to amend TULRCA 1992, Sch A1 under paras 166A–166B and 169A–169C.

4.189   Further, detailed powers are now included under TULRCA 1992, Sch A1, para 170A for CAC case managers to request information from employers, unions and applicant workers in relation to matters relating to TULRCA 1992, Sch A1.

Chapter 5

WORKER CONSULTATION

5.1 One of the main areas of development in the area of collective employment law since 1997 has been the growth in the importance of collective worker consultation otherwise than through trade unions. This new form of worker consultation has been prompted largely at a European level, reflecting the greater willingness of employers in mainland Europe to allow worker representation in the running of businesses. This has resulted in two Directives being passed in Europe, the European Union Works Council Directive[1] (the EWC Directive) and the Information and Consultation of Employees Directive[2] (the ICE Directive) which, in both cases, have been enacted under United Kingdom national law (by means of the Transnational Information and Consultation of Employees Regulations 1999[3] (TICE 1999) in the case of the former, and by the Information and Consultation of Employees Regulations 2004[4] (ICE 2004) in the case of the latter).

5.2 These two sets of regulations have entered into national law by different routes (under the European Communities Act 1972, s 2(2) in the case of TICE 1999 and under the Employment Relations Act 2004 (ERA 2004), s 42 in the case of ICE 2004).

5.3 The two sets of regulations have different scopes. In the case of TICE 1999, the focus is on large, pan-European undertakings with the purpose of those provisions being to provide a better flow of information to employees in pan-European undertakings and to enable them to be consulted with at a transnational level. By contrast, ICE 2004 focuses on national businesses (including small to medium-sized businesses) and aims to allow the provision of information to, and consultation with, employees in those undertakings, on an ongoing basis (rather than in one-off situations, as occurs, for example, in the case of collective redundancies[5] or on the transfer of an undertaking[6]).

5.4 This chapter will look at each of the provisions in turn.

---

[1]   Directive 94/45/EC.

[2]   Directive 2002/14/EC.

[3]   SI 1999/3323.

[4]   SI 2004/3426.

[5]   See the provisions of the Trade Union and Labour Relations (Consolidation) Act 1992 (TULRCA 1992), s 188 et seq.

[6]   See the provisions of Transfer of Undertakings (Protection of Employment) Regulations 1981 (TUPE 1981), SI 1981/1794, regs 10 and 11.

EUROPEAN WORKS COUNCILS

Relationship between the EWC Directive and existing legislation

5.5   The purpose of the EWC Directive is to establish a mechanism for informing and consulting with employees of pan-European undertakings and is seen as a means of complementing, rather than replacing, existing obligations regarding the provision of information to employee representatives and consultation with them in specific circumstances where this is already required by European or national law.

5.6   The EWC Directive, Art 12 states that the Directive applies without prejudice to the Collective Redundancies Directive[7] and the Acquired Rights Directive[8] (as amended by the Business Transfers Directive[9]). Art 12 also states that the EWC Directive is without prejudice to rights of information and consultation of employee representatives under national law.

5.7   Unlike the information and consultation provisions of the Collective Redundancies Directive and the Acquired Rights Directive, which contain a specific framework of information to be provided, a timescale for provision and the requirement for sanctions for non-compliance, the approach to the EWC Directive is aspirational and, for the most part, flexible, rather than prescriptive. The EWC Directive, Art 9 states with some idealism that the central management and the European works council 'shall work together in a spirit of co-operation with due regard to their reciprocal rights and obligations'.

Who falls within the provisions of the Directive?

5.8   The EWC Directive was adopted by the Council of Ministers on 22 September 1994. It came into existence through the use of procedures in the Agreement on Social Policy annexed to the Treaty on European Union (the Maastricht Treaty). Following the passing of the EWC Directive, Member States were obliged to transpose the Directive into national laws by no later than 22 September 1996. The EWC Directive aimed to have transposing laws coming into force simultaneously.

5.9   The European Union initially estimated that some 1,500 multinational undertakings would be affected in the European Union.

5.10   At the time of the EWC Directive being passed, the United Kingdom was not a signatory to the Social Chapter (under which the Directive was passed) and therefore the EWC Directive did not apply in the United Kingdom. However, following a change of government in 1997, the incoming Labour Government adopted the Social Chapter and the package of measures that existed under the Social Chapter, including the European Union Works Council Directive. TICE 1999 was laid before Parliament on 14 December 1999 and came into force on 15 January 2000. It largely adopts its central concepts from the EWC Directive.

---

[7]   Directive 75/129/EEC.
[8]   Directive 77/187/EEC.
[9]   Directive 92/56/EEC.

5.11 The preamble to the EWC Directive sets out its objectives. These state that the functioning of the European internal market involves concentrations of undertakings, mergers, joint ventures and a transnationalisation of undertakings. Further, the preamble notes that the pre-existing procedures for informing and consulting employees were essentially nationally based and not geared to transnational entities: those legal provisions stopped at the national frontier.

5.12 Furthermore, it was recognised that employees of an entity which is part of a group of undertakings in one Member State may be affected by the decisions made by a head office or by a controlling undertaking based outside that state, which could therefore bypass purely national consultation procedures. This could lead to unequal treatment as between group employees in different Member States. In order to address this problem, the preamble to the EWC Directive states that if economic activities are to develop in a harmonious fashion, undertakings in two or more Member States must inform and consult representatives of all employees who may be affected.

Basic definitions under TICE 1999

5.13 The EWC Directive declares in Art 1 that its purpose is to improve the right to information and to consultation of employees in two types of transnational undertakings, these being defined as Community-scale undertakings (CSU) and Community-scale groups of undertakings (CSGU).

5.14 An immediately noticeable point is that both CSUs and CSGUs are large-scale concerns. This reflects the fact that the Social Chapter requires that Directives made under it should avoid administrative, financial and legal constraints being imposed which would hold back the creation and development of small and medium-sized undertakings. In the light of the objectives of the EWC Directive, it does not apply to undertakings or groups within just one Member State (even though the undertaking or group may employ many more than the threshold numbers mentioned): this is the provenance of the ICE Directive.

5.15 Employees are defined under TICE 1999, reg 2(1) as to mean employees employed under a contract of employment (including for the purposes of TICE 1999, reg 41 an individual who has ceased to work under a contract of employment). 'Contract of employment' is defined under TICE 1999, reg 2(1) as to mean a contract of service or apprenticeship, whether express or implied, and (if express) whether oral or in writing.

5.16 The means by which the objective of information and consultation is to be met is through European works councils (EWCs). These are defined by TICE 1999, reg 2(1) as to mean councils, established under and in accordance:

- with TICE 1999, reg 17 or 18 and the provisions of the Schedule; or
- where appropriate, the provisions of the law or practice of a Member State other than the United Kingdom which are designed to give effect to the EWC Directive, Art 6 or 7 and Annex,

with the purpose of informing and consulting employees.

5.17 Further, the definition of EWCs also requires that they consist of 'employee representatives' to meet with central management of the undertaking and discuss and consult with regard to a range of topics arising in relation to the business of the undertaking.

5.18   The EWC Directive speaks throughout of 'employee representatives'. It does not mention trade unions and makes no assumption in this regard, leaving this to be dealt with by national laws and practices. In the United Kingdom, 'employee representatives' are defined under TICE 1999, reg 2(1) as to mean:

- if the employees are of a description in respect of which an independent trade union is recognised by their employer for the purpose of collective bargaining, representatives of the trade union who normally take part as negotiators in the collective bargaining process; and
- any other employee representatives elected or appointed by employees to positions in which they are expected to receive, on behalf of the employees, information:
  - which is relevant to the terms and conditions of employment of the employees; or
  - about the activities of the undertaking which may significantly affect the interests of the employees,

but excluding representatives who are expected to receive information relevant only to a specific aspect of the terms and conditions of employment, or interests of, the employees, such as health and safety or collective redundancies.

5.19   The EWC Directive and TICE 1999 are largely procedural in their content and their provisions are largely intended to promote a general improvement in information and consultation provision in the workplace.

5.20   Turning to CSGUs, these are defined under TICE 1999, reg 2(1) as to cover a group of undertakings with at least 1,000 employees in the Member States, at least two group undertakings in different Member States and at least two different group undertakings each employing 150 or more employees. CSGUs comprise a 'controlling undertaking' which can exercise a 'dominant influence' over other undertakings (the controlled undertakings) (TICE 1999, reg 3(1)), and 'controlled undertakings' (being undertakings over which that dominant influence can be exercised).

5.21   The arithmetic for ascertaining whether workforces meet these criteria is to be based on the average number of employees, including part-time employees, employed during the previous 2 years, calculated in accordance with national legislation or practice (TICE 1999, reg 6(1) and (2)). TICE 1999, reg 6(3) provides that part-time workers working 75 hours or less per month for a whole month, may be treated as being half a person for each such month.

5.22   'Dominance' for these purposes arises through direct or indirect ownership of capital or voting rights or financial participation (TICE 1999, reg 3(1)). Under TICE 1999, reg 3(2), there is a rebuttable presumption that dominance exists where one undertaking directly or indirectly holds the majority of the issued share capital of another undertaking or controls a majority of voting rights or can appoint more than half of the management or other supervisory body. Conversely, a dominant influence is not presumed to be exercised solely by virtue of the fact that an office holder is exercising functions, according to the law of a Member State, relating to liquidation, winding-up, insolvency, cessation of payments, compositions of creditors or analogous proceedings (TICE 1999, reg 3(5)).

5.23   Ultimately, however, whether an undertaking is a 'controlling undertaking' is a matter of national law (TICE 1999, reg 3(6)).

5.24 In seeking to ascertain whether a CSGU exists, the European Court of Justice (ECJ) has held that it is not possible for an undertaking which may be part of a CSGU to claim that it has not yet been established that a CSGU exists having a controlling undertaking within the group, and therefore for the undertaking of which the request has been made to refuse to pass information relating to the numbers of employees and structure of the undertakings (as is required under the EWC Directive, Arts 2(1) and 11)[10] to the employees concerned or their representatives so as to avoid the establishment of an EWC.[11] The ECJ added that a right to information enabling the workers concerned to determine whether they have the right to demand the opening of negotiations with central management is a necessary prerequisite for determining whether a CSU or CSGU exists (which itself is a prerequisite for establishing an EWC or an employee information and consultation procedure (ICP)). The ECJ further added that communication of documents clarifying and explaining the information which is indispensable for that purpose may also be required insofar as their communication is necessary in order that the employees concerned or their representatives may gain access to information enabling them to determine whether or not they are entitled to request the opening of negotiations.

Scope of TICE 1999

5.25 TICE 1999, reg 4 deals with the circumstances in which TICE 1999 applies generally. Regulation 4(1) provides that TICE 1999, regs 7–41 and 46 apply in relation to a CSU or CSGU only where, in accordance with reg 5, the 'central management' is situated in the United Kingdom.

5.26 Further, TICE 1999, reg 4(2) provides that in relation to a CSU or CSGU, whether or not the central management is situated in the United Kingdom, the following provisions of TICE 1999 apply:

- TICE 1999, regs 7 and 8(1), (2) and (4) (provision of information on employee numbers);
- TICE 1999, regs 13–15 (United Kingdom members of the special negotiating body);
- TICE 1999, reg 18 to the extent it applies the Schedule, paras 3–5 (United Kingdom members of the EWC);
- TICE 1999, reg 23(1)–(5) (breach of statutory duty);
- TICE 1999, regs 25–33 (protections for members of an EWC etc);
- TICE 1999, regs 34–39 (enforcement bodies) to the extent they relate to applications made or complaints presented under any of the other regulations referred to in this paragraph; and
- TICE 1999, regs 40 and 41 (restrictions on contracting out).

Multinational corporations with headquarters outside the European Union

5.27 The EWC Directive and TICE 1999 have an indirect application to multinational companies with headquarters outside the European Union.

---

[10] In respect of which the ECJ held in *Betriebsrat der Firma ADS Anker Gmbh v ADS Anker Gmbh* ECJ (C-349–01) (2004) IDS Brief B763/11 that these obligations also entail obligations to provide details of the employees' representative bodies and the names of the representatives who would be acting on their behalf in establishing an EWC.

[11] *Betriebsrat der Brofrost Josef H Boquoi Deutschland West GmbH & Co KG v Brofrost Josef H Boquoi Deutschland West GmbH & Co KG* [2001] IRLR 403.

Undertakings with an operational presence of the requisite scale in the Member States are obliged to comply with the EWC Directive in respect of their European Union workforces. The EWC Directive requires action on the part of 'central management' of an undertaking for the purposes of creating the conditions and means necessary for an EWC or ICP.

5.28 'Central management' for the purposes of TICE 1999 is loosely defined under TICE 1999, regs 2(1) and 5(1). Under TICE 1999, reg 2(1), 'central management' is stated to be the central management of a CSU or a CSGU. Beyond this, no definition is provided.

5.29 More particularly, TICE 1999, reg 5(1)(a) covers the situation where the central management is located in the United Kingdom.

5.30 The EWC Directive, Art 4(2) and TICE 1999, reg 5(1) cover the situation where central management is not situated in a Member State but where the central management has delegated that a representative agent designated by the central management will discharge the obligations of the central management for creating the EWC or ICP under the EWC Directive. In such a case, it is necessary to determine whether the representative agent is situated in the United Kingdom or another Member State. In the case of the former, TICE 1999, reg 5(1)(b) applies and the United Kingdom is deemed to be the seat of the central management. In the case of the representative agent having its seat in another Member State, the national law enactment of the EWC Directive of that Member State applies to the central management.

5.31 Additionally, under TICE 1999, reg 5(1)(c), where neither the central management nor a representative agent are located in a Member State but in the case of:

- a CSU, there are employed in an establishment situated in the United Kingdom, more employees than are employed in any other establishment which is situated in a Member State; or
- in the case of a CSGU, there are employed in a group undertaking situated in the United Kingdom, more employees than are situated in any other Member State,

and the central management initiates or is required to initiate by TICE 1999, reg 9(1), negotiations for an EWC or an ICP, the central management is deemed to be in the United Kingdom. Where the CSU or CSGU has more employees located in another Member State, then that Member State's enactment of the EWC Directive applies to the matter.

Establishing an EWC

5.32 The EWC Directive lays down a procedure through which employees of CSUs can establish EWCs or an ICP. This is contained in the EWC Directive, Arts 4–7 which are incorporated in TICE 1999, Part II.

5.33 Central management can of its own initiative initiate negotiations for establishing an EWC or an ICP (TICE 1999, reg 9(5)). However, under TICE 1999, reg 9(1) and (2), the central management of a CSU must initiate negotiations at the written request of at least 100 employees or their representatives in at least two undertakings or establishments in at least two different Member States. In this regard, it is not possible for a CSU or CSGU to avoid the application of the deeming provisions under TICE 1999, reg 5 by arguing that the actual central management of the CSU or CSGU is not located in a European Union Member State. The ECJ has held in this regard that where the actual central management of a CSGU is not located in a European Union Member State and fails to make available to the deemed central management information required by employees' representatives for opening negotiations for the establishment of an EWC, the EWC Directive, Art 4(1) requires the deemed central management to request that information from other undertakings in the CSGU which are situated in the Member States. It is also the obligation of the management of each of the undertakings within the CSGU in the other Member States to supply the deemed central management with the information concerned where that information is either in their possession or under their control.[12]

5.34 In order for a written request or requests to be valid, the request(s) must be sent to the central management or the local management, specify the date on which the request was sent and, where appropriate, be made after the expiry of a period of 2 years commencing on the date of a decision under TICE 1999, reg 16(3) unless the special negotiating body (SNB) to be established for the purposes of negotiating the EWC and the central management has agreed otherwise (TICE 1999, reg 16(3)).

5.35 Where there is a dispute as to whether a valid request for an EWC or ICP has been made in the United Kingdom, it is possible for the central management to apply to the Central Arbitration Committee (CAC) for a declaration on the matter (TICE 1999, reg 10(1)). Under TICE 1999, reg 10(2), the CAC can only consider an application for a declaration if:

● the application is made within a 3-month period beginning on the date when a request (or the first of a number of such requests) was made for the purposes of TICE 1999, reg 9 (it is irrelevant whether that request or the first such request was a valid request);
● the application is made before central management takes any step to initiate negotiations for the establishment of an EWC or an ICP; and
● at the time when the application is made, there has been no application by the central management for a declaration under TICE 1999, reg 10(3).

5.36 If the central management considers for any reason that the obligation under TICE 1999, reg 9(1) did not apply to it on the relevant date, it may apply to the CAC for a declaration as to whether this is the case and has a 3-month period for doing so (TICE 1999, reg 10(3)). Where the date on which a valid request is made is a date before an application for a declaration under TICE 1999, reg 10, the time periods under TICE 1999, reg 18 (the statutory default EWC procedure) are suspended for a period of time commencing on the date of the application and ending on the date of the declaration (TICE 1999, reg 10(4)). If the CAC believes that the employer's application is frivolous, vexatious or otherwise unreasonable, the CAC is required to make a declaration to that effect and state that the time-limit adjustments under TICE 1999, reg 10(4) do not apply (TICE 1999, reg 10(5)).

---

[12] *Gesamtbetriebsrat Der Kuhne & Nagel AG & Co KG v Kuhne & Nagel AG & Co KG* [2004] IRLR 332. See too *Betreibsrat der Firma ADS Anker GmbH v ADS Anker GmbH* ECJ (C-349–01) (2004) IDS Brief B763/11.

5.37   In order to facilitate negotiations for the establishment of either an EWC or ICP, the EWC Directive and TICE 1999, Part III provide for the establishment of an SNB. Under TICE 1999, reg 11 the SNB is given the task of determining in a written agreement with the central management, the scope, composition, functions and term of office of a EWC or the arrangements for implementing an ICP (TICE 1999, reg 11).

5.38   The EWC Directive, Art 5(2) provides that an SNB must comprise at least three and not more than 18 members. The EWC Directive, Art 5(2)(a)–(c) lays down guidelines in this connection, as follows:

- Each Member State is to determine how SNB members from its territory are to be elected or appointed.
- It is obligatory for Member States to ensure that where employees have no representatives in an undertaking 'through no fault of their own', they are to be given the right to elect or appoint members of the SNB.
- The election or appointment procedure must ensure that the SNB has at least one member from each Member State in which the CSU has one or more establishments, or the CSGU has one or more controlled undertakings, and also that 'supplementary members' are elected or appointed in proportion to the number of employees within a Member State, as laid down by the legislation of the Member States in which the central management is located (in cases where the territory concerned is the United Kingdom or a non-European Union territory, this will be the territory in which the representative agent is situated). Accordingly, the total could vary from SNB to SNB, depending on the geographical and head count spread of workers in the various Member States.

5.39   TICE 1999 provides for the composition of the SNB at TICE 1999, reg 12(2) and (3) which states that there must be:

- at least one member representing each Member State in which a CSU has one or more establishments, or in which a CSGU has its controlling undertaking or one or more controlled undertakings;
- one additional member from a Member State in which there are employed 25 per cent or more but less than 50 per cent of the employees of the undertaking or group of undertakings who are employed in the Member States;
- two additional members from a Member State in which there are employed 50 per cent or more but less than 75 per cent of the employees in the undertaking or group of undertakings who are employed in the Member States; and
- three additional employees from a Member State in which there are employed 75 per cent or more of the employees in the undertaking or group of undertakings who are employed in the Member States.

5.40   Further, the SNB, once it is composed, is required to inform the central management and local management of the composition of the SNB (TICE 1999, reg 12(4)).

5.41   In order to provide for the election of members of the SNB, balloting arrangements are provided by TICE 1999, regs 13 (balloting arrangements) and 14 (conduct of ballot). These provide for the following matters.

5.42 As regards balloting arrangements under TICE 1999, reg 13, the United Kingdom members of the SNB (ie any of the employees lawfully working in the United Kingdom) are required to be elected by a ballot of the United Kingdom employees (reg 13(1)). The obligation to arrange for the holding of a ballot falls on the United Kingdom management (reg 13(2)) and the ballot must be undertaken in accordance with TICE 1999, reg 13(3), which provides as follows:

- The ballot must be a single ballot which may comprise separate ballots of employees in discrete constituencies as the United Kingdom management may determine where the number of United Kingdom members of the SNB to be elected is more than one and the United Kingdom management believes that having separate ballots would better reflect the interests of the United Kingdom employees as a whole.
- United Kingdom employees of either CSUs or CSGUs on the day of a ballot have the right to vote in the ballot.
- Any United Kingdom employee or United Kingdom employee representative in either a CSU or CSGU immediately before the latest time at which a person may become a candidate in a ballot is entitled to stand for election as a representative of an SNB.[13]
- The United Kingdom management must appoint an independent ballot supervisor (defined under TICE 1999, reg 13(7) as being someone whom the United Kingdom management reasonably believes will be independent and who will carry out his functions independently), to supervise the conduct of the ballot of the United Kingdom employees. In the case of multiple ballots, it is possible to appoint a separate independent ballot supervisor for each such ballot.
- The United Kingdom management must make final arrangements for the conduct of the ballot, must publish those final arrangements in such a manner as will, so far as reasonably practicable, bring them to the attention of the United Kingdom employees and the United Kingdom employees' representatives. Further, before publishing the final arrangements, the United Kingdom management is required to consult with the United Kingdom employees' representatives on the proposed arrangements.

5.43 A right of complaint to the CAC exists in the event that a United Kingdom employee or United Kingdom employees' representative believes that the balloting arrangements are defective. In such a case, a complaint may be presented within 21 days of the United Kingdom management publishing the final arrangements (TICE 1999, reg 13(4)). TICE 1999, reg 13(8) specifically provides that final arrangements for the ballot will be defective where any of the requirements in TICE 1999, reg 13(3)(b)–(f) are not complied with or where in a case where separate ballots are to be conducted in relation to different parts of the workforce, these do not adequately reflect the interests of the United Kingdom employees as a whole.

---

[13]   In *European Commission v Austria*, C-465–01, [2004] 3 CMLR 1268, the ECJ held that to deny a foreign national working legally in a Member State the right to stand for election as an employee representative in a works' council, trade union or other workers' representative body on the basis of his nationality is discriminatory and operates to deny free movement of workers contrary to the EC Treaty, Art 39.

5.44   As regards the conduct of the ballot, TICE 1999, reg 14 provides that the United Kingdom management must:

- ensure that an appointed ballot supervisor carries out his functions under TICE 1999, reg 14 and that there is no interference with the carrying out of those functions from the United Kingdom management, or the central management (where it is not also the United Kingdom management); and
- comply with all reasonable requests made by a ballot supervisor for the purposes of, or in connection with, the carrying out of those functions.

5.45   Further, TICE 1999, reg 14(2) provides in relation to a ballot supervisor's appointment that he:

- must supervise the conduct of the ballot, or the separate ballots, he is being appointed to supervise, in accordance with the arrangements for the ballot of the United Kingdom employees published by the United Kingdom management under TICE 1999, reg 13(3)(f) or, where appropriate, in accordance with the arrangements as required to be modified by an order made as a result of a complaint presented under TICE 1999, reg 13(4);
- does not conduct the ballot or any of the separate ballots before the United Kingdom management has satisfied the requirement specified in TICE 1999, reg 13(3)(e) and:
  - where no complaint has been presented under TICE 1999, reg 13(4), before the expiry of the 21-day period beginning on the date on which the United Kingdom management published its final ballot arrangements under TICE 1999, reg 13(3)(f); or
  - where a complaint has been presented under TICE 1999, reg 13(4), before the complaint has been determined and, where appropriate, the arrangements have been modified as required by an order made as a result of the complaint;
- conducts the ballot, or each separate ballot, so as to secure that:
  - so far as reasonably practicable, those entitled to vote are given the opportunity to vote;
  - so far as reasonably practicable, those entitled to stand as candidates are given the opportunity to stand;
  - so far as is reasonably practicable, those voting are able to do so in secret; and
  - the votes given in the ballot are fairly and accurately counted.

5.46   If the CAC upholds the complaint, it may make a declaration to that effect and make an order specifying amendments to the final arrangements requiring the United Kingdom management to modify the arrangements so as to satisfy the requirements of TICE 1999, reg 13 (TICE 1999, reg 13(5) and (6)).

5.47   Under TICE 1999, reg 14(3), as soon as reasonably practicable after the holding of the ballot, the ballot supervisor must publish the results of the ballot in such manner as to make them available to the United Kingdom management and, so far as reasonably practicable, the United Kingdom employees entitled to vote in the ballot and the persons who stood as candidates in the ballot.

5.48   Under TICE 1999, reg 14(4), the ballot supervisor must publish an 'ineffective ballot report' where he considers (whether or not on the basis of representations made to him by another person) that:

- any of the requirements under TICE 1999, reg 14(2) were not satisfied with the result that the outcome of the ballot would have been different; or
- there was interference with the carrying out of his functions or a failure by management to comply with all reasonable requests made by him with the result that he was unable to form a proper judgment as to whether each of the requirements referred to under TICE 1999, reg 14(2) was satisfied in relation to the ballot.

5.49 Where a ballot supervisor publishes an ineffective ballot report, the report must be published within a period of one month commencing on the date on which the ballot supervisor publishes the results of the ballot under TICE 1999, reg 14(3).

5.50 Under TICE 1999, reg 14(6), the ballot supervisor is required to publish an ineffective ballot report in such manner as to make it available to the United Kingdom management and, so far as reasonably practicable, the United Kingdom employees entitled to vote in the ballot and the persons who stood as candidates in the ballot.

5.51 If the ballot supervisor publishes an ineffective ballot report, then, if there has been a single ballot or an ineffective ballot report has been published in respect of every separate ballot, the outcome of the ballot or ballots shall have no effect and the United Kingdom management shall again be under the obligation in TICE 1999, reg 13(2). However, if there have been separate ballots, the United Kingdom management shall arrange for the separate ballot or ballots in respect of which an ineffective ballot report was issued to be re-held in accordance with TICE 1999, regs 13 and 14, and no such ballot shall have effect until it has been re-held and no ineffective ballot report has been published in respect of it.

5.52 Under TICE 1999, reg 14(8), all costs relating to the holding of a ballot, including payments made to the ballot supervisor for supervising the conduct of the ballot, are required to be borne by the central management (whether or not an ineffective ballot report has been made).

5.53 TICE 1999, reg 15 provides for 'consultative committees'. Consultative committees are defined by TICE 1999, reg 15(5) as being a body of persons:

- whose normal functions include or comprise the carrying out of an information and consultation function;
- which is able to carry out its information and consultation function without interference from the United Kingdom management, or from the central management (where it is not also the United Kingdom management);
- which, in carrying out its information and consultation function, represents all the United Kingdom employees; and
- which consists wholly of persons who were elected by a ballot (which may have consisted of a number of separate ballots) in which all the employees who, at the time, were United Kingdom employees entitled to vote.

5.54 The 'information and consultation function' is defined by TICE 1999, reg 15(5) as being the function of receiving, on behalf of all the United Kingdom employees, information which may significantly affect the interests of the United Kingdom employees, but excluding information which is relevant only to a specific aspect of the interests of the employees, such as health and safety or collective redundancies, and being consulted by the United Kingdom management or the central management (where it is not also the United Kingdom management) on that information.

5.55   Under TICE 1999, reg 15(1), where a consultative committee exists no United Kingdom member of the SNB may be elected by a ballot of the United Kingdom employees, except in accordance with TICE 1999, reg 15(2), (3) or (9) (see **5.56**) and the consultative committee is entitled to nominate from its number the United Kingdom members of the SNB.

5.56   As to the exceptions in relation to the case in which there is a consultative committee in existence but where United Kingdom members of the SNB may be elected nonetheless, these are:

- under TICE 1999, reg 15(2), where the consultative committee fails to nominate any United Kingdom members of the SNB, all of the United Kingdom members of the SNB are to be elected by a ballot of the United Kingdom employees in accordance with TICE 1999, regs 13 and 14;
- under TICE 1999, reg 15(3), where the consultative committee nominates such number of persons to be a United Kingdom member, or United Kingdom members, of the SNB, which is less or more than the number of United Kingdom members of the SNB required, the consultative committee shall be treated as having failed to have nominated any United Kingdom members of the SNB; or
- under TICE 1999, reg 15(9), where the CAC has made a declaration under TICE 1999, reg 15(8) that no nomination made by the consultative committee shall have effect, all of the United Kingdom members of the SNB are then required to be elected by a ballot of the United Kingdom employees in accordance with TICE 1999, regs 13 and 14.

5.57   Under TICE 1999, reg 15(6), the consultative committee must publish the names of the persons whom it has nominated to be United Kingdom members of the SNB in such a way as to bring them to the attention of the United Kingdom management and, so far as reasonably practicable, the United Kingdom employees and United Kingdom employees' representatives.

5.58   Further, under TICE 1999, reg 15(7), where the United Kingdom management, a United Kingdom employee or a United Kingdom employees' representative believes that either the consultative committee does not satisfy the requirements in TICE 1999, reg 15(4) or any of the persons nominated by the consultative committee is not entitled to be nominated, then that person or body, may, within 21 days beginning on the date on which the consultative committee published the names of persons nominated under TICE 1999, reg 15 (6), present a complaint to the CAC. Where the CAC finds the complaint well founded it shall make a declaration to that effect. In such a case, no nomination made by the consultative committee shall have effect (TICE 1999, reg 15(8)).

5.59   Where the consultative committee nominates any person to be a United Kingdom member of the SNB, the nomination has effect where no complaint has been presented under TICE 1999, reg 15(7), after the expiry of a period of 21 days beginning on the date on which the consultative committee published the names of persons nominated under TICE 1999, reg 15(6). Alternatively, where a complaint has been presented under TICE 1999, reg 15(7), the nomination has effect after the complaint has been determined without a declaration under TICE 1999, reg 15(8) having been made.

Establishment of EWCs and ICPs

5.60 TICE 1999, Part IV deals with the establishment of EWCs and ICPs. In this regard, TICE 1999, reg 16(1) provides that the central management is to convene a meeting of the SNB, informing local management with a view to reaching a written agreement (under TICE 1999, reg 17) with central management, as to the scope, composition, functions and term of the EWC or, as an alternative, other arrangements for implementing an ICP.

5.61 TICE 1999, reg 16(3) provides that by a two-thirds majority, the SNB may decide not to open negotiations or to terminate negotiations already opened, in which case all procedures towards establishing an EWC come to an end and the fall-back provisions, described at **5.70** et seq, do not come into effect. Once that has happened, no new request for the SNB to be convened can be made within 2 years, unless the parties otherwise agree a shorter period (TICE 1999, reg 16(4)).

5.62 For the purpose of the negotiations, the SNB may be assisted by experts of its choice (TICE 1999, reg 16(5)). Further, the central management is required to pay for any reasonable expenses relating to the negotiations that are necessary to enable the SNB to carry out its functions in an appropriate manner. However, where the SNB is assisted by more than one expert the central management is not required to pay any expenses in respect of more than one such expert (TICE 1999, reg 16(6)).

5.63 The content of the 'written agreement' is outlined in the EWC Directive, Art 6, which is incorporated in to United Kingdom law as TICE 1999, reg 17. Essentially, the SNB and management are left with considerable autonomy to negotiate 'in a spirit of co-operation' with a view to reaching agreement on detailed arrangements for information and consultation of employees (TICE 1999, reg 17(1)). Unless a wider scope is provided for in the agreement, the powers and competence of an EWC and the scope of an ICP shall, in the case of a CSU, cover all the establishments located within the Member States and, in the case of a CSGU, all group undertakings located within the Member States (TICE 1999, reg 17(1)).

5.64 In particular, under TICE 1999, reg 17(4) the agreement may determine:

- which undertakings of the CGSU or which establishments of the CSU are to be covered by the agreement;
- the composition of the EWC, in particular, its members, seat allocations and the term of office of its members;
- the scope and functions of the EWC and the procedures for informing it and consulting with it;
- the venue, frequency and duration of EWC meetings;
- the financial and material resources to be allocated to the EWC; and
- how long the agreement is to last and the procedure for its renegotiation.

5.65 It is envisaged, therefore, that the agreement under TICE 1999, reg 17 may not be permanent. However, it is up to management and the EWC to determine the extent of details, whether these are very detailed or very broad brush. It would be possible for the SNB to agree with central management to include within the scope of the EWC, United Kingdom undertakings and that United Kingdom employees should form part of the membership of the EWC.

5.66   As mentioned at **5.60**, under TICE 1999, reg 17(5) central management and the SNB can decide to establish one or more ICPs instead of an EWC. Neither the EWC Directive nor TICE 1999 contains any guidance as to the nature and scope of an ICP other than TICE 1999, reg 17(5) stating two things. First, such an alternative agreement must stipulate how the employee representatives are to have the right to meet and discuss information conveyed to them. Secondly, the information is to relate in particular to transnational questions which significantly affect workers' interests. By contrast, this is not a mandatory feature of an EWC agreement. Obviously the SNB will no doubt be aware of the alternative of going for an EWC and this may well condition their thinking as to what is an acceptable alternative. Further, an agreement to create an ICP is stated specifically *not* to be subject to the provisions of TICE 1999, Schedule (which provides for a default constitution for an EWC in the event that the parties are unable to agree a constitution), save to the extent that the parties agree that any of those provisions shall apply TICE 1999, reg 17(6).

5.67   Where a CSGU comprises one or more undertakings or groups of undertakings which are themselves CSUs or CSGUs, the EWC shall be established at the level of the highest-level CSGU, unless the negotiated agreement under TICE 1999, reg 17(4) provides otherwise (TICE 1999, reg 17(7)).

5.68   There is, moreover, a time pressure under TICE 1999, reg 18, in that in three sets of circumstances, a fall-back provision comes into operation where agreement on the formation of a EWC or ICP cannot be reached. These circumstances are where:

- central management and the SNB so agree;
- central management refuses to begin negotiations within 6 months of being requested to do so by the requisite 100 employees in two establishments in at least two Member States; or
- central management accedes to the request to begin negotiations but after 3 years no agreement has been made (and the SNB has not decided to abandon negotiations under TICE 1999, reg 16(3)).

5.69   In any of those circumstances there will come into operation what are termed the 'subsidiary requirements'. Member States are obliged to adopt legislation for such subsidiary requirements, which must effectively meet standards laid down in an Appendix to the EWC Directive. TICE 1999 provides for this under TICE 1999, reg 18(1).

5.70   The system envisaged by TICE 1999, Schedule is both prescriptive and detailed, in contrast with the relatively free hand given to central management and SNB to agree such matters for themselves. While it will apply only in the circumstances described, it may have an influence on negotiations and on agreements reached thereby. If employee representatives and central management know that in the fullness of time they are going to have the subsidiary requirements or nothing, that may be a spur for both sides towards agreement. They will also no doubt serve as a bench-mark for negotiation.

5.71   The competence of the EWC under the subsidiary requirements in TICE 1999, Schedule is prescribed and not negotiable. Also, under the subsidiary requirements in the Schedule, the competence of an EWC for an undertaking or group of undertakings having central management outside the European Union is limited to matters concerning *all* their establishments within the

Member States or at least two establishments or group undertakings in different Member States (TICE 1999, Schedule, para 6). It is therefore a good deal more specific and limited in scope than might be the case with an EWC established through negotiated agreement. Further, the provisions of the Schedule apply for a period of 4 years before they are reviewed to see whether either an employer-specific EWC constitution is to be negotiated thereafter, or whether the provisions of the Schedule are to continue to apply (TICE 1999, Schedule, para 10).

5.72 The scheme of the subsidiary requirements in TICE 1999, Schedule is that the EWC shall consist of between three and 30 members (TICE 1999, Schedule, para 2(1)), who are to be employees of the undertaking elected or appointed by the employees' representatives or in the absence of such representatives, by the entire body of employees (para 3). Many of the features of TICE 1999, Schedule are similar to provisions that exist under the EWC Directive with regard to the creation of the EWC under the Schedule (for example, with regard to the countries from where members of the EWC are to be drawn (para 2); the election and appointment of members of the EWC (para 3); and balloting arrangements and the conduct of the ballot (paras 4 and 5)).

5.73 Further, the EWC has the right to meet with central management once a year and to be informed and consulted with by central management (TICE 1999, Schedule, para 7). This information and consultation must be on the basis of a report to be prepared by central management on the business or prospects of the CSU or CSGU. The annual meeting has to relate in particular to the structure, economic and financial situation (presumably of all of the CSU), probable business development and production and sales, and employment situation and trends. Also to be covered under para 7 are organisational changes, new working methods, transfer of production, cut-backs, closures of undertakings, establishments and collective redundancies.

5.74 The EWC will have the right to meet and receive, on an ad hoc basis, information about exceptional circumstances, significantly affecting the employees' interest, particularly, relocations, closure of establishments or undertakings or collective redundancies. It is expressly stated that 'this meeting shall not affect the prerogatives of the central management' (TICE 1999, Schedule, para 8).

5.75 The EWC adopts its own rules of procedure (TICE 1999, Schedule, para 9(3)). Like the SNB, the EWC will have to have at least one member from each Member State where the undertaking has an establishment, with supplementary members to reflect the proportions of the undertaking's employees in each Member State. Where the size of the EWC requires, it must elect a select committee of not more than three members.

5.76 The EWC members from the Member States directly concerned are entitled to form the select committee for this purpose (TICE 1999, Schedule, para 9(1)).

5.77 The EWC may be assisted by experts of its choice, so far as necessary to enable it to carry out its functions (TICE 1999, Schedule, para 9(4)). All costs of operation of the EWC are to be borne by the employer, although it is possible to limit funding to one expert (para 9(5)). Central management is in particular to meet the cost of organising meetings and arrangement interpretation facilities, accommodation and travel expenses (para 9(6)).

5.78   The task of communicating to representatives of employees in the CSUs the content and outcome of the information and consultation procedures is that of the members of the EWC (TICE 1999, Schedule, para 9(2)).

5.79   Once the EWC is established, TICE 1999, reg 19 provides that the central management and the EWC are under a duty to work in a 'spirit of cooperation' with due regard to their reciprocal rights and obligations. This duty is stated specifically to the central management and information and consultation representatives.

Failure to establish an EWC or ICP

5.80   Where the parties have reached agreement on the establishment of a EWC or ICP, or TICE 1999, Schedule is deemed to apply to the parties, and, because of a 'failure' of the central management, the EWC or ICP has not been established either in whole or in part in accordance with the terms of the agreement under TICE 1999, reg 17 or in accordance with the provisions of the Schedule, a complaint may be presented to the Employment Appeal Tribunal (EAT) by a 'relevant applicant' (TICE 1999, reg 20(1)). A failure is defined by TICE 1999, reg 20(2) as to mean an act or omission and a failure by the local management shall be treated as a failure by the central management.

5.81   Further, a 'relevant applicant' is stated by TICE 1999, reg 20(3) to be either, in a case where a special negotiating body exists, the SNB or, in a case where an SNB does not exist, an employee, employees' representative or person who was a member of the SNB (if the SNB existed previously).

5.82   Where the EAT finds the complaint well founded it shall make a decision to that effect and may make an order requiring the central management to take such steps as are necessary to establish the EWC or ICP in accordance with the terms of the agreement under TICE 1999, reg 17 or, as relevant, to establish a EWC in accordance with the provisions of the Schedule (TICE 1999, reg 20(4)). Any such order must specify:

- the steps which the central management is required to take;
- the date of the failure of the central management; and
- the period within which the order must be complied with.

5.83   Further, under TICE 1999, reg 20(7) if the EAT makes a decision under TICE 1999, reg 20(4) that the employer has failed to comply with its obligations under TICE 1999 it is also required to issue a written penalty notice to the central management requiring it to pay a penalty to the Secretary of State. This is so unless the EAT is satisfied, on hearing the representations of the central management, that the failure resulted from a reason beyond the central management's control or that it has some other reasonable excuse for its failure (TICE 1999, reg 20(8)).

5.84   Under TICE 1999, reg 20(5), it is specifically stated that the EAT shall not find a complaint to be well founded either where:

- the central management made no application in relation to the request under TICE 1999, reg 10(1), or where the request consisted of separate requests and, due to the 3-month time-limit under TICE 1999, reg 10(2)(a) the central management was unable to make an application in relation to a particular request, and the central management shows that the request was not a valid request because a requirement of TICE 1999, reg 9(2) or (3) was not satisfied; or

● the central management made no application under TICE 1999, reg 10(3) but shows that the obligation in TICE 1999, reg 9(1) did not, for any reason, apply to it on the relevant date.

5.85 Similar provisions apply under TICE 1999, reg 21 where the central management is in default of an obligation under either TICE 1999, reg 17 negotiated constitution, or TICE 1999, Schedule in relation to the operation of the EWC or ICP. As with a failure to establish an EWC or ICP, an application can be made to the EAT against the 'defaulter', defined by TICE 1999, reg 21(3) as being either the central management or the EWC (in the case of a failure relating to an EWC), or in the case of a failure concerning an ICP, either the central management or any one or more of the information and consultation representatives.

5.86 TICE 1999, reg 22 deals with penalty notices. TICE 1999, reg 22(1) provides that a penalty notice shall specify the amount of the penalty which is payable, the date before which the penalty is payable and the failure and the period to which the penalty relates. Further, TICE 1999, reg 22(2) states that the amount of the penalty cannot exceed £75,000. In determining the amount of the penalty, under TICE 1999, reg 22(3), the EAT is specifically required to take into account the following points:

● the gravity of the failure;
● the period of time over which the failure occurred;
● the reason for the failure;
● the number of employees affected by the failure; and
● the number of employees of the CSU or CSGU in the Member States.

5.87 An unpaid penalty (whether in whole or in part) is stated to be recoverable by the Secretary of State as a civil debt (TICE 1999, reg 22(5)).

Confidential information

5.88 The confidential information and trade secrets of any business are of crucial importance to it, not least due to the damage which the business may suffer if that type of information and secrets of that nature are disclosed without authority, either generally or specifically (so as to be made of use by competitors or would-be competitors).

5.89 Further, given the potentially very wide-reaching disclosures that have to be made (either under an EWC with an agreed constitution, or under a constitution governed by TICE 1999, Schedule or through an ICP), it is likely that information that will have to be disclosed to an EWC or though an ICP may well include very sensitive commercial intelligence. This is a point that was recognised by the EWC Directive, Art 8(1) of which provides that Member States shall provide that members of SNBs and EWCs, together with any experts assisting them, are not authorised to reveal any information which has expressly been provided to them in confidence. This provision has been included as TICE 1999, Part VI, the key features of which are as follows.

5.90 First, TICE 1999, reg 23(1) and (2) provide that any person who is or was a member of an SNB; an ICP representative; or an expert assisting an

SNB, an EWC, its select committee or information and consultation representatives (a 'recipient'), shall not disclose any information or document which is or has been in his possession by virtue of the recipient's position as described, where that information or document has entrusted it to the recipient requiring it to be held in confidence. This obligation is stated by TICE 1999, reg 23(3) to be a duty owed to the central management and is specifically stated to be actionable as a breach of statutory duty. The duty not to disclose is stated expressly to be subject to the right to make 'protected disclosures', ie to act as a 'whistle-blower' for the purposes of the Employment Rights Act 1996 (ERA 1996) (TICE 1999, reg 23(5)).

5.91 In order to prevent central management from needlessly labelling information or documents entrusted to a recipient as being 'confidential', a recipient is given the right to make an application to the CAC for a declaration as to whether it was reasonable for central management to have described the information as confidential (TICE 1999, reg 23(6)). If the CAC considers that the disclosure of the information or document would not, or would not be likely, to prejudice or cause serious harm to the undertaking, it is required to make a declaration to this effect (TICE 1999, reg 23(7) and (8)).

5.92 Further, a safeguard for employers is that the EWC Directive, Art 8(2) provides that central management is not to be obliged to transmit information when its nature is such that according to 'objective criteria' it would seriously harm the functioning of the undertakings concerned or be prejudicial to them. This requirement is transferred through into national law as TICE 1999, reg 24(1). The reference to 'objective criteria' was specifically included to protect against possible abuses by central management.

5.93 In the event that a dispute arises as to whether information or a document which the central management has failed to provide is of a confidential nature, it is possible either for central management or a would-be recipient of the information to apply to the CAC under TICE 1999, reg 24(2). If the CAC makes a declaration that the disclosure of the information or document in question would not, according to objective criteria, seriously harm the functioning of, or be prejudicial to, the undertaking or group of undertakings concerned, the CAC is required to issue an order that the information or document shall be disclosed by central management (TICE 1999, reg 24(3)). Under TICE 1999, reg 24(4)), any such order is required to specify:

- the information or document to be disclosed;
- the recipient or recipients to whom the information or document is to be disclosed;
- any terms on which the information or document is to be disclosed; and
- the date before which the information or document is to be disclosed.

Protection of members

5.94 The EWC Directive, Art 10 provides that employees who are EWC members or involved with an ICP are to enjoy the same protection relating to the carrying out of their function as employee representatives have under national laws in their country of employment. Article 10 adds that this applies in particular to attendance at SNB or EWC meetings. In order to provide this protection under United Kingdom national law, various rights are provided under TICE 1999, Part VII for certain categories of employees, these being:

- a member of a special negotiating body;
- a member of an EWC;
- an information and consultation representative; or
- a candidate in an election in which any person elected will, on being elected, be such a member or representative.

5.95 These groups of employees are provided with:

- The right to take reasonable time off from the employee's working hours in order to perform their functions as such a member, representative or candidate (TICE 1999, reg 25(1)). Time off work is time that the employee would otherwise be required to be at work (TICE 1999, reg 25(2)).
- The right to be paid remuneration by his employer for the time taken off at the 'appropriate hourly rate', which is the amount of one week's pay divided by the number of normal working hours in a week for that employee when employed under the contract of employment in force on the day when the time is taken. A week's pay for these purposes is calculated in accordance with ERA 1996, Part XIV, Chapter II (TICE 1999, reg 26(1)–(3)). In the event that an employer has unreasonably refused to allow an employee to take time off under TICE 1999, reg 25, or to be paid for that time off under TICE 1999, reg 26, a claim may be presented to an employment tribunal within the period of 3 months beginning with the date on which it is alleged that the failure to allow time off should have been permitted (or such longer period as the employment tribunal considers reasonable in a case where it was not reasonably practicable for the complaint to have been presented) (TICE 1999, reg 27).
- The right not to be unfairly dismissed or dismissed by reason of redundancy which applies in two broad groups of situations for the purposes of TICE 1999, regs 28 and 29, these being:
  - where the employee falls within the four protected categories outlined at **5.94** where the reason or principal reason for the dismissal is that the employee performed any functions or activities as such a member, representative or candidate, or the employee or a person acting on the employee's behalf made a request to exercise an entitlement conferred on the employee by TICE 1999, reg 25 or 26; or
  - where the employee is not within the protected categories outlined in **5.94**, but is dismissed solely or principally because the employee:
    - (i) took, or proposed to take, any proceedings before an employment tribunal to enforce a right or secure an entitlement conferred on him under TICE 1999;
    - (ii) exercised, or proposed to exercise, any entitlement to apply or complain to the EAT or the CAC, or in Northern Ireland the Industrial Court, conferred by TICE 1999;
    - (iii) requested, or proposed to request, information in accordance with TICE 1999, reg 7;
    - (iv) acted with a view to securing that an SNB, EWC or ICP did or did not come into existence;
    - (v) indicated that he supported or did not support the coming into existence of an SNB, EWC or ICP;
    - (vi) stood as a candidate in an election in which any person elected would, on being elected, be a member of an SNB or EWC, or an information and consultation representative;

(vii)   influenced or sought to influence the way in which votes were to be cast by other employees in a ballot arranged under TICE 1999;

(viii)   voted in such a ballot;

(ix)   expressed doubts, whether to a ballot supervisor or otherwise, as to whether such a ballot had been properly conducted; or

(x)   proposed to do, failed to do, or proposed to decline to do, any of the things mentioned above.

- The right not to be subjected to a detriment short of dismissal (under TICE 1999, reg 31). This will apply to the same two categories of employees as for the case of the right not to be unfairly dismissed (see the point above).

5.96   TICE 1999, reg 40 provides restrictions on contracting out of the provisions of TICE 1999 (other than TICE 1999, Part VII, in respect of which contracting out under the terms of a compromise agreement executed in accordance with the provisions of TICE 1999, reg 41 is possible).

5.97   Finally, there are a number of exceptions to the general provisions of TICE 1999 under, respectively:

- TICE 1999, reg 42 in relation to agreements for the establishment of either an EWC or ICP under the EWC Directive, Art 6, under the provisions of the laws of another Member State, notwithstanding that the central management is situated in the United Kingdom;
- TICE 1999, reg 43 in relation to EWCs established under the EWC Directive, Art 7 prior to the commencement date of TICE 1999 where the central management is situated in the United Kingdom but the EWC is established under the laws of another Member State;
- TICE 1999, reg 44 in relation to agreements under the EWC Directive, Art 3 in connection with agreements in a CSU or CSGU providing for the transnational information and consultation of employees covering the entire workforce entered into prior to 16 December 1999;
- TICE 1999, reg 45 in relation to agreements under the EWC Directive, Art 13 in connection with agreements in a CSU or CSGU providing for the transnational information and consultation of employees covering the entire workforce entered into prior to 23 September 1996 in the Member State (other than the United Kingdom) whose national law governs the agreement; and
- TICE 1999, reg 46, which provides that no long haul crew member shall be a member of an SNB or EWC, or an information and consultation representative unless permitted by central management.

ICE 2004

Introduction

5.98   The second area of formal employee consultation is also a European measure and, initially, is in relation to the information and consultation of employees in undertakings employing more than 150 employees, this being under the ICE Directive,[14] which came into force on 23 March 2002. The United Kingdom's method of implementation was in the form of ICE 2004.[15] In the case of large employers, ICE 2004 will radically extend their legal obligations to inform and consult employees far beyond what was previously required under United Kingdom law. As is clear elsewhere in this book, obligations to consult collectively with employees were previously limited to particular and relatively narrow situations, such as the transfer of undertakings and collective redundancies. In summary, ICE 2004 will eventually require employers with at least 50 employees to establish machinery for informing and consulting employees, where a substantial proportion of employees want the employer to do so, albeit that the initial request for such information and consultation machinery can be made by a relatively small proportion of the employees in the workforce (in respect of which see **5.107**).

5.99   The ICE Directive states that a particular objective of the EC is to promote 'social dialogue' between management and labour. The ICE Directive sets out a framework for informing and consulting employees in this context. The means that the European Union has chosen to promote such dialogue, using a standing body of employee representatives (where employees request such a body), which has not, historically, been a feature in United Kingdom industrial relations: the more traditional model in the United Kingdom has been collective bargaining between trade unions and management. Indeed, structures for the involvement of employees, or bodies representing employeeʼs, in management is more commonly found in other European Union Member States. For example, in France, Sweden and Italy, works councils exist with guaranteed trade union involvement. Conversely, the limited cases where United Kingdom employers have been obliged to carry out collective consultation by law have resulted from the need to comply with other European Union employment Directives.

5.100   The Department of Trade and Industry (DTI) accepted this concept of 'social dialogue' in its discussion paper 'High Performance Workplaces: The role of employee involvement in a modern economy' (2002), stating that it considers that involving employees more in understanding the business they work in can be an important factor in achieving 'high performance workplaces'.

5.101   The ICE Directive and ICE 2004 impose obligations beyond those previously in existence in the United Kingdom. As stated at **5.4** et seq, the largest employers with substantial operations in the European Union and other European Union Member States are already affected by the existing EWC Directive, which provides for employees in community-scale undertakings (those that employ at least 1,000 employees, with an minimum of 50 employees in each of two Member States) to be able to initiate negotiations for an agreement for an EWC or ICP. However, the extension under ICE 2004 now requires information to be provided, and consultation to be undertaken, with workforces of a sufficient size where sufficient numbers of the workforce meet the thresholds to require that their employer informs and consults with them.

---

[14]   Directive 2002/14/EC.
[15]   SI 2004/3426.

5.102   Prior to implementing ICE 2004, the Government raised the issue of the impact of information and consultation arrangements on existing collective agreements in place with the trade unions. The Government accepted that employers who recognise trade unions in relation to some, but not all, of their employees may be faced with the possibility both of providing information and undertaking consultation under such a pre-existing collective agreement.

Implementation of ICE 2004

5.103   Under ICE 2004, regs 3 and 4 and Sch. 1, the reach of ICE 2004 will extend by stages as follows:

(i) for undertakings with 150 or more employees – 6 April 2005;
(ii) for undertakings with 100 or more employees – 6 April 2007; and
(iii) for undertakings with 50 or more employees – 6 April 2008.

5.104   These thresholds apply just to *employees*, disregarding other types of 'workers' (ICE 2004, regs 2 and 3(1)(a)).

5.105   To determine the number of employees in an 'undertaking' for these purposes, ICE 2004, reg 4(1) and (2) provides that an average is to be taken of the number of employees employed in an undertaking in the previous 12 months by determining the number of employees in each of those months, adding the figures together and dividing by 12. Further, where an employee works 75 hours or less per month (excluding overtime and absences from work and assuming the month to have 21 working days), the employee may be counted as being half an employee for calculation purposes (ICE 2004, reg 4(3)). Where an undertaking has been in existence for less than 12 months, the 12-month period is reduced to the number of months that the undertaking has been in existence (ICE 2004, reg 4(4)).

5.106   ICE 2004, reg 2 defines an undertaking as a public or private undertaking carrying on an economic activity whether or not operating for gain. The Government stated in its consultation paper 'High Performance Workplaces Informing and Consulting Employees' (2002), that it is its belief that an undertaking is a legal entity, such as a company. This appears to be a narrower interpretation of 'undertaking' than an 'economic entity' which has evolved for TUPE 1981 purposes. It remains to be seen whether this interpretation is correct and it will certainly be open to challenge.

5.107   Employees or their representatives are entitled to request, in writing, data from their employer as to the number of employees employed in the relevant calculation periods. Any such request must be dated (ICE 2004, reg 5(1) and (2)). The employer must provide the employee or the employees' representative who made the request with data to enable the employee or employee representative to make the ICE 2004, reg 4 calculation and determine for the purposes of ICE 2004, reg 7(2) what number of employees constitutes 10 per cent of the employees in the undertaking.

5.108   In the event that an employer does not provide the information or provides false or incomplete information, an employee or employer representative may, within one month of requesting the information from the employer, apply to the CAC which has a power to order the information to be disclosed (ICE 2004, reg 6(1) and (3)). Any such order must state the data in respect of which the CAC finds that the complaint is well founded and which is to be disclosed to the complainant, the date (or if more than one, the earliest date) on

the employees of the relevant undertaking. Further, any employee or employees' representative who believes that the arrangements for a ballot held under ICE 2004, reg 8 or 9, as the case may be, did not satisfy one or more of the requirements set out in ICE 2004, reg 8(4) may, within 21 days of the date of the ballot, present a complaint to the CAC. If the CAC finds the complaint to be well founded, it can make an order requiring the employer to initiate negotiations or to comply with the balloting requirements (as appropriate) (ICE 2004, reg 10(3)).

5.118 For the purposes of ICE 2004, reg 12(1), no employee request or employer notification is valid if it is made or issued:

● where a negotiated agreement applies, within a period of 3 years from the date of the agreement or, where the agreement is terminated within that period, before the date on which the termination takes effect;
● where the standard information and consultation provisions apply within a period of 3 years from the date on which they started to apply; or
● where the employer has held a ballot under ICE 2004, reg 8, or was one of the employers who held a ballot under ICE 2004, reg 9 and the result was that the employees did not endorse the valid employee request, within a period of 3 years from the date of that request.

5.119 Further, ICE 2004, reg 12 does not apply where there are material changes in the undertaking during the applicable period having the result that where a ballot under ICE 2004, reg 8 or 9 has been held, the ballot is no longer valid, or where a negotiated agreement under ICE 2004, reg 16 has been concluded, it no longer covers all of the employees of the undertaking.

5.120 Under ICE 2004, reg 13(1), it is possible for the employer to question whether a valid request has been presented to it. The circumstances where the employer can do this are limited to cases where the employee request does not satisfy the requirements of ICE 2004, reg 7, or was prevented from doing so under ICE 2004, reg 12, or because the undertaking was not one to which ICE 2004 applied (under ICE 2004, reg 3) on the date that the employee request was made. Likewise, under ICE 2004, reg 13(2), if an employee or an employees' representative considers that an employer notification was not valid because it did not comply with one or more of the requirements in ICE 2004, reg 11(2), or was prevented from being valid by ICE 2004, reg 12, that person may apply to the CAC for a declaration as to whether the notification was valid. In any such case, the employer may make an application to the CAC.

5.121 Under ICE 2004, reg 13(3), the CAC may only consider an application for such a declaration if the application is made within a one-month period beginning on the date of the employee request or the date on which the employer notification is made.

The negotiating process

5.122 Under ICE 2004, reg 14(1), in order to start negotiations, employers must arrange for all employees in the undertaking to be able to elect 'negotiating representatives', inform the employees in the undertaking who the negotiating representatives are and then invite the negotiating representatives to begin negotiations for a negotiated agreement on information (an Information and Consultation Agreement).

5.123   In this regard, the election or appointment of the representatives must be arranged in such a way that, following their election or appointment, all employees of the undertaking are represented by one or more representatives. Further, all employees of the undertaking must be entitled to take part in the election or appointment of the representatives and, where there is an election, all employees of the undertaking on the day on which the votes may be cast in the ballot, or if the votes may be cast on more than one day, on the first day of those days, must be given an entitlement to vote in the ballot (ICE 2004, reg 14(2)).

5.124   Generally, ICE 2004 envisages a period of 6 months (commencing 3 months after the date of the employee request for the negotiations) for an Information and Consultation Agreement to take place, but this period may be extended by agreement (ICE 2004, reg 14(3) and (5)). However, certain periods of time are expressly excluded as counting towards the 6-month period, these being:

- under ICE 2004, reg 14(3) and (4), where the employer holds a ballot under ICE 2004, reg 8 or 9, the period between the employer notifying the employees of its decision to hold such a ballot and whichever of the following dates is applicable:
    - where there is no complaint to the CAC under ICE 2004, reg 10, the date of the ballot;
    - where there is a complaint to the CAC under ICE 2004, reg 10, and the complaint is dismissed by the CAC or on appeal, the date on which it is finally dismissed;
    - where there is a complaint to the CAC and the outcome, whether of the complaint or of any appeal from it, is an order to hold the ballot under ICE 2004, reg 8 or 9, the date of the ballot that most recently took place; or
    - where there is a complaint to the CAC under ICE 2004, reg 10 and the outcome, whether of the complaint or of any appeal from it, is an order requiring the employer to initiate negotiations in accordance with ICE 2004, reg 7(1), the date on which the order is made;
- where an application for a declaration is made to the CAC pursuant to ICE 2004, reg 13, the period between the date of that application and the final decision of the CAC or any appeal from that decision;
- where a complaint about the election or appointment of negotiating representatives is presented pursuant to ICE 2004, reg 15, the time between the date of the complaint and the determination of the complaint, including any appeal and, where the complaint is upheld, the further period until the negotiating representatives are re-elected or reappointed; and
- where a complaint about the ballot for employee approval of a negotiated agreement is presented pursuant to ICE 2004, reg 17, the time between the date the complaint is presented to the CAC and the determination of the complaint (including any appeal and, where the complaint is upheld, the further period until the re-holding of the ballot).

5.125   In the event that an employee or employee representative considers that any of these requirements have not been satisfied he may, within 21 days of the election or appointment, make a complaint to the CAC which may order the employer to rectify this (ICE 2004, reg 15(1)). In such a case, where the CAC finds the complaint to be well founded, it is required to make an order requiring the employer to arrange for the election or appointment of negotiating representatives to take place again within such period as the order shall specify (ICE 2004, reg 15(2)).

5.126 In spite of appearances to the contrary, ICE 2004 is not actually very prescriptive: it does not lay down any detailed requirements as to the information and consultation process. This is left for agreement between the employer and the employees' negotiating representatives. However, under ICE 2004, reg 16(1), the Information and Consultation Agreement must set out the circumstances in which employees are to be informed and consulted, be in writing, be dated, be otherwise approved in accordance with **5.127**, be signed by or on behalf of the employer and either provide:

• for the appointment or election of information and consultation representatives to whom the employer must provide the information and whom the employer must consult; or
• that the employer must provide information directly to the employees to which it relates and consult those employees directly.

5.127 Whether or not it comprises one or more than one different parts, for a negotiated Information and Consultation Agreement to be valid, under ICE 2004, reg 16(3) and (4), it must:

• cover all of the employees in the undertaking;
• be approved by all of the negotiating representatives, or a majority of the negotiating representatives and at least 50 per cent of the employees employed in the undertaking, either in writing or via a ballot. Specifically, where an Information and Consultation Agreement comprises more than one part, each such part must satisfy this test.

5.128 In the case of an employer being required to undertake a ballot for the purposes of ICE 2004, reg 16, under ICE 2004, reg 16(5) it is necessary for the ballot to comply with the following requirements:

• the employer is required to make such arrangements as are reasonably practicable to ensure that the ballot is fair;
• all employees of the undertaking or, as the case may be, to whom the part of the agreement relates, on the day on which the votes may be cast in the ballot, or if the votes may be cast on more than one day, on the first day of those days, must be given an entitlement to vote in the ballot; and
• the ballot must be conducted so as to secure that so far as is reasonably practicable, those voting do so in secret and the votes given in the ballot are accurately counted.

5.129 Furthermore, under ICE 2004, reg 16(6), where the employer holds a ballot it must, as soon as reasonably practicable after the date of the ballot, inform the employees entitled to vote of the result.

5.130 ICE 2004, reg 17(1) provides a right for any negotiating representative who believes that the balloting arrangements did not satisfy one or more of the requirements to present a complaint to the CAC, which must be presented within 21 days of the date of the ballot. In such a case, where the CAC finds the complaint well founded, it is required to make an order requiring the employer to hold the ballot again within such a period as is specified by the CAC in the order (ICE 2004, reg 17(2)).

5.131 Additionally, under ICE 2004, reg 18(1)(a), where after the making of a valid employee request or issue of a valid employer notification to initiate negotiations for an Information and Consultation Agreement, the employer does not do so, the 'standard information and consultation provisions' under ICE 2004, reg 20 are deemed to apply from the later of the date:

- which is 6 months from the date on which the valid employee request was made or the valid employer notification was issued; or
- information and consultation representatives are elected under ICE 2004, reg 19.

5.132 A similar provision applies under ICE 2004, reg 18(1)(b) in the case where the parties do not agree terms for an Information and Consultation Agreement, save that the two dates upon which the 'standard information and consultation provisions' apply are either the date:

- which is 6 months from the date of the time-limit under ICE 2004, reg 14(3) (or if the parties agreed to extend the period of 6 months under ICE 2004, reg 14(5), that later date); or
- on which information and consultation representatives are elected under ICE 2004, reg 19.

5.133 For the purposes of ICE 2004, reg 19(1), where the 'standard information and consultation provisions' apply, before they start to apply, the employer must arrange for the holding of a ballot of its employees to elect the relevant number of information and consultation representatives in respect of the undertaking. Under ICE 2004, Sch 2, para 15, the employer is required to meet all of the costs relating to the holding of the ballot.

5.134 ICE 2004, reg 19(2) provides for detailed balloting requirements to be observed under ICE 2004, Sch 2 in relation to that ballot, as follows:

- The ballot must comprise a single ballot unless the employer decides to hold separate ballots of employees, in such constituencies as the employer determines, because the employer decides that the information and consultation representatives to be elected would better reflect the interests of the employees as a whole than if a single ballot were held.
- If it becomes clear that the number of people standing as candidates in the ballot are equal to or less than the 'required number of information and consultation representatives' (being one representative per 50 employees or part thereof, with at least two and not more than 25, per ICE 2004, reg 19(3)), the obligation to hold the ballot ceases and the candidates become the information and consultation representatives.
- All employees of the undertaking must be given an entitlement to vote in the ballot on the day on which the votes are cast in the ballot, or if the votes are cast on more than one day, on the first of those days.
- Any employee who is an employee of the undertaking at the latest time at which it is possible to become a candidate as an information and consultation representative, is entitled to stand.
- The employer must appoint an independent ballot supervisor to supervise the conduct of the ballot. Further, the employer must ensure that the independent ballot supervisor carries out his functions and that there is no interference with the carrying out of those functions. The employer is also required to comply with all reasonable requests made by the ballot supervisor for the purposes of or in connection with the carrying out of

the ballot supervisor's functions (ICE 2004, Sch 2, para. 8). For these purposes, a person is taken to be independent where the employer:

- reasonably believes that that person will carry out any functions conferred on him in relation to the ballot competently; and
- has no reasonable grounds for believing that that person's independence might reasonably be called into question (ICE 2004, Sch 2, para 6),

• After the employer has formulated proposals as to the arrangements for the ballot and before it has published the final arrangements in accordance with ICE 2004, Sch 2, the employer must, so far as is reasonably practicable, consult with employees' representatives or, if no such representatives exist, the employees, on the proposed arrangements for the ballot.

• The employer must publish the final arrangements for the ballot in such manner as to bring them to the attention of, so far as reasonably practicable, its employees and, where they exist, the employees' representatives.

5.135 ICE 2004, Sch 2, para 3 provides that any employee or an employees' representative who believes that the arrangements for the ballot are defective may present a complaint to the CAC, provided that the complaint is presented within 21 days of the date on which the employer published the final arrangements for the ballot. If the CAC finds the complaint well founded, it is required to make a declaration to that effect and may make an order requiring the employer to modify the arrangements it has made for the ballot or to satisfy the balloting requirements under ICE 2004, Sch 2. Any order so made must specify the modifications to the arrangements which the employer is required to make and the requirements it must satisfy (ICE 2004, Sch 2, paras 4 and 5).

5.136 As regards the functions undertaken by an independent ballot supervisor, under ICE 2004 Sch 2, para 9 these require that the ballot supervisor:

• supervises the conduct of the ballot in accordance with the arrangements for the ballot published by the employer or as modified by the CAC (para 9(a));

• does not conduct the ballot before the employer has satisfied the requirement to publish the final arrangements for the ballot and where no complaint has been presented to the CAC, within 21 days of the date on which the employer published the arrangements. Where a complaint is made to the CAC and determined by it, the ballot supervisor cannot conduct the ballot until the complaint has been determined by the CAC and any requirements ordered by the CAC have been complied with by the employer (para 9(b));

• conducts the ballot so as to secure that:
  - so far as reasonably practicable, those entitled to vote are given the opportunity to do so;
  - so far as reasonably practicable, those entitled to stand as candidates are given the opportunity to stand;
  - so far as reasonably practicable, those voting are able to do so in secret; and
  - the votes given in the ballot are fairly and accurately counted (para 9(b)).

5.137 Further, as soon as reasonably practicable after the date of the ballot, the ballot supervisor is required to publish the results of the ballot in such a way as to make them available to the employer and, so far as reasonably practicable, the employees entitled to vote in the ballot and the persons who stood as candidates in the ballot (ICE 2004, Sch 2, para 10).

5.138   Under ICE 2004, Sch 2, paras 11–13, the ballot supervisor is required to publish 'an ineffective ballot report' (which must be published within a period of one month commencing on the date on which the ballot supervisor publishes the results of the ballot), and publish it in such a way as to make it available to the employer and, so far as reasonably practicable, the employees entitled to vote in the ballot and the persons who stood as candidates in the ballot, where the ballot supervisor considers that:

●   any of the requirements of the employer in connection with the ballot under ICE 2004, Sch 2, para 2 were not satisfied with the result that the outcome of the ballot would have been different; or

●   there was interference with the carrying out of the ballot supervisor's functions, or a failure by the employer to comply with all reasonable requests made by the ballot supervisor, with the result in either case that the ballot supervisor was unable to form a proper judgment as to whether each of the requirements in ICE 2004, Sch 2, para 2 were satisfied in the ballot.

5.139   Under ICE 2004, Sch 2, para 14, the outcome of an ineffective ballot report is that the ballot is rendered void, the employer is required to arrange for the ballot or ballots in respect of which the ineffective ballot report has been issued to be re-held in accordance with ICE 2004, reg 19 and no such ballot takes effect until it has been validly re-held by the employer.

5.140   If the employer and the negotiating representatives fail to reach agreement then statutory information and consultation procedures will apply by default under ICE 2004, reg 20(1) and (3), in relation to the information and consultation representatives. The employer will then have to:

●   provide them with information on the recent and probable development of the activities and economic situation of the undertaking in which they work;

●   inform and consult with them on the situation, structure and probable development of the undertaking and on any measures envisaged, in particular where there is a threat to employment;

●   inform and consult with them on decisions likely to lead to substantial changes in work organisation or in contractual relations (including in relation to TULRCA 1992, ss 188–192 and under TUPE 1981, regs 10–12). Under this head ICE 2004, reg 20(3) provides that consultation must be with a view to reaching agreement. In effect, the scope of the statutory consultation under those other provisions can be extended. However, under ICE 2004, reg 20(5), the duties to inform and consult the information and consultation representatives on decisions falling within this provision cease to apply once the employer is under the relevant duty to consult under TULRCA 1992, ss 188–192 or TUPE 1981, regs 10–12 (respectively) and the employer has notified the information and consultation representatives in writing that it will be complying with its duty under those other provisions instead of under ICE 2004, provided that the notification is given on each occasion on which the employer has become, or is about to become, subject to the particular duty to consult. In other words, there may be an overlap between the competing duties to consult under, respectively, ICE 2004, TUPE 1981 and TULRCA 1992, and the employer cannot escape its duty to consult under ICE 2004 simply because other specific duties also apply. Indeed, it is possible to envisage a situation where there is a transfer governed by the provisions of TUPE 1981, following which collective redundancies for the purposes of TULRCA 1992 may be entailed at the transferor's residual undertaking, where the transferor is subject to an Information and Consultation Agreement: in such a case all three statutory consultation regimes potentially apply.

5.141   For these purposes, under ICE 2004, reg 20(4), consultation is required to be undertaken:

* in such a way as to ensure that the timing, method and content of the consultation are appropriate;
* on the basis of the information supplied by the employer to the information and consultation representatives and of any opinion which those representatives express to the employer;
* in such a way as to enable the information and consultation representatives to meet the employer at the relevant level of management depending on the subject under discussion and to obtain a reasoned response from the employer to any such opinion; and
* in relation to matters falling within ICE 2004, reg 20(1)(c), with a view to reaching agreement on decisions within the scope of the employer's powers.

5.142   ICE 2004, reg 20(6) specifically provides that where there is an obligation on the employer to inform and consult with its employees, a failure on the part of a person who controls the employer (either directly or indirectly) to provide information to the employer does not constitute a valid reason for the employer failing to inform and consult.

The duty of co-operation

5.143   In order to make the Information and Consultation Agreements work once they have been either agreed or imposed, ICE 2004, reg 21 states that the parties are under a duty, when negotiating or implementing an Information and Consultation Agreement, or when implementing the standard information and consultation provisions, to work in a 'spirit of co-operation' with due regard for their reciprocal rights and obligations, taking into account the interests of both the undertaking and the employees. This is very broad in its terms and it will be interesting to see how this requirement is construed in practice. Disputes could arise as to the degree of co-operation being given by the parties. For example, it is unclear how far the duty to co-operate may mean that employers will have to take employees' interests into account. Although there is a good argument that employers should not have to change business decisions which they propose to take just because employees are strongly opposed to them, it is not clear how far employers are expected to go towards meeting those concerns.

Penalties

5.144   Member States are permitted under the ICE Directive to make provision for any business decision taken which contravenes the information and consultation provisions of the ICE Directive to be void. This caused quite understandable concern to businesses when the provision was included in the ICE Directive. However, the provision is currently of academic interest only in the United Kingdom as this option was not taken up in ICE 2004. Instead, disputes in connection with a negotiated agreement or under the standard information and consultation provisions are to be referred to the CAC under ICE 2004, reg 22, which provides for the CAC to have a power to make an order requiring a party to comply with the terms of an Information and Consultation Agreement or the standard information and consultation provisions, as relevant (ICE 2004, reg 22(4)). Any such complaint must be brought within a period of 3 months commencing with the date of the alleged act or omission. The CAC's order must specify what is to be done and by when.

5.145   Further, under ICE 2004, reg 22(6), if the CAC makes a declaration under ICE 2004, reg 22(4), the applicant may, within the period of 3 months beginning with the date on which the declaration is made, make an application to the EAT for a penalty notice to be issued against the employer. Where such an application is made, under ICE 2004, reg 22(7), the EAT must issue a written penalty notice to the employer requiring it to pay a penalty (recoverable as a civil debt: ICE 2004, reg 23(5)) to the Secretary of State of up to £75,000 in respect of the failure unless satisfied, on hearing representations from the employer, that the failure resulted from a reason beyond the employer's control or that the employer has some other reasonable excuse for its failure. Under ICE 2004, reg 23(3), when issuing a penalty notice the EAT is specifically required to take into account the following matters:

- the gravity of the employer's failure;
- the period of time over which the failure occurred;
- the reason for the failure;
- the number of employees affected by the employer's failure; and
- the number of employees employed by the undertaking or, where an Information and Consultation Agreement covers employees in more than one undertaking, the number of employees employed by all of those undertakings.

5.146   Any penalty levied under ICE 2004, reg 23 is not a criminal sanction and, quite apart from the right not to disclose information and/or documents to employee representatives which exists in certain circumstances under ICE 2004, reg 26 (see **5.147** et seq), some employers may consider that it is worth not disclosing or consulting in certain circumstances if the potential maximum exposure of £75,000 would be outweighed by the benefit of not disclosing information and/or documents.

Protection of confidential information

5.147   The fact that employees will be entitled to be given information about the business in which they work, and are, in certain cases, to be consulted about that information, may create potential problems as regards confidential information. Indeed, some of the information which it is envisaged will be disclosed under the statutory information and consultation procedures is by its very nature information of a highly confidential, and, in the case of public companies, possibly also price-sensitive, nature. Consequently, it was necessary in the drafting of ICE 2004 for there to be provisions relating to employees and their representatives to whom such information is entrusted, to receive that information subject to a duty of confidentiality. ICE 2004, regs 25 and 26 do this at two levels, first, by providing that any information so disclosed is subject to a statutory duty of confidentiality and, secondly, by providing that an employer does not have to disclose information where its disclosure would harm the legitimate interests of the undertaking. Each of these points is considered in turn.

5.148   First, ICE 2004, reg 25(1) provides that a person to whom the employer entrusts any information or document under ICE 2004, where the information or document is disclosed on terms requiring it to be held in confidence, must not disclose that information or document except, where the terms of disclosure from the employer permit that person to do so, in accordance with those terms. In this regard, under ICE 2004, reg 25(3), the obligation to comply is stated to be a duty owed to the employer, and a breach of the duty is actionable as a breach of statutory duty (subject to the defences and other incidents applying to actions for breaches of statutory duty). Consequently, anyone breaching the duty of confidence may be liable to the full extent of any loss suffered by their employer. How effective this will be in deterring employee representatives from disclosing confidential information remains to be seen, but it is doubtful whether such an action could remedy the damage which an employer's business might suffer due to the wrongful disclosure of confidential information given that most employers will have the assets to make good what may be huge damages.

5.149   The duty under ICE 2004, reg 25 does not override any other statutory rights or duties (in particular, rights in relation to 'whistle-blowing' under the ERA 1996) (ICE 2004, reg 25(4) and (5)).

5.150   Furthermore, so as to prevent an employer from simply labelling information as 'confidential' and thereby preventing employees or their representatives from disclosing non-confidential information which could otherwise be freely disclosed, a right exists under ICE 2004, reg 25(6) for a recipient of any information or document disclosed on terms requiring it to be held in confidence to ask the CAC for a declaration as to whether it was reasonable for the employer to require the recipient to hold the information or document in confidence. In such a case, where the CAC considers that the disclosure of the information or document by the recipient would not, or would not be likely to, harm the legitimate interests of the undertaking, it must make a declaration that it was not reasonable for the employer to require the recipient to hold the information or document in confidence and the information is then treated as not having been disclosed in confidence (ICE 2004, reg 25(7) and (8)).

5.151   As regards information which is genuinely confidential which the employer does not wish to disclose to employee representatives, ICE 2004, reg 26(1) provides that the employer is not required to disclose any information or document to any person where the nature of the information or document is such that, according to 'objective criteria', the disclosure of the information or document would seriously harm the functioning of, or would be prejudicial to, the undertaking. Under ICE 2004, reg 26(2), if there is a dispute between the employer and, in a case where information and consultation representatives have been elected or appointed, those representatives, or in a case where they have not been elected, any employee of the undertaking, either the employer or any employee representative or employee (as the case may be) may apply to the CAC for a determination of the matter. Upon hearing the matter, the CAC is required to make a declaration and, if it is in favour of disclosing the information or document, the CAC is required to make an order to that effect (ICE 2004, reg 26(3)). In making its decision, it seems that the CAC must consider the matter on the basis of the 'objective criteria' referred to in ICE 2004, reg 26(1); in other words, the CAC must consider whether it was reasonable for the employer not to disclose. No guidance is given as to what amounts to 'objective criteria' for the purposes of ICE 2004, reg 26(1); however, this is likely to be considered on a case-by-case basis by the CAC.

5.152   In the event that the CAC makes an order requiring the employer to disclose information or a document, under ICE 2004, reg 26(4), the order must state:

- the information or document to be disclosed;
- the person or persons to whom the information or document is to be disclosed;
- any terms on which the information or document is to be disclosed; and
- the date before which the information or document is to be disclosed.

Rights of negotiating representatives and information and consultation representatives

5.153   Negotiating representatives and information and consultation representatives are given certain rights and protections in relation to the performance of their duties. First, under ICE 2004, reg 27(1), such representatives have the right to paid time off work during their 'working hours' to carry out their duties. Working hours for these purposes are defined as being any time when, in accordance with the representative's contract of employment, the representative is required to be at work (ICE 2004, reg 27(2)). This is likely to be construed in accordance with the similar provisions for paid time off for carrying out the duties of a trade union official under TULRCA 1992, s 168.[16]

5.154   Further, any such time off from working hours as is granted to representatives is required to be paid under ICE 2004, reg 28 at the employee's appropriate hourly rate (as determined in accordance with ERA 1996, Part XIV, Chapter II).

5.155   Under ICE 2004, reg 29(1), representatives are provided with the right to present a claim to an employment tribunal in respect of any breach of the rights to time off or pay for that time off. Any such claim is required to be presented within a period of 3 months from the date on which it is alleged that the paid time off should have been granted (ICE 2004, reg 29(2)).

5.156   Further, employees are provided with the right not to be unfairly dismissed or unfairly dismissed by reason of redundancy under ICE 2004, regs 30(1), (2) and 31, for certain reasons relating to ICE 2004 where the employees fall into any of the following categories:

- employees' representatives;
- negotiating representatives;
- information and consultation representatives; or
- candidates in an election in which any person elected will, on being elected, be such a representative.

---

[16]   In connection with which see, for example, *Hairsine v Kingston upon Hull City Council* [1992] IRLR 211.

5.157 The reasons in which a dismissal in respect of ICE 2004 might be unfair are provided under ICE 2004, reg 30(3) as being any of the following:

- an employee performed or proposed to perform any functions or activities as such a representative or candidate;
- the employee exercised or proposed to exercise an entitlement to time off to perform duties as representatives under ICE 2004, reg 27 or 28; or
- the employee (or a person acting on his behalf) made or proposed to make a request to exercise such an entitlement.

5.158 Further, under ICE 2004, reg 30(6), irrespective of whether an employee is a representative and has any of the rights set out below (provided that the employee acts in good faith), the employee is treated as being unfairly dismissed where the reason for the dismissal is any of the following:

- the employee took, or proposed to take, any proceedings before an employment tribunal to enforce a right or secure an entitlement conferred on him by ICE 2004;
- the employee exercised, or proposed to exercise, any entitlement to apply or complain to the CAC or the EAT conferred by ICE 2004 or to exercise the right to appeal in connection with any rights conferred by ICE 2004;
- the employee requested, or proposed to request, data in accordance with ICE 2004, reg 5;
- the employee acted with a view to securing that an agreement was or was not negotiated or that the standard information and consultation provisions did or did not become applicable;
- the employee indicated that he supported or did not support the coming into existence of a negotiated agreement or the application of the standard information and consultation provisions;
- the employee stood as a candidate in an election in which any person elected would, on being elected, be a negotiating representative or an information and consultation representative;
- the employee influenced or sought to influence by lawful means the way in which votes were to be cast by other employees in a ballot arranged under ICE 2004;
- the employee voted in a ballot arranged under ICE 2004;
- the employee expressed doubts, whether to a ballot supervisor or otherwise, as to whether any such ballot had been properly conducted; or
- the employee proposed to do, failed to do, or proposed to decline to do, any of the things mentioned in the preceding six points.

5.159 Where the dismissal falls within any of these reasons set out at **5.158**, the minimum period of qualification for the right not to be unfairly dismissed and the upper age limit for the right are removed by ICE 2004, reg 31(2) and (3).

5.160 Similar provisions to those relating to unfair dismissal also exist with regard to employees being subjected to action short of dismissal for a reason related to ICE 2004, with reasons being identical but being set out in ICE 2004, reg 32(3) and (6).

Current effect of ICE 2004

5.161 Under ICE 2004, reg 3 and Sch 2, with effect from 6 April 2005 employers employing at least 150 employees in their undertaking became subject to ICE 2004. ICE 2004 is phased so that on 6 April 2007, employers employing 100 employees, and on 6 April 2008, employers employing 50 or more employees, are affected. Employers having information and consultation procedures in place which comply with the requirements of ICE 2004 prior to their coming into effect will be fully compliant and the only way in which such pre-existing procedures can be upset is by using the procedures under ICE 2004, reg 8. Indeed, in such a case, it is open to the employer to use the confirmatory ballot procedure under ICE 2004, reg 8(2) so as to ask employees to approve the employer's pre-existing arrangements.

5.162   Other than this, although it is possible for the employer to take the initiative in instigating an Information and Consultation Agreement under ICE 2004, reg 11, no action is required in the absence of a valid request for an agreement: employers can therefore just await events.

5.163   For those employers without information and consultation arrangements already in place, there may be both advantages and disadvantages in instigating an Information and Consultation Agreement. Many factors need to be considered by employers in this regard.

5.164   The advantage to employers in establishing information and consultation arrangements before a request is made is that such arrangements can be designed to suit the employer's needs, in particular, in determining in which areas it is prepared to inform and consult, how it is prepared to inform and consult and what it considers to be confidential information. Employers who wait for a formal request to be made under ICE 2004 may be forced to negotiate an Information and Consultation Agreement and if agreement is not reached, the employer will find the more stringent standard information and consultation provisions under ICE 2004, reg 20 imposed upon it. However, to pre-empt for consultation will require for the top management of an undertaking to decide upon a plan for information and consultation arrangements, to communicate the plan to employees, to arrange for the election of negotiating representatives, to prepare the agreement and negotiate it to a successful conclusion. There is also the risk that having set the ball rolling with regard to information and consultation arrangements, employers may not be able to stop it and may find themselves facing a truculent workforce which will not accept less than the statutory minimum standard information and consultation provisions.

Chapter 6

TRADE UNION OBLIGATIONS

TRADE UNION MEMBERS AND TRADE UNIONS

6.1 By means of the common law and by statute, trade union members now have a substantial degree of control over the union of which they are a member. At common law, the trade union rulebook is treated as a contract of membership between members of the trade union and the union itself. As such, it is subject to interpretation by the court in the same way as other contracts. In this regard, of particular use to trade union members is the power of the courts to imply terms into the rulebook, as a contract, and the use by the courts of the doctrine of public policy to override terms in trade union rulebooks which may be unfair to members.

6.2 This has not always been the case though and has arisen in the case of statutory rights largely as a result of changes to government policy since 1979.

Common law rights of trade union members

6.3 The vast majority of the jurisprudence concerning the common law construction of trade union rulebooks by the courts has arisen out of either the disciplinary function exercised by trade unions or as a result of the (now historical) concept of the closed shop. The method by which trade union rulebooks should be construed has been the subject of a number of competing theories. First, in *Bonsor v Musicians Union*,[1] the claimant was expelled from membership of the defendant trade union for failing to pay a weekly union subscription to the defendant. The claimant sued, alleging breach of contract on the part of the defendant and sought an injunction preventing his expulsion. In construing the rulebook, the Court of Appeal held that trade union rules were:[2]

'... not so much a contract, ... but ... more a legislative code laid down by some members of the union to be imposed on all members of the union. They are more like bye-laws than a contract.'

The court then held that, as such, the rulebook was judicially reviewable and that trade unions could be held to account when acting outside their authority in the same way as could a public body.

---

[1]   [1954] 1 All ER 822.
[2]   [1954] 1 All ER 822 at 825.

6.4   This 'by-law' theory was subsequently rejected by the House of Lords in the case of *Faramus v Film Artistes Association*.[3] Here, the facts concerned the exclusion from membership of a purported member of the defendant trade union on the grounds that he was ineligible for membership prior to having 'joined' the union. The House of Lords held:[4]

> '... that there is here no true analogy between the rules of this union and the bye-laws of some corporation which would entitle the Court to treat the rule (as they could treat a bye-law) as ineffective and invalid if outside the law-making power conferred on the makers of the rules.'

6.5   To the extent that *Faramus*[5] dealt with the issue of joining a trade union rather than actual membership itself, it is uncertain how far it goes in the destruction of the by-law theory.

6.6   The better theory relating to the construction of trade union rulebooks is the 'contract theory'. This theory treats the rulebook as a contract of membership which should be construed in the same way as any other contract. It was initially disputed as a valid theory but is now the accepted doctrine. One of the first cases to examine the theory was *Lee v Showmen's Guild of Great Britain*,[6] where the claimant had been fined for breaking the defendant union's rules on competition, having not surrendered a fairground pitch to a rival upon being ordered to do so by the union. The claimant was then fined, refused to pay the fine and was expelled from the union pursuant to an automatic expulsion clause within the union's rulebook. The claimant sued the defendant for breach of contract. On appeal to the Court of Appeal, the court appeared to reject the notion of the contract theory, holding that:[7]

> '... [trade unions] wield power as great, if not greater, than any exercised by Courts of law. They can deprive a man of his livelihood ... They are usually empowered to do this for any breach of rules which ... they impose and which he has no real opportunity of accepting or rejecting. In theory their powers are based on contract. The man is supposed to have contracted to give them these great powers; but in practice he has no choice in the matter.'

6.7   However, the House of Lords subsequently confirmed that it is proper to construe union rulebooks as contracts. In *British Actors Equity Association v Goring*, the House of Lords was faced with the construction of certain rule changing provisions within a union rulebook and held that:[8]

> 'While it cannot be said that the rules are a fine example of legal drafting, [we] do not think that, because they are the rules of a union, different cannons of construction should be applied to them than are applied to any written documents. Our task is to construe them so as to give them a reasonable interpretation which accords with what in our opinion must have been intended.'

---

3   [1964] 1 All ER 25.
4   [1964] 1 All ER 25 at 30.
5   *Faramus v Film Artistes Association* [1964] 1 All ER 25.
6   [1952] 2 QB 329.
7   [1952] 2 QB 329 at 342.
8   [1978] ICR 791 at 794.

6.8 In order to reach an understanding of what the parties were taken to have intended, regard must be had to the particular circumstances of each case including the nature and size of the union and formal reliance on rules and resources open to a particular union. Likewise, the courts should not give an overly sophisticated construction to the rules. As was stated by the House of Lords in *Heaton's Transport (St Helens) Limited v TGWU*:[9]

'... trade union rulebooks are not drafted by parliamentary draftsmen. Courts of law must resist the temptation to construe them as if they were; for that is not how they would be understood by the members who are the parties to the agreement of which the terms, or some of them, are set out in the rulebook, ... Furthermore, it is not to be assumed, as in the case of a commercial contract which has been reduced into writing, that all the terms of the agreement are to be found in the rulebook alone; particularly as respects the discretion conferred by the members upon committees or officials of the union as to the way in which they may act upon the union's behalf. What the members understand as to the characteristics of the agreement into which they enter by joining a union is well stated in the section of the TUC handbook on the Industrial Relations Act [Industrial Relations Act 1971] which gives advice about the content and operation of unions' rules. Paragraph 99 reads as follows: " ... Custom and practice may operate either by modifying a union's rules as they operate in practice, or by compensating for the absence of union rules. Furthermore, the procedure which custom and practice lays down very often vary from workplace to workplace within the same industry, and even within different branches of the same union." '

6.9 Therefore, in examining trade union rulebooks the following points need to be addressed:

● trade union rulebooks are to be construed as contracts made between trade unions and their members;
● in arriving at the correct construction of a rulebook, the courts are to have regard to all the circumstances surrounding the particular case including external evidence of terms which are unwritten and may arise from custom and practice of the union and its members; and
● courts should arrive at a construction that members would have understood and not be over-reliant upon strict legal construction of the wording.

Ouster clauses

6.10 Trade union rulebooks may contain clauses which attempt to make a trade union the final arbiter of any disputes that occur as between a member of the trade union and that union. The problem that arises in relation to these clauses is one of public policy. The courts are the proper forum for the resolution of a legal matter and, as such, have often intervened in disputes in all areas of the law when a challenge to their jurisdiction arises. The law in relation to trade unions rulebooks is no different. What needs to be examined, however, is what is being potentially excluded from the jurisdiction of the court. Ouster clauses essentially fall into three categories:

---

[9]   [1972] ICR 308 at 393.

- clauses that attempt to remove totally the court's jurisdiction on matters of fact;
- clauses which seek to remove the court's jurisdiction to hear disputes on points of law; and
- clauses which attempt to delay access to the courts until internal remedies have been exhausted by trade union members.

6.11   As to the first of these categories, there is, prima facie, nothing wrong with clauses that make trade unions the sole arbiter of questions of fact in relation to disputes between trade unions and their members. In *Lee v Showmen's Guild of Great Britain*, the Court of Appeal held that:[10]

'... [Trade unions and their members] can, of course, agree to leave questions of law as well as questions of fact, to the decision of the domestic tribunal. They can, indeed, make the tribunal the final arbiter on questions of fact ...'

6.12   As to ouster clauses purporting to restrain the court from examining a question of law, the Court of Appeal also considered these in *Lee*:[11]

'... [Trade unions and their members] cannot make the [domestic tribunal] final arbiter on questions of law. They cannot prevent its decisions being examined by the Courts. If parties should seek, by agreement, to take the law out of the hands of the Courts and put it into the hands of a private tribunal, without recourse at all to the Courts in case of any error of law, then the agreement is to that extent contrary to public policy and void.'

6.13   Clauses which seek to influence the time at which a trade union member can have recourse to the courts are slightly more problematic. The courts' approach to these clauses is dealt with in the cases of *White v Kuzych*[12] and *Leigh v NUR*.[13] In the former case, the Privy Council held that internal remedies should be exhausted if a requirement exists in the union rulebook to that end. However, in the latter case, the High Court took a more pragmatic approach, holding that:[14]

' ... [Wh]ere there is an express provision in the rules that the claimant must exhaust his domestic remedies, the Court is not absolutely bound by that because its jurisdiction cannot be ousted, but the [claimant] will have to show cause why it should interfere with the contractual position ... [In] the absence of such a provision the Court can readily, or at all events, more readily, grant relief without prior recourse to the domestic remedies, but may require the [claimant] to resort first to those remedies.'

6.14   This approach was endorsed by the Court of Appeal in *Longley v NUJ*[15] where the court emphasised that a claimant would have to show cause in order to invoke the aid of a court prior to exhausting internal remedies afforded

---

10   [1952] 2 QB 329 at 392.
11   *Lee v Showmen's Guild of Great Britain* [1952] 2 QB 329 at 342.
12   [1951] 2 All ER 435.
13   [1970] Ch 326.
14   [1970] Ch 326 at 334.
15   [1987] IRLR 109.

under the union's rulebook. Cause might, for example, amount to the disciplinary committee of a trade union refusing to allow a member a right of
appearance.

6.15 To the extent that a claimant cannot show cause allowing him to apply
to the courts prior to exhausting internal remedies, then, ordinarily, the proper
course for a court is to stay proceedings issued by the employee until the matter
has been resolved by the union's domestic tribunal concerned.

6.16 The common law is subject to statutory intervention. The Trade Union
and Labour Relations (Consolidation) Act 1992 (TULRCA 1992), s 63 deals
with clauses delaying access to the courts. This section is primarily aimed at
internal union proceedings taking an unnecessarily long time to be resolved.
Under TULRCA 1992, s 63(2), where proceedings take more than 6 months to
resolve, then a claimant member has a right to have the dispute heard by a
court. This is so notwithstanding that the proceedings are almost complete. The
right of access to the courts is not an absolute right though. To the extent that
the court finds that a member has contributed to the delay in proceedings as a
result of his unreasonable conduct, the court can extend the 6-month period of
investigation for such length of time as it considers appropriate (TULRCA
1992, s 63(4)).

6.17 It is possible to apply to the courts in a dispute arising out of a trade
union rulebook prior to a trade union tribunal being commenced, although in
the light of the foregoing, such cases will be rare.

Construction of rulebooks

6.18 Once it is accepted that trade union rulebooks are contracts in the same
way as other contracts, the courts are then faced with the task of construing
them. Whilst there is a substantial body of case law in this area, it is now of
much reduced significance due to the statutory rights that were granted to trade
union members during the reforms of the 1980s and also as a result of the
closed shop reforms of the same era which substantially reduced the number of
legal challenges to the way in which trade unions acted in reliance on their
rulebooks. This said, the common law principles are still of importance due to
the remedies that are available in breach of contract cases (most notably the
ability for courts to grant injunctions).

6.19 In considering how to construe a particular union rulebook, the courts
will pay attention to any express terms, any implied terms and also the impact
of public policy in a given case. Each will be looked at in turn.

Express terms

6.20 The starting principle is that the courts are required to construe a union
rulebook as it would appear to the reasonable trade union member. Of
particular use to trade union members in this regard will be the help that can be
derived from the construction of rules for election of candidates to minor
offices of a union. As will be seen at **6.153** et seq, trade union members are
entitled to stand as candidates in elections for the major offices of their trade
union and cannot be unreasonably excluded from doing so (TULRCA 1992,
s 47). However, this statutory right only extends to such major offices. There is
no similar statutory provision in relation to minor offices for which a member
may wish to stand, such as that of shop steward. To the extent that a trade

union rulebook provides that any class of member can stand as a candidate for elections, the exclusion of members who satisfy the class requirements under the rulebook is capable of being unlawful. In such circumstances, the courts may be able to provide a remedy to a member who is so prejudiced. For example, in *Leigh v NUR*,[16] the claimant successfully obtained an injunction preventing the defendant trade union from refusing to allow him to stand as a candidate in elections for the post of union president after he had shown that he met the candidacy requirements. A similar result was achieved in *Ecclestone v National Union of Journalists*,[17] a case where the claimant had alleged that the defendant had breached a rule which provided that:

> '... the NEC shall prepare a shortlist of applicants who have the required qualifications ...'

by devising a qualification to exclude the claimant from standing, this being that all candidates should have the confidence of the NEC. In this regard, the High Court held that the NEC was required to act rationally, fairly and in accordance with good employment practice in setting the qualifications for candidature. The court then held that good employment practice required that the selection criteria should be laid down in advance of their application so as to avoid the danger that they will be applied arbitrarily in order to exclude a particular candidate. As the procedure adopted by the union was outside the scope of good employment practice, it was outside the discretion given to the union under the union rules.

6.21   Further, in *Annamunthodo v Oilfield Workers' Trade Union*,[18] the appellant had been expelled from the defendant trade union on the grounds that he had publicly alleged embezzlement of union funds by the president of the union. As a result, the appellant had been charged with four counts of breach of union rules, each of which provided for a maximum penalty of a fine, but was expelled from membership of the union under a provision which he had not been charged with. The Privy Council ordered the expulsion to be set aside on the grounds that it was not open to the defendant to impose a harsher penalty than that expressly provided for under the rules.

6.22   Other examples of terms that have been judicially considered are:

- a rule requiring compulsory attendance at union branch meetings;[19]
- a purported alteration of trade union rules in defiance of a court order;[20] and
- strike balloting rules contained in the union rulebook.[21]

Implied terms in rulebooks

6.23   As contracts, trade union rulebooks can have terms implied into them in the same way as any other contracts. Terms can be implied on an ad hoc basis

---

16   [1970] Ch 326.
17   [1999] IRLR 166.
18   [1961] 3 All ER 621.
19   *MacLelland v NUJ* [1975] ICR 116.
20   *Clarke v Chadburn* [1984] IRLR 350.
21   *Taylor v NUM (Derbyshire)* [1984] IRLR 440.

or as a result of the particular nature of the rulebook as a contract of membership. However, not every term claimed to be implied will be held to be implied by the courts.

6.24 The existence of an implied term in the rulebook can be argued by both union and member alike. However, when looking at the rulebook, the tendency of the courts has been to give the rulebook as a contract a meaning that is most favourable to the member rather than to extend the powers of the union over the member. Following this principle, as a general rule, the courts will not imply a power for trade unions to discipline their members.[22]

6.25 However, not every implied term alleged by a member to exist will be held to exist. In deciding issues in relation to the construction of union rulebooks, the courts are required to take into account the fact that unions exist primarily to promote the greater good of their collective membership. For example, in *Iwanuszezak v GMBATU*,[23] the defendant had negotiated revised work patterns with an employer which were to the benefit of a majority of the defendant's members working for the employer. However, the claimant argued that the agreement breached an implied term of the union's rulebook, this being that the union was required to act for his benefit, and this term had been breached since the claimant had been adversely affected by the changes. On appeal, the Court of Appeal held that whilst the union was required to look after the interests of its members, the order of those interests was collective interests first and individual interests second. It was therefore possible for the union to put the collective interests of its members before those of the claimant and, accordingly, there had been no breach of the implied term.

6.26 Likewise, in *AB v CD*,[24] the High Court was called upon to consider whether there could be implied into the rulebook of the National Union of Rail, Maritime and Transport Workers, a term to the effect that a single transferable vote from previous rounds of voting should be allowed in the case of a dead heat in a final vote for election to trade union office, a method of deadlock resolution suggested in a booklet of the Electoral Reform Society (ERS), the union's ballot scrutineer of many years' standing. The court held that this was possible, adding that in order to give the rulebook sense, it was necessary to imply a means of dealing with the deadlock. In this regard, the court then held that a tie-break rather than a re-ballot was the obvious method of dealing with the deadlock. Further, all editions of ERS guidance recommended this method of tie-break and this was the most obvious and straightforward way of dealing with the matter. Accordingly, the union's basis for deciding the matter in this way was approved by the court.

6.27 This said, it has been held that express terms in trade union rulebooks empowering a committee of a union to act in a particular fashion can be tempered by the requirement of reasonableness. For example, in *Esterman v*

---

[22] See in this regard *Spring v NASDS* [1956] 1 WLR 585; *Luby v Warwickshire Miners Association* [1912] 2 Ch 371; and also *Leigh v NUR* [1970] Ch 326. To contrary effect, see *McVitae v Unison* [1996] IRLR 33 where it was held that a union had an implied power to discipline members in respect of matters arising prior to the creation of the union from three separate unions
[23] [1988] IRLR 219.
[24] [2001] IRLR 808.

NALGO,[25] the defendant union had voted on taking industrial action. When the result of the vote was published, only 49 per cent of those members of the union voting had voted in favour of industrial action. Notwithstanding this, the union resolved to take industrial action and instructed members not to take part in the administration of local elections. The claimant refused to co-operate with the instruction of the union, was disciplined and found guilty of breaching a rule under the rulebook which provided:

'Any member who disregards any regulation issued by the branch or is guilty of conduct which, in the opinion of the executive committee, renders him unfit for union membership, shall be liable to expulsion.'

6.28 The claimant presented a claim for breach of contract. The High Court granted an injunction, holding:[26]

'An Act of Parliament carries penalties for its breach, but it is a fallacy to assume that every democratically elected body is entitled to obedience to every order on pain of being found guilty of being unfit to be a member of an association. It must depend on the order and it must depend on the circumstances and, in my judgment, if implicit obedience is to be exacted, those who issue the order must make quite sure that they have the power, that no reasonable man could be in doubt that they have the power and that they are making a proper exercise of the power, and that no reasonable man could say to himself that "this is an order which I have no duty to obey".'

Trade union rulebooks and public policy

6.29 The terms of union rulebooks are subject to the requirements of public policy. Not every provision contained in a trade union rulebook will be binding on the members of the union, even if members of the union signify their consent in writing to such terms. Further, unions may be required to observe basic principles of natural justice in the treatment of their members. Natural justice requires, in general terms, that a member of a trade union has the right to a hearing before any disciplinary action is taken against the member, that any such hearing is free from bias and that a trade union cannot act as judge and jury in its own cause.

6.30 Whilst the concept of natural justice is derived from the area of public law, any suggestion of supposed control of the workings of a domestic tribunal (such as a trade union disciplinary committee) has traditionally been frowned upon by the courts. To this end, public law remedies are not available in the context of union rulebook disputes. As trade union rulebooks operate as contracts, public policy can either be incorporated into the rulebook as an implied term or it can operate as a device to strike down express terms within rulebooks where such terms seek to deny the operation of natural justice.

6.31 Natural justice in relation to union rulebooks is of particular importance when considering the issue of disciplining members of a union and, historically, it has been important in relation to the use of closed shops by which trade unions were able to deny employees the ability to work for a living.

---

[25]   [1974] ICR 625.
[26]   *Esterman v NALGO* [1974] ICR 625 at 635.

As can be seen in **Chapter 9**, the use of closed shops is now no longer possible in practical terms due to the legislative reforms of the 1980s. However, trade union membership can still be beneficial to individuals and the courts are prepared to intervene in order to ensure that unions behave fairly towards their members. For example, in *Breen v AEU*, the Court of Appeal stated that trade unions are:[27]

> '... domestic bodies which control the destinies of thousands ... They can make or mar a man by their decisions. Not only by expelling him from membership, but also by refusing to admit him as a member ... Often their rules are framed so as to give them a discretion. They claim that it is an unfettered discretion. They go too far ... They are not above the law, but subject to it. Their rules are said to be a contract between the members and the union. So be it. If they are a contract, then it is an implied term that the discretion should be exercised fairly. But the rules are in reality more than a contract. They are a legislative code laid down by the council of the union for the benefit of the members ... Even though its functions are not judicial or quasi-judicial, but administrative, still it must act fairly.'

6.32   The proposition derived from *Breen*[28] is that trade union rulebooks are open to challenge by the courts either on the basis of an implied term requiring unions to act fairly or by means of public policy to strike out express terms. Each will be considered in turn.

Public policy as an implied term in trade union rulebooks

6.33   The implied term theory works on the basis that a reasonable man would conclude that the principles of natural justice would not be excluded from operating in relation to trade union rulebooks. For example, natural justice requires that where a union member is subject to discipline or expulsion, he should have the right to a hearing. Likewise, it is necessary that a person facing disciplinary charges should know what those charges are, a point illustrated by *Annamunthodo v Oilfield Workers' Trade Union*[29] and *Lee v Showmen's Guild of Great Britain*.[30]

Avoidance of rulebook terms by operation of public policy

6.34   The courts are also prepared to strike out express terms in trade union rulebooks due to their failure to comply with public policy. To the extent that a trade union rulebook operates to exclude any aspect of natural justice, this form of provision has consistently been held to be void. For example, in *Edwards v SOGAT*,[31] the union's rulebook contained a term providing that, to the extent that a temporary member of the union was more than 6 weeks in arrears with subscriptions, that member was to be automatically expelled from the union with no right of appeal. The claimant, through an oversight by a union official, did not have his subscriptions collected and was expelled under the rule. The claimant presented a claim for breach of contract. On appeal, the

---

27   [1971] 2 QB 175 at 190.
28   *Breen v AEU* [1971] 2 QB 175.
29   [1961] 3 All ER 621.
30   [1952] 2 QB 329.
31   [1971] 1 Ch 354.

Court of Appeal found for the claimant, holding that once a member had been admitted to a trade union, there was no right for the union to expel the member in an arbitrary fashion not in accordance with the principles of natural justice.

6.35   Further, in *Roebuck v NUM*,[32] the claimants had appeared as witnesses against the defendant union in a libel action brought by the union's president against a local newspaper. The union's rulebook contained a term providing that members could be disciplined by the area executive committee for action which, in the opinion of that committee, was likely to be detrimental to the union. The president of the union brought charges against the claimants and personally presented the charges to the committee. The committee, which was also chaired by the president, found the charges to have been proved and imposed sanctions accordingly. The members sought a declaration that the finding was in breach of the principles of natural justice, notwithstanding the proper constitution of the meeting. The High Court found for the claimants, holding that disciplinary proceedings had to be constituted so as to avoid the appearance of bias to a reasonable man. This requirement had evidently not been complied with.

6.36   Not every claim by a member of a trade union that the union has failed to comply with the principles of natural justice will succeed. For example, in *Cheall v APEX*,[33] the claimant had been a member of a union with which he had become disenchanted. Consequently, he joined the defendant union but, on joining, he did not reply to a question raised which asked whether he had belonged to any other unions. Both his previous union and the defendant union were governed by the Bridlington Principles (which regulate relationships between trade unions including, inter alia, the recruitment of members between unions). It subsequently came to the attention of the defendant that the claimant had not declared his membership of his former union. The claimant's former union referred the matter to the TUC Disputes Committee, which found the defendant union to have improperly recruited the claimant contrary to the Bridlington Principles and recommended that the claimant should be expelled from the defendant's membership. This penalty was imposed whereupon the claimant sued claiming that his inability to appear before the TUC Disputes Committee to argue his case amounted to a denial of natural justice. The matter was appealed to the House of Lords which dismissed the claim, holding that there was no principle of public policy to which the Bridlington Principles were contrary and, in any event, to the extent that the claimant was not faced with the loss of his job as a result of his expulsion, he had no cause of action. See **6.46** et seq with regard to the statutory positions dealing with the right not to be expelled from membership of a trade union.

Shortcomings of the rulebook as a contract of membership

6.37   The principal shortcoming of construing the union rulebook as a contract of membership is that a contract would require there to have been a valid agreement in place between member and union. Where such agreement is missing, no common law rights can be claimed under the rulebook. For

---

[32]   [1978] ICR 676.
[33]   [1983] ICR 398.

example, in *Faramus v Film Artistes Association*,[34] the defendant union's rulebook contained a rule requiring that, in order to be eligible for membership of the union, applicants for membership must have had no criminal convictions. The claimant, had, in his youth, been sentenced to a custodial prison sentence. He did not enter this conviction on his application for membership and was admitted to the union. After 8 years of membership, the claimant's conviction came to light whereupon the defendant purported to revoke his membership. The claimant sought an injunction to prevent his expulsion from the union by revocation of his membership, which he claimed would be in breach of the rules of natural justice. Ultimately, the House of Lords refused to grant the application holding that no right of natural justice could be implied as the claimant had never validly been a member of the union under its membership requirements. It followed that he was not being expelled, since he did not qualify as a member in the first place and there was therefore no term which he could argue had been breached, since he was unable to rely upon the rulebook as a contract. Despite the many changes which have been made relating to the right to seek membership of a trade union, *Faramus* would be likely to be decided in the same way today.

6.38 The shortcomings of construing union rulebooks as contracts are, in practice, less obvious today as a result of the reform of the closed shop, due to the decreased significance of trade union membership in relation to obtaining employment.

Contractual remedies for breaching terms of the rulebook

6.39 The usual common law rules in relation to remedies for breach of contract will be applied to the case of a breach of contract arising from a trade union rulebook. Therefore, depending on the consequences of a breach of the rulebook by a union, a union member may be able to recover damages, alternatively gain an injunction, and, in either case, has the possibility of obtaining a declaration as to rights and duties under the rulebook as follows.

Damages

6.40 A member of a trade union will be able to recover damages to the extent that he has suffered a loss arising from a breach by the union of which he is a member of the union's rulebook to the extent that such loss is reasonably foreseeable.[35]

6.41 In awarding damages, the court is not required to take into account any injury to feelings that the union member may have suffered, this being in line with the general rule in relation to commercial contracts as set down in *Addis v The Gramophone Co Limited*.[36] Further, a union member who is able successfully to present a claim for breach of contract will be required to take reasonable steps to mitigate his loss and, to the extent that this does not happen, no damages can be awarded for the loss representing that part of the loss attributable to the failure to mitigate.[37]

---

[34]   [1964] 1 All ER 25.
[35]   Per *Bonsor v Musicians' Union* [1955] 3 All ER 518.
[36]   [1909] AC 488.
[37]   *Edwards v SOGAT* [1971] Ch 354.

6.42   Unlike damages awarded against a trade union in the commission of an industrial/economic tort, there is no limit to the potential liability of a union for breach of contract (per TULRCA 1992, s 20(1)).

Injunctions

6.43   An injunction may be an important remedy for a trade union member, particularly one facing expulsion from his union. Injunctions can be gained at an interim stage under the principles set down in *American Cyanamid Co v Ethicon Limited*.[38] Accordingly, from the point of view of a trade union member trying to enforce a term or terms of the rulebook, no more than a serious question as to a breach of the terms of the rulebook needs be shown coupled with a consideration of where the balance of convenience lies in relation to granting the injunction. The courts are prepared in an appropriate case to grant an injunction in favour of a trade union member to uphold membership rights under the rulebook. For example, in *Porter v NUJ*,[39] the House of Lords granted an injunction when considering an application brought by the claimant to prevent his expulsion from the defendant union arising out of the claimant's failure to take part in industrial action.

6.44   To the extent that an injunction is granted at an interim stage, two practical benefits will arise for the member seeking the injunction. First, many of the cases brought against trade unions for breach of rights in relation to the union rulebook do not proceed to trial with the result that the member will retain his union membership following the successful obtaining of an interim injunction. Secondly, the injunction can force the union to take back a member or risk contempt proceedings with the possible fines, imprisonment and sequestration that this form of enforcement can bring with it (regard should be had to RSC Ord 45, r 5, carried over into CPR, Sch 1). Reinstatement is not available as a remedy under the provisions for expulsion from a union contained under TULRCA 1992, s 174 et seq.

Declarations

6.45   A declaration as to the rights of the parties is obtainable as a final remedy in a case for breach of contract. At an interim stage however, it is rarely, if ever, available. In *International General Electric Co of New York Limited v Commissioners of Customs and Excise*,[40] the Court of Appeal held that an interim remedy declaring the rights of the parties could not exist except perhaps in an exceptional case. However, *Clarke v Chadburn (No 2)*[41] appears to have been such a case. Here, the High Court granted an interlocutory declaration coupled with an injunction to prevent an unlawful change of union rules purportedly taken by the NUM on the grounds that a substantial number of members would have been affected by the proposed change which thereby justified the sparing use of the court's available discretion.

---

[38]   [1975] AC 295.
[39]   [1980] IRLR 404.
[40]   [1962] Ch 784.
[41]   [1984] IRLR 350.

RIGHTS IN TORT OF TRADE UNION MEMBERS AGAINST THEIR UNION

6.46 The rights that a trade union member has against his trade union are covered by general principles of the law of tort. In this regard, the High Court has held that the extent of a trade union's duty to its member in relation to the tort of negligence is to use ordinary care and skill in advising or acting for a member in an employment dispute. In the case of a union obtaining external representation for a member, there is a break in any chain of causation once the external representative is appointed and the liability of the trade union falls away and passes to the external representative.[42]

STATUTORY RIGHTS OF TRADE UNION MEMBERS AGAINST THEIR UNION

6.47 The rights given to trade union members have been expanded progressively, commencing in the 1980s. The following rights are now available for members against their union or proposed union:

- not to be unjustifiably excluded or expelled from the union;
- not to be unjustifiably disciplined;
- to a ballot prior to the taking of industrial action;
- to vote on the existence of a union political fund;
- to abstain from contributions to the union political fund;
- to inspect union accounts;
- to have regular elections for union officials;
- to stand as a candidate for union office; and
- to prevent unlawful use of union property.

THE RIGHT NOT TO BE EXCLUDED OR EXPELLED FROM A TRADE UNION

6.48 The right not to be excluded or expelled from a trade union was one of the inroads made into the freedom of trade unions to manage their own affairs during the 1980s. The right, whilst doubtless still important to aggrieved individual members, is, perhaps, of less importance today than when the closed shop operated, where denial of trade union membership could lead to the inability to secure employment.

6.49 The right not to be excluded or expelled from a trade union cuts back greatly the concept of freedom of association. It is, however, a long-standing inroad into the concept of freedom of association and a right not to be unreasonably excluded from membership has been present for trade union members in one form or another since the Industrial Relations Act 1971 (IRA 1971) (apart from a short period between 1976 and 1980 when the Trade Union and Labour Relations (Amendment) Act 1976 removed any such right). The right in its original formulation focused upon the reasonableness of the action on the part of a trade union in excluding a member. However, this formulation was replaced by the Trade Union Reform and Employment Rights Act 1993 (TURERA 1993), s 14, which introduced new substantive provisions in the form of TULRCA 1992, ss 174–177. The right in its current form cuts back the

---

[42]   *Friend v Institution of Professional Managers and Specialists* [1999] IRLR 173.

effect of the old-style Bridlington Principles, which allowed the TUC Disputes Committee to recommend that a trade union member be expelled from his union in a case where rival trade unions were in dispute over the membership of that member.[43] Following the introduction of TURERA 1993, s 14, the Bridlington Principles were revised and it is now no longer possible for the TUC Disputes Committee to recommend the expulsion of a member.

6.50   The effect of TULRCA 1992, ss 174–177 is that a trade union now has no automatic right to deny membership or expel members, notwithstanding contrary provisions in the union's rulebook. There are, however, a number of cases in which it is still possible to deny membership of a trade union by means of exclusion or expulsion.

6.51   TULRCA 1992, s 174(1) creates the right not to be excluded or expelled from a trade union unless the exclusion or expulsion is permitted by s 174(2), which will be allowed where:

- A member of a trade union no longer satisfies an enforceable membership requirement under the union's rules. An enforceable membership requirement is defined in TULRCA 1992, s 174(3), by means of a closed class of cases, these being:
    - restrictions on membership by virtue of any or all of employment in a particular trade, industry or profession;
    - an occupational description (including grade level or category of appointment); and/or
    - possession of specialist skills or qualifications.
- A member no longer qualifies for membership as a result of having moved out of a particular geographical boundary relevant for trade union membership.
- A union regulates the affairs of members with one particular employer or group of employers and the member ceases to work for that employer or group of employers.
- The exclusion or expulsion is entirely due to the member's conduct. Conduct is defined in TULRCA 1992, s 177(1)(b) as including any statements, acts or omissions on the part of an employee. However, conduct is inadmissible as a reason for excluding or expelling a union member under s 174(4)(a) it is 'protected conduct', ie it relates to the claimant being or ceasing to be, or having been or having ceased to be:
    - a member of a trade union;
    - an employee employed at a particular place; or
    - a member of a political party (under TULRCA 1992, s 174(4A)). (However, membership of a political party is not 'protected conduct' where it falls within the definition of 'excluded conduct' under TULRCA 1992, s 174(4B), this being in the case of activities undertaken by an individual as a member of a political party. This last point was inserted by the Employment Relations Act 2004 (ERA 2004) as a means of allowing trade unions to expel or exclude individuals who have taken part in activities which may be contrary to the union's political beliefs.)

---

[43]   See *Cheall v APEX* [1983] IRLR 215 for an example of the operation of the old-style Bridlington Principles.

6.52 Further, conduct to which TULRCA 1992, s 65 applies (this being essentially the individual acting in his own interest rather than the collective interest of the union: TULRCA 1992, s 174(4)(b)), cannot be used by a union to justify exclusion or expulsion from trade union membership.

6.53 To the extent that a trade union can show that a member's conduct contravenes the union's rulebook and is otherwise outside the protected categories of conduct set out at **6.51**, then the common law construction of the rulebook will be the only available help to such a member faced with exclusion or expulsion.

6.54 Exclusion and expulsion are partly defined in TULRCA 1992, s 177(2)(a) and (b). Section 177(2)(a) deals with deemed exclusion from membership and covers the situation where an applicant for union membership is not informed one way or the other as to whether he is to be granted membership of the union, but there has been such an inordinate delay in notifying the applicant from the date upon which it could be reasonably expected that the applicant's application had been received by the union, that the delay would reasonably appear to amount to an exclusion from membership.[44]

6.55 Under TULRCA 1992, s 177(2)(b), expulsion includes an automatic termination of membership of a trade union upon the occurrence of a condition subsequent under the union's rules triggered by a member.

6.56 To the extent that a trade union has unlawfully excluded or expelled an individual, the individual has an initial right to present a claim to an employment tribunal under TULRCA 1992, s 174(5).

Procedure and remedies

6.57 A claimant must lodge a complaint to the employment tribunal either within 6 months of an exclusion or expulsion, or within such other extended period as the tribunal considers reasonable in all the circumstances (TULRCA 1992, s 175).

6.58 If the employment tribunal finds that the union has excluded or expelled the claimant for a reason under TULRCA 1992, s 174(4) or (4A) it must make a declaration to that effect (TULRCA 1992, s 176(1) or (1A), respectively).

6.59 If, in making a declaration under TULRCA 1992, s 174(4A) the employment tribunal finds that the conduct to which the exclusion or expulsion was attributable consisted wholly or mainly of conduct of the claimant which was contrary to a rule or objective of the union, the tribunal is required to make a declaration to that effect (TULRCA 1992, s 176(1B)). However, the tribunal is not allowed to make such a declaration unless the union shows that, at the time of the conduct of the claimant which was contrary to the objective in question, it was reasonably practicable for that objective to be ascertained if the claimant was not at that time a member of the union, by a member of the general public, and if he was at that time a member of the union, by a member of the union (TULRCA 1992, s 176(1D)). In this regard, it is immaterial

---

[44] See, for example, *NACODS v Gluchowshi* [1996] IRLR 252.

whether the claimant was a member of the union at the time of the conduct contrary to the rule or objective (TULRCA 1992, s 176(1C)).

6.60   In the event of the employment tribunal upholding a claim, much will turn upon the union's reaction to the tribunal's decision. Under TULRCA 1992, s 176(3), a claimant cannot take further steps in pursuing his remedy for a period of 4 weeks after the initial declaration has been made by the employment tribunal. This period is to allow the union to review the exclusion or expulsion and, hopefully, to revoke that action.

6.61   If the union does not revoke an exclusion or expulsion, the claimant can press forward to a compensation hearing at an employment tribunal or, if the union does not admit or re-admit the member, the Employment Appeal Tribunal (EAT) (TULRCA 1992, s 176(2)). Compensation is awarded on a just and equitable basis (TULRCA 1992, s 176(4)). Under TULRCA 1992, s 176(6), the maximum amount of compensation to be awarded at a compensation hearing cannot exceed the aggregate of an amount equal to 30 times the limit for the time being imposed by the Employment Rights Act 1996 (ERA 1996), s 227(1)(a) (the maximum amount of a week's pay for basic award in unfair dismissal cases) and an amount equal to the limit for the time being imposed by ERA 1996, s 124(1) (maximum compensatory award in unfair dismissal cases). Further, in the case of an award of compensation by the EAT, the award is not allowed to be less than £6,100 (TULRCA 1992, s 176(6)).

6.62   Both the EAT and an employment tribunal can make such deduction from an award of compensation as they see fit on the basis of a claimant's contributory fault (TULRCA 1992, s 176(5)).

6.63   As to whether it is possible to be compensated for injury to feelings in an award of compensation in such cases, this was considered in *Bradley v NALGO*[45] where the EAT held that an award of compensation could be made, but would be modest and only possible in cases where the sole cause of the injury to feelings was the expulsion itself and not some other cause.

6.64   Two final points should be noted. First, the statutory right not to be excluded or expelled from trade union membership is expressly declared to be in addition to any pre-existing rights that a claimant may have under the common law to challenge a union's action (TULRCA 1992, s 177(5)), in respect of which see **6.39** et seq.

6.65   Secondly, neither employment tribunals nor the EAT have the power to order a trade union's unlawful action in the form of exclusion or expulsion to be rescinded. This is unlike the common law which can achieve rescission of action through an injunction preventing breach or purported breach of the rulebook.

THE RIGHT NOT TO BE UNJUSTIFIABLY DISCIPLINED BY HIS TRADE UNION

6.66   The right for a trade union member not to be unjustifiably disciplined by his trade union was one of the more controversial rights introduced in the trade union reforms of the 1980s. It was originally introduced under the

---

[45]   [1991] IRLR 159.

Employment Act 1988 (EA 1988), s 3. At the time of its introduction it was condemned for undermining the collective position of organised labour by giving individual trade union members a right not to strike if they so choose, notwithstanding a properly conducted strike ballot. To this end, it has been labelled a 'scab's charter'.[46]

6.67 The right not to be 'unjustifiably disciplined' is provided by TULRCA 1992, s 64, albeit that this is something of a misnomer in that there is no need for an objective determination as to whether disciplinary action taken by a trade union against a member is reasonable: instead, regard is had as to whether action falls within an exhaustive list of automatically unjustifiable reasons.

6.68 Discipline for these purposes is defined under TULRCA 1992, s 64(2) as being any of the following matters:

- expulsion from a trade union, branch or section of that union;
- a requirement to pay a sum of money to a trade union or to a branch or section of a trade union or to any other person;
- treating as unpaid, or as paid for a different purpose, any sum of money paid by a member to a trade union in respect of any union subscription or obligation;
- the deprivation from, or denial of access to, any trade union benefit, service or facility which would otherwise be available to a member of that trade union as a result of membership of the union or a branch or section of the union;
- a recommendation by a trade union to another trade union, or section or branch of that other trade union, that a member should not be granted membership of that other trade union; or
- the subjection by a trade union of a member of that union to any other detriment.

Detriment

6.69 As to what amounts to a 'detriment', this is not defined by TULRCA 1992 but was considered in *NALGO v Killorn and Simm*,[47] where a member of the defendant union was named as a strike-breaker in a list published by the union so as to cause the member embarrassment. This was held by the EAT to be a 'detriment' to the claimant.

Unjustifiable discipline

6.70 As to when discipline is unjustifiable, this is defined in the form of an exclusive list under TULRCA 1992, s 65(1), (2) and (4). The list was extended by TURERA 1993, s 16 and now extends to cover any conduct, or preparation towards such conduct, or matters which are believed by a trade union to amount to conduct, under TULRCA 1992, s 65(2), as follows:

- failure to participate in, or support a strike or other industrial action, or an

---

[46] See McKendrick 'The Rights of Trade Union Members – Part I of the Employment Act 1988' (1988) ILJ 141 at pp 149–150.
[47] [1990] IRLR 464.

indication of a lack of support or opposition to such action, whether the action is taken by the member's union or another;

- failure by a claimant to contravene some requirement under a contract of employment for a purpose connected with a strike or industrial action;
- an assertion by a member, whether or not it is done through legal proceedings or otherwise, that a union, an official or representative of it, or any trustee of union property, has contravened, or is proposing to or likely to contravene, some rule of the union, enactment or other rule of law;
- encouraging or assisting other employees of an employer either to carry out lawfully imposed obligations under their contracts of employment or to make the type of claims listed in the point immediately above;
- contravening a requirement imposed by, or as a result of, a determination which infringes an individual's right not to be disciplined;
- failing to allow an employer to deduct from a member's wages such sums as would represent the member's subscriptions to a union pursuant to a check-off agreement to deduct those sums;
- resigning or proposing to resign from a union or another union, or joining or proposing to join another union, or refusing to join another union, or being a member of another union;
- working or proposing to work or not work with members of another union;
- working for, or proposing to work for, an employer who does, has or will or will not employ trade union labour, whether they be members of an individual's own union or members of another union; and
- making a union do some act which it is required to do on a ballot of members under TULRCA 1992.

6.71   As to what amounts to 'other industrial action' in the first point listed at **6.70**, some guidance was given by the EAT in *Fire Brigades Union v Knowles*,[48] where two full-time firemen accepted additional part-time employment as retained part-time fire fighters. They were subsequently expelled by the defendant for contravening union policy on such posts. The officers claimed that the union policy amounted to 'other industrial action' but the EAT held otherwise, stating:[49]

> 'Not all things which seek to put pressure on an employer will automatically and ipso facto amount to industrial action, even though the employer may feel himself inhibited as a result of the pressure. The lay members of this appeal tribunal emphasise that if the industrial tribunal's approach were correct, it would lead to many negotiating sessions between employers and unions amounting to "other industrial action", because those negotiations regularly involve the application of pressure on employers by the union side threatening to take strike action or some other form of action and the employers' freedom of action is often constrained by the knowledge of such threats.'

6.72   Further, if a trade union member makes any false allegation against a union or persuades another person to do so and as a result thereof the union

---

[48]   [1996] IRLR 337. The decision of the case was subsequently upheld by the Court of Appeal ([1996] IRLR 617).

[49]   [1996] IRLR 337 at 340.

takes disciplinary action against the member, that action by the union is justifiable under TULRCA 1992, s 65(5).

6.73 Where a breach of the right occurs, a right of complaint lies to an employment tribunal provided that the complaint is lodged within 3 months or such other period as the tribunal thinks is reasonable in all the circumstances (TULRCA 1992, s 66(1) and (2)).

6.74 If the act of discipline complained of lies in expelling a member of the union, the right that must be pursued is under TULRCA 1992, s 174 (the right not to be excluded or expelled from a trade union: see **6.48** et seq) and not the right not to be unlawfully disciplined.

Remedies

6.75 If an employment tribunal finds that a complaint is well founded, it is required to make a declaration to that effect (TULRCA 1992, s 66(3)). As with the right not to be unlawfully excluded or expelled from a trade union, much will then turn upon how the union reacts to the declaration. TULRCA 1992, s 67 provides a further remedy in the form of compensation for a claimant. A compensation award hearing must be sought within 6 months of the date of the declaration, although a compensation award hearing cannot take place until 4 weeks have expired from the date of the declaration by the employment tribunal (TULRCA 1992, s 67(3)).

6.76 During the 4-week period from the date of the declaration, the union is implicitly required to consider whether it wants to punish the member. If the union fails to rescind the disciplinary action which is the subject of the complaint, a compensation hearing is heard by the EAT and if the disciplinary action is rescinded, by the employment tribunal (TULRCA 1992, s 67(2)). Compensation is awarded on a just and equitable basis[50] subject to the duty to mitigate (TULRCA 1992, s 67(5) and (6)). The maximum amount of compensation is capped at the amount of the aggregate of 30 times the amount of a 'week's pay' for the purposes of ERA 1996, s 228 and the maximum of the compensatory awards for unfair dismissal (TULRCA 1992, s 67(5) and (8)). However, under TULRCA 1992, s 67(8), the EAT must impose a minimum award of at least £6,100. Further, under TULRCA 1992, s 67(8A), if on the date on which the application was made the determination infringing the claimant's right not to be unjustifiably disciplined has not been revoked, or the union has failed to take all the steps necessary for securing the reversal of anything done for the purpose of giving effect to the determination, the amount of compensation awarded must be at least £6,100.

6.77 The alternative course of action for a union which does not want to face the minimum award of compensation is to retract the disciplinary action which is the subject of the complaint within the required 4-week period. Where this happens, the compensation hearing is heard by an employment tribunal

---

[50] In respect of which the EAT has held in *Beaumont v Amicus MSF* EAT (0122/03), that awards for injury to feelings can be made under TULRCA 1992, s 67. In so finding, the EAT held that injury to feelings compensation had to be awarded in line with the guidelines set out in *Vento v Chief Constable of West Yorkshire Police (No 2)* [2003] IRLR 102 and rejected an argument that injury to feelings compensation should not be awarded under the principle in *Dunnachie v Kingston upon Hull City Council* [2004] IRLR 727.

(TULRCA 1992, s 67(2)). The employment tribunal is not bound to make an order for a minimum award though and the award to a claimant could therefore be nil.

6.78   To the extent that an employment tribunal finds that a claimant caused or contributed to disciplinary action taken by a union, it can reduce an award of compensation that it would otherwise make by such sum as it thinks is just and equitable (TULRCA 1992, s 67(7)).

6.79   Finally, there is no power for employment tribunals to order that disciplinary action imposed by a trade union must be revoked. In such a case, a union member's only recourse in seeking to have disciplinary action revoked is to seek a common law remedy in respect of any breach of the union rulebook, which are discussed at **6.39** et seq.

THE RIGHT TO A BALLOT BEFORE THE TAKING OF INDUSTRIAL ACTION

6.80   The duty of trade unions to hold a ballot prior to taking industrial action will be examined in greater detail in **Chapter 7**. The right of individual trade union members to challenge the legality of industrial action taken or proposed to be taken by the union of which they are a member was created by EA 1988 and is now carried over into TULRCA 1992, s 62.

6.81   For the purpose of TULRCA 1992, s 62(2), industrial action is deemed to be unlawful where:

- it is taken by a trade union without the majority support of a properly conducted ballot (including with regard to the appointment of an independent scrutineer and the use of proper ballot papers), of members of the union (all of whom were afforded an equal and unhindered entitlement to vote), at each workplace at which it is proposed to call industrial action, where the members of the union have been advised of the outcome as soon as reasonably practicable thereafter and in relation to which all of the procedural requirements in relation to the ballot have been complied with at the correct time for compliance; or
- industrial action is taken in spite of a properly conducted ballot of members of the union which has resolved not to take industrial action of the type to which the complaint relates.

6.82   Industrial action will be deemed to have been taken by a trade union where either a trade union has itself caused industrial action to be taken, or where the union is vicariously liable for the acts of any of the groups of union officials listed in TULRCA 1992, s 20(2).[51]

6.83   A member of a trade union may present a complaint to the High Court that the union of which he is a member has, or is likely to take, industrial action to induce members of the union (including the claimant) to take industrial action which does not have the support of a ballot (TULRCA 1992, s 62(1)). If the court upholds the complaint it may take such measures as it thinks fit under TULRCA 1992, s 62(3) to ensure that:

---

[51]   In respect of which see **Chapter 9** for more detailed commentary.

- there is no, or any further, inducement of the union's members to take part, or continue, the industrial action; and
- no member of the union takes industrial action after the order as a result of having been induced to do so by the union before the grant of the order.

6.84 It is also possible for the court to grant an interim injunction if it thinks necessary under TULRCA 1992, s 62(4).

6.85 Further, under TULRCA 1992, s 63 trade union members are granted the right not to be denied access to the courts notwithstanding anything in the rules of the union or in the practice of any court. In this regard, if a member or former member of the union begins proceedings in a court with respect to a matter to which TULRCA 1992, s 63 applies, then if the member has previously made a valid application to the union for the matter to be submitted for determination or conciliation in accordance with the union's rules, and the court proceedings are begun after the end of the period of 6 months (beginning with the day on which the union received the application), the rules requiring or allowing the matter to be so submitted, and the fact that any relevant steps remain to be taken under the rules, are deemed to be irrelevant to any question whether the court proceedings should be dismissed, stayed or sisted, or adjourned (as relevant).

THE RIGHT TO A VOTE ON THE EXISTENCE OF A UNION'S POLITICAL FUND

6.86 It has been lawful for trade unions to have a political fund since the Trade Union Act 1913 which repealed the decision of the House of Lords in *ASRS v Osbourne*,[52] holding that the use of funds for political purposes was ultra vires the statutory object of trade unions under the Trade Union Acts 1871–1876.

6.87 When the Trade Union Act 1984 (TUA 1984) was commenced, it sought to curb the ability of trade unions to have a political fund as of right, on the basis that the existence and use of such funds was not necessarily representative of the wishes of union members. TUA 1984 therefore introduced the concept of an initial ballot for the establishment of new political funds and periodic balloting for the continued existence of such funds and for funds which existed at the commencement of TUA 1984.

Political objects

6.88 The starting-point in relation to political funds is TULRCA 1992, s 71 which imposes a prohibition on the use of trade union funds for 'political objects' unless a political fund resolution has been passed by the union. Furthermore, under TULRCA 1992, s 71(1)(b) a union must draw up rules approved by the Certification Officer in relation to the use of the political fund. These rules must deal with the issues of the creation of a separate political fund and the ability of members to contract out of payment into the political fund if they so choose. The prohibition of using funds for political objects in the absence of a valid political fund resolution is widely drafted under TULRCA 1992, s 71(2) and would catch the transfer of funds from one trade union to

---

[52]   [1910] AC 87.

another where the latter union had a valid political fund resolution, so that the latter union could use those funds for political objects.

6.89   Political objects are broadly defined under TULRCA 1992, s 72(1) and cover such matters as:

- contributions or payments directly or indirectly made to political parties;
- the provision of services or property for a political party;
- the registration of electors or the candidature of any person, the selection of candidates or the holding of a ballot by the union in connection with the election of any person to a political office;
- the maintenance of the holder of any political office;
- the holding of any conference or meeting the main purpose of which is the transaction of business in connection with a political party; or
- the production, publication or distribution of any literature, document, film, sound recording or advertisement the main purpose of which is to persuade people to vote or not to vote for a particular political party or candidate.

6.90   This last point is highly significant since, for example, if a union uses the media to publicise the need for its members' jobs, that publicity will be outside the scope of the political fund and expenditure in such a case can come from general union funds. However, if a union strays into the realms of seeking to influence voters in political elections by using publicity, for example, advertisements, those advertisements must be paid for by the political fund. For example, in *Paul and Frazer v NALGO*,[53] the defendant union had no political fund and the claimants sought to challenge the use of general union funds by the defendant for its media campaign entitled 'Make People Matter'. The campaign sought to focus public attention on the treatment of public sector employees by the Government. No other government or political party was referred to in the advertisements. The defendant advanced the argument that, since the advertisements bore a disclaimer to the effect that it was not trying to influence voters, the advertisements did not amount to a political object of the union. The High Court was not persuaded and noted that the advertising campaign took place immediately prior to local and general elections. Consequently, to the extent that the Government was the target of the advertisements to the exclusion of any other political party, then, despite the disclaimer, the effect of the advertisements would be to put a message to the public that the Government should not be voted for and, therefore, the campaign was in reality a political one. The court concluded by stating that if the campaign had taken place at a time when no elections were happening, it could not have influenced voters to vote or not vote for a person or party and would not have fallen within TULRCA 1992, s 72(1)(f).

6.91   Further, TULRCA 1992, s 72(2) provides that if a person attends a political conference or meeting as a delegate or otherwise as a participant, any expenditure that he incurs is deemed to be expenditure for political purposes.

6.92   Following amendments made to TULRCA 1992 under the Employment Relations Act 1999 (ERA 1999), s 29, it is possible for an application to be made by a trade union member to the Certification Officer in respect of trade

---

[53]   [1987] IRLR 413.

union funds which are used for political purposes in the absence of a valid political fund resolution (TULRCA 1992, s 72A(1)). Upon such an application being made, the Certification Officer:

- must make such inquiries as he thinks fit;
- must give the applicant and the union an opportunity to be heard;
- must ensure that, so far as is reasonably practicable, the application is determined within 6 months of being made;
- may make or refuse the declaration requested;
- must, whether he makes or refuses the declaration, give reasons for his decision in writing; and
- may make written observations on any matter arising from, or connected with, the proceedings.

6.93   Further, under TULRCA 1992, s 72A(3) and (4), in the event that the Certification Officer makes a declaration that funds have been so used unlawfully, the Certification Officer's declaration must:

- specify the provisions of TULRCA 1992, s 71 which have been breached;
- specify the amount of the funds applied in breach; and
- if the Certification Officer is satisfied that the union has taken or agreed to take steps with a view to remedying the declared breach, or securing that a breach of the same or any similar kind does not occur in future, specify those steps in making the declaration.

6.94   Furthermore, under TULRCA 1992, s 72A(5), if the Certification Officer makes such a declaration he may also make an order for remedying the breach in such terms as he thinks just in the circumstances. The Certification Officer may also request that he is provided with information in relation to questions raised by him (although he has no power to enforce that answers are provided, save that he may proceed in the absence of any answers to move on to his declaration (TULRCA 1992, s 72A(6)). Both declarations and orders of the Certification Officer are treated as if they had been issued by the courts and may be enforced in the same way through the courts by members of the trade union against the union (TULRCA 1992, s 72A(7)–(9)).

Political fund resolutions

6.95   A political fund resolution needs to be passed under TULRCA 1992, s 73(1) in order to approve a political fund. Every trade union must have a fresh ballot at least once every 10 years in order to maintain its political fund. If a ballot for a political fund is not held, then under TULRCA 1992, s 73(3), the previous resolution ceases to have effect on the tenth anniversary of the date of the last ballot.

6.96   If a ballot is held and a simple majority of those voting on the resolution approve it, the resolution is passed and takes effect as a substantive rule of the union which can be rescinded under the union's constitution in the same way as any other union rule (TULRCA 1992, s 73(2)). Upon the passing of a new political fund resolution, the previous political fund resolution automatically ceases to have effect. If, however, a ballot for a political fund does not pass the resolution, the old political fund resolution continues after the ballot for a further period of 2 weeks (TULRCA 1992, s 73(4)). It is possible in that period for the union to continue to apply the political fund for political purposes.

Voting on political fund resolutions

6.97   Under TULRCA 1992, save for overseas members of a union (TUL-RCA 1992, s 94(l)), every member of the union is entitled to have an equal vote in a ballot for a political fund resolution (TULRCA 1992, s 76).

6.98   Trade unions are required to submit to, and have approved by, the Certification Officer, a set of rules for the purpose of a political fund resolution ballot (TULRCA 1992, s 74(1)). Under TULRCA 1992, s 73(2), such rules must be submitted afresh on each and every occasion that a political fund resolution ballot is held notwithstanding the fact that previous sets of rules have passed the Certification Officer's scrutiny.

6.99   Prior to holding a political fund resolution ballot, TULRCA 1992, s 75 requires that a union must appoint a suitably qualified independent scrutineer who the union believes to be competent and independent to oversee the whole voting process. Regulations may be passed laying down the necessary qualifications for independent scrutineers.[54]

6.100   The independent scrutineer's terms of appointment will include, inter alia, all the matters contained within TULRCA 1992, s 75(3), as amended by TURERA 1993, together with any such other terms of appointment as the appointing union may specify. As a minimum therefore, independent scruti-neers are responsible for:

● supervising the production and distribution of voting papers;
● inspecting the register of members to ensure that the same is accurate and up to date. In this regard, members of the union may request the independent scrutineer to carry out this task if the members believe that the register of members is out of date (TULRCA 1992, s 75(3A)). A union is bound to comply with any request of an independent scrutineer to produce the register of members and allow the independent scrutineer to inspect the same, irrespective of the format of the register (for example, computerised or hard copy) (TULRCA 1992, s 75(5A) and (5B));
● taking such preliminary steps as are necessary to compile a statutory report on the conduct of a ballot;
● making the report to the trade union as soon as reasonably practicable after the last date for the return of voting papers;
● retaining custody of voting papers used in the ballot and a copy of the register of members for a period of one year beginning on the day that the result of the ballot is published and thereafter destroying the ballot papers.

6.101   Under TULRCA 1992, s 75(4), the trade union is required to ensure that nothing in the terms of the independent scrutineer's appointment is such as to make it reasonable for any person to call the independent scrutineer's independence in relation to the union into question and to ensure that the independent scrutineer carries out his functions without any interference which would make the carrying out of those functions liable to call his independence into question (TULRCA 1992, s 75(6)). Further, before the independent scrutineer begins to carry out his functions, the union is required under

---

[54]   See in this regard the Trade Union Ballots and Elections (Independent Scrutineer Qualifications) Order 1993, SI 1993/1909 and the Trade Union Ballots and Elections (Independent Scrutineer Qualifications) Order 1993 (Amendment) Order 2002, SI 2002/2267.

TULRCA 1992, s 75(5) either to send a notice stating the name of the independent scrutineer to every member of the union to whom it is reasonably practicable to send the notice, or take all such other steps for notifying members of the name of the independent scrutineer as it is the practice of the union to take when matters of general interest to all its members need to be brought to their attention. Finally, the union is required to comply with all reasonable requests of the independent scrutineer for the purposes of, or in connection with, the carrying out of his functions in relation to the ballot.

6.102 The ballot itself is dealt with under TULRCA 1992, s 77. The method of voting is by a voting paper marked by the voter (TULRCA 1992, s 77(1)). Voting papers must specify the name of the independent scrutineer and the date and address for return of the voting papers, together with an individual number from a block of consecutive whole numbers (TULRCA 1992, s 77(2)).

6.103 Voters must be able to vote without interference from any trade union official, member or employee of the union and must be free to vote, as far as is reasonably practicable, without cost to the member. A ballot should be, as far as is reasonably practicable, a postal ballot, thereby helping to ensure that it is secret (TULRCA 1992, s 77(3) and (4)).

6.104 Counting of the ballot is required to be undertaken by independent persons. To this end, TULRCA 1992, s 77A(1) and (2) requires that a union must ensure that it engages either an independent scrutineer or some other person who the union believes to be both competent and independent, to store, distribute and count the voting papers. If that person appointed is not the independent scrutineer for the ballot, then it will be necessary to ensure that the person who counts the voting papers returns them to the independent scrutineer as soon as possible after the result of the ballot (TULRCA 1992, s 77A(5)).

6.105 After the result of the political fund resolution ballot is known, the independent scrutineer is responsible for preparing a report on the ballot under TULRCA 1992, s 78, which must comment upon the following:

- The number of voting papers returned to the independent scrutineer together with the number of spoilt and valid votes cast.
- The name of the independent person who counted the votes.
- Whether or not the independent scrutineer was satisfied that the preparation, storage, distribution and return of the voting papers and the vote itself were carried out fairly and without contravention of any statute and whether the independent scrutineer believes that he was allowed to carry out his task without interference.
- Where the independent scrutineer has inspected or asked to inspect the register of members, whether he did so himself or was asked to do so as a result of a members request and, if so, the independent scrutineer must state whether or not he declined the request. If the independent scrutineer did inspect the register of members, he must state whether or not he believed the same to be a fair reflection of the membership of the union at the time he inspected it (TULRCA 1992, s 52(2A)).

Remedy for failure to comply with the balloting process

6.106 If a union fails to comply with the requirements of its approved balloting rules, or fails to comply with the result of a political fund resolution ballot, then under TULRCA 1992, s 79, a member of the union may apply either to the Certification Officer (TULRCA 1992, s 80) or the High Court (TULRCA 1992, s 81) for a declaration that the union has so failed to comply. Further, following changes made under ERA 1999, both the Certification Officer and the court (TULRCA 1992, ss 80(5A)–(5C) and, s 81(4) respectively) may issue an Enforcement Order by which the union can be compelled to:

- secure the holding of a ballot in accordance with the order;
- take such other steps to remedy the declared failure as may be specified in the order; and/or
- abstain from such acts as may be so specified with a view to securing that a failure of the same or a similar kind does not occur in future.

6.107   In either case, under TULRCA 1992, s 79(3), an application must be made within one year of the ballot result being published.

6.108   Where an Enforcement Order has been made, any person who is a member of the union and was a member at the time it was made is entitled to enforce obedience of the order as if he had made the complaint on which it was made (TULRCA 1992, ss 80(5C) and 81(6) in the case of orders made by the Certification Officer and the courts respectively).

Political funds

6.109   The main rules relating to political funds are contained in TULRCA 1992, ss 82–83. Under TULRCA 1992, s 82, union rules must provide for:

- payment for political objects out of a separate political fund;
- exemption from paying into the fund by those members who give notice in accordance with TULRCA 1992, s 84;
- the right not to be excluded from any union right or benefit for those members of the union who have given notice of exemption from paying into the political fund; and
- not making contributions to a political fund a condition precedent to joining a union.

6.110   To the extent that such rules do not exist, a union member is allowed to challenge his union's rules by presenting a claim to the Certification Officer who may make such order as he thinks fit so as to enable any breach of TULRCA 1992, s 82 to be remedied by the union (TULRCA 1992, s 82(2) and (3)). In this regard, the Certification Officer is specifically provided with a power to make such inquiries as he thinks fit (TULRCA 1992, s 82(2A)) and may make a decision in the absence of replies to those inquiries on the basis of the information available to him (TULRCA 1992, s 82(3A)). Where an order is made by the Certification Officer, any person who is a member of the union and was a member at the time it was made is entitled to enforce obedience of the order as if he had made the complaint on which it was made (TULRCA 1992, s 82(4A)). Such an order can be enforced in the same way as an order of the County Court (TULRCA 1992, s 82(4B)).

6.111   If a trade union has a political fund resolution enabling it to create a political fund, TULRCA 1992, s 83(1) and (2) deal with the assets of the fund. The political fund must be a wholly independent fund which cannot draw upon any sources other than contributing members' subscriptions to the fund, and other property that accrues to the fund in the course of administering the assets of the fund (for example, interest or dividends on the capital of the fund)

(TULRCA 1992, s 83(2)). Further, where a political fund resolution is not renewed, members of the union cannot be required to contribute to the assets of the political fund after the political fund resolution ceases to be valid (TULRCA 1992, s 83(2)).

6.112 If a trade union incurs liabilities as a result of its political objects (for example, expenditure on publicity campaigns), the only union assets available to meet those liabilities will be the assets of the political fund (TULRCA 1992, s 83(3)). This is so notwithstanding that a liability may have been contractually incurred on the basis that general union funds will be available to satisfy the liability or that a charge has been granted over any other union asset. Further, it is possible to recover assets improperly applied from other union funds under TULRCA 1992, s 16.

Unspent surplus following the rejection of a political fund resolution

6.113 To the extent that a political fund resolution ballot resolves against the retention of a political fund, the union concerned has three options with regard to any surplus that may still remain in the political fund. First, the union may carry on using the fund for political purposes for a 6-month period beginning with the day on which the ballot was held. It can use this 6-month period to run down the fund if it so chooses. It cannot, however, use the running-down provision to incur a deficit or increase one if one already exists (TULRCA 1992, s 89(2)).

6.114 Secondly, a union may transfer the surplus in the political fund to general union funds and use them for the purpose of the particular fund or funds into which they are subsequently transferred (TULRCA 1992, s 89(4)).

6.115 Thirdly, the union can keep the surplus frozen pending a re-ballot at some point in the future but the union must ensure that no additions are made to the fund, save to the extent that they result either from normal investment activity (for example, by way of interest or dividends), or as a result of contributions that were collected prior to the political fund resolution ballot (TULRCA 1992, s 89(3)).

6.116 If a union attempts to carry on collecting subscriptions from its members for the political fund or otherwise contravenes any of the requirements set out above, members of the union may apply to the court for a declaration that the union is acting unlawfully (TULRCA 1992, s 90(4)). If such an application is successful, the court may, if it thinks it necessary to ensure that additions to the political fund are stopped, make an order to that effect (TULRCA 1992, s 90(5)).

THE RIGHT TO ABSTAIN FROM MAKING CONTRIBUTIONS TO THE POLITICAL FUND

6.117 Trade union members have had the right to contract out of paying into union political funds since the passing of the Trade Union Act 1913. The scheme of the Trade Union Act 1913 was kept substantially in place until being replaced by TUA 1984, the provisions of which are now carried over into TULRCA 1992, Chapter VI, Part I, which works on a contracting out basis instead of those wishing to contribute to union funds being required to contract in. Upon the implementation of TUA 1984, the TUC gave undertakings to the then Government in respect of the reforms to ensure that the contracting out system would be operated fairly. The necessity for these undertakings lies in the apathy towards contracting out expressed by trade union members who are bound by a political fund resolution where the use of the political funds might not necessarily accord with the beliefs of individual trade union members.[55]

Substantive provisions

6.118 The main provisions relating to contracting out of political fund contributions are in TULRCA 1992, ss 84–88. TULRCA 1992, s 84(1) provides for a model form that members of a union can use to give notice to their union of their objection to making payments to the union political fund. The form is only a model and provided that the content is substantially the same, minor variations in individual cases will not matter. As a bare minimum, the form should contain a statement as to a member's unwillingness to pay into the political fund and the fact that the member is therefore exempt from payment into the political fund. The notice is applicable in respect of members wishing to contract out of an existing fund and also, under TULRCA 1992, s 84(2), in respect of the adoption of a new political fund resolution by a trade union.

6.119 If a trade union has passed a new political fund resolution it is required to give notice in an appropriate form to its members advising them that they can contract out of payments to the political fund and also the place at which a contracting out form can be obtained, this being either the head office of the union, any of its branch offices or directly from the Certification Officer (TULRCA 1992, s 82(2)(b)).

6.120 TULRCA 1992, s 84(3) specifies that the manner in which the notice is to be given to members is to be in accordance with the rules of the union as approved by the Certification Officer and that the Certification Officer is to have regard to the existing character and status of the union on a case-by-case basis in approving the draft rules submitted.

6.121 The consequence of a member serving an exemption notice on his trade union is that after a new political fund resolution has been adopted by the union, the member will be exempt from contributions from the date on which that resolution was passed, provided that he has given notice within one month of the date of passing of that resolution (TULRCA 1992, s 84(4)(a)). If, however, the member takes longer than one month to notify the union, or notifies the union during the period of validity of an existing political fund resolution, then under, s 84(4)(b), the member will only become exempt from contributions to the political fund as from 1 January in the year following the giving of that notice. In all cases, under TULRCA 1992, s 84(5), the exemption notice, once given and binding, will continue in force until it is withdrawn by the member.

6.122 Under TULRCA 1992, s 85, an exemption from contributions to the political fund is all-embracing. It therefore does not matter that a union chooses to have a separate political fund levy from members or deducts a fractional contribution from the general subscription that each member pays to

---

55   See research to this end, Ewing 'Trade union political funds: the 1913 Act revisited' (1984) ILJ 221.

the union. If the latter method is used, members who have served an exemption notice will be entitled to a reduced subscription to the extent of the political fund fraction of the subscription. The union rulebook is required to take this into account and must also, so far as is practical, show exempt members the fraction of general subscription that is put towards the political fund (TULRCA 1992, s 85(2)(b)).

Effect of contracting out upon employers

6.123 TULRCA 1992, s 86 applies to employers in relation to contracting out and provides that employers are bound by the contracting out provisions to the extent that they are responsible for collecting political fund subscriptions either as a separate levy or rolled up in a general union subscription. If a union member wishes to contract out of making payments to his union's political fund, the member is required to certify in writing to his employer that he is exempt from the political fund levy and has notified his union in writing of this fact. Once this certification has been provided, an employer is bound from the first day that it is reasonably practicable to comply after receiving notice of that certification (TULRCA 1992, s 86(2)).

6.124 Furthermore, an employer is not entitled to refuse to deduct any contributions from members who are exempt from contributing to the political fund, as might occur, for example, as a result of the increased administration cost of treating contributing and non-contributing members differently. TULRCA 1992, s 86(3) effectively provides that deductions by way of check-off to the extent that they are made by an employer, should be correct in law for each member. This may well pose a problem to a union since the employer carrying out the check-off function will have the option of refusing to make check-off deductions across the board if the administration involved becomes burdensome and may pass the administration of deductions (and associated cost) back to the union.

Remedy for unlawful contributions/failure to deduct

6.125 Where an employer makes deductions from an employee's salary in spite of receiving a properly certificated objection from an employee, the employee's remedy lies in making a claim to an employment tribunal under TULRCA 1992, s 87. A claim has to be presented within 3 months of the deduction or the last of a series of such deductions or such longer period as the tribunal considers reasonable in a case where it was not reasonably practicable to have presented a claim earlier (TULRCA 1992, s 87(2)). The employer is provided with a defence under TULRCA 1992, s 87(3) to the effect that it did not receive the employee's certification. However, the burden of proof in relation to this matter lies on the employer. If the employment tribunal is satisfied that the employer has failed to comply with its duty, it is required to make a declaration to this effect and make an order requiring the employer to pay the sum incorrectly deducted to the employee within a time specified in the order. The employment tribunal can also order that the employer does not make any future such deductions (TULRCA 1992, s 87(4)). In the event that the employer fails to comply with an order, the employee may present a further complaint to the employment tribunal at any time in the period commencing after 4 weeks have elapsed from the date of the original order and ending 6 months after the date of the original order, which, if the employment tribunal finds in favour of the claimant in respect of that claim, must make an order requiring the employer to pay to the employee a sum equal to 2 weeks' pay (as determined under the ERA 1996, s 225) as compensation (TULRCA 1992, s 87(5)–(8)).

INSPECTION OF TRADE UNION ACCOUNTS

6.126   Trade union members have wide powers to inspect the accounts of their union. The right to inspect trade union accounts was increased following the Miners' Strike 1984–1985 which highlighted the inadequacies of the old accounting regime under which trade unions operated (which did not require proper records of assets and liabilities to be maintained). The right to inspect trade union accounts is now set out in TULRCA 1992, Chapter III, Part I.

The duty to keep proper accounting records

6.127   This duty is provided under TULRCA 1992, s 28(1) and requires trade unions to keep proper records of their assets and liabilities. Trade unions are also required to establish a satisfactory system of controlling accounting records, cash holdings, receipts and remittances. Records must be kept for a period of 6 years (TULRCA 1992, s 29(1)).

6.128   The duty to keep proper accounts is compounded under TULRCA 1992, s 32 which requires an annual return dealing with the matters set out under TULRCA 1992, s 32(3) to be filed with the Certification Officer by 1 June in the calendar year following that to which it relates (TULRCA 1992, s 32(2)). Copies of trade union annual returns are available from the union to members of the public free of charge (TULRCA 1992, s 32(5)). The Certification Officer is also required to keep copies of all annual returns submitted to the Certification Officer and these can be inspected by members of the public at all reasonable hours either free or on payment of a reasonable charge (TULRCA 1992, s 32(6)).

6.129   Further, trade unions are required to provide their members with a statement of the content of their annual return within 8 weeks of the date upon which the annual return was sent to the Certification Officer (TULRCA 1992, s 32A(1)). The statement must either be an individual statement to each member or must be distributed in any other way that the union commonly uses to bring matters of general interest to the attention of its members (TULRCA 1992, s 32A(2)). The statement must deal with the matters referred to in TULRCA 1992, s 32A(3)–(5), these being:

- the total income and expenditure of the union during the year;
- how much of the income relates to membership subscriptions;
- the total income and expenditure of any political fund;
- the income received by the president, general secretary and each committee member of the union;
- the report made by the auditors of the union together with their names and addresses;
- any other matter that a union thinks is of importance in helping its members to reach a balanced view of the union's financial affairs; and
- a statement in the form set out in TULRCA 1992, s 32A(6) advising union

members that they can take up irregularities in the annual return with any of the union, its officials, trustees, auditors, the Certification Officer or the police.

6.130 The Certification Officer must be sent a copy of any such statement and the Certification Officer is required to make a copy of such a statement available free of charge to any union member for the period of 2 years after delivery of the statement (TULRCA 1992, s 32A(7)–(9)).

6.131 Under TULRCA 1992, s 33, trade unions are also required to appoint auditors who are required to report each year on the annual return (TULRCA 1992, s 36). Auditors are granted rights of inspection as set out under TULRCA 1992, s 37, being the rights of access to records of the union and explanations from officers of the union, the right to attend any general meeting of the union and the right to be heard at such a meeting.

6.132 TULRCA 1992, s 34 provides conditions of eligibility for appointment to the post of auditor and the right to appoint and remove auditors from their post is dealt with under TULRCA 1992, s 35. Trade unions must also comply with their duties under TULRCA 1992, s 37 to provide assistance to their auditors in the performance of their duties (both in respect of providing access to financial records and explanations from officers of the union).

THE RIGHT TO INSPECT TRADE UNION ACCOUNTS

6.133 TULRCA 1992, s 30 creates a right for a member of a trade union to have access to the accounting records of his union. Former union members are able to inspect the records of their former union for any period during which they were a member (TULRCA 1992, s 30(1)). Where a member of a union makes a request to inspect union accounts, the union must, within 28 days from the day on which that request was made, allow the member access to the accounts. Further, the union must allow the member to have an accountant present if he so wishes, and allow the member to take away copies of the accounts (TULRCA 1992, s 30(2)). The right of an accountant to be present can be refused if the member has refused to enter into any reasonable request for confidentiality concerning the accounts that the union may require (TULRCA 1992, s 30(3) and (5)). Furthermore, a trade union is allowed to make a reasonable administrative charge for granting access to records and providing copies of records. However, in making a charge for granting access and providing copies, the union must provide the principles upon which the charge is to be made (TULRCA 1992, s 30(6)).

Enforcement of the right

6.134 If a trade union fails to comply with a valid request by a member or former member of a union to inspect the union's accounts two consequences arise. First, under TULRCA 1992, s 31(1), the member or former member making the request may apply to the High Court or the Certification Officer. In the case of an application to the court, this is dealt with under TULRCA 1992, s 31(2), and if the court finds in favour of the applicant, it may grant such an order as the court considers appropriate with regard to providing access to the records, allowing an accountant to accompany the member or former member and/or allowing the member or former member to take copies or extracts from the records. The court may also grant injunctive relief in an appropriate case (TULRCA 1992, s 31(3)).

6.135 In the case of an application to the Certification Officer, under TULRCA 1992, s 32(2A), the Certification Officer must make such inquiries as he thinks fit, and give the applicant and the trade union an opportunity to be heard. Where the Certification Officer makes inquiries of a party which go unanswered, the Certification Officer has no power to compel that a reply is provided but may determine the application notwithstanding that the information has not been provided to him (TULRCA 1992, s 32(4)). Further, under TULRCA 1992, s 32(2B), where the Certification Officer is satisfied that the claim is well founded he must make such an order as he considers appropriate for ensuring that the applicant is allowed to inspect the records requested, is allowed to be accompanied by an accountant when making the inspection of those records and is allowed to take, or is supplied with, such copies of, or of extracts from, the records as he may require. Any order of the Certification Officer may be enforced in the same way as an order of the court (TULRCA 1992, s 32(5)).

6.136 Additionally, the refusal by a trade union to comply with a valid request to inspect such records is a criminal offence under TULRCA 1992, s 45(5).

Financial investigations by the Certification Officer

6.137 The Certification Officer is empowered to require trade unions to produce documents and to appoint inspectors from his staff to investigate the financial affairs of unions. These powers were introduced by TURERA 1993, which inserted them as TULRCA 1992, ss 37A–37E.

Production of documents

6.138 The power of the Certification Officer to call for the production of relevant documents is provided under TULRCA 1992, s 37A. Relevant documents are defined as being those documents relating to the financial affairs or accounts of a trade union (TULRCA 1992, s 37A(6)).

6.139 The power to require production of documents allows the Certification Officer to call for documents to be produced if he thinks that there is good reason (TULRCA 1992, s 37A(1)).[56] The power extends to production by a trade union, or a branch or a section of a trade union.

6.140 The order to produce should specify the documents to be produced and a time and a place for the documents to be produced at (TULRCA 1992, s 37A(1)). The Certification Officer is also empowered to authorise members of his staff to attend at a union and require immediate production of relevant documents on production of evidence of authority (TULRCA 1992, s 37A(2)). Any such production of documents takes place without prejudice to any lien

---

[56]   See also TULRCA 1992, s 37E(1) in relation to the duty to consider the exercise of the power where an auditor does not certify the accounts to be true and fair or where an auditor has been hindered in carrying out his functions.

that is asserted over a relevant document (TULRCA 1992, s 37A(4)). Production of documents for these purposes includes taking copies or extracts from documents (TULRCA 1992, s 37A(5)). A person is not allowed to refuse to produce documents on the grounds that production would tend to expose the person to the risk of criminal proceedings (TULRCA 1992, s 37A(7)). This said, any such statement by a person as to this likelihood cannot be used in evidence against the maker of the statement unless in the course of a criminal investigation into a union's affairs the maker of the statement is prosecuted for making a false statement or makes a further inconsistent statement dealing with the same point (TULRCA 1992, s 37A(7)).

6.141 Documents that are the subject of legal professional privilege or the subject of a banker's duty of confidence cannot be required to be produced by the Certification Officer (TULRCA 1992, s 37E(3)–(4)).

Investigation by inspectors appointed by the Certification Officer

6.142 The power of the Certification Officer to appoint investigators is dealt with by TULRCA 1992, ss 37B–37D. Such an appointment can only occur where there are circumstances suggesting fraud or financial mismanagement on the part of a trade union or where a union has failed to comply with its statutory or contractual financial obligations (TULRCA 1992, s 37B(2)).

6.143 An investigator so appointed can request production of any document relating to a union's financial affairs or any other document that is relevant to an investigation, can require attendance before the inspector and can require all reasonable assistance with his investigation generally (TULRCA 1992, s 37B(3)–(5)).

6.144 As with the power to request production of documents, there is no right to withhold documents on the grounds that they tend to incriminate the producer of the document (TULRCA 1992, s 37B(6)).

6.145 Where an inspector is appointed, the inspector has a duty to prepare a report (either in writing or printed) at the discretion of the Certification Officer (TULRCA 1992, s 37C(1)). The Certification Officer can request a discontinuance of an investigation where a criminal investigation is to be conducted or for any other reason (TULRCA 1992, s 37C(4)).

6.146 At the outcome of an investigation, the Certification Officer is required to publish a report and must make available copies of the report free of charge to the union under investigation, to an auditor of the union if the auditor so requests, and to any member of the union who has caused that investigation to be undertaken by making a complaint and requesting a copy of the report (TULRCA 1992, s 37C(6) and(7)).

6.147 A certified copy of the report is admissible as evidence in any legal proceedings (TULRCA 1992, s 37C(8)).

ELECTION OF TRADE UNION OFFICIALS

6.148 Most trade unions have a provision in their rulebooks covering the holding of elections for union officials. To the extent that a trade union's rulebook deals with this matter, it is possible to challenge a failure to hold elections in accordance with those rules as a breach of contract.[57]

6.149   However, the problems involved with elections for the posts of officials of a union have traditionally arisen in cases where there has been a strong figurehead controlling a given union. This was recognised by the Government in the early 1980s during its extensive reform of trade union law and, as a consequence, TUA 1984 was enacted to provide for elections to all the voting posts of a trade union's executive committee. However, the figurehead problem was not adequately resolved by TUA 1984. Unions were able to bypass the election requirement by providing for non-voting membership of their executive committees with the consequence that such figureheads were not caught by the statutory requirements. Matters came to a head during the Miners' Strike 1984–1985 when in 1985, the NUM, in order to remove their President from the ambit of TUA 1984, held a vote to change its constitution so as to make the President's position a non-voting one. As a consequence of these avoidance tactics, EA 1988 was passed which introduced the requirement that any position on a trade union executive committee should be an elected one. The changes under EA 1988 are now incorporated as TULRCA 1992, Chapter IV, Part I and they apply notwithstanding any rules to the contrary within a union's rulebook (albeit that some exceptions have been created to this rule, most recently under ERA 2004).

Election requirements

6.150   TULRCA 1992, s 46(1) imposes a duty for unions to hold elections at least every 5 years for the positions of:

- membership of the executive committee;
- any position by virtue of which a person is a member of the executive committee;
- president; and
- general secretary.

6.151   To the extent that the office of president or general secretary is a non-voting position which cannot be occupied by an incumbent for more than 13 months, and was not so occupied by an incumbent for more than one period of 13 months, there is no requirement to hold elections for such a position (TULRCA 1992, s 46(4)). Likewise, under TULRCA 1992, s 46(4A) (inserted by ERA 2004), there is no application of the provisions to a president if:

- the holder of that position was elected or appointed to it in accordance with the rules of the union;
- at the time of his election or appointment as president he was an elected member of the union's executive, otherwise held an elected position on the executive or was secretary of the union;
- it is no more than 5 years since either he was elected, or re-elected, to the position mentioned in the above point which he held at the time of his election or appointment as president, or he was elected to another position of the above-mentioned kinds at a qualifying election held after his election or appointment as president of the union; and

---

[57]   See, for example, *Leigh v NUR* [1970] Ch 326.

- he has, at all times since his election or appointment as president, held the position above by virtue of having been elected to it at a qualifying election.

6.152 Membership of a trade union executive committee is defined to cover any person who, under the rules or practices of a union, is able to attend or speak at meetings of the executive otherwise than simply to provide factual information to it (TULRCA 1992, s 46(3)). The executive committee for these purposes is defined under TULRCA 1992, s 119 as being the principal committee of the union exercising executive functions.

Candidates for elections to union offices

6.153 TULRCA 1992, s 47(1) provides the right for each member of a trade union not to be excluded unreasonably from standing as a candidate for election to union office. In this regard, a direct or indirect requirement that a candidate should be a member of a political party is expressly described as being an unreasonable ground (TULRCA 1992, s 47(2)). An indirect requirement for these purposes would include, for example, a requirement to attend as a delegate at the annual conference of a political party.

6.154 Trade unions are otherwise free to impose reasonable restrictions on candidature due to a proposed candidate's membership of a class of members defined by union rules. A class cannot be imposed on an ad hoc basis by a union (TULRCA 1992, s 47(3)) but can, for example, allow a union to impose restrictions on members from one particular trade in a large, multi-traded union or allow restrictions upon candidates from a particular geographical region. Restrictions of this type serve to make national, multi-traded unions representative of the membership of the union as a whole.

Election addresses

6.155 A complement to the right to stand as a candidate for election to trade union office is the right for a candidate to have an election address published by the union (TULRCA 1992, s 48(1)). A union is allowed to limit the length of an election address but the limit cannot be less than 100 words. A union may also specify a deadline for the submission of election addresses by all candidates. Further, unions are allowed an unfettered choice in deciding what, if any, non-written matter is included with an election address (TULRCA 1992, s 48(2), (3) and (4)).

6.156 Trade unions are not allowed to alter the copy submitted for an election address except to the extent that a candidate submitting the copy consents to the alteration or insofar as it is necessary to make a minor alteration for the purposes of printing the address (TULRCA 1992, s 48(4)). Additionally, unions must ensure that the same production method is used for all candidates who stand (TULRCA 1992, s 48(5) and (6)). Unions must meet the cost of production of election address for each candidate in their election (TULRCA 1992, s 48(7)).

6.157 Finally, it should be noted that the only person liable (whether the liability is civil or criminal) for the content of an election address is the candidate causing the election address to be published, not the union publishing the address (TULRCA 1992, s 48(8)).

Conduct of elections for union offices

6.158   If an election for trade union office is uncontested, there is no requirement to hold a ballot (TULRCA 1992, s 53). However, if an election is contested, the union is required to hold a procedurally complex ballot in order to ensure a fair and independent election process.

6.159   Under TULRCA 1992, s 49(1), prior to holding an election for the offices of its officials, a union is required to appoint an independent scrutineer whose task is to ensure that the election is fairly carried out. The union must ensure that the independent scrutineer is fully independent and it must believe that the scrutineering process will be carried out competently. The functions of the independent scrutineer can be limited to that required under TULRCA 1992 or can be expanded by agreement with the independent scrutineer if a union so chooses. Regulations may be passed dealing with the suitability of persons to act as independent scrutineers.[58] Specifically, the functions of an independent scrutineer are set out under TULRCA 1992, s 49(3), as follows:

- The production and, if an independent scrutineer is also appointed to carry out the counting of the ballot, distribution of the voting papers. If an independent person is called upon to supervise the count of the ballot, the independent person will also carry out the distribution of the voting papers. The independent scrutineer is also required to provide the name of the person to whom the voting papers should be returned by those voting.
- To inspect the register of members to ensure that the same is reasonably complete and up to date and reflects the union's membership.
- To take such steps as appear to be reasonably necessary to compile the statutory report required by TULRCA 1992, s 52.
- To retain custody of the voting papers once they are received, for a period of one year, and, thereafter, if no complaint has been lodged with the High Court or Certification Officer concerning the conduct of the election, to dispose of the same.

6.160   Before the independent scrutineer commences his functions, the union is required to send a written notice to its members notifying them of the name of the independent scrutineer (TULRCA 1992, s 49(5)). Upon appointing an independent scrutineer, as far as is reasonably possible, a union is required to ensure that each member of the union is notified of the name of the independent scrutineer and is required to supply to the independent scrutineer a copy of the up-to-date register of members in a legible form (TULRCA 1992, s 49(5A)). If the union has a cut-off deadline by which members should have joined in order to be eligible to vote in an election for officials of the union, the register should be up to date as at this date. A union member may request that the independent scrutineer inspects the register of members if the member believes the register does not accurately reflect union membership (TULRCA 1992, s 49(3A)).

6.161   Unions are also required to ensure that nothing is done to compromise the independence of an independent scrutineer (TULRCA 1992, s 49(6) and (7)).

---

[58]   See the Trade Union Ballots and Elections (Independent Scrutineer Qualifications) Order 1993, SI 1993/1909 and Trade Union Ballots and Elections (Independent Scrutineer Qualifications) Order 1993 (Amendment) Order 2002, SI 2002/2267, to this end.

6.162 Unions are free to impose restrictions on those classes of its membership who are eligible to vote for the election of its officials. Therefore, whilst the general rule under TULRCA 1992, s 50(1) is that each member is entitled an equal right to vote (subject to unions having a right under TULRCA 1992, s 60(1) to exclude overseas members from voting under union rules), there is provision for a class of excluded categories and a class of restricted categories. As regards the permitted categories of members who are excluded from voting under a union's rules, TULRCA 1992, s 50(2) provides that these are:

● unemployed members of the union;
● members of the union who are in arrears in respect of any subscription or contribution which is lawfully due to a union; and
● members of the union who are apprentices, students, trainees or new members of the union.

6.163 As regards those members of the union who can be restricted from voting, under TULRCA 1992, s 50(3), these are such classes as the union may determine by reference to:

● a trade or occupation;
● a geographical area; and
● those members of the union who under union rules are treated as a separate section within the union.

6.164 The restrictions under TULRCA 1992, s 50(3) are therefore aimed at national and multi-traded unions in order to maintain a fair cross-section of the union being elected for office. It is not possible to have a valid class restriction which would stop a union member from voting at all elections for union office save to the extent that the class restriction is based on the excluded categories under TULRCA 1992, s 50(2) (TULRCA 1992, s 50(4)).

6.165 Voting papers are subject to certain prescribed requirements to eliminate interference in the voting process. Voting papers should be individually numbered from a series of consecutively whole-numbered papers. Each paper must bear upon it the name of the independent scrutineer and the address to which the voting paper is to be returned (TULRCA 1992, s 51(2)). The prescribed method of voting is by placing a mark upon the voting paper (TULRCA 1992, s 51(1)).

6.166 Voting should be secret so far as is possible, without cost to the voting member, by post and without interference to members from the union, its members or employees (TULRCA 1992, s 51(3)). As regards the cost of the ballot to members, in *Paul and Frazer v NALGO*,[59] it was held that this requirement is satisfied by providing a reply-paid envelope to a member.

6.167 The result of a ballot is obtained by counting the number of direct votes (which includes a single transferable vote method of counting, ie ranking candidates by order of preference received by a candidate: TULRCA 1992, s 51(6) and (7)). The restriction was introduced to stop such practices as block voting and electoral colleges. In *R v Certification Officer, ex p EPEA*,[60] the House of Lords held that where a trade union rulebook contained a restriction

---

[59] [1987] IRLR 413.
[60] [1990] IRLR 398.

upon more than three members from one geographical area serving on the executive committee, this did not infringe TULRCA 1992, s 51(6). The effect of the rule was that only the first three members 'past the post' in a particular area were entitled to a seat on the executive committee, notwithstanding that a fourth member from the same area polled a greater number of votes than a candidate from another area.

6.168   TULRCA 1992, s 51A(1) and (2) also requires that the storage, distribution and counting of the voting papers is carried out by an independent person. This can either be the independent scrutineer or some other independent person in relation to whom the union has no reason to doubt either his independence or competence to carry out the task.

6.169   An independent person is required to carry out his duties so as to ensure that the procedure is carried out in a manner which is as fair as possible. In doing so, he should attempt to ensure that his function is not contravened or subjected to malpractice or unfairness (TULRCA 1992, s 51A(3)). The independent person, if appointed separately from the independent scrutineer, must return the voting papers to the independent scrutineer as soon as is reasonably practical after the completion of the counting of the voting papers (TULRCA 1992, s 51A(5)).

6.170   Trade unions are not allowed to do anything which might compromise the independence of the independent person by reference to his terms of appointment or by interfering, directly or indirectly, with the way in which the tasks of the independent person are carried out. Trade unions are also required to carry out any reasonable request by an independent person to enable the proper completion of the vote count (TULRCA 1992, s 51A(6)).

6.171   After a ballot has been completed and the voting papers returned to the independent scrutineer, the independent scrutineer is required to complete a report under TULRCA 1992, s 52. The report must address similar matters to those detailed at **6.105** in relation to the ballot on trade union political funds under TULRCA 1992, s 78.

6.172   A trade union is not allowed to release the result of a ballot until such time as it has received a copy of the independent scrutineer's report. Once the result has been received, the union must take such steps as are reasonably practicable to ensure that within 3 months of receipt of the report, each member of the union receives a copy of it. Alternatively, a union must distribute the content of the report by taking all such steps as it is the practice of the union to take in bringing to the attention of its members matters of general importance. A union can, in addition, on request from a member of the union, release a copy of the report for free or upon payment of a reasonable fee (TULRCA 1992, s 52(3)–(6)).

Remedies for failure to comply with election requirements

6.173   TULRCA 1992 provides a remedy for a trade union member, or a person who was so at the time of an election for trade union office, and who feels that the union has not complied with the statutory election requirements. Under TULRCA 1992, s 54(1), a trade union member may make an application for a declaration that the union has failed to comply with the statutory election requirements. The application can be made to either the Certification Officer (TULRCA 1992, s 55) or to the High Court (TULRCA 1992, s 56). Where an election has been held, no application under TULRCA 1992, s 55 or 56 with respect to that election may be made after the end of the period of one year beginning with the day on which the union announced the result of the election (TULRCA 1992, s 54(3)).

6.174 The making of an application to the Certification Officer under TULRCA 1992, s 55 does not prevent the making of a subsequent application to the High Court in respect of the same matter (TULRCA 1992, s 54(1)), although the court is bound to have regard to any findings by the Certification Officer (TULRCA 1992, s 56(2)). No right of appeal lies from a decision of the Certification Officer although there remains the possibility of judicially reviewing a decision or making an application to the High Court.

6.175 Under TULRCA 1992, s 55(2), on an application being made to him, the Certification Officer must, so far as possible within 6 months of an application being made to him (TULRCA 1992, s 55(6)), make such inquiries as he thinks fit, give the applicant and the trade union an opportunity to be heard, and may make or refuse the declaration asked for and provide written reasons for his decision (together with any written observations relating to the process) (TULRCA 1992, s 55(5)).

6.176 If the Certification Officer makes a declaration he shall specify in it the provisions with which the trade union has failed to comply (TULRCA 1992, s 55(3)). Further, where a declaration is made and the Certification Officer is satisfied that steps have been taken by the union with a view to remedying the declared failure, or securing that a failure of the same or any similar kind does not occur in future, or that the union has agreed to take such steps, the Certification Officer must specify those steps in the declaration (TULRCA 1992, s 55(4)). Furthermore, under TULRCA 1992, s 55(5A), the declaration is to be accompanied by an Enforcement Order imposing on the union one or more of the following requirements:

- the securing of the holding of a properly compliant election in accordance with the Enforcement Order within a stated time-limit;
- the taking of such other steps to remedy the declared failure as may be specified in the Enforcement Order within a stated time-limit; and
- a requirement to abstain from such acts as may be so specified with a view to securing that a failure of the same or a similar kind does not occur in future.

6.177 A declaration and an Enforcement Order are treated as if they were issued by the court (TULRCA 1992, s 55(8) and (9)) and in the case of an Enforcement Order under TULRCA 1992, s 55(5C), may be enforced by any person who is a member of the union and was a member at the time the order was made, or any person who is or was a candidate in the election in question.

6.178 Similar rights to apply for declarations and an Enforcement Order lie in the case of an application to the High Court under TULRCA 1992, s 56.

6.179 Any error in the counting of a ballot by an independent person will not be sufficient to require a fresh ballot to be held if the error is an accidental one and would not influence the result of the election (TULRCA 1992, s 51(5)(b)).

6.180 To the extent that an official is elected in an election which is subsequently found to have a material procedural irregularity, anything done by the elected official on behalf of the union between the result of the ballot and the subsequent declaration of invalidity will still be treated as a valid act of the union (TULRCA 1992, s 61(2)).

THE RIGHT TO PREVENT MISUSE OF TRADE UNION PROPERTY

6.181   Two discreet rights are covered under this head, these being the right to prevent a trade union from granting unlawful indemnities in respect of its members, and the right of a trade union member to prevent a trustee of union property from acting improperly in relation to that property. The theme of the legislation under this head is to make trade unions accountable to their members.

The right to prevent unlawful indemnities

6.182   The right is provided under TULRCA 1992, s 15(3) and covers the case where, for example, a trade union uses its assets to pay a fine imposed upon a union member as a result of some unlawful offence or contempt of court whilst the member was taking part in activities of the union.

6.183   The common law previously allowed the payment of fines incurred by a member of a trade union if the union's rulebook made specific provision for payment in such cases. The provision was held to cover only such fines as had actually been incurred by members of the union, and the union was not allowed prospectively to authorise payment for offences which might be committed by members of the union at some future point in time.[61]

6.184   The position now is that TULRCA 1992, s 15(1) states the following acts to be unlawful uses of a union's property:

- the payment for an individual of a penalty which has been or may be imposed on him for an offence or for contempt of court;
- the securing of any such payment; and
- the provision of anything for indemnifying an individual in respect of such a penalty.

6.185   If a trade union applies its property for any of the purposes listed under TULRCA 1992, s 15(1), any member receiving the benefit of union property in those circumstances becomes liable to account to the union for the value of the property received by him, or applied for his benefit (TULRCA 1992, s 15(2)). To the extent that a union fails to institute proceedings to recover the property, under TULRCA 1992, s 15(3), an individual member may institute proceedings on behalf of the union to recover the property so applied.

Action against trustees of trade union property

6.186   A right of action exists against trade union trustees under TULRCA 1992, s 16 for any member of a trade union who claims that a trustee of the union has either:

---

[61]   See, for example, *Drake v Morgan* [1978] ICR 56; and *Thomas v NUM (South Wales Area)* [1985] ICR 136.

- carried out the trustee's functions so as to enable either an unlawful use of the union's property to take place; or
- complied with an unlawful direction with regard to the use of the union's property.

6.187   The position under TULRCA 1992, s 16(1) and (2) is that an application to the court may be made by any member of the union who was a member at the time that the property was misapplied or was so when a direction to use the property improperly was complied with. The court may make such orders as it thinks fit for the removal of one or more of the trustees of the union and can compel the trustees to initiate action to recover the property which has been misapplied (TULRCA 1992, s 16(3)).

6.188   The right under TULRCA 1992, s 16 is available in addition to any other cause of action that may exist for breach of trust on the part of the trustees (TULRCA 1992, s 16(6)).

Chapter 7

TRADE UNION-RELATED EMPLOYMENT RIGHTS

7.1 This chapter will focus upon the rights that exist for both trade union members and those wishing to abstain from such membership, in respect of their employment. As with so much of recent trade union law, this area has been developed radically over the past 25 years, in particular in relation to the existence of the closed shop. Two principal groups of rights exist, these being the right to associate (or to dissociate) with a trade union and the right to participate in the activities of a trade union.

THE RIGHT TO ASSOCIATE

Trade union members

7.2 As was stated in **Chapter 1**, the main thrust of trade union law in the last century until 1979 was aimed at attempting to let trade unions and employers regulate their own affairs through legal abstention in the arena of industrial relations. Trade unions were seen as a valuable force in regulating industrial relations and to this end, the closed shop, ie the right of one or more trade unions to insist that employees employed by a particular employer were members of that or those trade unions, was encouraged. However, this position changed upon the enactment of the Industrial Relations Act 1971 (IRA 1971), which provided a right not to be unfairly dismissed where the dismissal was in connection with a closed shop practice. This right was repealed under the Trade Union and Labour Relations Act 1974 (TULRA 1974) and a new right was subsequently provided so that it became automatically fair to dismiss in connection with a closed shop.

7.3 As a result of legislative changes in the 1980s, trade union membership became a neutral factor in the workplace through which now no advantages arise from either belonging or not belonging to a trade union.

7.4 The law has moved further than just providing a right not to be unfairly dismissed and the position as it now stands is that the following rights exist for an employee against his employer in the context of trade unions and employment:

- the right not to be refused employment for a trade union-related reason;
- the right not to have action short of dismissal taken against an employee for a trade union-related reason;
- the right not to be unfairly dismissed for a trade union-related reason;
- the right not to be made redundant for a trade union-related reason;

- the right not to be unfairly dismissed in connection with certain types of industrial action; and
- the right not to be 'blacklisted' by an employer for a trade union-related reason,

each of which will be examined in turn.

REFUSAL TO OFFER EMPLOYMENT FOR A TRADE UNION-RELATED REASON

7.5   The right not to be discriminated against in relation to an offer of employment being made for a trade union-related reason was one of the last changes made to the closed-shop reforms of the 1980s and early 1990s and was introduced by the Employment Act 1990 (EA 1990). Following the consolidation of trade union law generally into the Trade Union and Labour Relations (Consolidation) Act 1992 (TULRCA 1992), the provision was carried over as TULRCA 1992, s 137 and provides as follows:

'(1)   It is unlawful to refuse a person employment—

(a)   because he is, or is not, a member of a trade union, or
(b)   because he is unwilling to accept a requirement—
   (i) to take steps to become or cease to be, or to remain or not to become, a member of a trade union, or
   (ii) to make payments or suffer deductions in the event of his not being a member of a trade union.'

7.6   The right is widely drafted. A number of points need to be considered in relation to the right.

7.7   First, the concept of 'employment' for the purposes of the right is narrow: under TULRCA 1992, s 143(1), 'employment' means employment under a contract of employment. For the purposes of TULRCA 1992, Crown servants and those employed by the House of Commons and the House of Lords are deemed to be employees (TULRCA 1992, ss 273(4) and (5), 278(4) and (5) respectively). Certain categories of workers are specifically excluded from protection, as follows:

- police officers (TULRCA 1992, s 280);
- share fishermen (TULRCA 1992, s 284); and
- overseas employees (TULRCA 1992, s 285(1)), although employees on British-registered ships are not excluded from protection (TULRCA 1992, s 285(2)).

7.8   Secondly, TULRCA 1992, s 137 defines extensively what amounts to refusing to employ as follows:

'(5)   A person shall be taken to be refused employment if he seeks employment of any description with a person and that person—

(a)   refuses or deliberately omits to entertain and process his application or enquiry, or
(b)   causes him to withdraw or cease to pursue his application or enquiry, or
(c)   refuses or deliberately omits to offer him employment of that description, or

(d) makes him an offer of such employment the terms of which are such as no reasonable employer who wished to fill the post would offer and which is not accepted, or

(e) makes him an offer of such employment but withdraws it or causes him not to accept it.

(6)   Where a person is offered employment on terms which include a requirement that he is, or is not, a member of a trade union, or any such requirement as is mentioned in subsection (1)(b), and he does not accept the offer because he does not satisfy or, as the case may be, is unwilling to accept that requirement, he shall be treated as having been refused employment for that reason.'

7.9   Further, TULRCA 1992, s 137(3) deals with the situation where an employer places or causes to be placed, an advertisement which is discriminatory for a trade union-related reason. It provides:

'(3)   Where an advertisement is published which indicates, or might reasonably be understood as indicating—

(a) that employment to which the advertisement relates is open only to a person who is, or is not, a member of a trade union, or

(b) that any such requirement as is mentioned in subsection (1)(b) will be imposed in relation to employment to which the advertisement relates,

a person who does not satisfy that condition or, as the case may be, is unwilling to accept that requirement, and who seeks and is refused employment to which the advertisement relates, shall be conclusively presumed to have been refused employment for that reason.'

7.10   It is not a criminal offence to place an advertisement offering employment to trade union or non-trade union member employees (contrast the position under the Sex Discrimination Act 1975, s 38(5) and the Race Relations Act 1976, s 29(5), although not the Disability Discrimination Act 1995, the Employment Equality (Religion or Religious Belief) Regulations 2003[1] or the Employment Equality (Sexual Orientation) Regulations 2003[2]).

7.11   Furthermore, in the event that a trade union is offered the chance to vet applicants for employment with an employer (as used to happen, for example, in much of the printing industry), and it considers or approves only members of the union, this practice is outlawed under TULRCA 1992, s 137(4), which provides:

'(4) Where there is an arrangement or practice under which employment is offered only to persons put forward or approved by a trade union, and the trade union puts forward or approves only persons who are members of the union, a person who is not a member of the union and who is refused employment in pursuance of the arrangement or practice shall be taken to have been refused employment because he is not a member of the trade union.'

---

[1]   SI 2003/1660.
[2]   SI 2003/1661.

7.12   Additionally, the concept of 'trade union membership' for the purposes of the rights under TULRCA 1992, s 137 is defined under TULRCA 1992, s 143(3), which provides as follows:

'(3)   References in sections 137 to 143 to being or not being a member of a trade union are to being or not being a member of any trade union, of a particular trade union, or of one of a number of particular trade unions.'

7.13   Accordingly, it is not open to an employer to argue that it does not object to employing trade union members generally, but that it objects to employing employees who are members of a particular union.

7.14   One of the problems that has arisen from the drafting of TULRCA 1992, s 137 is that, unlike TULRCA 1992, ss 146 and 152 (dealing with action short of dismissal for a trade union-related reason and unfair dismissal where the reason for the action is a trade union-related reason), TULRCA 1992, s 137 does not cover the concept of refusing to employ due to a person taking part in trade union-related activities. This point has been discussed in *Discount Tobacco and Confectionery Limited v Armitage*;[3] *Associated Newspapers Limited v Wilson and Associated British Ports v Palmer*;[4] *Harrison v Kent County Council*;[5] and *Speciality Care plc v Pachela*.[6] Unfortunately, many of these cases do not deal directly with the pre-employment right not to be discriminated against.

7.15   The *Discount Tobacco* case[7] arose from the claimant enlisting the help of a trade union official to obtain a copy of her terms and conditions of employment. Before receiving this information, the claimant was dismissed for what was described by her employer as her lack of suitability for the job. The claimant presented proceedings against her employer claiming that she had been unfairly dismissed and that the real reason for her dismissal was her trade union membership. An industrial tribunal held that the claimant had been dismissed because of her trade union membership. The employer appealed alleging that there was a difference between dismissing because of an employee's status as a trade union member and taking part in the activities of a trade union. On appeal the Employment Appeal Tribunal (EAT) held that:[8]

'We find ourselves unconvinced of [the] distinction. In our judgment, the activities of a trade union officer in negotiating and elucidating terms of employment is, to use a prayer book expression, the outward and visible manifestation of trade union membership. It is an incident of union membership which is, if not the primary one, at any rate, a very important one and we see no genuine distinction between membership of a union on the one hand and making use of the essential services of a union, on the other.

Were it not so, the scope of [TULRCA 1992, s 152] would be reduced almost to vanishing point, since it would be only just the fact that a person

---

3   [1990] IRLR 15.
4   [1995] IRLR 258.
5   [1995] ICR 43.
6   [1996] IRLR 248.
7   *Discount Tobacco and Confectionery Limited v Armitage* [1990] IRLR 15.
8   [1990] IRLR 15 at 16.

was a member of a union, without regard to the consequences of that membership, that would be the subject matter of that statutory provision and, it seems to us, that to construe that paragraph so narrowly would really be to emasculate the provision altogether.'

7.16 The problem with this case is that in the context of the right under TULRCA 1992, s 137, it is merely obiter. Further, the credibility of the EAT decision in the *Discount Tobacco* case[9] was undermined by the decision of the House of Lords in the joint appeals of *Associated Newspapers Limited v Wilson and Associated British Ports v Palmer*[10] (*'Wilson and Palmer'*).

7.17 The *Wilson and Palmer* cases[11] concerned proceedings brought in relation to the right not to have action short of dismissal taken against an employee for a trade union-related reason. During proceedings in *Wilson and Palmer* before the House of Lords, their Lordships considered the *Discount Tobacco*[12] decision and held that it was a case concerning trade union membership. Their Lordships also held that there ought to be a distinction drawn between trade union membership per se, on the one hand, and taking part in the activities of a trade union, on the other. In particular, Lord Bridge stated that the decision in *Discount Tobacco* provided, at best, an unnecessary gloss on the language of TULRCA 1992 and, at worst, distorted the meaning of TULRCA 1992. Lord Slynn, who dissented on this point, held that:[13]

'... I do not consider that action "preventing or deterring" someone from being a member of a trade union or penalising him for doing so is limited to action taken in respect of his status as a member; the fact that he has or wants to have a union membership card. It may include action to prevent or deter him from, or action penalising him for, exercising his rights as a member of a trade union. The exercise of such rights is not necessarily included in the phrase "taking part in the activities" of a trade union, words more apt to cover such activities as attending union meetings or acting as an official of the union.'

7.18 Lord Browne-Wilkinson, who also dissented on this point in *Wilson and Palmer*[14] did not express an opinion although he added that he did not share Lord Bridge's view.

7.19 However, *Wilson and Palmer*[15] was subsequently successfully appealed to the European Court of Human Rights (ECHR) and the right not to have action short of dismissal taken for a trade union-related reason was then amended under the Employment Relations Act 2004 (ERA 2004) (see **7.37** et seq). Consequently, the House of Lords decision in *Wilson and Palmer* insofar as it interprets *Discount Tobacco*,[16] may well be of little use in providing guidance in relation to the right under TULRCA 1992, s 137 not to suffer pre-employment discrimination for a trade union-related reason.

---

9   *Discount Tobacco and Confectionery Limited v Armitage* [1990] IRLR 15.
10   [1995] IRLR 258.
11   [1995] IRLR 258.
12   *Discount Tobacco and Confectionery Limited v Armitage* [1990] IRLR 15.
13   [1995] IRLR 258 at 265.
14   [1995] IRLR 258.
15   [1995] IRLR 258.
16   *Discount Tobacco and Confectionery Limited v Armitage* [1990] IRLR 15.

7.20   *Harrison v Kent County Council*[17] specifically deals with TULRCA 1992, s 137. Here, the EAT dealt with an appeal by the claimant against the decision of an industrial tribunal refusing his claim that he had been discriminated against on grounds of his trade union membership prior to employment. The claimant was a social worker who had been a trade union member and had taken part as a trade union official in organising industrial action. He applied to the respondent for a job and was rejected on the ground that because of his previous trade union activity, he was likely to be unco-operative given his past anti-management style. The EAT allowed the appeal holding that the industrial tribunal had misdirected itself as to the law, stating:[18]

> 'The industrial tribunal's construction of section 137(1) of the Act of 1992 [TULRCA 1992, s 137(1)] takes a narrower view of the conceptual limits of membership of a trade union than is expressed by the ordinary and natural meaning of the section. The fallacy in the tribunal's approach is to proceed by analogy with section 146(1) and section 152(1), to draw a rigid distinction between, on the one hand, membership of a trade union and, on the other hand, taking part in the activities of a union. Although membership and activities are specified in separate paragraphs of section 146(1) and section 152(1), it does not follow that they are self-contained, mutually exclusive categories or concepts ...

> The construction adopted by the [tribunal] would have a consequence inconsistent with promoting the purpose of the provision. The purpose of section 137(1)(a) of the 1992 Act is to protect a person from being discriminated in access to employment on grounds related to union membership. In reality, the persons most likely to be discriminated against are those who have been most active in membership.'

7.21   The point that comes out of these cases is that the protection provided under TULRCA 1992, s 137 is different to that provided under TULRCA 1992, ss 146 and 152 (respectively, the rights not to suffer action short of dismissal or to be discriminated against for a trade union-related reason). Whilst the House of Lords in the in *Wilson and Palmer*[19] cast doubts on the view that a person's status as a trade union member and their activities are one and the same, it seems clear that the purposive construction in *Harrison*,[20] which directly addresses the point at issue under TULRCA 1992, s 137, is to be preferred in this regard.

Causation

7.22   One last avenue that is open to an employer who has failed to employ a person due to a trade union-related reason is to argue that there is no causal link between membership of the trade union and the failure to employ the job applicant: the trade union-related reason must be the proximate cause of the failure to employ the job applicant. Therefore, if an employer can prove that another reason existed for failing to employ a job applicant (for example, because the job applicant had lied about being a member of a trade union and

---

[17]   [1995] ICR 434.
[18]   [1995] ICR 434 at 444.
[19]   [1995] IRLR 258.
[20]   *Harrison v Kent County Council* [1995] ICR 434.

the employer genuinely and reasonably believed that such behaviour would undermine the employer's trust and confidence in the working relationship), the employer may be able to defend an action presented under this head.[21]

Employment agencies

7.23   The duty not to discriminate against a job applicant is also extended by TULRCA 1992, s 138 to cover the conduct of employment agencies instructed by an employer. TULRCA 1992, s 138(1) provides that it is unlawful for an employment agency to refuse to provide any of its services to a person because that person is or is not a trade union member or because that person is unwilling to take steps to become or cease to be a member of a trade union.

7.24   As to when an employment agency is taken to have refused to provide a service, TULRCA 1992, s 138(4) states that this occurs where an employment agency:

●   refuses or deliberately omits to provide the service to a claimant;
●   causes the claimant not to avail himself of the services or to cease using the services of the agency; or
●   provides the claimant with a different service or with a service on different terms to those that it would provide to others.

7.25   An employment agency is also taken to have discriminated against a person seeking to use its services where it makes an offer to provide services to that person but does so only under condition that one of the prohibited grounds under TULRCA 1992, s 138(1) is satisfied and the person to whom the offer is made refuses to comply with that condition (TULRCA 1992, s 138(5)).

7.26   Additionally, where an employment agency publishes an advertisement which could reasonably be taken to indicate that its services would not be available to a person who is or is not a trade union member, or is or is not willing to take steps to become or cease to be such a member, it is deemed to have acted unlawfully to the extent that such a person applies to the agency to use its services and the agency refuses to provide the services for the reasons stated in TULRCA 1992, s 137 (TULRCA 1992, s 138(3)).

7.27   Where an employment agency issues an advertisement which causes a person not to apply to the agency in the first place (thereby negating a claim under TULRCA 1992, s 138(3)), this will amount to causation for the purposes of TULRCA 1992, s 138(4)(b) (ie the duty for the employment agency not to discriminate on grounds of trade union status).

Procedure

7.28   In a case where either an employer or an employment agency unlawfully discriminates on grounds of a person's trade union membership against an applicant for, respectively, employment or the provision of an employment agency's services (as set out above), a claim will lie to an employment tribunal under, respectively, TULRCA 1992, ss 137(2) and 138(2). A claim made in either case must be presented to the employment tribunal within 3 months of

---

[21]   See, for example, *Fitzpatrick v British Railways Board* [1991] IRLR 376 on this point.

the unlawful conduct or within such further period as the tribunal considers to be reasonable (TULRCA 1992, s 139(1)).

7.29   The date of conduct giving rise to a claim for the purposes of TULRCA 1992, s 137 is defined by TULRCA 1992, s 139(2) as being:

'(a) in the case of an actual refusal, the date of the refusal;
(b) in the case of a deliberate omission—
    (i) to entertain or process the complainant's application or enquiry, or
    (ii) to offer employment,
the end of the period within which it was reasonable to expect the employer to act;
(c) in the case of conduct causing the complainant to withdraw or cease to pursue his application or enquiry, the date of that conduct;
(d) in a case where an offer was made but withdrawn, the date when it was withdrawn;
(e) in any other case where an offer was made but not accepted, the date on which it was made.'

7.30   For the purposes of discrimination by an employment agency under TULRCA 1992, s 138, the date of conduct giving rise to the claim is defined by TULRCA 1992, s 139(3) as being:

'(a) in the case of an actual refusal, the date of the refusal;
(b) in the case of a deliberate omission to make a service available, the end of the period within which it was reasonable to expect the employment agency to act;
(c) in the case of conduct causing the complainant not to avail himself of a service or to cease to avail himself of it, the date of that conduct;
(d) in the case of failure to provide the same service, on the same terms, as is provided to others, the date or last date on which the service in fact was provided.'

7.31   Where a person considers making an allegation against both a prospective employer and an employment agency arising out of the same facts, the application can be made jointly against the prospective employer and the employment agency or against either of them (TULRCA 1992, s 141(1)). An employment tribunal dealing with a dispute must join the employer or the employment agency (as the case may be) to the proceedings where a request to join is made at any time prior to the hearing of the case (although employment tribunals can refuse to do so after a hearing has started). An employment tribunal is not allowed to join a party to a case after it has decided on the issue of liability in a dispute (TULRCA 1992, s 141(2)).

7.32   It is also possible for an employment tribunal to which a claim has been presented under TULRCA 1992, s 137 or 138 to join as a third party to the proceedings any trade union or other person who has called, organised, procured or financed a strike or other industrial action, or has threatened to do so where the purpose of that person's action is to induce an employer or employment agency to behave in a discriminatory fashion for the purposes of TULRCA 1992, s 137 or 138. The application can be made by either the claimant or any of the respondents to an action (TULRCA 1992, s 142(1)). As with joining employers or employment agencies, it is possible for an application to join a third party to be made at any time prior to the commencement of a hearing whereupon the employment tribunal must allow the application. If an application to join a third party is made after a case has commenced, the tribunal may reject the application and if it has already decided the outcome of the case, it must reject the application (TULRCA 1992, s 142(2)).

Remedies

7.33 An employment tribunal hearing a claim under TULRCA 1992, s 137 or 138 which finds for the claimant must make a declaration to that effect. In addition, if and to the extent that the employment tribunal considers just and equitable, the tribunal can make an award of compensation and/or make a recommendation that the respondent takes such action as is necessary, within a specified period, to reduce the adverse effect of the discrimination to the claimant (TULRCA 1992, s 140(1)).

7.34 In making an award of compensation, an employment tribunal must apply the rules relating to damages for breach of statutory duty and it may make an award to reflect injury to feelings suffered by the claimant (TULRCA 1992, s 140(2)).

7.35 As to cases concerning injury to feelings in other areas of discrimination, regard should be had to *Vento v Chief Constable of West Yorkshire Police (No 2)*,[22] which provides guidance as to the bands of compensation which are recoverable for injury to feelings (broadly, three bands, depending upon the seriousness of the employer's default being £1,000–£5,000 for minor injury to feelings; £5,000–£15,000 for more serious cases); and £15,000–£25,000 for the most serious cases. *Orlando v Didcot Power Station Sports & Social Club*[23] sets down the principles which employment tribunals should take into account in awarding compensation under this head. Unlike cases involving other forms of unlawful discrimination (compensation for which is not subject to any statutory cap on the amount of compensation to be awarded), trade union-related discrimination cases are subject to a cap on the maximum amount of compensation that can be awarded, this being the same as the cap on compensation for unfair dismissal under the Employment Rights Act 1996 (TULRCA 1992, s 140(4)).

7.36 Where proceedings have been presented jointly against an employer and an employment agency and an employment tribunal finds in favour of the claimant, it can award compensation to be paid by either or both respondents in such amounts as it thinks fit (TULRCA 1992, s 141(3)). Further, where a third party has been joined to the proceedings under the provisions of TULRCA 1992, s 142 an employment tribunal can make an award of compensation against any or all of the employer, employment agency or third party as the tribunal thinks fit in all the circumstances of the case (TULRCA 1992, s 142(3)–(4)).

DETRIMENT IMPOSED FOR A TRADE UNION-RELATED REASON

7.37 The right for an employee not to have action short of dismissal taken against him for a reason related to his trade union membership is one that has existed in statutory form in one shape or another since IRA 1971. When it was

---

[22]   [2003] IRLR 102.
[23]   [1996] IRLR 262.

introduced under IRA 1971, s 5, the right was for an employee either to be or not be a member of a registered trade union under IRA 1971 and, if the employee was a member of such a union, to take part in the activities of the union at an appropriate time. IRA 1971 was repealed and replaced by TULRA 1974. The provision under IRA 1971, s 5 was replaced by the Employment Protection Act 1975 (EPA 1975), s 53 (which was itself subsequently incorporated into the Employment Protection (Consolidation) Act 1978 (EPCA 1978) as s 23). As EPCA 1978, s 23, the purpose of the provision changed to provide a right to take part in trade union activities and not to be forced into joining an employer's staff association. EPCA 1978, s 23 was then itself changed during the course of the early 1980s trade union reforms under, variously, the Employment Act (EA) 1980, EA 1982 and EA 1988 before being consolidated into TULRCA 1992, s 146. Further changes were then incorporated into TULRCA 1992, s 146 by the Trade Union Reform and Employment Rights Act 1993 (TURERA 1993), s 13, and the Employment Relations Act 1999 (ERA 1999), s 2 and Sch 2. Most recently, amendments have been made to TULRCA 1992, s 146 by ERA 2004 as a result of the decision of the ECHR in the joint application of *Wilson and Palmer v The United Kingdom*[24] ('*Wilson and Palmer No 2*'), including, in particular, the creation of a new right not to have inducements being made to a worker as a result of his status as a member or non-member of a trade union (under TULRCA 1992, s 145A et seq, in respect of which, see **7.74** et seq).

7.38   The formulation of the right not to suffer action short of dismissal due to an worker's status as a member or non-member of a trade union is now provided under TULRCA 1992, s 146. The right is neutral in that its formulation requires that an employer shall not take action taken against a person because he is or is not a union member or a member of a particular union or takes part in the activities of an independent trade union at an appropriate time.

7.39   The right is not available to share fishermen (TULRCA 1992, s 284) or overseas employees (TULRCA 1992, s 285, although it is available to workers on British registered ships under TULRCA 1992, s 285(2)). Crown servants, House of Lords and House of Commons staff are specifically granted the right under TULRCA 1992, s 146 (per TULRCA 1992, ss 273, 277 and 278 respectively).

Scope of the right

7.40   TULRCA 1992, s 146 provides the following:

'(1)   A worker has the right not to be subjected to any detriment as an individual by any act, or any deliberate failure to act, by his employer if the act or failure takes place for the sole or main purpose of—

(a)   preventing or deterring him from being or seeking to become a member of an independent trade union, or penalising him for doing so,

(b)   preventing or deterring him from taking part in the activities of an independent trade union at an appropriate time, or penalising him for doing so,

---

[24]   [2002] IRLR 568.

(ba) preventing or deterring him from making use of trade union services at an appropriate time, or penalising him for doing so, or

(c) compelling him to be or become a member of any trade union or of a particular trade union or of one of a number of particular trade unions.'

7.41 TULRCA 1992, s 146(1) was amended following changes introduced by ERA 2004, the reason for which will become clear in the following paragraphs. A number of the points in this definition require explanation, as follows.

Action

7.42 The right under TULRCA 1992, s 146 can be breached by an employer in any of the four ways listed above. In connection with these different ways of breaching the right, the first point is where an employer takes 'action' against a worker. The question of what amounts to 'action' for these purposes has been the subject of protracted litigation in *Wilson and Palmer*[25] and *Wilson and Palmer No 2*.[26]

7.43 Prior to the *Wilson and Palmer* litigation,[27] the accepted meaning of the word 'action' in relation to this right was as set down in *Ridgway v National Coal Board*.[28] *Ridgway* concerned a dispute arising out of the aftermath of the Miners' Strike 1984–1985. At the end of this strike, the National Coal Board (NCB) entered into negotiations with a newly created union, the Union of Democratic Mineworkers (UDM), for the purposes of setting wage levels in the coal mining industry. The negotiations resulted in UDM members being granted similar wages to employees who were members of the National Union of Mineworkers (NUM). However, at one colliery, members of the UDM were paid enhanced salaries but members of the NUM were not. The claimant, who was an NUM member, presented a claim under EPCA 1978, s 23, claiming that by not giving him similar wages to employees who were UDM members, the NCB had taken action short of dismissal in order to make him become a member of the UDM. The NCB defended the action claiming that they had not taken 'action' against the claimant but had merely omitted to grant him a pay rise. On appeal, the Court of Appeal held that the omission to grant a pay rise to members of the NUM amounted to 'action' for the purposes of EPCA 1978, s 23, stating that:[29]

'... to draw the suggested distinction between action and omission would produce absurd results. Take the case of an employer who provides car parking permits for employees but not as part of the terms of their employment. If he were to give permits to only such of his employees as did not belong to a trade union, for the purpose of penalising other employees for belonging to a union, on the Coal Board's argument the failure to provide car parking permits for the union members could only

---

25 [1995] IRLR 258.
26 [2002] IRLR 568.
27 *Associated Newspapers Limited v Wilson and Associated British Ports v Palmer* [1995] IRLR 258; *Wilson and Palmer v The United Kingdom* [2002] IRLR 568.
28 [1987] IRLR 80.
29 [1987] IRLR 80 at 87.

constitute an "omission" if the union members had a reasonable expectation that they too would receive the permits. But if the sequence of events were altered, and all employees had received car parking permits and then for the purpose of penalising the union members, the employer withdrew their permits, that would constitute "action" and would be remediable under [TULRCA 1992, s 146] regardless of whether the complainants had any reasonable expectation that they would continue to hold the permits. That cannot be right ...

It is natural for lawyers to think of omissions in terms of failure to perform a duty. That is how omissions feature in the law of negligence. It is also an acceptable dictionary definition. But it is not a necessary definition. An omission need be no more than a mere failure or neglect to act. This, I think, is the natural meaning here, where "omission" appears as the simple converse of "action". No notion of duty or obligation attaches to the concept of "action". Nor should it, I think, to the concept of action. If, of course, that which the employer has omitted to do is something which he would not have been expected to do and would not in the ordinary way have done, a Tribunal is unlikely to conclude that the omission was for an objectionable purpose within the subsection. I do not, however, think that there is a reason for giving this familiar word anything other than what seems to me its natural and straightforward meaning.'

7.44   Importantly, the case was decided on the basis of the word 'action' as defined in EPCA 1978, s 153, which provided that 'action' included an omission. The problem was enlarged in that, due to the convoluted legislative history of what is now TULRCA 1992, s 146, upon the right being consolidated into EPCA 1978, this was the first time that a definition of 'action' had been provided by the legislation under which the provision arose: neither IRA 1971 nor EPA 1975 had contained a definition of action.

7.45   The position was reviewed in the *Associated Newspapers* case. The facts of the case were that the employer, the owner of a newspaper, had decided to scrap collective bargaining in order to pursue pay reviews on an individual basis. The claimant, who was a journalist employed by Associated Newspapers, was a member of the National Union of Journalists (NUJ). The NUJ was one of the unions that would be affected as a result of the abolition of collective bargaining by the employer. In order to achieve its aim of individual negotiations, the employer offered a 4.5 per cent pay rise to all employees prepared to negotiate individually. Those employees not accepting individual bargaining did not get the pay rise. The claimant contended that this was action short of dismissal. He succeeded in proceedings before the industrial tribunal, lost on appeal in the EAT[30] and further succeeded in the Court of Appeal[31] (where his claim was joined with *Palmer v Associated British Ports* to become *Wilson and Palmer*[32]). After the claimant succeeded in the Court of Appeal, the Government introduced changes in the form of TURERA 1993, s 13 which amended the evidence that employment tribunals could take into account in reaching a decision so as to allow them to look at whether an employer was seeking to

---

[30]   [1992] IRLR 440.

[31]   [1993] IRLR 336.

[32]   *Associated Newspapers Limited v Wilson and Associated British Ports v Palmer* [1995] IRLR 258.

further a change with a class of his employees even though this might otherwise contravene TULRCA 1992, s 146. An employment tribunal hearing a case was then obliged to examine the employer's reason for promoting the change and, unless it was action such that no reasonable employer would take, the tribunal was to disregard the fact that it would otherwise be action short of dismissal.[33]

7.46 The employer then appealed the case to the House of Lords.[34] The House of Lords, by a majority, held that the employer had not taken 'action' against the claimant. Their Lordships so held on the basis that, although reliance was placed on the meaning of the word 'act' as defined by EPCA 1978, s 153 (now carried over as TULRCA 1992, s 298) which includes an omission to act, since the original enactment of the provision under IRA 1971 did not contain a definition of what amounts to action, the definition of 'act' provided under EPCA 1978, s 153 could not be used in construing the meaning of the word 'act'. This was because EPCA 1978 was a consolidation and the accepted convention in relation to consolidations is that they would not have been expected to alter the pre-existing law. Accordingly, the majority of the House of Lords felt free to approach the question as to what amounted to 'act' as a new point of law. The majority of their Lordships held that action meant positive acts and not omissions. It followed from this that since an omission rather than a positive course of action had taken place, no claim would arise unless the claimant could show that the purpose of the employer had been to penalise him for being a member of a trade union or to deter him from being a union member (as opposed to deterring him from making use of the services of a union), which, on the facts, he could not.

7.47 Following the House of Lords decision in *Wilson and Palmer*,[35] it became extremely difficult for an employee to succeed in a claim brought under TULRCA 1992, s 146 where the employer invoked a policy of trade union derecognition (coupled with 'sweeteners' to persuade employees to deal on an individual basis) because of the combined effect of *Wilson and Palmer* and the changes incorporated by the amendments in TURERA 1993 resulting in the (now repealed) TULRCA 1992, s 148(3)–(5).

7.48 However, an application was then made to the ECHR against the United Kingdom in *Wilson and Palmer No 2*[36] by the claimants on the basis that the United Kingdom had failed in its positive obligation under the European Convention on Human Rights, Art 11 to protect the claimants rights to freedom of peaceful assembly, freedom of association and the right to join a trade union by allowing employers to use financial incentives to induce employees to surrender important trade union rights. The ECHR found for the claimants and awarded them €7,730 each by way of compensation.

7.49 Following the ECHR victory for the claimants in *Wilson and Palmer No 2*,[37] the Government amended the principles under TULRCA 1992, s 146 in connection with the right not to have action short of dismissal taken against an employee for a trade union-related reason. The Government did this by

---

[33] This was previously provided under the now repealed TULRCA 1992, s 148(3)–(5).
[34] [1995] IRLR 258.
[35] [1995] IRLR 258.
[36] [2002] IRLR 568.
[37] [2002] IRLR 568.

introducing amendments to TULRCA 1992 under ERA 2004 in relation to the right not to have to have action short of dismissal taken against an employee (see **7.50** et seq) and, by introducing new rights not to have to suffer inducements due to a worker's trade union status (discussed at **7.74**).

7.50   The amendments made under ERA 2004 initially made two substantial amendments to the scope of the right not to have to suffer action short of dismissal for a trade union-related reason. First, the scope of the right was extended from covering only 'employees' to covering 'workers'. Secondly, the nature of the right was extended from covering 'action short of dismissal' to workers suffering a 'detriment'. Consequently, older case law in the area must now be treated with a degree of caution as it may not take in all of the new concepts in relation to the right.

7.51   Although the main formulation of the right of a worker not to suffer a detriment for a trade union-related reason is set out at **7.40**, under TULRCA 1992, s 146(3) a worker has the right not to be subjected to any detriment as an individual by any act, or any deliberate failure to act, by his employer if the act or failure takes place for the sole or main purpose of enforcing a requirement (whether or not imposed by a contract of employment or in writing) that, in the event of his not being a member of any trade union or of a particular trade union or of one of a number of particular trade unions, he must make one or more payments. This might arise, for example, where a trade union requires that non-members pay a sum in lieu of the value of a trade union subscription to a third party.

7.52   Further, a claimant has to be subjected to a detriment 'as an individual', in order for a claim under TULRCA 1992, s 146 to arise. This point was considered by the Court of Appeal in *FW Farnsworth Limited v McCoid*,[38] a case involving the derecognition pursuant to a collective agreement by the respondent of a trade union member in his capacity as a shop steward on grounds that the claimant's conduct had come into question. The Court of Appeal held that action taken by the respondent which affected the claimant only arose from his position as shop steward. The court held that the inclusion of the words 'as an individual' in the formulation of TULRCA 1992, s 146 was for the purpose of excluding collective disputes from the ambit of TULRCA 1992, s 146. The court added that derecognition of a shop steward was severely damaging to an individual and should give rise to an action to see if the respondent was justified in doing what did.

7.53   Under TULRCA 1992, s 146(4) any deduction made by an employer from the remuneration payable to a worker in respect of his employment, if it is attributable to his not being a member of any trade union or of a particular trade union or of one of a number of particular trade unions, is deemed to be a detriment to which he has been subjected as an individual by an act of his employer taking place for the sole or main purpose of enforcing a requirement under TULRCA 1992, s 146(3).

Detriment resulting from taking part in trade union activity at an appropriate time

7.54   A further case in which the provisions of TULRCA 1992, s 146(1) are important is in the case where an employer takes action against workers for taking part in the 'activities of independent trade union' at an 'appropriate time'.

---

[38]   [1999] IRLR 626.

Activities of an independent trade union

7.55   In considering what amounts to taking part in the activities of an independent trade union, a distinction needs to be drawn between action taken against a worker for undertaking activities on his own account and action which is taken against a worker for undertaking activities which have a genuine connection with a trade union. A good illustration of this point under older case law is *Chant v Aquaboats Limited*,[39] a case decided on the basis of a similar provision in connection with unfair dismissal. The claimant was a member of a union, UCATT, and had organised a petition during his working time, claiming that working conditions were unsafe. His employer dismissed him for incapability due to the slowness of his work (which, unsurprisingly, was slowed down by his organising the petition). On appeal, the employee's claim that he was carrying out the activities of an independent trade union at an appropriate time was rejected by the EAT which held that the expression 'activities of an independent trade union' did not include the claimant's activities as a trade union member in organising a petition, notwithstanding that this was something that a trade union might seek to do.

7.56   For the purposes of the right not to suffer a detriment under TULRCA 1992, s 146, the provisions of TULRCA 1992, s 146(2A)–(2D) need to be considered in cases arising after 1 October 2004. In this regard, TULRCA 1992, s 146(2A) provides that 'trade union services' means services made available to the worker by an independent trade union by virtue of his membership of the union. Further, references to a worker's 'making use' of trade union services include his consenting to the raising of a matter on his behalf by an independent trade union of which he is a member.

7.57   Additionally, under TULRCA 1992, s 146(2B), if an independent trade union of which a worker is a member raises a matter on the worker's behalf (with or without his consent), and the worker's employer penalises the worker for that, this is specifically stated to be penalising the worker for the purposes of the right not to suffer a detriment as mentioned in TULRCA 1992, s 146(1)(ba). Furthermore, under TULRCA 1992, s 146(2C), workers also have the right not to be subjected to any detriment as an individual by their employer by any act, or any deliberate failure to act, if the act or failure takes place because of the worker's failure to accept an offered inducement made in contravention of TULRCA 1992, s 145A or 145B (this directly addressing the form of discrimination arising under *Wilson and Palmer No 2*[40]). Particularly, not conferring a benefit that, if the offer had been accepted by the worker, would have been conferred on him under the resulting agreement is stated to be a detriment and to be a deliberate failure to act (TULRCA 1992, s 145(2D)).

7.58   Further examples under older case law of what amounts to the activities of an independent trade union have included:

- *Miller v Rafique*[41] (taking part in a trade union meeting);
- *Marley Tile Co Limited v Shaw*[42] (consulting a shop steward or other trade union official); and

---

39   [1978] ICR 643.
40   [2002] IRLR 568.
41   [1975] IRLR 70.
42   [1978] ICR 828.

- *Dixon v West Ella Developments Limited*[43] (recruiting trade union members).

7.59   By way of contrast, in *Lyon and Scherk v St James Press Limited*,[44] the EAT held that where the claimants had been dismissed for secretly organising a chapel of the National Union of Journalists, the dismissal was fair since, on the facts, the act of organising the chapel, at what was a small employer which ran its business openly and informally with its workforce, amounted to a wholly unreasonable act on the part of the members. However, this decision should be followed with caution and is unlikely to have withstood the amendments to TULRCA 1992, s 146 following 1 October 2004 as it does not make a distinction between whether employees behave reasonably or unreasonably; rather it focuses upon whether an employee has taken part in the activities of an independent trade union and it is therefore highly probable that this case is now wrong in law.

'Appropriate time'

7.60   The phrase 'appropriate time' is defined by TULRCA 1992, s 146(2) as to mean:
    '(a) a time outside the worker's working hours, or
    (b) a time within his working hours at which, in accordance with arrangements agreed with or consent given by his employer, it is permissible for him to take part in the activities of a trade union or (as the case may be) make use of trade union services;

    and for this purpose 'working hours', in relation to an worker, means any time when, in accordance with his contract of employment (or other contract personally to do work or perform services), he is required to be at work.'

7.61   Two issues arise here, these being, first, what is meant by the expression 'worker's working time' and, secondly, at what point an employer is taken to provide its consent.

Worker's working time

7.62   One of the problems facing employers is whether a worker's break times from work are within his normal working hours. This was considered by the EAT in *Zucker v Astrid Jewels Limited*.[45] The case was brought under the similar provisions relating to the unfair dismissal of an employee for taking part in the activities of an independent trade union at an appropriate time. The claimant had discussed trade union membership with fellow employees whilst on her lunch and tea breaks. Her employer thought that this was not at an appropriate time for her to be canvassing trade union membership support since the employee was within her working hours (and was still at work), there had been no consent provided to the employee to canvass membership and so the employer believed that it was entitled to dismiss the employee. On appeal, the EAT held that an employee's working hours were those when the employee should actually be working. Consequently, since the employee was not required

---

43   [1978] ICR 856.
44   [1976] IRLR 215.
45   [1978] ICR 1088.

to work during her breaks, she was outside her working hours, albeit that the breaks were a part of her working day when she was required to be on the employer's premises.[46]

7.63 However, it is unlikely that a worker would be able to argue successfully that taking industrial action during the course of a worker's working hours is an 'appropriate time'.[47]

7.64 As to when consent is provided, quite apart from cases where consent is expressly provided, it is possible for consent to be implied.[48] However, it is for those asserting that implied consent exists to prove it has been provided. Ultimately, if an employer has provided consent for a worker to take part in trade union activities, it is possible for an employer to terminate the right on giving notice either under the terms of a collective agreement or reasonable notice in the event that any such collective agreement or ad hoc arrangement is silent with regard to notice or there is no such agreement.

7.65 Finally, if the complaint is that the worker is an employee and the detriment suffered is that the employee has been dismissed, under TULRCA 1992, s 146(5A) the employee cannot claim to have a suffered a 'detriment' under TULRCA 1992, s 146; instead, the employee must pursue a claim under TULRCA 1992, s 152 (unfair dismissal).

Enforcement and procedure

7.66 Where a worker alleges that the right under TULRCA 1992, s 146 has been breached the worker may present a claim to an employment tribunal (TULRCA 1992, s 146(5)). Any claim must be presented within 3 months of the action or the last in any series of actions taken against the worker, or within such other period as an employment tribunal hearing a claim thinks reasonable if it was not reasonably practicable to present a claim within the time-limit (TULRCA 1992, s 147).

7.67 Employers are required to show the sole or main purpose for which any action or failure to act took place (TULRCA 1992, s 148(1)). It is expressly provided that employers are unable to argue that the reason for taking action or failing to act was that they were pressurised into taking action against a claimant by the threat or taking of industrial action (for example, by a trade union) (TULRCA 1992, s 148(2)).

7.68 If action or a failure to act by an employer has occurred in respect of an employee due to pressure from a third party, it is possible to join the third party to the proceedings (TULRCA 1992, s 150(1)). Where an application to join a third party to proceedings is presented before the hearing of a case, an employment tribunal must order the third party to be joined. If a hearing has begun, the tribunal has a discretion to refuse an application to join a third party and once a case has been decided, the tribunal is bound to refuse an application (TULRCA 1992, s 150(2)).

---

[46] See too the decision in *Post Office v Crouch* [1974] ICR 378 dealing with the repealed IRA 1971, s 5 on the same point.
[47] *Brennan v Ellward (Lancs) Limited* [1976] IRLR 378.
[48] *Marley Tile Co Limited v Shaw* [1978] ICR 828.

Remedies

7.69 Where an employment tribunal finds for a claimant in a claim under
TULRCA 1992, s 146, the tribunal is required to make a declaration to that
effect and may make an award of compensation (TULRCA 1992, s 149(1)).
Compensation is awarded in such sum as the tribunal considers to be just and
equitable in the circumstances of a case taking into account the loss suffered by
the claimant. There is no limit to the amount of compensation that can be
awarded.

7.70 Compensation must take account of the costs that have been reasonably
incurred as a consequence of the right being infringed together with the loss of
any benefits that have arisen as a result of the claim (TULRCA 1992, s 149(3)).
It appears that it is possible to recover compensation for injury to feelings
claimed as non-pecuniary loss in a case of trade union-related discrimination.
In *Brassington v Cauldon Wholesale Limited*[49] and *Cheall v Vauxhall Motors
Limited*,[50] the claimant recovered compensation for non-pecuniary loss that
had been suffered. Subsequently, the correctness of these decisions was challenged in *Ridgway v National Coal Board*[51] but the Court of Appeal left the
matter open in that case. In *Cleveland Ambulance NHS Trust v Blane*,[52] the
EAT reaffirmed that it is possible to make an award for non-pecuniary losses.
Further, in *London Borough of Hackney v Adams*,[53] the EAT held that there
was no reason to treat claims of trade union discrimination differently to
claims of sex or race discrimination with regard to award compensation for
injury to feelings. The EAT held further that whilst injury to feelings would
often flow inevitably from an act of sex or race discrimination, the same might
not be true of trade union-related discrimination and that each case would have
to be considered on its own merits with regard to an award of compensation for
injury to feelings. The EAT has also revisited the matter, albeit obiter, in *Virgo
Fidelis Senior School v Boyle*.[54] Here, the EAT was required to consider the case
of a teacher who was dismissed for raising concerns about difficult pupils in a
situation where, inter alia, the teacher had sought to invoke union help in
dealing with the matter. In a very thorough review of the authorities in the area
(including a consideration of the categories of compensation for injury to
feelings in other areas of discrimination law), the EAT discussed fully the issue
of injury to feelings compensation in trade union-related discrimination cases
and held that the *Vento*[55] categories of compensation should be applied to all
cases involving a detriment being suffered by a claimant (including trade union
cases where compensation falls to be awarded under TULRCA 1992, s 149).

7.71 The problem with making an award for non-pecuniary loss under this
head is that it would allow an employee to recover more than he would be able
to recover in the event of his being unfairly dismissed since, following the case
of *Norton Tool Co Limited v Tewson*,[56] it has consistently been held (most

---

[49] [1977] IRLR 479.
[50] [1979] IRLR 253.
[51] [1987] IRLR 80.
[52] [1997] IRLR 332.
[53] [2003] IRLR 402.
[54] [2004] IRLR 268.
[55] *Vento v Chief Constable of West Yorkshire Police (No 2)* [2003] IRLR 102.
[56] [1972] IRLR 86.

recently by the House of Lords in *Dunnachie v Kingston Upon Hull City Council*[57]) that there is no right to compensation for injury to feelings as a result of the manner in which a dismissal is effected by an employer if the statute creating the right does not specifically provide for it. This point was discussed in the *Cleveland Ambulance* case,[58] *London Borough of Hackney v Adams*[59] and *Virgo Fidelis Senior School v Boyle*,[60] all of which accepted that the ambit of the words under TULRCA 1992, s 146 are broad enough to encompass a claim for injury to feelings. However, on the basis that these cases are correct[61] then, following *Dunnachie*, this would produce the anomalous result that an employee who has action short of dismissal taken against him for a trade union-related reason and successfully presented a claim under TULRCA 1992, s 146 would be able to recover compensation for injury to feelings, yet if the employee was dismissed in an otherwise similar factual matrix and had to proceed for a claim of unfair dismissal under TULRCA 1992, s 152 (due to TULRCA 1992, s 146(5A)), the employee would be denied compensation for injury to feelings under *Dunnachie*. However, in the related area of claims for injury to feelings in the context of unjustifiable discipline by a trade union towards one of its members, the EAT has considered the *Dunnachie* argument and rejected it.[62]

7.72 An employment tribunal is also bound to take account of a claimant's duty to mitigate his loss (TULRCA 1992, s 149(4)) and may reduce any compensation that it would otherwise award due to the fact that the claimant has either caused or contributed to his own loss (TULRCA 1992, s 149(6)).

7.73 If action or a failure to act by an employer was prompted due to pressure from a third party who has been joined to the proceedings and an employment tribunal finds for the claimant, it may order that any compensation is payable by the employer or the third party or both, in such amounts as it thinks fit (TULRCA 1992, s 150(3)).

THE RIGHT NOT TO HAVE TO SUFFER TRADE UNION-RELATED INDUCEMENTS

7.74 As stated above, this right was introduced by the Government under ERA 2004 following the decision of the ECHR in *Wilson and Palmer No 2*.[63] The right introduced is for a worker not to have inducements made to him as a result of his status as a member or non-member of a trade union (TULRCA 1992, s 145A et seq). The new right is the counterpart to the right not to have suffer a detriment for a trade union-related reason. In this regard, TULRCA 1992, s 145A(1) provides:

---

[57]   [2004] IRLR 727.
[58]   *Cleveland Ambulance NHS Trust v Blane* [1997] IRLR 332.
[59]   [2003] IRLR 402.
[60]   [2004] IRLR 268.
[61]   Which, following the case of *Skiggs v South West Trains Limited* [2005] IRLR 459 in relation to compensation awarded for injury to feelings under TULRCA 1992, s 172 for failing to allow an employee to take time off for trade union duties, appears to be correct.
[62]   *Beaumont v Amicus MSF*, EAT, 4 August 2004 (0122/03).
[63]   [2002] IRLR 568.

'(1)   A worker has the right not to have an offer made to him by his employer for the sole or main purpose of inducing the worker—

(a) not to be or seek to become a member of an independent trade union,
(b) not to take part, at an appropriate time, in the activities of an independent trade union,
(c) not to make use, at an appropriate time, of trade union services, or
(d) to be or become a member of any trade union or of a particular trade union or of one of a number of particular trade unions.'

7.75   For the purposes of TULRCA 1992, s 145A(2), 'an appropriate time' means either a time outside a worker's working hours, or a time within his working hours at which, in accordance with arrangements agreed with or consent given by his employer, it is permissible for the worker to take part in the activities of a trade union or make use of trade union services. Further, under TULRCA 1992, s 145A(3), 'working hours' are defined to mean any time when, in accordance with his contract of employment (or other contract personally to do work or perform services), he is required to be at work.

7.76   The concepts of what is 'an appropriate time' and what are the worker's 'working hours' are likely to be considered in the same way as the provisions relating to the right not to have action short of dismissal taken against a worker for a trade union-related reason (see **7.60** et seq).

7.77   For the purposes of TULRCA 1992, s 145A(4), 'trade union services' means services made available to the worker by an independent trade union by virtue of his membership of the union, and references to a worker's 'making use' of trade union services include his consenting to the raising of a matter on his behalf by an independent trade union of which he is a member.

7.78   In the event that an employer breaches the right under TULRCA 1992, s 145A(1), a worker or former worker may present a claim to an employment tribunal (TULRCA 1992, s 145A(5)).

7.79   Additionally, the Government introduced under ERA 2004 a new TULRCA 1992, s 145B(1), being the right for workers who are members of a trade union recognised by an employer, or which is seeking to be so recognised, not to have an offer made to them if acceptance of the offer, together with other workers' acceptance of offers which the employer also makes to them, would have a 'prohibited result', and the employer's sole or main purpose in making the offers is to achieve that result. For these purposes, a 'prohibited result' is defined under TULRCA 1992, s 145B(2) to mean that the workers' terms of employment, or any of those terms, will not (or will no longer) be determined by collective agreement negotiated by or on behalf of the union. In this regard, under TULRCA 1992, s 145B(4), having terms of employment determined by collective agreement is specifically stated not to be regarded for the purposes of TULRCA 1992, ss 145A, 146 (action short of dismissal) or 152 (unfair dismissal) as making use of a trade union service. In the event that the employer breaches the right under TULRCA 1992, s 145B(1), a worker or former worker may present a complaint to an employment tribunal in respect of that breach (TULRCA 1992, s 145B(5)). TULRCA 1992, s 145F(4) provides that a claim to the employment tribunal is the only remedy available in this respect.

7.80 Under TULRCA 1992, s 145C, any claim under TULRCA 1992, s 145A or 145B must be presented to an employment tribunal before the end of the period of 3 months beginning with the date when the offer was made or, where the offer is part of a series of similar offers to the claimant, the date when the last of them was made, or such further period where the tribunal is satisfied that it was not reasonably practicable for the complaint to be presented in time.

7.81 In respect of claims under TULRCA 1992, s 145A, TULRCA 1992, s 145D(1) provides that it is for the employer to show what was its sole or main purpose in making the offer. Likewise, in respect of a claim under TULRCA 1992, s 145B it is for the employer to show what was its sole or main purpose in making the offers under that section (TULRCA 1992, s 145D(2)). In determining any cases under TULRCA 1992, s 145A or 145B, employment tribunals are not allowed to take account of any pressure which was placed on the employer by calling, organising, procuring or financing a strike or other industrial action, or by threatening to do so. Where pressure was so brought to bear, employment tribunals must ignore it (TULRCA 1992, s 145D(3)).

7.82 Under TULRCA 1992, s 145D(4), in determining whether an employer's sole or main purpose in making offers was the purpose mentioned in TULRCA 1992, s 145B(1), the matters taken into account must include any evidence:

- that when the offers were made, the employer had recently changed or sought to change, or did not wish to use, arrangements agreed with the union for collective bargaining;
- that when the offers were made the employer did not wish to enter into arrangements proposed by the union for collective bargaining; or
- that the offers were made only to particular workers, and were made with the sole or main purpose of rewarding those particular workers for their high level of performance or of retaining them because of their special value to the employer.

7.83 Under TULRCA 1992, s 145E, where an employment tribunal finds for a claimant under TULRCA 1992, s 145A or 145B, the tribunal must make a declaration to that effect, and must make an award to be paid by the employer to the claimant in respect of the offer complained of. TULRCA 1992, s 145E(3) states that the amount of the award shall be £2,500 (subject to any adjustment of the award that may fall to be made under EA 2002, Part 3). Any award of compensation can be adjusted for an employee's contributory fault (TULRCA 1992, s 145E(6)).

7.84 TULRCA 1992, s 145E(4) provides that where an employer grants additional rights where it makes an offer to workers in contravention of TULRCA 1992, s 145A or 145B which is accepted, the employer cannot enforce the agreement to vary, or recover any sum paid or other asset transferred by it under the agreement to vary. Further, where the worker's terms and conditions of employment are so varied, nothing in TULRCA 1992, s 145A or 145B makes the variation unenforceable by either party.

7.85 TULRCA 1992, s 145F makes certain provisions in relation to interpretation of the rights under TULRCA 1992, ss 145A and 145B. In particular, it provides that any references in TULRCA 1992, ss 145A–145E to being or becoming a member of a trade union include references to being or becoming a member of a particular branch or section of that union, and to being or becoming a member of one of a number of particular branches or sections of that union (TULRCA 1992, s 145F(1)). Further, TULRCA 1992, s 145F(2) provides that references in TULRCA 1992, ss 145A–145E to taking part in the activities of a trade union, and to services made available by a trade union by virtue of membership of the union, are to be construed in accordance with TULRCA 1992, s 145F(1).

UNFAIR DISMISSAL FOR A TRADE UNION-RELATED REASON

7.86   The right not to be dismissed unfairly for a trade union-related reason is another of the rights that was both eroded and expanded during the trade union law reforms of 1979–1997. This section will not focus on the principles that underpin unfair dismissal generally; regard should be had to more mainstream employment texts for these principles. Instead, it will focus on the ways in which unfair dismissal differs in trade union cases.

7.87   The right not to be unfairly dismissed for a trade union-related reason was introduced by IRA 1971. Following the repeal of IRA 1971 and enactment of TULRA 1974 as part of the 'Social Contract' package of measures, the right not to be unfairly dismissed for a trade union-related reason was carried over under TULRA 1974. As originally enacted under IRA 1971, if an employee was dismissed for a trade union-related reason, the dismissal was automatically unfair. Given that the agenda of IRA 1971 was the promotion of collective bargaining through means of the closed shop, it is not surprising that this was so.

7.88   The right not to be dismissed for a trade union-related reason has been remodelled in a number of ways overtime, most recently to take account of the decision of the ECHR in *Wilson and Palmer No 2*[64] and the changes made under ERA 2004 in the light of that decision.

7.89   The provisions relating to the right not to be unfairly dismissed for a trade union-related reason under TULRCA 1992, ss 152 and 153, are now as follows:

'**152 Dismissal of employee on grounds related to union membership or activities**

(1)   For purposes of Part X of the Employment Rights Act 1996 (unfair dismissal) the dismissal of an employee shall be regarded as unfair if the reason for it (or, if more than one, the principal reason) was that the employee—

(a) was, or proposed to become, a member of an independent trade union,
(b) had taken part, or proposed to take part, in the activities of an independent trade union at an appropriate time,
(ba) had made use, or proposed to make use, of trade union services at an appropriate time,
(bb) had failed to accept an offer made in contravention of section 145A or 145B, or
(c) was not a member of any trade union, or of a particular trade union, or of one of a number of particular trade unions, or had refused, or proposed to refuse, to become or remain a member.

---

[64]   [2002] IRLR 568.

(2)   In subsection (1) "an appropriate time" means—

(a) a time outside the employee's working hours, or
(b) a time within his working hours at which, in accordance with arrangements agreed with or consent given by his employer, it is permissible
for him to take part in the activities of a trade union or (as the case
may be) make use of trade union services;

and for this purpose "working hours", in relation to an employee, means
any time when, in accordance with his contract of employment, he is
required to be at work.

(2A)   In this section—

(a) "trade union services" means services made available to the employee
by an independent trade union by virtue of his membership of the
union, and
(b) references to an employee's "making use" of trade union services
include his consenting to the raising of a matter on his behalf by an
independent trade union of which he is a member.

(2B)   Where the reason or one of the reasons for the dismissal was that an
independent trade union (with or without the employee's consent) raised a
matter on behalf of the employee as one of its members, the reason shall
be treated as falling within subsection (1)(ba).

(3)   Where the reason, or one of the reasons, for the dismissal was—

(a) the employee's refusal, or proposed refusal, to comply with a requirement (whether or not imposed by his contract of employment or in
writing) that, in the event of his not being a member of any trade
union, or of a particular trade union, or of one of a number of
particular trade unions, he must make one or more payments, or
(b) his objection, or proposed objection, (however expressed) to the
operation of a provision (whether or not forming part of his contract
of employment or in writing) under which, in the event mentioned in
paragraph (a), his employer is entitled to deduct one or more sums
from the remuneration payable to him in respect of his employment,

the reason shall be treated as falling within subsection (1)(c).

(4)   References in this section to being, becoming or ceasing to remain a
member of a trade union include references to being, becoming or ceasing
to remain a member of a particular branch or section of that union or of
one of a number of particular branches or sections of that trade union.

(5)   References in this section—

(a) to taking part in the activities of a trade union, and
(b) to services made available by a trade union by virtue of membership of
the union,

shall be construed in accordance with subsection (4).

153 Selection for redundancy on grounds related to union membership or activities

Where the reason or principal reason for the dismissal of an employee was
that he was redundant, but it is shown—

(a) that the circumstances constituting the redundancy applied equally to one or more other employees in the same undertaking who held positions similar to that held by him and who have not been dismissed by the employer, and

(b) that the reason (or, if more than one, the principal reason) why he was selected for dismissal was one of those specified in section 152(1),

the dismissal shall be regarded as unfair for the purposes of Part X of the Employment Rights Act 1996 (unfair dismissal).'

The reason for dismissal

Trade union membership

7.90   Once an employment tribunal has held that an employee has been dismissed for one of the reasons in TULRCA 1992, s 152, the dismissal will be automatically unfair. It is no defence for an employer to say that it did not intend to dismiss for a trade union-related reason. The question to be asked is whether, objectively on the facts, an employee has been so dismissed. A good example is *Dundon v GPT Limited*,[65] where the claimant was a trade union representative who over the course of his 20 years' employment with the employer, had taken on more and more trade union-related business as part of his working day. At the time of the claimant's dismissal he contributed only about 20 per cent of his working time to the business of his employer with the rest of his working time being taken up by trade union duties. The employer selected the claimant for redundancy with one of the redundancy selection criteria being employee productivity. The claimant scored very badly under this head and was dismissed. The industrial tribunal held that the employer had not meant to select him for a trade union-related reason and therefore the dismissal was fair. On appeal, however, the EAT held that if the employer had selected the claimant for redundancy because of his work output, it must be connected to the claimant's trade union work and therefore the reason that he had been selected was because he was a member of a particular trade union.

Exercising trade union membership rights

7.91   Prior to amendments made under ERA 2004 following the decision of the ECHR in *Wilson and Palmer No 2*,[66] the main cases in relation to exercising trade union membership rights were *Discount Tobacco and Confectionery Limited v Armitage*[67] and *Associated Newspapers Limited v Wilson*[68] (which have been examined at **7.14** et seq in relation to employers discriminating against a job applicant, or a worker suffering an inducement or detriment, for a trade union-related reason). However, the confusion which had been created by these cases was swept away following creation of the new rights not to be dismissed for having used or proposing to use the services of a trade union and/or failing to accept an offer in contravention of TULRCA 1992, s 145A or 145B (respectively, TULRCA 1992, s 152(1)(ba) and (bb)).

---

[65]   [1995] IRLR 403.
[66]   [2002] IRLR 568.
[67]   [1990] IRLR 15.
[68]   [1995] IRLR 258.

7.92 Furthermore, under the new TULRCA 1992, s 152(2A) and (2B) (see **7.89**), there is now considerable scope for employees to argue that they have 'made use' of the services of an independent trade union. Whilst the definition of 'making use' of trade union services is very broad under TULRCA 1992, s 152(2A)(b) (and will doubtless result in litigation as employers try to argue that an employee in a given case was not 'making use' of such services), following the post-ERA 2004 changes to TULRCA 1992, s 152, a case such as *Discount Tobacco and Confectionery Limited v Armitage*[69] would now clearly be an unfair dismissal for a trade union-related reason due to TULRCA 1992, s 152(2B) providing that the raising of a matter on behalf of a member of a trade union is deemed to be 'making use' of the services of a trade union. It also seems that under the definition in TULRCA 1992, s 152(2A)(a) it is open to a trade union to certify what its membership services are.

Taking part in union activities at an appropriate time

7.93 As to what amounts to an appropriate time and whether an employer has provided consent, the law in relation to this head has already been discussed under the identical provisions relating to having action short of dismissal taken against an employee on grounds of his trade union membership at **7.60**.

Payments in lieu of membership

7.94 Under TULRCA 1992, s 152(3), a dismissal is unfair in respect of an employee where the employee refuses to agree, or objects, to a deduction from his wages in the event of his not being a member of a trade union. This provision has been in effect since EA 1980.

Selection for redundancy

7.95 Selection for redundancy on the basis of a trade union-related reason is dealt with by TULRCA 1992, s 153. The criteria for establishing unfair dismissal under this provision are that:

- a redundancy situation existed in an 'undertaking';
- it applied equally to the claimant and one or more other employees in the same 'position' as the claimant; and
- the key factor in the claimant's dismissal is one of the reasons set out in TULRCA 1992, s 152(1).

7.96 In establishing this ground it needs to be considered what amounts to a claimant's 'position' and what is meant by an 'undertaking'.

7.97 The current definition of what amounts to a claimant's 'position', is provided by Employment Rights Act 1996 (ERA 1996), s 235. By way of legislative history, the definition of a 'trade union', in relation to unfair dismissal-related redundancies, used to exist as EPCA 1978, s 59. Further, EPCA 1978, s 153 provided a definition of 'position' in terms of status, nature of work and terms and conditions of employment as a whole. This definition of 'position' was not transposed to TULRCA 1992 when the right not to be unfairly dismissed for a trade union-related reason was consolidated into

---

[69]   [1990] IRLR 15.

TULRCA 1992. However, the definition of 'position' was subsequently carried over into ERA 1996 upon consolidation of the other individual employment rights legislation.

7.98   The definition of what amounts to an employee's 'position' was discussed in *O'Dea v ISC Chemicals Limited*.[70] Here, the claimant was employed as a technical services operator but spent half of his working time undertaking trade union activities and the other half as a packing operator. As such, he occupied a unique role in the context of the business. The claimant was selected for redundancy when his department closed down and he was not considered for one of the other available posts with the employer. The claimant presented a claim for unfair dismissal on the basis of his unfair selection for redundancy on the grounds of his trade union activities under EPCA 1978, s 59 (now TULRCA 1992, s 153), which the industrial tribunal rejected, holding that he occupied a special 'position' in the workforce. However, the tribunal then awarded the claimant compensation for unfair dismissal on the grounds that his employer had failed to inform those making the job appointments to other departments that his trade union activities should be disregarded. This award was then reduced by 80 per cent to take account of the fact that the claimant probably would not have been selected for one of the posts. On appeal, it was argued by the claimant to the Court of Appeal that the industrial tribunal should have focused on his contractual title of 'technical services operator' rather than his actual work as a packing operator. The court rejected this argument holding that to do so:[71]

> '... would require the Industrial Tribunal to ignore not merely what the [claimant] did as a shop steward but also what work he did as an employee as well as the terms and conditions of his employment. There is no justification for this in the language of [the Act]. Indeed it would render any meaningful comparison futile in circumstances such as the present.'

7.99   The Court of Appeal added that what amounts to an employee's 'position' will be a question of fact for the tribunal hearing the case to determine.[72]

7.100   The concept of 'an undertaking' is not defined by TULRCA 1992 but the phrase almost certainly takes on the accepted definition of what amounts to an undertaking within the meaning of the Transfer of Undertakings (Protection of Employment) Regulations 1981[73] (TUPE 1981), reg 2(1) and regard should be had to more mainstream employment law texts on this point.

Unfair dismissal following 'other industrial action'

7.101   The right not to be unfairly dismissed for taking 'other industrial action' is another of the rights that has been heavily modified as a result of the trade union law reforms of the period 1979–1997. The right was introduced

---

[70]   [1996] ICR 222.

[71]   [1996] ICR 222 at 230.

[72]   Other cases dealing with the concept of what amounts to an employee's 'position' are *Britool Limited v Roberts* [1993] IRLR 481; *CGB Publishing v Killey* [1993] IRLR 520; and *Dundon v GPT Limited* [1995] IRLR 403.

[73]   SI 1981/1794.

under IRA 1971 and covered the situation where one or more employees were dismissed for taking part in industrial action but their employer had subsequently taken steps selectively to rehire from amongst the dismissed employees and had excluded from re-employment, for example, the ringleaders of the industrial action giving rise to the dismissals. Upon the repeal of IRA 1971, the right was carried over into TULRA 1974 and was then carried through into EPCA 1978. The right was subsequently heavily modified by EA 1982, EA 1990 and TURERA 1993. The right has also been modified more recently by ERA 1999 and ERA 2004.

7.102 The main provisions in relation to the right not to be unfairly dismissed for taking 'other industrial action' exist under TULRCA 1992, ss 237 and 238 which provide as follows:

'**237 Dismissal of those taking part in unofficial industrial action** (1)   An employee has no right to complain of unfair dismissal if at the time of dismissal he was taking part in an unofficial strike or other unofficial industrial action.

(1A)   Subsection (1) does not apply to the dismissal of the employee if it is shown that the reason (or, if more than one, the principal reason) for the dismissal or, in a redundancy case, for selecting the employee for dismissal was one of those specified in or under—

(a)   section 98B, 99, 100, 101A(d), 103, 103A or 104C of the Employment Rights Act 1996 (dismissal in jury service, family, health and safety, working time, employee representative, protected disclosure and flexible working cases),

(b)   section 104 of that Act in its application in relation to time off under section 57A of that Act (dependants).

In this subsection "redundancy case" has the meaning given in section 105(9) of that Act; and a reference to a specified reason for dismissal includes a reference to specified circumstances of dismissal.

(2)   A strike or other industrial action is unofficial in relation to an employee unless—

(a)   he is a member of a trade union and the action is authorised or endorsed by that union, or

(b)   he is not a member of a trade union but there are among those taking part in the industrial action members of a trade union by which the action has been authorised or endorsed.

Provided that, a strike or other industrial action shall not be regarded as unofficial if none of those taking part in it are members of a trade union.

(3)   The provisions of section 20(2) apply for the purpose of determining whether industrial action is to be taken to have been authorised or endorsed by a trade union.

238 Dismissals in connection with other industrial action

(1)   This section applies in relation to an employee who has a right to complain of unfair dismissal (the "complainant") and who claims to have been unfairly dismissed, where at the date of the dismissal—

(a)   the employer was conducting or instituting a lock-out, or

(b) the complainant was taking part in a strike or other industrial action.

(2) In such a case an employment tribunal shall not determine whether the dismissal was fair or unfair unless it is shown—

(a) that one or more relevant employees of the same employer have not been dismissed, or
(b) that a relevant employee has before the expiry of the period of three months beginning with the date of his dismissal been offered re-engagement and that the complainant has not been offered re-engagement.

(2A) Subsection (2) does not apply to the dismissal of the employee if it is shown that the reason (or, if more than one, the principal reason) for the dismissal or, in a redundancy case, for selecting the employee for dismissal was one of those specified in or under—

(a) section 98B, 99, 100, 101A(d), 103 or 104C of the Employment Rights Act 1996 (dismissal in jury service, family, health and safety, working time, employee representative and flexible working cases),
(b) section 104 of that Act in its application in relation to time off under section 57A of that Act (dependants).

In this subsection 'redundancy case' has the meaning given in section 105(9) of that Act; and a reference to a specified reason for dismissal includes a reference to specified circumstances of dismissal.

(2B)   Subsection (2) does not apply in relation to an employee who is regarded as unfairly dismissed by virtue of section 238A below.'

7.103   In this regard it is necessary to consider when or what industrial action is 'unofficial' which is dealt with under TULRCA 1992, s 237. Unofficial industrial action in respect of a trade union is taken to be all industrial action that is taken without the authorisation or endorsement of the trade union where it has members engaged in the industrial action (TULRCA 1992, s 237(2)–(3)). It is important to note that this does not mean that the industrial action necessarily has the endorsement of a properly conducted ballot: that is dealt with under TULRCA 1992, s 238A. It means authorisation or endorsement within the contemplation of TULRCA 1992, s 20(2).[74] Consequently, even if no ballot has taken place and the union endorses industrial action taken in its name, that is sufficient for TULRCA 1992, s 237 to hold that the action is not 'unofficial'. If an individual is not a trade union member and takes part in industrial action which has trade union members involved in it whose union has authorised or endorsed that action then, notwithstanding that the individual is not a member of that trade union, the industrial action will not be 'unofficial' as regards that individual. In other words, the same industrial action can be classed both as not being unofficial and unofficial depending on

---

[74]   See in this regard the EAT's decision in *Balfour Kilpatrick Limited v Acheson* [2003] IRLR 683, where the EAT considered the context of a repudiation industrial action which had not been properly effected and held that since this was so, employees who had withdrawn their labour were still taking industrial action that was not unofficial and therefore could present claims that they had been unfairly dismissed.

the identity of an individual, a consideration of whether that individual is a member of a trade union and, if so, whether that union has balloted in favour of taking industrial action.

7.104   For example, if an employee is a member of trade union X, a fellow employee is a member of trade union Y and a further employee is not a trade union member, then, to the extent that union X endorses industrial action through means of a strike ballot and union Y does not, any action taken by all three employees will not be unofficial as regards the member of union X and the non-unionised employee, but unofficial as regards the member of union Y. The result is capricious. Further, it cannot be avoided by the hypothetical union Y member resigning his membership of that union during the course of action. This is because TULRCA 1992, s 237(6) provides that employees who cease to be trade union members during the course of industrial action are deemed to retain their membership for the purposes of determining whether industrial action is unofficial until the end of that round of industrial action. The effect is that the only way for a person to take part in industrial action which is not unofficial where his trade union refuses to authorise or endorse the proposed action, is to resign from the trade union prior to taking part in that action.

7.105   Further, where employees of an employer are not members of a trade union and take industrial action, TULRCA 1992, s 237 does not apply to them (unless other employees who are trade union members take part in the same industrial action) (TULRCA 1992, s 237(2)). Their action will neither be official nor unofficial since these are concepts relevant to unionised employees only.

Unfair dismissal for taking industrial action

7.106   Under TULRCA 1992, s 237(1), if industrial action is unofficial it does not matter that an employer is selective in whom it chooses to dismiss. The employer can be as arbitrary as it wishes in such a situation and may decide to 'shoot a few generals' as an example to the rest of the workforce. If that is the case, those employees so dismissed have no recourse unless they can show that the reason or primary reason for the dismissal was for a reason under TULRCA 1992, s 237(1A), namely dismissal for undertaking jury service, family, health and safety, working time, employee representative, protected disclosure, flexible working cases or for taking time off to care for dependants.

7.107   If an employee falls into the category of industrial action that is other than unofficial (or as the heading to TULRCA 1992, s 238 calls it, 'other industrial action'), then an employer choosing to dismiss those taking part in such action is left with an all or nothing election; the employer cannot pick and choose who to dismiss from amongst those taking part (TULRCA 1992, s 238(2)(a)). If an employer decides to dismiss employees from amongst those taking part in that 'other industrial action', then the employer will have to dismiss *all* of the employees taking part in the action and recruit a new labour force to replace them. If an employer decides to dismiss employees taking part in industrial action, it cannot selectively re-employ from those he has dismissed unless it does so no earlier than the period of 3 months after the last of the dismissals (TULRCA 1992, s 238(2)(b)).

7.108   If an employee has been dismissed for taking part in 'other industrial action', unless the employee can show (as with those taking part in unofficial industrial action) that the reason for the dismissal is actually due to another statutorily protected reason, no claim can be heard by an employment tribunal (TULRCA 1992, s 238(2) and (2A)). Further, under TULRCA 1992, s 238(2B), TULRCA 1992, s 238(2) does not apply in relation to an employee who is regarded as unfairly dismissed by virtue of TULRCA 1992, s 238A, protected industrial action (discussed at **7.127**).

7.109   Consequently, it is up to an employee who has been dismissed to show that his employer dismissed him for an automatically unfair reason or that the employer was undertaking a lock-out. Alternatively, the employee will have to show that he was taking part in 'other industrial action' (within the meaning of TULRCA 1992, s 238) and that his employer had either not dismissed all relevant employees or had done so but had then selectively re-engaged within 3 months of the employee's dismissal.

7.110   This therefore begs the following questions:

- What is meant by a lock-out?
- When is an employee taking part in 'other industrial action'?
- At what time can an employer legitimately dismiss employees?
- When does selective re-engagement occur?

Each will be looked at in turn.

Lock-outs

7.111   No statutory definition exists as to what is meant by a lock-out. The best judicial definition of the phrase is probably that provided by the Court of Appeal in *Express and Star Limited v Bunday*, where it was held that:[75]

> '... the Shorter Oxford Dictionary ... defines a "lock-out" as "an act of locking-out a body of operatives; i.e. a refusal on the part of an employer, or employers acting in concert, to furnish work to their operatives except on conditions to be accepted by the latter collectively." For [our] part [we] would again be prepared to accept this dictionary definition as at least a reliable indication of what does constitute a lock-out in modern industrial relations. Nevertheless, [we] think that it would be wrong to treat the dictionary definition as if it were expressly contained in the statute and to seek to apply it word for word to any problem that may arise in this context. As has already been pointed out, each of these cases must be decided on its own facts and merits and, as will appear, subject to what [we] have already said, [we] have no doubt that the best appreciation of what is or is not a strike or lock-out will come from either an [Employment] Tribunal, or on appeal the Employment Appeal Tribunal, highly experienced in these matters as these bodies respectively are.'

Industrial action

7.112   Industrial action in this context is either a strike or other industrial action. The term 'strike' is defined by TULRCA 1992, s 246 as being a concerted stoppage of work. As to what amounts to other forms of industrial action, the law reports provide many different examples, for example,

---

[75]   [1987] IRLR 422 at 425.

go-slows;[76] refusal to work overtime;[77] and, indeed, any other form of withdrawal of goodwill.[78] It has also been held[79] that an employee who refused to cross a picket line for fear of harassment was involved in a strike and that her motive for refusing to cross was irrelevant. Further, it has been held that industrial action that has been deliberately provoked by an employer is caught by the provisions of TULRCA 1992, s 238.[80] However, there may in cases be a thin line, easily crossed, between, for example, taking part in a trade union meeting at an appropriate time (dismissal for which would be dealt with under TULRCA 1992, s 152, in respect of which see **7.89**) and taking part in a trade union meeting, permission for which has been refused by an employer, and which may therefore be taking unofficial industrial action, dismissal for which would be covered under TULRCA 1992, s 238.[81]

7.113   As to whether a particular employee was engaged in industrial action taking place, this is a question of fact and it is up to the claimant to show that he was ready, willing and able to carry out the terms of his contract of employment both to the letter and the spirit of the contract. However, if an employee is legitimately absent from work but nevertheless takes part in industrial action, the employee may still be treated as engaged in the industrial action. The matter was considered in *Bolton Roadway Limited v Edwards* where it was held:[82]

> 'Whether an employee is taking part in strike action is, as we have said, a question of fact. Whether an employee's activity represents a breach of his obligation to attend work, may be relevant to the question whether he is taking part in a strike, but it is not in our view an essential ingredient. We would take, as an example, the case of an employee who is for the time being on holiday or away sick. That employee by reason of his holiday entitlement or his sickness would not be in breach of his contractual obligation to work; but if he associated himself with the strike, attended at the picket line or took part in the other activities of the strikers with a view to furthering their aims, he would, in our view, be capable of being held to be taking part in the strike. Any other view would be to make nonsense of the plain language of the phrase "taking part in the strike or other industrial action".'

7.114   Therefore, where an employee does not attend for work for a reason that is unconnected with any industrial action which is taking place, the prudent employer cannot simply assume that the employee is in breach of contract; rather the employer should carry out an investigation into the reason for any non-attendance in the same way as he would for any other absenteeism.[83]

---

76   *Secretary of State for Employment v ASLEF (No 2)* [1972] ICR 19.
77   *Power Packing Case makers Limited v Faust* [1983] ICR 292.
78   *Ticehurst v British Telecommunications plc* [1992] IRLR 219.
79   *Coates v Modern Methods and Materials Limited* [1982] IRLR 318.
80   See in this regard *Wilkins v Cantrell & Cochrane (GB) Limited* [1978] IRLR 483; and *Marsden v Fairey Stainless Limited* [1979] IRLR 103.
81   These facts are similar to *Rasool v Hepworth Pipe Co Limited* [1980] IRLR 88.
82   [1987] IRLR 392 at 396.
83   See further in this regard *Hindle Gears Limited v McGinty* [1984] IRLR 477; *Manifold*

The time of dismissal

7.115   In order for an employer to be able to present a defensible position in relation to unfair dismissal claims when dismissing employees taking part in 'other industrial action' within the meaning of TULRCA 1992, s 238, the employer must only dismiss employees who are actually taking part in the relevant action at the time that they are taking part. This point is quite complex. To start with, it needs to be shown that employees who are dismissed are taking part in industrial action. If the employer 'jumps the gun' by dismissing prior to industrial action being taken or dismisses after such action has been taken and is concluded, the dismissals will be unfair.

7.116   Two difficult examples of employers dismissing prior to action being taken are *Midland Plastics v Till*[84] and *Lewis v E Mason & Sons Limited*.[85] In *Midland Plastics*, the employer had dismissed certain of its trade union member employees after they notified the employer that it was their intention to take industrial action unless certain demands were met by the employer. The employees claimed that they had been unfairly dismissed and submitted a claim to the industrial tribunal. It was alleged by the employer that the tribunal had no jurisdiction to hear the case because the employees had been dismissed for taking part in industrial action. The tribunal disagreed and found for the employees. The employer appealed to the EAT. The EAT declined the employer's appeal on the grounds that it was necessary to distinguish between a threat to take industrial action and the taking of the action itself, which was causally the point in time at which, what is now TULRCA 1992, s 238, operated. The EAT held:[86]

> '... if the employers are to succeed, as it seems to us they must be able to show that the threat of taking industrial action can itself amount to taking industrial action. We reject that view ... [w]e cannot accept ... that because the threat to take industrial action imposed pressure on the employers, such threat itself constituted the taking of industrial action.'

7.117   However, in the *Lewis* case,[87] another division of the EAT reached the opposite conclusion holding that notice of proposed industrial action could amount to industrial action. *Lewis* is probably wrongly decided and the better view is that employers cannot rely on industrial action being taken until such time as the employees in question have breached the letter and spirit of their employment contracts. Put another way, the employees have not at that point crossed the Rubicon; they are free not to follow through with their threat.

7.118   As to the issue of employees being dismissed after action has ceased, regard should be had to the decisions in *Heath v JF Longman (Meat Salesman) Limited*[88] and *Mainland Car Deliveries Limited v Cooper*.[89] In both cases it was held that once an employer knows that industrial action is finished and then

---

  Industries Limited v Sims [1991] IRLR 242; *Jenkins v P & O European Ferries (Dover) Limited* [1991] ICR 652; and *Rogers v Chloride Systems* [1992] ICR 198.

84   [1983] IRLR 9.
85   [1984] IRLR 4.
86   [1983] IRLR 9 at 11.
87   *Lewis v E Mason & Sons Limited* [1984] IRLR 4.
88   [1973] IRLR 214.
89   Unreported (EAT 492/96).

dismisses employees for taking part in that action, the employer loses the protection that would otherwise be available under what is now TULRCA 1992, s 238.

Selective re-engagement

7.119   As has been noted above, an employee will be able to claim that he has been unfairly dismissed where his employer selectively re-engages 'relevant' fellow employees who have been dismissed with the claimant for taking part in the same industrial action. This begs the following questions:

- Who is a 'relevant' fellow employee?
- When do the employees take part in the 'same industrial action'?
- At what time must it be shown that a comparator remained in employment?
- What constitutes an offer of re-employment?

7.120   As to who are 'relevant' fellow employees, the starting-point is TULRCA 1992, s 238(3) which provides that relevant employees means in relation to a lock-out, employees who were directly interested in the dispute in contemplation or furtherance of which the lock-out occurred, and in relation to a strike or other industrial action, those employees at the establishment of the employer at or from which the claimant works who at the date of his dismissal were taking part in the action. TULRCA 1992, s 237(3) also provides that nothing in TULRCA 1992, s 237 (which relates to dismissal of those taking part in unofficial industrial action) affects the question who are relevant employees for the purposes of TULRCA 1992, s 238. This provision effectively ties the place of employment down to that at which the claimant works and has the effect, for example, of allowing an employer with many different sites to negotiate different terms with each different place of employment, or to dismiss the employees at those establishments. It further narrows the pool of relevant employees by requiring that relevant employees are those who are taking part in the industrial action at the date of dismissal. It follows that if an employer issues an ultimatum to return to work which is complied with by some employees and not complied with by others, and after the date on which the ultimatum expires the employer dismisses those still taking industrial action, the pool of relevant employees is those employees still taking industrial action at that date but not those employees who have returned to work prior to the deadline.

7.121   As to when the 'same industrial action' takes place, this was discussed in *McCormick v Horsepower Limited*.[90] Here, the claimant was one of a group of employees who took part in a strike aimed at securing better terms and conditions of employment. A fellow employee, B, chose not to cross a picket line and stayed away from work. In doing so, B failed to inform the employer as to his reasons for non-attendance. After a period of time, B attended for work. He was not dismissed along with the claimant who submitted that B was a relevant employee taking part in action who had not been dismissed. On appeal, the Court of Appeal held that B was not engaged in the industrial action and was not taking any other form of industrial action by staying away

---

[90]   [1981] ICR 535.

from work. It followed that, since B was not taking part in the 'same industrial action' as the claimant, he was not a 'relevant employee' for the purposes of what is now TULRCA 1992, s 238(3), and therefore the claim failed.

7.122   As to what is the relevant time for showing that a claimant's comparator has not been dismissed, it was held by the Court of Appeal in *P & O European Ferries (Dover) Limited v Byrne*[91] that the relevant time is the end of the hearing at which the employment tribunal is required to consider whether it has jurisdiction. According to the court, the purpose of that hearing is to allow an employer to know what the case is against him. The by-product of the *Byrne* decision is that it allows an employer to defeat a claim by dismissing the comparator employees prior to the end of the jurisdiction hearing. This said, if an employer makes offers of re-engagement to all of the dismissed employees within a 3-month period of a claimant's dismissal, no claim can arise even if the offers of re-engagement are staggered throughout the period.[92]

7.123   When considering what amounts to an offer of re-engagement to a comparator, if a claimant is allowed to pursue a claim under TULRCA 1992, s 238, the comparator must be offered re-engagement within 3 months of the dismissal of the claimant. No formal written offer is required to be made to the comparator.[93]

7.124   Once an offer of re-engagement has been made by an employer to a comparator, it is no defence for the employer to say that it did not mean to make the offer. In *Bigham v GKN Kwikform Limited*,[94] the EAT held that, where an offer was inadvertently made by the employer to a comparator within the restricted 3-month period, even though the employer subsequently re-dismissed the comparator when it found out about the mistake, it was still possible for the claimant to bring a claim under TULRCA 1992, s 238(2)(b). It was pointed out by the EAT in that case that the comparator had no intent to defraud the employer. Where such intent is present (for example, in a very large organisation with a high labour turnover, where an employee applies to work under a false name), the employer may have a defence to a claim by arguing that any offer of employment was made by it on the basis of a unilateral mistake (as to the identity of the employee), and the acceptance of the offer by the comparator would be voidable at the election of the employer with the result that the contract of employment would be treated as not having existed and therefore the conditions of TULRCA 1992, s 238 would not be triggered. This said, it will be possible for an employer to show that it has made an offer to all employees including the claimant even where the claimant is not individually notified by the employer. For example, in *Marsden v Fairey Stainless Limited*,[95] the employer inadvertently wrongly addressed an offer of re-engagement to the claimant after having orally advised the claimant of a position for him. It was held by the EAT that since the claimant knew that an offer of re-engagement had been made to him in any event, the lack of formal written notice was of no importance.

---

[91]   [1989] ICR 779.
[92]   *Highland Fabricators Limited v McLaughlin* [1984] IRLR 482.
[93]   *Marsden v Fairey Stainless Limited* [1979] IRLR 103.
[94]   [1992] IRLR 4.
[95]   [1979] IRLR 103.

7.125 Likewise, it will be a defence for an employer to show that there is another potentially fair reason under ERA 1996, s 98 as to why an offer of re-engagement has not been made to a claimant. This is because, unlike unfair dismissal under TULRCA 1992, ss 152 and 153, it is not automatically unfair selectively to re-engage employees. Instead, a claimant's case locks into the provisions of ERA 1996 by virtue of TULRCA 1992, s 239(1) and therefore an employer may be able to show any of the full range of potentially fair reasons under ERA 1996 as being the reason or principal reason that the employer dismissed or failed to offer re-engagement.

7.126 Further, in connection with the time-limits for presenting a claim in respect of a dismissal under TULRCA 1992, s 238 or 238A (see **7.127**), under TULRCA 1992, s 239(2), these are extended from the usual 3-month period under ERA 1996, s 111 to either 6 months or where the employment tribunal is satisfied that it was not reasonably practicable for the complaint to be presented before the end of that period, within such further period as the tribunal considers reasonable.

7.127 Following changes implemented by ERA 1999, a new right not to be unfairly dismissed for participation in 'protected industrial action' was created and inserted as TULRCA 1992, s 238A. The right contemplates that where employees are taking part in industrial action which has the support of a properly conducted ballot, it should be unlawful in the first instance to dismiss employees who may have a legitimate grievance with their employer and are effectively taking action of last resort during the continuance of their working relationship with the employer to resolve that grievance. The right was modified under ERA 2004 so as to extend the period of time during which employees enjoy protection under the right. TULRCA 1992, s 238A provides as follows:

'238A Participation in official industrial action

(1) For the purposes of this section an employee takes protected industrial action if he commits an act which, or a series of acts each of which, he is induced to commit by an act which by virtue of section 219 is not actionable in tort.

(2) An employee who is dismissed shall be regarded for the purposes of Part X of the Employment Rights Act 1996 (unfair dismissal) as unfairly dismissed if—

(a) the reason (or, if more than one, the principal reason) for the dismissal is that the employee took protected industrial action, and
(b) subsection (3), (4) or (5) applies to the dismissal.

(3) This subsection applies to a dismissal if it takes place the date of the dismissal is within the period of eight weeks beginning with the day on which the employee started to take protected industrial action within the protected period.

(4) This subsection applies to a dismissal if—

(a) it takes place the date of the dismissal is after the end of that period, and
(b) the employee had stopped taking protected industrial action before the end of that period.

(5)   This subsection applies to a dismissal if—

(a) it takes place the date of the dismissal is after the end of that period,
(b) the employee had not stopped taking protected industrial action before the end of that period, and
(c) the employer had not taken such procedural steps as would have been reasonable for the purposes of resolving the dispute to which the protected industrial action relates.

(6)   In determining whether an employer has taken those steps regard shall be had, in particular, to—

(a) whether the employer or a union had complied with procedures established by any applicable collective or other agreement;
(b) whether the employer or a union offered or agreed to commence or resume negotiations after the start of the protected industrial action;
(c) whether the employer or a union unreasonably refused, after the start of the protected industrial action, a request that conciliation services be used;
(d) whether the employer or a union unreasonably refused, after the start of the protected industrial action, a request that mediation services be used in relation to procedures to be adopted for the purposes of resolving the dispute;
(e) where there was agreement to use either of the services mentioned in paragraphs (c) and (d), the matters specified in section 238B.

(7)   In determining whether an employer has taken those steps no regard shall be had to the merits of the dispute.

(7A)   For the purposes of this section "the protected period", in relation to the dismissal of an employee, is the sum of the basic period and any extension period in relation to that employee.

(7B)   The basic period is twelve weeks beginning with the first day of protected industrial action.

(7C)   An extension period in relation to an employee is a period equal to the number of days falling on or after the first day of protected industrial action (but before the protected period ends) during the whole or any part of which the employee is locked out by his employer.

(7D)   In subsections (7B) and (7C), the "first day of protected industrial action" means the day on which the employee starts to take protected industrial action (even if on that day he is locked out by his employer).

(8)   For the purposes of this section no account shall be taken of the repudiation of any act by a trade union as mentioned in section 21 in relation to anything which occurs before the end of the next working day (within the meaning of section 237) after the day on which the repudiation takes place.

(9)   In this section "date of dismissal" has the meaning given by section 238(5).'

7.128   The right created is quite complex, but can be stated as covering the following points. First, under TULRCA 1992, s 238A(1), the gateway to the right is entered by industrial action being taken which would not be actionable in tort under TULRCA 1992, s 219, that is lawful industrial action having the support of a properly constituted ballot for the purposes of TULRCA 1992. Further, TULRCA 1992, s 238A(7) states that the merits of the dispute giving rise to the protected industrial action are not to be considered when determining whether a dismissal for taking part in the protected industrial action is unfair. Furthermore, in the event that a union repudiates protected industrial action after it has commenced, the industrial action does not cease to be protected until the next working day (TULRCA 1992, s 238A(8)), which therefore allows those taking protected industrial action to return to work once their union has withdrawn its support without the risk of the employees being dismissed lawfully by the employer on a day which had commenced as being protected.

7.129   Where this gateway is entered, under TULRCA 1992, s 238A(2), the dismissal of an employee for taking part in that industrial action is automatically unfair for the purposes of ERA 1996 if the principal reason for the dismissal is that the employee was taking part in that industrial action and the dismissal:

- takes place within 8 weeks of the 'protected period';
- takes place after the end of the 'protected period' and the employee had stopped taking protected industrial action before the end of the 'protected period'; or
- takes place after the end of the 'protected period', the employee had not stopped taking protected industrial action before the end of the 'protected period' and the employer had not taken 'reasonable procedural steps' to resolve the dispute to which the industrial action relates.

7.130   Pausing there, three points arise. First, since TULRCA 1992, s 238A(2) states that the principal reason for the dismissal has to be the taking part in protected industrial action, if an employer can show that the principal reason for the dismissal was another, fair reason (for example, the employer discovers that the employee had been engaged in gross misconduct and dismissed the employee fairly for that reason), then notwithstanding that the employee may also have been taking part in protected industrial action at the time of the dismissal, the dismissal may be fair.

7.131   Secondly, the protected period has been amended following changes made by ERA 2004. Under TULRCA 1992, s 238A(7A)–(7D), the protected period now comprises the period of 12 weeks beginning with the first day of protected industrial action (ie the day on which the protected industrial action, or a lock-out by the employer, commenced), together with any period of extension thereto after the first day of the protected industrial action during the whole or any part of which the employee is locked-out by his employer (TULRCA 1992, s 238A(7C)).

7.132   Thirdly, the concept of what are 'reasonable procedural steps' is dealt with under TULRCA 1992, ss 238A(6) and 238B. In this regard, employment tribunals must consider whether:

- the employer or a union had complied with any procedural requirements established under any applicable collective agreement;
- the employer or a union had offered or agreed to commence or resume negotiations after the start of the protected industrial action;
- the employer or a union had unreasonably refused a request to use conciliation services after the start of the protected industrial action;

- the employer or a union had after the start of the protected industrial action refused a request that mediation be used in relation to procedures for resolving the dispute; or
- where there was an agreement for conciliation or mediation to be used, TULRCA 1992, s 238B applied.

7.133   In relation to the matters under TULRCA 1992, s 238B(2)–(5), the employment tribunal is required to consider whether the employer or union:

- at meetings arranged by the conciliator or mediator, was represented by an 'appropriate person';
- at meetings arranged by the conciliator or mediator, co-operated in the making of arrangements for meetings to be held with the conciliator or mediator to the extent requested;
- fulfilled any commitment given by it during the provision of the service to take particular action; and
- at meetings arranged by the conciliator or mediator between the parties making use of the service, the representatives of the employer or union answered any reasonable question put to them concerning the matter subject to conciliation or mediation.

7.134   The 'appropriate person' is defined under TULRCA 1992, s 238B(6) as being either, in the case of the employer, the person with authority to settle the matter on behalf of the employer or a person authorised by such a person to make recommendations with regard to the settlement. In the case of a trade union, the appropriate person is the person responsible for handling the matter on the union's behalf.

7.135   So as to ensure that mediation and conciliation are conducted in a 'without prejudice' environment, TULRCA 1992, s 238B(8) specifically provides in relation to conciliator or mediator that:

- the notes taken by or on behalf of conciliator or mediator are not admissible in evidence before an employment tribunal;
- the conciliator or mediator must refuse to give evidence as to anything communicated to him in connection with the performance of his functions as a conciliator or mediator if, in his opinion, to give the evidence would involve his making a 'damaging disclosure'; and
- the conciliator or mediator may refuse to give evidence as to whether, for the purposes of TULRCA 1992, s 238B(5), a particular question was or was not a reasonable one.

7.136   In summary, the right not to be dismissed for taking protected industrial action is procedurally complex and is designed, as with much modern employment law, to keep disputes within the workplace or, at any rate, out of the employment tribunals. Inevitably, given the complexity of these provisions, litigation involving TULRCA 1992, s 238A is likely to be complex and probably costly as a result.

Trade union-related unfair dismissal procedure

7.137   The procedural aspects of trade union-related unfair dismissal claims are dealt with at one of two levels depending upon whether the dismissal is automatically unfair as a result of it being a dismissal within either TULRCA 1992, ss 152–153 or whether it is an unfair dismissal dealt with by TULRCA 1992, ss 238–238B. Each of the two different areas will be examined in turn and will assume an understanding of the basic principles of the law of unfair dismissal. It should be noted generally that in automatically unfair dismissal claims, the provisions of TULRCA 1992 lock into those existing under ERA 1996, Part X, albeit in a modified form and are to be construed as one with ERA 1996, Part X (TULRCA 1992, s 167(2)).

Procedure in automatically unfair dismissal claims

7.138 The first procedural modification is under TULRCA 1992, s 154(1) which removes the requirement for a claimant to have completed one year's continuous employment with the employer prior to dismissal and also removes the upper age limit of 65 in relation to unfair dismissal claims.

7.139 Secondly, unlike ordinary unfair dismissal claims, in the case of TULRCA 1992, s 152 unfair dismissal claims (but not claims for unfair dismissal due to unfair selection for redundancy under TULRCA 1992, s 153), an employment tribunal has the power, under TULRCA 1992, s 161, to make an Interim Continuation Order the effect of which is to require that an employee's employment with the dismissing employer is deemed to continue pending the outcome of the substantive unfair dismissal claim. An application for such an order must be made to the employment tribunal within the 7 days immediately following the effective date of dismissal, although it is specifically provided that an application can be made before, or after the effective date of dismissal (TULRCA 1992, s 161(1) and (2)). The application should state why it is believed that the claim falls within TULRCA 1992, s 161.[96] Where the interim continuation is followed, there is deemed to be compliance with the statutory dismissal procedures implemented under EA 2002.[97]

7.140 The date of dismissal for these purposes is taken to be either the date on which notice was given to an employee to terminate a contract of employment or in any other case the effective date of termination (TULRCA 1992, s 161(6)).

7.141 Under TULRCA 1992, s 161(3), in order for an application to be considered by an employment tribunal, a certificate in writing must be provided by an authorised official of the independent trade union to which the claimant belongs stating that:

- on the date of dismissal the employee was or proposed to become a member of the union; and
- there appear to be reasonable grounds for supposing that the reason or principal reason for the claimant's dismissal were the grounds set out in the claim.

7.142 There are statutory presumptions that documents purporting to be an authorisation for a trade union official to act and to be a certificate under TULRCA 1992, s 161(3) are such documents unless the contrary is proved (TULRCA 1992, s 161(5)). It is not necessary that an express appointment to a post as an authorised official of a trade union exists and this can be inferred from the status of an official.[98] To the extent that a trade union official is

---

[96] Per *Stone v Charrington & Co* [1977] ICR 248.
[97] Employment Act 2002 (Dispute Resolution) Regulations 2004, SI 2004/752, reg 5(1)(b).
[98] Per *Farmeary v Veterinary Drug Co Limited* [1976] IRLR 322.

challenged to prove that he is an authorised person for these purposes and fails to do so, this amounts to a material defect in a claim for an Interim Continuation Order and will remove an application from the jurisdiction of an employment tribunal hearing the application.[99]

7.143   The point of the interim continuation procedure is to resolve a dispute at an early stage before the damage to trust and confidence in the working relationship caused by a dismissal becomes irreversible. To this end, when an application is made under TULRCA 1992, s 162, an employment tribunal receiving an application is required to determine the application as soon as is reasonably practicable after receiving the application and certificate (TULRCA 1992, s 162(1)). Further, once a hearing date has been set, the date should not be postponed unless 'special circumstances' exist (TULRCA 1992, s 162(4)).

7.144   An employment tribunal is required to give an employer not less than 7 days notice of the date, time and place of a hearing together with a copy of the application (TULRCA 1992, s 162(2)). If a third party to a dispute is being joined to an action for unfair dismissal, the third party is also entitled to receive notice of the time, date and place of the hearing and a copy of the application.

7.145   At the hearing of a claim under TULRCA 1992, s 161, in the event that an employment tribunal finds it 'likely' that it will find a claimant unfairly dismissed at the substantive unfair dismissal hearing, it can then go on to make an Interim Continuation Order under TULRCA 1992, s 163(1). 'Likely' for these purposes was defined by the EAT in *Taplin v C Shippam Limited*,[100] as to mean a 'pretty good' chance of success. The EAT accepted that the industrial tribunal chairman in the case had not erred in law by deciding that this equated to a 51 per cent or more chance of success.

7.146   An employment tribunal is required to announce its findings at the hearing and explain to both parties if they are present the powers that it may exercise. It is also required to ask the employer if it is present whether it is willing, in the period between the hearing under TULRCA 1992, s 161 and the substantive unfair dismissal hearing, to reinstate, or alternatively, to re-engage, the claimant on terms not less favourable than those enjoyed by the claimant prior to the dismissal giving rise to the claim (TULRCA 1992, s 163(2) and (3)).

7.147   Where the employer is prepared to reinstate the employee under an Interim Continuation Order, the employment tribunal will grant the order (TULRCA 1992, s 163(4)). If the employer proposes to re-engage the employee in another job in the period between the interim continuation hearing and the substantive unfair dismissal hearing, and the employer specifies the terms and conditions of the new job, the employment tribunal is required to put the proposed new working conditions to the claimant (TULRCA 1992, s 163(5)(a)). The claimant then has the opportunity either of accepting the job (whereupon the employment tribunal will make an Interim Continuation Order in those terms) or rejecting the job. If, in the opinion of an employment tribunal, the employee reasonably rejects the offer of re-engagement in alternative employment made by an employer, the employment tribunal is bound to make an Interim Continuation Order based on the terms and conditions

---

[99]   Per *Salemany v Habib Bank Limited* [1983] ICR 60.
[100]   [1978] ICR 1068.

enjoyed by the employee prior to dismissal (TULRCA 1992, s 163(5)(b)). If the employment tribunal is of the opinion that a claimant has unreasonably rejected an offer of alternative employment made by the employer, it must not make an Interim Continuation Order (TULRCA 1992, s 163(5)). In the event that either an employer refuses to attend the hearing or does so but advises the employment tribunal that it is not minded to re-employ a claimant, then the employment tribunal is bound to make an Interim Continuation Order (TULRCA 1992, s 163(6)).

7.148 The provisions of Interim Continuation Orders are dealt with by TULRCA 1992, s 164. The effect of such an order is that it provides that the contract of employment in connection with which it is made is deemed to continue in force from the date of the initial dismissal until the determination of the substantive unfair dismissal hearing or settlement of the claim (TULRCA 1992, s 164(1)). The Interim Continuation Order is effective with regard to matters such as pay or any other benefit derived from employment, seniority, pension rights and other such matters, and also is effective with regard to determining the period of continuous employment (TULRCA 1992, s 164(1)(a) and (b)). An employment tribunal is specifically required to state in an Interim Continuation Order the amount of pay to be paid in a normal pay period or part thereof falling to be paid between the date of dismissal and the Interim Continuation Order hearing (TULRCA 1992, s 164(2)). To the extent that an employer has given an employee pay in lieu of notice or a lump sum as compensation for dismissal, this must be set off against any entitlement to remuneration arising under an Interim Continuation Order (TULRCA 1992, s 164(5) and (6)).

7.149 Once an Interim Continuation Order has been made, it is possible for either party to apply to an employment tribunal to vary or revoke the order due to a relevant change of circumstances since the making of the order (TULRCA 1992, s 165(1)). This hearing can be heard by a different employment tribunal to that which made the Interim Continuation Order.[101] The procedure to be adopted in such cases is similar to that needed for the grant of an Interim Continuation Order save that no trade union certificate needs to supplied.

7.150 In the event that an employer fails to comply with the terms of an Interim Continuation Order, then upon an application being made by an employee under TULRCA 1992, s 166(1), an employment tribunal can award such sum as compensation as it thinks just and equitable in all the circumstances as a result of an employer's refusal to comply (TULRCA 1992, s 166). The tribunal is entitled to take into account consequential loss suffered by the employee (TULRCA 1992, s 166(1)).

Remedies in automatically unfair dismissal claims

7.151 The usual remedies of reinstatement, re-engagement and compensation for unfair dismissal are available in automatically unfair trade union-related dismissals under TULRCA 1992, ss 152–153, but these will not be discussed in this book and regard should be had to mainstream employment law works for a full discussion of this area generally. In addition there is an entitlement to

---

[101] Per *British Coal Corporation v McGinty* [1988] IRLR 7.

receive a minimum basic award under TULRCA 1992, s 156. The minimum basic award is necessary given that it is possible to claim unfair dismissal for a trade union-related reason without an employee meeting the usual one-year continuous service requirement with the employer, or for employees aged over 65 who would not otherwise receive an entitlement to a basic award under ERA 1996 (TULRCA 1992, s 154). The amount of the award is set by TULRCA 1992, s 156(1) and is currently £3,800. Reductions can be made from the basic award where the basic award is made under TULRCA 1992, s 153 for contributory fault on the part of the employee (TULRCA 1992, s 156(2)).

Liability of third parties

7.152   A third party who induces a dismissal to take place for a trade union-related reason can be joined as a party to an unfair dismissal action. This occurs under TULRCA 1992, s 160 which applies where an employer has been induced by a third party (typically a trade union) to dismiss an employee by threatening or causing a strike or other industrial action due to the employee's membership or non-membership of a trade union or one or more particular trade unions (TULRCA 1992, s 160(1)). The request to join a third party can be made by either a claimant or an employer (TULRCA 1992, s 160(1)) and must be granted if made at any time prior to a substantive unfair dismissal hearing. A request to join a third party can be refused after the hearing has started and must be refused after liability has been determined (TULRCA 1992, s 160(2)).

7.153   Where a third party is joined to successful proceedings for a trade union-related unfair dismissal, it is possible for either or both of the employer and the third party to be held liable to pay compensation (TULRCA 1992, s 160(3)).

Procedure and remedies in industrial action-related unfair dismissal claims

7.154   The procedure and remedies for claims under this head are dealt with under TULRCA 1992, s 239(1) which ties into the provisions of ERA 1996. The effect is that such claims are dealt with in the same way as non-trade union unfair dismissal claims. This said, two caveats need to be observed, these being in relation to the time-limit for presenting an application to an employment tribunal and in relation to what amounts to contributory fault for the purposes of deductions from an award of compensation under ERA 1996. Each will be examined in turn.

7.155   First, the time-limit for a claim arising under TULRCA 1992, s 238 is extended from the normal period of 3 months (under ERA 1996, s 111(2)) to 6 months by TULRCA 1992, s 239(2). The reason for this extension is to allow a dismissed employee to see whether any discriminatory re-engagement of other employees occurs for the purposes of TULRCA 1992, s 238(2)(b).

7.156   With regard to deductions for contributory fault, the House of Lords has held in *Crossville Wales Limited v Tracey (No 2)*[102] that when an employment tribunal is determining whether to make a deduction for contributory fault in the case of selective re-engagement unfair dismissals, it is to take no

---

[102]   [1997] IRLR 691.

account of the fact that employees have taken industrial action. Their Lordships stated that the reason for this is because of the impossibility of attaching
blame individually to particular actors in collective industrial action. Their
Lordships went on to say that if an individual actor is shown specifically to
have engaged in conduct over and above the industrial action generally, then
the particular fault can be used to reduce an award of compensation.

THE RIGHT NOT TO BE BLACKLISTED FOR TAKING PART IN TRADE UNION-RELATED ACTIVITIES

7.157   This right is an adjunct of the principle of freedom of association as
discussed in the foregoing paragraphs. The right was created under ERA 1999,
s 3 and provides for the Secretary of State to implement regulations prohibit-
ing:

- the compilation of lists which contain details of members of trade unions
  or persons who have taken part in the activities of trade unions, and are
  compiled with a view to being used by employers or employment agencies
  for the purposes of discrimination in relation to recruitment or in relation
  to the treatment of workers; and
- the use, or the sale or supply of such lists.

7.158   Such regulations are specifically allowed to cover such matters as:

- conferring jurisdiction (including exclusive jurisdiction) on employment
  tribunals and on the EAT;
- including provision for or about the grant and enforcement of specified
  remedies by courts and tribunals;
- including provision for the making of awards of compensation calculated
  in accordance with the regulations;
- including provision permitting proceedings to be brought by trade unions
  on behalf of members in specified circumstances;
- including provisions about cases where an employee is dismissed by his
  employer and the reason or principal reason for the dismissal, or why the
  employee was selected for dismissal, is a blacklisting-related reason; and
- creating criminal offences in respect of blacklisting punishable by a fine up
  to level 5 on the standard scale (including in relation to a person who aids
  the commission of the offence or to a person who is an agent, principal,
  employee, employer or officer of a person who commits the offence).

7.159   Currently, no such regulations are in force although draft regulations
were prepared in 2003.

PARTICIPATION RIGHTS OF TRADE UNION MEMBERS

7.160   Participation rights in the activities of a trade union are contingent
upon a trade union being independent and recognised by a particular employer;
these rights cannot exist simply due to membership of a trade union. There are
two participation rights: first, the right of a trade union official to take paid
time off work to carry out trade union duties and, secondly, the right for trade
union members to take time off work to take part in the activities of a trade

union. The statutory rights are also supplemented by the Advisory, Conciliation and Arbitration Service (ACAS) Code of Practice No 3, *Time Off for
Trade Union Duties and Activities* (2003). Each of the rights will be looked at in
turn.

Paid time off for trade union officials

7.161   The provisions relating to the rights for trade union officials and trade
union learning representatives to have paid time off work are set out in
TULRCA 1992, ss 168–169. The rights to paid time off work for trade union
officials are set out in TULRCA 1992, s 168(1)–(2) and TULRCA 1992,
s 168A, which provide:

'168 Time off for carrying out trade union duties

(1)   An employer shall permit an employee of his who is an official of an
independent trade union recognised by the employer to take time off
during his working hours for the purposes of carrying out any duties of
his, as such an official, concerned with—

(a)   negotiations with the employer related to or falling within section 178(2) (collective bargaining) in relation to which the trade union
is recognised by the employer,

(b)   the performance on behalf of employees of the employer of functions
related to or connected with matters falling within that provision
which the employer has agreed may be so performed by the trade
union,

(c)   receipt of information from the employer and consultation by the
employer under section 188 (redundancies) or under the Transfer of
Undertakings (Protection of Employment) Regulations 1981.

(2)   He shall also permit an employee to take time off during his working
hours for the purpose of undergoing training in aspects of industrial
relations—

(a)   relevant to carrying out of such duties as are mentioned in subsection (1), and

(b)   approved by the Trade Union Congress or by the independent trade
union of which he is an official.

...

168A Time off for union learning representatives (1)   An employer shall
permit an employee of his who is—

(a)   a member of an independent trade union recognised by the employer,
and

(b)   a learning representative of the trade union,

to take time off during his working hours for any of the following
purposes.

(2)   The purposes are—

(a)   carrying on any of the following activities in relation to qualifying
members of the trade union—
(i) analysing learning or training needs,

(ii) providing information and advice about learning or training matters,

(iii) arranging learning or training, and

(iv) promoting the value of learning or training,

(b) consulting the employer about carrying on any such activities in relation to such members of the trade union,

(c) preparing for any of the things mentioned in paragraphs (a) and (b).

...

(10) In subsection (2)(a), the reference to qualifying members of the trade union is to members of the trade union—

(a) who are employees of the employer of a description in respect of which the union is recognised by the employer, and

(b) in relation to whom it is the function of the union learning representative to act as such.'

Time off work for trade union duties

7.162 The rights under TULRCA 1992, s 168 are tightly prescribed turning, first, on the matter for which an employee who is a trade union official is to be allowed time off work, being matters related to or connected with performing trade union representative statutory duties. If that aspect of the right is satisfied, then there are two sets of circumstances in which the right can be exercised, essentially for 'performance' (TULRCA 1992, s 168(1)), or for 'educational' (TULRCA 1992, s 168(2)), purposes.

7.163 Prior to the commencement of EA 1988, s 14, the right to paid time off work for the performance of trade union duties was wider in scope and allowed trade union officials time off for any duties connected generally with industrial relations. Any cases prior to the commencement of this amendment are therefore of limited help in defining the current scope of the right.

7.164 The performance limb of the right under TULRCA 1992, s 168(1) allows a trade union official time off work to prepare and take part in collective bargaining arrangements falling within TULRCA 1992, s 178 on behalf of employees, to exercise functions granted by such collective agreements on behalf of fellow employees, or to participate for the purposes of collective consultation under TULRCA 1992, s 188, or under TUPE 1981, in cases where the union is recognised by the employer.

7.165 The right only applies where a trade union has granted an official of it authority to act in respect of those matters. This is a matter to be agreed between a relevant official and his trade union. A trade union official cannot claim paid time off from work if he is usurping a duty which does not fall within the authority granted expressly or impliedly by his union. In *Ashley v Ministry of Defence*,[103] the EAT held that attendance by a trade union official at an unofficial meeting of trade union representatives to ensure a common approach on pay and allied terms prior to an official meeting did not fall within the right to paid time off work. The EAT concluded that unless the official's union had authorised the meeting (which, on the facts it had not), it could not

---

[103]   [1984] IRLR 57.

be said that the official was acting within his duty. It follows that where a trade union has authorised an official to act and he is preparing for that action, this will ordinarily be caught within TULRCA 1992, s 168(1)(a) by virtue of being 'connected with' the matter.[104]

7.166   The educational purpose of the right under TULRCA 1992, s 168(2) allows a trade union official paid time off work for training in aspects of industrial relations connected with matters under TULRCA 1992, s 168(1) or in respect of matters approved by the TUC or by his union. In this regard, it is necessary that the duties performed or to be performed by the official fall within the express or implied authority granted by his union. It follows from this that the right to paid time off for this purpose will turn on the circumstances and status of a particular official. For example, in *Menzies v Smith and McLaurin Limited*,[105] a claim for paid time off work was held by the EAT correctly to have been refused. The claimant had asked for paid time off to attend a course on job security. At the time of his request, his employer was negotiating redundancies. However, the EAT held that the course was too general in nature and would not have had any direct impact on his ability to negotiate in the particular circumstances. It was also felt that it was designed for a higher level of official than the claimant. It follows from this latter point that, although approval may be granted to a course by either the TUC or a particular trade union, it is still necessary for the course to be relevant to the claimant's circumstances.

Time off for union learning representatives

7.167   The right to paid time off for union learning representatives was introduced under EA 2002. The right is available to an employee who meets the double qualification under TULRCA 1992, s 168A(1) of being a member of an independent trade union recognised by the employee's employer, and being a trade union-approved learning representative. The latter point can be proved by the union showing that the employee was so appointed or elected in accordance with the union's rules (TULRCA 1992, s 168(11)).

7.168   Additionally, under TULRCA 1992, s 168A(7), if an employer is required to permit an employee to take time off under TULRCA 1992, s 168A(1), the employer must also permit the employee to take time off during his working hours for the purposes of:

● undergoing training which is relevant to his functions as a learning representative, and

● where, in the last 6 months, in relation to the employee, the trade union has given the employer notice that the employee will be undergoing sufficient training to enable him to carry on trade union learning activities, undergoing that training.

---

[104]   An example of this point is *London Ambulance Service v Charlton* [1992] IRLR 510, which approved a number of the pre-1990 cases, notably *Sood v GEC Elliot Process Automation Limited* [1979] IRLR 416; *Beal v Beacham Group Limited* [1982] IRLR 192; and *British Bakeries (Northern) Limited v Adlington* [1988] IRLR 177.

[105]   [1980] IRLR 180.

7.169   Under TULRCA 1992, s 168A(1), time can be taken off work by a learning representative for any of the purposes under TULRCA 1992, s 168A(2), as set out at **7.161**.

7.170   Under TULRCA 1992, s 168A(3), the right for learning representatives to paid time off is only available where a trade union has given the employee's employer written notice that the employee is a learning representative of the union and one of the 'training conditions' of TULRCA 1992, s 168A(4) are met in relation to the employee, these being that:

- The employee has undergone sufficient training to enable him to carry on trade union learning activities and the trade union has given the employer notice in writing of this.
- The trade union has in the last 6 months given the employer notice in writing that the employee will be undergoing such training. In this regard, TULRCA 1992, s 168A(5) provides that only one such notice can be given to the employer.
- Within 6 months of the trade union giving the employer notice in writing that the employee will be undergoing such training, the employee has done so, and the trade union has notified this to the employer.

7.171   As with time off for trade union duties, the right is to time off during the employee's working hours (in respect of which see **7.173**).

The amount of time off under the rights

7.172   The amount of time off to be granted is dealt with under TULRCA 1992, s 168(3) (in the case of time off for trade union duties) and TULRCA 1992, s 168A(8) (in the case of time off for learning representatives), which provide that an employee is entitled to such time off as is reasonable in all the circumstances. Further, both TULRCA 1992, ss 168(3) and 168A(8) provide that it is necessary for employers to consider the relevant provisions of the ACAS Code of Practice No 3, *Time Off for Trade Union Duties and Activities* (2003). Two points arise in this regard: first, what are the employee's working hours and, secondly, whether there is any judicial guidance as to what is reasonable time off.

The employee's working hours

7.173   The rights to paid time off under TULRCA 1992, ss 168 and 168A only allow an employee time off during his working hours. The concept of the employee's working hours is defined under TULRCA 1992, s 173(1) as being any time that an employee is required by his contract of employment to be at work. It follows that if, for example, an employee attends a course or a meeting outside his working hours, he will have no right to claim a corresponding amount of time off from his working hours. This said, if the course or meeting is outside his working hours but the employee is required to travel in working hours to get to it, the employee will be allowed time off for the travelling since this is likely to be 'reasonable' under TULRCA 1992, s 168(3). For example, in *Hairsine v Kingston Upon Hull City Council*,[106] the claimant was required to work on a shift basis. He was allocated an afternoon and evening shift by his

---

[106]   [1992] IRLR 211.

employer on a day when he was due to attend a course in the morning and afternoon. As the claimant was rostered to attend at work for the afternoon and evening shift, but worked the latter only, he argued that he should have been paid on the basis that he had worked a full day during the morning and afternoon and was entitled to pay for a full day for that session (ie his evening shift was effectively overtime). The employer paid the claimant for the afternoon and evening shift only. The claim was rejected by both the industrial tribunal and the EAT, with the EAT holding that time off must be part of the claimant's 'working hours', which is to be given a literal meaning. Since the claimant had not been rostered to work during the morning, he had no right to payment for it.

Time off to be reasonable

7.174   In relation to time off for trade union activities, TULRCA 1992, s 168 provides that the time to be taken off must be reasonable. In assessing the question of the reasonableness of a request, an employer can take into account the amount of time off that is being requested, the purpose for which it is being taken and the occasions on which it is being requested together with any conditions that have been laid down by the employer (TULRCA 1992, s 168(3)).

7.175   In the case of time off for trade union learning representatives, under TULRCA 1992, s 168A(8), the amount of time off which an employee is to be permitted to take off and the purposes for which, the occasions on which and any conditions subject to which time off may be taken are stated to be those that are reasonable in all the circumstances having regard to the ACAS Code of Practice No 3, *Time Off for Trade Union Duties and Activities* (2003).

7.176   A question arises as to what test is to be applied to the question of reasonableness in this context, ie should it be a subjective view of reasonableness from the point of view of the employer at the time of refusal, or an objective view determined by an employment tribunal subsequently. In *Ministry of Defence v Crook*,[107] the EAT held that the test was to consider whether the employer had behaved within a band of reasonable responses to the request for time off (ie the same test as that for unfair dismissal). This view has been endorsed in *Wignall v British Gas Corporation*[108] and in *Hairsine v Kingston Upon Hull City Council*.[109]

Refusal of time off

7.177   Where an employer refuses an employee the right to take time off work under TULRCA 1992, s 168 or 168A, the employee is left with a difficult choice. The employee must either forego taking the time off work and present a claim under TULRCA 1992, s 168(4) or 168A(9) (as the case may be) for pay, or take the time off and make a claim under TULRCA 1992, s 169(5) (which allows an employee to be paid for the time off if his employer subsequently refuses to pay him for legitimately taking time off work under either TULRCA 1992, s 168 or 168A). In the event that the employee takes time off in defiance

---

[107]   [1982] IRLR 488.
[108]   [1984] IRLR 493.
[109]   [1992] IRLR 211.

of an employer's instruction, the result may well be a breach of contract on the employee's part since the employee could be argued to be failing to follow a lawful and reasonable instruction. This said, it may be possible to show that the employer has behaved so unreasonably as to undermine trust and confidence in the working relationship leading to a 'who breached the contract' dispute. If the employer were to dismiss unfairly in such circumstances, it would be automatically unfair by virtue of TULRCA 1992, s 152, although this may well be small consolation to the employee who has been so constructively dismissed. In such circumstances, employees may well be best advised to miss the course and make a claim for compensation to an employment tribunal under TULRCA 1992, s 168(4).

Right to pay for time off

7.178   Where an employee has taken time off under TULRCA 1992, s 168 or 168A, an employer is bound to pay the employee for the time so taken under TULRCA 1992, s 169(1). The amount of pay is dealt with by TULRCA 1992, s 169(2)–(4) and is stated to be such sum as an employee would ordinarily be paid during the working time that the employee is absent. If an employee is entitled by his contract of employment to be paid for time off, the sums that he would be entitled to under the statutory right are set off under TULRCA 1992, s 169(4). In the case of part-time employees exercising the right, they have the right to be paid on the same basis as their full-time counterparts when attending union-run courses away from their work.[110]

Enforcing the rights

7.179   To the extent that an employer unreasonably refuses to allow an employee to take time off work, or unreasonably refuses to pay for the working time that has taken been taken off, a claim can be presented to an employment tribunal under, respectively, TULRCA 1992, s 168(4) or 168A(9), or 169(5). A claim must be made within 3 months of the date on which the failure occurred or within such further period as the tribunal thinks fit where it has decided that it was unreasonable to present the claim within the 3-month time period (TULRCA 1992, s 171). In order for a claim to be presented, the employee has to establish on the balance of probabilities that he in fact made a request for paid time off to the employee's employer.[111]

7.180   Where a claim is upheld by an employment tribunal the tribunal is bound to make a declaration to that effect and may award compensation of such sum as the tribunal considers just and equitable in all the circumstances having regard to the employer's default in failing to permit time off to be taken by the employee and to any loss sustained by the employee which is attributable to the matters complained of (TULRCA 1992, s 172(1) and (2)). In *Skiggs v*

---

[110]   See in this regard *Davies v Neath Port Talbot County Borough Council* [1999] IRLR 769, which disapproves the earlier decision of *Manor Bakeries Limited v Nazir* [1996] IRLR 604. *Davies* is still of use notwithstanding the introduction of the Part-time Workers (Prevention of Less Favourable Treatment) Regulations 2000, SI 2000/1551, which only provides the basis of a claim for a part-time worker receiving less favourable terms than a full-time worker in a situation where the full-time worker undertakes comparable work to the part-time worker.

[111]   *Ryford Limited v Drinkwater* [1996] IRLR 16.

South West Trains Limited,[112] the EAT was required, inter alia, to consider whether the provisions of TULRCA 1992, s 172 allowed a claimant, who had suffered no financial loss as a result of an employer's decision not to allow the employee paid time off to undertake trade union duties, to recover compensation for injury to feelings. The EAT held that the wording of TULRCA 1992, s 172, which provides for compensation to be awarded for the employee's loss, is drafted so as to allow an employment tribunal to award compensation for loss beyond mere financial loss and therefore envisages that sums for injury to feelings may be recovered.

7.181 Where a claim is made under TULRCA 1992, s 169, the remedy is a declaration and an order of compensation for the value of the wages which have not been paid (TULRCA 1992, s 172(3)).

TIME OFF FOR TRADE UNION ACTIVITIES

7.182 The right for employees to take time off work to take part in trade union activities is set out in TULRCA 1992, s 170, which provides as follows:

'(1) An employer shall permit an employee of his who is a member of an independent trade union recognised by the employer in respect of that description of employee to take time off during his working hours for the purpose of taking part in—

(a) any activities of the union, and
(b) any activities in relation to which the employee is acting as a representative of the union.

(2)   The right conferred by subsection (1) does not extend to activities which themselves consist of industrial action, whether or not in contemplation or furtherance of a trade dispute.'

7.183 The right is very widely defined. However, the EAT has sought to limit the scope of the right in *Luce v London Borough of Bexley*.[113] Here, the claimant sought time off work to attend a union lobby of Parliament. His employer refused the request for time off whereupon the claimant presented proceedings in the industrial tribunal claiming that he should have been allowed to attend. The tribunal rejected the claim on the grounds that it was necessary to consider whether it was a reasonable activity, which it found it was not. The EAT rejected an appeal, holding, that:[114]

'... although we do not consider that the phrase [any activities] should be understood too restrictively, we are satisfied that it cannot have been the intention of Parliament to have included any activity of whatever nature.'

7.184 It is submitted that this position is not correct. TULRCA 1992, s 170 requires only that an employee takes part in any of the activities of an independent trade union recognised by his employer; there is no qualification apart from that relating to industrial action and as such the case must be wrong

---

[112]   [2005] IRLR 459.
[113]   [1990] IRLR 422.
[114]   [1990] IRLR 422 at 425.

in law. Indeed, for either an employer or an employment tribunal to second-guess what a trade union believes is necessary for its members would seem to extend the law far beyond that which is set out in TULRCA 1992, s 170.

7.185 Following amendments made under EA 2002 to introduce the new learning representative rights, amendments were made to TULRCA 1992, s 170. These provide that the right to time off for trade union activities does not extend to time off for the purpose of acting as, or having access to services provided by, a learning representative of a trade union (TULRCA 1992, s 170(2A)). Further, employers are required to permit their employees who are members of an independent trade union recognised by the employer to take time off during their working hours for the purpose of having access to services provided by a person in his capacity as a learning representative of the trade union where the learning representative would be entitled to time off under TULRCA 1992, s 168A(1) for the purpose of undertaking learning activities.

7.186 As with the right for employees to time off work for undertaking trade union duties, an employer can consider whether a request is reasonable (TULRCA 1992, s 170(3)).

Enforcing the right

7.187 It is possible to present a claim to an employment tribunal within 3 months of an employer's refusal to allow time off work (TULRCA 1992, ss 170(4) and 171). Where an employment tribunal allows a claim, the tribunal must make a declaration to that effect and, where appropriate, make an order for compensation reflecting the loss suffered (TULRCA 1992, s 172(1)).

Chapter 8

THE INDUSTRIAL TORTS AND BREACH OF CONTRACT

INTRODUCTION

8.1   Industrial action has for a long time been the means that trade unions have adopted, usually as a last resort, to bring about change in the workplace. As set out in **Chapter 1**, industrial action has been a legitimate part of the industrial negotiating machinery since approximately the last quarter of the nineteenth century. Industrial action places two collectives (capital and labour) against each other and allows the collectives to engage in a process of attrition to bring about a new industrial order. Up until the start of the 1970s, this was the natural way of industrial negotiation. Indeed, various judgments over the course of the twentieth century reflected the importance of the right to take industrial action. For example, in *Crofter Hand Woven Harris Tweed Co Limited v Veitch*, Lord Wright stated:[1]

> 'In commercial affairs each trader's rights are qualified by the right to compete. Where the rights of labour are concerned, the rights of the employer are conditioned by the rights of the men to give or withhold their services. The right of workmen to strike is an essential element in the principle of collective bargaining.'

8.2   This statement is very much representative of the high point of what became known as the 'collective *laissez faire*' school of thought.

8.3   The current view of this area of the law, however, is that there is no right to strike, merely immunity from the tortious consequences of industrial action when it is taken. Further, in the event that individual employees withdraw their labour, this can amount to a breach of their contracts of employment, although the Employment Rights Act 1996 (ERA 1996), s 216 recognises that the continuity of employment of an employee who chooses to strike will be maintained during the course of such action until such time as the employee either returns to work or is dismissed. To the extent that an employee engages in industrial action and his wages are reduced to reflect the value of services lost by his employer as a result of the industrial action, no claim for the lost wages exists under ERA 1996, Part II (the provisions dealing with the unlawful deduction of wages). Other statutory employment rights that can be lost for taking industrial action are the right to receive a statutory redundancy payment

---

1   [1942] AC 435 at 463.

(ERA 1996, s 140) and the right to receive guarantee payments (ERA 1996, s 29). Furthermore, the question of entitlement to social security benefits is also tied into the issue of industrial action and the absence of a 'right to strike' is reflected in the fact that it is not possible to claim jobseekers allowance during the course of industrial action (Jobseekers Act 1995, s 14) or statutory sick pay (Social Security Contribution and Benefits Act 1992, Sch 11, paras 2 and 7).

INDUSTRIAL ACTION AND THE LAW OF TORT

8.4   The purpose of industrial action is that by the use of collective force, employees can bring about work-related changes. However, deliberately harming the legitimate interests of an employer may amount to tortious conduct, and there is no doubt that in many cases industrial action can be seen as a deliberate attempt to harm the legitimate interests of an employer (even if this view is only held by the employers affected by such action). The problem for employers, however, is that when considering the legality of industrial action, trade unions enjoy a degree of immunity in tort. This said, in certain circumstances, the immunity enjoyed by trade unions can be removed. Therefore, in the context of the legality of industrial action the following issues arise:

• Has a tort been committed in the course of the industrial action?
• Does an immunity exist in law for the tort committed?
• Has the immunity been removed?
• Does a remedy exist, to any extent, against the union?

8.5   This chapter will focus on the first of those issues, **Chapter 9** will focus on the second and third issues and **Chapter 10** will discuss the issue of remedies.

THE INDUSTRIAL TORTS

8.6   The main torts that will be committed during the course of industrial action are economic torts, ie the harm resulting from these torts is economic in nature rather than the result of the tort being some form of personal or property damage. In this regard, a number of torts have evolved over the years, some or all of which may be committed during the course of industrial action, as follows:

• conspiracy, (both simple and by using unlawful means);
• directly or indirectly inducing breach of contract;
• using unlawful means to interfere with a contract, trade or business;
• intimidation;
• harassment; and
• other torts committed during picketing.

Each of the torts will be examined in turn.

Simple conspiracy

8.7   After the introduction of the Conspiracy and Protection of Property Act 1875, s 3 which provided:

'An agreement or combination by two or more persons to do or procure to be done any act in contemplation or furtherance of a trade dispute ... shall not be indictable as a conspiracy if such act committed by one person would not be punishable as a crime ...'

it was assumed that it was no longer possible for a trade union to be thwarted in its attempts to attempt to negotiate work-related change by means of a concerted withdrawal of labour. The problem was that the Conspiracy and Protection of Property Act 1875 expressly dealt with the concept of criminal conspiracy only: it did not address conspiracy as it arose in the form of the law of tort for a good reason, namely, that it was a little used tort. Indeed as the High Court observed in *Midland Bank Trust Co Limited v Green (No 3)*:[2]

'As regards the tort of conspiracy ... very little is heard of it until the 19th Century when it was brought into prominence as a result of the legislature having, in 1875, enacted that combinations in furtherance of trade dispute should not be indictable ...'

8.8 After the passing of the Conspiracy and Protection of Property Act 1875, a number of cases were brought using the tort of conspiracy as a cause of action, the three most prominent of which were *Mogul Steamship Co Limited v McGregor Gow & Co*;[3] *Allen v Flood*;[4] and *Quinn v Leathem*.[5]

8.9 The *Mogul* case[6] concerned a shipowners' trade association. The association had decided that its members should reach an agreement on the number of ships to be sent to particular ports, the rates that would be charged for cargo and the rebates that would be given to cargo owners who agreed to use associated members exclusively as their shipping agent. The claimant was a shipowner who had been excluded from the association. It sent its ships to ports at which the defendant operated in order to source cargoes. The defendant discovered that the claimant was operating in one of its ports and promptly sent more of its members' ships to the port. It underbid the claimant at prices which were uneconomic for the journeys being undertaken. Further, it instructed agents operating for it that they would be dismissed if they gave cargoes to the claimant and told customers that the rebates that were provided would be removed from customers who used the claimant for the provision of services. The claimant commenced proceedings claiming that the concerted action of the association amounted to a conspiracy to injure the claimant. The House of Lords held in relation to the claim that:[7]

'... [a]s the law is now settled, [we] apprehend that in order to substantiate their claim, the appellants must shew, either that the object of the agreement was unlawful, or that illegal methods were resorted to in its prosecution. If neither the end contemplated by the agreement, nor the means used for its attainment were contrary to the law, the loss suffered by the appellants was damnum sine injuria.'

8.10 The House of Lords went on to hold that a combination to trade and offer discounts for doing so, even if it might be harmful, did not amount to an actionable conspiracy in law.

---

2   [1979] Ch 496 at 523.
3   [1892] AC 25.
4   [1898] AC 1.
5   [1901] AC 495.
6   *Mogul Steamship Co Limited v McGregor Gow & Co* [1892] AC 25.
7   [1892] AC 25 at 41.

8.11   *Mogul*[8] was followed in 1898 by *Allen*.[9] The importance of *Allen* can be seen by the length of the case (189 pages of the Appeal Cases) and the fact that it was argued twice before the House of Lords (the second occasion being in front of nine Law Lords and an advisory body of eight High Court judges). The facts of the case were, of themselves, quite simple. The claimants were shipwrights who had been employed to carry out work on the repair of a ship. The defendant was an ironworker and union official. The trade union to which he belonged operated a closed shop at the Glengall Iron Company's shipyard. The defendant informed the employer that, unless the claimant was dismissed, his trade union would call a strike of its members working for the employer. In the face of this threat, the employer succumbed and dismissed the claimant who sued the defendant claiming that he had conspired with members of the trade union to injure the claimant's interests. At trial, the claim was rejected by the High Court, which held that there was no evidence of conspiracy, coercion, intimidation or breach of contract on the part of the defendant. However, a jury found that the defendant had maliciously caused the employer to dismiss the claimant and awarded damages of £40. The decision was then affirmed by the Court of Appeal. On appeal, the House of Lords, through a majority decision (6–3), found in favour of the defendant. Lord Watson (in the majority), stated:[10]

> 'It is, in my opinion, the absolute right of every workman to exercise his own option with regard to the persons in whose society he will agree or continue to work. It may be deplorable that feelings of rivalry between different associations of working men should run ever so high as to make members of one union seriously object to continue their labour in company with members of another trade union; but so long as they commit no legal wrong, and use no means which are illegal, they are at perfect liberty to act upon their own views.'

8.12   The majority of their Lordships also went on to hold that the conduct of the defendant was not actionable, even if it was motivated by malice or bad motive; there had been no conspiracy. To put the matter in a different way, if no tort had been committed, the defendant was perfectly entitled to do something that he had a lawful right to do and to do it with bad grace.

8.13   The decision in *Allen*[11] was followed shortly afterwards by the third of the cases in the simple conspiracy trilogy, *Quinn v Leathem*.[12] In *Quinn*, the claimant was a Belfast butcher who employed the defendants (who were members of a trade union). One of the trade union's objects was to help promote the interests of other members of the trade union at the expense of non-members. To this end, the defendants organised a closed shop. The claimant also employed a butcher who was not a trade union member. The claimant was visited by the defendants who informed him that, if he continued to employ the non-trade union member employee, they would cause one of his clients not to take meat from him any more by informing the customer that

---

8   *Mogul Steamship Co Limited v McGregor Gow & Co* [1892] AC 25.
9   *Allen v Flood* [1898] AC 1.
10   [1898] AC 1 at 98.
11   *Allen v Flood* [1898] AC 1.
12   [1901] AC 495.

their members in the customer's employment would refuse to handle the meat delivered by the claimant. The claimant lost the customer and, additionally, was put on 'blacklists' in the Belfast area by the union. As a result of the action taken by the union, the claimant sued for damages caused by the conspiracy. On appeal, the matter was heard by the House of Lords. Their Lordships held for the claimant and, in doing so, distinguished *Allen v Flood*. According to their Lordships, the chief distinction between the two cases was that in *Allen*, the mere presence of threats existed which were not carried into effect by the defendants. However, in *Quinn*, the defendants had gone further in their actions. They had threatened the claimant with a potential loss of business and then carried the threat into effect. The matter was addressed by Lord Brampton in this fashion:[13]

'A conspiracy consists of an unlawful combination of two or more persons to do that which is contrary to law, or to do that which is wrongful and harmful towards another person. It may be punishable criminally by indictment, or civilly by an action on the case in the nature of conspiracy if damage has been occasioned to the person against whom it is directed. It may also consist of an unlawful combination to carry out an object not in itself unlawful by unlawful means. The essential elements, whether of a criminal or actionable conspiracy, are, in my opinion, the same, though to sustain an action special damage must be proved.'

8.14 At first glance, the decisions in *Mogul*,[14] *Allen*[15] and *Quinn*[16] are irreconcilable in that they appear to decide the same point in differing fashions. However, the accepted point of reconciliation between the three cases is that *Mogul* decided that it is not unlawful to carry out acts that harm another where the acts complained of are not unlawful in themselves and will further the interests of those combining; *Allen* decides that an act that is not carried into effect in the form of a conspiracy and which is of itself lawful is not actionable; and *Quinn* holds that a combination to injure another, which is not in the trade interests of those combining, can be actionable where it is either unlawful action, or is lawful action but is carried into effect with the aim of harming the victim provided that the victim can show special damage. This position has been endorsed in a number of subsequent judgments.[17]

Elements of a simple conspiracy

8.15

The elements of the tort of simple conspiracy are that a claimant must show the following the things:

- a combination of two or more persons;
- an agreement between the members of the combination to do an act or cause an act to be done to the victim of the conspiracy;

---

13 [1901] AC 495 at 528.
14 *Mogul Steamship Co Limited v McGregor Gow & Co* [1892] AC 25.
15 *Allen v Flood* [1898] AC 1.
16 *Quinn v Leathem* [1901] AC 495.
17 See, for example, *Ware and De Freville v Motor Trade Association* [1921] 3 KB 40; *Sorrell v Smith* [1925] AC 700; and *Crofter Hand Woven Harris Tweed Co Limited v Veitch* [1942] AC 435.

- an intention to injure the claimant; and
- a predominant purpose of injuring the claimant.

Each will be looked at in turn.

The combination

8.16   One of the problems that exists in establishing a conspiracy in the context of industrial action is whether for the purposes of membership of a conspiracy, trade unions can count as a person for the purposes of the numbers necessary to make up a conspiracy. As was seen in **Chapter 2**, trade unions do not have legal personality save to the extent that they are granted status by the Trade Union and Labour Relations (Consolidation) Act 1992 (TULRCA 1992), s 10. However, as regards a union's ability to be a conspirator, it must be doubtful that the alleged conspirators in an action could be both an official of the union (for example, a shop steward) and the trade union itself. Indeed, if the language of TULRCA 1992, s 20 (the section attaching liability in tort to a trade union) is examined, TULRCA 1992, s 20(1)(b) states that:

> '(1)   Where proceedings in tort are brought against a trade union—
>
> ...
>
> (b) in respect of an agreement or combination by two or more persons to do or to procure the doing of an act which, if it were done without any such agreement or combination, would be actionable in tort on such a ground,
>
> then, for the purpose of determining in those proceedings whether the union is liable in respect of the act in question, that act shall be taken to have been done by the union if, *but only if* [emphasis added], it is to be taken to have been authorised or endorsed by the trade union in accordance with the following provisions.'

8.17   TULRCA 1992, s 20(2) requires that another person or group of persons, who hold positions of authority in the trade union, must act to make the union liable. Consequently, since TULRCA 1992 requires the conspiracy to have taken place before liability can attach to a trade union, it would seem that the union cannot itself be a conspirator.

8.18   Another more fundamental problem exists in any event and that is the question of how it is to be determined whether a body that is, at best, quasi-corporate, can have the mental capacity to enter into a conspiracy. This said, it has been held that corporate bodies can conspire with directors of corporations.[18]

Agreement

8.19   An agreement for the purposes of a conspiracy can be express or implied. It must, however, be present. It is not enough that the alleged conspirators have independently done the same thing to the victim. An agreement may, however, be implied from the circumstances of the action taken

---

[18]   See, for example, *Belmont Finance Corporation v Williams Furniture Limited (No 2)* [1980] 1 All ER 393; and *Prudential Assurance Co Limited v Newman Industries (No 2)* [1982] Ch 204.

against a claimant, for example, where all unionised employees at an establishment walk out on strike at the same time. A conspiracy may not take place though where, for example, individuals break their contracts of employment by refusing to cross an unlawful picket line.

8.20 This said, it is not necessary for conspirators to reach agreement at the same time: it is possible for a person to become a conspirator after a wrongful common venture has been embarked upon by a group of tortfeasors where the wrongful act is still continuing, for example, where an employee joins an unlawful strike after it has begun.

8.21 Further, it is possible to have a conspiracy where one of the parties taking part in the conspiracy could not actually carry the conspiracy into effect himself. In *Rookes v Barnard*,[19] industrial action was threatened to enforce a closed shop the result of which was the dismissal of the claimant, a non-trade union member employee. Part of the claimant's claim alleged a conspiracy. One of the alleged conspirators involved in the threat to break contracts of employment was a trade union official not actually employed by the employer. The House of Lords nonetheless held that he could be involved in the conspiracy.

8.22 Once the conspiracy has been established, the law treats an act done by one of the conspirators as an act of them all if the act is in furtherance of the objects of the conspiracy.[20]

Intention to injure

8.23 With every conspiracy there must be an intention to cause wrongful harm to the claimant.[21] In the case of a simple conspiracy, the wrongful harm is found in the malicious purpose, being the doing of the act to the claimant.[22] As to what amounts to intention on the part of the tortfeasors, it would appear to amount to the same test as intention under the criminal law, ie that wrongful harm to the claimant is the natural and probable consequence of the actors action.[23]

Predominant purpose

8.24 As has been stated at **8.14**, the key distinction between the cases of *Allen v Flood*[24] and *Quinn v Leathem*[25] is that in order for liability to attach against conspirators, an act must actually be done; a threat will not suffice. The most obvious form of act will be a withdrawal of labour on the part of the conspirators. Moreover, it is the manner in which the conspiracy is delivered. The conspirators must behave maliciously towards the victim; they must know what they are doing, know that they are behaving oppressively towards the

---

19 [1964] AC 1129.
20 *DC Thomson & Co Limited v Deakin* [1952] Ch 646.
21 *Lonrho Limited v Shell Petroleum Co* [1982] AC 173; and see also the further decision of the House of Lords in *Lonrho plc v Fayed* [1992] 1 AC 448.
22 *Crofter Hand Woven Harris Tweed Co Limited v Veitch* [1942] AC 435.
23 *R v Hancock* [1986] AC 455.
24 [1898] AC 1.
25 [1901] AC 495.

victim and must do so in the absence of a lawful defence. To the extent that a lawful defence can be established, no tort will have been committed.[26]

Defence

8.25   A defence exists to a claim for simple conspiracy. The tort requires a predominant purpose on the part of the conspirators to injure the interests of the claimant. This predominant purpose was rather taken for granted by the courts in earlier cases where a simple conspiracy was alleged, until the landmark case of *Crofter v Veitch*.[27] Here, the claimant was a manufacturer of tweed cloth on the Scottish mainland. Members of the defendant trade union were dockers on the island of Lewis. Millowners on the island had agreed with the defendant to operate a closed shop if the union could stop the import of cloth from the Scottish mainland. The dockers managed to do this by refusing to handle the cloth which needed to be finished on the island in order to be sold as Harris tweed. The claimant sought an injunction and damages for alleged simple conspiracy. On appeal to the House of Lords, their Lordships held that, when looking at industrial disputes, the predominant purpose of a trade union will usually be an attempt to enforce a change in the terms and conditions of employment for the benefit of the union's members. A trade union may well intend to cause harm to an employer to achieve that purpose; but that is a side issue. To this end, trade unions will have a defence in many cases of simple conspiracy on this basis.

8.26   Other cases in point are *DC Thomson & Co Limited v Deakin*;[28] *Scala Ballroom (Wolverhampton) Limited v Ratcliffe*;[29] and *JT Stratford & Son Limited v Lindley*.[30] *Thomson* concerned an attempt made by the printing union, NATSOPA, to make an employer abandon its policy of employing non-union labour. This was held to be a legitimate purpose in establishing a defence to an action based upon a simple conspiracy. Likewise, in the *Stratford* case, an attempt to gain trade union collective bargaining rights was held to be a valid primary purpose for the purposes of establishing a defence to a simple conspiracy. Furthermore, *Scala* is a case that shows the flexibility of the concept introduced by *Crofter*.[31] Here, the removal of a colour bar at a ballroom was the object of a boycott by the Musicians' Union. This, too, was held to be a lawful defence to an action for simple conspiracy even though it did not translate into detailed financial benefits for the union's members.

8.27   However, in *Huntley v Thornton*,[32] a decision was granted against the defendant trade union. The case turned on a decision to expel the claimant from trade union membership for refusing to support a 24-hour strike over a claimed pay rise. Initially, the trade union was intent merely on disciplining the claimant. The claimant, however, left a disciplinary meeting convened in relation to his action before the conclusion of that meeting. Consequently, the

---

[26]   *Mogul Steamship Co Limited v McGregor Gow & Co* [1892] AC 25.
[27]   [1942] AC 435.
[28]   [1952] Ch 646.
[29]   [1958] 1 WLR 1057.
[30]   [1965] AC 269.
[31]   *Crofter v Veitch* [1942] AC 435.
[32]   [1957] 1 WLR 321.

local committee of the trade union decided to recommend to the unions' executive council the expulsion of the claimant; this recommendation was refused by the executive committee. In the meantime, the claimant had left his original employment and was seeking fresh employment. The local committee was successful in blocking this with employers operating closed shops. The claimant tried to make amends with the local committee of the trade union but they refused to accept his apology and resolved to expel the claimant, which, under the union's rules, was ultra vires. The claimant sued alleging a conspiracy and was successful in the High Court which held that the predominant purpose in this case was not the interests of the trade union but an attempt to appease the local committee's 'ruffled dignity'.

Burden of proof

8.28 The burden of proof in a case of simple conspiracy will lie on the claimant who must establish all elements of the tort, including a predominant purpose on the part of the tortfeasors to behave maliciously towards the claimant.[33] It will commonly be the case that, as to the issue of a trade union's predominant purpose, a defendant may adduce evidence in rebuttal by showing that, whilst it may be taken to have intended to harm the claimant, the trade union's purpose was to secure a legitimate aim.[34]

Problems with simple conspiracy

8.29 It has been suggested that the tort of simple conspiracy is an anomaly. The problem lies in the comparison between *Allen v Flood*[35] and *Quinn v Leathem*[36] in that if one takes the view that *Allen* is a case involving an individual acting on his own as opposed to a conspiracy, the question that arises is why it is unlawful to do a thing in concert with another which would, if done by an individual actor, be lawful. This issue was addressed by the House of Lords in *Lonrho Limited v Shell Petroleum Co Limited (No 2)*,[37] which concluded that the tort was too well established to be discarded however anomalous it may seem today.

CONSPIRACY USING UNLAWFUL MEANS

8.30 Whereas the tort of simple conspiracy focuses upon a wrongful motive for the doing of an act causing harm, conspiracy using unlawful means focuses upon the means adopted to cause harm. The elements which are required to establish the tort are the following:

- a combination of two or more persons;
- an agreement between the members of the combination to injure the claimant;
- the collective performance by, or at the behest of, the combination of an act which is itself unlawful; and
- an intention to injure the claimant in the performance of the act.

---

33   *Crofter Hand Woven Harris Tweed Co Limited v Veitch* [1942] AC 435.
34   *Sorrell v Smith* [1925] AC 700.
35   [1898] AC 1.
36   [1901] AC 495.
37   [1982] AC 173.

Unlawful acts

8.31 Unlawful acts for the purposes of this species of conspiracy can be broken down essentially into three categories, these being criminal acts, tortious acts and acts that consist of a breach of contract on the part of the tortfeasor. Each will be considered in turn.

Criminal acts

8.32 It is generally accepted that where a combination of workers commits a criminal act against a claimant, that act will be actionable as a conspiracy in tort. However, this view is reached against the background of the difficult decision in *Lonrho Limited v Shell Petroleum Co Limited (No 2)*.[38] Prior to this case, the House of Lords had accepted that a conspiracy which had at its root a criminal act aimed at the claimant was actionable under the tort of conspiracy using unlawful means.[39]

8.33 The *Lonrho* case[40] arose out of the economic blockade of the former Southern Rhodesia which was implemented by the British Government. The blockade was imposed by an Order in Council which was enforceable by criminal sanctions against any person breaking the boycott. The claimant, as part of its trading operations, carried on the business of oil suppliers. It brought proceedings against the defendants claiming that Shell and BP had conspired between them to carry on supplying oil to Southern Rhodesia in breach of the boycott. The claimant alleged that this directly affected its business interests. To the extent that the claimant could establish a tortious conspiracy, the conspiracy would have been one arising through the use of unlawful means. However, the claimant had problems in establishing such a conspiracy. First, whilst it was alleged that the defendants may have conspired to commit criminal acts, the acts were not aimed at causing harm to the claimant. This of itself was fatal to the claimant being able to establish a conspiracy using unlawful means. However, the House of Lords also held that it is not possible to frame a civil action out of the breach of a criminal statute unless either the statute provides for enforcement through the civil courts, or the claimant is someone who suffers particular harm as a result of a breach of the statute. Since the claimant did not fall into either category, the claim failed.

8.34 Another example of the tort in action is *Gouriet v Union of Post Office Workers*.[41] Here, the claimant was a member of the Freedom Association. He objected to a threatened boycott of mail to South Africa by postal workers and claimed that the boycott would result in a criminal offence under the Post Office Act 1953, s 58. The claimant sought an injunction to prevent the proposed action. On appeal, the House of Lords refused to grant the injunction. Their Lordships held that the courts would not grant civil remedies to uphold penal statutes unless the claim was brought either by the Attorney-General in the public interest or because the claimant would suffer personal hardship as a result of the criminal action.

---

[38]   [1982] AC 173.
[39]   See, for example, *Sorrell v Smith* [1925] AC 700; and *Rookes v Barnard* [1964] AC 1129.
[40]   *Lonrho Limited v Shell Petroleum Co Limited (No 2)* [1982] AC 173.
[41]   [1978] AC 435.

8.35   After *Lonrho v Shell*,[42] it seemed that it would not be possible to use criminal wrongdoing as a means for launching a claim of civil conspiracy unless the claimant fell into either or both of the *Lonrho v Shell* categories. However, in *Lonrho plc v Fayed*,[43] the House of Lords reviewed the law relating to conspiracy using unlawful means and held that all that was decided by *Lonrho v Shell* was that in every conspiracy, an intent to injure the claimant must be shown and therefore the long-standing views of the House of Lords in *Sorrell v Smith*[44] and *Rookes v Barnard*[45] still hold good.

Tortious acts

8.36   It is possible to allege that a combination of workers has agreed to commit other torts against a claimant. In such a case, there is a genuine question as to whether or not the allegation of conspiracy actually adds anything to the overall litigation or amounts to 'belt and braces' litigation. Certainly, the view of the House of Lords in *Sorrell v Smith* was that an allegation of conspiracy in such circumstances added nothing to a claimant's case.[46]

Breach of contract

8.37   It is still debatable whether a breach of contract amounts to unlawful means for the purposes of this form of conspiracy and in this regard, two cases on the point are highly pertinent, these being *Rookes v Barnard*[47] and *Barretts & Bairds (Wholesale) Limited v IPCS*.[48] In *Rookes*, the claimant sued the defendant on account of his dismissal by his employer. The dismissal had arisen due to the employer operating a closed shop. The claimant was not a member of the trade union of which the defendants were members, and as a result, officials of the trade union threatened the employer with strike action unless the claimant was dismissed. The claimant sued, alleging, inter alia, that he had been the victim of a civil conspiracy using unlawful means, this being the threat to break the contracts of employment of the union members employed by the employer. The House of Lords left open the point as to whether a conspiracy to break contracts of employment was actionable with Lord Devlin stating:[49]

> 'I am not saying that a conspiracy to breach a contract amounts to the tort of conspiracy; that point remains to be decided. I am saying that in the tort of intimidation a threat to break a contract would be a threat of an illegal act. It follows from that that a combination to intimidate by means of a threat of a breach of contract would be an unlawful conspiracy; but it does not necessarily follow that a combination to commit a breach of contract simpliciter would be an unlawful conspiracy.'

---

42   *Lonrho Limited v Shell Petroleum Co Limited (No 2)* [1982] AC 173.
43   [1992] 1 AC 448.
44   [1925] AC 700.
45   [1964] AC 1129.
46   [1925] AC 700 at 716.
47   [1964] AC 1129.
48   [1987] IRLR 3.
49   [1964] AC 1129 at 1210.

8.38   With this point left open by the House of Lords, it was not until 1987 that the point was revisited in the *Barretts & Bairds* case.[50] This case is, regrettably, only a first instance decision. It concerned a dispute arising between fatstock officers staffing private abattoirs. A dispute arose between the officers and their employer, the Meat and Livestock Commission. An abattoir owner affected by the dispute presented brought proceedings in the High Court for an injunction alleging that the action being taken amounted to a conspiracy using unlawful means. Although the case was decided on other grounds, the High Court held, inter alia, that there was an arguable case for finding that a breach of contract could amount to unlawful means for the tort of conspiracy.

8.39   In summary, as the law currently stands, it is uncertain whether breach of contract does amount to unlawful means, but for the sake of consistency with other torts, there is a strong argument that it should do.

Predominant purpose

8.40   The matter of the conspirators' state of mind in the commission of the tort of conspiracy using unlawful means was addressed in *Lonrho plc v Fayed*.[51] The case arose out of the aborted take-over of the House of Fraser group of companies by the claimant. The claimant had been prevented from assuming control of the group pending the outcome of a Monopolies and Mergers Commission (MMC) investigation, which might have released the claimant from undertakings that it had given to the Secretary of State in the event that the Secretary of State had accepted the MMC report. In the meantime, the House of Fraser Group attracted a rival bid from the defendants. Allegedly, the defendants, in order to avoid having themselves referred to the MMC, made various untrue representations to the Secretary of State dealing with such matters as their source of funding and commercial background. The result of the alleged statements was that the Secretary of State did not refer the defendants' bid to the MMC and the sale was allowed to go ahead. The claimant sued claiming that the defendants had conspired using unlawful means to injure its business interests. The House of Lords was asked to consider as an interim point whether it was necessary to show that the defendants had a predominant purpose of injuring the claimant in the course of their action. Their Lordships held that, in a case of conspiracy to use unlawful means, the motive (ie the predominant purpose) of the conspirators was irrelevant. All that was necessary was that an intention of harming the claimant be shown.

Damage

8.41   It appeared to be settled as early as *Quinn v Leathem*[52] that in order to establish a conspiracy of either variety, a claimant was required to establish that he has suffered pecuniary loss. The point was challenged though in *Lonrho plc v Fayed (No 5)*[53] where the Court of Appeal drew a distinction between a claimant being able to assess financial loss arising as a result of a

---

50   *Barretts & Bairds (Wholesale) Limited v IPCS* [1987] IRLR 3.
51   [1992] 1 AC 448.
52   [1901] AC 495.
53   [1994] 1 All ER 188.

conspiracy (which could be assessed with some degree of precision), and that loss which arose in a more general fashion (for example, in *Lonrho plc v Fayed (No 5)*, damages for loss of reputation). Indeed, in *Lonrho plc v Fayed (No 5)*, the Court of Appeal stated, albeit obiter, that it would usually expect to see a calculation of loss being pleaded.

INDUCING BREACH OF CONTRACT

8.42   The tort of inducing a breach of contract owes its origins to the old law of master and servant and was derived from the employer's status in society, rather than from any more rational explanation. The historical view of the relationship was that a servant was essentially a chattel of his master and therefore the law should protect the relationship in favour of a master by preventing outside interference.[54] The tort has now been re-rooted in modern times to cover a right generally not to have contracts interfered with by outsiders and it matters not whether the claimant is an employer, employee or is suing to prevent a wrong arising in relation to some other form of contract. The tort can be committed in two forms, these being by means of a direct inducement to breach, or indirectly. Each will be considered in turn.

Direct inducement to breach a contract

8.43   Direct inducement to breach a contract is the older and simpler form of the tort. Its origins lie in the case of *Lumley v Gye*,[55] which concerned a theatre manager who had contracted to hire the services of an opera singer for a fixed term of 3 months. One of the terms of the singer's contract of engagement was that she would not sing elsewhere during the term of the contract without the consent of the claimant. During her contractual term, the singer was approached by the defendant, the owner of a rival music hall, who offered her the chance to sing at his establishment on better terms. The singer subsequently left the claimant's establishment in breach of contract to undertake the more advantageous engagement and the claimant sued the defendant for inducing a breach of contract on the part of the singer. The High Court held that the claimant could succeed in his claim, with the court effectively reshaping the pre-existing law that a master had a cause of action against a person who procured a servant of the master to leave the master's employment. The action did not require that there should be a strict relationship of employment. As the court put the matter:[56]

'... the class of cases referred to ... rests upon the principle that the procurement of [a] violation of [a] right is a cause of action, and that, when this principle is applied to a violation of a right arising upon a contract of hiring, the nature of the service contracted for is immaterial. It is clear that the procurement of the violation of a right is a cause of action in all instances where the violation is an actionable wrong ...'

---

54   See the judgment of Lord Sumner in *Commissioner for Executing the Office of Lord High Admiral v SS Amerika* [1917] AC 38 at 60, in this regard.
55   (1853) 2 E & B 216.
56   (1853) 2 E & B 216 at 231.

8.44 *Lumley v Gye*[57] was viewed at the time as a huge extension of trade union liability and the tort was vigorously used as a cause of action against trade unions for the reason that organisers of industrial action invariably cause employees to abstain from working in breach of their contracts of employment. By inducing a breach of contract in this way, the commission of the tort of inducing breach of contract is inevitable.

Elements of the tort

8.45 In order to establish the tort of directly inducing a breach of contract, a claimant is required to prove a number of points, these being illustrated in the decision of the Court of Appeal in *DC Thomson & Co Limited v Deakin*,[58] as follows:

- a contract must exist which is the subject of the dispute;
- the tortfeasor must have knowledge of the existence of the contract to be breached;
- an intention must exist on the part of the tortfeasor to induce a breach of the contract to the detriment of the claimant;
- an inducement to breach the contract must be provided by the tortfeasor to the person contracting with the claimant; and
- a breach of the contract must arise from the inducement of the tortfeasor,

each of which will be examined in further detail.

Existence of the contract

8.46 The tort generally occurs only where a contract is currently in existence. It had been suggested at the inception of the tort that it could be committed where a person induced another into not entering in to a contract with a person in the first place. In this regard, the Court of Appeal commented in *Temperton v Russell*, that:[59]

> 'The next point is, whether the distinction ... between the claim for inducing persons to break contracts already entered into with the [claimant] and that for inducing persons not to enter into contracts with the [claimant] can be sustained, and whether the latter claim is maintainable in law. I do not think that the distinction can prevail. There was the same wrongful intent in both cases, wrongful because malicious. There was the same kind of injury to the [claimant]. It seems a rather fine distinction to that, where a defendant maliciously induces a person not to carry out a contract already made with the [claimant] and so injures the [claimant], it is actionable, but where he injures the [claimant] by maliciously preventing a person from entering a contract with the [claimant], which he would otherwise have entered into, it is not actionable.'

---

[57] (1853) 2 E & B 216.
[58] [1952] Ch 646.
[59] [1893] 1 QB 715 at 728.

8.47   In *Allen v Flood*,[60] on the question of extending liability to cases where a contract has not yet been entered into, the House of Lords stated of the observations in *Temperton v Russell*,[61] that:[62]

> 'It seems to have been regarded as only a small step from the one decision to the other, and it was said that there seemed to be no good reason why, if an action lay for maliciously inducing a breach of contract, it should not equally lie for maliciously inducing a person not to enter into a contract. So far from thinking it a small step from the one decision to the other, I think there is a chasm between them. The reason for a distinction between the two cases appears to me to be this: that in the one case the act procured was the violation of a legal right, for which the person doing the act that injured the [claimant] could be sued as well as the person who procured it; whilst in the other case no legal right was violated by the person who did the act from which the [claimant] suffered ...'

8.48   This view was endorsed by the High Court in *Midland Cold Storage Limited v Steer*.[63]

8.49   This said, it has been held that an action will lie in a case where no contract exists but a tortfeasor has indicated that if one were to come into existence he would induce a breach of it. In *Torquay Hotel Co Limited v Cousins*,[64] the claimant owned a hotel that was affected by secondary industrial action brought by the Transport and General Workers Union. In order to further its cause (gaining a union foothold at the claimant's hotel), the union asked its members at an oil supply company not to supply fuel oil to the hotel. The hotel therefore decided to contact another fuel supplier to arrange delivery. Prior to a contract with the new supplier being concluded with the claimant, the defendants found out about the proposed contract and told the new supplier that the claimant had been 'blacked' and that there would be serious repercussions for the supplier if it dealt with the claimant. The claimant sought injunctions preventing an induced breach of the existing oil supply contract and the proposed alternative oil supply contract (which had yet to be concluded). The Court of Appeal held for the claimant in respect of both the existing contract and with regard to the proposed alternative oil supply contract, notwithstanding that the existence of a contract had not been proved in the latter case. The defendants had shown by their conduct that they would have attempted to breach the contract and that was found to be enough for the purposes of granting an injunction.

Knowledge of the contract on the part of the tortfeasor

8.50   It has consistently been held by the courts that knowledge of a contract to be breached has to exist on the part of the tortfeasor if an actionable inducement is to be established. For example, in *Rookes v Barnard*,[65] the House of Lords stated that an act of inducement is not by itself actionable. Further, in

---

60   [1898] AC 1.
61   [1893] 1 QB 715.
62   [1898] AC 1 at 121.
63   [1972] Ch 630.
64   [1969] 2 Ch 106.
65   [1964] AC 1129.

British Industrial Plastics Limited v Ferguson,[66] the House of Lords held that knowledge of the contract is an 'essential ingredient' to the cause of action.

Knowledge

8.51   First, it needs to be addressed whether the knowledge to fix the liability of a tortfeasor is knowledge of the terms of the contract or simply knowledge of the existence of a contract between the claimant and another. The answer is now clearly the latter of these two formulations. However, this was not always so. As recently as 1965 it was argued that a tortfeasor would only be liable where he had precise knowledge of the existence of a contract and the terms to be breached under it. This proposition was finally put to rest in *JT Stratford & Son Limited v Lindley.*[67] Here, the claimant company was associated with another company, Bowker and King Limited (Bowker), via a controlling third party. The claimant carried on the business of repairing and hiring barges. Bowker was approached by several unions for the purposes of securing recognition (the Transport and General Workers (TGWU) and the Watermen's Union). Bowker rejected the recognition requests of both unions initially. Ultimately, it afforded recognition to the TGWU. The result of this was that the Watermen's Union decided to 'black' the barges of the claimant after off-loading any cargoes that they might be carrying with the result that the claimant's barges were effectively immobilised. The claimant sued claiming that the Watermen's Union had induced breaches of the barge charterers' contracts. It was also argued that no immunity was available to the Watermen's Union since the breaches of contract were not breaches of contracts of employment committed in contemplation or furtherance of a trade dispute. An argument was advanced by the defendants that they did not have knowledge of the precise terms of hire and therefore they could not have committed the tort of inducing breach of the charters. An interim injunction was initially granted in favour of the claimant but the Court of Appeal overturned this holding that:[68]

> '... [The] breaches were due, no doubt, to the embargo imposed by the union. But are the defendants guilty of the tort of inducing the breaches of contract? For this purpose it must be shown that the defendants knew of the relevant terms of the contract and intended to procure breaches of them ...'

8.52   The majority of the Court of Appeal then went on to hold that it had not been shown that the union had knowledge of the relevant terms of the charters.

8.53   If this requirement had prevailed, the tort would quickly have become redundant as regards inducing breaches of sale or supply contracts or indeed contracts of employment. In most cases a trade union will not know the detailed content of a contract between an employer and a customer or supplier and to have such a precise formulation of liability would act substantially to the detriment of an employer. As it happened, a reversal of the decision was swift. The House of Lords in the appeal in *Stratford v Lindley* reversed the knowledge requirement and went on to hold that all that was necessary to attach liability

---

[66]   [1940] 1 All ER 479.
[67]   [1965] AC 269.
[68]   [1965] AC 269 at 288.

to a trade union with regard to the requirement of knowledge was knowledge of the factual existence of the contract, not the terms of it, their Lordships holding that:[69]

> 'The respondents knew that barges were always returned promptly on completion of the job for which they had been hired, and it must have been obvious to them that this was done under contracts between the appellants and the barge hirers. It was argued that there was no evidence that they were sufficiently aware of the terms of these contracts to know that their interference would involve breaches of these contracts. But I think at this stage that it is reasonable to infer that they did know that ...
>
> Did the defendants have sufficient knowledge of the terms of the hirers' contracts? It is no answer to a claim based on wrongfully inducing a breach of contract, to assert that the defendants did not know with exactitude all the terms of the contract. The relevant question is whether they had sufficient knowledge of the terms to know that they were inducing a breach of contract.'

8.54 This position has been followed consistently since *Stratford v Lindley*.[70] Whilst the courts require that there must be knowledge of the contract, it seems at times that they pay mere lip service to the requirement and are ready to infer the existence of knowledge on the part of a tortfeasor. For example, in *Associated Newspapers Group v Wade*,[71] action taken to enforce trade union recognition by means of refusing to handle advertisements from particular advertisers was held to amount to inducing breach of contract. The argument that the defendant, who had caused the advertising contracts to be breached, had no knowledge of them, was dealt with in short order by the Court of Appeal which concluded that as a trade union representative who had dealt in the claimant's line of business for many years, he must be taken to have known that advertising contracts were secured well in advance of publication.

Actual or constructive knowledge?

8.55 The second point is whether knowledge of the existence of a contract can be imputed to a tortfeasor who is genuinely ignorant of the existence of a contract that is being breached. The answer is that in an appropriate case knowledge will be imputed to such a person. As *Associated Newspapers Group v Wade*[72] shows, in some cases, it simply defies belief that a person cannot have knowledge of the existence of a contract. Moreover, if a person were to choose to avoid the existence of a contract coming to his attention, then this would give him an advantage that would not be available to more honest tortfeasors. So in *Emerald Construction Co Limited v Lowthian*,[73] where a large power station was to be built using a particular contractor and the contractor had subcontracted out part of the work to the claimant who operated a policy of union labour-only subcontracting, the contractor was visited by an official of

---

[69]   *JT Stratford & Son Limited v Lindley* [1965] AC 269 at 332.
[70]   *JT Stratford & Son Limited v Lindley* [1965] AC 269.
[71]   [1979] ICR 664.
[72]   [1979] ICR 664.
[73]   [1966] 1 WLR 691.

the Amalgamated Union of Building Trade Workers who informed the contractor that, unless the subcontract was terminated, their bricklayer members would not operate on the site. The claimant therefore sought an injunction preventing the defendants from inducing breach of contract. The defendants admittedly knew of the existence of the subcontract but not its precise terms. On the issue of the union's knowledge, the Court of Appeal held:[74]

> 'If the officers of the trade union, knowing of the contract, deliberately sought to procure a breach of it, they would do wrong ... Even if they did not know of the actual terms of the contract but had the means of knowledge – which they deliberately disregarded – that would be enough. Like the man who turns a blind eye. So here, if the officers deliberately sought to get this contract terminated, heedless of its terms, regardless whether it was terminated by breach or not they would do wrong. For it is unlawful for a third person to procure a breach of contract knowingly, or recklessly, indifferent whether it is a breach or not.'

8.56   Regard should also be had to *NWL Limited v Woods*;[75] *Merkur Island Shipping Corporation v Laughton*;[76] *Express Newspapers Limited v McShane*;[77] and *Dimbleby & Sons v NUJ*,[78] all of which show the ease of inferring knowledge on the part of trade union officials.

8.57   Conversely, in *Timeplan Education Group Limited v National Union of Teachers*,[79] the Court of Appeal held in a case concerning the provision of Antipodean supply teachers paid at rates by the claimant below the School Teachers' Pay and Conditions Act 1991, that when the defendant wrote to the New Zealand Education Institute (NZEI) to advise it that it 'might consider it inappropriate to carry Timeplan advertising in future' this did not amount to an unlawful interference with a contract. The reason for this was that, although the High Court had held that the defendant must have been aware of some contractual relationship between the claimant and NZEI, the Court of Appeal held that this was an incorrect assumption on the facts. Further, the court held that it could not be spelt out from the defendant's letter to NZEI that there was any intention to persuade, procure or induce NZEI to break the contract with the claimant (the existence of which the defendant was unaware).

8.58   Since many claimants will seek an injunction against a tortfeasor at an early stage in a dispute where a tort is being committed in circumstances where the tortfeasor may not be protected by a statutory immunity, an interim injunction will often be sought. Following the case of *American Cyanamid Co v Ethicon Limited*,[80] the test for granting an interim injunction has focussed on proving that a serious question exists to be tried. This, of course, will be established on the basis of witness statement evidence, which does not reveal as much as cross examination at a trial. Given the inferences that courts draw as

---

[74]   [1966] 1 WLR 691 at 700.
[75]   [1979] 1 WLR 1294.
[76]   [1983] 2 AC 570.
[77]   [1980] AC 672.
[78]   [1984] 1 WLR 427.
[79]   [1997] IRLR 457.
[80]   [1975] AC 396.

to the knowledge of trade union officials, the hurdle of establishing liability on the part of a tortfeasor by a claimant is a relatively low one to negotiate.

8.59   The corollary of the above point is that where a defendant is genuinely and honestly ignorant of the existence of a contract that is being breached, no liability in tort can attach. The point was taken to its logical conclusion in *Smith v Morrison*,[81] where the question at issue was whether a defendant had an honest doubt as to the existence of a contract. According to the trial judge, where an honest doubt exists no liability can attach. However, to escape liability doubt must exist as to the fact of the contract and not as to the effect of its breach.[82]

Intention to harm the claimant

8.60   It has been said that the requirement on the part of the defendant of an intention to injure the claimant is tied up with knowledge of the contract to be breached.[83] However, it is uncertain just how far this requirement extends. A debate existed until relatively recently as to whether the intention was to be defined in the manner of 'wilful blindness' or whether the tort can only be committed where the predominant purpose of the tortfeasor is to cause injury to the claimant. The first of these propositions was considered in *Falcolner v ASLEF and NUR*,[84] which concerned an action brought by the claimant as a passenger of British Rail against the defendant railway unions on the grounds that they had not complied with the procedural requirements under the Trade Union Act 1984, ss 10 and 11 prior to commencing industrial action. As a result of the industrial action, the claimant had been stranded in London and forced to incur expenditure on a hotel, as well as suffering general inconvenience. In their defence, the defendant unions argued, inter alia, that they had not intended to harm the claimant; rather they wished to put pressure on the employer of their members, British Rail. The matter was heard in the county court before His Honour Judge Henham. In response to the union defence, Judge Henham held:[85]

> 'As to the need to prove the defendants intended to procure a breach of, or interference with the performance of, those contracts, I find no sympathy for the argument that the [claimant] was not the object or instrument of the action taken when the strike was called. Undoubtedly it was the intention of the defendants to cause the BR Board to be rendered incapable of performing its contractual obligations with the [claimant] and other passengers but to suggest that the effect upon them (ie the passengers) was merely consequential is, in my view, both naive and divorced from reality. It was clearly the intention of the defendants in calling the strike to direct its effect upon the [claimant] and others and thus to induce the Board to accede to the defendants' wishes.'

---

81   [1979] 1 WLR 659.
82   See in this regard *Pritchard v Briggs* [1980] Ch 338 at 413; and *Metropolitan Borough of Solihull v National Union of Teachers* [1985] IRLR 211.
83   See, for example, the comments of Lord Diplock in *Merkur Island Shipping Corporation v Laughton* [1983] 2 AC 570 at 608–609.
84   [1986] IRLR 331.
85   [1986] IRLR 331 at 333.

8.61   In other words, the only possible effect of the action would have been to harm people in the position of the claimant, and the defendant unions had deliberately turned a blind eye to the contracts of travelling members of the public and were therefore liable for the effects of breaches of those contracts.

8.62   Against this view was a decision of the High Court in *Barretts & Bairds (Wholesale) Limited v Institution of Professional Civil Servants*,[86] in which the court refused to continue to uphold an interlocutory injunction, holding that in order to establish liability under the tort of interfering with a contract, it was necessary to show on the part of the tortfeasor a predominant purpose of injuring the claimant. In so holding, the court based its decision on the House of Lords decision in *Lonrho Limited v Shell Petroleum Co Limited (No 2)*.[87]

8.63   In any event, pending any appeal to the House of Lords, the matter has seemingly been laid to rest by the decision of the Court of Appeal in *Mainstream Properties Limited v Young*.[88] Although the case does not turn on the issue of industrial action (relating to an alleged inducement by a property development company (the defendant) to employees of another property development company (the claimant) to divert contracts for the development of land away from the claimant), the case is nonetheless relevant as it was brought under this head of tort. The Court of Appeal considered another recent authority on the matter (*Douglas v Hello!*,[89] a case about as far removed from the cut and thrust of industrial relations as it is possible to get, concerning the publication of wedding photographs from a celebrity marriage). In this regard, the court held, first, that for the tort to be committed, once knowledge of the existence of the contract to be breached was proved, it was necessary for the claimant to show that the defendant had a specific subjective intention to cause harm to the claimant. In this regard, the court held that there were strong policy reasons why the law should restrict the ambit of the tort in this way, since to allow the tort to be extended by its commission through recklessness, or even further, negligence, would carry with it the risk of inhibiting competition and entrepreneurship by third parties to contracts. The Court of Appeal then specifically addressed the issue of the tort being committed through a reckless disregard of the claimant's contractual rights, holding that what was needed to establish liability was a positive intention on the part of the defendant, not a mere failure to take into account the claimant's potential rights. The court concluded by saying that there is nothing in the policy of the tort which prevents a defendant from showing why he or she acted in a particular way based on a mistake of law. As matters stand following *Mainstream Properties*, the less action a defendant takes to establish whether a third party potential claimant will be affected by his or her acts, the more chance there is that the claimant will not be able to establish the tort, a somewhat curious state of affairs. Indeed, as Sedley LJ noted in *Mainstream Properties*, with regard to the reckless potential tortfeasor, it is akin to allowing them to put a telescope to a blind eye with regard to the motive for acting. Whether the policy of the law will change on appeal remains to be seen.

---

[86]   [1987] IRLR 3.
[87]   [1982] AC 173.
[88]   [2005] EWCA Civ 861, [2005] All ER (D) 148 (Jul).
[89]   [2005] EWCA Civ 595, [2005] 2 FCR 487.

Inducement

8.64   The third element that has to be proved in the tort is that of inducement. According to Evershed MR in *DC Thomson & Co Limited v Deakin*,[90] inducement can take effect in three ways: these being pressure, persuasion or procuration.

Pressure

8.65   Numerous examples exist of what amounts to 'pressure' on the part of a tortfeasor. Pressure essentially amounts to threats made to a contracting party that some undesirable consequence will happen in the event of dealing with the claimant. In *DC Thomson v Deakin*,[91] the pressure consisted of informing a supplier of the claimant that the supplier would experience industrial action of its own if it carried on dealing with the claimant. As a result, the supplier stopped supplying the claimant. In that case, an interim injunction was not granted since the affidavit evidence did not establish evidence of direct procurement of a wrongful act on the part of the supplier. However, in *JT Stratford & Son Limited v Lindley*,[92] the House of Lords held, obiter, that pressure had been applied to a trade association where it was informed of the possibility of the barges which were operated through it being 'blacked'. Although language contained in a letter from the union to the association was couched in neutral terms, the clear inference from it was that there was an embargo on the boats which would be enforced.[93]

8.66   Pressure must be distinguished from the mere giving of advice to a person not to deal with another. It has been commented that it is very difficult to draw a line between the giving of advice and pressure.[94]

Persuasion

8.67   Persuasion will commonly occur where a trade union asks its members to take part in strike or other industrial action in breach of the notice requirements provided for by their contracts of employment. Again, as with pressure, a distinction needs to be drawn between persuasion and advice. Advising as to the consequences of a continued course of dealings with a person is not unlawful. However, there is again a thin line between advice and persuasion. In the *Torquay Hotels* case,[95] the 'advice' given by the Transport and General Workers Union to its members as to the existence of a dispute with the claimant, was held to amount to persuasion.

8.68   It is no defence to an allegation that an inducement has occurred through persuasion that the party who has been persuaded to break the contract was easily persuaded. In *Thomson v Deakin*, the Court of Appeal dealt with this point in the following way:[96]

---

[90]   [1952] Ch 646 at 686.
[91]   *DC Thomson & Co Limited v Deakin* [1952] Ch 646.
[92]   [1965] AC 269.
[93]   See, too, in relation to this area generally *Torquay Hotel Co Limited v Cousins* [1969] 2 Ch 106.
[94]   See Coleridge J in *Lumley v Gye* (1853) 2 E & B 216 at 252; *Camellia Tanker Limited SA v International Transport Workers Federation* [1976] ICR 274; and *Timeplan Education Group Limited v NUT* [1997] IRLR 457.
[95]   *Torquay Hotel Co Limited v Cousins* [1969] 2 Ch 106.
[96]   [1952] Ch 646 at 694.

'... the contract breaker may himself be a willing party to the breach, without any persuasion by the third party, and there seems to be no doubt that if a third party, with knowledge of a contract between the contract breaker and another, has dealings with the contract breaker which the third party knows to be inconsistent with the contract, he has committed an actionable interference ... The inconsistent dealing between the third party and the contract breaker may, indeed, be commenced without knowledge by the third party of the contract thus broken; but, if it is continued after the third party has notice of the contract, an actionable interference has been committed by him ...'

8.69   Other cases which deal with parties willing to breach a contract include *British Motor Trade Association v Salvadori*[97] and *Sefton v Tophams Limited*[98] (later reversed by the House of Lords on other grounds).

Procuring

8.70   Inducement can also occur by giving some form of consideration to the contract breaker not to fulfil his obligations, ie by procuring. For example, in *Lumley v Gye*,[99] money was paid to an opera singer to induce her to breach her contract of engagement and in *British Motor Trade Association v Salvadori*,[100]money was paid to car dealers to supply cars to a second-hand car dealer in breach of a re-sale agreement.

Breach of the contract

8.71   As can be seen above, in most cases it is necessary that for the tort of inducing breach of contract to be committed, the contract must actually be breached before all elements of the tort are finally established.[101] An exception to this rule exists were a tortfeasor threatens to breach a contract as soon as it is concluded.[102] To the extent that a contract is caused to be breached in circumstances where a break clause could have been validly operated instead of the contract being breached, it is no defence to say that the contract could have been so lawfully terminated.[103] This will commonly occur where unionised employees are called upon to take industrial action since, although an employee's contract of employment can lawfully be brought to an end upon the giving of proper notice, a call to such action, whilst possibly being accompanied by strike notice (ie notice that the employee will not work during the period of industrial action), will not usually be accompanied by notice of termination of the contract of employment. This is true even where the strike notice is of equivalent length to the notice required lawfully to terminate the contract of employment. In *Rookes v Barnard*, Lord Devlin said of this point:[104]

---

[97]   [1949] Ch 556.
[98]   [1965] Ch 1140.
[99]   (1853) 2 E & B 216.
[100]   [1949] Ch 556.
[101]   See, for example, *Midland Cold Storage Limited v Steer* [1972] 630 at 644–645.
[102]   See *Torquay Hotel Co Limited v Cousins* [1969] 2 Ch 106; and *Brekkes Limited v Cattel* [1972] Ch 105.
[103]   *Emerald Construction Co Limited v Lowthian* [1966] 1 WLR 691.
[104]   [1964] AC 1129 at 1204.

'It is not disputed that the notice constituted a threat of breach of contract by the members of AESD. It is true that any individual employee could lawfully have terminated his contract by giving seven days' notice and if the matter is looked at in that way, the breach might not appear to be a very serious one. But that would be a technical way of looking at it. As Donovan LJ said in the Court of Appeal, the object of the notice was not to terminate the contract either before or after the expiry of seven days. The object was to break the contract by withholding labour but keeping the contract alive for as long as would tolerate the breach without exercising their right of recession.'

8.72 The matter was put more succinctly in *Barretts & Bairds (Wholesale) Limited v Institution of Professional Civil Servants* where Henry J in the High Court observed that no one today gives their notice before striking.[105]

Defences

8.73 To the extent that a claimant can establish the elements of the tort and, assuming that no immunity is available to the defendant, it is necessary to consider whether the defence of justification is available to the tortfeasor. It is doubtful whether in fact the defence does still exist today and it has only ever been successfully raised in one case, *Brimelow v Casson*,[106] and that was not a typical trade union dispute. Here, the claimant was a theatre manager and was suing the defendants for inducing a breach of contract. The claimant had organised a number of theatrical reviews at different theatres. The defendant, in his capacity as a trade union official, had discovered that due to the very low wages that were being paid by the claimant, female members of the theatre's chorus line were resorting to prostitution. The defendant contacted the theatres that the claimant had booked and requested that they refuse to honour the agreements that they had with the claimant, which some of them duly did. The case was dealt with by the High Court which held that the defendant was justified in procuring the breach as a result of a duty that was owed to his profession to prevent the chorus girls from being corrupted as a result of their insufficient income.

8.74 Subsequently, in *South Wales Miners Federation v Glamorgan Coal Co*,[107] the House of Lords held that there was no justification involved in a trade union trying to obtain better wages for members of the union, even where the union believed that higher wages would ultimately benefit the employer as well. Further, it is difficult to see how a repeat of *Brimelow v Casson*[108] could arise today given the requirement for employers to pay the National Minimum Wage.

---

[105] [1987] IRLR 3 at 8.
[106] [1924] 1 Ch 302.
[107] [1905] AC 239.
[108] [1924] 1 Ch 302.

8.75   Indeed, in cases that have followed *Brimelow*,[109] judges have stated that the defence only succeeded on the basis of a moral duty that was owed to the members of the chorus line.[110]

INDIRECT INDUCEMENT TO BREACH A CONTRACT

8.76   Unlike direct inducement to breach, indirect inducement to breach a contract requires that the defendant:

- has knowledge of the existence of a contract between a third party, (T1), and the claimant;
- induces another person, T2 (commonly an employee of T1), to do an unlawful act to T1 thereby causing T1 to break the contract that T1 has with the claimant; and
- must intend to cause harm to the claimant as a result of an act of inducement.

Development of the tort and the concept of unlawful means

8.77   The first case dealing with the tort of indirect inducement was *DC Thomson & Co Limited v Deakin*,[111] where trade union officials called its members to subject the claimant company to a boycott (the reason for which was to seek to introduce a closed shop with the claimant). In order to enforce the boycott, the defendant officials contacted lorry driver members of their union who handled supplies of paper from a company, Bowaters, to the claimant. The defendants warned the union members that the claimant was the subject of a boycott and that they were not to carry out further deliveries. Bowaters refused to allow their drivers to handle the paper deliveries fearing reprisals if they carried on with supplying the claimant. The claimant sued for an injunction preventing breach of the commercial contract which was refused at first instance and then again in the Court of Appeal. The court held that in order to establish the tort of indirect inducement to breach a contract, it was necessary to prove that the contracts of employment of the lorry drivers at Bowaters had actually been breached. However, since the drivers were not ordered to load the lorries of the defendant, it was not possible to make out this limb of the tort and therefore the claim failed.

8.78   Shortly after *DC Thomson & Co Limited v Deakin*,[112] the House of Lords was to develop the tort of indirect inducement to breach a contract in *JT Stratford & Son Limited v Lindley*.[113] As stated above, the case concerned a refusal by watermen to return barges to their owner after cargoes of goods had been delivered. This action was undertaken to ensure that trade union recognition took place at a company associated with the claimant. The House of Lords, after first having redefined what was meant by 'knowledge' of a contract on the part of a tortfeasor in the context of inducing breach of contract, went on to find that the watermen were in breach of their contracts of employment

---

[109]   *Brimelow v Casson* [1924] 1 Ch 302.
[110]   See, for example, the judgment of Stuart-Smith LJ in *Edwin Hill & Partners v First National Finance Corporation* [1988] 3 All ER 801 at 806.
[111]   [1952] Ch 646.
[112]   [1952] Ch 646.
[113]   [1965] AC 269.

and that this constituted 'unlawful means' for the purposes of indirectly inducing a breach of contract. The decision was subsequently followed by the House of Lords in *Merkur Island Shipping Corporation v Laughton*,[114] where the principle was used to place liability on the defendants for requesting tugmen to refuse to service ships operated under flags of convenience. It was also used in *Dimbleby & Sons Limited v National Union of Journalists*,[115] where liability under the tort was extended to cover journalists who would not supply news copy to their employer due to the employer's insistence on using a particular printer. It was held that a refusal to supply copy amounted to a breach of contract.

8.79   What is now beyond doubt is that it is necessary to establish unlawful means if this form of the tort of inducing breach of contract is to be established. It is, however, this requirement that has provided a small degree of salvation to trade unions, faced with the reality of the restrictions on the taking of industrial action following the reforms of the law relating to industrial action between 1979 and 1997. As was shown in the case of *Middlebrook Mushrooms Limited v Transport and General Workers Union*,[116] where a mushroom grower which was involved in a trade dispute with staff in relation to overtime payments. Industrial action was taken and the defendant, through its regional officer, announced that its members would attend at supermarkets supplied by the claimant to hand out leaflets informing the public of the dispute. The leaflets concluded with a call from the trade union for the public to boycott the claimant's mushrooms. The claimant argued that the defendant was inducing the supermarkets to which it supplied to breach their supply contracts with the claimant. An interim injunction was granted by the High Court preventing the action. On appeal, the Court of Appeal reversed the decision. It held that the High Court had incorrectly treated the case as one of direct inducement to breach a contract. The Court of Appeal went on to hold that, unlike cases such as *Merkur Island Shipping*[117] or *Stratford v Lindley*,[118] the defendant probably had no knowledge of the mushroom supply contracts. Mushrooms were oversupplied and had a very short shelf life. It was open to the union to conclude that no long-term supply contracts existed and contracts were more likely to be ad hoc. If this was the case, it was difficult to see how the defendant could have knowledge of such contracts.

8.80   In any event, the facts did not support the allegation of direct inducement to breach the supply contracts since it was supermarket shoppers and not the supermarkets themselves who were being targeted. The tort was therefore one of indirect inducement if it was anything at all. It followed that if customers were being targeted then, in the ordinary course of things, they would be able to make up their own minds whether or not to buy mushrooms (unless unlawful means were used against the customers which would have to be proved by the claimant). Ultimately, the claimant did not have evidence of

114   [1983] 2 AC 570.
115   [1984] 1 WLR 427.
116   [1993] IRLR 232.
117   *Merkur Island Shipping Corporation v Laughton* [1983] 2 AC 570.
118   *JT Stratford & Son Limited v Lindley* [1965] AC 269.

this. The handing out of leaflets amounted to nothing more than free speech and could not be considered to be unlawful. As Hoffmann LJ stated:[119]

'The fact that the defendant has communicated to the contracting party the information that consequences will follow if he does not break his contract does not necessarily mean that the communication is the cause of the contract being broken. That is the equivalent of killing the messenger. I suppose there may be a case in which the defendant's force of personality is such that his mere communication of a request not to perform the contract, unaccompanied by any express or implied intimation of favourable consequences if he does so, or adverse consequences if he does not, is in itself sufficient to cause the contract to be broken. It is more usual, however, for the contracting party to be told expressly or impliedly that some action will be taken if or unless he breaks the contract. In such a case it is the occurrence or apprehension of that action which causes the contract to be broken, not the communication. To decide whether the inducement was direct or indirect, one therefore has to ask whether the actual or apprehended action was on the part of the defendants or persons for whom they were in law responsible.'

8.81   It followed that since the leafleting of members of the public was not aimed directly at the supermarket, no direct inducement had been made out and it was impossible to make out a case of indirect inducement since the customers were able to make up their minds whether they wanted to enter into contracts to buy mushrooms.

Causation

8.82   In order for a claimant to prove the tort of indirect inducement to breach a contract, causation must be established. In *DC Thomson & Co Limited v Deakin*, the Court of Appeal stated that breach of contract must follow as a 'necessary consequence' of the breach, holding that:[120]

'... the expression "necessary consequence" used here and elsewhere in this judgment, [means] that it must be shown that, by reason of the withdrawal of the services of the employees concerned, the contract breaker was unable, as a matter of practical possibility, to perform his contract; in other words, ... the continuance of the services of the particular employees concerned must be so vital to the performance of the contract alleged to have been interfered with as to make the effect of their withdrawal comparable, for practical purposes, to a direct invasion of the contractual rights of the party aggrieved under the contract alleged to have been interfered with, as for example, (in the case of a contract for personal services), the physical restraint of the person by whom such services are to be performed.'

8.83   It follows, that if the contract breaker has a free choice in the matter (for example, as in *Middlebrook Mushrooms*,[121] where the supermarkets might have

---

[119]   *Middlebrook Mushrooms Limited v Transport and General Workers Union* [1993] IRLR 232 at 237.

[120]   [1952] Ch 646 at 697.

[121]   *Middlebrook Mushrooms Limited v Transport and General Workers Union* [1993] IRLR 232.

responded to perceived commercial pressure from their customers), no causation will be established and therefore neither will the tort.

Defence

8.84 As with the direct version of the tort, it is conceivably possible that the defence of justification, to the extent that it still exists (see **8.73** et seq), is available in the case of the indirect version.

INTERFERING WITH A CONTRACT, TRADE OR BUSINESS USING UNLAWFUL MEANS

8.85 The tort of interfering with a contract, trade or business is an evolutionary one that has come into being through refinement of the tort of inducing breach of contract (in both of its forms). The tort was unheard of until 1969 when it was first promulgated in the case of *Torquay Hotel Co Limited v Cousins*.[122] The facts of this case are fully stated above (at **8.49**), but in brief the claimant's supplier of fuel oil had been told by the Transport and General Workers Union that the hotel had been 'blacked' for refusing to recognise it. In the hotel's fuel oil supply contract, there was a *force majeure* clause which included as one of its triggers, prevention of oil supply due to industrial action. On appeal, one of the points facing the Court of Appeal was whether or not there had been a breach of contract which could give rise to liability under the tort of inducing breach of contract. The decision of the Court of Appeal was that the union which had engineered industrial action could not take advantage of the *force majeure* clause so as to deny the existence of a tort which it had itself committed. The Court of Appeal was therefore prepared to hold that the tort that had in fact been committed was one of indirect inducement to breach. However, Lord Denning MR was prepared to go further, stating:[123]

> 'The principle of *Lumley v Gye*[124] ... is that each of the parties to a contract has a right to the performance of it: and it is wrong for another to procure one of the parties to break it or not to perform it. That principle was extended a step further by Lord MacNaghten in *Quinn v Leathem*[125] ... so that each of the parties has a right to have his "contractual relations" with the other duly observed. It is ... a violation of legal right to interfere with contractual relations recognised by law if there be no sufficient justification for the interference ... The time has come when the principle should be extended further to cover "deliberate and direct interference with the execution of a contract without that causing any breach." That was a point left open by Lord Reid in *Stratford v Lindley*[126] ... But the common law would be seriously deficient if it did not condemn such interference.'

8.86 Lord Denning's remarks, albeit obiter in the *Torquay Hotel* case,[127] were used in the subsequent cases of *Hadmor Productions Limited v Hamilton*[128]

---

[122] [1969] 2 Ch 106.
[123] [1969] 2 Ch 106 at 138.
[124] (1853) 2 E & B 216.
[125] [1901] AC 495.
[126] *JT Stratford & Son Limited v Lindley* [1965] AC 269.
[127] *Torquay Hotel Co Limited v Cousins* [1969] 2 Ch 106.
[128] [1983] 1 AC 191.

(where the House of Lords confirmed the existence of the tort) and in *Merkur Island Shipping Corporation v Laughton*.[129] The *Merkur Island* case concerned a blockade of a ship operating under flags of convenience. The claimant was a shipowner operating a ship which was registered in Liberia. The boycott arose due to the International Transport Workers Federation (the ITF) receiving a complaint about poor employment conditions from one of the workers on the ship. Prior to the complaint, the ITF was already pursuing a campaign against ships that operated under flags of convenience due to the poor conditions of employment that prevailed on such ships.

8.87   The claimant chartered the ship prior to the dispute and it was then subsequently sub-chartered. One of the clauses of the charter provided that payment under the charter should cease for time lost due to boycotts and that if more than 10 days were lost, the master of the ship would have the option of terminating the charter altogether.

8.88   The ITF discovered that the *Hoegh Apapa* had been chartered and was due to load at Liverpool in 1982. It instructed its members in Liverpool not to take the ship out to sea at which point the claimant sued the defendant alleging interference with their contracts, trade or business.

8.89   The appeal was heard by the House of Lords who had to decide whether an injunction could be granted preventing the action. Lord Diplock (who gave the only substantive judgment in the case) adopted further remarks of Lord Denning MR in the *Torquay Hotel* case. In that case, Lord Denning, whilst defining the elements of the tort of interfering with a contract, trade or business, stated that:[130]

> '... there must be interference in the execution of a contract. The interference is not confined to the procurement of a breach of contract. It extends to a case where a third person prevents or hinders one party from performing his contract, even though it be not a breach.'

8.90   Lord Diplock approved this comment and also went on to approve the four-stage classification put forward by Jenkins LJ in *Thomson v Deakin*[131] in relation to inducing breach of contract. Lord Diplock stated that the tort of interfering with a contract, trade or business had the same elements as inducing breach of contract but that, instead of having as one of its central elements a requirement that a tortfeasor should intend breach of contract, there should be substituted a requirement that the tortfeasor induced interference with performance of the contract, trade or business, thereby covering acts that fell short of breach of contract. This substitution, he added, would not apply in cases where the wrongdoing consisted of employees breaking their own contracts of employment and thereby having a knock-on effect of interfering with the performance of a claimant's contract.

Elements of the interfering with a contract, trade or business

8.91   As the tort has the same elements as that of inducing breach of contract (but for the substitution of a requirement for the tortfeasor to intend to

129   [1983] 2 AC 570.
130   *Torquay Hotel Co Limited v Cousins* [1969] 2 Ch 106 at 138.
131   *DC Thomson & Co Limited v Deakin* [1952] Ch 646.

interfere with performance as opposed to breach a contract), it can be committed both directly and indirectly. If the tort is committed indirectly, unlawful means must be used in its commission.

8.92 As with inducing breach of contract, following the decision of the Court of Appeal in *Mainstream Properties Limited v Young*,[132] it is clear that the intention to injure the claimant on the part of the tortfeasor is a specific subjective intention in the form of a predominant purpose rather than mere wilful blindness.

Scope of interfering with contract, trade or business

8.93 It is still uncertain exactly how wide the ambit of the tort of interfering with a contract, trade or business is. To this end, each case must proceed very much on its own particular facts whilst attempting to derive help from the cases already handed down. Examples of cases where the tort has been used are:

- *Hadmor Productions Limited v Hamilton*,[133] where the claimant claimed a right to be able to have its films transmitted without interference from a film technicians union. Although the House of Lords recognised the existence of the tort, they felt that it had not been established that the defendants were not protected by statutory immunity from the consequences of the tort that they had committed.
- *Messenger Group Newspapers Limited v NGA (1982)*,[134] where a campaign of writing letters to potential advertisers in a free newspaper discouraging them to advertise was held to fall foul of the tort.
- *Meade v Haringey London Borough Council*,[135] where inducing breach of statutory duty was held to be capable of being the unlawful means behind the commission of the tort.[136]

Defences

8.94 It would appear that the defence of justification should be available to this tort in the same way that it is available to the tort of inducing breach of contract, to the extent that the defence still exists (in respect of which see **8.73**).

INTIMIDATION

8.95 The tort of intimidation is probably the oldest of the recognised economic torts. This said, it took substantial litigation in the 1960s to establish that the tort still existed since it had been unused as a cause of action of between the end of the eighteenth century and 1964 when the House of Lords confirmed that the tort had not lapsed in *Rookes v Barnard*.[137]

8.96 Prior to *Rookes*,[138] the case of *Tarleton v McGawley*[139] was the last reported incidence of the tort. That case concerned two ships attempting to

---

[132] [2005] EWCA Civ 861, [2005] All ER (D) 148 (Jul).
[133] [1983] 1 AC 191.
[134] [1984] IRLR 397.
[135] [1979] ICR 494.
[136] See also the comments of the Court of Appeal in *Associated British Ports v Transport and General Workers' Union* [1989] IRLR 305.
[137] [1964] AC 1129.
[138] *Rookes v Barnard* [1964] AC 1129.

carry out trade off the coast of Cameroon. One of the ships, the *Tarleton*, had
sent out a smaller vessel to trade with the local inhabitants who had come out
to meet the ship in a canoe. Seeing this, the captain of the other ship fired a
cannon across the bow of the canoe to dissuade the locals from trading, with
the result that one of its occupants was killed. Unsurprisingly, the remainder of
the crew of the canoe turned the canoe around and headed back for the coast
with the result that no trade took place with the *Tarleton*. The *Tarleton's* owners
sued for the loss of the value of the trade. They recovered damages with
Lord Kenyon holding that it was unlawful for the defendants to threaten those
who tried to let trade take place.

8.97   Following *Tarleton v McGawley*,[140] the next reported example of the
principle in operation was *Rookes*.[141] The case concerned a designer working
for BOAC. The claimant was not a trade union member, having recently
resigned from the union of which he had been a member. BOAC had an
informal agreement with that trade union under which a closed shop was
established. As a result of the claimant's resignation and in order to ensure that
the closed shop was maintained, the defendants, who were union officials,
informed BOAC that unless the claimant was dismissed, the other members of
the design office in which the claimant worked would go on strike. As a result
of this pressure, BOAC suspended the claimant and then terminated his
employment on notice. The claimant sued the defendants, claiming amongst
other things, that he had been the victim of the tort of intimidation. At first
instance, he was successful in his claim and damages were awarded against the
defendants, it being accepted that the immunity in tort provided by the Trade
Disputes Act 1906 did not cover intimidation. On appeal, the Court of Appeal
refused to recognise that the tort covered threats relating to industrial action
and held that, to the extent that it still existed, the tort was confined to cases
where the wrongful action amounted to threats of physical violence. The Court
of Appeal went so far as to label the tort as 'a rare and peculiar cause of
action'.[142]

8.98   The claimant appealed to the House of Lords, in particular against the
proposition that only threats of physical violence provided the basis for the
tort. The House of Lords allowed the appeal and went some considerable way
to rejecting the Court of Appeal's decision. For example, Lord Reid stated:[143]

> 'Intimidation of any kind appears to me to be highly objectionable. The
> law was not slow to prevent it when violence and threats of violence were
> the effective means. Now that subtler means are at least equally effective I
> see no reason why the law should have to turn a blind eye to them.'

8.99   Lord Hodson, on the type of threat needed to establish the tort,
added:[144]

> 'It would be strange if threats of violence were sufficient and the more
> powerful weapon of a threat to strike were not, always provided that the

---

139   (1793) 1 Peake 270.
140   (1793) 1 Peake 270.
141   *Rookes v Barnard* [1964] AC 1129.
142   [1963] QB 623 at 688.
143   [1964] AC 1129 at 1169.
144   [1964] AC 1129 at 1201.

threat is unlawful. The injury and suffering caused by a strike is very often widespread as well as devastating, and a threat to strike would be expected to be certainly no less serious than a threat of violence.'

8.100 Lord Devlin added further:[145]

'I find therefore nothing to differentiate between a threat of a breach of contract from a threat of physical violence or any other illegal threat. The nature of the threat is immaterial ... All that matters to the [claimant] is that, metaphorically speaking, a club has been used. It does not matter what the club is made of – whether it is a physical club or an economic club, a tortious club or an otherwise illegal club. If an intermediate party is improperly coerced, it does not matter to the [claimant] how he is coerced.'

8.101 Lord Pearce concluded the judgment by stating:[146]

'Businesses are run on the basis of contracts. The threat by an important supplier to withhold the supplies under a long term contract on which a manufacturer relies might be tantamount to a threat of ruin and compel him to the supplier's demands. It would seem strange if the law should disregard intimidation by such potent contractual weapons, while taking cognisance of less potent tortious weapons.'

8.102 It is clear from the speeches that the nature of a threat made to a person is immaterial. It follows that in almost every single case where economic pressure is exerted in the context of an industrial dispute, the tort will be committed.

Elements of the tort

8.103

According to Lord Denning MR in *Morgan v Fry*,[147] the essential elements of the tort are:
- a threat by a person;
- the use of unlawful means;
- an intention on the part of the tortfeasor to compel a third party to obey the tortfeasor's wishes; and
- the causation of loss to the claimant as a result of a third party at whom the threat is aimed submitting to the same in order to prevent the threat being carried into effect.

Each of these elements will be looked at in turn.

Threats

8.104 The nature of threats has been discussed above. As Lord Devlin stated in *Rookes*,[148] the nature of the threat is immaterial. The threat can be either express or it can be implied from a reasonable man's expectation of a tortfeasors's likely conduct. To qualify as a threat, a demand must contain an element of compulsion. The High Court in *Camellia Tanker Limited v*

---

[145] [1964] AC 1129 at 1209.
[146] [1964] AC 1129 at 1234.
[147] [1968] 2 QB 710.
[148] *Rookes v Barnard* [1964] AC 1129.

ITWF,[149] held that a threat should be designed so as to compel an employer to come to its senses. It follows that, in the absence of a threat, where all that is present is the mere communication of information from a trade union to an employer, the tort cannot be made out.[150]

8.105   The problem of the distinction between threats and communications lies in the fact that it is very difficult to divorce the reality of a situation from the way in which a comment relating to it is delivered. In other words, what might be perceived as information being conveyed in the eyes of a trade union might be construed as a threat in the eyes of an employer. For example, in *Beaverbrook Newspapers Limited v Keys*,[151] a comment by a trade union official to an employer that: 'You have the law on your side, but I have common sense on mine. If you go down that road, I will close you down ...', was held to amount to a threat.[152]

Unlawful means

8.106   In order for a threat to be actionable in the tort of intimidation, it must contain an intimation that unlawful means will be used against the victim so as to provide a benefit to the tortfeasor. A threat to carry into effect lawful action cannot amount to a threat for the purpose of establishing the tort. The view that taking action by lawful means could provide the basis of a claim in tort was dismissed in the case of *Sorrell v Smith*[153] where it was described by the House of Lords as 'the leading heresy'.

8.107   Lord Reid took this point further in *Rookes v Barnard*, stating that:[154]

'So long as the defendant only threatens to do what he has a legal right to do he is on safe ground. At least if there is no conspiracy he would not be liable to anyone for doing the act, whatever his motive may be, and it would be absurd to make him liable for threatening to do it but not for doing it. But I agree with Lord Herschell (*Allen v Flood* [1898] AC 1, 121) that there is a chasm between doing what you have a legal right to do and doing what you have no legal right to do, and there seems to me to be the same chasm between threatening to do what you have a legal right to do and threatening to do what you have no legal right to do.'

8.108   Unlawful means now covers:

- threats to commit a breach of contract (per Lord Devlin in *Rookes*[155]);
- torts (per Lord Reid in *Rookes*[156]);
- criminal acts (per Lord Evershed in *Rookes*[157]),

---

[149]   [1976] ICR 274.
[150]   See in this regard the comments of Lord Donovan in *JT Stratford & Son Limited v Lindley* [1965] AC 269 at 340.
[151]   [1978] ICR 582.
[152]   See also *News Group Newspapers Limited v SOGAT (No 2)* [1986] IRLR 337, with regard to other 'information' delivered in the context of industrial action.
[153]   [1925] AC 700.
[154]   [1964] AC 1129 at 1168.
[155]   *Rookes v Barnard* [1964] AC 1129 at 1209.
[156]   [1964] AC 1129 at 1167; and see too *Morgan v Fry* [1968] 2 QB 710.
[157]   [1964] AC 1129 at 1182; and see too *Tarleton v McGawley* (1793) 1 Peake 270.

and it may well cover a threat to breach an equitable obligation.[158]

8.109   On the other hand, it has been held in *Morgan v Fry*[159] that where employees give notice to their employer equivalent in length to that required properly to terminate their contracts of employment in the form of 'strike notice', this will not amount to unlawful means. This decision is hard to reconcile with subsequent cases such as *Simmons v Hoover*,[160] and the better view is probably that workers do not mean to give notice to terminate their contracts and therefore must simply be taken as giving notice to an employer of a wrong that is to be committed by them. Indeed, as is stated at **8.62**, the view of the High Court in *Barretts & Bairds (Wholesale) Limited v Institution of Professional Civil Servants*[161] is that strike notice simply is not given these days.

Intention of coercing the victim of the threat

8.110   The tort of intimidation is an intentional tort.[162] As with the other economic torts which are committed intentionally, the problem arises as to whether intention must rank as predominant purpose on the part of the tortfeasor, or whether it is enough that the tortfeasor is wilfully blind to the consequences of his action. This point is discussed above at **8.60** et seq in the case of the nature of the intention required to induce or interfere with a contract, trade or business. For reasons of consistency, it would be surprising if the concept of intention bore a different meaning in relation to the tort of intimidation.

Loss

8.111   It is necessary for the claimant to show that he has suffered a loss as a result of the threat made and that the loss is causally related to the threat. In *Messenger Newspapers Group Limited v NGA (1982)*,[163] it was held that the claimant was able to recover for the costs involved in preventing a threat from becoming acted upon where the costs were causally related to the threat.

COMMON LAW HARASSMENT

8.112   Common law harassment is one of the newer industrial torts and is a product of the courts dealing with violent industrial conflict in the 1980s. Disputes such as the Miners' Strike of 1984–1985 and the Wapping *Times* Newspapers dispute, resulted in threats of violence and the throwing of missiles at strike-breakers who crossed the picket lines in those disputes. As a result of this form of pressure, action was taken by the employers to stop the threats and violence. In doing so, the employers relied upon the Code of Practice on Picketing issued by the Secretary of State. As stated in **Chapter 1**, the Code of Practice on Picketing was originally issued under the Employment Act 1980, s 3 which gave the Secretary of State a power to issue Codes of Practice where it

---

[158]   See *Prudential Assurance Co Limited v Lorenz* (1971) 11 KIR 78.
[159]   [1968] 2 QB 710.
[160]   [1977] ICR 61.
[161]   [1987] IRLR 3.
[162]   See, in this regard, the comments of Lord Evershed in *Rookes v Barnard* [1964] AC 1129 at 1183 and those of Lord Devlin at 1205.
[163]   [1984] ICR 435.

was necessary to give guidance to promote industrial relations. The Code of Practice is not legally binding (as it states itself at section A, para 8 of the current Code of Practice (1st Revision, 2002), but it provides evidence of what is good industrial practice. Paragraph 31 of the original Code of Practice[164] stated:

> 'Large numbers on a picket line are … likely to give rise to fear and resentment amongst those seeking to cross that picket line, even where no criminal offence is committed. They exacerbate disputes and sour relations not only between management and employees but between the pickets and their fellow employees. Accordingly, pickets and their organisers should ensure that in general the number of pickets does not exceed six at any entrance to a workplace. Frequently a smaller number would be appropriate.'

8.113   One of the first cases to test the effect of the Code of Practice was *Thomas v NUM (South Wales Area)*,[165] which involved picketing at a number of collieries in Wales during the Miners' Strike 1984–1985. The picketing was both abusive and violent towards strike-breakers, and the houses of the strike-breakers were also picketed by those on strike. An action was brought by the claimants (who were strike-breakers), alleging that they were the victim of harassment and nuisance, the nuisance being in respect of picketing at their homes. The defendants claimed that they were immune from an action being brought against them under the statutory immunity granted for peaceful picketing. The matter was heard by the High Court which had to consider whether the case was an appropriate one for the grant of an interim injunction. The court dealt first with the contention that the union was immune from action in tort by questioning whether the presence of such large number of pickets was reasonably necessary for the purposes of peacefully communicating with people entering the workplace. The court held that there was no need for such large number to have congregated; communication with those seeking to enter the workplace could easily have taken place with the recommended six pickets (or less) under the Code of Practice. The court then went on to consider the issue of what torts had been committed. The court rejected claims by the claimants that the actions of the pickets amounted to assault, obstruction of the highway, unlawful interference with the contracts of the strike-breakers or intimidation (in the sense of attempting to compel employees not to work). However, the court held that a species of the tort of nuisance might have been committed by the pickets, holding that:[166]

> 'The working miners are entitled to use the highway for the purpose of entering and leaving their respective places of work. In the exercise of that right they are at present having to suffer the presence and behaviour of the pickets and demonstrators. The law has long recognised that unreasonable interference with the rights of others is actionable in tort. The law of nuisance is a classic example … It is, however, not every act of interference with the enjoyment by an individual of his property rights that will be actionable in nuisance. The law must strike a balance between conflicting

---

[164]   Now section E, para 51 of the Code of Practice, 1st Revision.
[165]   [1985] IRLR 136.
[166]   [1985] IRLR 136 at 149.

rights and interests ... Nuisance is strictly concerned with, and may be regarded as confined to, activity which unduly interferes with the use of land or of easements. But there is no reason why the law should not protect on a similar basis the enjoyment of other rights. All citizens have the right to use the public highway. Suppose an individual were persistently to follow another on a public highway, making rude gestures or remarks in order to annoy or vex. If continuance of such conduct were threatened no one can doubt but that a civil court would, at the suit of the victim, restrain by injunction the continuance of the conduct. The tort might be described as a species of private nuisance, namely unreasonable interference with the victim's right to use the highway. But the label for the tort does not, in my view matter ... A decision whether in this, or in any other similar case, the presence or conduct of pickets represents a tortious interference with the right of those who wish to go to work to do so without harassment must depend on the particular circumstances of the particular case. The balance to which I have earlier referred must be struck between the rights of those going to work and the rights of the pickets.'

8.114   Having held that the rights of the claimants were being interfered with under this tort, and in respect of the nuisance that they were suffering at their homes, the High Court then went on to grant an interim injunction limiting the number of pickets in attendance to six, notwithstanding that the claimant could not show that harm was being suffered over and above the volley of abuse from six such strikers.

Criticism of the tort of common law harassment

8.115   After the decision in *Thomas v NUM (South Wales Area)*,[167] the next case to deal with the issue of whether a tort of common law harassment existed was *News Group Newspapers Limited v SOGAT (No 2)*,[168] where the High Court was asked to consider whether it would grant an injunction to prevent the disputes occurring at the *Times* Newspaper plant at Wapping, inter alia, on grounds of common law harassment. The court addressed the matter stating that:[169]

'The defendants criticise [the statement of law at **8.113**]. They submit that Scott J should not have invented a new tort and that it is not sufficient to found liability that there has been an unreasonable interference with the rights of others, even though when a balance is struck between conflicting rights and interests the scale comes down heavily in favour of the [claimants], unless those rights are recognised by the law and fall within some accepted head of tort.

I am bound to say that, with all respect to Scott J, I think there is force in these criticisms, especially where it does not appear that damage is a necessary ingredient of the tort. If, of course, damage peculiar to the [claimant] is established, then the tort is that of nuisance.'

---

167   [1985] IRLR 136.
168   [1986] IRLR 337.
169   [1986] IRLR 337 at 348.

8.116   The High Court then went on to hold that a nuisance had been made out in the *News Group* case[170] and intimidation had been threatened. There was therefore no need to deal with the tort of common law harassment.

8.117   In the other main case to have discussed the tort of common law harassment and its existence, *Khorasandjian v Bush*[171] (a case of stalking arising from harassment by persistent telephone calls), Peter Gibson J (sitting as a judge of the Court of Appeal) agreed with the comments of the High Court in the *News Group* case.[172] However, the comments of Peter Gibson J are merely obiter as he went on to hold that there was no need to decide the case before him on the basis of the alleged tort and neither of the other judges in the case addressed the matter. Consequently, it would appear that the weight of judicial opinion seems to be against the existence of a tort of common law harassment, not that this matters much now due to the statutory tort of harassment under the Prevention from Harassment Act 1997.

HARASSMENT UNDER THE PROTECTION FROM HARASSMENT ACT 1997

8.118   Harassment under the Protection from Harassment Act 1997 when introduced was aimed at unlawful harassment arising from such matters as rave parties and stalking of individuals. However, there is nothing in the make up of the tort that prevents it from being used as a cause of action in the context of industrial action. Indeed, it is well suited to dealing with matters such as harassment of strike-breakers.

Elements of the tort

8.119   The tort is committed under the Protection from Harassment Act 1997 (PHA 1997), s 1(1) where a person pursues a course of conduct:

- which amounts to harassment of another, and
- which he knows or ought to know amounts to harassment of the other.

8.120   Under PHA 1997, s 1(2), a person whose course of conduct is in question (the harasser) 'ought to know' that the conduct amounts to harassment of another if a reasonable person in possession of the same information as the harasser would think the course of conduct amounted to harassment of the other.

8.121   Under PHA 1997, s 7, references to 'harassing a person' are stated to include alarming the person or causing the person distress. Furthermore, under PHA 1997, s 7(3), a 'course of conduct' must involve conduct on at least two occasions. Further, under PHA 1997, s 7(4), 'conduct' is stated to include speech.

8.122   Harassment under PHA 1997 is specifically stated to give rise to a civil claim under PHA 1997, s 3. PHA 1997, s 3(1) provides that a claim can arise in a case where an actual or apprehended breach of PHA 1997, s 1 exists by the person who is or may be the victim of the course of conduct in question. In the

---

[170]   *News Group Newspapers Limited v SOGAT (No 2)* [1986] IRLR 337.
[171]   [1993] 3 All ER 669.
[172]   *News Group Newspapers Limited v SOGAT (No 2)* [1986] IRLR 337.

event of such a claim, PHA 1997, s 3(2) provides that damages may be awarded for (among other things) any anxiety caused by the harassment and any financial loss resulting from the harassment. Further, under PHA 1997, s 3(3) where in a civil claim a court grants an injunction for the purpose of restraining the harasser from pursuing any conduct which amounts to harassment, and the victim considers that the harasser has done anything which he is prohibited from doing by the injunction, the victim may apply for the issue of a warrant for the arrest of the harasser.

8.123   Additionally, under PHA 1997, s 3(6), where a court grants an injunction under PHA 1997, s 3(3)(a), and without reasonable excuse the harasser does anything which he is prohibited from doing by the injunction, that is stated to amount to a criminal offence. In the event of a conviction of the harasser for such an offence, PHA 1997, s 3(7) provides that the conduct is not punishable as a contempt of court. However, under PHA 1997, s 3(9) where the harasser is found guilty of an offence under PHA 1997, s 3(6), the harasser will be liable on conviction on indictment, to imprisonment for a term not exceeding 5 years, or a fine, or both, or on summary conviction, to imprisonment for a term not exceeding 6 months, or a fine not exceeding the statutory maximum, or both.

8.124   Finally, since the tort of harassment under PHA 1997 is not one of the torts for which an immunity is granted in tort under the provisions of TULRCA 1992, s 219, to the extent that the tort is proved by a claimant, the tortfeasor is liable to the full extent of the loss suffered by the claimant. It is also possible for the employer of a tortfeasor to be vicariously liable for the tortfeasor's breach of duty under PHA 1997.[173]

OTHER TORTS COMMITTED DURING PICKETING

8.125   This section will do no more than briefly examine certain other torts which may be committed during the course of picketing and regard should be had to more mainstream works on the law of tort in relation to these torts generally. In this regard, the main torts which can be committed in the course of industrial action are the following:

- trespass to the highway;
- private nuisance; and
- public nuisance,

each of which will be dealt with briefly below.

Trespass to the highway

8.126   Trespass to the highway can be committed in the context of picketing by a person who uses a highway for any purpose outside that which is prescribed by law. Public highways provide a right for the public to pass along them for the purposes of travel.[174] To the extent that a public highway is used for purposes other than this, the persons so misusing it may be liable in tort for either damages or an injunction.

---

[173]   See *Majrowski v Guy's and St Thomas's NHS Trust* [2005] EWCA Civ 25, dealing with vicarious liability in a bullying, intimidating and harassment case brought in respect of an employee's line manager.

[174]   *Harrison v Duke of Rutland* [1893] 1 QB 142.

8.127   The main problem arising in relation to this tort is that most highways are these days owned by local authorities who have little interest in claiming damages or seeking an injunction in the course of industrial action (unless, perhaps, it is their own premises which are the subject of the industrial action). In *Hubbard v Pitt*,[175] the claimant was an estate agent who was being picketed by local residents. An action was brought by the agent to prevent the picketing which, it was alleged, was causing harm to the claimant's business. The High Court granted an interlocutory injunction on the grounds of nuisance, stating:[176]

> 'The law appears ... to be clear: At common law, the use of the highway for picketing is illegal as it is a use not responsive to the purposes for which the highway was dedicated. It is, therefore, at least a trespass. It may also be an unreasonable user of the highway and therefore a common law nuisance. This will always be a question of fact, and what is or is not a reasonable user of the highway will be determined by reference to the purposes for which the highway was dedicated. As picketing is a use of the highway wholly unconnected with the purposes of dedication and is, in fact, designed to interfere with the rights of an adjoining owner to have unimpeded access from the highway, it is likely to be found to be an unreasonable user unless it is so fleeting and so insubstantial that it can be ignored under the de minimis rule ... Put shortly, therefore, the use of the highway for picketing is illegal unless – (1) it is in contemplation or furtherance of a trade dispute in the circumstances set out in the statute, or (2) it is found as a fact to be insubstantial in the sense that I have mentioned.'

Private nuisance

8.128   The tort of private nuisance is committed where a person is caused to suffer an unreasonable and unlawful interference with the use or enjoyment of his property caused by another.[177] In the context of industrial disputes this may occur where, for example, pickets congregate outside a workplace in such number as to provide an unreasonable obstruction to an employer's business.

8.129   Various cases have shown that an employer may use the tort to prevent picketing. In *Hubbard v Pitt*,[178] an injunction was awarded on the grounds of a nuisance being occasioned by the pickets. Likewise, in *News Group Newspapers Limited v SOGAT (No 2)*,[179] the High Court was prepared to hold that the activity of pickets in the *Times* Newspapers Wapping dispute amounted to nuisance due to their obstruction of, and abusive behaviour on, the highway resulting in the claimant being unable to use its land reasonably and lawfully.[180] In *Gate Gourmet Limited v Transport and General Workers Union*,[181] the High

---

[175]   [1975] ICR 77; affirmed [1975] ICR 308.
[176]   [1975] ICR 77 at 91.
[177]   See, for example, *Cunard v Antifyre Limited* [1933] 1 KB 551.
[178]   [1975] ICR 308.
[179]   [1986] IRLR 337.
[180]   Other examples of the tort are *Mersey Dock and Harbour Co v Verrinder* [1982] IRLR 152; *Norbrook Laboratories Limited v King* [1982] IRLR 456; and *Thomas v NUM (South Wales Area)* [1985] IRLR 136.
[181]   [2005] EWHC 1889 (QB).

Court, when faced with a case involving multiple pickets at two different sites, one of which was at the side of a public highway, relied upon the right of freedom of assembly (as provided under the European Convention on Human Rights, Art 11), to allow an unrestricted right to continue picketing peacefully by the side of the public highway, whilst limiting the number of pickets who could be in attendance at the entrance of the employer's premises.

8.130 In *Hubbard v Pitt*, Lord Denning MR in the Court of Appeal gave a strong dissenting judgment attacking the view that picketing will of itself be a nuisance stating that:[182]

'... [P]icketing is not a nuisance in itself. Nor is it a nuisance for a group of people to attend at or near the [claimant]'s premises in order to obtain or communicate information or in order to peacefully persuade. It does not become a nuisance unless it is associated with obstruction, violence, intimidation, molestation or threats.'

8.131 Cases since *Hubbard v Pitt*[183] have tended not to follow Lord Denning's view as to the legality of picketing and have instead focused on the view of the majority of the Court of Appeal. It follows that in most industrial disputes where picketing takes place, there is a good chance that the tort may be committed but it needs to be remembered that if the picketing is lawful and within the immunity for peaceful picketing under TULRCA 1992, s 220, it will be protected and there will be no cause of action in this regard. Much will depend therefore upon the conduct of the pickets in each case and, if there are large number of pickets involved, the effect of the Code of Practice on Picketing.

PUBLIC NUISANCE

8.132 The tort of public nuisance is committed where an act or omission takes place which unreasonably causes harm or potential harm to a class of the Crown's subjects.[184] In order for a claimant to establish liability for the tort, he must show that he has suffered special damage himself over and above that suffered by the public generally as a result of the tort being committed. In *News Group Newspapers Limited v SOGAT (No 2)*,[185] the High Court held that the tort had been committed by pickets unreasonably obstructing the highway and causing the claimant substantial expense in the form of having to arrange buses to bring journalists and other employees into the plants affected. Public nuisance is also a crime at common law.

INDUSTRIAL ACTION AND BREACH OF CONTRACT

8.133 Where employees take industrial action, the action so taken is likely to amount to a breach of contract. In deciding whether or not contracts of employment have been breached, much will depend upon the nature of the

---

[182] [1975] ICR 308 at 317.
[183] [1975] ICR 308.
[184] Per Denning LJ in *Southport Corporation v Esso Petroleum Co Limited* [1954] 2 QB 182, who added at 196 that it is a concept that '... covers a multitude of sins, great and small'.
[185] [1986] IRLR 337.

industrial action being taken. This section will focus on the particular quirks of the law of contract when applied to industrial action.

8.134   Breach of contract is an action available to employers and employees alike. It follows that if industrial action is taken by employees in response to the unreasonable action of an employer, those affected by the industrial action may be able to sue for breach of contract.

Industrial action taken by employees

8.135   In determining whether or not employees have committed a breach of contract when undertaking industrial action, the nature of the industrial action that has been taken by the employees involved needs to be considered. Industrial action can be divided into two categories, being those cases where employees totally withdraw their services to an employer and those cases where employees provide lesser services than the employer is entitled to expect under the terms of the contract of employment.

Total withdrawal of labour

8.136   The most common situation where this occurs is in the case of a strike. Strikes are defined by TULRCA 1992, s 246 as 'any concerted stoppage of work'. It used to be thought that, provided employees gave notice equivalent in length to that which would lawfully bring about the termination of their contract, they were committing no breach of contract in withdrawing their labour and notice of this type earned the description 'strike notice'. Lord Denning MR discussed the concept of strike notice in *Morgan v Fry*:[186]

> 'It has been held for over 60 years that workmen have a right to strike ... provided that they give sufficient notice beforehand: and a notice is sufficient if it is as least as long as the notice required to terminate the contract.'

8.137   This view of strike notice as being a right that employees have to withhold labour but maintain the contract of employment has lost favour in the courts. Lord Reid stated of the concept of strike notice in *Rookes v Barnard*:[187]

> 'The object of [strike] notice was not to terminate the contract either before or after the expiry of the seven days. The object was to break the contract by withholding labour but keeping the contract alive for as long as the employers would tolerate the breach without exercising their right of rescission.'

8.138   The matter was subsequently taken further by Phillips J, in *Simmons v Hoover Limited*, who said:[188]

> '... a settled, confirmed and continued intention on the part of the employee not to do any of the work which under his contract he had engaged to do; which was the whole purpose of the contract ... appears ... to be repudiatory of the contract of employment.'

---

[186]   [1968] 2 QB 710 at 725.
[187]   [1964] AC 1129 at 1204.
[188]   [1977] ICR 61 at 76.

8.139 Most recently, there are the comments of Henry J in *Barretts & Bairds (Wholesale) Limited v Institution of Professional Civil Servants*,[189] where he observed, 'no-one today gives their notice before striking'.

8.140 The position is therefore that employees who strike, unless it is the case that either:

- they are striking in response to a breach of contract on the part of their employer; or
- they have a term in their contracts of employment allowing them to suspend the contract through the giving of strike notice,

will themselves commit a breach of contract and open themselves to the potential for action to be taken against them by their employer.

Partial withdrawal of services by employees

8.141 Where employees decide to carry on working for their employer but to deny the employer of the benefit of a particular function of their employment, they may commit a breach of contract. In deciding whether or not this is the case, it needs to be considered whether the service that is being denied to the employer is contractual or non-contractual.

8.142 Examples of cases where a service has been denied to an employer and has been held to be contractual are:

- *Secretary of State for Employment v ASLEF (No 2)*,[190] a withdrawal of labour in a work to rule;
- *Cresswell v Board of Inland Revenue*,[191] where employees refused to adapt to computerised working methods requested by the employer and continued to operate in accordance with the way in which they had traditionally performed their duties;
- *Miles v Wakefield Metropolitan District Council*,[192] where a council officer failed to work 3/37ths of his monthly hours whilst involved in an industrial dispute; and
- *Ticehurst v British Telecommunications plc*,[193] where a refusal to give an undertaking to work normally and not take part in further industrial action was held to be a breach of the implied term of trust and confidence.

8.143 In order to escape liability for failing to provide a benefit, the duty which the employee ceases to provide in the context of industrial action must genuinely be a voluntary one. This point was considered in *Metropolitan Borough of Solihull v National Union of Teachers*,[194] where teachers engaged in industrial action refused to supervise pupils during lunch periods or provide

---

[189] [1987] IRLR 3.
[190] [1972] ICR 19. The qualification of this case by the Privy Council in *Burgess v Stevedoring Services Limited* [2002] IRLR 810 should be noted: the opinion of the Privy Council was that an overtime ban of itself did not amount to a breach of contract where the employees conducting the overtime ban otherwise performed their contractual duties in accordance with their contracts of employment.
[191] [1984] IRLR 190.
[192] [1987] ICR 368.
[193] [1992] IRLR 219.
[194] [1985] IRLR 211.

lunchtime activities so as to provide cover for colleagues who were ill. The High Court found that the action taken by the teachers amounted to a breach of contract and that an injunction could be issued against the teachers taking industrial action since no ballot had been taken prior to the action.

8.144　What will amount to voluntary activity will depend upon the facts of any particular case but could, for example, cover such matters as teachers refusing to supervise after-school sports activities. Where an employee holds a position of responsibility, for example, managers, under the principle in *Ticehurst v British Telecommunications plc*,[195] it will probably be no defence for the employee to finish work according to the stipulated hours of his contract and claim that any extra services are voluntary. Indeed, it seems that it is open to the employer to require employees to confirm that they will not act in a way that withdraws the employee's goodwill from the employment relationship as there is expected to be some flexibility in the working relationship. On this basis, the higher up in an employer's organisation that an employee is, the greater is the degree of flexibility that can be expected from that employee.

Breach of contract by the employer

8.145　In the same way that employees can commit breaches of their contracts of employment, employers may also commit breaches. In the context of industrial action, this may take the form, for example, of a lock-out by the employer so as to force employees to accept changes to their terms and contracts of employment imposed upon them against their will. However, lock-outs are a rare luxury for employers today and are very much a tactic of days gone by. In *Express Newspapers Limited v Bunday*, lock-outs were defined by the Court of Appeal in the following way:[196]

> 'Since there is no [statutory] definition of the word "lock-out" ... , it must be given its ordinary meaning ... What is material is that in my view the ordinary meaning of the word "lock-out" comprehends not merely the act of the employer in refusing to allow his employees to work, but the reason why he refuses.'

8.146　Lock-outs may amount to a breach of contract on the part of an employer who instigates a lock-out without giving employees their proper contractual notice before embarking upon this course of action,[197] or they may amount to a reasonable response by an employer to breaches of contract that have been committed by its employees.[198]

8.147　It follows that, since there may be a considerable overlap between a strike and a lock-out, it will be necessary to decide who committed the first breach of contract when determining whether to grant a remedy in a particular dispute.

8.148　If an employer stages a lock-out in breach of contract, the employer may find itself open to the usual remedies available in the case of breach of contract, (a declaration, damages for breach of contract, an injunction to

---

[195]　[1992] IRLR 219.
[196]　[1987] IRLR 422 at 427.
[197]　See, for example, *Saunders v Neale* [1974] ICR 565.
[198]　See, for example, *Express Newspapers v Bunday* [1987] IRLR 422.

prevent breach or further breaches of the contract or a claim for unfair dismissal). However, if employees are seeking to bring an action for damages arising out of their loss of salary during the period when a lock-out takes place, it is incumbent upon them to show that they were ready and willing to work for the employer if the employer had allowed them to work.[199]

8.149 The remedies open to an employer faced with industrial action are considered more fully below in **Chapter 10**.

---

[199] See, in this regard, *Henthorn v Central Electricity Generating Board* [1980] IRLR 361.

Chapter 9

TRADE UNION IMMUNITY, LOSS OF IMMUNITY AND COLLECTIVE RESPONSIBILITY

INTRODUCTION

9.1   This chapter will focus upon the issues of when a trade union is immune from the consequences of industrial action taken in its name and, if not, when it can be held liable for the consequences of such industrial action. It will also examine vicarious liability, in particular, when a trade union can be liable for the actions of its officials.

Establishing immunity from action in tort

9.2   The immunities in tort that are provided to trade unions exist under the Trade Union and Labour Relations (Consolidation) Act 1992 (TULRCA 1992), ss 219–220. A number of points can be made about the immunities. First, where immunity exists in tort, it is available only in respect of the tortious consequences of industrial action. There is no defence to an action for breach of contract that may be taken against an individual worker.

9.3   Secondly, immunity in tort can exist irrespective of whether or not a defence exists for a tort or torts committed during the course of industrial action.

9.4   Thirdly, in order for an immunity to be granted, those seeking the immunity must show that they have complied with a precise formulation of what the law takes to be protected industrial action: it is not enough that a trade union or group of workers claims that they are involved in industrial action with their employer. The nature of this formulation has changed over the years, most notably during the period 1979–1997. Therefore, care needs to be taken when relying on old case law in this regard as some cases may not be decided in the same way today in the light of the more restrictive immunities which now exist.

The 'Golden Formula'

9.5   The term the 'Golden Formula' is often used to describe the statutory formulation found in the immunities granted by TULRCA 1992, ss 219 and 220 and is believed to have been coined by Professor Lord Wedderburn.[1]

9.6   Under the Golden Formula, trade unions are immune from liability in tort where the torts to which TULRCA 1992, ss 219 and 220 apply are committed against a claimant wholly or mainly 'in contemplation or further- ance of a trade dispute'.

9.7   A 'trade dispute' is defined by TULRCA 1992, s 244(1), as follows:

'(1)   In this Part a "trade dispute" means a dispute between workers and their employer which relates wholly or mainly to one ore more of the following—

(a)   terms and conditions of employment, or the physical conditions in which any workers are required to work;
(b)   engagement or non-engagement, or termination or suspension of employment or the duties of employment, of one or more workers;
(c)   allocation of work or the duties of employment between workers or groups of workers;
(d)   matters of discipline;
(e)   a worker's membership or non-membership of a trade union;
(f)   facilities for officials of trade unions; and
(g)   machinery for negotiation or consultation, and other procedures, relating to any of the above matters, including the recognition by employers or employers' associations of the right of a trade union to represent workers in such negotiation or consultation or in the carry- ing out of such procedures.'

9.8   There are numerous case law examples of whether a matter genuinely falls to be classified as a 'trade dispute' within the meaning of TULRCA 1992, s 244. Indeed, given the multiple hurdles which must now be negotiated by a trade union seeking to undertake industrial action, challenges to whether a matter falls within the categories outlined under TULRCA 1992, s 244 are becoming more common. In this regard, examples of matters which have been alleged to be the subject of a trade dispute are:

•   Industrial action taken by schoolteachers in protest about a decision of a school's board of governors to allow a disruptive pupil back into general schooling.[2] It was held that a dispute as to the reasonableness of the instruction could amount to a dispute as to terms and conditions of employment under TULRCA 1992, s 244(1)(a).
•   A dispute relating to the introduction of a productivity scheme on a voluntary basis for certain workers in a much wider workforce.[3] It was held that this was a dispute as to terms and conditions of employment under TULRCA 1992, s 244(1)(a).

---

[1]   See Wedderburn *The Worker and the Law* (Penguin, 1st edn, 1965) at p 222.
[2]   *P v National Association of Schoolmasters/Union of Women Teachers* [2001] IRLR 532.
[3]   *British Telecommunications plc v Communication Workers Union* [2004] IRLR 58.

- A dispute arising from the proposed outsourcing of a hospital's undertaking for a period of 30 years in circumstances where the employer refused to seek a guarantee from the transferee that terms and conditions of employment would be protected pursuant to the Transfer of Undertakings (Protection of Employment) Regulations 1981[4] (TUPE 1981) during that period.[5] The Court of Appeal held that this was not a dispute as to terms and conditions of employment under TULRCA 1992, s 244(1)(a) since it related to a dispute about whether workers' terms and conditions of employment might change after their employment with the employer subject to the dispute had ceased, ie after the transfer pursuant to TUPE 1981 had occurred. Although the union subsequently presented a challenge to the European Court of Human Rights (ECHR)[6] on the basis that the grant of an injunction to prevent the union taking industrial action was contrary to the European Convention on Human Rights, Art11(1) (with which the ECHR agreed), the ECHR went on to hold that the provisions under TULRCA 1992 regulating the undertaking of industrial action were 'necessary in a democratic society', satisfied the provisions of European Convention on Human Rights, Art11(2) and therefore the Court of Appeal was justified in upholding the injunctive order against the claimant.
- A dispute arising from the outsourcing of a local authority's housing assessment and advice unit where a union sought to ballot its members in relation to the intention of the local authority to cease being the employer of its members employed in the local authority's housing assessment and advice unit.[7] The Court of Appeal held that the dispute, relating as it did to the change in the identity of the employer, was one amounting to a trade dispute.

THE GOLDEN FORMULA EXAMINED

The person committing the tortious act

9.9 The formulation of the Golden Formula is neutral as regards who may claim the benefit of the immunity in tort: it allows the immunity to be claimed by any one of the potential tortfeasors (worker, trade union official or trade union) who may commit a tort in the course of industrial action.

The time for of the commission of the tort

9.10 The Golden Formula places a temporal limit on the availability of immunity by requiring that immunity can only be claimed where industrial action is committed 'in contemplation or furtherance' of a trade dispute. Lord Loreburn, in *Conway v Wade*,[8] when speaking of the original formulation of the immunities under the Trade Disputes Act 1906, said that the requirement applies where:[9]

---

4   SI 1981/1794.
5   *University College Hospital NHS Trust v UNISON* [1999] IRLR 31.
6   *UNISON v The United Kingdom* [2002] IRLR 497.
7   *Westminster City Council v UNISON* [2001] IRLR 524.
8   [1909] AC 506.
9   [1909] AC 506 at 512.

'... either a dispute is imminent and the act is done in expectation of and with a view to it, or ... the dispute is already existing and the act is done in support of one side to it.'

9.11   In *Conway v Wade*,[10] the claimant sued his former trade union in respect of the union inducing his former employer to dismiss him for failing to pay trade union subscriptions. The union argued that it was acting in contemplation or furtherance of a trade dispute and that it was therefore immune from action in tort. The House of Lords held that no trade dispute existed or was contemplated. The action taken by the union was vindictive and aimed at ensuring that the claimant paid his subscriptions. It followed that as the action taken was not within the Golden Formula, it could not be the subject of the immunity. This said, each case will turn very much on its own facts. In trying to establish that a trade dispute is contemplated, it is not necessary that battle lines should be drawn: as the matter was put in *Beetham v Trinidad Cement Limited*:[11]

'By definition a trade dispute exists wherever a "difference" exists; and a difference can exist long before the parties become locked in combat. It is not necessary that they should have come to blows. It is sufficient that they should be sparring for an opening.'

9.12   The matter was also considered in *Bent's Brewery Co Limited v Hogan*,[12] where a questionnaire sent out by a trade union official to pub managers in Liverpool requesting details of their working conditions so as to enable the union to plan a programme for obtaining better wages and conditions for its members. The claimant argued that the letter constituted an inducement to its managers to breach their contracts of employment with the claimant since many of those contracts contained confidentiality clauses. The defendant claimed that the information was being collected in contemplation of a trade dispute and therefore he was immune from action in tort. The High Court held:[13]

'The ... question [the court has] to decide is whether the document was sent out by the defendant, or on his behalf, in contemplation or furtherance of a trade dispute ... No demand has been made for either better conditions or increased wages by any manager to any of the plaintiff brewery companies. No such demands had been made by the plaintiff, or his union on behalf of such managers ... In [the court's] opinion, a dispute cannot exist unless there is a difference of opinion between two parties as to some matter. There is no evidence before [the court] that any dispute existed. The highest that can be put on the evidence in favour of the defendant is that the document was sent out to obtain information which, after consideration of the information obtained, might lead to a request which, if not granted, might result in a dispute.'

9.13   It follows that a dispute must be objectively ascertainable on the facts, ie within the contemplation of both parties on the evidence available, if the immunity is to be claimed on the basis of contemplating a trade dispute.

---

[10]   [1909] AC 506.
[11]   [1960] AC 132 at 143.
[12]   [1945] 2 All ER 570.
[13]   [1945] 2 All ER 570 at 579.

9.14   A case that illustrates the point the other way is *Health Computing Limited v Meek*.[14] Here, a public sector trade union had issued notices to its members operating in the National Heath Service instructing them not to work with the claimant, which had been requested to advise local health authorities on the installation of computerised medical services. At the time of the union members' instruction, no jobs were directly threatened. The claimant sought an injunction and argued that the union was not protected under the Golden Formula as no trade dispute was contemplated. The High Court held on the evidence that some of the health authorities might tend to use the services of the claimant and, as a result, this could bring the defendant union into dispute with the claimant. Consequently, it was reasonable to infer that a dispute was contemplated.

9.15   A comparison between the *Health Computing*[15] and *Bent's Brewery*[16] cases shows that they are materially different in nature. In *Bent's Brewery*, the information requested was to see if a dispute *might* arise if pub managers' terms and conditions of employment were not as the union would have liked. Any potential trade dispute was effectively two steps removed (these being the receipt of information and then deciding whether to act upon it). However, in *Health Computing*, the possibility of job losses had already been foreseen (although not confirmed), and the dispute was therefore only one step away (ie the likelihood of conflict). It was therefore sufficiently proximate for a trade dispute to be contemplated.

9.16   In *Conway v Wade*, Lord Shaw said of the meaning of the words 'in contemplation or furtherance' that:[17]

'... they do not cover the case of coercive interference in which the intervener may have in his own mind that if he does not get his own way he will thereupon take ways and means to bring a trade dispute into existence. To "contemplate a trade dispute" is to have before the mind some objective event or situation with those elements of fact or probability to which I have averted, but it does not mean a contemplation, mediation or resolve in regard to something as yet wholly within the mind and of a subjective character.'

9.17   This said, once the facts giving rise to the dispute have been objectively established, it does not matter that the person acting takes a decision which he thinks will help further his objectives but which in reality would not do so. Thus the test as to whether the action taken is in contemplation or furtherance of the dispute is a subjective one. This was shown in *Express Newspapers Limited v MacShane*,[18] where the National Union of Journalists (NUJ) was in dispute with certain regional newspapers and called on journalists who were with the Press Association to join the dispute. When the Press Association journalists did not comply fully with the request, the NUJ asked its members working for national newspapers (including the claimant) to boycott Press Association copy. In the Court of Appeal, an interim injunction was granted

14   [1980] IRLR 437.
15   *Health Computing Limited v Meek* [1980] IRLR 437
16   *Bent's Brewery Co Limited v Hogan* [1945] 2 All ER 570.
17   [1909] AC 506 at 522.
18   [1980] IRLR 35.

against the union on the grounds that the activity of the union would not be capable of helping it reach its stated objectives.

9.18   The problem with the decision of the Court of Appeal was that it made the action of trade union officials reviewable by the courts, and therefore the decision as to what action could be taken by a trade union was reviewable too. On appeal, a majority of the House of Lords agreed that the test of whether action was likely to further a person's position in the course of a trade dispute was a subjective one for the person taking the action. Their Lordships were of the view that in some cases, action taken by trade union officials might tend to be out of proportion to the benefit that was provided by the taking of the action. Lord Diplock stated that it was this situation that caused the subjective test to 'stick in judicial gorges'. His Lordship added that the effect of the statute on a plain and literal reading meant that the words 'an act done by a person in furtherance or contemplation of a trade dispute' referred to the state of mind of the doer of the act, concluding:[19]

> 'My Lords, ... [the objective test has] ... the effect of enabling the court to substitute its own opinion for the bona fide opinion held by the trade union or its officers, as to whether action proposed to be taken or continued for the purpose of helping one side or bringing pressure to bear upon the other side to a trade dispute is likely to have the desired effect. Granted bona fides on the part of the trade union or its officers this is to convert the test from a purely subjective to a purely objective test and for the reasons I have given I do not think the wording of the section permits of this. The belief of the doer of the act that it will help the side he favours in the dispute must be honest; it need not be wise, nor need it take account of the damage it will cause to innocent and disinterested third parties.'

9.19   The other main issue needing to be addressed in relation to the Golden Formula is when action will be taken to 'further' a trade dispute. It is clear that once a dispute has been settled by agreement subsequent action cannot be related to that resolved dispute.[20] One issue that could possibly allow an old dispute to be reopened is, as with the common law generally, where the resolution of the dispute has been achieved by fraud or misrepresentation. This said, in the absence of a written agreement, it may be difficult to point to the precise time when a trade dispute has ceased. It is in these grey area cases that the courts may intervene so as to decide whether there is a trade dispute.[21]

9.20   The final point in relation to action taken in 'contemplation or further-ance' of a trade dispute is to consider the position of action taken by a person where that person knows that the other side to a potential trade dispute will give in at the possibility of pressure being exerted. The position at common law was that such action was not regarded as taken in 'contemplation' of a trade dispute. As Buckley LJ put it in *Cory Lighterage Transport Limited v Transport and General Workers Union*,[22] how can an act be done in contemplation of a trade dispute where the actor knows that no dispute will arise?

---

19   *Express Newspapers Limited v MacShane* [1980] IRLR 35 at 40.
20   See, for example, *Stewart v AUEW* [1973] IRLR 57.
21   See, for example, *JT Stratford & Co Limited v Lindley* [1965] AC 269; and *Newham London Borough Council v NALGO* [1993] IRLR 83 in this regard.
22   [1973] IRLR 152.

9.21   However, the law is now clear that such action will be deemed to be in contemplation of a trade dispute as TULRCA 1992, s 244(4) provides:

> 'An act, threat or demand done or made by one person or organisation against another which, if resisted, would have led to a trade dispute with that other, shall be treated as being done or made in contemplation of a trade dispute with that other, notwithstanding that because that other submits to the act or threat or accedes to the dispute no dispute arises.'

9.22   In other words, a trade dispute is not prevented from being so simply because the other party does not want a dispute.

The target of industrial action

9.23   TULRCA 1992, s 244(1) requires that where industrial action is taken it should be in support of a trade dispute between workers and their employer. The police (TULRCA 1992, s 280) and armed services (TULRCA 1992, s 296(1)(c)) are excluded from the definition of 'worker' under TULRCA 1992, s 296(1). Further, in the context of trade disputes, the general definition of a 'worker' is restricted by TULRCA 1992, s 244(5) which provides that a worker:

> '... in relation to a dispute with an employer, means—
> (a) a worker employed by that employer; or
> (b) a person who has ceased to be so employed if his employment was terminated in connection with the dispute or if the termination of his employment was one of the circumstances giving rise to the dispute.'

9.24   Therefore, workers are those who are in employment or were in employment with the employer immediately before the commencement of a trade dispute. It is not possible to argue that a trade dispute exists with a prospective employer as, for example, where a transfer of an undertaking is proposed and it causes resentment among the workforce: in such a situation it will be possible to be in dispute with the transferring employer but not the prospective transferee employer.[23]

9.25   In considering the statutory definition of 'worker' for these purposes, a Minister of the Crown is treated as being an employer where the dispute arises from the minister's portfolio of responsibility notwithstanding that the minister is not a de facto employer of those taking part in the action (TULRCA 1992, s 244(2)).

9.26   Other than this, the question as to whether the parties to a trade dispute fall within the Golden Formula is one of fact. Two issues need to be examined in looking at this relationship. The first is whether a trade union's reasons for seeking to induce its members to take industrial action are 'wholly or mainly' related to one or more of the reasons under TULRCA 1992, s 244(1) as is required under that section. Secondly, there is the issue of whether a trade union can pierce the veil of incorporation in determining in relation to a group of companies, of which one has a genuine trade dispute, whether others can legitimately be the subject of industrial action within the Golden Formula.

---

[23]   See *Westminster City Council v UNISON* [2001] IRLR 524.

The reason for industrial action

9.27   Generally, it will be impossible to distinguish the objects of a trade union from those of its members. In some trade union recognition disputes, the courts have held that industrial action called by a trade union is called for a reason independent to that of the union's members and is therefore outside the Golden Formula,[24] ie the action is not 'wholly or mainly' related to the matters under TULRCA 1992, s 244. Good examples of this are the cases where the courts have held that a trade union is acting to promote its own political objects or where a trade union is essentially taking revenge against an employer for its conduct in relation to another matter.

Politically motivated industrial action

9.28   The starting point in this area is what amounts to politically motivated industrial action. In *Sherrard v AUEW*, Roskill LJ held that:[25]

> 'Although the phrase "political strike" has from time to time been used in reported cases, it is to my mind a phrase which should be used, at any rate in a court of law, with considerable caution, for it does not lend itself to precise or accurate definition. It is all too easy for someone to talk of a strike as being a "political strike" when what that person really means is that the object of the strike is something that he as an individual subjectively disapproves.'

9.29   It follows that whether a strike or other industrial action is aimed at attempting to change policy rather than influencing matters within the workplace is something that has to be judged from the facts of a given case. A good example is the case of *Mercury Communications Limited v Scott-Garner*,[26] where the second defendant was the Post Office Engineering Union which opposed the idea put forward by the Government to privatise the United Kingdom telephone system. Consequently, the union instructed its members not to help the claimant by connecting them to the telephone network. The claimant sued and the union defended on the basis that it was involved in a trade dispute and was therefore immune from the consequences of its action. The defence was based upon concerns that the union had regarding job losses. The Court of Appeal held that a dispute could exist between British Telecommunications and the defendant but that it did not do so on the facts which showed that the objections of the union actually related to the principle of privatisation rather than any imminent job losses resulting from privatisation. It was shown that British Telecommunications anticipated that any job losses that were likely to arise would be lost either through natural wastage or retirements. A fundamental problem for the union was that they knew this and, as such, could not genuinely have believed that jobs would be lost.

9.30   However, in *London Borough of Wandsworth v National Association of Schoolmasters/Union of Women Teachers*,[27] the claimant sought an injunction against the defendant union on the grounds that it had induced workers of the

---

24   See, for example, *JT Stratford & Co Limited v Lindley* [1965] AC 269.
25   [1973] IRLR 188 at 190.
26   [1983] IRLR 494.
27   [1983] IRLR 344.

claimant to breach their contracts of employment. The dispute between the parties arose as a result of balloted industrial action which had asked the following question of the union's members:

> 'In order to protest against the excessive workload and unreasonable imposition made upon teachers, as a consequence of the national curriculum and testing, are you willing to take action, short of a strike?'

9.31 The request had arisen out of the union's protest at the hours that were being required of school teaching staff. The union had also voiced concerns about the educational quality of the proposed new national curriculum. In response to the ballot question, an 88 per cent majority was returned which resulted in a boycott of all elements of the national curriculum considered by the union to be unnecessary. In defence of the litigation arising from the boycott the union argued the statutory immunity under the Golden Formula. Both the High Court and the Court of Appeal agreed with the union's claim to immunity. In the Court of Appeal, Neill LJ stated:[28]

> 'We have come to a clear conclusion in this case ... It seems to us to be quite clear that looking at the history since 1990 there has been increasing concern expressed by the union on behalf of its members with regard to working time. This concern came to a head as the date for the key stage 3 testing approached. It is quite clear that members of the union have criticisms to make of the national curriculum educational grounds. This was recognised by Mr de Gruchy in paragraph 3 of his affidavit, but he added: "Of most concern to the union in relation to its members is the excessive and unnecessary workload that the national curriculum imposes on teachers".
>
> That statement, which remains uncontradicted, is to be read in the context as referring primarily to the extra time which teachers have to work. Furthermore, we attach considerable importance to the wording of the question posed in the ballot paper ... In our judgment the dispute does mainly relate to the terms and conditions of employment of the union's members and is a trade dispute ...'

9.32 Therefore, it is not enough that a trade union has expressed concern over government policy; it is important to remember that the key question to be addressed is whether the dispute relates wholly or mainly to the matters set down in TULRCA 1992, s 244(1). If this question is properly considered then it does not matter that a trade union has a dispute with the government as an employer, even though the dispute may appear to arise out of a matter connected with government policy. By way of further example, in *Sherrard v AUEW*,[29] the claimant sought an injunction to prevent his union from taking strike action in protest over what might have appeared to be Government prices and incomes policy. The protest was launched by members of the union employed by the Government who objected to a pay freeze arising under the Counter Inflation (Temporary Provisions) Act 1972. The injunction was refused. The Court of Appeal held that there was enough evidence to suggest

---

28   *London Borough of Wandsworth v National Association of Schoolmasters/Union of Women Teachers* [1983] IRLR 344 at 350.
29   [1973] IRLR 188.

that the dispute arose as a consequence of a protest about wage fixing. That was enough to bring the dispute within the Golden Formula.

9.33   Other examples of cases that have been held to be prompted by political objects rather than for reasons connected with a trade dispute are:

- *Associated Newspaper Group Limited v Flynn*,[30] a case concerning industrial action taken in defiance of the introduction of the Industrial Relations Act 1971.
- *BBC v Hearn*,[31] a case concerning a trade union's dissatisfaction over the South African Government's apartheid policy.
- *NWL Limited v Nelson*,[32] a case concerning an allegation that a trade union was embarking upon a political crusade against ships bearing flags of convenience rather than caring for its members wages. This argument was rejected by the House of Lords which held that a connection with an external political purpose was irrelevant.
- *Express Newspapers Limited v Keys*,[33] a protest over the Government's economic policy.
- *Hadmor Productions Limited v Hamilton*,[34] where the defendant trade union was found to have a genuine concern about possible job losses for its members if independent television companies were used to produce television programmes.
- *Associated British Ports v Transport and General Workers Union*,[35] a case concerning the abolition of the National Dock Labour Scheme (NDLS), which would have directly affected the rights of registered dock workers, but which was also set against a background of political objection by the union to the Government's proposed abolition of the NDLS. At first instance, the High Court refused to grant an injunction holding that the union's reasons for calling industrial action were different to those in the *Mercury Communications* case,[36] centring as they did on the removal of the NDLS which provided a unique status and certain special employment privileges for the union's members who were members of the NDLS: the High Court was categorical that the dispute related to terms and conditions of employment. On appeal, the Court of Appeal overturned the decision on other grounds.
- *University College London Hospital NHS Trust v UNISON*,[37] a case involving a proposed 30-year outsourcing of hospital services, where it was held that it was possible for a trade union to have more than one purpose at any given time in the context of taking industrial action. Here the Court of Appeal held, first, that a union could have 'a root and branch' policy of opposition to a particular course of political activity and, secondly, that it was possible at the same time for a union to have a more limited objective as the reason for seeking industrial action, namely, to alleviate the adverse

---

[30]   (1970) 10 KIR 17.
[31]   [1977] IRLR 273.
[32]   [1979] IRLR 478.
[33]   [1980] IRLR 247.
[34]   [1982] IRLR 102.
[35]   [1989] IRLR 399.
[36]   *Mercury Communications Limited v Scott-Garner* [1983] IRLR 494.
[37]   [1999] IRLR 31.

consequences to its members' interests that the union anticipates will flow from the political policy to which it is objecting: in other words that where a trade union has a particular political agenda, this will not always mean that the union's predominant purpose is the promotion of the political object and the union may be 'mainly' acting for the purposes of its members in relation to one or more of the matters under TULRCA 1992, s 244(1).

● *Westminster City Council v UNISON*,[38] another case involving outsourcing, where the Court of Appeal held that a trade union's objection to the outsourcing of a local authority's housing assessment and advice unit, relating as it did to the identity of its members' employer, although in line with the union's policy of objecting to outsourcing, was a case where the union was also seeking to further the interests of its members. In short, whether a trade union is acting wholly or mainly in its own interests, the interests of its members, or both, is a question of fact to be examined against the full facts of a given case.

Revenge cases

9.34   As stated above, the other common example of cases held not to be predominately connected with a trade dispute as defined by TULRCA 1992, s 244 are those where a trade union has acted out of a sense of vengeance. Examples of this are *Torquay Hotel Co Limited v Cousins*[39] (in respect of which see **Chapter 8** generally); and *Universe Tankships Inc of Monrovia v ITWF*,[40] which arose from the ITWF's campaign against ships operating under a flag of convenience. The ITWF had agreed to release the claimant's ship from being 'blacked' on condition that the claimant paid a sum of money to the union's welfare fund. Having paid the requested sum, the claimant sought to recover the money under the law of restitution. The case raises an interesting point as to when hard bargaining on the part of a union becomes economic duress. The House of Lords was prepared to find that this case crossed the line into duress. Further, since the case was based in restitution rather than tort, it followed that the immunities in tort would not apply to help the union.

Piercing the veil in industrial action

9.35   Whether the courts will allow a trade union to pierce the veil of incorporation in the context of industrial action being taken within a group of companies depends upon whether the veil of incorporation is being used as a sham device to defeat a trade union's claim to immunity or whether the employer which is the target of the industrial action has a legitimate commercial reason for having a number of companies. In *Examite Limited v Whittaker*,[41] and *The Marabu Porr*,[42] it was held to be possible to take industrial action against a company other than that at which the dispute had originated.

---

38   [2001] IRLR 524.
39   [1969] 2 Ch 106.
40   [1982] IRLR 200.
41   [1977] IRLR 312.
42   [1979] 2 Lloyd's Rep 331.

9.36   However, in *Dimbleby & Sons Limited v National Union of Journalists*,[43] the contrary position was the outcome. In *Dimbleby*, industrial action was taken by the union against a printing company, T Bailey Foreman Limited (TBF). At the time of the dispute, secondary picketing was still lawful against customers of a party involved in a trade dispute. The union believed that the claimant had its printing carried out by TBF. However, the reality was that a subsidiary, T Bailey Foreman (Printers) Limited, carried out the work. The union therefore caused its members at the claimant not to send copy to TBF, thereby inducing them to breach their contracts of employment. The result was that the claimant sued and the union defended claiming reliance on the statutory immunity from action. The matter reached the House of Lords where their Lordships refused to hold that a dispute with TBF necessarily meant that the union also had a dispute with T Bailey Foreman (Printers) Limited.

Legitimate purposes

9.37   Industrial action will be carried out for a legitimate purpose if it is taken in respect of any of the matters listed in TULRCA 1992, s 244(1) (in connection with which see **9.7**). This is so notwithstanding that the matter to which the dispute relates takes place outside the United Kingdom (per TULRCA 1992, s 244(3)) so long as the person or persons whose actions in the United Kingdom are said to be in contemplation or furtherance of a trade dispute relating to matters occurring outside the United Kingdom are likely to be affected in respect of one or more of the matters arising under TULRCA 1992, s 244(1)(a)–(g) by the outcome of the dispute.

THE SCOPE OF THE IMMUNITIES UNDER THE GOLDEN FORMULA

9.38   The scope of the immunities in tort are provided by TULRCA 1992, ss 219 and 220. The immunities work by protecting only primary industrial action, ie disputes between workers and their employer. This said, in the case of lawful picketing, it is possible for the secondary consequences of such primary action to be protected.

Protection from liability in tort

9.39   TULRCA 1992, 219 provides that:

'(1)   An act done by a person in contemplation or furtherance of a trade dispute is not actionable in tort on the ground only—

(a) that it induces another person to break a contract or interferes or induces another person to interfere with its performance, or

(b) that it consists in his threatening that a contract (whether one to which he is a party or not) will be broken or its performance interfered with, or that he induce will another person to break a contract or interfere with its performance.

(2)   An agreement or combination by two or more persons to do or procure the doing of an act in contemplation or furtherance of a trade

---

43   [1984] IRLR 161.

dispute is not actionable in tort if the act is one which if done without any such agreement would not be actionable in tort.'

9.40   The definition essentially provides a list of the characteristics of torts that are protected under TULRCA 1992, s 219. It follows that if a claim is either:

- not brought in tort;[44] or
- brought under a tort which is not listed,[45]

the action taken will not be immune from action in tort.

9.41   Assuming that they are committed in contemplation or furtherance of a trade dispute, torts to which the immunity apply have one characteristic in common and that is they are all required to be committed against the victim of the tort using lawful means. Consequently, only certain variants of the torts discussed in **Chapter 8** are protected, as follows:

- Inducement to breach a contract. Direct inducement is covered by TULRCA 1992, s 219(1)(a) and indirect inducement is covered by TULRCA 1992, s 219(1)(b). However, if the means used against a third party who interferes with a contract are unlawful, no immunity is available under TULRCA 1992, s 219.
- Interfering with a contract, trade or business. As with inducing breach of contract, liability for the direct form of the tort is covered by TULRCA 1992, s 219(1)(a) and indirect inducement is covered by TULRCA 1992, s 219(1)(b) to the extent that the tort is not committed by the use of unlawful means.
- Intimidation. The immunity here is provided by TULRCA 1992, s 219(1)(b) provided that the threats made in the commission of the tort relate solely to breach of contract and not to threats of other unlawful conduct.
- Simple conspiracy, covered by TULRCA 1992, s 219(2).
- Conspiracy using unlawful means, provided that the unlawful means are the torts already discussed and that these torts are themselves committed in a way that does not involve the use of unlawful means; where a tort is committed in this way, it would make the tort 'not actionable' for the purposes of TULRCA 1992, s 219. If, however, the conspiracy in question is one to commit a tort that does not enjoy the benefit of statutory immunity under TULRCA 1992, s 219, for example, statutory harassment under the Protection from Harassment Act 1997, then since the primary tort's unlawful means are not protected, the conspiracy cannot be protected either.

9.42   TULRCA 1992, s 219(3) adds that if a tort is committed in the course of picketing, the tortfeasor will only be immune under TULRCA 1992, s 219 from the consequences of the tort if the tort is committed in the course of peaceful picketing.

---

[44]   See *Universe Tankships Inc of Monrovia v ITWF* [1982] IRLR 200, where the claim was brought in restitution; and *Prudential Assurance Co Limited v Lorenz* (1971) 11 KIR 78, where the claim was based upon the equitable duty to account.

[45]   See *Rookes v Barnard* [1964] AC 1129, a claim under the tort of intimidation, (which is now covered by TULRCA 1992, s 219(1)(b)); and *Thomas v NUM (South Wales Area)* [1985] IRLR 136, a claim in the tort of common law harassment (to the extent it exists).

Liability in connection with peaceful picketing

9.43	TULRCA 1992, s 220 provides:

'(1)	It is lawful for a person in contemplation or furtherance of a trade dispute to attend—

(a)	at or near his own place of work, or
(b)	if he is an official of a trade union, at or near the place of work of a member of the union whom he is accompanying and whom he represents,

for the purpose only of peacefully obtaining or communicating information, or peacefully persuading any person to work or abstain from working.'

9.44	TULRCA 1992, s 220 provides a complex set of hurdles to be overcome if the immunity which it provides is to be obtained, as follows.

Geographical restrictions

9.45	First, the immunity under TULRCA 1992, s 220 is limited geographically and requires that peaceful picketing is committed at or near a person's place of work. Expanded definitions of this phrase are provided for workers who have a number of possible places of employment (TULRCA 1992, s 220(2)) and for dismissed workers (TULRCA 1992, s 220(3)). The expanded definition allows the former category of workers to picket any place at which they work or from which their work is administered for the purposes of the immunity. Former workers can picket at the place that they used to work at prior to their employment terminating for the purposes of the immunity.

9.46	In all cases, a worker's place of work must be as defined by TULRCA 1992, s 220 if the immunity for peaceful picketing is to be relied on. For example, the High Court was asked to consider in *News Group Newspapers Limited v SOGAT (No 2)*[46] whether ex-workers can picket their ex-employer's new place of business. The court held that it was not possible to transfer a picket line since the pickets had not worked at the new plant and this was not covered by the literal reading of TULRCA 1992, s 220.[47] Likewise in *Gate Gourmet Limited v Transport and General Workers Union*,[48] the High Court was prepared to hold that a largely peaceful secondary assembly some 500 metres from an employer's place of business (at which a primary picket line of up to 25 dismissed employees was assembled) was capable of being 'near' the employer's place of business and therefore potentially fell within the scope of TULRCA 1992, s 220.

9.47	However, in *Rayware Limited v Transport and General Workers Union*,[49] where workers had set up a picket line at the nearest point of access to their employer's business that they were lawfully able to attend without going on to

---

[46]	[1986] IRLR 337.
[47]	A similar result occurred in *Union Traffic Limited v Transport and General Workers Union* [1989] IRLR 127.
[48]	[2005] EWHC 1889 (QB).
[49]	[1989] IRLR 134.

private land (so as to avoid trespassing), the Court of Appeal held that the picketing was lawful on the basis of the words 'at *or near* his own place of work'.

9.48 The definition under TULRCA 1992, s 220 may also allow trade union officials to claim the benefit of the immunity if they are accompanying members of their union.

Purpose of the picket

9.49 The immunity under TULRCA 1992, s 220 is only provided for limited purposes, these being where the purpose of the picket is peacefully to communicate and receive information or to attempt to make people work or prevent them from doing so. The courts have traditionally taken a hard line as to when these purposes have been exceeded. For example, in *Tynan v Balmer*,[50] the Divisional Court held that the lawful purposes under TULRCA 1992, s 220 had been exceeded by trade union members who, in the course of a picket, had attempted to seal off a public highway. The case also shows the link between the immunity under TULRCA 1992, s 220 which, if complied with, is a full immunity in tort only, and the powers of the police; since the police enjoy a considerable discretion in moving pickets on to prevent *criminal* consequences arising from picketing (see **Chapter 11**), the right to attend for the purposes of peaceful picketing is a limited one. Furthermore, there is the possibility that, simply through weight of numbers, a picket line may be unlawful.[51]

LOSS OF IMMUNITY

9.50 In the event that a prima facie tortious act is granted the benefit of immunity under TULRCA 1992, s 219 or 220, it does not follow that the person committing the tort will always remain protected from the consequences of tort. TULRCA 1992 has a number of provisions built in which operate to disapply the immunities that would otherwise be granted. Many of these provisions are used to enforce duties that are owed by a trade union to an employer. The immunities will be removed where:

- no ballot takes place prior to the taking of industrial action;
- notice of industrial action is not given to an employer prior to the action being taken;
- industrial action is taken by a workforce to enforce trade union membership;
- industrial action is taken in support of workers who were dismissed for taking unofficial industrial action;
- secondary industrial action is being taken;
- industrial action is being taken to enforce recognition of a trade union in relation to a supply contract; or
- industrial action is being taken by pickets acting otherwise unlawfully,

each of which will be examined in turn.

---

[50] [1967] 1 QB 91.
[51] See, for example, *Thomas v NUM (South Wales Area)* [1985] IRLR 136.

Balloting prior to the taking of industrial action

9.51   Since the Trade Union Act 1984 (TUA 1984), trade unions have been obliged to hold secret postal ballots for the taking of industrial action, in order for the union to retain the benefit of immunity under TULRCA 1992, ss 219–220. However, it was not until the Employment Act 1988 (EA 1988) that members of trade unions were given the right to demand that a ballot should be held prior to the taking of industrial action. The provisions relating to the balloting of industrial action have been heavily modified by the Employment Relations Act 1999 (ERA 1999) and the Employment Relations Act 2004 (ERA 2004).

9.52   If a trade union does not hold such a ballot, it can be prevented from taking industrial action, or further industrial action by any one of three interested parties, these being:

- an employer affected by the action (under TULRCA 1992, s 226);
- a member of the union (under TULRCA 1992, s 62, see **Chapter 6**); or
- any third party who suffers as a result of the unlawful action (under TULRCA 1992, s 235A).

9.53   In this regard, TULRCA 1992, s 226 provides as follows:

'(1)   An act done by a trade union to induce a person to take part, or continue to take part, in industrial action—

(a) is not protected unless the industrial action has the support of a ballot, and

(b) where section 226A falls to be complied with in relation to the person's employer, is not protected as respects the employer unless the trade union has complied with section 226A in relation to him.

In this section "the relevant time", in relation to an act by a trade union to induce a person to take part, or continue to take part, in industrial action, means the time at which proceedings are commenced in respect of the act.

(2)   Industrial action shall be regarded as having the support of a ballot only if—

(a) the union has held a ballot in respect of the action—
(i) in relation to which the requirements of section 226B so far as applicable before and during the holding of the ballot were satisfied,
(ii) in relation to which the requirements of sections 227 to 231 were satisfied, and
(iii) in which the majority voting in the ballot answered "Yes" to the question applicable in accordance with section 229(2) to industrial action of the kind to which the act of inducement relates;
(b) such of the requirements of the following sections as have fallen to be satisfied at the relevant time have been satisfied, namely—
(i) section 226B so far as applicable after the holding of the ballot, and
(ii) section 231B;
(bb) section 232A does not prevent the industrial action from being regarded as having the support of the ballot; and
(c) the requirements of section 233 (calling of industrial action with support of ballot) are satisfied.

Any reference in this subsection to a requirement of a provision which is disapplied or modified by section 232 has effect subject to that section.

(3)   Where separate workplace ballots are held by virtue of section 228(1)—

(a) industrial action shall be regarded as having the support of a ballot if the conditions specified in subsection (2) are satisfied, and
(b) the trade union shall be taken to have complied with the requirements relating to a ballot imposed by section 226A if those requirements are complied with,

in relation to the ballot for the place of work of the person induced to take part, or continue to take part, in the industrial action.

(3A) If the requirements of section 231A fall to be satisfied in relation to an employer, as respects that employer industrial action shall not be regarded as having the support of a ballot unless those requirements are satisfied in relation to that employer.

(4)   For the purposes of this section an inducement, in relation to a person, includes an inducement which is or would be ineffective, whether because of his unwillingness to be influenced by it or for any other reason.'

9.54   The purpose of these provisions is to secure a situation in which those who will actually be induced to take industrial action have the opportunity to take part in the ballot which authorises that action so that workers are not put in a situation where if they value their standing among their fellow workers, they have to take part in industrial action in relation to which they have not been balloted.[52] In short, the requirements that need to be complied with for the purposes of ensuring that industrial action is lawful are that:

• a trade union needs properly to have called industrial action which it is proposing to take;
• the ballot paper in relation to the proposed industrial action must be correct in all material respects;
• notice of the ballot must have been given to the employer and a sample of the ballot paper must have been disclosed to the employer;
• those members of the trade union being balloted must be the correct community of the trade union's total membership;
• the ballot itself must be properly conducted; and
• every employer of the workers voting whom it is reasonable for the trade union to notify, must be notified.

9.55   The foregoing requirements do not need to be observed either where the number of members entitled to vote in the ballot, or, in a case where separate workplace ballots need to be held under TULRCA 1992, s 228(1), the aggregate number of members entitled to vote in the ballot, is less than 51 (per TULRCA 1992, s 226C).

9.56   Trade unions should also attempt to comply with the Code of Practice, *Industrial Action Ballots and Notice to Employers* (2000) issued by the Secretary

---

[52]   *National Union of Rail, Maritime and Transport Workers v Midland Mainline Limited* [2001] IRLR 813.

of State. The Code of Practice, as with other Codes of Practice, is non-statutory guidance in nature but, inevitably, it will weigh heavily on the minds of any court dealing with a dispute in respect of which there has been failure to follow any relevant provisions of the Code, as the Code is admissible as evidence of good industrial relations practice under TULRCA 1992, s 207.

Balloting of industrial action

9.57　When a trade union is considering taking industrial action, it is necessary to specify on the ballot paper by which the union proposes to call industrial action, a person who is authorised (either actually, or as a result of being deemed to be authorised under TULRCA 1992, s 20(2)) to call the industrial action on behalf of the union (TULRCA 1992, s 233(1) and (4)). Further, the ballot must comply with the conditions under TULRCA 1992, s 233(3), these being that:

- there must not have been a call by the union to take part or continue to take part in the industrial action to which the ballot relates, or any authorisation or endorsement by the union of any such industrial action, before the date of the ballot; and
- the industrial action to which the call relates must begin before the ballot ceases to be effective in accordance with TULRCA 1992, s 234.

9.58　If the foregoing requirements are not complied with, any industrial action taken in breach is deemed to be unauthorised and those workers taking part in the industrial action will not enjoy any immunity from liability in tort that might otherwise be available. Further, workers taking part in such industrial action may be lawfully dismissed in certain cases by their employer (see generally **Chapter 7** in this regard).

9.59　Industrial action must be taken within the time allowed before a ballot authorising the taking of such action becomes stale, whereupon a fresh ballot will be required (TULRCA 1992, ss 233(3)(b) and 234). Under TULRCA 1992, s 234(1), this time-limit is either 4 weeks or 8 weeks if the union and the employer have agreed a longer period. The period begins in either case with the date of the ballot and ends at midnight on the last night of that relevant period.[53] Under TULRCA 1992, s 234(2), it is possible to apply to the court for an order declaring that a period of time does not count towards the particular relevant period where for the whole or part of that period the calling or organising of industrial action is prohibited either by virtue of:

- a court order which subsequently lapses or is discharged, recalled or set aside; or
- an undertaking given to a court by any person from which that person is subsequently released or by which he ceases to be bound.

Issues with the ballot paper

9.60　A ballot paper used for the calling of industrial action must comply with a number of requirements under TULRCA 1992, s 229(1A), as follows:

---

[53]　Per *RJB Mining (UK) Limited v NUM* [1995] IRLR 556.

- It must contain the name of an independent scrutineer who is required to oversee the balloting process and the address to which the ballot paper is to be returned by post.[54]
- It must state the number of the ballot paper, which must be one of a number of consecutive whole numbers.
- It must contain a question that can be answered either 'Yes' or 'No'. The question can be specific to any given factual situation but it must deal with either the issue of whether those voting wish to take part in a strike or, alternatively, whether they wish to take part in industrial action short of a strike (TULRCA 1992, s 229(2)). TULRCA 1992, s 229(2A) makes it clear that call-out bans and overtime bans constitute industrial action. To the extent that a trade union puts to its members eligible to vote both options as alternatives, it must ask both questions. For example, in *Post Office v Union of Communication Workers*,[55] the trade union had asked only one question of its members this being whether its members were 'willing to take industrial action up to and including strike action'. An injunction was sought by the claimant alleging that the proposed action (which had the support of 51 per cent of those voting) was unlawful. The Court of Appeal granted an injunction to prevent the threatened industrial action holding that it was not clear what action the union's members were authorising the union to call. However, in *British Telecommunications plc v Communication Workers Union*,[56] the High Court held that an incorrect assumption by the defendant that the legal definition of 'strike action' was broad enough to cover all forms of withdrawal of labour (including working to rule, overtime bans and non-cooperation), was not sufficiently misleading to that part of the union being balloted with regard to industrial action as to render the ballot void. It was reasonably clear to the court that the members of the union being balloted appreciated that if they approved the call to industrial action, a strike could be undertaken.
- It must contain the following statement:

> 'If you take part in a strike or other industrial action, you may be in breach of your contract of employment.
> However, if you are dismissed for taking part in strike or other industrial action which is called officially and is otherwise lawful, the dismissal will be unfair if it takes place fewer than eight twelve weeks after you started taking part in the action, and depending on the circumstances may be unfair if it takes place later.'

9.61   This last requirement is laid down by TULRCA 1992, s 229(4), as amended by ERA 2004. It is not possible to qualify or comment upon the statement in any way on the ballot paper. This is true even if the form of industrial action proposed would not result in workers acting in breach of contract. Consequently, so as to avoid the possibility of an invalid ballot, if a trade union wishes to comment on the content of the statutory statement

---

[54]   NB: if the voters are merchant seamen, the address to which the ballot paper should be returned is taken out of the requirements and the name of the ship to which the crew belongs should be inserted instead (TULRCA 1992, s 229(1A)). Other detailed balloting requirements apply to merchant seamen under TULRCA 1992, s 230(2A).

[55]   [1990] IRLR 143.

[56]   [2004] IRLR 58.

(particularly with regard to whether members of the union may be acting in breach of contract with regard to the nature of any particular proposed course of industrial action), as a matter of good practice, the union should do so in a separate form of address that is not sent to the members to be balloted with the ballot paper.

The proportion of the union to be balloted

9.62   Those members of a trade union entitled to vote on the taking of industrial action are dealt with under TULRCA 1992, s 227. This provides that all members of the union who it is reasonable at the time of the ballot for the union to believe will be induced by the union into taking part or continuing with the industrial action proposed or commenced are entitled equally to vote on the taking of that industrial action (TULRCA 1992, s 227(1)). In essence, two questions are asked under TULRCA 1992, s 227: first, which employees did the union believe at the time of the ballot would be induced into taking industrial action and, secondly, was that belief a reasonable one on the part of the trade union.[57]

9.63   It is therefore up to each trade union to decide the class of members that it is seeking to canvass with a view to taking industrial action. The union can choose between different classes of members at one employer provided that it makes reasonable efforts to approach all workers in that class. It can also choose to ballot all workers of a particular description at different employers nationally if there is genuinely a trade dispute with all the different employers.[58] A union may also ballot all members of a national workforce. In doing so, strict adherence to TULRCA 1992, s 227 is required.[59]

Conduct of the ballot

9.64   Under TULRCA 1992, s 230(1), every person who is entitled to vote in the ballot must be allowed to vote without interference from, or constraint imposed by, the union or any of its members, officials or employees and, so far as is reasonably practicable, be enabled to do so without incurring any direct cost to himself. Further, under TULRCA 1992, s 230(2), except in relation to merchant seamen (dealt with under the specific provisions of TULRCA 1992, s 230(2A)–(2C)), so far as is reasonably practicable, every person who is entitled to vote in the ballot must have a voting paper sent to him by post at his home address or any other address which he has requested the trade union in writing to treat as his postal address, and be given a convenient opportunity to vote by post.[60] Whether a trade union has attempted to take proper account of those entitled to vote is dealt with under TULRCA 1992, s 230(4). This requires that ballots are to be secret and conducted in such a way as to ensure that they are

---

[57]   *National Union of Rail, Maritime and Transport Workers v Midland Mainline Limited* [2001] IRLR 813.

[58]   See, for example, *University of Central England v NALGO* [1993] IRLR 81.

[59]   See, for example, *RJB Mining (UK) Limited v NUM* [1997] IRLR 621.

[60]   In this regard, the union is not required to secure that the ballot paper arrives at the property provided that it sends it out properly. However, the union should take reasonable steps to ensure that members of the union keep the union informed as to their changes of address and must properly record those changes of address (*National Union of Rail, Maritime and Transport Workers v Midland Mainline Limited* [2001] IRLR 813).

fair and accurate and that any minor errors are to be disregarded if they are accidental and would not make a significant difference to the result.

9.65   A complication arises in relation to members of a trade union who have commenced employment with an employer after the holding of an industrial action ballot and who are asked to take part in that industrial action. Whether a ballot is valid in such a case was addressed by the Court of Appeal in three cases, these being *British Railways Board v NUR*,[61] *Post Office v Union of Communication Workers*[62] and *London Underground v National Union of Rail, Maritime and Transport Workers*.[63]

9.66   In the *Post Office* case, the Court of Appeal held that:[64]

'The union clearly cannot identify and ballot those of its members who are not employees of the employer at the time of the ballot, but who will, in the event, join the workforce at a later date. It would seem to follow that any call for industrial action following a ballot should be expressly limited to those who were employed by the employer, and given an opportunity of voting, at the time of the ballot.'

9.67   In the *London Underground* case,[65] the defendant union had enjoyed a large increase in membership after a call for industrial action and subsequent ballot in favour of industrial action. The claimant argued that, given the upturn in membership, the defendant might not have a ballot that had a majority of its membership working for the employer who were in favour of taking action and sought an injunction to prevent the threatened industrial action. The High Court granted the injunction requested but on appeal, the Court of Appeal overturned the injunction holding that:[66]

'There is nothing in the very detailed requirements which Parliament has laid down for the conduct of the ballot which compels the union to restrict its call for industrial action to those of its members who were members at the date of the ballot and were given the opportunity to take part in it. Parliament must be taken to have appreciated that there would be constant changes in the membership of a large union, and that by normal accretion alone significant numbers of new members might join the union between the date of the ballot notice given to the employer ... and the holding of the ballot, and between the holding of the ballot and the taking of industrial action. In the case of a lengthy dispute, the numbers in the latter case could be very large indeed.'

9.68   The court went on to consider the position of extending industrial action to a new class of members of the union employed by the employer holding that:[67]

---

[61]   [1989] IRLR 349.
[62]   [1990] IRLR 143.
[63]   [1995] IRLR 636.
[64]   *Post Office v Union of Communication Workers* [1990] IRLR 143 at 147.
[65]   *London Underground v National Union of Rail, Maritime and Transport Workers* [1995] IRLR 636.
[66]   [1995] IRLR 636 at 639.
[67]   *London Underground v National Union of Rail, Maritime and Transport Workers* [1995] IRLR 636 at 639.

'If [the union] changes its mind and decides to extend the industrial action to members who were members of the union at the time when the ballot was held but who were not balloted, then it must hold a fresh ballot.'

9.69   Whilst these cases apparently conflict, they can be reconciled in that, as the Court of Appeal pointed out in the *London Underground* case,[68] the *Post Office* case[69] appears to discuss changes to an employer's workforce rather than to the membership of a union and it is therefore presumably dealing with persons who were members of the union taking industrial action, prior to those members being employed by the employer subject to the industrial action, with the members subsequently coming to be employed by that employer: consequently, it was quite correct in such a situation that those members should be balloted.

9.70   As the Court of Appeal pointed out in the *London Underground* case,[70] no reference is to be found in TULRCA 1992, s 227 to a definition of the employer against whom action is taken. Further, since Lord Donaldson was not supported by the other members of the Court of Appeal in the *Post Office* case,[71] the better view is that his remarks were merely obiter dicta.

9.71   Conversely, the *British Railways Board* case[72] makes the point that if changes to membership between a ballot and industrial action called following the ballot are de minimis, they will not be allowed to invalidate the ballot.

9.72   Following the amendment to TULRCA 1992, s 227 by ERA 2004 (dealing with the entitlement of all members of the union induced by the union to take part in the industrial action), and the insertion of TULRCA 1992, ss 232A and 232B by ERA 1999, industrial action is not be regarded as having the support of a ballot if, in respect of any member of the union induced by the union to take part, or to continue to take part, in the industrial action who is not afforded the opportunity to vote in the ballot on industrial action, it was reasonable at that time for the union to believe that the member would be induced to take part in, or to continue to take part in, the industrial action (TULRCA 1992, s 232A)). However, under TULRCA 1992, s 232B(1), small accidental failures in relation to balloting are to be disregarded if the failure is, or failures are, accidental and on a scale which is unlikely to affect the result of the ballot.[73] In particular, the provisions which are stated to be covered by the

68   *London Underground v National Union of Rail, Maritime and Transport Workers* [1995] IRLR 636.
69   *Post Office v Union of Communication Workers* [1990] IRLR 143.
70   *London Underground v National Union of Rail, Maritime and Transport Workers* [1995] IRLR 636.
71   *Post Office v Union of Communication Workers* [1990] IRLR 143.
72   *British Railways Board v NUR* [1989] IRLR 349.
73   See in this regard *P v National Association of Schoolmasters/Union of Women Teachers* [2001] IRLR 532, where an inadvertent failure to send ballot papers to two workers in a ballot pool of 28 workers was held to be covered under TULRCA 1992, s 232B where the ballot produced a result of 25:1 in favour of taking industrial action. Conversely, in *National Union of Rail Maritime and Transport Workers v Midland Mainline Limited* [2001] IRLR 813, a ballot population of 91 was balloted. Twenty-five workers voted in favour of strike action, 17 voted against and 49 abstained. After the ballot, it transpired that a further 25 members of the union had not been balloted, 11 of whom the union had not updated its records to show as being in the relevant grades for industrial action; 10 of whom the union wrongly believed to

small, accidental failure provision under TULRCA 1992, s 232B are TULRCA 1992, ss 227(1), 230(2), 230(2A), 230(2B) and 232A(c)). Since TULRCA 1992, s 232A is specifically stated to cover members of the union, rather than members of the union employed by an employer at the time of a ballot on industrial action, it is possible that union members not employed by an employer at the time of a ballot whom it is reasonable to believe will become so employed and subsequently do become employed, may taint the outcome of a ballot already held when they become employed.

9.73 TULRCA 1992, ss 228 and 228A (as modified by ERA 1999) provide as follows:

> '**228 Separate workplace ballots** (1)   Subject to subsection (2), this section applies if the members entitled to vote in a ballot by virtue of section 227 do not all have the same workplace.
>
> (2)   This section does not apply if the union reasonably believes that all those members have the same workplace.
>
> (3)   Subject to section 228A, a separate ballot shall be held for each workplace; and entitlement to vote in each ballot shall be accorded equally to, and restricted to, members of the union who—
>
> (a)   are entitled to vote by virtue of section 227, and
>
> (b)   have that workplace.
>
> (4)   In this section and section 228A "workplace" in relation to a person who is employed means—
>
> (a)   if the person works at or from a single set of premises, those premises, and
>
> (b)   in any other case, the premises with which the person's employment has the closest connection.
>
> **228A Separate workplaces: single and aggregate ballots**
>
> (1)   Where section 228(3) would require separate ballots to be held for each workplace, a ballot may be held in place of some or all of the separate ballots if one of subsections (2) to (4) is satisfied in relation to it.
>
> (2)   This subsection is satisfied in relation to a ballot if the workplace of each member entitled to vote in the ballot is the workplace of at least one member of the union who is affected by the dispute.
>
> (3)   This subsection is satisfied in relation to a ballot if entitlement to vote is accorded to, and limited to, all the members of the union who—
>
> (a)   according to the union's reasonable belief have an occupation of a particular kind or have any of a number of particular kinds of occupation, and

---

be in arrears of subscriptions, three of whom had ballot papers sent to the wrong addresses and one member who had erroneously not been sent a ballot paper. The Court of Appeal held that the ballot was not properly constituted because the union should not be able to rely upon its own defective administrative processes to rely upon the inconsequential failures provisions of TULRCA 1992, s 232B to escape its strict statutory obligations under TULRCA 1992, s 232A.

(b) are employed by a particular employer, or by any of a number of particular employers, with whom the union is in dispute.

(4) This subsection is satisfied in relation to a ballot if entitlement to vote is accorded to, and limited to, all the members of the union who are employed by a particular employer, or by any of a number of particular employers, with whom the union is in dispute.

(5) For the purposes of subsection (2) the following are members of the union affected by a dispute—

(a) if the dispute relates (wholly or partly) to a decision which the union reasonably believes the employer has made or will make concerning a matter specified in subsection (1)(a), (b) or (c) of section 244 (meaning of "trade dispute"), members whom the decision directly affects,
(b) if the dispute relates (wholly or partly) to a matter specified in subsection (1)(d) of that section, members whom the matter directly affects,
(c) if the dispute relates (wholly or partly) to a matter specified in subsection (1)(e) of that section, persons whose membership or non-membership is in dispute,
(d) if the dispute relates (wholly or partly) to a matter specified in subsection (1)(f) of that section, officials of the union who have used or would use the facilities concerned in the dispute.'

9.74   In broad terms, the above requirements are that a trade union is required to hold a separate industrial action ballot at each different workplace at which members of the union who may be asked to take part in industrial action with an employer or employers are employed, unless it is the case that the union reasonably believes that proposed industrial action will be confined to one workplace (TULRCA 1992, s 228(1)–(3)). In practical terms, this requires a union to interrogate its membership records where there is a possibility that industrial action may spill over into more than one workplace with a common employer, so as to ensure that there is no possibility that its members who may take part in that industrial action at other workplaces of the employer are not excluded from the ballot: a union's membership records are likely to provide the best source of objective verification for the reasonableness of the union's belief.

9.75   Further, TULRCA 1992, s 228(3) contemplates the situation where a worker works from more than one set of premises for an employer. This is an important provision in the case of a workforce becoming increasingly more flexible in its working patterns, but is also apt to cover more traditional multi-site workers, such as delivery drivers and transport workers.

9.76   TULRCA 1992, s 228A, provides for a number of exceptions to the requirement to hold separate workplace ballots and for there to be substituted a single ballot, or several ballots, instead.

The majority for a ballot in favour of industrial action

9.77   A further issue to be considered is that of the size of the majority required in a ballot on the taking of industrial action. In this regard TULRCA 1992, s 226(2)(a)(iii) requires there to be a 'majority' of those voting in the ballot who have answered 'Yes' to the question applicable under TULRCA 1992, s 229(2) with regard to the type of industrial action proposed to be taken.

In deciding what amounts to a majority for these purposes, two questions need to be asked, being, first, whether the majority is of all those entitled to vote or a majority of valid votes cast and, secondly, whether account should be taken of spoilt ballot papers in determining the size of a majority. Both questions were addressed by the Court of Appeal in *West Midlands Travel Limited v Transport and General Workers Union*,[74] where, a majority of just over 50 per cent had been achieved on the basis of valid votes cast but, if spoilt ballot papers had been taken into account, only 48 per cent of those 'voting in the ballot' would have voted in favour of industrial action. The court held that for the purposes of TULRCA 1992, s 226(2)(a)(iii), those 'voting in the ballot' meant those validly casting votes. As such, a majority had been achieved.

Conduct of industrial action ballots

9.78 The conduct of ballots on the taking of industrial action is dealt with by TULRCA 1992, s 230. This provides that every person entitled to vote is allowed to do so free from constraint or interference by the union or anyone acting for it (although it is conceivably possible for an employer to attempt to interfere with the outcome of a ballot), and the ballot is required, so far as is reasonably practicable, to be at no direct cost to the member (TULRCA 1992, s 230(1)). Further, TULRCA 1992, s 230(2) requires that ballots are to be by post, so it follows that this will require unions to send out pre-paid return envelopes to comply with this requirement.[75] TULRCA 1992, s 230 also contains separate provisions dealing with the balloting of merchant seamen and TULRCA 1992, s 232 has special provisions relating to the balloting of overseas members of trade unions.

Notice of ballot and copy of ballot paper to employer

9.79 The voting procedure in the case of a ballot prior to the taking of industrial action requires that the employer must be provided with notice of the taking of a ballot on industrial action. The notice requirements are extremely complex and amongst the most heavily modified requirements of a difficult area, the thought behind this area seeming to be the prevention of the taking of industrial action in the first place by allowing employers the ability to seek injunctive relief at a very early stage, to draw matters to the attention of that part of its workforce which is being balloted in relation to the taking of industrial action to try to dissuade them from taking industrial action, and the mitigation of the impact of industrial action on the employer by allowing the employer to take steps, if necessary, to recruit or train an alternative work-force.[76] The notice requirements are provided under TULRCA 1992, s 226A, which provides as follows:

'**226A Notice of ballot and sample voting paper for employers**

---

[74] [1994] IRLR 578.
[75] NB: if a trade union has members who are merchant seamen special provisions apply allowing them to vote on their ship if the ship is likely to be outside Great Britain during the period for industrial action, in relation to which see TULRCA 1992, s 230(2A) and (2B).
[76] See in this regard the comments of the Court of Appeal in *National Union of Rail Maritime and Transport Workers v London Underground Limited* [2001] IRLR 228.

(1) The trade union must take such steps as are reasonably necessary to ensure that—

(a) not later than the seventh day before the opening day of the ballot, the notice specified in subsection (2), and

(b) not later than the third day before the opening day of the ballot, the sample voting paper specified in subsection (3) subsection (2F), is received by every person who it is reasonable for the union to believe (at the latest time when steps could be taken to comply with paragraph (a)) will be the employer of persons who will be entitled to vote in the ballot.

(2) The notice referred to in paragraph (a) of subsection (1) is a notice in writing—

(a) stating that the union intends to hold the ballot,

(b) specifying the date which the union reasonably believes will be the opening day of the ballot, and

(c) containing—

   (i) the lists mentioned in subsection (2A) and the figures mentioned in subsection (2B), together with an explanation of how those figures were arrived at, or

   (ii) where some or all of the employees concerned are employees from whose wages the employer makes deductions representing payments to the union, either those lists and figures and that explanation or the information mentioned in subsection (2C).

(2A) The lists are—

(a) a list of the categories of employee to which the employees concerned belong, and

(b) a list of the workplaces at which the employees concerned work.

(2B) The figures are—

(a) the total number of employees concerned,

(b) the number of the employees concerned in each of the categories in the list mentioned in subsection (2A)(a), and

(c) the number of the employees concerned who work at each workplace in the list mentioned in subsection (2A)(b).

(2C) The information referred to in subsection (2)(c)(ii) is such information as will enable the employer readily to deduce—

(a) the total number of employees concerned,

(b) the categories of employee to which the employees concerned belong and the number of the employees concerned in each of those categories, and

(c) the workplaces at which the employees concerned work and the number of them who work at each of those workplaces.

(2D) The lists and figures supplied under this section, or the information mentioned in subsection (2C) that is so supplied, must be as accurate as is reasonably practicable in the light of the information in the possession of the union at the time when it complies with subsection (1)(a).

(2E) For the purposes of subsection (2D) information is in the possession of the union if it is held, for union purposes—

(a) in a document, whether in electronic form or any other form, and
(b) in the possession or under the control of an officer or employee of the union.

(2F) The sample voting paper referred to in paragraph (b) of subsection (1) *is*—

(a) a sample of the form of voting paper which is to be sent to the employees concerned, or
(b) where the employees concerned are not all to be sent the same form of voting paper, a sample of each form of voting paper which is to be sent to any of them.

(2G) Nothing in this section requires a union to supply an employer with the names of the employees concerned.

(2H) In this section references to the "employees concerned" are references to those employees of the employer in question who the union reasonably believes will be entitled to vote in the ballot.

(2I) For the purposes of this section, the workplace at which an employee works is—

(a) in relation to an employee who works at or from a single set of premises, those premises, and
(b) in relation to any other employee, the premises with which his employment has the closest connection.

(3A) These rules apply for the purposes of paragraph (c) of subsection (2)—

(a) if the union possesses information as to the number, category or work-place of the employees concerned, a notice must contain that information (at least);
(b) if a notice does not name any employees, that fact shall not be a ground for holding that it does not comply with paragraph (c) of subsection (2).

(3B) In subsection (3) references to employees are to employees of the employer concerned.

(4) In this section references to the opening day of the ballot are references to the first day when a voting paper is sent to any person entitled to vote in the ballot.

(5) This section, in its application to a ballot in which merchant seamen to whom section 230(2A) applies are entitled to vote, shall have effect with the substitution in subsection (3) subsection (2F), for references to the voting paper which is to be sent to the employees, of references to the voting paper which is to be sent or otherwise provided to them.'

9.80 In broad terms, it can be seen that these requirements are for a trade union undertaking a ballot on industrial action to provide information, which it reasonably believes to be correct, to the employer, by no later than 7 days before ballot papers are first sent out, of the fact that the ballot is to be held, when the union believes that it will hold the ballot (TULRCA 1992, s 226A(1), (2)(a) and (b) and (4)), and to provide the employer with lists and figures relating to the total number of employees being balloted, the number of employees in each category of employee being balloted, the places of their employment and the number of each employee at each workplace (TULRCA 1992, s 226A(2)(c)–(2D) and (2I)). There is no requirement for the union to provide the employer with the names of its members on such a list (TULRCA 1992, s 226A(2G)). Interestingly, the requirement is limited to the provision of information in the lists and figures concerning 'employees' and not the broader categorisation of 'workers'. As to the requirement of reasonable belief on the part of a union, this is unlikely to be satisfied by a union unless it has carried out, at the very least, a full review of its membership records in relation to the disclosures required of the union.

9.81   The employer must also be provided with a sample of the ballot paper not less than 3 days before the holding of the ballot (TULRCA 1992, s 226A(1)(b) and (2F)), the reason for this is to allow the employer to examine whether the question posed with regard to the calling of industrial action could reasonably give rise to the inference that the purpose of the proposed industrial action is otherwise than in relation to a trade dispute under TULRCA 1992, s 244.[77]

Independent scrutineers

9.82   As with nearly all other forms of voting in relation to trade unions, under TULRCA 1992, s 226B, the voting procedure in the case of a ballot prior to the taking of industrial action requires that an independent scrutineer must be appointed to observe the conduct of the ballot. TULRCA 1992, s 226B provides as follows:

'226B Appointment of scrutineer

(1)   The trade union shall, before the ballot in respect of the industrial action is held, appoint a qualified person ("the scrutineer") whose terms of appointment shall require him to carry out in relation to the ballot the functions of—

(a) taking such steps as appear to him to be appropriate for the purpose of enabling him to make a report to the trade union (see section 231B); and

(b) making the report as soon as reasonably practicable after the date of the ballot and, in any event, not later than the end of the period of four weeks beginning with that date.

(2)   A person is a qualified person in relation to a ballot if—

(a) he satisfies such conditions as may be specified for the purposes of this section by order of the Secretary of State or is himself so specified; and

(b) the trade union has no grounds for believing either that he will carry out the functions conferred on him under subsection (1) otherwise than competently or that his independence in relation to the union, or in relation to the ballot, might reasonably be called into question.

---

[77]   See, for example, the consideration of this point by the Court of Appeal in *London Borough of Wandsworth v National Association of Schoolmasters/Union of Women Teachers* [1993] IRLR 344.

An order under paragraph (a) shall be made by statutory instrument which shall be subject to annulment in pursuance of a resolution of either House of Parliament.

(3) The trade union shall ensure that the scrutineer duly carries out the functions conferred on him under subsection (1) and that there is no interference with the carrying out of those functions from the union or any of its members, officials or employees.

(4) The trade union shall comply with all reasonable requests made by the scrutineer for the purposes of, or in connection with, the carrying out of those functions.'

9.83 The independent scrutineer is appointed to oversee the balloting procedure so as to ensure that it is properly carried out without interference from the union, its members or employees, including with regard to his own function (TULRCA 1992, s 226B(3)).

9.84 Under TULRCA 1992, s 231 as soon as reasonably practicable after holding the ballot, the union is required to inform all persons entitled to vote in the ballot of the number of:

- votes cast in the ballot;
- individuals answering 'Yes' to the question, or to each question on industrial action;
- individuals answering 'No' to the question, or, as the case may be;
- to each question; and
- spoiled voting papers.

9.85 Likewise, under TULRCA 1992, s 231A, as soon as reasonably practicable after the holding of the ballot, the union must take such steps as are reasonably necessary to ensure that every relevant employer in respect of which the ballot is held, is informed of the matters mentioned under TULRCA 1992, s 231 notified to those members of the union entitled to vote in the ballot.

9.86 Under TULRCA 1992, ss 226B(1) and 231B(1), within 4 weeks of a ballot, the independent scrutineer appointed to supervise it is required to prepare a report stating:

- whether he is satisfied that no enactment was contravened during the balloting procedure;
- that appropriate arrangements were made for handling the voting papers through to their being counted; and
- whether the independent scrutineer was interfered with in any way by the trade union, its officials or employees.

9.87 Under TULRCA 1992, s 231B(1), to the extent that the independent scrutineer is not able to confirm any of these points, he is required to particularise the problems that incurred.

9.88 The independent scrutineer is also required to make available to any person entitled to vote in the ballot, or the employer of such a person, a copy of his report for a period of 6 months after the ballot. The independent scrutineer may charge a reasonable fee for providing a copy of the report (TULRCA 1992, s 231B(2)).

9.89   As regards the persons qualified to be an independent scrutineer under TULRCA 1992, s 226B(2), this is dealt with under delegated legislation.[78]

Notice of industrial action to an employer

9.90   The notice provisions for the taking of industrial action arose out of a campaign of industrial action taken in relation to London Underground. The requirements were introduced by the Trade Union Reform and Employment Rights Act 1993, s 21 and are now contained in TULRCA 1992, s 234A. The purpose of this notice is to inform an employer as to the areas of its business that will be affected by the industrial action and to allow the employer to plan what steps, if any, the employer can take, to mitigate the consequences of the industrial action. The provisions have been very heavily modified in recent times by ERA 1999 and ERA 2004 with regard to the content of the written notice which trade unions are required to give to employers before industrial action is taken; consequently, case law in this area prior to the implementation of ERA 2004 needs to be followed with caution. Indeed, under TULRCA 1992, s 234A(1), the immunity in tort that would otherwise be available in respect of a properly balloted strike is removed where a trade union fails to take such steps as are reasonably necessary to ensure that the employer receives relevant notice within the 'appropriate period'. In this regard, an exception is provided under TULRCA 1992, s 234A(2) where it would be unreasonable for the union to believe, at the latest time when steps could be taken to ensure that the employer receives such a notice, that the employer is the employer of any person who will be or have been induced to take part, or continue to take part, in the industrial action.

9.91   Under TULRCA 1992, s 234A(5A), the written notice is required in relation to those employees of the employer who the union reasonably believes will be induced by the union, or have been induced, to take part or continue to take part in the industrial action (these employees being defined under TULRCA 1992, s 234A(5C) as 'affected employees'), and the notice must:

- contain the lists and figures under TULRCA 1992, s 234A(3A) and (3B) and provide an explanation of how those figures were arrived at, or where some or all of the affected employees are employees in respect of whom the employer operates a check-off arrangement, contain either those lists and figures and that explanation or the information required to provided in the alternative under TULRCA 1992, s 234A(3C);
- state whether industrial action is intended to be continuous or discontinuous and specify where the industrial action is to be continuous, the intended date for any of the affected employees to begin to take part in the action, or where the industrial action is to be discontinuous, the intended dates for any of the affected employees to take part in the action; and
- state that the notice is given under TULRCA 1992, s 234A.

9.92   As regards the lists to be contained under TULRCA 1992, s 234A, under TULRCA 1992, s 234A(3A) these are lists of the categories of employee to which the affected employees belong, and of the workplaces at which the

---

[78]   Trade Union Ballots and Elections (Independent Scrutineer Qualifications) Order 1993, SI 1993/1909 and Trade Union Ballots and Elections (Independent Scrutineer Qualifications) Order 1993 (Amendment) Order 2002, SI 2002/2267 (made under TULRCA 1992, s 226B(2)).

affected employees work. Further, under TULRCA 1992, s 234A(3B), the figures required to be provided are the total number of the affected employees, the number of the affected employees in each category of employees and the number of the affected employees who work at each workplace at which it is proposed to take industrial action. Additionally, under TULRCA 1992, s 234A(3C), the information to be provided in a check-off case is that information that will enable the employer readily to deduce the total number of affected employees, the categories of employee to which the affected employees belong and the number of affected employees in each of those categories, and the workplaces at which the affected employees work and the number of them who work at each of those workplaces. Under TULRCA 1992, s 234(3F), trade unions are not required to supply the employer with the names of the affected employees.

9.93 Where lists, figures and/or information are supplied in such a notice, the union is required to ensure that any such lists, figures and/or information are as accurate as is reasonably practicable in the light of the information in the possession of the union at the time when it is required to comply with TULRCA 1992, s 234A.

9.94 The 'appropriate period' is defined under TULRCA 1992, s 234A(4) as the period beginning with the day when the union notifies the employer of the result of the ballot under TULRCA 1992, s 231A, and ending with the seventh day before the day, or before the first of the days, specified in the relevant notice. In other words, the employer faced with the prospect of industrial action is entitled to a clear 7 days' notice before the industrial action bites.

9.95 Under TULRCA 1992, s 234A(5), where notice is correctly served on an employer under TULRCA 1992, s 234A, it will cover acts done by the union if the employee induced falls within a notified category of employee and the workplace at which he works is a notified workplace in relation to either continuous industrial action (provided there is no participation by any such employee in that industrial action before the date specified in the notice), or discontinuous industrial action (provided that there is no participation by the employee in the industrial action on a day not specified by the union to be an industrial action day under the relevant notice). Continuous and discontinuous industrial action are defined under TULRCA 1992, s 234(6).

9.96 Similar provisions to those under TULRCA 1992, s 226A apply under TULRCA 1992, s 234A(5A)–(5D) with regard to the place of work at which an employee works and with regard to notified workplaces at which it is proposed to take industrial action.

9.97 It is possible for a union to decide not to proceed with the taking of industrial action after a ballot in favour of industrial action has been held, or to suspend the taking of industrial action. The provisions dealing with this arise under TULRCA 1992, s 234A(7)–(7B). These provide that where industrial action ceases to be authorised or endorsed by a trade union, or where such authorisation or endorsement is suspended any industrial action taking place after the revocation of the authorisation or endorsement, or during a period of suspension having been first properly authorised, that industrial action is treated as not having a valid notice of industrial action properly served upon the employer.

9.98   As to when industrial action is treated as being authorised or endorsed by a trade union, this is dealt with under TULRCA 1992, s 234A(8) and (9), which provides that the questions as to whether persons or committees whose acts were authorised or endorsed by the union are to be determined in accordance with TULRCA 1992, s 20(2)–(4) (ie the provisions dealing with the liability in tort of a trade union).

9.99   The effect of TULRCA 1992, s 234A when combined with the length of the balloting process and the requirement for the union to notify the employer before the holding of a ballot in relation to proposed industrial action under TULRCA 1992, s 226A, is to allow employers a clear window of opportunity to mitigate the hardships which they might otherwise face in relation to proposed industrial action by arranging cover for those workers taking part in the industrial action; in other words to import, or train from existing staff, strikebreakers.

Action taken to enforce a closed shop

9.100   As was seen in **Chapter 1**, much of the thrust of the reform of trade union law in the period 1979–1997 was aimed at bringing to an end the practice of the closed shop (which was seen as uncompetitive, in restraint of trade and responsible for setting wages above what would otherwise be the market level). If a trade union now uses tortious means to ensure that a closed shop is established, no immunity is available to that union in respect of that action taken by the union under TULRCA 1992, s 222, which provides as follows:

'(1)   An act is not protected if the reason, or one of the reasons, for which it is done is the fact or belief that a particular employer—

(a)   is employing, has employed or might employ a person who is not a member of a trade union, or
(b)   is failing, has failed or might fail to discriminate against such a person.

(2)   For the purposes of subsection 1(b) an employer discriminates against a person if, but only if, he ensures that his conduct in relation to—

(a)   persons, or persons of any description, employed by him, or who apply to be, or are, considered by him for employment, or
(b)   the provision of employment for such persons,

is different in some or all cases, according to whether or not they are members of a trade union, and is more favourable to those who are.

(3)   An act is not protected if it constitutes, or is one of a number of acts which together constitute, an inducement or attempted inducement of a person—

(a)   to incorporate in a contract to which that person is a party, or a proposed contract to which he intends to be a party, a term or condition which is or would be void under section 144 (union membership requirement in contract for goods or services), or
(b)   to contravene section 145 (refusal to deal with person on grounds relating to trade union membership).'

9.101   The removal of immunity from action in tort is all-embracing and covers situations where pressure is brought to bear upon an employer who does not want to have a closed shop (TULRCA 1992, s 222 (1) and (2)). It also covers the situation of attempts to extend a union's influence to suppliers of the employer (TULRCA 1992, s 222(3)).

9.102   Industrial action is not protected if a trade union seeks to induce an employer to favour union members over non-union (TULRCA 1992, s 222(2)). However, it would seem that the immunity will not be removed where a trade union is protesting about pay increases awarded to non-trade union employees of an employer (for example, in contravention of TULRCA 1992, s 146 and the union is seeking to merely obtain parity for its members).

Support of employees dismissed for taking unlawful industrial action

9.103   The main thrust of removing the immunity in this case is to discourage unofficial industrial action being taken. The measure was introduced by the Employment Act 1990 (EA 1990) and was carried over into TULRCA 1992, s 223; this removes immunity from action in tort where the commission of a tort, or one of the reasons for its commission, is to support workers who have been dismissed for taking unlawful industrial action. In this regard the immunity will be removed where one of the reasons (even if it is not the predominate reason) for industrial action is to support workers who it is believed have been dismissed for taking unofficial industrial action (as defined under TULRCA 1992, s 237).

Secondary industrial action

9.104   The removal of the immunities in tort under this head was introduced as one of the first reforms of trade union law in 1980. Prior to this, it was not unlawful to take industrial action against another employer who might not be connected with a dispute.

9.105   The first attempt to reform was in the form of the Employment Act 1980 (EA 1980), s 17, which allowed certain secondary action to be undertaken in relation to commercial contracts in three situations, these being where:

●   there was a direct contractual relationship between the victim of the secondary industrial action and the victim of the primary industrial action, for example, suppliers of a party involved in a trade dispute;
●   where the victim of the secondary industrial action was an associated employer of the victim of primary industrial action, or was a customer or supplier of the associated employer; or
●   where the industrial action was taken by a person lawfully picketing at his own place of work or a trade union official accompanying such a person (see now TULRCA 1992, s 220(4) as to this last point).

9.106   EA 1990, s 4 removed the first two of those exceptions and replaced them with what is now TULRCA 1992, s 224, which provides as follows:

'(1)   An act is not protected if one of the facts relied on for the purpose of establishing liability is that there has been secondary action which is not lawful picketing.

(2)   There is secondary action in relation to a trade dispute when, and only when, a person—

(a) induces another to break a contract of employment or interferes or induces another to interfere with its performance, or

(b) threatens that a contract of employment under which he or another is employed will be broken or its performance interfered with, or that he will induce another to break a contract of employment or to interfere with its performance,

and the employer under the contract of employment is not the employer party to the dispute.

(3)   Lawful picketing means acts done in the course of such attendance as is declared lawful by section 220 (peaceful picketing)—

(a) by a worker employed (or, in the case of a worker not in employment, last employed) by the employer party to the dispute, or

(b) by a trade union official whose attendance is lawful by virtue of subsection (1)(b) of that section.

(4)   For the purposes of this section an employer shall not be treated as a party to a dispute between another employer and workers of that employer; and where more than one employer is in dispute with his workers, the dispute between each employer and his workers shall be treated as a separate dispute.

In this subsection "worker" has the same meaning as in section 244 (meaning of "trade dispute").

(5)   An act in contemplation or furtherance of a trade dispute which is primary action in relation to that dispute may not be relied on as secondary action in relation to another trade dispute.

Primary action means such action as is mentioned in paragraph (a) or (b) of subsection (2) where the employer under the contract of employment is the employer party to the dispute.

(6)   In this section "contract of employment" includes any contract under which one person personally does work or performs services for another, and related expressions shall be construed accordingly.'

Scope of the immunity

9.107   The reason for the changes under EA 1990 (as incorporated in TULRCA 1992, s 224) above was largely the complexity of the legislation that preceded it.[79] The legislation in its old form pre-EA 1990 allowed for a degree of balance between the interests of a trade union in being able to make its point by means of industrial action against an employer and the right of third parties not to become embroiled in a dispute which was nothing to do with them. The formulation as it now stands under TULRCA 1992, s 224 has the advantage of simplicity over its predecessor (all secondary action is unlawful, save for peaceful picketing at a worker's own place of work where the employer being picketed is a legitimate party to a trade dispute): thus, all that is protected now in the form of secondary action is the secondary effect of primary industrial

---

[79]   For an example of a failed attempt to take advantage of the old immunity, see *Dimbleby & Sons Limited v National Union of Journalists* [1984] IRLR 161.

action, ie attempting to persuade the suppliers, customers and other workers of the employer in dispute not to deal with the employer provided that lawful means are adopted in the course of persuading such third parties.

9.108 Finally, TULRCA 1992, s 224 does not distinguish between commercial and non-commercial contracts (unlike its predecessor, EA 1980, s 17).

Industrial action taken to impose trade union recognition at suppliers

9.109 The removal of immunity in the above circumstances was initially introduced under the Employment Act 1982. It is now dealt with under TULRCA 1992, s 225 which provides as follows:

'(1) An act is not protected if it constitutes, or is one of a number of acts which together constitute, an inducement or attempted inducement of a person—

(a) to incorporate in a contract to which that person is a party, or a proposed contract to which he intends to be a party, a term or condition which is or would be void by virtue of section 186 (recognition requirement in contract for goods or services), or

(b) to contravene section 187 (refusal to deal with person on grounds of union exclusion).

(2) An act is not protected if—

(a) it interferes with the supply (whether or not under a contract) of goods or services, or can reasonably be expected to have that effect, and

(b) one of the facts relied upon for the purposes of establishing liability is that a person has—
   (i) induced another to break a contract of employment or interfered or induced another to interfere with its performance, or
   (ii) threatened that a contract of employment under which he or another is employed will be broken or its performance interfered with, or that he will induce another to break a contract of employment or to interfere with its performance, and

(c) the reason, or one of the reasons, for doing the act is the fact or belief that the supplier (not being the employer under the contract mentioned in paragraph (b)) does not, or might not—
   (i) recognise one or more trade unions for the purpose of negotiating on behalf of workers, or any class of worker, employed by him, or
   (ii) negotiate or consult with, or with an official of, one or more trade unions.'

9.110 The provision is a mirror image of the duty not to attempt to impose recognition requirements in supply contracts (dealt with in **Chapter 11**). The removal of immunity in this case does not cover the position where a trade union is seeking to gain a foothold of recognition at the place of employment of the workers taking industrial action, provided that the workers taking industrial action confine their activity to seeking recognition for themselves only.

Ancillary unlawful industrial action taken by pickets

9.111 Over and above all of these possible grounds for the loss of immunity will be the loss of immunity where any ancillary industrial action taken by pickets is unlawful. This requires that not only must the industrial action be properly called (ie following a ballot approving the action) and for a proper purpose, it must be properly carried out. The requirement is provided under TULRCA 1992, s 219(3) which provides as follows:

> 'Nothing in subsections (1) and (2) prevents an act done in the course of picketing from being actionable in tort unless it is done in the course of attendance declared lawful by section 220 (peaceful picketing).'

9.112   It will be remembered that TULRCA 1992, s 219(1) and (2) establishes the general immunity from action for trade unions in the circumstances specified thereunder.

ESTABLISHING COLLECTIVE RESPONSIBILITY

9.113   The law relating to the liability of trade unions and employers' associations operates by making such bodies liable for:

- their own wrongful acts,
- for the wrongful acts of their officials; and
- potentially for acts of their members of such bodies.

9.114   The rules relating to the liability of a trade union for its members are essentially a function of 'good housekeeping'. Trade unions should operate lawfully and should require their officers and members to do so. This section will focus upon, first, trade union liability and, secondly, the liability of employers' associations.

Trade union liability

9.115   The history of trade union liability has been extensively dealt with in **Chapter 1**. It has been possible to take legal proceedings against a trade union in its own name since the case of *Taff Vale Railway Co v Amalgamated Society of Railway Servants*.[80] This position has been codified by statute and is now carried over as TULRCA 1992, s 10. Once it is established that there is a prima facie case against a trade union, it is necessary to consider the nature of the harm that has been committed. This will determine whether the general common law rules relating to the attachment of liability apply or whether special statutory rules apply instead.

Civil wrongs committed by a trade union

9.116   In the context of industrial action, torts fall into two categories, those being the industrial/economic torts (in respect of which there may exist a prima facie immunity in tort), and other torts.

Liability in respect of the industrial/economic torts

9.117   As regards this category of torts, liability can be established by either a trade union acting unlawfully itself (primary liability) or by the law deeming the union liable for the acts of its officials or making it vicariously liable for the acts of its members.

---

[80]   [1901] AC 426.

9.118   As regards primary liability, this will arise under TULRCA 1992, s 20(2)(a) where a trade union has rules which authorise the taking of industrial action in the name of the union. The union rules for these purposes are defined as being a union's written rules or any other written provisions forming part of the union rulebook or wider contract of membership. It follows from this that it is not possible to have an oral rule agreed by members of a trade union that would have the effect of binding the union so as make it primarily liable.

9.119   It is also possible for a trade union to be held liable for the acts of its officials, which for these purposes are being defined as the principal executive committee, the president or the general secretary of the union (TULRCA 1992, s 20(2)(b)). This remains the case even if the union rulebook or a wider membership contract purports to exclude liability for unlawful acts taken by such persons (TULRCA 1992, s 20(4)).

9.120   A trade union may also be vicariously liable for the acts of a committee of the union or any other official of the union, whether or not the official is employed by the union (TULRCA 1992, s 20(2)(c)). This is capable of including minor officials of a union, such as shop stewards and other branch-level officials.

9.121   A committee of a trade union for the purposes of TULRCA 1992, s 20(2)(c) is defined in TULRCA 1992, s 20(3)(a) as meaning any group of persons constituted in accordance with the rules of the union.

9.122   For these purposes, an act is taken to be done, authorised or endorsed by an official of a trade union if it was carried out by any such committee of the union having as one of its purposes the organising and co-ordinating of industrial action if the official was a member of the committee at the material time (TULRCA 1992, s 20(3)(b)). This provision is potentially the most damaging to trade unions in the context of the loss of the immunities in tort and it requires the greatest diligence on the part of trade unions in terms of its policing. Where liability potentially arises under this provision, trade unions are left with the option of either taking responsibility for the acts of their members in these circumstances or they can repudiate these acts (TULRCA 1992, s 20(4)).

9.123   Repudiation of acts taken in the name of a union must take place following the statutory formula set out under TULRCA 1992, s 21 which requires that repudiation of the acts of minor officials or committees must be undertaken by any of the executive committee, president or general secretary of the union. Repudiation must be implemented as soon as reasonably practicable after the unlawful act giving rise to the potential liability comes to the attention of any of the union via those officials (TULRCA 1992, s 21(1)).

9.124   The form which repudiation is to take is dealt with under TULRCA 1992, s 21(2). This requires that written notice of repudiation must be given to the official or committee without delay. It also requires the union to do its best to ensure that written notice is given to each member of the union who is taking part, or might want to take part, in the action and to the employer of such persons. The notice must be given without delay. Under TULRCA 1992, s 21(3), the notice is required to contain a specified form of wording, as follows:

> 'Your union has repudiated the call (or calls) for industrial action to which this notice relates and will give no support to unofficial industrial action

taken in response to it (or them). If you are dismissed while taking unofficial industrial action, you will have no right to complain of unfair dismissal.'

9.125 To the extent that the repudiation is not carried out in this fashion, it is ineffective and the union will be liable for the consequences of industrial action taken in its name notwithstanding that the union has so attempted to repudiate the action of the official or committee concerned in other ways (TULRCA 1992, s 21(4)).[81] Furthermore, even if a union does comply with the letter of the law in terms of the form of its repudiation, the union cannot attempt to defeat the spirit of the law; if at any time after a valid repudiation has taken place in the prescribed form, the executive committee, president or general secretary behaves in a manner inconsistent with that repudiation, the repudiation is deemed to be ineffective (TULRCA 1992, s 21(5)). Likewise, if the tortious act consists of the interfering with a commercial contract (as defined in TULRCA 1992, s 21(7) as to exclude contracts of employment or for the personal performance of work or services), and a party to the contract has not received written notice of the repudiation within 3 months of requesting it, the repudiation is deemed to be ineffective (TULRCA 1992, s 21(6)).

Other tortious acts committed by unions

9.126 To the extent that torts are committed by a union other than prima facie immune industrial/economic torts, the ordinary law of vicarious liability will apply in determining whether a union is responsible for consequential loss. The leading case on the point in the context of trade unions is *Heaton's Transport (St Helens) Limited v Transport and General Workers Union*,[82] where the defendant union had adopted a policy of ensuring that sea containers should only be loaded and unloaded by persons registered under the statutory dock labour scheme. If employers refused to honour this policy, their lorries were 'blacked' by the union. In this regard, shop stewards at two ports established unofficial committees to ensure that such 'blacking' took place. When the claimants sued, the union contended that it was not liable for the acts of the unofficial committees. The House of Lords rejected this argument holding:[83]

> 'No new development is involved in the law relating to the responsibility of a master or principal for the act of a servant or agent. In each case the test to be applied is the same: was the servant or agent acting on behalf of, and within the scope of authority conferred by the master or principal ... Usually a servant, as compared with an agent, has wider authority because his employment is more permanent and he has a larger range of duties as he may have to exercise discretion in dealing with a series of situations as they arise. The agent in an ordinary case is engaged to perform a particular

---

[81]   The provision is also relevant in the context of whether industrial is unofficial for the purposes of TULRCA 1992, s 237. For example, in *Balfour Kilpatrick Limited v Acheson* [2003] IRLR 683, where a trade union failed to repudiate industrial action in accordance with TULRCA 1992, ss 20 and 21, the industrial action was held not to be unofficial for the purposes of TULRCA 1992, s 237, with the result that union members dismissed in the course of that industrial action were entitled to pursue claims for unfair dismissal.

[82]   [1972] IRLR 25.

[83]   [1972] IRLR 25 at 28.

task on a particular occasion and he has authority to do whatever is required for that purpose but has no general authority.'

9.127 The House of Lords went on to add that unless the union had taken steps that could objectively be construed as forbidding the members concerned form taking industrial action (for example, withdrawing their credentials), the union would be bound by the action taken.[84]

Torts committed by employers' associations

9.128 Employers' associations can be sued in the same way as any other company (if they are incorporated) or, in the case of an unincorporated association, under TULRCA 1992, s 127(2)(b). No special rules exist with regard to liability being fixed on such associations. Furthermore, although there is no cap on the quantum of damages that can be awarded against an employers' association (see **Chapter 10** for the position relating to trade unions), if damages are awarded against an employers' association, the award can only be enforced against the property of the association. In the case of an unincorporated association, the personal property of the members of the employers' association is specifically excluded from being subject to enforcement proceedings (TULRCA 1992, s 130).

---

[84] See for further examples of common law liability being extended to trade unions *Thomas v NUM (South Wales Area)* [1985] IRLR 136; and *News Group Newspapers Limited v SOGAT 82 (No 2)* [1986] IRLR 337.

Chapter 10

REMEDIES AGAINST TRADE UNIONS

10.1 This chapter will focus upon the remedies that can be awarded against a trade union in the context of industrial disputes. In this regard, the general rules relating to both equitable and common law remedies are modified in certain respects. The general position with regard to remedies will be examined initially and thereafter the particular modifications that exist in the context of industrial relations.

EQUITABLE REMEDIES

Specific performance

10.2 Specific performance compels a party in breach of contract to honour its obligations under the terms of the contract. As it is a final remedy (ie available after the conclusion of a trial to establish liability), it is likely to be inappropriate in most employment disputes where a remedy may be needed quickly to prevent an unlawful strike adversely affecting an employer due to the length of time which often elapses between the commencement of proceedings and establishing liability at the trial of an action.

10.3 The general position in relation to specific performance is that, as with all equitable remedies, it is granted at the discretion of the court and the discretion will only be exercised in relation to a contract having a specific, as opposed to a general, property.

10.4 Further, specific performance will not be granted where damages are an adequate remedy. Since in many employment cases it may well be possible to find adequate replacement labour, the courts are unlikely to exercise their discretion so as to grant an order for specific performance.

10.5 Over and above this, the courts have taken the general view that specific performance should not lie as a remedy in employment cases. The reason for this was set down in *De Francesco v Barnum*,[1] which held that the courts:[2]

> '... should be very unwilling to extend decisions the effect of which is to compel persons who are not desirous of maintaining continuous personal relations with one another to continue those personal relations ... the courts are bound to be jealous lest they should turn contracts of service

---

[1]   (1890) 45 Ch D 430.

[2]   (1890) 45 Ch D 430 at 438.

into contracts of slavery ... and ... should lean against the extension of the doctrine of specific performance and injunction in such a manner.'

10.6   In *CH Giles & Co Limited v Morris*,[3] the High Court held that the proposition advanced in *De Francesco*[4] was an absolute one and held that:[5]

'... [T]he reasons why the court is reluctant to grant a decree of specific performance of a contract for personal services (and I would regard it as a strong reluctance rather than a rule) are, I think, more complex and more firmly bottomed on human nature. If a singer contracts to sing, there could no doubt be proceedings for committal if, ordered to sing, the singer remained obstinately dumb. But if instead the singer sang flat, or sharp, or too fast, or too slowly, or too quietly, or too loudly, or resorted to a dozen of the manifestations of temperament traditionally associated with some singers, the threat of committal would reveal itself as a most unsatisfactory weapon: for who could say whether the imperfections of performance were natural or self-induced? To make an order with such possibilities of evasion would be vain; and so the order will not be made.'

10.7   Ultimately, given the views advanced in the *CH Giles* case,[6] the law was changed by statute and is now consolidated as the Trade Union and Labour Relations (Consolidation) Act 1992 (TULRCA 1992), s 236, which provides as follows:

'No court shall, whether by way of—

(a) an order for specific performance or specific implement of a contract of employment, or
(b) an injunction or interdict restraining a breach or threatened breach of such a contract,

compel an employee to do any work or attend at any place for the doing of any work.'

10.8   The position now is that specific performance does not lie as a remedy in employment cases.

Injunctions

10.9   Injunctions are orders which have the effect of prevent a state of affairs being carried into effect or from continuing in effect where, in either case, the state of affairs amounts, or could amount, to an actionable civil wrong.

10.10   The power of the courts to grant injunctions is now derived from the Supreme Court Act 1981, s 37 which provides that:

'(1) The High Court may by order (whether [interlocutory] or final) grant an injunction ... in all cases in which it appears to the court to be just and convenient to do so.

(2) Any such order may be made either unconditionally or on such terms and conditions as the court thinks just.'

3   [1972] 1 WLR 307.
4   *De Francesco v Barnum* (1890) 45 Ch D 430.
5   [1972] 1 WLR 307 at 318.
6   See too, *Hill v CA Parsons & Co Limited* [1972] Ch 305.

10.11   Injunctions can be of either an interim or final nature. The principles applicable to each will be dealt with in turn.

Interim injunctions

10.12   The starting point in relation to interim injunctions is to consider their use in the context of employment disputes. The big advantage of an interim injunction is the relative speed with which it can obtained.[7] This may well be of importance in the context of threatened industrial action or industrial action which has commenced without proper statutory compliance.

'Without notice' interim injunctions

10.13   In general terms, it is possible to obtain an interim injunction without notice, thus making it an extremely effective remedy for an employer threatened with a trade dispute. When an application is made without notice it involves only one party being heard; in these circumstances, this is usually the employer. Consequently, such an injunction can only be granted where full and frank disclosure is made by the party seeking the order (ie it must include all matters relevant to the granting of the interim injunction, including matters which may be injurious to the claimant's case), and will only be granted where the case is an urgent one in which the claimant would otherwise suffer irreparable harm if forced to go through the procedure for obtaining a normal interim injunction under CPR Part 25. It is also usual for a claimant to be required to provide a cross undertaking in damages sufficient to cover any damage which may be suffered as a result of an injunction being wrongfully granted. Security for such a cross undertaking may be required. Such injunctions may, it seems, be granted against 'persons unknown' in the course of large-scale industrial action.[8]

10.14   As to the High Court procedure relevant to the granting of an interim injunction, regard should be had to the Civil Procedure Rules 1998[9] (CPR) Part 25 and the very detailed CPR PD 25, a full discussion of which is beyond the scope of this work.

10.15   An interim injunction using the procedure under CPR Part 25 and CPR PD 25 will require the claimant to put both sides of the case (CPR PD 25, para 3.3). The general rule in relation to without notice injunctions is that they are granted until a stated return day, at which point both parties to the dispute can return to address the court on the merits of the injunction. At that subsequent hearing, the injunction can either be continued pending a trial on the merits or lifted pending trial (which for the purposes of an employment dispute in either case usually results in the interim injunction being used as a final determination of the matter).

10.16   The County Court Act 1984, s 38 deals with the power of the county court to grant injunctions.

---

7   See, for example, *Gate Gourmet Limited v Transport and General Workers Union* [2005] EWHC 1889 (QB), where an injunction was granted over the course of a weekend in the court's summer break in an urgent, high-profile industrial dispute.

8   See, again, *Gate Gourmet Limited v Transport and General Workers Union* [2005] EWHC 1889 (QB).

9   SI 1998/3132.

10.17　The problem with using without notice injunctions in the context of employment disputes arises under TULRCA 1992, s 221 which states:

'(1)　Where—

(a) an application for an injunction or interdict is made to a court in the absence of the party against whom it is sought or any in representative of his, and

(b) he claims, or in the opinion of the court would be likely to claim, that he acted in contemplation or furtherance of a trade dispute,

the court shall not grant the injunction or interdict unless satisfied that all steps which in the circumstances were reasonable have been taken with a view to securing that notice of the application and an opportunity of being heard with respect to the application have been given to him.'

10.18　Due to the speed with which the remedy of a without notice injunction can be obtained, TULRCA 1992, s 221 allows the court to consider whether a trade union would be likely to claim the benefit of the immunities from action in tort provided by TULRCA 1992, ss 219–220 (see more generally **Chapter 9**) in the absence of the union being represented in court.

10.19　If a union does, in fact, allege that it is entitled to the benefit of such an immunity (or the court is satisfied that the trade union would claim to be entitled to the benefit of the immunity in the absence of the union actually being present), the result of TULRCA 1992, s 221(1) is that, save where all reasonable steps have been taken to bring an application for an injunction to the attention of a trade union so as to try and bring it into the proceedings, a without notice injunction is unlikely to be granted in a case involving a trade dispute.[10]

10.20　TULRCA 1992, s 221 has profound consequences for employers seeking to gain a tactical advantage over employees or trade unions taking industrial action since the employer will not be so readily able to 'spike the guns' of potential strikers in the same way that the employer could with any another third party seeking to commit an economic tort against the employer.

General interim injunctions

10.21　TULRCA 1992 adds to the position under the general law in relation to the grant of interim injunctions. The general position governing the grant of such injunctions was considered by the House of Lords in *American Cyanamid Co v Ethicon Limited*, where their Lordships held that:[11]

'... when an application for an [interim] injunction to restrain a defendant from doing acts alleged to be in violation of the [claimant]'s legal right is made upon contested facts, the decision whether or not to grant an [interim] injunction has to be taken at a time when ex hypothesi the existence of the right or the violation of it, or both, is uncertain and will remain uncertain until final judgment is given in the action. It was to

---

[10]　See, for example, *United Biscuits (UK) Limited v Fall* [1979] IRLR 110; *Barretts and Bairds (Wholesale) Limited v IPCS* [1987] IRLR 3; and the comments in *Gate Gourmet Limited v Transport and General Workers Union* [2005] EWHC 1889 (QB).

[11]　[1975] AC 396 at 406.

mitigate the risk of injustice to the [claimant] during the period before that uncertainty could be resolved that the practice arose of granting him relief by way of [interim] injunction; but since the middle of the 19th century this has been subject to his undertaking to pay damages to the defendant for any loss sustained by reason of the injunction if it should be held at the trial that the [claimant] had not been entitled to restrain the defendant from doing what he was threatening to do. The object of the [interim] injunction is to protect the [claimant] against injury by violation of his right for which he could not be adequately compensated in damages recoverable in the action if the uncertainty were resolved in his favour at the trial; but the [claimant]'s need for such protection must be weighed against the defendant's corresponding need to be protected against injury resulting from his having been prevented from exercising his own legal rights for which he could not be adequately compensated under the [claimant]'s undertaking in damages if the uncertainty were resolved in the defendant's favour at the trial. The court must weigh one need against the other and determine where the "balance of convenience" lies.'

10.22 Their Lordships then considered how to assess the strength of a case on the evidence available at an interim hearing, stating:[12]

'*Hubbard v Vosper* [1972] 2 QB 84 was treated by Graham J and the Court of Appeal in the instant appeal as leaving intact the supposed rule that the court is not entitled to take account of the balance of convenience unless it has first been satisfied that if the case went to trial upon no other evidence than is before the court at the hearing of the application the [claimant] would be entitled to judgment for a permanent injunction in the same terms as the [interim] injunction sought.

Your Lordships should in my view take this opportunity of declaring that there is no such rule. The use of such expression as "a probability," "a prima facie case," or "a strong prima facie case," in the context of the exercise of a discretionary power to grant an [interim] injunction leads to a confusion as to the object sought to be achieved by this form of temporary relief. The court no doubt must be satisfied that the claim is not frivolous or vexatious; in other words that there is a serious question to be tried.

It is no part of the court's function at this stage of the litigation to try to resolve conflicts of evidence on affidavit as to facts on which the claims of either party may ultimately depend nor to decide difficult questions of law which call for detailed arguments and mature considerations.'

10.23 The House of Lords then addressed the issue of granting an injunction at the request of a claimant, holding that:[13]

'... the governing principle is that the court should first consider whether, if the [claimant] were to succeed at trial in establishing his right to a permanent injunction, he would be adequately compensated by an award of damages for the loss he would have sustained as a result of the defendant's continuing to do what was sought to be enjoined between the time of the application and the time of the trial. If damages in the measure

---

[12]   [1975] AC 396 at 407.
[13]   [1975] AC 396 at 408.

recoverable at common law would be an adequate remedy and the defendant would be in a financial position to pay them, no [interim] injunction should normally be granted, however strong the [claimant]'s claim appeared to be at that stage. If, on the other hand, damages would not provide an adequate remedy for the [claimant] in the event of his succeeding at the trial, the court should then consider whether, on the contrary hypothesis that the defendant were to succeed at the trial in establishing his right to do that which was sought to be enjoined, he would be adequately compensated under the [claimant]'s undertaking as to damages for the loss he would have sustained by being prevented from doing so between the time of the application and the time of the trial. If damages in the measure recoverable under such an undertaking would be an adequate remedy and the [claimant] would be in a financial position to pay them, there would be no reason upon this ground to refuse an [interim] injunction.

It is where there is doubt as to the respective remedies in damages available to either party or to both, that the question of balance of convenience arises. It would be unwise to attempt even to list all the various matters which may need to be taken into consideration in deciding where the balance lies, let alone to suggest the relative weight to be attached to them. These will vary from case to case.

Where other factors appear to be evenly balanced it is a counsel of prudence to take such measures as are calculated to preserve the status quo.'

10.24   Their Lordships added that only in the last resort should regard be had to the relative strength of the parties' cases as revealed in the witness statement evidence.

10.25   The position generally, therefore, is first, to consider the implications of damages. If that is not conclusive, secondly, the court should consider the balance of convenience with regard to the granting of the injunction or maintaining the status quo and, thirdly, only then should the court consider the relative strength of each side's case as they appear on the face of the witness statements.

10.26   The position is modified in relation to injunctions in the context of industrial action by TULRCA 1992, s 221(2). This provides:

'Where—

(a) an application for an [interlocutory] injunction is made to a court pending the trial of an action, and
(b) the party against whom it is made claims that he acted in contemplation or furtherance of a trade dispute,

the court shall, in exercising its discretion whether or not to grant the injunction, have regard to the likelihood of that party's succeeding at the trial of the action in establishing any matter which would afford a defence to the action under section 219 (protection from certain tort liabilities) or section 220 (peaceful picketing).'

10.27 This provision, together with the law as stated in *American Cyanamid*[14] raises a number of issues in the context of industrial action injunctions. First, the question of whether damages awarded against a union for tort (see **10.80**) will be adequate to compensate an employer for the harm that occurs to him as a result of torts committed against him. Given that damages are capped under TULRCA 1992, s 22, it is conceivable that, for example, in a long-running trade dispute with a large trade union, or, for that matter, a short-running dispute with a small union, damages may not be adequate to compensate an employer. This factor ought to weigh on the mind of a court hearing an application for an injunction.[15]

10.28 Secondly, the general law is modified by TULRCA 1992, s 221(2). This requires the court to consider the likelihood of the defence to an action provided under the 'Golden Formula' (ie that the action has been taken or is proposed to be taken in furtherance or contemplation of a trade dispute). This requirement has been considered by the House of Lords in *NWL Limited v Nelson*[16] and in *Dimbleby and Sons Limited v NUJ*,[17] on each occasion the lead judgment being given by Lord Diplock. In the *NWL case*, his Lordship held that, if a defendant could show that it was likely that immunity in tort could be established under (what is now) TULRCA 1992, ss 219–220, an application for an injunction would probably be refused albeit that there may be cases where the seriousness of the consequences were such that a higher degree of probability should be required: in such cases the likelihood of the defence succeeding could only be viewed as one factor in deciding where the balance of convenience lay with regard to the grant of an injunction. Their Lordships were firmly of the view that the judge hearing the application should normally refuse to grant an injunction where the defendant proved the likelihood of his success on the balance of probabilities since Parliament had intended a wide immunity under (what is now) TULRCA 1992, ss 219 and 220.

10.29 The third issue to be considered is whether, over and above the provisions of TULRCA 1992, s 221(2), there is a power for courts to grant injunctions even if it is possible in a given case to establish immunity under the Golden Formula. The answer appears to be yes. In *Duport Steels Limited v Sirs*,[18] the House of Lords overturned the grant of an interim injunction to prevent a strike of steelworkers, the injunction having been granted on the grounds that the steelworkers' activity was potentially threatening to the national economy. Although the injunction was quashed, their Lordships held that the courts have a residual discretion to grant injunctions notwithstanding the likelihood of a trade dispute defence succeeding at trial, but that residual power requires an exceptional case where the consequences of the threatened act might be disastrous. Their Lordships went on to hold that the case they were faced with, although undoubtedly very serious, was not in itself exceptional and industrial action would not cause immediate serious danger to public safety or health.

---

14 *American Cyanamid Co v Ethicon Limited* [1975] AC 396.
15 See *Dimbleby and Sons Limited v NUJ* [1984] IRLR 161 on this point; and also the reasoning of Sir John Donaldson MR in *Mercury Communications Limited v Scott-Garner* [1984] IRLR 494.
16 [1979] IRLR 478.
17 [1984] IRLR 161.
18 [1980] ICR 161.

10.30   Further, in *Express Newspapers Limited v MacShane*,[19] Lord Scarman in the House of Lords, stated, obiter dicta, that an interim injunction might be granted where industrial action endangers the nation or puts at risk such fundamental rights as the right of the public to be informed and the freedom of the press.[20] However, if this view is correct then, as Lord Wedderburn[21] has pointed out, the result is that the granting of injunctions so as to protect the public interest, is a way of bypassing the statutory immunities under TULRCA 1992, ss 219 and 220.

10.31   Fourthly, over and above the law as stated in *American Cynamid*[22] and modified by TULRCA 1992, s 221(2), there is a question as to whether a harsher principle applies in any event. This is due to the fact that, since *American Cyanamid* was decided, the effect of that decision has been watered down by subsequent cases. In many cases involving industrial action, it is unlikely that a dispute will go to a full trial of the merits. In such cases, it was held by the Court of Appeal in *Cayne v Global Natural Resources plc*[23] that where the grant or refusal of an interim injunction would have the practical effect of putting an end to the action, the court should approach the case on the broad principle of what it can best do to avoid injustice, and to balance the risk of doing an injustice to either party. In such a case the court must bear in mind that to grant an interim injunction may mean giving the claimant judgment against the defendant without permitting the defendant the right of trial. Accordingly, the *American Cyanamid* guidelines, requiring the court to look at the balance of convenience when deciding whether to grant or refuse an interim injunction, would not apply in such a case, since, whatever the strengths of either side, the defendant should not be precluded by the grant of an interlocutory injunction from disputing the claimant's claim at trial. Consequently, the better view of the law is that of the House of Lords in *NWL Limited v Nelson*,[24] ie that the relative strength of the parties cases should be looked at. The Court of Appeal held in *Cayne* that *American Cyanamid* was mere guidance from the House of Lords and was not to be rigidly applied in every case.[25]

10.32   Finally, it needs to be borne in mind that TULRCA 1992, s 221(2) applies only to the economic torts. If other torts are alleged to have been committed in the course of industrial action, TULRCA 1992, s 221(2) does not apply and the court is free to determine any dispute on the basis of the general common law principles.

---

[19]   [1980] AC 672.
[20]   See too the Court of Appeal decision in *Beaverbrook Newspapers Limited v Keys* [1978] IRLR 34.
[21]   *The Worker and the Law* (Penguin, 3rd edn, 1986).
[22]   *American Cyanamid Co v Ethicon Limited* [1975] AC 396.
[23]   [1984] 1 All ER 225.
[24]   [1979] IRLR 478.
[25]   Regard should also be had to the subsequent cases of *Cambridge Nutrition Limited v BBC* [1990] 3 All ER 523; and *Lansing Linde Limited v Kerr* [1991] IRLR 80 and to like effect.

Mandatory injunctions

10.33   Mandatory injunctions are orders requiring the party subject to the order to do a stated thing by a stated time. The High Court has held[26] that where mandatory interim injunctive relief is sought, a more onerous test generally applies than that of whether the claimant has a good arguable claim that there is a serious question to be tried (as laid down under the *American Cyanamid*[27] test). Accordingly, the High Court concluded that unless there are special circumstances, a mandatory interim injunction which, if granted, would amount to a major part of the relief claimed, should be granted only in a clear case.[28] Consequently, given the problems in enforcing them, and the more general problems that such orders create in the context of industrial relations, the general rule in relation to mandatory injunctions is that they should be awarded in exceptional cases only.[29]

Injunctions and the proper claimant

10.34   When considering whether to pursue a claim for an injunction in the context of industrial action, it is necessary to consider which person or persons should be the defendant. If industrial action undertaken against a person is taken by a union and some or all of its members and/or officials, it needs to be considered whether it is possible to request an injunction restraining a class or classes of the potential defendants from committing tortious acts. The answer to the question is still undecided. The Court of Appeal in *M Michaels (Furriers) Limited v Askew*[30] held that it is possible to allow a representative action against a group of unnamed pickets protesting about cruelty in the fur trade. However, in the context of industrial action, the High Court has held that this approach is not correct: in *News Group Newspapers Limited v SOGAT 82*,[31] Stuart-Smith J (in relation to what is now CPR 19.6) stated that the potential defendants must have the same interest in the proceedings.[32] They cannot have the same interest if different members of a union have different defences. Consequently, in the case that the judge was dealing with, the members of the defendant union could not be the subject of a representative action since individual members of the unions had different defences to the claim against them.

10.35   A fundamental principal relating to the grant of an injunction is that a claimant must have a legal interest that can be protected by the injunction being sought. In short, the claimant must face loss or harm as a result of a threatened wrong at the hands of a tortfeasor. Generally, this will be evident from the

---

26   *Jakeman v South West Thames Regional Health Authority* [1990] IRLR 62.
27   *American Cyanamid Co v Ethicon Limited* [1975] AC 396.
28   The High Court adopted the reasoning of the Court of Appeal in *Locabail International Finance Limited v Agroexport* [1986] 1 WLR 657.
29   See for examples of this point *Austin Rover Group Limited v AUEW (TASS)* [1985] IRLR 162; *Parker v Camden London Borough Council* [1986] Ch 162; and *Kent Free Press v NGA* [1987] IRLR 267.
30   (1983) Sol Jo 597.
31   [1986] IRLR 337.
32   This was confirmed by the High Court in *Gate Gourmet Limited v Transport and General Workers Union* [2005] EWHC 1889 (QB).

circumstances surrounding an application. However, a problem arises in the case of a claimant seeking to enforce the criminal law by means of an injunction.

10.36   As has been seen above in relation to the industrial torts (see **Chapter 8**) and as can be seen below in relation to the commission of criminal offences in the context of industrial action (see **Chapter 12**), a number of criminal offences may be committed in the course of industrial action that can give rise to civil consequences. The question arises as to whether a claimant can use the civil courts to enforce the criminal law and thereby minimise the consequences of industrial action.

10.37   The leading case on the point is *Gouriet v Union of Post Office Workers*.[33] Here, the claimant was an individual who objected to a boycott of South African post by the defendant union on account of South Africa's apartheid policy. The claimant initially contacted the Attorney-General to seek his permission to bring a relator action on the basis that the postal workers were contravening the offence under the Post Office Act 1953, s 58 of wilfully delaying or detaining any postal packet. The Attorney-General refused to provide his consent. The claimant therefore commenced proceedings to obtain an injunction. The application was refused at first instance but then granted on appeal by the Court of Appeal. One of the defendant unions was joined ex parte on the grounds that, since the conduct of the union was outside the Golden Formula, TULRCA 1992, s 221(1) (as it now is) did not provide the union with immunity. The Attorney-General appealed to the House of Lords where their Lordships held that, in order to establish a cause of action in tort, the claimant would have to show that he was personally suffering special damage as a result of the defendant's conduct. As he could not do so, his claim in tort was dismissed.[34]

10.38   The only alternative for the claimant was to seek to enforce the criminal law through the civil courts by means of an injunction preventing its breach, a matter which would require the Attorney-General's permission (which had already been refused). Furthermore, their Lordships considered that it would be an exceptional case that allowed the Attorney-General to use an injunction to protect the public interest since a failure to follow the court's direction would allow the court to use its civil jurisdiction to enforce the criminal law through committal proceedings. *Gouriet*[35] is still good law on the availability of injunctive relief to enforce the criminal law generally.

Enforcing injunctions

10.39   Injunctions are remedies that are aimed against a particular person or persons. The terms of an injunction must be strictly obeyed by a defendant and to the extent that a defendant breaches an injunction, he will be in contempt of

---

[33]   [1978] AC 435.

[34]   However, this last point is no longer good law following *Re F (mental patient: sterilisation)* [1990] 2 AC 1, where the House of Lords held the courts may adjudicate justiciable issues, but there need not be a right which is, or is claimed to be, vested in a claimant himself. Instead, three points must be satisfied, these being whether there is a real question to be decided, whether the claimant has a real interest in the matter, and that the matter is properly argued before the court.

[35]   *Gouriet v Union of Post Office Workers* [1978] AC 435.

court. Contempt of court is a criminal offence under the Contempt of Court Act 1981. A person who commits a contempt of court may be sent to prison for a term not exceeding 2 years (Contempt of Court Act 1981, s 14(1)).

10.40 The criminal standard of proof (ie proof beyond a reasonable doubt), is applicable by the court before a claimant can succeed in establishing that a contempt of court has occurred.[36]

10.41 The Court of Appeal has held in *Director General of Fair Trading v Smiths Concrete Limited*[37] that in the context of breaching a civil court order, the mens rea is that the defendant must have acted knowingly. This rationale has been adopted by the House of Lords in *Attorney-General v Punch Limited and Others*.[38]

10.42 It is possible for a defendant to breach an order for an injunction in a number of different ways. These are:

● simple breach by the person to whom the order is addressed;
● vicarious liability on the part of the defendant as a result of a breach of the order by a third party for whom the defendant is legally responsible; and
● liability arising from the interference of a third party.

Breach of an injunctive order by the defendant

10.43 The starting-point is that a defendant is bound by a court order from the moment that he has knowledge of its existence. In *Kent Free Press v NGA*,[39] an injunction had been served on the defendant union to prevent it from 'blacking' the claimant's printing work at a typesetter unconnected with the dispute then in progress between the claimant and the defendant. The defendant was informed of the content of the order by a telephone call but did not comply with the order until 2 days after receiving a copy of it. At a subsequent hearing for contempt of court, the High Court held that by not following the terms of the order as soon as the union had received notice (ie when it had notice by telephone), the union committed a contempt of court. The court added that in an appropriate case, it may be possible for a defendant to wait until he has sight of an order before acting upon the same, but this will not usually be the case were a defendant is an experienced litigant (for example, a large union), well used to the content of injunctive orders and the implications of failing to comply with them. Consequently, liability will arise when the defendant knows of that which he has to do with sufficient certainty and in sufficient detail rather than forthwith from personal service of an injunctive order. The court added that were this not the case, it would give advantage to those who avoided service, and would encourage trickiness by defendants.

10.44 Usually contempt of court will be committed where a defendant fails to follow a court order to the letter of the order. In *Howitt Transport Limited v*

---

[36] *Attorney-General v Newspaper Publishing plc* [1988] Ch 333.
[37] [1992] ICR 229.
[38] [2002] UKHL 50, [2003] 3 WLR 49.
[39] [1987] IRLR 267.

Transport and General Workers Union, the National Industrial Relations Court (NIRC) dealt with the question of the forms in which contempt may occur holding:[40]

> 'It may, at the top end of the scale, consist of a flat defiance of the court's authority. Going down the scale, it may not amount to flat defiance but rather to a passive ignoring of the court's Order. Going down the scale further, it may amount to a half-hearted or, perhaps, colourable attempt to comply with the court's Order, and at the bottom end of the scale, there may have been a genuine, whole hearted use of the best endeavours to comply with the Order which, nevertheless, has been unsuccessful. In each case there is a breach of the court's Order. In each case, to use the technicalities of the law, there is "contempt of court", but the quality of the non-compliance varies over an enormous range.'

10.45   In *Express and Star Limited v National Graphical Association (1982)*,[41] the defendant union was found to be in contempt of court for failing to comply with the substance of an injunction. The defendant had allowed industrial action to continue in the face of an injunctive order despite making a sham attempt at compliance with the order by issuing instructions to its members to comply with the order but then failing to distribute the instructions. In short, there must be compliance in full with the terms of an order and the spirit of the order, not the paying of mere lip service to the order.

10.46   As Sir John Donaldson stated in *Howitt Transport*,[42] any failure to comply with an injunctive order is technically a contempt of court. This begs the question of what happens to a defendant who has attempted substantially to comply with the terms of an order. In *Express Newspapers Limited v Mitchell*,[43] the defendants threatened to take industrial action in support of workers in the health service, which would have amounted to unlawful secondary action, and an injunction was sought and granted which required the defendants to desist from taking such action and to ensure that their members were contacted to prevent them from taking part in such action. One of the defendants issued a statement to the members of his union that 'strongly recommended' that industrial action should not be taken. The union had some 1,300 members employed in the area of the dispute at the time that the statement was issued. The acts of the official were still held to be inadequate to comply with the terms of the injunctive order, although it was accepted that the defendant's conduct amounted to a form of mitigation when considering the penalty to be imposed upon him.

10.47   In *Austin Rover Group Limited v AUEW (TASS)*,[44] the defendant union failed to comply with the terms of a mandatory interim injunction made against it which prevented the union from taking industrial action without first holding a ballot in relation to that industrial action. The union continued in its course of action and contended in the subsequent contempt proceedings that it was not bound to hold a ballot because the injunctive order was defective and

---

[40]   [1973] IRLR 25 at 26.
[41]   [1986] ICR 589.
[42]   *Howitt Transport Limited v Transport and General Workers Union* [1973] IRLR 25.
[43]   [1982] IRLR 465.
[44]   [1985] IRLR 162.

the union could not therefore comply with the order. Unsurprisingly, the High Court held that the proper course of action in such a situation was to appeal the terms of the order, not to protest by failing to comply with its terms.

10.48 It seems that in a court hearing, contempt of court proceedings will assume that the original order was valid when made.[45]

Vicarious liability in respect of injunctive orders

10.49 A trade union can be made vicariously liable for the acts of it members. The test will be that adopted under TULRCA 1992, s 20 in relation to the torts committed by the union or in its name (see further **Chapter 9**). A union may be able to repudiate liability for the actions of its minor officials provided it acts in accordance with the requirements for such repudiation set out in TULRCA 1992, s 21 (in respect of which see **Chapter 9**).

Liability arising from third-party interference

10.50 A third party can become liable for committing acts that are the subject of an injunction where that third party has knowledge of the injunction. The principle is best illustrated by the case of *Attorney-General v Newspaper Publishing plc*.[46] The case arose out of the *Spycatcher* book litigation. During the course of the litigation, the Attorney-General was granted an injunction against *The Observer* and *The Guardian* newspapers preventing them from printing extracts of the book *Spycatcher*, which it was alleged breached the Official Secrets Act 1911. Other national newspapers later printed extracts from the book, although they were not themselves parties to the original injunction. The Attorney-General subsequently brought contempt of court proceedings against the other newspapers. At first instance, the High Court held that since the other newspapers were not parties to the initial action and not subject to the order, they could not be the subject of committal proceedings brought in relation to that injunction. However, on appeal, the Court of Appeal over-turned the decision and held that a third party may be liable for breaching the terms of an injunctive order even though the third party was not a party to the order, provided that the third party had knowledge of the terms of the order being breached and knew that it would be interfering with the administration of justice by committing those breaches of that order.

10.51 In respect of liability for contempt of court under this head, if a third party acts at the request of a defendant union, the third party itself can be liable for the act as a *criminal* contempt (rather than a civil one), since the third party is not a party to the order, but has nevertheless carried into effect the defendant's actions.

Penalties for contempt of court

10.52 Where a trade union or one or more of its officials commits a contempt of court, much will turn upon the circumstances of the case in

45 See *Richard Read (Transport) Limited v National Union of Mineworkers (South Wales Area)* [1985] IRLR 67; and *Isaacs v Robertson* [1985] AC 97 on this point.
46 [1988] Ch 333. See also *Attorney-General v Times Newspapers Ltd* [1992] 1 AC 191; *Attorney-General v Newspaper Publishing plc* [1997] 1 WLR 927; and *Attorney-General v Punch Limited and Others* [2002] UKHL 50, [2003] 3 WLR 49.

deciding how the contempt will be punished. The power of the court to punish for contempt is dealt with under CPR, Sch 1, which carries over RSC Ord 52 (together with the introduction of a Practice Direction). A court has three ways in which to punish contempt of court, these being by imposing a fine or imprisonment (in the case of an individual) and, in the case of a trade union or a corporate body, by sequestrating the assets of that body.

10.53   In the case of sequestration, upon the contempt being purged, the contemnor's assets are returned to the contemnor less the cost of the sequestration and any fine that is imposed. Costs are often substantial.

10.54   Where a Sequestration Order is granted, sequestrators are entitled to receive information relating to assets to be sequestered from third parties, notwithstanding that the third party does not personally hold any of the contemnor's assets. Guidance in this area was provided by the NIRC in *Eckman v Midland Bank Limited*, where the court held:[47]

> 'In our judgment, the position of a third party in relation to a writ of sequestration is analogous to that of a third party in relation to an injunction, namely, that he is subject to a duty not knowingly to take any action which will obstruct compliance by the sequestrators with the terms of the writ of sequestration which require them to take possession of the assets.'

10.55   This approach was confirmed by the Court of Appeal in *Messenger Newspapers Group Limited v National Graphical Association (1982)*.[48]

10.56   Finally, it should be noted that only the specific assets of the contemnor (not those jointly owned with others) can be sequestrated.[49]

Purging contempt

10.57   The method by which a contempt of court is purged will vary according to the nature of the penalty in respect of contempt that has been imposed by the court. Usually the contemnor will be required to apologise to the court for his actions. Indeed, the court may refuse to hear any application made by the contemnor until such time as it is satisfied that the contemnor recognises the authority of the court.[50] An apology must amount to an admission of wrongdoing on the part of the contemnor: an 'apology' that is phrased as a non-admission of liability will be ineffective.[51]

10.58   A fine can be levied as penalty for contempt of court. If a fine has been imposed by the court, it does not matter that it is not paid by the contemnor. All that matters is that the fine has been paid. It should be noted that fines are not subject to the cap on damages that can be awarded against a union under TULRCA 1992, s 22.

---

[47]   [1973] ICR 71 at 80.
[48]   [1984] ICR 345.
[49]   For an example of this point, see *News Group Newspapers Limited v SOGAT 82* [1986] IRLR 227.
[50]   See for, example, *Clarke v Heathfield* [1985] ICR 203; and *Clarke v Heathfield (No 2)* [1985] ICR 606.
[51]   See, for example, *Mirror Group Newspapers Limited v Harrison* (unreported) November 1986.

10.59 In a case where an apology is not forthcoming, imprisonment for contempt may be appropriate for an individual. In such a situation, it is possible to release a contemnor notwithstanding that he does not apologise since it has to be remembered that the purpose of the imprisonment is punishment. This is as true of committal to prison as it is in the case of a union failing to apologise before having its assets returned.[52]

DAMAGES

10.60 The quantum of damages in tort is be assessed by reference to the rule set out by Lord Blackburn in *Livingstone v Rawyards Coal Co* where his Lordship held that this would be:[53]

'... that sum of money which will put the party who has been injured, or who has suffered, in the same position as he would have been in if he had not sustained the wrong for which he is now getting his compensation or reparation.'

10.61 The potential claimants that might bring an action against a trade union will usually fall into one of four categories, these being:

- employers;
- workers;
- commercial third parties; and
- third-party consumers.

10.62 The loss that each of the above groups may suffer will vary from case to case but may typically include the following types of loss:

- loss of profit;
- consequential loss;
- injury to feelings; and/or
- damages for loss caused by contempt of court.

10.63 In addition, it needs to be considered whether exemplary damages can be awarded in appropriate cases so as to make an example of the union. Each of these points will be considered in turn.

Loss of profit

10.64 In most industrial/economic tort actions, it will be necessary to show that the claimant has suffered a loss. If the alleged loss is based upon the loss of a potential profit from commercial activity, a problem may lie in attempting to prove the amount of profit that would have been earned but for the commission of the tort. However, the courts have consistently been ready to infer that the opportunity to earn a profit has been lost in industrial tort cases. For example, in *Goldsoll v Goldman*, the High Court held:[54]

---

[52] See, in this regard, the comments of Scott J in *Richard Read (Transport) Limited v National Union of Mineworkers (South Wales Area)* [1985] IRLR 67.

[53] (1880) 5 App Cas 25 at 39.

[54] [1914] 2 Ch 603 at 615. See, too the comments of the Court of Appeal in *Exchange Telegraph Co v Gregory* [1896] 1 QB 147; and *British Industrial Plastics v Fergusson* [1938] 4 All ER 504 both of which support this proposition.

'... damage may be inferred, that is to say, that if the breach which has been procured by the defendant has been such as must in the ordinary course of business inflict damage upon the [claimant], then the [claimant] may succeed without proof of any particular damage which has been occasioned to him.'

10.65   Further, in the case of *Bent's Brewery Co v Hogan*,[55] the High Court was prepared to hold that loss of profit could arise as a result of unlawfully disclosed information revealed by questionnaires that related to pub managers' salaries which was used by the defendant union to exert pressure on the claimant in order to attempt to effect salary rises (thereby having the effect of reducing the claimant's profit as a consequence of the extra wages which would have to be paid). The High Court was prepared to find for the claimant in this case even though loss had yet to be incurred, since it was sufficient to infer that loss would arise.

10.66   Loss of profit can be claimed by an employer who is the victim of unlawful industrial action or by a commercial third party who suffers as a result, for example, as a consequence of the loss of a supply contract due to unlawful industrial action being threatened against the supplier.

Consequential loss

10.67   As a general statement, any consequential loss that flows as a result of tortious misconduct on the part of a defendant can be recovered as damages from the defendant provided that the loss is foreseeable and not too remote.

10.68   In *British Motor Trade Association v Salvadori*,[56] the defendant induced breaches of covenants not to re-sell cars at a premium to certain persons, including the defendant. In the course of litigation against the defendant, the claimant sought from the defendant, as consequential loss, the cost of setting up an inquiry system set up to investigate the breaches of covenant that had been induced by the defendant. In approving the claim for this head of loss, could the High Court held that it could:[57]

'... see no reason for not treating the expenses so incurred as which could not be recovered as part of the costs of the action as directly attributable to the tort or torts. That these expenses cannot be precisely quantified is true, but it is also immaterial.'

10.69   More recently, in *Messenger Newspapers Group Limited v National Graphical Association (1982)*,[58] so as to keep on producing its newspapers in the face of industrial action being organised by the defendant, the claimant was forced to organise transport to drive its staff across a picket line. The defendant was held to be liable to pay damages for these costs and for the costs incurred in order to protect the claimant's business generally from harm which might be committed by the defendant's members during the course of the industrial action.

---

55   [1945] 2 All ER 570
56   [1949] Ch 556.
57   [1949] Ch 556 at 569.
58   [1984] IRLR 397.

Injury to feelings

10.70 It has been consistently held by the courts that in order to ground an action for any of the economic torts, financial loss must be shown to have been suffered by the claimant. Further, it seems that, whilst mere injury to feelings is not of itself enough to such ground an action, if other harm attributable to the defendant's conduct has been occasioned, then this may be recoverable too.[59] The upshot of this is that the court may take account of deliberate malice in the way that industrial action is taken by a trade union by awarding aggravated damages.[60]

10.71 Furthermore, this head of loss may be pleaded by an individual who is the victim of unlawful tortious conduct committed by a trade union.[61]

Damages arising from a contempt of court

10.72 It is not possible for damages to be awarded for a contempt of court. The proper method of enforcing a court order in the face of a refusal by a party to comply with the terms of the order is by committal proceedings.[62]

Exemplary damages

10.73 The purpose of exemplary damages is to provide an award over and above that merely compensating a victim of a tort: it is to punish a tortfeasor for the way in which he has committed the tort. To this end, such an award deviates from the general purpose of the law of tort stated in *Livingstone v Rawyards Coal Co*,[63] that being to compensate and to put the claimant in the position as if the tort had not been committed. Prior to *Rookes v Barnard*,[64] an apparently common feature of the law of tort was the willingness of the courts to award a sum to a claimant for the way in which a tort had been committed. The House of Lords held in *Rookes* that no award of exemplary damages should be made save in three specific categories of cases, as follows:

- where such an award is expressly authorised by statute;
- where the award is to punish oppressive conduct by a government official; or
- where the conduct of the tortfeasor is intended to produce a profit for the tortfeasor as a result of the tort.

10.74 As Lord Devlin said in *Rookes*, such a result would:[65]

> '... remove from the law a source of confusion between aggravated and exemplary damages which has troubled the learned commentators on the subject. Otherwise, it will not, I think, make much difference to the substance of the law or rob the law of the strength which it ought to have.

---

59   See, for example, *Pratt v British Medical Association* [1919] 1 KB 244; and *Quinn v Leathem* [1901] AC 495.
60   See, for example, *Messenger Newspapers Group Limited v National Graphical Association (1982)* [1984] IRLR 397.
61   As *Pratt v British Medical Association* [1919] 1 KB 244 shows.
62   *Re Hudson* [1966] Ch 207.
63   (1880) 5 App Cas 25.
64   [1964] AC 1129.
65   *Rookes v Barnard* [1964] AC 1129 at 1230.

Aggravated damages in this type of case can do most, if not all, of the work that can be done by exemplary damages. In so far as they do not, assaults and malicious injuries to property can generally be punished as crimes.'

10.75   Although the principle in *Rookes*[66] was subsequently challenged by the Court of Appeal in a libel case, *Broome v Cassell & Co*[67] (where the Court of Appeal tried to reverse the decision in *Rookes* on the ground that it had been arrived at per incuriam and that the three categories propounded by the House of Lords were illogical, arbitrary and restrictive), the House of Lords confirmed the *Rookes* categories in the subsequent appeal in *Broome*.[68]

10.76   This begs the question as to whether exemplary damages can be awarded in industrial disputes. In *Messenger Newspapers Group Limited v National Graphical Association (1982)*,[69] the High Court made an award of exemplary damages against the defendant trade union expressly relying on *Rookes*.[70]

10.77   The position, it seems, is that, where a trade union has deliberately taken steps by means of a tort unprotected by a statutory immunity to further the interests of itself and/or its members, and provided further that the claimant is the victim of such behaviour, and that an award of exemplary damages if made is moderate, exemplary damages can be awarded against a trade union.

TULRCA 1992 MODIFICATIONS TO COMMON LAW DAMAGES PRINCIPLES

10.78   TULRCA 1992 modifies the common law position with regard to the award of damages for torts in two ways. First, it imposes a cap on the amount of damages that can be awarded against a trade union which has committed a tort which is unprotected by the statutory immunity. Secondly, it limits the assets of a trade union which can be the subject of enforcement proceedings.

The cap on damages

10.79   The maximum amount of damages that can be awarded against a trade union in tort is capped by TULRCA 1992, s 22, which applies where any proceedings are brought in tort against a trade union save for proceedings:

- for personal injury as a result of negligence, nuisance or breach of duty imposed by either the common law or statute;
- for breach of duty in connection with the ownership, occupation or possession of property; or
- brought in respect of defective products under the Consumer Protection Act 1987, Part I.

---

[66]   *Rookes v Barnard* [1964] AC 1129.
[67]   [1971] 2 QB 354.
[68]   [1972] AC 1027.
[69]   [1984] IRLR 397.
[70]   *Rookes v Barnard* [1964] AC 1129.

10.80 Under TULRCA 1992, s 22(2) the statutory cap on damages works by limiting liability according to the size of membership that a union has. The following limitations apply:

Number of members in union	Capped amount of damages
Less than 5,000	Up to £10,000
5,000 or more but less than 25,000	Up to £50,000
25,000 or more but less than 100,000	Up to £125,000
100,000 or more	Up to £250,000

10.81 Two things should be noted about the statutory cap on damages. First, the cap applies only to damages that are awarded against the union and does not apply to interest on damages or fines made against a union.[71] Secondly, the Secretary of State has a power to vary from time to time the level of the cap on damages that can be awarded under TULRCA 1992, s 22(3).

Restrictions on enforcing awards against certain property of a union

10.82 In addition to the cap on the amount of damages that can be awarded against a trade union under TULRCA 1992, s 22, there is also a limit on the property that can be used to satisfy the enforcement of a judgment against a trade union. Under TULRCA 1992, s 23, any proceedings brought against a trade union to enforce an order for damages cannot be awarded against 'protected property' of the union, whether the action is in tort or otherwise, and whether the same represents damages, costs or expenses (TULRCA 1992, s 23(1)). The definition of when proceedings are brought against a trade union is wide and covers, for example, the situations where proceedings are brought against the union, trustees of a union holding property on trust for the union or where the proceedings are brought against members or officials of a union and are sued in a representative capacity for the union generally.

10.83 As to what amounts to 'protected property', this is defined under TULRCA 1992, s 23(2) as comprising:

- property belonging to trustees of a trade union otherwise than in their capacity as trustees;
- property belonging individually to members of a trade union;
- property belonging to an official of a trade union who is neither a member nor a trustee;
- property that is comprised in a trade union's political fund where there is a restriction in the union's rules preventing the fund from being used to finance strikes and it was in force at the time of the action that is the subject of the complaint; and
- property that is comprised in a trade union's provident benefit fund.

10.84 It should be noted that, although such property is protected as regards judgment debts, it can still be sequestrated in contempt of court proceedings.

---

[71] See, for example, *Messenger Newspapers Group Limited v National Graphical Association (1982)* [1984] IRLR 397, where both were included in the order made against the defendant.

EMPLOYERS' ASSOCIATIONS

10.85   In respect of the first three categories of property identified in **10.83**, under TULRCA 1992, s 130, employers' associations enjoy a similar (although slightly more limited) protection as to their property which can be safeguarded against enforcement of judgment proceedings. However, employers' associations do not receive the benefit of a corresponding provision to the cap on damages under TULRCA 1992, s 22.

Chapter 11

THIRD PARTY RELATIONSHIPS

11.1　This chapter will focus upon the relationships that exist between trade unions, employers' associations and third parties. These relationships can be divided into three categories, as follows:

- relationships with an employer's suppliers;
- relationships with an employer's customers; and
- relationships with other trade unions.

RELATIONSHIPS WITH AN EMPLOYER'S SUPPLIERS

11.2　This aspect of trade union law was heavily modified during the period 1979–1997. Prior to the reforms made during this period, the law was largely one of abstention in regulating the conduct of trade unions in relation to third parties. The law allowed a trade union to put pressure on an employer which recognised the union, to seek to extend such recognition through to the employer's suppliers or customers so as to promote closed shops at the suppliers or customers in one of two ways, these being either through the use of recognition clauses in supply contracts or through the use of union labour only clauses contained in such supply contracts. The purposes of these types of clause was to ensure that suppliers either recognised particular unions for the purposes of collective bargaining or that all employees working for an employer's suppliers or customers were members of one or more particular trade union.

11.3　The EA 1980 made inroads into these practices by removing immunity from the consequences of economic torts committed in the course of industrial action in relation to secondary industrial action and providing the right not to be unfairly dismissed as an employee of a supplier which was forced to recognise a trade union in such circumstances. The Employment Act 1982 followed on by providing that both union labour only clauses and union recognition clauses in supply contracts were deemed to be void. The Employment Act 1988 took matters further still and its provisions (discussed below) are now contained in the Trade Union and Labour Relations (Consolidation) Act 1992 (TULRCA 1992) with the effect now that any industrial action taken to enforce trade union membership through to an employer's suppliers or customers has no immunity in tort.

Union labour only clauses in supply contracts

11.4　The law relating to union labour only clauses in supply contracts acts comprehensively to defeat such clauses on all fronts. First, such clauses are deemed to be void under TULRCA 1992, s 144 which provides:

'A term or condition of a contract for the supply of goods or services is void in so far as it purports that the whole, or some part of, the work done for the purposes of the contract is done only by persons who are, or are not, members of trade unions or a particular trade union.'

11.5   The provision is phrased neutrally so that if an employer were to stipulate that no union labour was to be engaged by a supplier or potential supplier, this would be unlawful in the same way as a requirement that union labour only should be used.

11.6   Secondly, TULRCA 1992, s 145 provides a cause of action to a claimant in respect of a refusal to deal with the claimant because of the claimant's failure to operate in accordance with a union labour only clause between the claimant and the employer. Refusal to deal for these purposes is defined under TULRCA 1992, s 145(2)–(4) as occurring in one of three ways, these being:

- In the case where an employer operates an approved suppliers list and fails to enter a supplier, or prospective supplier of goods or services, on that list due to the supplier or prospective supplier failing to comply with a union labour only clause (TULRCA 1992, s 145(2)).
- Where the reason for the refusal to deal is the claimant's failure or proposed failure to comply with a union labour only clause in relation to a proposed contract for the supply of goods or services (TULRCA 1992, s 145(3)). A refusal to deal with a claimant will occur for these purposes where a person is:
  – excluded from a group of persons tendering for the contract;
  – refused permission to tender for goods or services; or
  – otherwise not dealt with in relation to a proposed contract.
- If an employer terminates a supply contract with a claimant because of a union labour only clause (TULRCA 1992, s 145(4)).

11.7   In the case of a supply contract which lapses and is not renewed because of a union labour only clause, this will probably amount to a case of otherwise determining not to enter into a contract for the purposes of TULRCA 1992, s 145(3)(c).

11.8   In relation to a refusal to deal with a supplier or prospective supplier of goods or services under TULRCA 1992, s 145(2)–(4), the cause of action for the claimant is breach of statutory duty and the usual defences and other legal incidents that would apply to claims for breach of statutory duty are expressly maintained (TULRCA 1992, s 145(5)).

Union recognition clauses

11.9   As with union labour only clauses, it is now unlawful for a trade union to attempt to impose union recognition clauses on an employer's suppliers. The provisions are similar in aim to those already looked at in **11.4** et seq, namely to extend the effect of trade union recognition through an employer's supply chain. Any such clause that is included in a supply contract is dealt with under TULRCA 1992, s 186, which provides as follows:

'A term or condition in a contract for the supply of goods or services is void in so far as it purports to require a party to the contract—

(a) to recognise one or more trade unions (whether or not named in the contract) for the purpose of negotiating on behalf of workers, or any class of worker employed by him, or

(b) to negotiate or consult with, or with an official of, one or more trade unions (whether or not so named).'

11.10 Where an employer seeks to include a union recognition clause in a supply contract and then refuses to deal with a supplier due to the supplier's reluctance to accept that clause, refusal to deal with the supplier is actionable under TULRCA 1992, s 187(l) and (2). The cause of action will either be a breach of contract (due to termination of the supply contract by the employer in purported reliance upon the void union recognition clause) or, alternatively, for breach of statutory duty under TULRCA 1992, s 187(3) where the employer refuses to enter into the supply contract in the first place.

11.11 As with union labour only clauses, the usual defences in relation to breach of statutory duty will apply (TULRCA 1992, s 187(3)).

11.12 Any industrial action taken by a trade union against an employer for the purposes of seeking to include or enforce union labour only clauses in the employer's supply contracts is action taken without the benefit of the immunities in tort under TULRCA 1992, ss 219 and 220 due to TULRCA 1992, s 225 which removes immunity in such cases.

Local government contracts and union labour recognition requirements

11.13 Over and above the general duties in relation to supply contracts in respect of the extension of trade union recognition which exist under TULRCA 1992, local authorities are specifically prohibited under the Local Government Act 1988, s 17(1) from taking account of non-commercial considerations when putting commercial contracts out to tender. Trade union labour or recognition requirements are both defined under the Local Government Act, s 17(5)(a) and (f) as being non-commercial matters.

RELATIONSHIPS WITH AN EMPLOYER'S CUSTOMERS

11.14 The concept of a duty being owed to an employer's customers emerged at common law through the case of *Falcolner v ASLEF*,[1] which established the common law right of a customer of an employer involved in a trade dispute not to have a contract to which the customer is a party interfered with by a third party (such as a trade union, in respect of which see **Chapter 8**). The right was put on a statutory footing under the Trade Union Reform and Employment Rights Act 1993 (TURERA 1993), s 22, becoming incorporated as TULRCA 1992, s 235A.

11.15 In this regard, the starting-point is TULRCA 1992, s 235A(1) and (2) which provides:

'(1) Where an individual claims that—

(a) any trade union or other person has done, or is likely to do, an unlawful act to induce any person to take part, or continue to take part, in industrial action, and

---

[1]   [1986] IRLR 331.

(b) an effect, or likely effect, of the industrial action is or will be to—
    (i) prevent or delay the supply of goods or services, or
    (ii reduce the quality of goods or services supplied,
to the individual making the claim,

he may apply to the High Court or the Court of Session for an order under this section.

(2) For the purposes of this section, an act to induce any person to take part, or to continue to take part, in industrial action is unlawful—

(a) if it is actionable in tort by one or more persons, or
(b) (where it is or would be the act of a trade union) if it could form the basis of an application by a member under section 62.'

11.16   The first point to note is that the provision applies where an *individual* suffers loss; thus, it is not a right that can be exercised by corporate customers of an employer. In *P v National Association of Schoolmasters/Union of Women Teachers*,[2] a claim was presented unsuccessfully on behalf of a school pupil where the pupil had been excluded from lessons with other children for disruptive behaviour but was readmitted to lessons with other pupils. The defendant union carried out a properly constituted ballot but it was alleged by the claimant, inter alia, that there was no trade dispute within the meaning of TULRCA 1992, s 244. On appeal, the Court of Appeal rejected the application on the basis that the dispute related to the reasonableness of the school governors' decision to readmit the excluded child into general teaching, which was capable of giving rise to a dispute relating to terms and conditions of employment.

11.17   Further, in order to be able to claim under TULRCA 1992, s 235A, the individual must show that the matter complained of is actionable in tort which will require the individual being able to prove not only that a tort has been committed, but that there is no immunity or defence available to the tortfeasor.

11.18   Furthermore, under TULRCA 1992, s 235A(6), it is necessary for the union to be liable for the industrial action so taken in accordance with the provisions of TULRCA 1992, s 20.

11.19   It does not matter that an individual presenting a claim under the provisions of TULRCA 1992, s 235A is a customer of an employer which is subject to industrial action, or has the right to be a customer of the employer affected by the unlawful industrial action taken (TULRCA 1992, s 235A(3)); rather, what must be shown under TULRCA 1992, s 235A(1) is that a consequence of the industrial action is that the industrial action will, or is likely to, affect the claimant. The term 'likely' is clearly capable of covering a wide range of meanings and as to when a likelihood will occur, this will be a question of fact in a particular case.

Orders to enforce the right

11.20   To the extent that a claimant in proceedings shows that the right under TULRCA 1992, s 235A has been breached, a court can grant an injunctive

---

[2]   [2001] IRLR 532.

order to prevent the industrial action continuing or to stop threatened industrial action occurring in the first place (TULRCA 1992, s 235A(4)).

RELATIONSHIPS WITH OTHER TRADE UNIONS

11.21 This area is substantially the largest of the three areas to be examined and largely covers the area of trade union mergers and de-mergers rather than causes of action which may exist as between trade unions. In this section the issue of mergers and de-mergers will be examined together with the rules relating to employers' associations on these points.

Mergers

11.22 Legislation relating to trade union mergers has been in effect since the Trade Union Act 1876, which contained complex procedural requirements having the effect of deterring trade unions from merging. The procedures under TULRCA 1992, ss 97–108 now, although simplified, are still quite complex and relate to trade union mergers occurring in one of two ways, these being by:

- amalgamation of the unions in question; or
- transferring the engagements of one union to another.

Amalgamation

11.23 Amalgamation is the process whereby two or more trade unions pool their collective assets and lose their individual identity to take on a new merged form representing the interests of all their combined constituent members. The process of amalgamation is overseen by the Certification Officer who has issued a booklet, 'Mergers – A guide to the statutory requirements for transfers of engagements and amalgamations of trade unions' (2005), which covers the process of merging.

11.24 The procedure to be adopted in the case of an amalgamation of two or more trade unions commences under TULRCA 1992, s 97, which requires that:

- an instrument of amalgamation is approved by the Certification Officer;
- notice of amalgamation is given to members of the merging trade unions; and
- a ballot is held amongst the union memberships and is passed with a majority in favour of the amalgamation (TULRCA 1992, s 97(1)).

The instrument of amalgamation

11.25 Instruments of amalgamation must be submitted to the Certification Officer for approval prior to a ballot being held in relation to a proposed merger by amalgamation (TULRCA 1992, s 98(1)). The provisions relating to amalgamations and transfers of engagements have been amended by the Employment Relations Act 2004 (ERA 2004). In particular, amendments have been made to TULRCA 1992, s 98 so that under TULRCA 1992, s 98(2) and (3), the Certification Officer must be satisfied that an instrument of amalgamation or a transfer complies with the requirements of any regulations in force in relation to amalgamations, and that the Certification Officer is not prevented from approving the instrument of amalgamation due to the proposed name of the amalgamated union being either the same, or so nearly resembling any such name as to be likely to deceive the public as the name under which another organisation:

- was on 30 September 1971 registered as a trade union under the Trade Union Acts 1871–1964;
- was at any time registered as a trade union or employers' association under the Industrial Relations Act 1971; or
- is for the time being entered in the list of trade unions or in the list of employers' associations.

11.26   For the avoidance of doubt, TULRCA 1992, s 98(4) provides that if the proposed name of the amalgamated trade union is the name of one of the amalgamating unions, that is not a ground for the Certification Officer to refuse to approve the instrument of amalgamation under TULRCA 1992, s 98(3).

11.27   The instrument of amalgamation is required to comply with any regulations that exist relating to the content of instruments of amalgamation. Currently, these are to be found in Trade Union and Employers' Associations (Amalgamations etc) Regulations 1975,[3] Sch 1. These require that the following matters should be contained in an instrument of amalgamation:

- a statement that the document is an instrument of amalgamation, together with the names of the organisations to be amalgamated and the fact that the amalgamated body will comply with the rules of the new body;
- either:
  - – the rules of the proposed new body; or
  - – a summary of the rules of the proposed new body having particular regard to the name and principal purposes of the body, the conditions of admission to membership, the methods of appointing its governing body and principal member and of changing its rules, and the contributions and benefits available to its members;
- details of the property held for the benefit of members of the amalgamating bodies that is not going to be applied in the amalgamated body, and a statement of what is to happen to it; and
- the proposed date of the amalgamation.

11.28   The matters set out above are the minimum that need to be included in an instrument of amalgamation and it is possible for such an instrument to include more than these minimum requirements. Once an instrument of amalgamation has been prepared, it must then be sent to the Certification Officer, having been signed by three members of the committee of management and the secretary of each of the amalgamating unions. The instrument of amalgamation must be sent to the Certification Officer on any form issued by him for these purposes from time to time and must be accompanied by the appropriate fee from time to time in force.

Notice to the members of the merging unions

11.29   The notice to be given to members is dealt with under TULRCA 1992, s 99, which provides that every voting paper sent out for the purposes of the

---

[3]   SI 1975/536.

ballot on the merger must be accompanied by a written notice approved by the Certification Officer (TULRCA 1992, s 99(1)). The notice must include either the full instrument of amalgamation or give a sufficient account of the instrument of amalgamation for members of the unions to make a reasonable judgment as to the effects of the proposed amalgamation or transfer (TULRCA 1992, s 99(2)).

11.30 To the extent that the full terms of the instrument of amalgamation are not set out in the notice, the notice must state where the full text of the instrument of amalgamation can be inspected by interested parties (TULRCA 1992, s 99(3)). The notice is not allowed to contain any views as to the desirability or otherwise of the proposed amalgamation or transfer (TULRCA 1992, s 99(3A)). Upon the notice being submitted to the Certification Officer, provided that it complies with the provisions of TULRCA 1992, the Certification Officer is bound to approve the notice (TULRCA 1992, s 99(5)). In the Certification Officer's booklet, 'Mergers – A guide to the statutory requirements for transfers of engagements and amalgamations of trade unions' (2005), guidance is provided as to the appropriate content of such notices, which states that notices are likely to be approved where they contain the following:

- a heading stating clearly that the document is a Notice to Members;
- a reference to TULRCA 1992, which imposes the notice requirement, either as a subheading to the notice or otherwise clearly at the forefront of the notice;
- a reference to the amalgamation or transfer and the statutory requirement to hold a ballot in relation to the amalgamation or transfer;
- a statement to the effect that either a simple majority, or such majority as the union rules require, is needed to approve the amalgamation or transfer;
- a statement to the effect that the instrument of amalgamation and the notice have both been received by the Certification Officer and approved by him; and
- the dates of the voting period and a statement that, in the case of voting papers sent out before the voting period, papers received prior to the commencement of that period shall be deemed to have been received during the voting period.

11.31 The booklet also purports to add to the statutory requirements by requiring that the start of the voting period is declared on the notice.

Balloting requirements

11.32 As with most matters relating to voting requirements in connection with trade unions, TULRCA 1992 sets down detailed provisions for balloting in connection with amalgamations. The starting-point is TULRCA 1992, s 100(1) which requires that a resolution approving the proposed transfer must be passed by ballot of the members of the unions to be amalgamated in accordance with TULRCA 1992, ss 100A–100E (inserted by TURERA 1993, s 4). A simple majority is required unless the rules of either amalgamating union expressly require a greater majority in favour of a merger (TULRCA 1992, s 100(2)).

11.33 TULRCA 1992, ss 100A–100E provide the process by which a ballot is to be held. TULRCA 1992, s 100A(1) provides for the appointment of a qualified independent scrutineer[4] to supervise an amalgamation ballot before the ballot is held and to carry out the statutory functions required and other functions specified in relation to his appointment. TULRCA 1992, s 100A(2) provides that prior to appointing an independent scrutineer, the appointing trade union must have no grounds for believing either that the independent scrutineer will carry out any functions conferred on him in relation to the ballot otherwise than competently, or that his independence in relation to the union, or in relation to the ballot, might reasonably be called into question. Further, under TULRCA 1992, s 100A(7), the trade union appointing an independent scrutineer must ensure that nothing in the terms of the independent scrutineer's appointment (including any additional functions specified in the appointment) is such as to make it reasonable for any person to call the independent scrutineer's independence in relation to the union into question.

11.34   Under TULRCA 1992, s 100A(3)(a) the independent scrutineer's appointment requires him to supervise the production and distribution of the voting papers and make provision for the return of the voting papers for counting. Further, under TULRCA 1992, s 100A(3)(a), the independent scrutineer is required to inspect the register of members of the trade union, or examine a copy of the register supplied to him by the union pursuant to its obligations under TULRCA 1992, s 100A(9)(a), whenever it appears to him appropriate to do so and, in particular, if a complaint is made to him by a member of the union that the member does not believe the register to be up to date. Such a complaint can be made at any time before the day before the independent scrutineer makes his report to the union (TULRCA 1992, s 100A(5)). The independent scrutineer must have carried out his obligation to inspect the register of members by either the date specified in the union's rules for determining who is entitled to vote in the ballot by reference to membership, or the last date on which voting papers are distributed for the purposes of the ballot (the relevant date) (TULRCA 1992, s 100A(13)).

11.35   The independent scrutineer is also required to compile a report with regard to the ballot (dealt with at **11.46**). TULRCA 1992, s 100A(3)(c) and (d) requires the independent scrutineer to take such steps as are appropriate for the purpose of enabling him to make his report and to make the report to the union as soon as reasonably practicable after the last date for the return of voting papers. Further, under TULRCA 1992, s 100A(3)(e), when the voting papers have been returned, the independent scrutineer is required to retain custody of all voting papers returned for the purposes of the ballot together with the copy of the register supplied to him by the union for a period of one year or until the Certification Officer or Employment Appeal Tribunal (EAT) authorises him to dispose of them in the event that a complaint is made about the conduct of the ballot.

11.36   The trade union's register of members is a sensitive document. In this regard, TULRCA 1992, s 100A(6) provides protection to a union having to

---

4   See the Trade Union Ballots and Elections (Independent Scrutineer Qualifications) Order 1993, SI 1993/1909 and the Trade Union Ballots and Elections (Independent Scrutineer Qualifications) Order 1993 (Amendment) Order 2002, SI 2002/2267 (made under TULRCA 1992, s 100A(2)), with regard to persons qualified to be an independent scrutineer.

disclose its register of members by providing that the independent scrutineer is bound by a duty of confidentiality in respect of the register.

11.37 Additionally, each of the trade unions appointing an independent scrutineer has certain functions to fulfil in relation to the appointment of the independent scrutineer, as follows:

- to ensure that they take steps either to notify their members individually of the appointment of the independent scrutineer, or to use the usual method that the union would adopt to bring matters of importance to the attention of members of the union (TULRCA 1992, s 100A(8));
- to supply the independent scrutineer with a copy of the register of their members' names and to comply with any requests that the scrutineer may have with regard to inspecting the register (TULRCA 1992, s 100A(9));
- to ensure that the independent scrutineer carries out his functions and that there is no interference with him during the carrying out of those functions which might compromise his independence (TULRCA 1992, s 100A(11)); and
- to comply with all reasonable requests made by the independent scrutineer for the purposes of, or in connection with, the carrying out of his functions (TULRCA 1992, s 100A(12)).

11.38 TULRCA 1992, s 100B deals with eligibility to vote and states that entitlement to vote in the ballot shall be accorded equally to all members of the trade union.

11.39 A question arises in the case of a trade union which has more than one class of members as to whether the union is entitled to specify which classes of members of the union are entitled to vote on a particular resolution, or whether all members of whatever class are entitled to vote. This point was addressed in *National Union of Mineworkers (Yorkshire Area) v Millward*,[5] where the EAT was required to consider whether unemployed members of the union who had the right to become full members again in the future if they found work in the mining industry, and had limited membership rights as a consequence, had a right to vote in a ballot. The Certification Officer held that the limited members were entitled to vote. The union appealed to the EAT which held that the correct approach is:[6]

> '... to ask how the language of [TULRCA 1992, s 100B] would be reasonably understood in the particular case by those to whom the section is addressed and whose affairs are to be affected by it ... [T]he crucial point in this case is that there is more than one class of persons described as members in the union rules: does, s 100B include all of them or only some of them? To determine the scope of the section it is necessary to examine the relationship between each class of members and the union with other members. Although they all belong to or form part of the union, there are significant differences between the different classes of members – in particular between the full members, on the one hand, and the rest of the members on the other hand, as well as between the different classes of other members.'

---

[5]   [1995] IRLR 411.
[6]   [1995] IRLR 411 at 415.

11.40   The EAT went on to conclude that the limited members were entitled to some fringe benefits of membership but not an entitlement to vote. The practical implications of this decision are that, first, it is the union itself that determines who has a right to vote and the Certification Officer should consider a particular union, and not unions generally, in determining whether all the members having the right to vote under union rules have had the chance to vote. Secondly, it follows from this that it is possible for a union to have different classes of members, some of whom may be entitled to have a greater say in the running of the union than others. Where this is the case for any given union, it is prudent for the union to ensure that its membership rules are clearly drafted so as to determine who will have voting rights in relation to the continued existence of the union and to exclude from voting those who have a lesser capacity (for example, retired, student or honorary members).

11.41   TULRCA 1992, s 100C covers voting in the case of an amalgamation or transfer ballot. Voting is carried out by the marking of a ballot paper by the person voting (TULRCA 1992, s 100C(1)). Voting papers are required to state the name of the independent scrutineer and the address to which the paper is to be returned together with the date by which it must be returned. Voting papers must be one of a number of consecutively whole-numbered papers (TULRCA 1992, s 100C(2)). Members are entitled to vote freely without interference or constraint, the ballot must be conducted at minimal cost to the members of the unions and must be carried out by post (TULRCA 1992, s 100C (3) and (4)). This will usually require the provision of a reply-paid envelope. Further, voting papers must not be sent with any direction or opinion from a union as to how to vote in the ballot (TULRCA 1992, s 100C(5)). If a voting paper is supplied with any other documents (other than the reply-paid envelope, TULRCA 1992, s 99 notice or the instrument of amalgamation), a member of the union may make a complaint to the Certification Officer under TULRCA 1992, s 103 who must ignore the result of the ballot (see **11.58**).

11.42   Finally, ballots are to be carried out so as to ensure, so far as is possible, that they are secret and fairly and accurately counted. Minor errors in counting which could not materially affect the outcome of a ballot are to be disregarded (TULRCA 1992, s 100C(6)).

11.43   Under TULRCA 1992, s 100D, voting papers are to be stored, distributed and counted by an independent person (who can be the independent scrutineer or another independent person) (TULRCA 1992, s 100D(1) and (2)). If the independent person is not the independent scrutineer, then the independent person is obliged to return the voting papers to the independent scrutineer as soon as reasonably practicable after counting the voting papers (TULRCA 1992, s 100D(5)). A trade union is not allowed to compromise the independence of the independent person; it is required to ensure that the independent person carries out his tasks without interference, and the trade union must also ensure that it complies with any reasonable request made of it by the independent person (TULRCA 1992, s 100D(6)).

11.44   Following the counting of the ballot, the independent scrutineer is required to prepare a report under TULRCA 1992, s 100E. A union is not allowed to publish the result of the ballot until such time as the independent scrutineer's report has been published (TULRCA 1992, s 100E(5)).

11.45   Under TULRCA 1992, s 100E(1), the independent scrutineer's report on the ballot is required to state the following information:

- the number of voting papers distributed for the purposes of the ballot;
- the number of voting papers returned to the scrutineer;
- the number of valid votes cast in the ballot for and against the resolution;
- the number of spoiled or otherwise invalid voting papers returned; and
- the name of the person (or of each of the persons) appointed under TULRCA 1992, s 100D to count the ballot, or if no person other than the independent scrutineer was appointed, that fact.

11.46   Further, under TULRCA 1992, s 100E(2) the independent scrutineer's report must also state whether the independent scrutineer is satisfied of the following:

- that there are no reasonable grounds for believing that there was any contravention of any statutory requirement in relation to the ballot;
- that the arrangements made with respect to the production, storage, distribution, return or other handling of the voting papers used in the ballot, and the arrangements for the counting of the votes, included all such security arrangements as were reasonably practicable for the purpose of minimising the risk that any unfairness or malpractice might occur in relation to the ballot; and
- that the independent scrutineer was able to carry out his functions without any such interference as would make it reasonable for any person to call his independence in relation to the union into question.

11.47   If the independent scrutineer is not satisfied as to any of the matters above, the report must give particulars of his reasons for not being so satisfied (TULRCA 1992, s 100E(2)).

11.48   Under TULRCA 1992, s 100E(3), the independent scrutineer's report must also include the following:

- Whether the scrutineer has inspected the register of names and addresses of the members of the trade union, or has examined the copy of the register as at the 'relevant date' (see **11.34**) supplied to him under TULRCA 1992, s 100A(9)(a).
- If the independent scrutineer has inspected the register of members, whether in the case of any inspection or examination he was acting on a request by a member of the trade union or at his own instance. In such a case, the report must not state the name of any member who has requested such an inspection or examination.
- Whether he declined to act on any such request.
- Whether any inspection of the register, or any examination of the copy of the register, has revealed any matter which the independent scrutineer considers should be drawn to the attention of the trade union in order to assist it in securing that the register is accurate and up to date.

11.49   Under TULRCA 1992, s 100E(4), where one or more persons other than the independent scrutineer is appointed to count the ballot under TULRCA 1992, s 100D the independent scrutineer's report must also indicate whether he is satisfied with the performance of the person, or each of them. If the independent scrutineer is not satisfied with the performance of any such person, the independent scrutineer must provide particulars of his reasons for not being so satisfied.

11.50   Under TULRCA 1992, s 100E(6), within 3 months of receiving the independent scrutineer's report, the union must:

- send a copy of the report to every member of the union to whom it is reasonably practicable to send it; or
- take all such other steps for notifying the contents of the report to the members of the union (whether by publishing the report or otherwise) as it is the practice of the union to take when bringing matters of general interest to all its members.

11.51   Under TULRCA 1992, s 100E(7), any such copy or notification is required to be accompanied by a statement that the union will, on request, supply any member of the trade union with a copy of the report, either free of charge or on payment of such reasonable fee as may be specified in the notification.

Registering the instrument of amalgamation

11.52   After a successful ballot, an instrument of amalgamation only takes effect when its registration takes place in accordance with TULRCA 1992, s 101. There is no duty to register the amalgamation if the parties to a proposed merger decide that they do not wish to complete the merger.

11.53   TULRCA 1992, s 101(2) provides that a merger is not to take effect until the expiry of 6 weeks from the date on which an application is made to the Certification Officer for registration of the amalgamation. This allows the Certification Officer to wait and see whether any challenges are mounted against the merger under the provisions of TULRCA 1992, s 103. Applications for registration cannot be made to the Certification Officer until such time as an independent scrutineer's report has been received by the unions concerned (TULRCA 1992, s 100E(6)).

11.54   Provisions have been implemented under ERA 2004 to deal with the situation of listing and certification after amalgamation and are incorporated as TULRCA 1992, ss 101A and 101B. Where an instrument of amalgamation is registered by the Certification Officer, each of the amalgamating unions is required to be entered in the list of trade unions under TULRCA 1992, s 101A(1). In such a case, under TULRCA 1992, s 101A(2), the Certification Officer must:

- enter, with effect from the amalgamation date, the name of the amalgamated union in the list of trade unions, and
- remove, with effect from that date, the names of the amalgamating unions from that list.

11.55   The Certification Officer must also issue a Certificate of Independence to the amalgamated union if when an instrument of amalgamation is registered by the Certification Officer each of the amalgamating unions has a Certificate of Independence which is in force (TULRCA 1992, s 101A(3) and (4)).

11.56   Further, under TULRCA 1992, s 101B(1) and (2), if an instrument of amalgamation is registered in respect of a union and the amalgamated union is entered in the list of trade unions under TULRCA 1992, s 101A, the amalgamated union is required to send to the Certification Officer the prescribed fee for registration from time to time and the following information in such a manner and form as the Certification Officer may require:

- a copy of the rules of the union;
- a list of its officers; and
- the address of its head or main office.

11.57 The information must be sent before the end of the period of 6 weeks beginning with the date on which the instrument of amalgamation takes effect or such longer period as the Certification Officer may specify if he considers that it is not reasonably practicable for the amalgamated union to send the information in that period (TULRCA 1992, s 101B(3)). A failure to comply with any of the requirements under TULRCA 1992, s 101B requires the Certification Officer to remove the amalgamated union's name from the list of trade unions (TULRCA 1992, s 101B(4)).

Complaints arising out of the amalgamation procedure

11.58 Complaints can be raised that a trade union has failed to comply with any of the requirements of TULRCA 1992, ss 99–100E, or in relation to a trade union's own rules relating to amalgamations. Under TULRCA 1992, s 103(1), such complaints are made to the Certification Officer. Indeed, TULRCA 1992, s 103(5) provides that a complaint to the Certification Officer is the only way that an amalgamation can be contested. Such a complaint must be made within 6 weeks beginning with the date on which an application to register a merger was sent to the Certification Officer (TULRCA 1992, s 103(2)). Where a complaint is made, the Certification Officer is required to make such inquiries as he thinks fit (TULRCA 1992, s 103(2A)). Where the Certification Officer makes any such inquiries, if the Certification Officer requests a person to provide information to him in connection with those inquiries, he must specify the date by which that information is to be furnished. However, unless the Certification Officer considers that it would be inappropriate to do so, he must nonetheless proceed with his determination of the application notwithstanding that the information has not been furnished to him by the specified date (TULRCA 1992, s 103(6)).

11.59 In the event that the Certification Officer upholds a complaint, he must make a declaration to that effect and may make an order specifying the steps to be taken before an application for registration will be accepted by him. In the event of such an order having been made, the Certification Officer cannot take any steps to formalise the amalgamation (TULRCA 1992, s 103(3)). Such an order can be enforced in the same way as a court order by any person who was a member of the union at the time the order was made (TULRCA 1992, s 103(8) and (9)). The Certification Officer is required to provide a statement, either orally or in writing, setting out the reasons for his decision (TULRCA 1992, s 103(4)).

11.60 Appeals lie from a decision of the Certification Officer to the EAT on a question of law only (TULRCA 1992, s 104).

TRANSFERS OF ENGAGEMENTS

11.61 The second method of trade union merger is by means of a transfer of engagement. This occurs where one trade union transfers its business to another which undertakes to carry out the engagements of the transferring union (TULRCA 1992, s 98(2)). In the case of a transfer of engagement, the procedure is less time-consuming in that only the transferring union needs to ballot its members prior to merger. Consequently, this makes it a more popular way of merging. The right to merge by transfer of engagement is dealt with by TULRCA 1992, s 97(2) which provides that a trade union may transfer its engagements to another union on condition that an instrument of transfer is drawn up in accordance with TULRCA 1992, s 98 and that notice is given to members prior to a ballot being held of the members.

The instrument of transfer

11.62 The instrument of transfer is required to comply with Trade Unions and Employers' Associations (Amalgamations, etc) Regulations 1975,[7] Sch 2, which requires that the following matters are incorporated into the instrument of transfer:

- a statement that the document is an instrument of transfer of the engagements of the transferring union and that upon the transfer taking effect the members of the transferor organisation will become members of the transferee union and will become subject to its rules;
- a statement as to: (i) what contributions and benefits will be applicable to members being transferred to the transferee union under that union's rules; (ii) the branch or section of the union that members are to be assigned to (if any); (iii) whether the transferee union's rules are to be changed prior to joining; and (iv) the effect of the changes and the date on which the transfer is to take effect; and
- any property that is not being transferred from the union being transferred together with a statement of what is to happen to that property.

11.63 The instrument of transfer must be signed by the management committee members of the transferor union and by the secretary of each of the unions. Usually, an instrument of transfer will have further clauses including an undertaking on the part of the transferee union to the effect that it will carry out the engagements of the transferor union. The instrument of transfer is required to be submitted to the Certification Officer before a ballot of members and must be approved by the Certification Officer prior to a ballot of the members of the transferring union taking place (TULRCA 1992, s 98(l)). The Certification Officer must approve the instrument of transfer if it meets with the criteria above (TULRCA 1992, s 98(5)).

Notice to members

11.64 Under TULRCA 1992, s 99 notice is required to be given to members of the transferor union in the same way as with a merger by amalgamation and regard should be had to **11.29** in this regard.

Balloting requirements

11.65 Further, similar balloting requirements to those that would be observed in the case of a merger by amalgamation apply in the case of a merger

---

[7]   SI 1975/536.

by transfer of engagement under TULRCA 1992, ss 100–100E and regard should be had to these provisions under **11.32**.

Alteration of the transferee union's rules

11.66 A power exists under TULRCA 1992, s 102 for a transferee union to alter its rules in relation to a forthcoming transfer of engagement in order to give effect to the transfer of engagement. The power is to be exercised by the committee of management or other governing body of the transferee union and an alteration is required to take place in the form of a written memorandum setting out the way in which the rules of the transferee have been changed (TULRCA 1992, s 102(1)). This power is only to be exercised where there is no express power in the transferee union's rules preventing the operation of TULRCA 1992, s 102(1).

11.67 The change of rules takes effect at the time the transfer becomes operative (TULRCA 1992, s 102(2)) and the power applies notwithstanding anything to the contrary in the rules of the transferee union (TULRCA 1992, s 102(3)). The amended rules should be sent to the Certification Officer for approval as a matter of good practice since he will be otherwise unable to review the instrument of transfer.

Registration

11.68 Once a trade union has complied with the requirements set out above and has a majority of members in favour of the change, it is possible to register the changes with the Certification Officer under TULRCA 1992, s 101(1). The same restrictions apply in relation to registration as apply in the case of an amalgamation (including the 6-week delay between receipt by the Certification Officer and registration coming into effect under TULRCA 1992, s 101(2)) and regard should be had to **11.53** with regard to registration generally.

Practical effect of mergers

11.69 When registration of a merger takes place a number of points arise. First, where, as a result of a merger, a trade union ceases to exist, final accounts for that union have to be prepared and returned to the Certification Officer. In the case of a newly formed trade union it will not have to submit a financial return until it has been in existence for 12 months (TULRCA 1992, s 43).

11.70 Secondly, the rules relating to leadership elections are changed. Where a person holding office in a union that is to be merged (whether by amalgamation or transfer of engagement) is appointed to an office in the new union, he is excused from having to submit to the usual union election requirements under TULRCA 1992, s 57(1)–(3) since a trade union created by merger is not required to hold leadership elections in the first year of its existence following merger, and as regards a union official carrying over his office into a new union, he is excused from having to stand for election until the expiry of the term of his original office (TULRCA 1992, s 57(2) and (3)). However, a duty to hold elections at an earlier point in time may exist under the union rulebook of the merged union.

11.71 Thirdly, the list of members of the merged trade union must be brought up to date under TULRCA 1992, s 24(1). An extension is granted to the period of time within which the list must be so amended in the case of an amalgamated union, and the newly merged union will have a period of one year within which to update the new list of members' names (TULRCA 1992, s 43(2)).

11.72   Fourthly, in the case of a merger by amalgamation, where both of the merging unions had in place a valid political fund resolution, the political fund resolution in effect in the amalgamated union will be deemed to be that resolution passed first in time by either of the combining unions (TULRCA 1992, s 93(1) and (2)). In the case of a transfer of engagements, if the transferee union has in existence a political fund resolution, the transferring members of the transferor union are bound by the transferee union's political fund resolution in the same way as other new joiners of the transferee union.

11.73   Finally, that property of merging unions (whether merging by transfer of engagements or amalgamation) which is to become comprised in the merged union transfers automatically under TULRCA 1992, s 105(1) without the need for any conveyance, assignment or assignation. However, TULRCA 1992, s 105 does not apply to property that is expressly excluded from the operation of a transfer by means of either the instrument of amalgamation or the transfer.

MERGERS OF EMPLOYERS' ASSOCIATIONS

11.74   The rules relating to the mergers of unincorporated employers' associations are similar to those relating to the merger of trade unions under TULRCA 1992, s 133, which provides as follows:

'(1)   Subject to subsection (2), the provisions of Chapter VII of Part I of this Act (amalgamations and similar matters) apply to unincorporated employers' associations as in relation to trade unions.

(2)   In its application to such associations that Chapter shall have effect—

(a)   as if in section 99(1) for the words from "that every" to "accompanied by" there were substituted the words "that, not less than seven days before the ballot on the resolution to approve the instrument of amalgamation or transfer is held, every member is supplied with",

(b)   as if the requirements imposed by sections 100A to 100E consisted only of those specified in sections 100B and 100C(1) and (3)(a) together with the requirement that every member must, so far as is reasonably possible, be given a fair opportunity of voting, and

(ba) as if the references in sections 101A and 101B to the list of trade unions were to the list of employers' associations, and

(c)   with the omission of sections 101(3), 101A(3) and (4), 103(2A) and (6) to (9) and 107.'

11.75   However, it can be seen that some differences do exist between the provisions relating to trade unions and those relating to employers' associations. First, there is the slight change in the formulation of the requirements relating to the giving of notice to employers' associations that would apply under TULRCA 1992, s 99(1) (under TULRCA 1992, s 133(2)(a)). Secondly, the detailed requirements with regard to the need to have an independent scrutineer and independent vote counter acting in connection with the ballot are swept away: the duties simply become a right for each member entitled to vote to have an equal vote (TULRCA 1992, s 100B), for the method of voting to be on voting papers marked by the voter (TULRCA 1992, s 100C(1)) and for each voter to be granted a right to vote without constraint and, so far as possible, at no cost to the voter (TULRCA 1992, s 100C(3)) ((TULRCA 1992, s 133(2)(b)). The other incidental provisions relating to the independent scrutineer, Certificate of Independence, inquiries of the Certification Officer upon a complaint in relation to a ballot and change of name in connection with a ballot under TULRCA 1992, Part I, Chapter VII are also removed (these being TULRCA 1992, ss 101(3), 101A(3), 103(2A) and (6)–(9), and 107, respectively).

11.76 In the case of an incorporated employers' association, any merger will be governed by the provisions of the Companies Acts 1985–1989.

HIVING OFF MEMBERS

11.77 An issue arises as to what happens to trade unions or employers' associations which have, for example, a large number of disaffected members who seek to break away and form their own trade union or employers' association. Three possibilities exist in such situations, these being:

- that the union or employers' association is subject to a breakaway;
- that a de-merger from the union or employers' association takes place; or
- that the union or employers' association decides to wind itself up,

each of which will be examined in turn.

Breakaways

11.78 When members of a trade union or employers' association decide to set up their own trade union or employers' association, the law relating to the position of the breakaway members is quite simple. TULRCA 1992 does not provide any special provisions for large-scale membership defection. However, in the case of trade union members, it does provide for individual trade union members to leave their union by means of resignation from that union upon members giving reasonable notice to the union to terminate their membership and otherwise complying with other reasonable conditions in relation to leaving the union (TULRCA 1992, s 69).

11.79 Consequently, there is no difference between one member of a trade union or employers' association resigning and a group of such members resigning together. In such circumstances, unless the rules of the union or employers' association provide otherwise the members will have no right to claim a share of the property of the union or employers' association which they are leaving as the property is held collectively for the union or employers' association and the members have a mere contractual right to enjoy that property in accordance with the rules of the union or employers' association during their period of membership. The right to enjoy such property use terminates on the members resigning their membership (unless specific provision otherwise exists in the rules of the union or employers' association).

De-merger

11.80 A de-merger from a previously merged trade union or employers' association can take place for any number of reasons. As with breakaways, there are no specific statutory provisions under TULRCA 1992 relating to this area. In considering whether and, if so, how, it is possible to de-merge, the starting-point, given the absence of statutory provisions in this regard, is the rulebook of the relevant trade union or employers' association. The rulebook is the contract that sets down the rights of members and/or particular groups of members, and it is therefore necessary to consider in each given case whether it makes express contractual provision concerning the possibility of a de-merger. A failure to follow rulebook de-merger provisions can result in the union or employers' association, or its members, seeking to prevent a de-merger by applying for an injunction to prevent breach of contract.[8]

11.81   In the absence of an express provision in the relevant rulebook, it is unlikely that a term will be implied into the rulebook allowing de-merger, especially, in the case of trade unions, given the existence of the statutory right[9] to resign from a trade union.

11.82   The only other ways of seeking a de-merger would be, first, to seek to change the relevant rulebook so as to include such a power by using any power to make changes to the rulebook contained in the rulebook itself, or, if there is no such power, by reaching a consensus of all members of the union or employers' association who will then be able to bring about such a change[10] (which may be impossible in the case of a large trade union or employers' association given that the vote of one member may scupper the process).

11.83   As to who owns the property of a trade union or unincorporated employers' association in the event of a de-merger, the starting-point is again to consider the rulebook of the relevant trade union or employers' association. If the rulebook provides for property to be granted to a section of the union or employers' association upon its de-merger, then the distribution of property must be dealt with in accordance with the rulebook. If, however, the rules do not provide for a division of property then, unless the de-merger is a friendly de-merger (in which case the rulebook can be amended as per **11.82**), that part of the union or employers' association de-merging may well have to do so without any property belonging to the union or employers' association from which it is de-merging. For example, in *Burnley Nelson Rossendale and District Textile Workers Union v Amalgamated Textile Workers Union*,[11] the claimant union de-merged from the defendant and claimed that it was entitled to an equitable proportion of the defendant union's funds. The High Court held that in the case of a hostile de-merger, the court had no inherent jurisdiction to rewrite the rules of a trade union where the de-merging union wanted to be provided with a proportion of the assets of the parent union from which it was de-merging where the parent union did not consent to the provision of assets. The court concluded that to hold otherwise would be an unjustified intervention into trade union affairs.

Dissolution

11.84   This area raises two fundamental questions, these being:

---

[8]   See, for example, *AUEW (TASS) v AUEW (Engineering Section)* [1983] IRLR 108.
[9]   Under TULRCA 1992, s 69.
[10]   See the common law position set down in *Dawkins v Antrobus (1881)* 17 Ch D 615.
[11]   [1986] IRLR 298.

- whether a trade union or unincorporated employers' association can dissolve itself; and
- what happens to the property of a trade union or unincorporated employers' association in the event of it being dissolved.

11.85 If a trade union or unincorporated employers' association contains within its rulebook a power allowing that body to be dissolved, then the rules should be followed in the event of the body seeking to dissolve itself.

11.86 However, if no such power exists, there are three other methods of dissolving a trade union or unincorporated employers' association. First, under the general common law, if all of the current members of an unincorporated association unanimously vote in a properly constituted meeting to dissolve the association of which they are members, then under the principle in *Dawkins v Antrobus*,[12] the association may be dissolved upon the passing of that vote.

11.87 Secondly, the High Court has an inherent jurisdiction to wind up an unincorporated association where no rule allowing this to be done by the members of the association exists in the constitution of such an association.[13]

11.88 Thirdly, an unincorporated association may dissolve itself where there are less than two members left in it under the principle in *Re Bucks Constabulary Widows' and Orphans' Fund Friendly Society (No 2)*,[14] on the basis that the very nature of an association is that it provides a facility for members of the association to associate with other members of the association. In other words, if there is only one member in the association (or, indeed, if there are no members), there is no one for a sole surviving member to associate with.

Distribution of funds upon dissolution

11.89 Assuming that a trade union or unincorporated employers' association is wound up by its members, the property of the body will, in the first instance, be distributed according to the rules of the body. However, where no provision exists with regard to the division of property, two possibilities arise. The first is that a resulting trust is created in favour of all members of the body in proportion to the contributions that they have made during their membership. It may also require that any donations that have been received from external sources for particular purposes are returned to those sources to the extent that they have not been exhausted by the body in the pursuit of the objectives for which the funds were raised.[15]

11.90 Problems exist with the resulting trust analysis though. It poses huge administrative problems in determining who has contributed to the funds of a trade union or employers' association, in what proportions over the years and how much of those funds can be earmarked as still in existence. The disposal of surplus assets to long-dead members of a trade union or employers' association whose next of kin may be difficult to trace is an additional problem even if the contributions and proportions can be determined.

---

[12] (1881) 17 Ch D 615.
[13] See, for example, *Keys v Boulter (No 2)* [1972] 1 WLR 642.
[14] [1979] 1 WLR 936.
[15] See, for examples of this general principle, *Re Gillingham Bus Disaster* [1958] Ch 300; and *Davis v Richard & Wallington Limited* [1990] 1 WLR 1511.

11.91   In any event, the resulting trust analysis was not favoured by the High Court in *Re Bucks Constabulary Widows' and Orphans' Fund Friendly Society (No 2)*,[16] which held that the better view is that a member of an unincorporated association (which may include a trade union or unincorporated employers' association) during a member's period of membership will usually be pursuant to a simple contractual relationship with the association. This will entail a right to use the facilities of the association (subject to the rules of the association) but not a right to claim a severable share of the assets of the association.[17]

11.92   Consequently, upon an unincorporated association being wound up, in the absence of any provision in the rules of the association to the contrary, individual members become entitled to a distribution of the assets of the association on the basis of an equal share in the assets with all other members of the association at the time of dissolution.[18]

11.93   To the extent that a trade union or unincorporated employers' association is moribund at the time of its dissolution, then assuming that it is governed by the usual contractual principles in relation to the membership of unincorporated associations, it seems likely that its property would fall to the Crown as bona vacantia under the principle in *Re Bucks Constabulary Widows' and Orphans' Fund Friendly Society (No 2)*.[19]

11.94   The provisions with regard to the dissolution of incorporated employers' associations would be dealt with under the Companies Act 1985, as amended and, in the case of an insolvent winding-up, the Insolvency Act 1986, as amended.

---

[16]   [1979] 1 WLR 936.
[17]   See also *Hughes v TGWU* [1985] IRLR 382.
[18]   See *Re Sick and Funeral Society of St John's Sunday School Golcar* [1973] Ch 51 in this regard. See too *Tierney v Tough* [1914] IR 142; *Re St Andrew's Allotment Association* [1969] 1 WLR 229; and *Re GKN Bolts and Nuts Limited Sports and Social Club* [1982] 1 WLR 774.
[19]   [1979] 1 WLR 936.

Chapter 12

TRADE UNIONS AND THE CRIMINAL LAW

INTRODUCTION

12.1   Trade union law has had a long history of regulation at the hands of the criminal law. **Chapter 1** describes, inter alia, how trade unions have, over time, become accepted as legal entities. However, there is still a large volume of legislation in existence which creates potential consequences under the criminal law for trade unions and their members. This legislation exists to ensure, inter alia, that regulatory matters and the provisions of the Trade Union and Labour Relations (Consolidation) Act 1992 (TULRCA 1992) are complied with, and for the protection of the public at large.

REGULATORY MATTERS

Record keeping offences

12.2   A number of offences exist in relation to the statutory record keeping duties of trade unions under TULRCA 1992, s 45 (see **Chapter 6** with regard to record keeping duties generally).

Refusal to comply with record keeping duties

12.3   The first of the offences is the failure to comply with record keeping duties under TULRCA 1992, s 45(1)–(3). This states:

'(1) If a trade union refuses or wilfully neglects to perform a duty imposed on it by or under any of the provisions of—
section 27 (duty to supply copy of rules),
sections 28 to 30 (accounting records),
sections 32 to 37 (annual return, statement for members, accounts and audit), or
sections 38 to 42 (member's superannuation schemes),

it commits an offence.

(2) The offence shall be deemed to have been also committed by—

(a) every officer of the trade union who is bound by the rules of the union to discharge on its behalf the duty breach of which constitutes the offence, or
(b) if there is no such officer, every member of the general committee of management of the union.

(3)   In any proceedings brought against an officer or member by virtue of subsection (2) in respect of a breach of duty, it is a defence for him to prove that he had reasonable cause to believe, and did believe, that some other person who was competent to discharge that duty was authorised to discharge it instead of him and had discharged it or would do so.'

12.4   The actus reus of the offence is the failure to perform any of the duties mentioned or referred to in TULRCA 1992, s 45(1).

12.5   The mens rea of the offence is either an intentional refusal to comply or wilful neglect to do so. An intentional refusal in this context or a failure to act which would give the impression that the union was refusing to act is capable of being an outright wilful failure to perform one of the duties under TULRCA 1992, s 45(1).

Potential defendants

12.6   Persons capable of committing the offence are a trade union itself as a primary defendant and also, under TULRCA 1992, s 45(2), officers of the union contractually bound by the rules of the trade union to carry out that function, or, alternatively, all members of the general management committee of the union. It should be noted that if a lower-level employee of the union refuses to comply with the duty, such a person does not commit the offence. The offence is drafted essentially to ensure that good housekeeping prevails on the part of trade unions and their officials.

Defences

12.7   A defence exists under TULRCA 1992, s 45(3) to an offence under TULRCA 1992, s 45(1) for an officer or member of the management committee of a union, but not the union itself. The defence requires that an officer or committee member has reasonable cause to believe, and did believe, that the duty imposed would be carried out by another person competent to discharge it.

12.8   As to what will amount to reasonable grounds, in accordance with the maxim that each case turns on its own facts, this will vary and is capable of amounting to such things as, for example, members of the management committee of a union being able to show that the union has a compliance officer who is ordinarily responsible for the duties subject to the offence under TULRCA 1992, s 45(1) and that it was the compliance officer who failed to act. In addition, a defendant will have to show subjectively that he believed that the duty was being carried out by that other person.

Penalty

12.9   To the extent that a person is convicted of an offence under TULRCA 1992, s 45(1), he will be liable to a fine not exceeding level 5 on the standard scale (per TULRCA 1992, s 45A(1)(a)).

Time-limit for prosecuting the offence

12.10   Time-limits are laid down under TULRCA 1992, s 45A(2) and (3) for the prosecution of an offence under TULRCA 1992, s 45. In order for a prosecution to be brought in relation to an offence of failing to send annual returns to the Certification Officer, it is possible to bring proceedings at any time within a 3-year period commencing with the date on which the offence was committed (TULRCA 1992, s 45A(2)). If the offence consists of any of the other offences under TULRCA 1992, s 45(1), proceedings can be commenced either within 6 months beginning on the date that the offence was committed, or within 12 months beginning with the date on which the Certification Officer had sufficient evidence to justify the proceedings. The time-limits are subject to the requirement that proceedings must, in any event, be brought within 3 years beginning with the date of the offence being committed (TULRCA 1992, s 45A(3)). The Certification Officer is allowed to provide a certificate stating the date on which he had sufficient information to prosecute an offence under TULRCA 1992, s 45 and this is conclusive proof of that fact (TULRCA 1992, s 45A(4)).

Wilful alteration of documents with intent to falsify

12.11 This offence is created by TULRCA 1992, s 45(4) which provides:

'A person who wilfully alters or causes to be altered a document which is required for the purposes of any of the provisions mentioned in subsection (1), with intent to falsify the document or to enable a trade union to evade any of those provisions, commits an offence.'

Actus reus

12.12 The actus reus of the offence requires the alteration of, or causing the alteration of, trade union accounting records, in either case so that the alteration is falsified. This limb of the actus reus is therefore capable of being committed by any person, whether or not they are members or officials of the union or whether they are third parties or are acting at the request of the union, for example, external accountants or auditors.

Mens rea

12.13 This comprises two limbs, the first being wilful knowledge of an alteration and, the second, an intention to falsify the document.

Potential defendants

12.14 The crime can be committed by anyone who carries into effect the falsification or causes this to happen (for example, by procuring that the alteration is carried into effect).

Defences

12.15 There are no statutory defences under TULRCA 1992, s 45(4) provided, however, where this is the case, all elements of the offence must be proven in the course of the prosecution and other defences may be raised according to instructions and the particular facts of the case.

Penalty

12.16 To the extent that a person is convicted of an offence under TULRCA 1992, s 45(4) he will be liable to either a maximum of 6 months' imprisonment, a fine not exceeding level 5 on the standard scale, or both (per TULRCA 1992, s 45A(1)(b)).

Hindering the Certification Officer in the investigation of financial affairs

12.17 This offence is directed at persons who prevent the Certification Officer from carrying into effect a financial investigation into the affairs of a union (see **Chapter 6** on this point). The offence is created by TULRCA 1992, s 45(5) which provides:

'(5)   If a person contravenes any duty, or requirement imposed, under section 37A (power of Certification Officer to require production of documents etc.) or 37B (investigations by inspectors) he commits an offence.'

Actus reus

12.18   The actus reus is committed by not carrying into effect a request from the Certification Officer or one of his officers, to produce a relevant document requested by him or them, or by otherwise hindering an investigation carried out by him or them.

Mens rea

12.19   The offence is one of strict liability and as such no mens rea is needed to commit the offence.

Potential defendants

12.20   TULRCA 1992, s 45(5) makes it an offence for any person to fail to comply with the requirements.

Defence

12.21   Two defences are provided under TULRCA 1992, s 45(6) being, first, that a defendant did not have the relevant document that he has been requested to supply or, secondly, that it was not reasonably practicable to expect him to comply with the requirement imposed.

Penalty

12.22   To the extent that a defendant is found guilty, he is subject to a fine not exceeding level 5 on the standard scale.

Destroying, mutilating or falsifying documents relating to the financial affairs of a union

12.23   This offence is created under TULRCA 1992, s 45(7), which provides:

'If an official or agent of a trade union—

(a) destroys, mutilates or falsifies, or is privy to the destruction, mutilation or falsification of, a document relating to the financial affairs of the trade union, or
(b) makes, or is privy to the making of, a false entry in any such document,

he commits an offence unless he proves that he had no intention to conceal the financial affairs of the trade union or to defeat the law.'

Actus reus

12.24   The actus reus can be committed in a number of different ways, being the defendant destroying, mutilating or falsifying relevant documents or where the defendant simply has knowledge of the destruction, mutilation or falsification of such a 'relevant document'. Relevant documents are those documents that relate to the financial affairs of a union.

Mens rea

12.25   This is an offence of strict liability and a defendant will be presumed guilty unless he can show the defence provided under TULRCA 1992, s 45(7).

Potential defendants

12.26   Persons liable to prosecution under this section are any 'officials or agents' of a trade union. Officials and agents are defined by TULRCA 1992, s 119 as to mean, first, in the case of an official, an officer of a union (including any member of a union's governing body or a trustee of unions funds), or a branch or section thereof, or a person elected or appointed in accordance with the rules of the union to be a representative of the union members to some degree. Agents are defined to mean bankers or solicitors of, or any persons employed by, a trade union or any branch or section of it. It should be noted that if such destruction as is contemplated by TULRCA 1992, s 45(7) takes place by someone who is not in such a position but who acts at the request of an official or agent of a union, the official or agent will be privy to the act and therefore liable for the commission of the offence.

Defence

12.27   A defence exists for a defendant charged under TULRCA 1992, s 45(7) where that person is able to show that he had no intention to conceal the financial affairs of the union, or, alternatively, to defeat the operation of the law.

Penalty

12.28   If convicted of an offence under TULRCA 1992, s 45(7), a person is liable either to a term of imprisonment not exceeding 6 months, a fine not exceeding level 5 on the standard scale, or both.

Fraudulent alteration or deletion of documents relating to the financial affairs of a union

12.29   This offence is created under TULRCA 1992, s 45(8) and provides as follows:

'If such a person fraudulently—

(a) parts with, alters or deletes anything in any such document, or
(b) is privy to the fraudulent parting with, fraudulent alteration of or fraudulent deletion in, any such document,

he commits an offence.'

Actus reus

12.30   The actus reus of this offence requires that a document relating to the financial affairs of a union is disposed of, altered, or deleted by, or with the connivance of, an official or agent of a union, as defined in TULRCA 1992, s 119.[1]

Mens rea

12.31   The mens rea to be shown is that for fraud, ie dishonesty. In this regard, see the Court of Appeal definition of dishonesty in *R v Ghosh*[2] which requires the application of a two-stage test, this being:

---

[1]   See **12.26** as to this definition.
[2]   [1982] QB 1053.

- whether according to the objective standards of honest people the conduct with which the defendant was charged was dishonest; and
- if so, whether the defendant subjectively knew this to be the case.

Potential defendants

12.32   As with the offence under TULRCA 1992, s 45(7), those who can be charged are officials or agents of a union.

Defence

12.33   No specific defence is provided in relation to this offence.[3]

Penalty

12.34   Upon summary conviction, it is possible to receive either up to 6 months' imprisonment, a fine not exceeding level 5 on the standard scale, or both.

False or misleading statements in the course of financial investigations

12.35   This offence is created under TULRCA 1992, s 45(9) and provides as follows:

'(9)   If a person in purported compliance with a duty, or requirement imposed, under section 37A or 37B to provide an explanation or statement—

(a) provides or makes an explanation or statement which he knows to be false in a material particular, or
(b) recklessly provides or makes an explanation or statement which is false in a material particular,

he commits an offence.'

Actus reus

12.36   The actus reus of the offence is to make a statement or provide an explanation to a question during the course of a financial investigation into the affairs of a trade union which is materially inaccurate.

Mens rea

12.37   The mens rea of the offence can be committed either by knowing that the statement is incorrect, or by being reckless as to the truth or otherwise of the statement.

Potential defendants

12.38   Any person who provides a materially false statement to a financial investigation into the affairs of a trade union can be charged with this offence.

Defence

12.39   Again, no statutory defence is provided There is no specific defence to an offence committed under TULRCA 1992, s 45(9), but see the general comments at **12.15** with regard to the need to prove an offence.

---

[3]   See, though, the general comments at **12.15**.

Penalty

12.40 If summarily convicted of an offence under TULRCA 1992, s 45(9), it is possible for a defendant to be sentenced to either 6 months' imprisonment, a fine not exceeding level five on the standard scale, or both.

Additional civil consequences of convictions of offences under TULRCA 1992, s 45

12.41 As well as being convicted under any of the offences above, a defendant who is so convicted can be disqualified from holding a 'senior office' in a trade union. If a conviction is obtained under TULRCA 1992, s 45(1) or (5), a person so convicted is not allowed to hold a senior position for a period of 5 years starting with the point in time immediately preceding the conviction (TULRCA 1992, s 45B(1)(a)). If the conviction is under TULRCA 1992, s 45(4), (7), (8) or (9), the period of disqualification is 10 years (per TULRCA 1992, s 45B(1)(b)).

12.42 Senior offices of a trade union for the purposes of **12.41** are defined by TULRCA 1992, s 45B(5) as any of the following:

- a member of the executive of a trade union (including any person who is entitled to attend at a union executive meeting for any reason other than the mere provision of information or professional or technical advice);
- any position by virtue of which a person is a member of the executive;
- the president of a union; or
- the general secretary of a union.

12.43 TULRCA 1992, s 45C(4) additionally provides for civil remedies and enforcement of a breach under TULRCA 1992, s 45B with TULRCA 1992, s 45C(1) providing that any member of a trade union who claims that the union has failed to comply with the requirement TULRCA 1992, s 45B may apply to the Certification Officer or to the court for a declaration to that effect. In the case of such an application, the Certification Officer:

- Must make such inquiries as he thinks fit. Under TULRCA 1992, s 45C(7), where the Certification Officer requests a person to furnish information to him in connection with inquiries made by him, the Certification Officer must specify the date by which that information is to be furnished and, unless he considers that it would be inappropriate to do so, must proceed with his determination of the application notwithstanding that the information has not been furnished to him by that specified date.
- Must give the applicant and the trade union an opportunity to be heard.
- Must ensure that, so far as is reasonably practicable, the application is determined within 6 months of being made.
- May make or refuse the declaration asked for.
- Must, whether he makes or refuses the declaration, give reasons for his decision in writing.

12.44 Further, under TULRCA 1992, s 45C(5) or (5A), where, respectively, the court or the Certification Officer makes a declaration, it or he must also, unless it or he considers that it would be inappropriate, make an order imposing on the trade union a requirement to take within such period as may be specified in the order such steps to remedy the specified declared failure. The applications are mutually exclusive in respect of a given applicant (TULRCA 1992, s 45C(5B) and (5C)), and if another applicant makes a later application in relation to the same matter, the court or the Certification Officer (as relevant) is required to have regard to the earlier decision of the court or Certification Officer (as relevant). Under TULRCA 1992, s 45C(6), where an order has been made under TULRCA 1992, s 45C(5) or (5A), any person who is a member of the trade union and was a member at the time the order was made is entitled to enforce the order as if he had made the application on which the order was made. Under TULRCA 1992, s 45C(8) and (9), a declaration made by the Certification Officer may be relied on as if it were a declaration made by the court, and an order made by the Certification Officer may be enforced in the same way as an order of the court. TULRCA 1992, s 45D provides that appeals from the Certification Officer lie to the Employment Appeals Tribunal on any question of law arising under TULRCA 1992, s 45C.

EMPLOYERS' ASSOCIATIONS

12.45   Unincorporated employers' associations are bound by similar record keeping obligations with regard to the information that they are bound to provide publicly (TULRCA 1992, s 131(1)) (incorporated employers' associations are bound by the record keeping duties under the Companies Act 1985). However, unlike trade unions, where a person is convicted of an offence under TULRCA 1992, s 45 in relation to an employers' association, there is no restriction placed on the offender preventing him from holding office within an employers' association.

Failure to provide information relating to collective redundancies

12.46   This offence has been examined briefly in **Chapter 3**. The offence is created under TULRCA 1992, s 194 where an employer fails to notify the Secretary of State of a collective redundancy as required by TULRCA 1992, s 193. The offence is one of strict liability and is committed where an employer fails to give the appropriate period of notice (being at least 90 days' notice where it is proposed to dismiss by reason of redundancy 100 or more employees, or 30 days' notice where it is proposed to dismiss by reason of redundancy 20 or more, but less than 100, employees).

12.47   Upon commission of an offence under TULRCA 1992, s 194, an offender can be sentenced on summary conviction to a fine not exceeding level 5 on the standard scale (TULRCA 1992, s 194(1)).

Restriction on prosecutions

12.48   Only the Secretary of State or a person authorised by him may prosecute an offence under TULRCA 1992, s 194 and any person so authorised is expressly prohibited from instructing counsel or a solicitor to act in the magistrates' court (TULRCA 1992, s 194(2)).

Potential defendants

12.49   Where an offence is committed by a body corporate under TULRCA 1992, s 194, it is also deemed to have been committed by any director, manager, secretary or other similar officer who consents, connives or is otherwise similarly neglectful in the commission of the offence (TULRCA 1992, s 194(3)).

GENERAL CRIMINAL OFFENCES

12.50   The range of criminal offences that can be committed by a trade union, or a member of one, during the course of industrial action is wide, but may be divided broadly into the following three categories:

- offences provided under TULRCA 1992;
- industry-specific offences; and
- general public order offences,

each of which will be examined in turn.

INDUSTRIAL ACTION OFFENCES UNDER TULRCA 1992

12.51   These offences are consolidated as TULRCA 1992, ss 240–241. They were originally enacted under the Conspiracy and Protection of Property Act 1875 but have been modified over the years to their current form. Two particular groups of offences are created under these two sections. TULRCA 1992, s 241 restricts the breaching of a contract of service or hiring where to do so could endanger human life or seriously damage valuable property. The second offence is, broadly speaking, criminal intimidation. Each will be examined in turn.

Breach of contract involving risk of injury to persons or property

12.52   The offence under TULRCA 1992, s 241 was originally enacted under the Conspiracy and Protection of Property Act 1875, s 5. It provides as follows:

'(1)   A person commits an offence who wilfully and maliciously breaks a contract of service or hiring, knowing or having reasonable cause to believe that the probable consequences of his doing so, either alone or in combination with others, will be—

(a) to endanger human life or cause serious bodily injury, or
(b) to expose valuable property, whether real or personal, to destruction or serious injury.

(2)   Subsection (1) applies equally whether the offence is committed from malice conceived against the person endangered or injured or, as the case may be, the owner of the property destroyed or injured, or otherwise.'

12.53   The offence has never actually been prosecuted since its introduction under the Conspiracy and Protection of Property Act 1875.

Actus reus

12.54   The actus reus of the offence occurs where as a result of breaching a contract of service or hiring, the probable consequence of that act is the risk of serious injury to persons or property as described. It should be noted that only a probable consequence (ie greater than 50 per cent chance, per Lord Diplock in *R v Sheppard*[4]), is required and not that the consequence has actually occurred.

---

[4]   [1981] 3 All ER 899.

Mens rea

12.55   The mens rea of the offence is twofold. It requires, first, that a contract of service or hiring is breached either wilfully or maliciously. Secondly, the defendant must know or have reasonable grounds to believe (ie it must be obvious to an honest and reasonable man) that the consequences of his action will be to cause damage to persons or property as defined.

Potential defendants

12.56   As stated above, the offence has never actually been prosecuted. It would seem that those most likely to commit the offence are in the emergency services, hospital workers or in those employed in the privatised utility companies. Further, it is difficult to see how the offence could be prosecuted privately. In order for a member of the public to prosecute a defendant in respect of an alleged offence under TULRCA 1992, s 240, he would have to be specifically affected by the crime or be granted the right to prosecute in the name of the Attorney-General.[5] By way of particular exception, the offence cannot be committed by seamen (TULRCA 1992, s 240(4)).

Defences

12.57   No specific defence to the offence is provided.

Penalty

12.58   If a person is convicted of an offence under TULRCA 1992, s 240, he is liable to receive either a 3-month term of imprisonment, a fine not exceeding level 2 on the standard scale, or both (TULRCA 1992, s 240(3)).

Criminal intimidation

12.59   The offence of criminal intimidation was originally enacted under the Conspiracy and Protection of Property Act 1875, s 7 and is now carried over into TULRCA 1992, s 241. The offence has been extensively used as a means of controlling breaches of public order in industrial action. The offence was prosecuted 275 times alone in the Miners' Strike 1984–1985. The offence is declared specifically to be an arrestable offence in the absence of a warrant of arrest (TULRCA 1992, s 241(3)).

12.60   Offences under TULRCA 1992, s 241 can be committed in a variety of different ways in the course of industrial action (though it should be noted that prosecutions under TULRCA 1992, s 241 are not confined solely to offences committed during the course of industrial action[6]).

12.61   TULRCA 1992, s 241 provides as follows:

'(1)   A person commits an offence who, with a view to compelling another person from doing or to do any act which that person has a legal right to do or to abstain from doing, wrongfully and without lawful authority—

(a)   uses violence to or intimidates that person or his wife or children, or injures his property,

(b)   persistently follows that person from place to place,

---

5   See, for example, *Gouriet v UPOW* [1978] AC 435 on this point.
6   *Todd v Director of Public Prosecutions* [1996] Crim LR 344.

(c) hides any tools, clothes or other property owned or used by that person, or deprives him or hinders him in the use thereof,

(d) watches or besets the house or other place where that person resides, works, carries on business or happens to be, or the approach to any such house or place, or

(e) follows that person with two or more other persons in a disorderly manner in or through any street or road.'

Actus reus

12.62   The actus reus of the offence can be committed in a variety of different ways. It is important for all of the variations of the offence that they are committed wrongfully and without lawful authority. This point was considered by the High Court in the civil case of *Thomas v National Union of Mineworkers*,[7] where the court concluded (after having reviewed *Ward, Lock & Co Limited v OPAS*[8]), that in order for conduct to be wrongful in this regard, it would have to be tortious. As to the remaining ways in which the actus reus of the offence can be committed, these will be considered separately.

Intimidation

12.63   The courts have consistently stressed that what amounts to intimidation is a question of fact to be decided on the basis of common sense in a particular case. For example, in *Connor v Kent*,[9] the defendant was a member of a different trade union to that of the victim. The victim had been told that a strike would occur unless he left his union and joined that to which the defendant belonged. No violence was threatened but, upon his refusing to join the union, he was dismissed by his employer. A summons was issued alleging that the defendant had committed the offence of intimidating the victim. The victim claimed that he was intimidated from working at anywhere where members of the defendant's union were numerically superior to his own. The defendant was convicted but then acquitted on appeal where it was held that the term intimidate:[10]

'... is not ... a term of art – it is a word of common speech and everyday use; and it must receive, therefore, a reasonable and sensible interpretation according to the circumstances of the cases as they arise from time to time.'

12.64   More recently, in *R v Jones*, the Court of Appeal partially defined the concept of intimidation as including:[11]

'... putting persons in fear by the exhibition of force or violence or the threat of force or violence, and there is no limitation restricting the meaning to cases of violence or threats of violence to the person.'

Persistent following

12.65   As with the previous head, the circumstances in which this part of the actus reus can be committed are legion. Indeed, in *Smith v Thomasson*,[12] it was

---

7   [1985] IRLR 136.
8   (1906) 22 TLR 327.
9   [1891] 2 QB 545.
10   [1891] 2 QB 545 at 559.
11   (1974) 59 Cr App R 120 at 125.
12   (1890) 62 LT 68.

held that it would be 'impossible' to provide a definition of this provision: consequently, each case in which a prosecution is brought therefore turns very much on its own facts.

Deprivation of property

12.66   This element of the offence was considered by the Court of Appeal in *Fowler v Kibble*,[13] The defendants were miners who were members of a trade union. They objected to working with other miners who were not union members. In order to prevent the non-union-member miners from working, they asked an employee of the mine owner not to give the non-union-member miners a safety lamp (the effect of which, for legislative reasons, denied them the ability to work). The non-union-member miners complained that they had been denied their property and that the offence had therefore been committed. The Court of Appeal, however, held that because the action taken was to promote a closed shop (a lawful act at that time), nothing unlawful was being done in preventing the miners from being given a safety lamp and therefore no offence was being committed. The important element of this case is that the safety lamps belonged to the employer and not to the miners themselves. If the safety lamps had in fact belonged to the miners, a trespass would have been committed (tortious) and since that is itself unlawful, the crime would have been committed.

Watching or besetting

12.67   The actus reus of watching or besetting is to be construed in line with the ordinary everyday meaning of the words.[14] As with the other forms of committing an offence under TULRCA 1992, s 241, any watching or besetting must be unlawful per se for an offence to be committed. If this is the case, it does not matter that a place that is watched or beset is that of a person who is not employed or who is not working for a particular employer. For example, in *Charnock v Court*,[15] a prosecution was successfully brought when unionised labourers 'watched' for potential non-union employees at railway stations around the country.

Following a person in a disorderly manner

12.68   What amounts to a 'disorderly fashion' will vary from case to case. In *R v McKenzie*,[16] it was held that a procedural requirement in order to prosecute the offence is that the nature of the conduct alleged to be disorderly must be specified in the charge before the court. It is not enough to state simply that a person has been followed. The full particulars of how the following is said to be disorderly must also be specified on the indictment.

Mens rea

12.69   The test is objective as regards an offence under TULRCA 1992, s 241 and is committed where a defendant has the purpose of compelling a person to do or refrain from doing that which he has a right not to do or to do. This,

13   [1922] 1 Ch 487.
14   *J Lyons & Sons v Wilkins* [1899] 1 Ch 811; and *Ward, Lock & Co Limited v OPAS* (1906) 22 TLR 327.
15   [1899] 2 Ch 696.
16   [1892] 2 QB 519.

according to the Divisional Court in *Director of Public Prosecutions v Fidler*,[17] means more than merely attempting to persuade. The prosecutor does not have to show that the compulsion was effective, merely that it was attempted.[18]

Potential defendants

12.70 No specific person is defined as being a defendant under TULRCA 1992, s 241 and the offence can therefore be committed by anyone.

Defences

12.71 No specific defence is provided to the offence. However, the conduct of a defendant must be unlawful in order for it to amount to an offence under TULRCA 1992, s 241. Therefore, it is necessary to remember that a defendant may be protected from the consequences of a potential tort being unlawful in the first place since it follows that, if a defendant is able to claim the immunity for peaceful picketing under TULRCA 1992, s 220, and if the immunity is not removed for other reasons (see **Chapter 9** generally), the action committed by a potential defendant will not be unlawful (one of the required elements of the actus reus), and the offence cannot be committed. Therefore, whilst TULRCA 1992, s 220 does not of itself provide a defence to criminal action, complying with the requirements of TULRCA 1992, s 220 will inevitably avoid successful criminal proceedings being brought for criminal intimidation under TULRCA 1992, s 241.[19]

Penalties

12.72 Offences under what is now TULRCA 1992, s 241 were prosecuted relatively lightly before the Miners' Strike 1984–1985. Due to its usefulness as a means of punishing public order offences in that trade dispute, it was amended by Public Order Act 1986, s 40(2), so that it could be punished by means of either a period of imprisonment not exceeding 6 months, a level 5 fine on the standard scale, or both (TULRCA 1992, s 241(2)).

Harassment

12.73 The offence of harassment was introduced by the Protection from Harassment Act 1997 (PHA 1997) to combat the problems faced by victims of 'stalking'. PHA 1997 creates offences if in relation to criminal harassment and also provides civil remedies in the form of both damages and an injunction. Further, upon conviction, breach of any sentence imposed may lead to further prosecution. In addition, unlike injunctions generally, if an offender shows contempt in the face of an injunctive Order granted in respect of a breach of PHA 1997, committal proceedings can be instituted, or the offender can be convicted of an offence under PHA 1997, s 3(6). Both forms of proceedings can result in imprisonment for a term not exceeding 5 years, a fine, or both where the offence is tried on indictment, or, if the offence is tried summarily, the offender can be sentenced to a term of imprisonment not exceeding 6 months, a fine up to the statutory maximum, or both. It is not possible to be

---

[17]   [1992] 1 WLR 91.
[18]   See in this regard *Agnew v Munro* (1891) 18 R (J) 22.
[19]   See in this regard *Tynan v Balmer* [1967] 1 QB 91; *Broome v DPP* [1974] ICR 84; and *Kavanagh v Hiscock* [1974] ICR 282.

committed for contempt and convicted of an offence in relation to failing to obey an injunction under PHA 1997 (PHA 1997, s 3(8)).

12.74 No full definition of harassment is provided but PHA 1997, s 7 provides that references to 'harassing' include alarming or causing distress to a person.

12.75 Offences under PHA 1997 could potentially occur in the course of industrial action.

Harassment under PHA 1997

Actus reus

12.76 The actus reus of the offence is committed where a person pursues a course of conduct which amounts to harassment of another. A course of conduct is defined in PHA 1997, s 7(2) as meaning conduct committed on at least two occasions and conduct is defined as including speech (PHA 1997, s 7(4)). The conduct must be such as to put the person in fear for his safety.

Mens rea

12.77 The mens rea of the offence is that an offender knows or ought to know that the conduct being committed amounts to harassment. As to when a person ought to know that conduct amounts to harassment, PHA 1997, s 1(2) provides that this will be where a reasonable person in possession of the same information would think that the course of conduct amounted to harassment. In other words, the test is objective.

Defences

12.78 Three specific defences are created under PHA 1997, s 1(3) these being where conduct is carried out in the investigation of a crime, where it takes place so as to comply with any enactment or rule of law, or where conduct is reasonable. In *Huntingdon Life Sciences Limited v Curtin*,[20] the High Court held that when an application for an injunction was made in connection with alleged harassment under PHA 1997, s 1, harassment did not occur where those allegedly committing the harassment were exercising a right of free speech in a matter of public interest or in a political demonstration.

Penalties

12.79 To the extent that a person is found guilty of an offence under PHA 1997, s 1, then under PHA 1997, s 2, the offender is liable to a term of imprisonment not exceeding 6 months, a fine not exceeding level 5 on the standard scale, or both.

Putting people in fear of violence under PHA 1997

Actus reus

12.80 The actus reus of the offence is committed where a person, on at least two occasions, causes another to fear that violence will be used against him as a result of the actor's conduct (PHA 1997, s 4(1)). Conduct includes speech for these purposes (PHA 1997, s 7(4)). If a defendant is found not guilty of an

---

[20]   (1997) *The Times*, 11 December.

offence at a trial on indictment, then under PHA 1997, s 4(5), a jury is entitled to return a guilty verdict in relation to the PHA 1997, s 1 offence of harassment, ie the lesser offence is an alternative verdict available to the court.

Mens rea

12.81 The mens rea is the same as for the offence of harassment under PHA 1997, s 4(2).[21]

Defences

12.82 The defences in respect of this offence are the same as for harassment save that the defence of reasonableness is qualified by the addition of a proviso that the conduct must be aimed at protecting the actor or another, or the actor or another's property (PHA 1997, s 4(3)(c)).

Penalties

12.83 To the extent that an offender is found guilty of this offence when tried on indictment, he can be sentenced to a term of imprisonment not exceeding 5 years or a fine, or both, or, when tried summarily, a term of imprisonment of a maximum of 6 months or a fine not exceeding the statutory maximum, or both. However, it is usual for these offences where the harassment alleged was non-violent, but prolonged that the court will impose an injunction aimed to prevent further incidents occurring between the parties.

GENERAL PUBLIC ORDER OFFENCES

12.84 This section will only highlight the public order-related offences that can be committed generally in the course of industrial action. Regard should be had to specialist criminal law reference works when looking in detail at the offences in this section. Offences exist at both common law (in the form of breach of the peace) and under statute (in the form of the Criminal Law Act 1977, the Highways Act 1980, the Public Order Act 1986 and the Police Act 1996). These two areas will be looked at in turn.

Breach of the peace

12.85 The usefulness of prosecuting pickets for threatening or causing a breach the peace was highlighted during the Miners' Strike 1984–1985 when in excess of 4,100 charges were presented concerning the offence during the course of that industrial dispute. The offence of threatening or causing a breach of the peace was defined in *R v Howell*, as occurring where:[22]

> '... harm is actually done or is likely to be done to a person or in his presence to his property or a person is in fear of being so harmed through an assault, an affray, a riot, unlawful assembly or other disturbance. It is for this breach of the peace when done in his presence or the reasonable apprehension of it taking place that a constable, or anyone else, may arrest an offender without warrant ...'

---

21 See **12.77**.
22 [1982] QB 416 at 427.

12.86   The usefulness of the offence of breach of the peace can be seen in cases such as *Piddington v Bates*[23] and *Kavanagh v Hiscock*[24] where it was used to restrict the numbers of pickets in attendance on a picket line. It was also used in *Moss v McLachlan*,[25] where police officers used the offence to arrest 'flying pickets' who travelled from Kent to coal mines in the Nottingham area in order to picket during the Miners' Strike 1984–1985. At the time of their arrest, the pickets were several miles from the Nottingham collieries. Their convictions were upheld by the Divisional Court. When arresting the would-be pickets, the police were held to be able to take into account their knowledge of the violent nature of the industrial dispute. The proximity of the would-be pickets to the collieries undoubtedly helped the police in that case. However, arrest for the offence was also used as a deterrent by police officers in turning back would-be pickets at the Dartford Tunnel during the same dispute, which is a far more doubtful use of the offence.

STATUTORY OFFENCES

Criminal conspiracy

12.87   Criminal conspiracy is regulated by the Criminal Law Act 1977, s 1(1). The offence of conspiracy will be committed where two or more persons combine to commit or to attempt to commit another substantive offence. The offence is indictable only and will be committed to the Crown Court as provided for by the Crime and Disorder Act 1998, s 51. However, limitations exist in relation to conspiracy in the context of industrial disputes. First, in order to prosecute conspiracy on indictment for a substantive offence that would be of itself only summary in nature, it is necessary to have the consent of the Director of Public Prosecutions under the Criminal Law Act 1977, s 4(1). Secondly, the maximum sentence that can be handed down is limited to that of the substantive offence (Criminal Law Act 1977, s 3). Thirdly, TULRCA 1992, s 242 creates a restriction on the prosecution of criminal conspiracy. Where the substantive offence is summary in nature and not punishable by imprisonment, it cannot be prosecuted as a criminal conspiracy.

Obstructing the highway

12.88   The offence is created under the Highways Act 1980, s 137, which provides:

> 'If a person, without lawful authority or excuse, in any way wilfully obstructs the free passage along a highway, he is guilty of an offence and is liable to a fine not exceeding level 3 on the standard scale.'

12.89   Wilful obstruction requires that an act is done deliberately and not through inadvertence.[26] In the context of industrial action, the offence may be committed, for example, where pickets prevent free passage in and out of an

---

[23]   [1961] 1 WLR 162.
[24]   [1974] ICR 282.
[25]   [1985] IRLR 76.
[26]   See in this regard *R v Senior* [1899] 1 QB 283.

employer's premises to either persons or vehicles. In *Broome v DPP*,[27] the defendant was convicted for refusing to allow a lorry access along a highway by standing in front of it during the course of a strike. The defendant appealed, unsuccessfully, to the House of Lords on the grounds that he was exercising his peaceful right to picket under what is now TULRCA 1992, s 220. In dismissing the appeal, their Lordships held that the peaceful picketing immunity did not provide a lawful right to obstruct the highway during the course of picketing, stating that:[28]

'... [the] words make it plain that it is nothing but the attendance of the pickets at the places specified that is protected; and then only if their attendance is for one of the specified purposes. The section gives no protection in relation to anything the pickets may say or do whilst they are attending if what they say or do is itself unlawful. But for the section, the mere attendance of pickets might constitute an offence under ... the [Highways Act 1980] ... or constitute a tort, for example, nuisance. The section therefore gives a narrow but nevertheless real immunity to pickets. It clearly does no more.'

Offences under the Public Order Act 1986

12.90 The Public Order Act 1986 (POA 1986) was enacted as a backlash to various high profile public order disturbances during the 1980s (not the least of which was the Miners' Strike 1984–1985). POA 1986 can be used specifically to control industrial action by its regulation of the rights of persons engaged in processions and static assemblies. POA 1986 has two main angles of attack so far as industrial action is concerned. These are, first, the specific public order offences that are created under POA 1986, ss 1–5 and, secondly, the control over processions and assemblies under POA 1986, ss 11–16.

12.91 The offences under POA 1986, ss 1–5 were introduced to repeal the previous common law offences of riot, rout, unlawful assembly and affray and also the offence under the Public Order Act 1936, s 5 of causing a breach of the peace by the use of threatening, abusive or insulting words or behaviour. In their place a graduated series of offences was created covering various forms of public disorder, as follows:

- *Riot* This offence arises under POA 1986, s 1 and is the most serious of the offences created by POA 1986. It requires that 12 or more persons who are present together simultaneously, intentionally or recklessly (POA 1986, s 6(1)), use or threaten unlawful violence for a common purpose (which can be inferred from the conduct of the actors (POA 1986, s 1(3)). The conduct of the actors when taken together must be such as to cause a notional person of reasonable firmness present at the scene to fear for his personal safety (POA 1986, s 1(1)). Riot can be committed in public or on private premises (POA 1986, s 1(5)). Riot is punishable by conviction on indictment to a maximum sentence of 10 years (POA 1986, s 1(6)). A prosecution for riot may not be brought without the permission of the Director of Public Prosecutions (POA 1986, s 7(1)).
- *Violent disorder* This offence arises under POA 1986, s 2. In order to

establish the offence, it is necessary to show that three or more persons who are present together, intentionally or recklessly (POA 1986, s 6(2)), use or threaten, unlawful violence so that the conduct of them, when taken together, is such as to cause a notional person of reasonable firmness present at the scene to fear for his personal safety (POA 1986, s 2(1)). It is immaterial whether the use or threat of violence is simultaneously carried into effect by the offenders for an offence under POA 1986, s 2(2) to be committed. The offence can be committed in public as well as in private places (POA 1986, s 2(4)). A person found guilty of violent disorder can, if convicted on indictment, be sentenced to up to 5 years' imprisonment, a fine, or both. Alternatively, if convicted at a summary trial that person may be imprisoned for up to 6 months, fined to the statutory maximum, or both (POA 1986, s 2(5)).

- *Affray* This offence arises under POA 1986, s 3, and is committed where a person, intentionally or recklessly, uses or threatens, unlawful violence towards another and his conduct is such as would cause a notional person of reasonable firmness present at the scene to fear for his safety (POA 1986, s 3(1)). Threats cannot be made by words alone if a defendant is to be charged with affray (POA 1986, s 3(3)). Affray can be committed in public and private places alike (POA 1986, s 3(5)). It is stated to be an arrestable offence under POA 1986, s 3(6). The penalty upon conviction on indictment is a term of imprisonment not exceeding 3 years, a fine, or both. If the conviction is in summary form, the maximum sentences are a term of imprisonment not exceeding 6 months, a fine up to the statutory maximum or both. There needs to be a hypothetical reasonable person who could be, but is not necessarily, at the scene of the offence.[29] In effect, no one need be present at the scene for the offence of affray to be made out.

- *Fear or provocation of violence* This offence arises under POA 1986, s 4, and is committed where a person intentionally or recklessly uses threatening, abusive or insulting words or behaviour towards another, or distributes or displays to another any writing, sign or other visible representation that is threatening, abusive or insulting. Further, it is necessary that the intention of the defendant should be such as to cause the victim to believe that immediate unlawful violence will be used against the claimant or against a third party, or would provoke it to be used (POA 1986, s 4(1)). The offence can be committed in public or in private (POA 1986, s 4(2)) and it is an arrestable offence (POA 1986, s 4(3)). The offence can only be tried summarily. There is a maximum sentence of 6 months' imprisonment, a fine not exceeding level 5 on the standard scale, or both for the offence (POA 1986, s 4(4)).

- *Intentional harassment, alarm or distress* This offence was created as POA 1986, s 4A by the Criminal Justice and Public Order Act 1994, s 154. The offence consists of intentionally causing harassment, alarm or distress by using threatening, abusive or insulting words or behaviour, or by distributing or displaying any written or visible representation that is threatening, abusive or insulting and would cause harassment, alarm or distress (POA 1986, s 4A(1)). The offence can be committed in public or in private (POA 1986, s 4A(2)), and it is an arrestable offence (POA 1986, s 4A(4)). The

---

[29]   *R v Davison* (1992) Crim LR 31, CA.

offence can only be tried summarily and a maximum sentence exists for the offence of 6 months' imprisonment, a fine not exceeding level 5 on the standard scale, or both (POA 1986, s 4A(5)).

- *Harassment, alarm or distress* This offence arises under POA 1986, s 5, and is committed where a person, within the sight or hearing of another, intentionally or recklessly, uses threatening, abusive or insulting words or behaviour, or distributes or displays any written or visible representation that is threatening, abusive or insulting which would cause harassment, alarm or distress (POA 1986, s 5(1)). The offence can be committed in public or in private (POA 1986, s 5(2)), and a power of arrest is provided if a person refuses to desist from the behaviour after having been warned by a constable (POA 1986, s 5(4)). The maximum penalty is a fine on summary conviction not exceeding level 3 on the standard scale (POA 1986, s 5(6)).

POA 1986 control of processions and assemblies

12.92 The controls that exist arise under POA 1986 at two levels, those relating to processions and those relating to assemblies. As to the first category, these are dealt with under POA 1986, ss 11–13. The powers allow the police to receive written notice of public processions intended to demonstrate support for a particular view, to publicise a cause or campaign or to mark a particular event (POA 1986, s 11(1)). The notice must inform the police of the route, the time and the date of the procession and also the name and addresses of the organisers of the procession (POA 1986, s 11(3)). Generally, 6 clear days' notice of a procession is required (POA 1986, s 11(5)). An exception exists in relation to spontaneous processions but these are unlikely to arise in the context of trade unions, which are required to comply with a clearly defined course of conduct in the context of industrial action (in relation to matters such as balloting and notifying employers) if they are to be immune from the tortious consequences of industrial action which they might take (see **Chapter 7** generally in this regard). Consequently, where a trade union proposes to undertake a procession in the course of industrial action, it should ensure that it has left sufficient time to provide the necessary information within the timescales envisaged under POA 1986, s 11.

12.93 Upon receiving notice of an intended procession, a chief officer of police can impose conditions on a procession, including refusing to allow the same to go ahead (POA 1986, ss 12–13). Failure to comply with any such requirements amounts to an offence which can lead to imprisonment for a period of up to 3 months or a fine not exceeding level 4 when tried summarily. Any person committing an offence by taking part in such a procession is liable to a fine not exceeding level 3 on the standard scale (POA 1986, ss 12(5)–(6) and 13(7)–(9) respectively).

12.94 The second set of requirements exists in relation to assemblies. Unlike processions, assemblies are static bodies, are easier to contain and therefore provide less of a public order problem. As a consequence of this, the requirements under POA 1986 are less detailed than in the case of processions.

12.95 POA 1986, s 14 deals with the area of restrictions on demonstrations. It allows a senior police officer to impose conditions on an assembly where he reasonably believes that the assembly may result in any of serious public disorder, serious damage to property or serious disruption to the life of the community. Conditions may also be imposed where a senior police officer reasonably believes that the purpose of those organising the assembly is to intimidate people into doing something that they have a right not to do or to do that which they have a right to abstain from doing.

12.96   Where any of the above conditions are satisfied, the senior police officer may make directions concerning the place at which the assembly is being, or is to be, held, its duration, and the maximum number of people who may take part in the assembly, in order to minimise the potential disorder, damage, disruption or intimidation (POA 1986, s 14(1)).

12.97   The practical implications of these provisions of POA 1986 are obvious given that one of the main purposes of industrial action is to make a person do that which he does not want to do. Further, given that the Code of Practice on Picketing PL928, 1st Revision (2002), makes express reference to the powers of the police (see paras 45–47) and contains section E entitled 'Limiting Numbers of Pickets' (which includes at para 51 a recommendation as to the maximum number of six pickets per workplace entrance), the potential for the police to exercise their discretion so as to dilute the effectiveness of a picket line is obvious.

BAIL CONDITIONS

12.98   If a person is arrested and charged for the alleged commission of an offence, the first stage in the criminal procedure that he will encounter after charge is consideration of bail. The right to bail is governed by the Bail Act 1976, as amended by the Criminal Justice and Public Order Act 1994, Part II, or, in the case of police bail, the Police and Criminal Evidence Act 1984, s 47, as amended by the Criminal Justice and Public Order Act 1994, s 27. The main constraint that can be imposed is in relation to conditions that can be attached to bail, in particular in the context of industrial action, a prohibition from attending the site of an industrial dispute. The lawfulness of this type of condition was challenged in *R v Mansfield Justices, ex p Sharkey*.[30] Here, the defendants were charged with offences committed during the course of picketing during the Miners' Strike 1984–1985. They were remanded on bail by magistrates who attached a condition that defendants were:

> '… [not] to visit any premises or place for the purpose of picketing or demonstrating in connection with the current trade dispute between the NUM and the NCB other than peacefully to picket or demonstrate at [their] usual place of employment.'

12.99   The defendants sought a review of the bail condition, asking that the condition attached should be quashed and that the magistrates should be directed to admit the applicants to unconditional bail. The matter was heard by the Divisional Court which refused the application. The court held that the Bail Act 1976, s 3(6) conferred a wide discretion on magistrates as to the conditions that they could attach. Magistrates were required to address the question of whether the condition was necessary to prevent the commission of further offences whilst the defendant was on bail. If they thought that a real risk existed that could be met by the imposition of conditions, then they would be justified in imposing a condition. The considerations which the magistrates'

[30]   [1984] IRLR 496.

must take into account were not only the commission of further offences, but also whether the conditions are necessary to prevent harm to the public and whether the defendant may fail to attend court on future occasions.

12.100   It does not follow from the foregoing that on every occasion where an offence has been committed in the course of industrial action bail conditions will be imposed. Nevertheless, what *Ex p Sharkey*[31] shows is that such conditions can be imposed and they are therefore another potential restriction that can arise in the context of industrial action.

CRIMINAL JUSTICE ACT 2003 (CJA 2003)

12.101   The Criminal Justice Act 2003 (CJA 2003), s 101 provides that a person's bad character may be adduced at trial in certain circumstances (ie previous convictions may be put before the jury). CJA 2003, s 101(1)(a)–(g) outlines the circumstances in which such an event can occur, but the provisions to be considered in this context are where it is important explanatory evidence (CJA 2003, s 101(1)(c)) and where it is relevant to an important matter in issue between the defendant and the prosecution (CJA 2003, s 101(1)(d)).

12.102   It may be possible that where a trade union official or a person undertaking industrial action is a regular attendee at picket lines and have previous convictions tending to show a propensity for unlawful behaviour on picket lines, it may be open to the Crown to make an application to adduce such evidence.

12.103   CJA 2003, s 101(2) provides:

> '... the Court must not admit evidence under subsection (1)(d) ... if on application by the Defendant to exclude it, it appears to the Court that the admission of the evidence would have such an adverse affect on the fairness of the proceedings that the Court ought not to admit it.'

12.104   Matters to be considered are the length of time which has elapsed between the similar offences and the current charges (CJA 2003, s 101(4)).

12.105   For full consideration of the application of these provisions, see the decision of the Court of Appeal in *R v Hanson, Gilmore and Pickstone*.[32]

---

[31]   *R v Mansfield Justices, ex p Sharkey* [1984] IRLR 496.
[32]   (2005) EWCA Crim 824, (2005) 169 JP 250.

INDEX

References are to paragraph numbers.